LATE MEDIEVAL ENGLAND 1399–1509

Pearson Education

We work with leading authors to develop the
strongest educational materials in history,
bringing cutting-edge thinking and best
learning practice to a global market.

Under a range of well-known imprints, including
Longman, we craft high quality print and
electronic publications which help readers to understand
and apply their content, whether studying or at work.

To find out more about the complete range of our
publishing, please visit us on the World Wide Web at:
www.pearsoneduc.com

LATE MEDIEVAL ENGLAND 1399–1509

A. J. POLLARD
UNIVERSITY OF TEESSIDE

An imprint of **Pearson Education**

Harlow, England · London · New York · Reading, Massachusetts · San Francisco
Toronto · Don Mills, Ontario · Sydney · Tokyo · Singapore · Hong Kong · Seoul
Taipei · Cape Town · Madrid · Mexico City · Amsterdam · Munich · Paris · Milan

Pearson Education Limited
Edinburgh Gate
Harlow
Essex CM20 2JE
England

and Associated Companies throughout the world

Visit us on the World Wide Web at:
http://www.pearsoneduc.com

First published 2000

ISBN 0 582 03135 4 PRR
ISBN 0 582 03134 6 CASED

British Library Cataloguing-in-Publication Data
A catalogue record for this book is available from the British Library

10 9 8 7 6 5 4 3 2 1
04 03 02 01 00

Typeset by 35 in 11/13pt Baskerville MT
Produced by Pearson Education Asia Pte Ltd.
Printed in Singapore

FOR SANDRA

CONTENTS

ILLUSTRATIONS

ABBREVIATIONS

The following abreviations are used in the notes and guide to further reading

BIHR   *Bulletin of the Institute of Historical Research*
BJRL   *Bulletin of the John Rylands Library*
CSPM   *Calendar of State Papers and Manuscripts existing in the Archives and Collections of Milan*, I, 1385–1618, ed. A. B. Hinds (1913)
EcHR   *Economic History Review*
EETS   Early English Text Series
EHD   *English Historical Documents, IV, 1327–1485*, ed. A. R. Myers (1969)
EHR   *English Historical Review*
Harleian MS 433   *British Library Harleian Manuscript 433*, ed. R. E. Horrox and P. W. Hammond, 4 vols (1979–83)
HJ   *Historical Journal*
HMC   Historic Manuscripts Commission
HR   *Historical Research*, formerly *Bulletin of the Institute of Historical Research*
JEH   *Journal of Ecclesiastical History*
JBS   *Journal of British Studies*
JMH   *Journal of Medieval History*
NH   *Northern History*
PL   *The Paston Letters*, 6 vols, ed. J. Gairdner (1904)
PP   *Past and Present*
PPC   *Proceedings and Ordinances of the Privy Council*, 7 vols, ed. A. H. Nicolas (1834–7)
Rot Parl *Rotuli Parliamentorum*, 6 vols, ed. J. Strachey and others (1767–77)
SH   *Southern History*
TRHS   *Transactions of the Royal Historical Society*
VCH   *Victoria History of the Counties of England*
YAJ   *Yorkshire Archaelogical Journal*

GENERAL EDITOR'S PREFACE

The Longman History of Medieval England covers the story of England from the end of the Roman occupation to the Reformation. The series describes and analyses the formative period of English history – one in which the peoples we now call the English arrived, settled, and gave their name to the whole country, a name and identity that were never displaced despite later conquests by other invaders. It is an absorbing story, and one which needs to be told afresh to take account of new research and new interpretations. Our series aims to do just that, while not losing sight of the need to carry the reader along: it is a prime aim that each volume is a pleasure to read.

Our intention is to explain *what* happened as well as *why* it happened. The series has a straightforward chronological framework, and puts a high value on readability and accessibility. That does not involve a purely narrative account, but one which integrates political, social, economic and other aspects to produce a richly-textured synthesis within a broad chronological survey. Each volume is the work of a specialist, using the latest research and making a substantial contribution to the study of his or her period rather than simply synthesising existing knowledge. Authors draw on their own findings as well as that of others, and point the way to fruitful approaches for further research.

It may be necessary, in the present climate of devolution and 'political correctness', to explain why the series covers English rather than British history. A. J. Pollard puts the case unanswerably: Britain was still a geographical expression at the end of the middle ages, and England, Scotland and Wales (not to mention Ireland) had their own histories. Although the kings ruling England gradually imposed their power over Wales and much of Ireland, they were never effectively British rulers in the post-1707 sense. On the other hand, rulers from 1016 onwards conquered England from overseas, and linked its destiny briefly to Denmark, and then for a much longer period to Normandy and other French provinces. A meaningful history of medieval England is, therefore, both more and less than a British history covering the same period.

In the rise of western Europe in the middle ages the importance of England was very great indeed. We may no longer believe, with some

Victorian historians, that medieval England and its institutions – such as parliament – were uniquely important, but they were certainly sufficiently distinctive to justify close study. England was arguably the earliest state in medieval Europe to develop a sophisticated, complex and centralised government, a system already evident well before the Norman Conquest. Despite many setbacks in later centuries, including the near-breakdown of government described in this volume, the institutions were to endure and to develop in an orderly way. If the government of modern Britain has evolved peacefully, without the upheavals suffered by its Continental neighbours since 1789, that can be attributed, in part at least, to the robust institutions laid down in the middle ages.

That is sufficient justification in itself of the importance of studying medieval England, not only for its own sake but also to understand the present. We should not succumb to the temporal parochialism which presents only the sixteenth century onwards as the focus of English and British history. The period spanned by these volumes was more than twice as long as that from Henry VIII to the present day, and during those nine centuries much that shaped English identity and institutions was created. To tell the story of those centuries is to face many challenges, and by doing so to remind ourselves of what has shaped England today. It is a story of perennial interest which will appeal to a wide readership.

A. J. Pollard's book re-tells and reinterprets the final section of that long story, a period still familiar to many from the sequence of Shakespeare's histories and from the tradition of historical interpretation which it reflected and reinforced. Much was wrong with that perspective, and in any case the flood of studies of fifteenth-century England, which shows no signs of abating, has meant that any interpretation of it must differ considerably from anything written before 1970. A. J. Pollard has an unrivalled knowledge of fifteenth-century England, as the author of many important studies over the past thirty years, and he is able to analyse the period in a masterly way, as well as retelling his story with wit and panache. He is able to present the men and women of that century in a convincing perspective, one which makes sense of both long-term change and short-term political revolutions, and one which distinguishes clearly between the elements of continuity and change at the end of the middle ages. It is a book which transforms our view of the period, and helps us to understand, as he puts it, 'the long transition from medieval to modern society.'

D. M. Palliser.

PREFACE

This book has been a long time in the making. I have found it more difficult than I expected to construct a detailed narrative history. Lying somewhere between a research monograph and a textbook, a traditional 'history' now seems to fit awkwardly between the two. While it in part derives from over thirty years of my own research on various aspects of fifteenth-century society, and my accumulated thought about the subject, it is neither the kind of book for which one undertakes a considerable body of new research nor that for which one merely summarises one's own current understanding of the topic. Rather it provides the opportunity to bring together the product of a good part of half a century's research undertaken by many historians and to take stock of where things now stand.

It is perhaps opportune that the book is being published at the beginning of the twenty-first century for, as I seek to show in my introductory chapter, the study of the fifteenth century has been utterly transformed since 1900, even since 1969, when the work which this follows on Longman's list, Wilkinson's *The Later Middle Ages in England*, was published. So rapidly has the academic and research historian's perception of the fifteenth century been transformed that one perhaps forgets that the general perception has changed much more slowly. A work such as this thus not only enables one to stand back and ponder the significance of recent research and to endeavour to bring the results together in a new synthesis, but it also aims to show those not so deeply familiar with, and close to, the field how much the understanding of the last century of the middle ages in England has changed in recent decades. How successfully this has been done the reader will judge.

A narrative History of Medieval England, of which this is the fourth and final chronological volume, might seem a somewhat passé project. Its scope and its focus might seem to be unnecessarily narrow. Why not a history of Britain, why yet another Anglo-centric narrative of political history? There are several answers to this question. One is that in the later middle ages England was the dominant political power within the British Isles. The kings of England controlled Wales, held Ireland loosely in sway, and claimed to be overlords of Scotland. Secondly a history of England in the fifteenth century is not restricted to the British Isles. In mid-century significant parts of northern and south-western France were part of the dominions of the king of England. A history of England in the fifteenth century touches as much on France as it does on Wales and parts of Ireland. Thirdly the fifteenth century witnessed an important stage in the growth of a sense of English identity, including it might be said the Englishman's (not necessarily the English woman's) misplaced sense of his superiority over his near neighbours. Britain was but a vague concept in the fifteenth century. A history of Britain, other than a discussion of the concept and its contemporary use, can be barely more than interlinked histories of its constituent 'nations'; and these have been well served in recent years.

The word 'England' meant both the person of the king and the realm over which he reigned. The contemporary doctrine of the separation of powers recognised the concept of the king's two bodies. One was the person of the king, which was mortal; the other was the body of the kingdom which was immortal. The King is Dead; Long Live the King. Politics focused on the person of the king, political history tends to focus on their reigns. Polydore Vergil in the early sixteenth century, drawing upon Roman imperial histories, was the first to construct a history of England based on the reigns of its kings. This work does the same. So central was the king that it is well-nigh impossible to construct a political narrative that does not focus on his person. But not all reigns are similar. It is considerably easier to write about the reign of a commanding king such as Henry V than about his son, Henry VI, who for much of his reign was incapable of ruling.

This is therefore in form largely a traditional, if not even old-fashioned, king-centred history of England. And inevitably it gives, as Jack Lander observed of general histories, a deceptively firm outline of political events. But the central chapters of the work escape from talk of court news, 'who loses and who wins; who's in, who's out', to try to find fifteenth-century England itself, its place within Britain, its institutions, its social structure, its peoples and their views of the world. It does not, however, extend to cultural history: it deals but cursorily with literature and the visual and performing arts. This is not to imply that they were unimportant or insignificant; indeed fifteenth-century England enjoyed a vibrant culture. It is rather that I am ill-equipped to give such an important aspect full justice.

England is easier to define than the fifteenth century, for which I have taken what one might call the conventional modern century. Its start is 1399, the deposition of Richard II and usurpation of Henry IV; its end 1509. But this is also the last volume in a series on medieval England and the death of Henry VII, any more than his accession in 1485, cannot be said to mark the end of the middle ages. I have therefore ended with a more general discussion of early Tudor England considering those developments and changes which might reasonably be said, together, to have brought one era to an end and opened another.

This book owes many debts of gratitude. First and foremost is to all those scholars working currently and in the recent past on fifteenth-century history. They know how much I owe to them, either from their works, correspondence or conversation. I have fallen out of the habit of asking friends to read drafts of my own writing, not I think out of arrogance, but out of laziness and cowardice. It is a fault for which I no doubt will suffer; but it does mean more than conventionally that the errors and inconsistencies are all my own. That said I would like particularly to thank Rowena Archer, Richard Britnell, Linda Clark, Anne Curry, Edwin and Anne De Windt, Keith Dockray, Ralph Griffiths, Steven Gunn, Michael Hicks, Michael Jones, Jenny Kermode and Colin Richmond, for their support and encouragement; the British Academy for a study leave award which did not quite lead, as intended, to early completion; my colleagues at the University of Teesside for allowing me further relief from teaching duties to do so; Robina Nixon for her invaluable assistance in the later stages with preparing the endnotes and bibliography; and Andrew McLennan and David Palliser for their patient, tactful and understanding editorial support. Above all, and more than conventionally, there is my wife Sandra. She has had to live with this project for almost a decade, and has put up with my distraction with the patience of Griselda. Words cannot express my gratitude. To her this book is dedicated with love.

ACKNOWLEDGEMENTS

We are grateful to the following for permission to reproduce copyright material:

The Bridgeman Art Library for Ms 265 f.IV Edward IV, with Elizabeth Woodville, *Edward V* and Richard, Duke of Gloucester, later Richard III, English, Dictes of Philosophers, (c. 1477), Lambeth Palace Library, London, UK/Bridgeman Art Library; *Effigy of Henry IV* (1367–1413) on his Tomb in Canterbury Cathedral, Kent, UK/Bridgeman Art Library; *Choosing the Red and White Roses* in the Temple Garden, 1910 by Henry A. Payne (Harry) (1868–1940), Houses of Parliament, Westminster, London, UK/Bridgeman Art Library, and *Court of the King's Bench*, Westminster Hall, from 'The Microcosm of London', engraved by J. Black (fl.1791–1831), pub. By R. Ackermann (1764–1834) 1808 (aquatint) by T. Rowlandson (1756–1827) and Pugin, A. C. (1762–1832), Private Collection/The Stapleton Collection/ Bridgeman Art Library; The British Library for *Knight's Yeoman/Robin Hood*, G. 11588; *The Empty Throne*, ms Harley 1319, f.57, and *John Talbot and Henry VI*, ms Royal 15 E VI, f.405: English Heritage Photographic Library for *Mount Grace Priory*, view of the Priory Church from the South West: National Gallery Company Ltd for The Virgin and Child with Saints and Donors (*The Donne Triptych*) by Hans Memlinc, © The National Gallery, London; National Monuments Record for *Thomas Paycocke's House*, Coggeshall, Essex, © Crown copyright, NMR, and *A Scolding Wife* (Henry VII Chapel, Westminster Abbey, © Crown copyright, NMR; National Portrait Gallery for *Henry V*, and *Henry VII*, by courtesy of the National Portrait Gallery, London; Royal Collection Enterprises for portrait of *Henry VI* by an unknown artist, RCIN 403442, OM 8 WC, The Royal Collection © 2000, Her Majesty Queen Elizabeth II; Society of Antiquaries of London for *Richard III*, and *Edward IV*, copyright Society of Antiquaries of London.

While every effort has been made to trace the owners of copyright, in a few cases this has proved impossible and we take this opportunity to offer our apologies to any copyright holders whose rights we have unwittingly infringed.

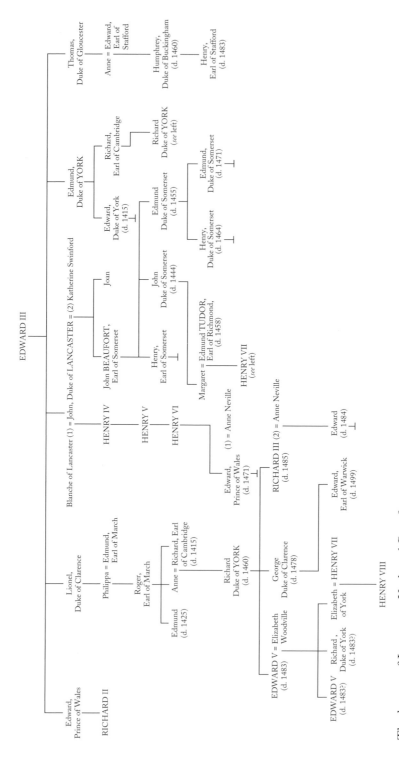

The houses of Lancaster, York and Beaufort

INTRODUCTION:
THE FIFTEENTH CENTURY IN HISTORY

The early tradition

In the Whig Interpretation of History, the 'metanarrative' which shaped perceptions of the history of England in the nineteenth and early twentieth centuries, the genius of the English was perceived to lie in their skill in steering a middle course between the extremes of anarchy and tyranny which characterised the histories of their inferior European neighbours. Only occasionally had the English regrettably fallen into either trap, and thankfully they had always been rescued by the innate moral rectitude and good sense of their ruling elites. Royal tyranny, in the early thirteenth, the late fourteenth and seventeenth centuries had tended to be the greater danger; but anarchy had prevailed in the fifteenth century. The fifteenth century was, as Sellars and Yeatman put it in their lampoon, an era of 'Sackage, Carnage and Wreckage';[1] it was *the* exemplar from English history of the dire consequences of weak government.

The view of the fifteenth century as an era of unprecedented and not to be repeated disorder has deep roots. It was fixed in the English historical imagination in the eight history plays of William Shakespeare which dramatised events from 1397 to 1485. Their central and connecting theme is the divine retribution visited on England for the crime committed by Henry IV in laying his hands on the Lord's anointed, Richard II; a sin not purged until Henry VII destroyed the malignant Richard III. All England, not just members of its ruling families, suffered as a consequence. In *Richard II* the bishop of Carlisle prophesies that;

> *Disorder, horror, fear and mutiny*
> *Shall her inhabit, and this land be call'd*
> *The field of Golgotha and dead men's skulls.*[2]

The prophecy is enacted in *Henry VI, Part II*; and Richmond reprises it at the end of *Richard III*:

England hath long been mad and scarred herself;
The brother blindly shed the brother's blood
The father rashly slaughter'd his own son,
The son, compell'd, been butcher to the sire.[3]

Could anything have been worse?

Shakespeare's historical cycle was a dramatisation of the received wisdom for popular entertainment. He was not writing Tudor propaganda. This is not to deny that this perception of the century had derived in part from such propaganda. But over a century after the accession of the first Tudor, what had once been propaganda had become embedded as accepted historical truth. One can easily trace the roots of Shakespeare's history through Holinshed, early Elizabethan writers such as Sir Thomas Smith, Edward Hall at the end of Henry VIII's reign, to Polydore Vergil thirty years earlier, to the propaganda deployed by Henry VII when he came to the throne and beyond. Sir Thomas Smith wrote in 1563 'They set the father against the son, and brother against the brother, the uncle slew the nephew and was slain himself. So blood pursued and ensued blood, till all the realm was brought to great confusion.'[4]

The cause was clear. It derived from dynastic dispute. Edward Hall in his preface to his 'Illustrious History of the Houses of Lancastre and Yorke', published in 1548, elaborated on examples, from the distant and recent past, of European civil wars, 'But', he stressed with fine rhetorical flourish, 'what misery, what murder and what execrable plagues and dissension this famous region [England] hath suffered by the division and dissension of the renowned houses of Lancaster and York, my wit cannot comprehend nor my tongue declare, neither yet my pen fully set forth.' Hall, as a servant of Henry VIII, dutifully stressed that all this had been 'suspended and apalled' in the person of Henry VIII, the true heir to both Lancaster and York, 'and by him clearly buried and perpetually extinct'.[5] And this notion itself derived from Henry VII's own conceit, deployed at the very beginning of his reign, that by marrying Elizabeth of York he had united the warring dynasties and brought civil war to an end.

But Henry VII was himself adapting the propaganda encapsulated twenty-five years earlier in Edward IV's parliamentary declaration of his title in 1461. It is in this remarkable, Yorkist, passage that one first sees almost in full the later Shakespearean vision:

Henry of Lancaster . . . Richard II, king annointed, crowned and
consecrated and his liege and most high lord in earth, against God's law,
man's liegance and oath of fidelity, with uttermost punishment and
tormenting, murdered and destroyed with most vile, heinous and
lamentable death.

Whereof this realm of England therefore hath suffered the charge of intolerable persecution, punishment and tribulation, whereof the like hath not been seen or heard in any other Christian realm by any memory or record, unrest, inward war and trouble, unrighteousness, shedding and effusion of innocent blood, abuse of the laws, partiality, riot, extortion, murder, rape and vicious living, have been the guiders and leaders of the noble realm of England.[6]

It is all there; except Edward IV proved to be a false saviour. Not until Henry VII did the true saviour descend on England and give us the leitmotif of the warring roses.

It is arguable that in essence Shakespeare dramatised Yorkist rather than Tudor propaganda. Its relevance to Shakespeare and his contemporaries, once more sharply in focus in the 1590s as Queen Elizabeth approached the end of her life with no declared heir apparent, was that it could easily happen again. As Sir Thomas Smith wrote in the early, uneasy years of the reign:

I am afraid to speak, and I tremble to think what murders and slaughters, what robbing and rifling, what spoiling and burning, what hanging and heading, what wasting and destroying, civil war should bring in, if ever it should come.[7]

Richmond's prayer for peace at the very end of *Richard III*, and thus at the very end of the cycle depicting eighty-eight years of disorder, spoke directly to contemporaries;

> *Abate the edge of traitors, gracious Lord*
> *That would reduce these bloody days again,*
> *And make poor England weep in streams of blood.*[8]

The plays were not about a remote and irrelevant past; they were about a possible present or near future. In the event James I succeeded Elizabeth I without conflict. Yet England wept in streams of blood forty years later.

In time other influences overlaid the immediately political foundation of the received view of the fifteenth century. The Reformation provided an additional reason for English men and women to distance themselves with relief from the world which preceded Henry VIII. For had not that king reformed religion, destroyed popery and driven out corruption and superstition? Fifteenth-century England had thus been morally and spiritually corrupt as well as politically self-destructive. Tyndale and Foxe, writing in the early Reformation, annexed Tudor propaganda to protestant propaganda, claiming, with little regard to historical accuracy, that the blood of Englishmen flowed from the rejection of Wycliffe and the murder of the king who had heeded him.[9]

The Renaissance, too, came to separate the fifteenth from later centuries. The triumph of the new learning, humanism, in the sixteenth century led generations of educated men and women to perceive the fifteenth century as marking the end of the middle ages; that dark and barbaric era that stretched interminably between the fall of Rome and the rebirth of learning (in England) in the early sixteenth century. A sharp line was drawn between the medieval and the modern. And, for convenience, the accession of Henry VII in 1485 neatly met requirements. Thereafter light followed dark, knowledge ignorance, and civilisation barbarity. By the eighteenth century the image was fixed of the fifteenth century as the nadir of the medieval centuries. The English had become a people incapable of civil government, sunk in superstition, living in a profound darkness. They were only to be rescued by the necessary corrective of Tudor firmness of purpose, the recovery of true religion and the restoration of learning.[10]

The Whig Interpretation

To this perception of a now distant past was added a further notion that England's growing commercial and industrial wealth had brought forward, even in the sixteenth century, a middle class which displaced the old feudal aristocracy. The fifteenth century was marked off by social change as well. It was the last of the feudal centuries. Even the counterbalance of romanticism, the gothic revival of the early nineteenth century, the High Church movement and renewed interest in the origins and development of the English constitution found the fifteenth century wanting. The heroic age of chivalry, the soaring achievements of cathedral architecture, the dedicated zeal of the monastic orders, and the foundations of representative government all lay earlier in the medieval centuries; the fifteenth by this comparison too was decadent, decayed and debased. All this was absorbed into what emerged as the 'Whig Interpretation', perceiving the past through the lens of the confident, reforming, middle-class, protestant Englishman of the mid-nineteenth century. Something of its nature is revealed in the dedicatory epistle, or brief historical essay, written by Bulwer Lytton as a preface to his novel on Warwick the Kingmaker, *The Last of the Barons*. Writing of the early sixteenth century he comments

> We behold in that social transition, the sober Trader – outgrowing the prejudices of the rude retainer or the rustic franklin, from whom he is sprung – recognising sagaciously and supporting sturdily the sectarian interests of the mighty Middle Class in which our modern civilisation . . . has established its stronghold.[11]

England was saved by the alliance of this mighty middle class with the new Tudor dynasty. The middle class, a champion of 'measured and thoughtful notions of liberty' (as opposed to 'the restless and ignorant movement of a democratic principle')[12] believed deeply in the force of progress, spiritual and moral as well as material, which it was England's destiny as God's chosen people to bring to the rest of the world. Against this the fifteenth century made a poor showing. Bishop Stubbs encapsulated the learned view of the century in a tortured passage at the very end of his *Constitutional History of England*, first published in 1878:

> The Historian turns his back on the middle ages with a brighter hope for the future . . . He recognizes the law of progress of this world, in which the evil and debased elements are so closely intermingled with the noble and beautiful. However progressive the evil might have been, the power of good is more progresive and more prolific . . . The most enthusiastic admirer of medieval life must grant that all that was good and great in it was languishing even to death; and the firmest believer in progress must admit that as yet there were few signs of returning health. The sun of the Plantagenets went down in clouds and thick darkness; the coming of the Tudors gave as yet no promise of light; it was 'as the morning spread upon the mountains', darkest before dawn.[13]

Stubbs's view of the fifteenth century drew heavily on received perceptions from the enlightenment, deploying the same metaphors of night and darkness, languishing and death before dawn and rebirth. Yet he was of the first generation of professional historians. The first university school of history was established in Oxford in 1850. Until then formal univeristy education in the arts had been solely in the classics, in which, of course, ancient Greek and Roman history was read. But English history was not perceived as a separate, rigorous discipline. It was written by essayists and men of letters, men such as Lytton or Macauley. But even before the school of history was established at Oxford, learned societies, most notably the Camden Society, were beginning to publish editions of medieval texts and the Rolls Series, established in 1857, began to publish and make available for research on a scholarly basis the materials deposited in the Public Record Office. Stubbs, a consummate researcher, drew upon a considerable body of new evidence. Nevertheless, his interest being firmly focused on the origin and development of the English constitution, a model for all the world, he found only evidence to confirm and enhance the view that the fifteenth century, after the failure of a premature Lancastrian Constitutional Experiment in its first decade, had been backsliding and regressive.[14]

The first fruits of modern historical research in the nineteenth century served only to entrench the historical tradition. Charles Plummer, in researching the background to Sir John Fortescue's *Governance of England*, found that the high ideals of feudalism had been debased by money payments and that a 'bastard' feudalism had emerged which only fostered corruption and undermined the rule of law. Fifteenth-century English society was morally degenerate and rotten to the core, a view popularised by William Denton in 1888.[15] The tradition had stood for almost four centuries; by the end of the nineteenth century it was stronger and more comprehensive than it had ever been. But whereas in 1600 the fifteenth century still represented a possible future, in 1900 it represented a shameful past from which the English nation had extricated itself and from which the rest of world could learn. If England had escaped from anarchy, superstition and barbarity, so too, under her stewardship, could the subject peoples of her Empire.

Twentieth-century revision

All flesh is grass; and so was the Empire. During the twentieth century the Whig Interpretation and much that it represented has withered. The fifteenth century has been revalued and reassessed. Many influences have been at work. One, and an element neither to be overlooked nor to be laboured, is the transformation of the world in which we live and think; phrases such as 'the decline of certainty' and 'post-industrial society' might come to mind. The twentieth century has been not a little unlike the fifteenth century of tradition, brutal and barbaric. It is inconceivable that at the end of one, the historian of the other could so effortlessly assume the smug superiority of a Victorian. But there are other more direct and measurable reasons for the wholesale revision which has engulfed, and continues unabated to engulf, the study of fifteenth-century English history.

While the traditional view of the century still dominated, and Stubbs occupied the moral high ground of constitutional history, others in the later nineteenth century, who were beginning to explore economic and social history, saw the century in a different light. It had been taken for granted, authenticated by such as Sir Thomas Smith, that the fifteenth century was an age of economic and social distress too. Smith colourfully wrote:

> England at the latter end of Henry VI's reign was almost a very chaos: parishes decayed, churches fell down, towns were desolate, ploughed fields waxed groves, pastures were made woods, almost half England by civil war slain, and those which remained not sure, but in moats and castles or lying in routs and heaps together.

Modern economic historians find the causes of the recession of which Smith was aware elsewhere than in the deposition of Richard II. They also stress that the civil wars largely passed by the common people. The roots of this reassessment lay in the concern for the condition of the working classes in the wake of industrialisation and in the rise of the labour movement. In 1874, J. R. Green, while acknowledging that 'there are few periods in our annals from which we turn with such weariness and disgust as from the Wars of the Roses', suggested that 'the trading and agricultural classes' enjoyed a general tranquillity and prosperity.[16] This was a view confirmed ten years later by J. Thorold Rogers, one of the first labour MPs, on the basis of an exhaustive study of records of wages and prices. What he revealed was that wage-earners in fifteenth-century England enjoyed a standard of living higher than it had ever been before and was again to be until the eighteenth century. This conclusion was reinforced in the early twentieth century by C. L. Kingsford who pointed out in an influential esssay entitled 'Social Life and the Wars of the Roses' that civil war barely touched most of the people most of the time; and has been subsequently expanded in a continuous series of local studies drawing upon surviving manorial records. It is now accepted that political upheaval, the strife between the houses of Lancaster and York, did *not* reduce England to 'a very chaos' and that, on the contrary, because of the relative shortage of labour and tenants, the standards of living of wage-earners and small-scale farmers improved.[17]

The early interest in the history of labour was, of course, linked to the 'ignorant movement' of socialism. It was soon subsumed in another meta-narrative: the Marxist interpretation. Karl Marx proposed that all history was the history of class struggle; that there were always at any one time two classes, one in control of the means of production, the other being exploited as the producers. In feudal society the aristocracy owned the land; the peasantry, unfree as serfs, worked it. This order was undermined by the growth of capitalism and the emergence of the bourgeoisie which in time displaced the feudal nobility. Marx's perception of the pattern of history, with its heightened awareness of the onward march of Lytton's 'mighty middle class' in the nineteenth century was one remove from the English Whig Interpretation. Marx too 'recognised the law of progress in this world', but it was a progess of a specific kind leading ultimately to the triumph of the proletariat.

Marx's theoretical framework was a major inspiration for several late-medieval historians in the early and mid twentieth century. Their principal concerns were to establish the mechanisms of class conflict and attempt to establish the precise stages of the transition from feudalism to capitalism, which complex process began to unfold in the later middle ages. Relatively straightforward was the decline of serfdom. It virtually disappeared during the fifteenth century. Peasants took advantage of favourable economic circumstances to assert their freedom, not primarily in major revolts, but day-to-day by local action and negotiation. But more problematic was the origin and roots of capitalism. Did it emerge from international trade and the creation of a mercantile elite, who nevertheless tended to use their wealth to buy themselves land, to abandon their bourgeois origins and join the aristocracy? Or did it emerge from within rural and small-town society as artisans and traders prospered from a marginal rise in consumer demand? And how did the landed elite react? Was its power, its social and political control in any way diminished at this stage?[18]

It was in addressing this last question, in undertaking an anatomy of the late-medieval landed elite as a social class, that K. B. McFarlane (1900–66), early in his career deeply influenced by Marxist thought, came to exert a fundamental influence on the interpretation of fifteenth-century political history. Educated himself in the Stubbsian tradition, he was profoundly distrustful of the notion that the era was debased or decayed and aware that, from the fifteenth-century perspective, the aristocracy had centuries of dominance ahead of them. Methodologically and conceptually he was most influenced by Lewis Namier, whose *Structure of Politics on the Accession of George III* was first published in 1929. Namier, working from collective biographies of the lords and commons, argued that party strife was of little relevance in 1760. The dynamics were provided by competing political connections seeking office and advancement; ideology played only a small role compared with the distribution of royal patronage by ministers of the crown. McFarlane saw parallels with the fifteenth-century world with which he was familiar; a world in which politicians were by historians as casually labelled Lancastrian or Yorkist as in the eighteenth century they were Whig or Tory. Moreover, he discerned the dominance of patronage and clientage. He reviewed and revised the concept of bastard feudalism, perceiving in the late-medieval baronial retinue a similar organism to the eighteenth-century connection. It was not the canker in the body politic perceived by Plummer.

The English nobility in the fifteenth century, McFarlane concluded, was neither divided against itself nor was it collectively destroyed by the Wars of the Roses. No middle class emerged to challenge its sway. No new monarchy emerged at the end of the century. Civil war had occurred because one particular king, Henry VI, was unfit for his office and lost his throne as a result; the restoration of royal authority was achieved by traditional means by kings (Edward IV and Henry VII) asserting their personal authority. Albeit that McFarlane's early intellectual stimuli were Marxist, his root and branch revision of the interpretation of late-medieval politics and society was essentially conservative. It emphasised the persistence of aristocratic dominance and the personal nature of political relationships. However, he neither encompassed his grand project of an anatomy of the late medieval nobility, nor completed the demolition of the Whig Interpretation of the fifteenth century. These tasks were left in the hands of those who followed in a transformed professional environment.[19]

Until the last third of the twentieth century, historical research in the field of fifteenth-century English history was restricted to a handful of scholars in barely more than three universities: Cambridge, London and Oxford. The opportunities for university education itself were severely limited. Only since 1964 have they expanded dramatically; with expansion has come a significant increase in the size of the academic historical profession. Concurrently the twentieth century has witnessed a transformation of training in historical research, adopted and adapted from German and French models, and focusing on the doctoral degree. The systematic analysis of documents this demands, has led to a more sceptical and probing approach to the quality of the evidence provided by them. It has also encouraged the development of new techniques and the application of concepts and approaches borrowed from related disciplines.

In the 1940s McFarlane established what today would be called a post-graduate school in late-medieval history at Oxford. His students, and their students (and now even the students' students) took up posts in the expanding university world. Consequently, the numbers of post-graduate students rose steadily in the 1960s, 70s and 80s. Thus from being a neglected and unregarded field of history in the early part of the century, with a few marginalised practitioners, as a result of the fortuitous conjunction of the growth of career opportunities and the influence of a particular scholar, fifteenth-century historical studies have flourished.

The fifteenth century is now one of the most intensely studied of the medieval centuries. Its transformation has been carried forward by the rapid expansion of academic publishing, and the particular interest of some of the newer presses. The volume of works written on fifteenth-century history in the last third of the twentieth century must surely surpass the volume of everything written in all the preceding years. One phenomenon has been the specially commissioned collection of essays, often the proceedings of conferences. Since 1972 at least forty collections of essays have been published which in their entirety, or in part, contain papers on the fifteenth century.

Another feature has been the multiplication of textbooks and general histories since the publication of E. F. Jacob's Oxford History, *The Fifteenth Century*, in 1961. Some encompass the century in general surveys of the later middle ages starting as early as the thirteenth century, notably M. H. Keen's *England in the Later Middle Ages* of 1973; others have focused only on part of the century, several on 'The Wars of the Roses'. Some take 1485 as the end, some 1509 and one, J. A. F. Thomson's *The Transformation of Medieval England* (1983), stretches it from 1370 to 1529. And yet others link the late fifteenth and early sixteenth centuries, most influentially C. S. L. Davies's *Peace, Print and Protestantism, 1450–1558*, published in 1976. The year 1969 marked a watershed. Up to and including Wilkinson's *The Later Middle Ages in England*, as the author revealed in his judgement on Henry IV that he had 'set England's face once more towards her destiny of reconciling liberty and order in the modern state',[20] the interpretation offered was traditional. Published also in 1969, the first edition of J. R. Lander's *Conflict and Stability in Fifteenth-Century England*, in its third edition still the best short introduction to the century, set out for the first time the new perception. A year later, F. R. H. Du Boulay's complementary positive assessment of late medieval English society, *An Age of Ambition*, carried an opening chapter entitled 'The Myth of Decline'.

The sources

A third reason for the explosion of fifteenth-century studies has been the availabilty of a rich seam of untapped source material. This might seem paradoxical, since the fragmentary and imperfect nature of the evidence has often been stressed. There is no single authoritative contemporary chronicle of the whole or greater part of the century to which the historian can turn for the central narrative. The great St Albans chronicle tradition was not sustained after the early part of the century. To some extent this is an advantage since a dominant voice, as that of Mathew Paris for the thirteenth century, can unwittingly mislead. The fifteenth-century historian has to reconstruct the narrative thread from what J. R. Lander vividly described as:

> a web of shreds and tatters, patched up from meagre chronicles and from
> a few collections of letters in which exaggerated gossip and wild rumours
> have been, all too often, confused with facts.[21]

But there are many narrative sources. They might be incomplete and unreliable, and, even after careful evaluation, leave uncertainty and contradiction, yet the essential chronology has been established from their pages. While, frustratingly, too little is often known about the motives of the principal protagonists, they can sometimes be deduced from their actions. The principal drawback of the narrative sources is that they reflect the partisanship of the times in which they were composed, usually a few years after the events. Thus the main accounts of the deposition of Richard II are Lancastrian in slant;

of the last years of Henry VI predominantly Yorkist; and of Richard III, as is well-known, Tudor. But in a more subtle way, the principal accounts of Henry V are slanted heavily in his favour. Because of the incompleteness and partiality of the narrative sources, interpretation of the history of the century cannot be anything but tentative, uncertain and sometimes controversial.[22]

Behind the narrative accounts lies the wealth of royal government records preserved in the Public Record Office, many of them printed. These include the archives of the great offices of state – Chancery, Privy Seal and Exchequer – copies of treaties and diplomatic correspondence, the official record of parliament and the law courts, and the financial accounts of the Crown's own estate, and estates which came into its hands. While this material exists in substantial quantity, it nevertheless remains incomplete. Thus the records of parliament do not include debates; they are largely the record of the acts passed. Only occasionally does more revealing information survive of what was discussed and said during an assembly. Fortunately minutes of council meeting of the minority and early majority of Henry VI have survived, but these were generated for exceptional circumstances, and for the most part the deliberations of the king's advisors are unrecorded. The surviving records of proceedings of the criminal law, much of them still to be examined in detail, are richer for the fifteenth than earlier centuries, but they are primarily copies of the indictments, or accusations; few cases for the defence or judgements are to be found. Nevertheless the public records are a rich source which amplify the narrative accounts of contemporaries. They frequently add detail to our knowledge of events and they occasionally enable us to correct, or resolve, contradictions concerning chronology. And they are full of detail of the routine relationships between Crown and subject which chroniclers rarely knew or were not interested in reporting.

Subjects kept records too. Landholders, lay and clerical, maintained archives in which they preserved their title deeds and related legal documents, the proceedings of their manorial courts and their estate accounts. Those of the laity, small as well as great, have survived in greater numbers for the fifteenth century than for earlier. And they wrote letters to each other. Four major collections of letters from the fifteenth century have survived, the earliest surviving family letters in England: those of the Celys (wool merchants), the Stonors, Plumptons and above all the Pastons (all gentry from different parts of the kingdom). And while their own copies, or drafts, have largely disappeared, proven copies of the wills of all classes of people are to be found in increasing number in the registers of the ecclesiasical probate courts. Religious houses, cathedral chapters, university colleges and boroughs kept records too, often preserved more carefully than by private individuals. Private records, like the public, but less frequently, amplify the political narrative. Their value, however, lies primarily in the broad field of economic and social history.

Recent trends

The fifteenth century nevertheless remains less fully documented than the sixteenth, let alone later centuries. But it is probably more broadly documented than the fourteenth or earlier centuries. It has been the realisation of the richness of these sources, unregarded by earlier generations, and their detailed exploration over the last four or five decades which has finally undermined the traditional picture of the fifteenth century. In using these sources late twentieth-century historians initially took two routes to which the documents led and McFarlane's work pointed. One has been to concentrate on the operation of patronage and clientage thoughout society; to take further the emphasis on politics, central and local, as the pursuit of self-interest and advancement. This has been done through the minute examination of the management of crown patronage from the public records and through the creation of detailed biographies of the pursuants and recipients. The stress has been functional and structural, stressing the timelessness and unexceptionality of fifteenth-century politics as the pursuit of power and the art of the possible. The other emphasis has been on local and provincial studies. It began with baronial families and moved on to counties as a focal point for studying the gentry. There is scarce a baronial family, or county, of fifteenth-century England which has not found its historian in the last thirty years. But again the emphasis has been on patronage and clientage, the operation of bastard feudalism, and the relationships between Crown and subject, court and country.[23]

In the last decade of the twentieth century, however, dissatisfaction has been expressed at what has been seen by some as an over-emphasis on patronage. A call has been made for a return to constitutional history and a fuller recognition of the role played by ideologies and principles in fifteenth-century politics. This is not an attempt to revive the traditional view, but primarily to warn that historians since the mid-twentieth century have gone too far down the road in perceiving the century in terms of the politics of the pork barrel. Fifteenth-century politicians, it is stressed, thought and acted within a clearly established constitutional framework. Issues like the effectiveness of law enforcement, or the legitimacy of the ruling dynasty's title to the Crown, or the Crown's capacity to serve the common weal were of political significance. In some quarters this has gone further to suggest that, especially in mid-century, the springs of political action were essentially altruistic; a point of view that is unlikely to receive universal support.[24]

Other new directions have also been taken. Recent interest in women's history, the recognition that the history of the fifteenth century, in common with other periods, has been written from the perspective of the male (by no means always by men), has made its mark. Women, the greater part of the population, were not just hidden from the history of the fifteenth century, they were to a large extent excluded, just as they were from its public life. Also believed to be excluded from the political process were the majority of men. This assumption too is now being challenged. Political participation extended down the social scale beneath the landed elite on which political history has always focused to middling sorts in town and country who were enjoying a degree of new prosperity in the century. Thirdly the spiritual and intellectual life of the century has been revalued in a more positive light, avoiding the hindsight and prejudice of protestants and humanists. Certain characteristics of English society in the century can be seen in a more forward-looking, even more 'progressive' slant, giving a new dimension to C. L. Kingsford's alternative whiggish thesis that the promise of the century ran counter to the prejudice of its traditional interpretation.[25]

Far more is now known of fifteenth-century England, provinces as well as the capital, country as well as the court, women as well as men, all social classes and not just the landed elite than was ever known before. Historians of the fifteenth century are agreed that the old Whig perception is no longer tenable. But they cannot now agree an alternative overview or paradigm, and they are unlikely to do so in the near future, especially on the balance between self-interest and ideology. Controversy is set to continue over major issues of interpretation; on whether, for instance, the descent into dynastic civil war which dominated the later fifteenth century was in part the result of worsening circumstances and weakening royal power, or entirely the consequence of the inadequacies of a particularly incompetent king.

One reason for continuing debate is that the sources do not answer all the questions. The career of Richard III is an obvious case. It is highly unlikely that new evidence will come to light to solve the mystery of the Princes in the Tower, or resolve the conundrum of his actions and motives. With other issues the difficulties lie in the sources themselves. The records of the criminal courts suggests an apparently alarming crime rate. But closer inspection reveals the record to be of reported alleged crime, not actual crime, often alleged in the graphic terms of riot (sometimes even collusively) so as to secure a speedier settlement of a property dispute than was available elsewhere. For a century which is a byword for lawlessness it is exceptionally difficult to gauge the exact level and scale of the problem. And what is one to make of the frequent recourse to arbitration during the century? Does this reveal a sophisticated awareness of the benefits of reconciliation over going to law? Or does it highlight the failure of the Crown to provide impartial justice?[26]

Regardless of the quality of the sources, however, it is in the nature of historical study that interpretation of the past is discussed, debated and disputed. No two historians will interpret the same evidence in identical ways. The greater the number of historians, the greater is the likely range of perceptions. The earlier concept of a 'scientific' history, whereby the facts were ultimately knowable, and there was always a right answer waiting to be found if not already known, has been discarded. The evidence of the past is being constantly reviewed and rethought in the light of the present. History is not the same as the past. What is past is done: the discourse of history, to use a fashionable late-twentieth-century formulation, is the sense that those in an ever-moving present make of the ever-growing past. While it is a commonplace of historical rhetoric to talk of studying the past on its own terms, or for its own sake, neither is possible; the claims are but devices to give greater credence to an historian's interpretation.

Recently this recognition of subjectivity, of the inseparability of the historian from the subject about which he or she writes, has been taken further under the influence of French linguistic theorists. Postmodernism has reduced all knowledge to the relative. The only reality is the language in which a text is written; nothing lies behind it other than what the reader discerns, not even what the author intended. Thus the reader of the text is the author of the text. This nostrum of Roland Barthes is applicable in the study of history equally to the sources which the historian uses as to all the writings drawing upon them. The past has no meaningful, independent, objective existence; and history is but another form of story-telling, its stories validated by reference to other stories which were constructed at the time. An historical narrative, such as that with which this work is largely concerned, is made up of a patchwork of such stories sewn together. And the construction of those stories is deeply influenced by our common stock of recurring stories and stereotypes. Any narrative, however, is also part of a metanarrative, either explicit or implicit, by which it is partly shaped. Thus the 'Whig Interpretation' of English history was such a metanarrative, into which the traditional narrative of the fifteenth century was fitted and by which it was shaped. So too was the Marxist interpretation; the revisionist view inspired by McFarlane; and now the newly proposed constitutional history. Any piece of historical writing, whether in its component parts or its grand sweep, is thus culturally determined.

In so far as the postmodern approach to historical knowledge is concerned, the reader of the above passage (as of the work as a whole) is, of course, the true author and will make of it what he or she will. The writer of this text, for his part, is not entirely convinced by postmodernism, although he has to admit to being attracted by metanarratives. He can, metaphysically as it were, see the logic of the argument. But while the past is clearly no longer in existence, it was once, and he still believes that it is the function of the historian to endeavour to understand that past and communicate his understanding to the reader. But it is only his, imperfect, understanding;

one understanding among many. It is this which he offers in the pages which follow.

The account of the last century or so of the middle ages which follows has been constructed in the light of, and with the benefit of, the work of innumerable scholars who have collectively reshaped our understanding of a century once considered too shocking for one's wives, or servants, to contemplate. It is an attempt to provide a summary of the state of learning on the subject as it stands at the end of the twentieth century. It is organised conventionally in three parts, the first offering a narrative of the politics of Lancastrian England, 1399–1461; the second a discussion of English society in the century; and the third the politics of Yorkist and Early Tudor England.

Notes and references

1   Sellar and Yeatman, *1066 and All That*, 54.

2   Shakespeare, *Richard II*, Act IV, Sc. I, 142–4.

3   Idem, *Richard III*, Act V, Sc. IV, 36–9.

4   Strype, *The Life of the Learned Sir Thomas Smith*, 221–2; cited by Aston, 'Wars of the Roses', 283.

5   Hall, *Lancastre and Yorke*, 1–2.

6   *Rot Parl*, 464.

7   Strype, *Sir Thomas Smith*, 216; Aston, 'Wars of the Roses', 283.

8   Shakespeare, *Richard III*, V, IV, 48–50.

9   Aston, 'Wars of the Roses', 292–5.

10   Watts, 'Introduction: History, the Fifteenth Century and the Renaissance', 8–18.

11   Lytton, *The Last of the Barons*, iv.

12   Ibid., v.

13   Stubbs, *The Constitutional History*, 3, 632.

14   Carpenter, 'Before and After McFarlane', 175–81.

15   Plummer, introduction to Fortescue, *Governance of England*, 1–30; Denton, *England in the Fifteenth Century*, 115–19.

16   Green, *History of the English People*, 288–90; Rogers, *Six Centuries*, 240–2, 326, 334.

17   Kingsford, *Prejudice and Promise*, 48–77.

18   See especially the work of Hilton, including *Bond Men Made Free, English Peasantry* and *Class, Conflict and the Crisis of Feudalism.*

19   Carpenter, 'Before and After McFarlane', 185–93; Cooper, 'Introduction' to McFarlane, *Nobility.* For a late example of the use of the terms 'Lancastrian' or 'Yorkist' to identify fiftenth-century MPs as members of one or other 'political party' see, Wedgwood, *History of Parliament. Biographies*, xiv.

20   Wilkinson, *Later Middle Ages*, 249.

21   Lander, *Crown and Nobility*, 94.

22   See further reading.

23   See below, pp. 243–51.

24   See below pp. 251–3.

25   See below chs 7, 8 and 9.

26   See below, pp. 241–2.

PART ONE

LANCASTER

CHAPTER ONE

The Lancastrian revolution, 1399–1403

The usurpation of the throne

John of Gaunt, duke of Lancaster, died on 3 February 1399. According to malicious gossip, he was wasted by syphilis and prematurely worn out by a life devoted to debauchery.[1] Clerical moralists may have drawn comfort from such apparently divine retribution, but the real significance of the event was political. Gaunt's death set in motion the course of events which led before the end of the year to the deposition of the king, Richard II, and the coronation of his son as Henry IV. A revolution followed which determined the shape and direction of English politics for more than a century.

The events of 1399 were far from inevitable. When his father died Henry Bolingbroke, duke of Hereford, was in exile. Bolingbroke's exile was the culmination of a long history of conflict between subject and king closely bound up with the political and constitutional crises that had dominated Richard II's reign since 1386. Henry had been one of the five Appellants (so called because they had 'appealed' the king's principal ministers of treason) who had sought to control the young king in 1386–8, even threatening to depose him. Although in more recent years the king had appeared more willing to forgive and forget the humiliation he had suffered at their hands, in 1397 he had struck back and had taken revenge on three of them – the duke of Gloucester, the earl of Warwick and Archbishop Arundel of Canterbury. Bolingbroke and Thomas Mowbray, duke of Norfolk, the other two, had sided with the king and had been rewarded with their dukedoms. A few months later, so Bolingbroke reported to the king, Mowbray suggested to him that they were to be the next victims and urged that they protect themselves. But Mowbray denied the accusation. Whether true or not, the king took advantage to punish them both. Before the issue could be settled by trial by combat, the king exiled Mowbray for life and Bolingbroke for ten years, reduced to six in response to Gaunt's plea. Bolingbroke's more lenient treatment owed much to the favour enjoyed by his father and to his own royal blood. His father was the second son of Edward III and the king's uncle. Royal clemency to Bolingbroke was extended further when he was issued letters patent authorising him to receive the income of his father's extensive estate should Lancaster die while he was still in exile. Nevertheless, the prospect of even six years comfortable exclusion from England did not endear the king to Bolingbroke who had not been proved guilty of any offence.[2]

John of Gaunt's death, following so soon after the exile of his son, presented Richard II with an uncomfortable dilemma. On the one hand he could honour his promise to Henry, now duke of Lancaster, and allow him to enjoy the wealth and power of his inheritance *in absentia*. But he would thereby expose himself to the risk that Lancaster would exploit his new position to raise rebellion. Alternatively he could break his word, deny Henry his inheritance, and seek to render him powerless. The second course had much to commend it. Since 1397 Richard, who had earlier in his reign found it difficult to establish his personal authority, had built up an apparently impregnable power in England. He had destroyed his magnate enemies. He had redistributed their estates and local power into the hands of a group of newly created dukes dependent on and loyal to him. He had secured the compliance of parliament and the vote of customs revenue for life. He was at peace with France and was unlikely in the foreseeable future to need to turn to parliament again for taxation. He had built up his own powerful retinue and in the Cheshire archers had recruited a small standing army. What was Bolingbroke against this?

Accordingly on 18 March Richard II revoked his letters guaranteeing the Lancastrian inheritance and banished Bolingbroke for life. At the same time he persuaded his ally at the French court, the duke of Burgundy, to place Henry under house arrest. The Lancastrian inheritance was confiscated and distributed among his prominent supporters, the dukes of Aumerle, Exeter and Surrey and the earl of Wiltshire. Lancaster's agents in England, seeking to secure the inheritance for their master, were denounced as tratiors. The destruction of Lancaster was intended to be the final step along the king's road to freedom from the magnate intervention and constraint that had plagued him for most of his reign. In fact it was destined to be the first step along the road to his own destruction.[3]

A combination of over-confidence, misjudgement and bad luck destroyed Richard II. He undertook an expedition to Ireland in the summer of 1399. In Ireland Richard had won something of the renown which his father and grandfather had enjoyed as military leaders. His previous expedition there and settlement in 1395 had offered some compensation for the setbacks in France. In 1398 a rebellion seriously threatened the achievement of 1395. In the spring of 1399, therefore, the king was preoccupied with raising a new army and mounting a new expedition to bring the Irish to heel. On 29 May he set sail, leaving his uncle Edmund, duke of York, as regent, utterly confident that Henry Bolingbroke was no threat.[4]

But even as Richard set sail for Ireland, events in France turned against him. The duke of Burgundy was ousted and his rival, the duke of Orleans, seized power at the court of Charles VI. Within two weeks Orleans and Bolingbroke formed an alliance. Orleans agreed to support Bolingbroke in an invasion of England; Bolingbroke agreed to make concessions in Aquitaine should he be successful. The expedition was quickly mounted to take advantage of Richard's absence in Ireland. It was therefore a tiny force that made its landing at Ravenspur at the mouth of the Humber at the very beginning of July. But it was skilfully and decisively led and enjoyed the initial advantage of surprise. The duke of York knew of the threat by 28 June when he took steps to strengthen the defences of the south coast. Bolingbroke encouraged him to expect a major landing in Sussex by installing Sir John Pelham in Pevensey. However Henry himself sailed to Yorkshire accompanied by the archbishop of Canterbury and his close companions in exile, Richard, earl of Arundel, Lord Cobham, Sir Thomas Erpingham, Sir John Norbury and Sir Thomas Rempston. They were welcomed by Sir Robert Waterton and other senior officials of the duchy of Lancaster in the county. Henry declared that he had returned solely to recover his right in the duchy and to reform the government. To emphasise the first he immediately marched north to secure Pickering, then west to Knaresbrough, before finally turning south to Pontefract. He faced little resistance, partly because the justness of his proclaimed cause was recognised and partly because in four months the new possessors of these Yorkshire lordships had not yet been able to install their own officers and win the loyalty of the tenants. At Pontefract thirty-seven knights and esquires of the Lancasrtrian retinue, summoned mainly from Yorkshire and Lancashire, mustered to proclaim their new duke and support his cause. A day or two later the army was reinforced at Doncaster by the earls of Westmorland and Northumberland and Northumberland's famed son, Sir Henry 'Hotspur' Percy. It was now a formidable force.

Richard II in Ireland heard news of his enemy's successful landing at about the time that Bolingbroke was at Doncaster. It was imperative for him to return to England as soon as possible. There is some evidence of divided counsel, indecision and unnecessary delay, but what defeated Richard was the sheer logistics of halting a campaign, regathering his forces, requisitioning ships and transporting his army back across the sea. It was probably because he appreciated the need to secure his stronghold in Cheshire and North Wales that he sent the earl of Salisbury ahead, while he set out from Waterford on 24 July with the main body. His intention seems to have been to land in South Wales and to join forces with the duke of York, raising troops in the southern counties. It was all to no avail. Not only did Bolingbroke intercept York before Richard landed, but also the royal fleet was scattered so that the king made landfall with only a remnant of his troops at Carmarthen on 29 July.

Henry likewise knew that speed was essential. While Richard was crossing the Irish Sea, he marched rapidly south for Bristol. On 27 July the duke of York and his army, perhaps outnumbered, certainly outmaneouvred, defected to him. Two days later Bristol fell and three of Richard's principal ministers, the earl of Wiltshire, Sir Thomas Bushy and Sir Henry Green were taken, summarily tried and executed. Wasting no time, the Lancastrian army immediatley turned north in a dash to secure Chester which they did on 8 August. Richard, in the meantime, made his way to Conway where, isolated and powerless, he rejoined the earl of Salisbury who had himself been unable to do no more than take control of North Wales for the king. By 10 August Henry of Lancaster controlled the kingdom. He had won a complete and almost bloodless victory. The king was at his mercy.

Richard II's rapid defeat in July and early August 1399 was first and foremost military and only secondly political. He had taken his most reliable troops to Ireland and had not been able to bring them back to England quickly enough to face Henry in the field. The duke of York had been able to raise his reserves in southern England. The king's retainers and many of his sheriffs had responded to the call to arms. But without the king himself to lead them, and faced with Henry's swift and determined action, they were not called upon to fight. There was sporadic resistance, especially in the Welsh marches, but it was unco-ordinated and too late. Richard's deputy, the unassertive duke of York, who may have had some sympathy for Bolingbroke's cause, preferred to resolve the crisis by compromise rather than confrontation. York may have been persuaded to adopt this stance by the presence of the earl of Northumberland in Henry's host. Northumberland had stood apart from the conflicts of Richard's reign, pursuing his own ambitions in the north. And, unlike Westmorland, he had never been close to the old duke of Lancaster. The duke's interference in the far north had seen to that. But Richard's recent policy in the marches had alienated him. In the last two years the king had sought to weaken the Percy grip on the Scottish borders and had put in his own trusted men.[5] In 1399 he paid the price. Percy support for Lancaster not only brought military strength but also added political respectability.

Whether or not Richard was also generally unpopular and his regime widely detested is hard to discern. It has been frequently argued that after two years of 'tyranny' Richard had alienated his subjects. There is little doubt that his ministers and immediate associates were disliked, as witness the fate of some of them at the hands of the mob early in 1400; that his high-handed actions since 1397 had been widely resented; and that his confiscation of the Lancastrian inheritance had sent shivers down the collective spine of the landed elite.[6] Yet there are reasons to suppose that the king himself nevertheless commanded support. The duke of York had no difficulty in raising an army to face Bolingbroke; what was missing was the king himself to lead them. Pro-Ricardian sentiment lingered long after he was dead, reflected in a sequence of sightings and masqueradings, which were from time to time to trouble Henry IV and which continued into the reign of Henry V. The issue is clouded by the fact that English accounts of his fall were written during the reign of Henry IV and are thus critical, if not hostile. It is possible, however, that many in 1399 were willing to back Bolingbroke in the belief that the king needeed to be curbed, who, had they realised at the time that his throne and life would also be at risk, might have acted in Richard II's defence.[7]

When Bolingbroke landed at Ravenspur he declared that he had come only to recover his duchy of Lancaster. Yet on 13 October he had himself crowned as Henry IV. It is unlikely that he had dissembled from the outset. At the beginning of July he launched on a desperate and speculative venture. He had nothing to lose. He could hardly have foreseen then that he would have had the kingdom in his grasp within six weeks. At first his ambitions were probably restricted, as he proclaimed, to recovering the duchy and securing control of the government. His programme harked back to the programme of the defeated Appellants. There is evidence to suggest that in the early stages of his campaign he intended to use the office of Steward of the Kingdom, to which he had succeeded, to justify his defiance of the king. There were constitutional precedents for the Steward to step in to 'protect' the kingdom from the worst abuses of a king. In so far as he had thought ahead as to what he would do should he defeat and capture the king, it is possible that he initially envisaged himself ruling in the king's name through such a device.[8]

Much was and has been made of Henry's perjury in July and August. On more than one occasion, it was later reported, he swore on oath that he did not seek the throne. In particular, four years later the rebellious Percys are supposed to have claimed that he had sworn such an oath in their presence at Doncaster. But this is a murky business. The evidence of the Percy claim is not contemporary.[9] Even if in 1403 the claim was made, there are obvious reasons why it might have been invented. And even if it is true, there is nothing in the behaviour of any of the Percys in the first year or so of Henry's reign to suggest that it troubled them a jot at the time. The earl of Northumberland, his brother and son were worldly politicans who knew precisely what was what in 1399.

Yet perjury almost certainly did occur in 1399, especially during the negotiations between Henry, Northumberland and Richard on 10–15 August, when the fate of the kingdom was decided. Having installed himself in Chester, Henry received messengers from the king, the dukes of Exeter and Surrey no less, and agreed to send Northumberland as his emissary. Northumberland set out charged to inform the king that Bolingbroke sought merely his reinstatement and the summoning of a parliament under the joint presidency of king and steward to reform the government. This in itself was an unprecedented demand which the king would never have accepted willingly. Only after receiving assurances from Northumberland that Henry did not seek to depose him, did Richard agree to meet him. On 14 August he set out for Chester. At Flint, on 15 August, Henry appeared in strength. Richard, once more assured, now by Archbishop Arundel, that no harm would be done to him, and by Lancaster himself that he only wished to help him govern the kingdom better, surrendered to the duke's protection. From that moment he was a prisoner. On 19 August a parliament was summoned to meet at Westminster on 30 September. Five days later, the administration of Chester having been purged, Lancaster set off for London with Richard under armed guard. Royal orders were now being issued 'by the advice' of the duke and the council; but before the end of August, Henry revealed his decision to depose the king, for a committee was appointed to examine evidence for 'the setting aside of King Richard and of choosing Henry, duke of Lancaster in his stead'. Having entered London in triumph on 1 September, Henry withdrew to Hertford to await the report of his committee.[10]

Henry Bolingbroke did not set out to take the throne in 1399. Perhaps he had not really thought through the possible consequences of his winning such an unexpectedly rapid and complete victory. Hard thinking at Chester in mid-August probably convinced him, however, that there was no sure political alternative to deposition. If he had learnt anything from the past, it was surely that no subject could rule Richard II indefinitely and that in time he would exact retribution for the wrongs done him. Bolingbroke had already gone too far to draw back. Now that he had power, the only chance he had of retaining it was to take the throne for himself and face the consequences. This is likely to have been the advice given by Thomas Arundel, the archbishop of Canterbury, who was constantly at his side throughout July and August. Thus it was only when Henry had Richard in his power that he set in motion the search for a plausible formulation of his legitimate right to be king of England. Had he intended from the outset to make himself king he would have had his claim ready.[11]

Having decided to usurp the throne and having the king in his possession, Henry had to find a fitting public justification and a plausible process by which the crown could be transferred to him. As far as possible the naked illegality of the act had to be clothed. He soon discovered, if he did not know it already, that he did not have a strong hereditary claim to the throne. A search through chronicles and all the other available historical record failed to produce sure evidence that he had a legitimate title. It is possible Henry had hoped that a thorough search might reveal that Edmund Crouchback, his ancestor as earl of Lancaster, had been the eldest son of Henry III. But this could not be proved. An alternative route was followed, so that when the peers and elected representatives gathered at Westminster on 30 September, Henry was ready to present his usurpation of the throne to the assembly. The throne was empty; Richard II, the throng in the hall was informed, had willingly abdicated the day before. What is more, according to the official record, he had told a deputation to the Tower that, had he the power to choose his successor, he would choose the duke of Lancaster. Thirty-two articles condemning Richard's regime were then read out; it was agreed by acclamation that the abdication should be accepted; and a formal deposition was enacted by representatives of the different estates.

Only then, on cue, did Henry of Lancaster come forward and claim that the vacant throne was rightfully his: 'In the name of Father, Son and Holy Ghost, I, Henry of Lancaster, challenge this Realm of England, and the Crown with all its members and appurtenances.' He gave three grounds for his claim. First, he was descended in the right line of blood from Henry III; second, 'through that right', God had sent him to recover it; and third, the realm was on the point of being undone for want of good government. The assembly, being asked individually and collectively to determine his claim, declared that he should be king.[12] Thereupon he occupied the throne. Writs were immediately issued for a new parliament to convene a week later in the same place. Legally, the assembly of 30 September had not been a parliament. It effectively reconvened as a parliament on 6 October. The proceedings of 30 September were then officially recorded.

Henry IV's accession to the throne was carefully stage-managed to give the appearance of strict legality and to maintain continuity from reign to reign. The deposition of Richard II had a clear precedent, on the similar grounds of misgovernment and willing abdication, in the deposition of Edward II. But the right of Henry IV to succeed him was tenuous to say the least. He did not claim to be next in line to the throne. As the son of John of Gaunt, he could have done so by claiming descent through an unbroken male line from Edward III, on the basis of his grandfather's settlement of the crown in tail male in the last year of his reign. But had he done so he would also have denied the right of descent through the female line which underpinned the English claim to the throne of France. In 1399 abandoning Edward III's claim to that throne was unimaginable and for Henry IV personally and politically unthinkable. Hence he resorted to a wide and undefined 'right' descent which carefully avoided direct reference to Edmund Crouchback while suggesting nevertheless that that was its basis. His title might have been strengthened had he been elected by parliament, but this would have entailed a surrender of prerogative that he could not contemplate. An assembly of the estates approved his assumption of the throne, it may indeed have welcomed it, but it did not itself confer the title.[13]

In the circumstances Henry probably secured the best title he could get and he made sure that he received full parliamentary approval for what he had done. Politically the usurpation was successful; the throne was transferred to him without dissent and with its prerogatives intact. Constitutionally the new king's title was fundamentally flawed. Henry himself knew this, and no fewer than four times in the first seven years of the reign sought to protect his legitimacy by parliamentary act. In October 1399 parliament declared that his son Henry, prince of Wales, was his right heir; in the spring of 1404 it swore assent to the principle that he should be succeeded by the issue of all his sons; in June 1406, since aspersions had recently been cast on his right to rule, it was ordained in parliament that he should be succeeded by only the male issue of his sons; and finally in December 1406 this ordinance itself was amended to re-admit the female issue of his sons. In 1404 and 1406 Henry was reacting to the Percy rebellions and attempts to depose him.

But lurking behind the threats of dissident noblemen was the awareness that Henry's title left others with at least as good a claim to the throne, especially the descendants of the earl of March, who before his death in 1398 Richard II had considered nominating his heir. By failing to rule out descent through the female line, and indeed by implicitly himself calling upon it through his own descent from Henry III through his mother Blanche of Lancaster, he left himself and his descendants vulnerable to the claim to a better descent by the Mortimer family through Philippa the daughter of Edward III's second son, Lionel of Clarence. In 1399 the eight-year-old Edmund earl of March could claim to be the legitimate heir of Richard II if, as Henry's challenge implied, descent through the female line were held to be superior to unbroken male descent. Fortunately for Henry the earl of March grew to be a man uninterested in his claim to the throne. However, after his death in 1425, the claim passed to his nephew Richard Plantagenet, third duke of York, who proved, in different circumstances, to be less reluctant to pursue it.

Securing control

The coronation took place with the customary splendour on St Edward the Confessor's day, Monday 13 October. The miraculous phial of oil said to have belonged to St Thomas Becket was used for the first time to anoint the king. The ceremony stressed for the world the divine approval of Henry's right to the throne.[14] At the subsequent banquet in Westminster Hall, the king's champion, Sir Thomas Dymock, clattered in on horseback to challenge any mere mortal who denied that right. According to Adam Usk, who was present, the king answered, 'If need be, Sir Thomas, I shall personally relieve you of that task.'[15] He was not called upon to do so there and then, but perhaps he knew in his bones that soon the need would arise.

Parliament had already assembled and on 14 October, immediately following the coronation, it sat down to business. It was an uncontroversial parliament. Perhaps the unanimity of the proceedings was asssisted by the continued presence of many of the troops who had served Henry in the summer. Henry was voted customs and subsidies for three years until Michaelmas 1402. He did not ask for a new tenth and fifteenth, but was given permission to collect outstanding sums from the last grant to Richard II. At the same time his representatives assured the convocation of Canterbury meeting at St Paul's that he would not tax the clergy unless he faced great necessity. The main business was to repeal the acts of Richard's last parliament and to put the principal supporters of the late king on trial. The dukes of Aumerle, Surrey and Exeter, the marquess of Dorset and the earls of Gloucester and Salisbury were arraigned on 29 October. They pleaded coercion and were treated with leniency. All were degraded and set at liberty. An act was passed condemning the deposed king himself to life imprisonment. Under the terms of the act he was soon moved to the Lancastrian stronghold of Pontefract. Finally Henry's son was created prince of Wales, duke of Cornwall and earl of Chester and took his seat in the Lords. Parliament formally acknowledged him to be heir to the throne.[16]

Parliament was dissolved on 19 November and the remaining companies of the king's armies were disbanded. The king himself withdrew to his manor of Kennington across the river in Surrey on 10 December and a week later travelled down to Windsor to celebrate Christmas.[17] But the king's peace of mind was broken on 4 January when news was brought to him, probably by the earl of Rutland, the duke of York's son, that the degraded lords were plotting to take advantage of a tournament at Windsor on 6 January to enter the castle and seize him and his family. Thus forewarned Henry raised troops in London. The rebels withdrew up the Thames valley. Although they proclaimed that King Richard had been released and was coming to join them, they failed to raise the country and their own troops began to desert them. At Cirencester on 8 January the townspeople turned on the earls of Kent and Salisbury and lynched them; Lord Despenser was killed by a mob in Bristol a week later; and the earl of Huntingdon was murdered at Pleshey. Other lesser participants were arrested and tried before the king at Oxford on 12 January. The Epiphany plot was a disastrous failure and the rising was quickly suppresseed, but its seriousness should not be under-estimated. Support was at hand. Troops were raised in Devon and Cornwall; four former captains of Richard's Cheshire archers raised the county on 10 January. It is puzzling that the plotters did not raise these troops in advance, for it is known that on 2 January Ralph Stathum of Morley in Derbyshire had forewarned various men of the locality to ride with him in the service of the earl of Huntingdon. Had more men been raised in advance, the rebellion might have come closer to success.[18]

The implications of the rebellion for Henry were ambiguous. His policy of leniency towards the erstwhile Ricardian courtiers had failed. Their opposition was no doubt intensified by the loss of favour, but it was founded on personal loyalty to the deposed king. Moreover, the rebellion had revealed that there were men in other parts of England who were prepared to rise in the name of Richard II, not only in the county of Chester. Yet the fate of the Hollands, Montagu and Despenser, murdered by mobs, indicated that the cause of Richard II excited little popular support in central southern England. Nevertheless the rebellion sealed the deposed king's fate. He died on or about 14 February. Adam Usk hinted that he starved himself to death, but the likelihood is that he was murdered.[19]

The Epiphany plot revealed how tenuously Henry held power and how narrowly based was his support. In the first three months the king went to great pains to present himself as a king who would rule with and through the consent of all his subjects. His chancellor had declared at the opening of parliament on 6 October 1399 that it was his will to be guided by the advice of the honourable, wise and discreet persons of his kingdom. First and foremost this implied the greater nobility, the dukes and earls. Yet, especially after the Epiphany plot, there was a notable shortage of such magnates on whom he could call. The duke of York was an ageing man (he died in 1402), and after the events of 1399 a broken reed. His son, Edward, earl of Rutland, was unreliable, as he was to demonstrate. The duke of Norfolk had died in exile in Venice; his son and heir Thomas was still a minor. The earldoms of Kent, Huntingdon and Salisbury were, after the rebellion of 1400, in the king's hands. The earls of Oxford and March were still minors, the earl of Devon was blind, the earl of Suffolk had withdrawn from politics, and Thomas Beauchamp, earl of Warwick, who died in 1401, was another spent force. The young earls of Arundel and Stafford were only just entering the political world. This left but three earls who played a full and active part from the beginning of the reign; the earls of Northumberland, Worcester and Westmorland, and their kinsmen, especially Northumberland's heir Sir Henry Percy (Hotspur) and Westmorland's brother Thomas, Lord Furnival – the Percys and Nevilles. To their number can be added John Beaufort, earl of Somerset, who was the king's half-brother and Westmorland's brother-in-law, and, although degraded in 1399, was quickly brought into favour as King's Chamberlain and proved himself a stalwart supporter of Henry IV. There was a handful of barons who actively supported the regime – Lords Grey of Codnor, FitzHugh, Roos and Willoughby especially – but Henry began his reign with a very small number of adult peers behind him. The same is true of the episcopal bench, with only Thomas Arundel, archbishop of Canterbury, and Henry Beaufort, bishop of Lincoln, closely connected with the Crown from the beginning.

In the circumstances, therefore, it is hardly surprising that Henry fell back on his own close associates of his days as earl of Derby and on the personnel of the duchy of Lancaster. Eight men, five of whom had shared exile with him, were of particular importance: Sir Peter Buckton, Sir Thomas Erpingham, John Norbury, Sir John Pelham, Sir Thomas Rempston, Philip Repington (his confessor), Sir Hugh Waterton and Robert Waterton. Erpingham was his righthand man and the chamberlain of the household. The household itself, with its chamber knights and esquires, drawn from the length and breadth of the kingdom, provided the vital link between court and country through which he could exercise power in the early days. Understandably central government was dominated by Henry's own men. While his first Keeper of the Privy Seal was Richard Clifford, dean of York, who remained in the office he had occupied since 1397, his choice as Chancellor fell on John Scarle, archdeacon of Lincoln, a relatively obscure career civil servant who had been Chancellor of the County Palatine of Lancaster from 1382 to 1395. John Norbury became Treasurer and Thomas Tutbury, one-time treasurer of John of Gaunt's household, was made Keeper of the Wardrobe. Membership of the continual council sitting at Westminster, into whose hands the routine administration of the kingdom was entrusted and to whom the king turned regularly for advice on key political issues, comprised the chief officers of state (chancellor, treasurer and privy seal) as well as John Prophet (Richard II's clerk of the council), the earls of Northumberland, Somerset, Westmorland and Worcester, and a group of knights and esquires of the household, prominent among whom in the early months were John Cheyne, John Doreward and Hugh Waterton, and when the king and his household were in the vicinity of London, Erpingham and Rempson. Three London merchants, William Brampton, John Shadworth and Richard Whittington, were also paid wages as councillors in the first eighteen months of the reign. Attendance, however, was irregular; surviving records suggest an average of seven or eight per meeting. The officers and household men carried the burden. England was controlled by the king's friends.[20]

The realm extended beyond the shores of England and Wales. Henry IV had equally to secure control of the English lordships in Ireland, Calais and Gascony. In 1399, despite the campaign conducted by Richard II in 1395, direct rule in Ireland was restricted to the counties of Dublin, Meath, Louth and Kildare, later formalised as the Pale, and the ports of Wexford, Waterford and Limerick. Beyond these enclaves, authority was exercised by the Anglo-Irish lords, most prominently the earls of Desmond and Ormonde, and further beyond their lordships to the north and west gaelic clans, who rejected English rule. Henry's first concern was to take control of the government in Dublin. On 10 December 1399 he removed John Holland, earl of Kent, and appointed Sir John Stanley as his lieutenant. Stanley had been Richard II's last controller of his household, but he had long-standing links with the new king, having been granted Henry's livery in 1386–7. The administration in Ireland, under the control of the deputy-lieutenant, the archbishop of Meath, had already accepted the new regime; and on 1 April 1400 Henry secured a temporary peace with the leading Irish chieftain, Ard Mac Murchadha, whose rebellion had drawn Richard II to Ireland in 1399, by ceding to him the annuity and inheritance witheld by the late king.[21]

Similarly Henry had no difficulty in securing control of Calais and its defences. Again he appointed a man who transferred his loyalty from Richard II – Sir Peter Courtenay – who took over the captaincy in August 1399, before Richard was deposed. However, Gascony, or those areas in the hinterland of Bordeaux, Bayonne and Dax, the Saintognes and Agenais which still remained in English possession, presented a greater problem. Matters were complicated by the fact that the leading nobles and burgesses of Gascony still loyal to the crown of England had resented the grant of the duchy to John of Gaunt in 1390, and had feared that it was the intention to separate it. Several men, especially prominent factions in Bayonne and Dax, were unwilling to accept the Lancastrian usurpation. Charles VI of France had hopes that there would be widespread defections to him. These did not materialise, but the uncertain situation explains why Henry took the unusual step of appointing a Gascon, Gaillard de Durfort, as his first seneschal. It was not until he and a small group of English officials sailed to Bordeaux in the spring of 1400 that Henry IV was able to assert his authority in the duchy, and even then his situation remained precarious as the French continued to suborn the Gascon nobility.[22]

The revolution threw Anglo-French relations into disarray. After long and exhausting negotiation Richard II had agreed terms with Charles VI at

Leulighem in 1396. The cornerstone of the truce had been the marriage between Richard and Charles' seven-year-old daughter Isabel. Isabel had come to England and instalments of her dowry had been paid; and commissioners had continued to meet regularly at Leulighem to monitor the truce. Charles VI refused to accept the deposition of his son-in-law and the degradation of his own daughter. He would not recognise Henry as king. And although the truce was confirmed by both sides – the French in January 1400, the English not until May – a state of undeclared war soon developed, both in Gascony and at sea, where freebooters and privateers were encouraged by the French. But while Isabel remained in England, and negotiations for her return and the repayment of her dowry dragged out during 1400, no overt breach occurred.[23]

The hostility of France made it all the more important for Henry rapidly to secure alliances with other powers. In the spring of 1401 he concluded a treaty for the marriage of his daughter Blanche with Louis, son and heir of the Holy Roman Emperor, Rupert II, and agreement was reached eighteen months later for the marriage of his youngest daughter, Philippa, with Eric, King of Denmark, the ruler of all Scandinavia. While this second marriage was not celebrated until 1406, Henry successfully established ties with the dominant powers of central and northern Europe, which, along with his renewal of the existing Portuguese alliance, effectively isolated the early threat from France. Thirdly, however, his own marriage by proxy on 3 April 1401 to Joan of Navarre, widow of the duke of Brittany and at the time regent of the duchy, did not bring any further diplomatic advantage because of swift French counter-measures.[24]

This left Scotland, relations with which rapidly deteriorated into open war. Henry declared his intention to invade Scotland before he dissolved parliament in November 1399. Early in October the Scots had taken advantage of the Lancastrian revolution to break the truce and to attack and slight the castle of Wark on Tweed. Negotiations failed when Robert III added insult to injury by addressing Henry as Duke of Lancaster. Henry formed an alliance with the dissident Scottish earl of March and plans were laid for a full-scale invasion, funded by clerical taxes, loans and service without pay by the lay lords. An army of just over 13,000 men (only slightly smaller than the armies which invaded Scotland in 1314, 1335 and 1385, and larger than most of the armies hitherto taken to France) mustered at York in June 1400. Twenty-four peers of the realm and at least 400 retainers, annuitants and fee-holders of the crown, all with their own detachments, as well as 244 men-at-arms of the king's own household in his personal company, were brought together. It was an impressive display of royal strength. In response to an eleventh-hour Scottish bid for peace, Henry ordered research into the English claim to sovereignty and advanced a new demand that the Scots do homage. The English army eventually crossed the Scottish border on 14 August and advanced unopposed to Edinburgh. No attempt was made on the castle and the army was restrained from excessive pillaging. With supplies running out and no enemy to engage, Henry retreated ignominiously back to England in September.[25]

It is not entirely clear why Henry went to war with Scotland in 1400. Possibly, although they insisted on a parliamentary declaration that it was entirely the king's decision, the Percys had pressed for a campaign in Scotland which would advance their own ambitions, thwarted by Richard. Bearing in mind that Henry owed a huge debt to them for their assistance in the usurpation of the throne, this seems a more likely explanation than the alternative that he intended a show of personal strength in the north to counter Percy domination. It is inconceivable that he mounted the expedition against Percy advice. It is likely too that he wished to make a demonstration to the world and his subjects not only that he was fully in command of his own kingdom, but was also the rightful overlord of Scotland. A decisive military victory, had it been achieved, would have cemented the success of his usurpation of the throne, paid the debt to the Percys, impressed his continental neighbours, and discouraged international intrigue. And it is to be remembered that Henry was himself an enthusiastic and renowned soldier.[26]

Parliament and Wales, 1400–2

Any initial optimism engendered by the success of the first year of the new reign was rapidly dispelled in the storm which subsequently engulfed the king. The revolution was almost overturned and the integrity of the kingdom all but destroyed as wave after wave of crises battered the regime after 1400. The troubles began innocuously enough in northern Wales. Using a quarrel with his English neighbour, Lord Grey of Ruthin, as a pretext, the Welsh squire, Owain Glyn Dŵr, heir to the Gruffudd dynasty, proclaimed himself prince of Wales in September 1400. Taking advantage of the absence of many of the local English on military service in Scotland, Owain and his associates attacked their settlements in Denbigh, Ruddlan, Flint, Hawarden, Holt, Oswestry and Welshpool. The king, fearing Ricardian sympathies, immediately on his return from the north conducted a three-week punitive raid through North Wales which, for the time being, restored order.[27]

The campaigns against Scotland and the Welsh proved expensive. Total expenditure in the first fifteen months of the reign had run at nearly £60,000 per annum, as much as in Richard II's last year. In the circumstances, and bearing in mind that Henry had consumed not only the customs revenue granted to him, but also the income from forfeited estates and even Queen Isabel's dowry in the process, it is not surprising that the perceived waste of the campaign was to rebound on him in his next parliament which assembled at Westminster in January 1401. At its opening the king drew attention to the great costs he had and would incur in the recovery of his throne, the Scottish expedition, his march into Wales and in maintaining the defence of France and Ireland. He asked for parliament's assistance, assuring those present that he had no intention to charge more than was absolutely necessary. Members of the commons, however, were unconvinced and after several weeks of haggling were only willing to renew the grant of customs and tunnage and poundage and to vote a subsidy of a tenth and fifteenth on an understanding that Henry would reform his administration. The commons objected to the manner in which Henry had come so rapidly to rely on his own trusted followers, who were inexperienced in royal government.

The concessions wrung from the king by early March were that the principal offices of the household and departments of state and the council seats would be occupied by men of 'honourable estate', who were to hold office until the next parliament and whose names would be declared to parliament. There followed a wholesale change of ministers. Out went the Chancellor, John Scarle, the Treasurer, John Norbury, the Treasurer of the Household, Thomas Tutbury (held principally responsible for the mismanagement of the finances), the Steward of the Household, Sir Thomas Rempson, and its Controller, Robert Litton. In came experienced administrators, all of whom had held office under Richard II: Edward Stafford, bishop of Exeter (Chancellor), Lawrence Allerthorpe (Treasurer), Thomas More (Treasurer of the Household), Thomas Percy, earl of Worcester (Steward of the Household), and Thomas Brounflete (Controller of the Household). These appointments were the king's, but the fact that he now called upon men who had been closely associated with his predecessor's regime, indicates the extent to which he accepted the criticism. Those removed from office, however, were not disgraced: especially Rempson, they continued in high favour.

By men of honourable estate the commons had the nobility and episcopate in mind. And although no list has survived of those nominated to the council by the king, evidence of attendance suggests that after March 1401 the earls of Northumberland, Worcester and Westmorland as well as the bishops of Bangor, Hereford and Rochester were more frequently present. And the establishment of a more aristocratic government is indicated by the appointments of the earl of Somerset as captain of Calais, the earl of Rutland as lieutenant of Guyenne and Prince Thomas as lieutenant of Ireland.[28]

It has been suggested that behind these changes lay something of a bloodless coup organised through parliament by the Percys, who particularly benefited.[29] But early in 1401 they had no need to force themselves on the king. They were still high in favour. Throughout 1400 Thomas, earl of Worcester, had been employed almost continually by the king either on embassies or at council. He appeared to one of the French envoys in November to be the leading councillor. His brother, the earl of Northumberland himself, was much engaged in the far north, but nevertheless had been present at a council that had met on the eve of parliament's assembly. It is more likely that Henry accepted the criticism and advice he received without resentment and acted accordingly. Indeed, the speaker of the house himself, Sir Arnald Savage, who had undertaken the negotiations on behalf of the commons, shortly afterwards entered royal service and was regranted an annuity paid by Richard II. Favour and trust were not imposed on the king.[30]

Another matter to which the king gave his atention during the parliament was the threat perceived to be posed by Lollardy. Lollardy was the heresy associated with the teachings of John Wycliffe (d. 1384) which had taken root in the last two decades. In the last week of February William Sawtry was tried and condemned in convocation as a relapsed heretic. At the same time the statute *De Heretico Comburendo* was passed through parliament to authorise his burning at Smithfield. Henry's willingness to put the state at the service of the Church was in part a concession to clerical support, and to Arundel in particular. It may also have been feared that the Lollards were inclined to favour the king's enemies (Sawtry had been implicated in the Epiphany plot); and playing up the danger of heresy to the political order may have been designed to buttress the legitimacy of the regime. Nevertheless, whatever the motivation behind the passage of the act, it did not lead to intensive persecution.[31]

By taking note of the anxieties of his supporters, lay as well as clerical, Henry secured the financial relief he needed. One necessity was to repay Queen Isabel's dowry and organise her return to France now that negotiations were finally being completed. The cost of escorting her to Leulighem on 31 July came to several thousand pounds. The truce between the two kingdoms was renewed two weeks later, but the return of Queen Isabel removed the principal constraint and the French attacks on English shipping intensified thereafter. While the undeclared war in the Channel and attacks on isolated English outposts in the marches of Gascony were a matter of concern for the government, its main preoccupation was the revolt in Wales which continued unabated.[32]

Over the winter of 1400–1 Hotspur, as Justiciar of North Wales and Chester, with the young prince of Wales in his company, had secured

North Wales. However a daring raid on Good Friday, 1 April, by which Gwilym and Rhys ap Tudor surprised and seized Conway castle, inspired further revolt among the northern Welsh resentful of a stengthened penal code recently imposed on them, and the firm enforcement of English authority by Hotspur and Prince Henry. Glyn Dŵr himself took to the field again in mid-Wales, but, after initial success, was checked by a force led by Edward Charlton, the lord of Powys. Henry himself followed up with a second punitive expedition in October. Glyn Dŵr refused to be drawn into combat, but some rebels were taken and executed, others submitted, the land was ravaged (including the abbey of Strata Florida). Finally the castles of Cardigan and Aberystwyth were reinforced, where the earl of Worcester, appointed lieutenant of South Wales, was left in command. But no sooner had Henry returned to England at the end of the month than Glyn Dŵr appeared again to threaten Welshpool and then Caernarvon and Harlech castles.[33]

The year 1401 drew to a close with the rebellion in Wales no nearer suppression. At this stage, however, the Crown had not lost control and it might still have been possible for Henry to have negotiated a settlement. Indeed contemporary reports suggest that this was the advice of the Percys: one story goes as far as to tell of the earl of Northumberland offering to plead for a pardon if Glyn Dŵr surrendered. It would not be surprising if earl and Hotspur were willing to appease. Their main interests lay in the north – Hotspur himself divided his time between his responsibilities in North Wales and the Scottish border. He had been given command in Wales and Chester to prevent a Ricardian rising, not to counter a Welsh revolt. A settlement with Glyn Dŵr would allow him to concentrate on his northern ambitions. It is possible that he did not press the recovery of Conway because he was prepared to negotiate a return to royal favour for the Tudor brothers who had been retained by Richard II. But for the marcher lords and the king (who was also a marcher lord, beside the father of the prince of Wales) concession was out of the question.[34]

Whatever hopes of a negotiated settlement there might have been evaporated in 1402. Glyn Dŵr won two significant victories: in April, during a raid on Ruthin he ambushed and captured his enemy Lord Grey and more significantly, on 22 June in a rare pitched batttle at Bryn Glas, near Knighton, he defeated and captured Sir Edmund Mortimer, the uncle of the earl of March and Hotspur's brother-in-law. Two months later he swept through South Wales for the first time where the people of Glamorgan and Gwent rose in support. Henry's response on hearing of Mortimer's defeat was to mount an ambitious three-pronged invasion – the prince of Wales in the north from Chester, he himself from Shrewsbury in the centre and the earl of Worcester in the south. The prince of Wales succeeded in revictualling the north Wales castles, but the king's advance was washed out by torrential rain. But it was the capture of Grey and Mortimer, not the king's further humiliation or the extension of the revolt to the south, which immeasurably strengthened Glyn Dŵr's hand. Grey was quickly ransomed, bringing a much-needed injection of cash to the cause. But Henry IV was less willing to bail Mortimer out. Dramatically, Mortimer threw in his lot with the rebels. He married one of Glyn Dŵr's daughters and in December declared in a letter to his tenants that he had joined the rebellion so as to restore Richard II, or if he were dead, recover the throne for the rightful heir, his nephew, the earl of March.[35]

In addition to becoming a dynastic challenge, the revolt also turned during 1403 into an overtly nationalist rising. Since the Edwardian conquest a century earlier Wales had been an occupied country controlled by an alien English aristocracy. Most of the land was held either by the English prince of Wales in the far west, or by marcher lords in the centre and eastern borders with England. Their ruthless exploitation of the native Welsh, intensified in the second half of the century, caused deep resentment. Henry himself, as lord of Brecon, had on his first visit in 1397 extracted a huge 'gift' of £1,000. As revenues from English resources declined towards the end of the fourteenth century, the greater English aristocrats, most of whom were marcher lords, squeezed compensation out of their Welsh tenants who themselves were denied the rights of English subjects. In fact the attempt was made to impose a form of *apartheid* on Wales. The English had established a number of boroughs to which settlers had been attracted. All rights to trade and civic authority were restricted to English burgesses; and a monopoly of all commercial activity in Wales was extended to these boroughs. One of the first reactions to the revolt in the Hilary parliament of 1401, and extended by council ordinances afterwards, was to sharpen these laws and to bring in new regulations curtailing the rights of the Welsh in England, even while offering further protection to the English in Wales. It was now forbidden for any Welsh man or woman to marry or 'consort' with an English woman or man. The Welsh, for their part, sustained their identity through their own flourishing mythical histories and prophetic tradition, kept alive by the bards, that looked back and forward to the days when the Britons had and would again dominate the Saxons.[36]

By the end of 1402 Henry IV was facing a revolt in Wales which threatened both his hold on the throne and the western periphery of his kingdom. For the time being he did not have the resources to support a sustained and systematic reconquest. Once the strategy of relying on the marcher lords and officers of the principality supported by occasional punitive raids proved inadequate, he placed Hotspur in command in the north and Worcester in the south, calling upon paid royal garrisons in the key border towns and fortresses. The emphasis was largely defensive; there was little that Henry could do for the time being except endeavour to contain the revolt.[37]

In the meantime other problems were mounting. Glyn Dŵr appealed to the Scots for help. Early in 1402, the duke of Albany, brother of Robert III, recently installed as the ailing king's lieutenant, sought to take advantage of Henry's difficulties. The earl of Crawford was sent to France to seek assistance which was readily given and a fleet was fitted out and set sail from Harfleur at the end of March. The main purpose of this fleet was not to carry reinforcements to Scotland, which it did, but to intensify the war at sea. An English fleet under the command of Sir Thomas Rempson also put to sea and in the months that followed merchant shipping on both sides, as well as neutrals suspected of trading with the enemy, were attacked with heavy losses to both sides. In Scotland the English had the better of cross-border raiding in June. In retaliation the earls of Douglas, Angus and Moray, with Albany's son and heir Murdoch, invaded Northumberland, reaching the gates of Newcastle before turning for home laden with booty. They were intercepted by the earl of Northumberland and Hotspur near Wooler and overwhelmed in the battle of Homildon Hill on 14 September. All the leaders were killed or taken prisoner. The victory secured the northern border.[38]

Two weeks later Henry's third parliament opened at Westminster. The victory at Homildon seems to have buoyed up the commons who effusively thanked the king for his great labours against the Welsh and Scots and particularly praised the earl of Northumber land, who on 20 October brought his prisoners into the parliament chamber formally to surrender them to the king. In this euphoric atmosphere, although still expressing reservation concerning the scale of royal annuities, the commons voted supply – the renewal of customs and tunnage and poundage and a subsidy of a tenth and a fifteenth – with little debate. When parliament was dissolved late in November, and after the king had graciously feasted all the members, Henry turned to the more relaxing business of welcoming his new queen, Joan of Navarre. Having been married on 7 February 1403 at Winchester, the royal couple travelled in state to Westminster where the queen was crowned amidst the conventional splendour and celebration. Soon after this interlude, however, Henry was suddenly faced by his most serious challenge – the revolt of the Percys – which came perilously close to toppling both him and his new queen.[39]

The Percy revolt

There can be no doubt that the Percys had been liberally rewarded by Henry. Within a month of his usurpation of the throne they had secured complete dominance of the border, the earl of Northumberland and Hotspur holding the west and east marches for ten years, Hotspur additionally being made captain of Roxburgh and granted the royal castle and lordship of Bamburgh for life. His father became constable of England, he was given control of North Wales with all the judicial and military offices in his hands. Financially, father and son were further rewarded with the custody of the Mortimer estates. The earl's brother, Thomas, close to the king at court, received his reward in the form of a £500 annuity. At both court and in the country the Percys were dominant throughout the first three years of the reign. Apart from the removal of Hotspur from the captaincy of Roxburgh early in 1402, at a time when Henry was endeavouring to strengthen the truce between England and Scotland, the king made no overt move to withdraw his favour or curtail his generosity. Certainly he had begun to promote and reward members of his own extended family, the Beauforts and the Nevilles, as well as to bring forward the young earls of Arundel, Stafford and Warwick, but this was to be expected. Ralph Neville, earl of Westmorland, was the king's own man in the north, generously rewarded by him. Although he was ultimately made captain of Roxburgh, succeeding Lord Grey of Codnor, it is noticeable that Henry did not as yet promote his brother-in-law and long-standing retainer to a position of outright challenge to Percy dominance.[40]

It is true that Northumberland and Hotspur had difficulty in securing full payment of their allowances and wages as wardens of the northern marches. Exchequer records show that they received nearly £40,000 in cash and assignments; the equivalent of payment in full for two years in time of truce and one and half years in time of war. A claim made by the earl in June 1403 that he and his son were owed £20,000 was exaggerated. This is not to say that there were not frustrations. Like all other officers and servants of the crown, they suffered from the chronic state of royal finances. They were frequently paid late and only by means of assignment on royal revenue which they had to collect and which all too often was non-existent. They faced a considerable cash-flow problem in paying royal troops under their command, which could only be solved by calling on their own private resources. And this was not all. During 1402 the Crown virtually became insolvent, the rate of default in assignments climbed and in the early months of 1403 they received very little. On the eve of their revolt, the wardens of the marches did have grounds for complaint. But then so did most of the king's servants.[41]

The key to the Percy rebellion lay less in their grievances against the king and more in their own ambition. The earl of Northumberland, a man in his early sixties, had picked his way with great skill through the political minefield of Richard II's reign. He had successfully avoided being too closely associated with either the court or its opponents, and, trusted by all, had built up his own reputation as a doughty warrior and man of integrity, whilst assiduously extending his own personal power in northern England. It was Richard II's attempt to break his monopoly in the last three years of the reign that had led him to support Henry Bolingbroke, even though in the past he had been no great friend of his family.[42] Percy support for the usurpation was given on the understanding that in return the earl would be able to resume and complete his control of the far north. And so he did. Because the family had no direct interest in Wales or the marcher lordships, it probably favoured concessions to Glyn Dŵr which would enable them, especially Hotspur, to concentrate on northern ambitions.

Two developments in 1402 opened a rift with Henry. One was the king's refusal to ransom Sir Edmund Mortimer, Hotspur's brother-in-law; the other was the victory at Homildon and its aftermath. Homildon greatly enhanced Percy standing and sealed their dominance in the north. A dispute over the prisoners created ill-feeling between king and subject. Henry, as was his right, demanded that the Scottish prisoners be handed over to him. The earl complied, but Hotspur, who had taken the earl of Douglas, refused. Yet, nevertheless, Henry, in an act of magnanimity at the time of his marriage celebrations in March 1403, relented, allowed Hotspur to keep his prisoners and granted to the earl and his heirs the greater part of the Douglas estates in southern Scotland.[43] The king had almost certainly capitulated to Percy pressure, for immediately Hotspur set about the task of invading southern Scotland and making good family control of Douglas lands. Had he succeeded he would have created a quasi-independent marcher lordship for his family carved out of the eastern border counties of both countries. This, it would appear, was the next stage of their aggrandisement. By June 1403 the Percys had led England into another war with Scotland which Henry had little choice but to support. On 10 July, shortly before he heard of Hotspur's rebellion, he was in the midlands raising troops for the campaign.[44]

On the eve of their rebellion the Percys were as high in favour with Henry as they had ever been. Indeed by appeasing Hotspur and endorsing the family's Scottish ambitions, Henry had made it seem that he was even more dependent on them. Yet in July they rebelled. When Hotspur defied the king, he declared his intention to depose Henry and instal the young earl of March as the legitimate king. The plot was well laid. Hotspur himself left the Scottish borders at the beginning of July, accompanied only by his regular bodyguard and prisoner, Douglas, so as not to arouse suspicion, but with the intention of raising troops in Cheshire and the Welsh marches in the name of Richard II's heir. He arrived by 9 July. Although Henry's administrators remained loyal to the Crown, he mobilised Richard II's Cheshire archers. Once he had raised an army, he set off immediately for

Shrewsbury to confront the prince of Wales. Hotspur had almost certainly come to an understanding with Glyn Dŵr through the good offices of Sir Edmund Mortimer. Glyn Dŵr launched a foray into South Wales, no doubt with the intention of drawing off some of the prince of Wales' men. The earl of Northumberland remained in the north. This was not because he failed to support his son. One reason was to guard the border against the duke of Albany who was gathering a substantial force to relieve Cocklaw and confront the English. Another was to divert the king.[45]

Henry IV had reached Nottingham on 12 July, but had turned back to Derby and Burton on Trent by 17 July, by which date he had news of Hotspur's rebellion and rumours of Northumberland's involvement. The plotters, who surely knew that Henry was making his way north, had probably calculated that Henry would be unable to reinforce Prince Henry, or would decide to prevent the earl linking with Hotspur. But they mistook their man. Raising the midland counties, Henry marched with all haste to Shrewsbury in time to reinforce his son on 20 July. On the following day the battle was fought about two miles north of the town. It was hard-fought. In the king's inititial advance, the commander of his vanguard, the young earl of Stafford, was killed. Several of the king's own knights and esquires died. But the royal assault pushed on and the battle was decided when Hotspur himself was shot down by an arrow. The earls of Worcester and Douglas were taken prisoner, Worcester being executed as a traitor two days later.

Northumberland himself still had to be faced. On 22 July letters were sent to the earl of Westmorland to suppress his rising. A few days later, Northumberland, who had perhaps advanced as far south as northern Yorkshire before hearing of his son's defeat and death, broke camp and fled back to his own county. The king himself marched north, reaching Pontefract early in August. On 11 August the earl submitted at York. He was taken into custody to face trial in parliament, stripped of his offices and ordered to surrender his Northumbrian castles to the king's men. No sooner had the north been pacified than Henry returned to confront the third party to the rebellion: Glyn Dŵr. By early September he was at Worcester where a great council convened. Later in the month he and his army advanced as far as Carmarthen, but yet again failed to bring any Welsh rebels to battle. Withdrawing to England, he nevertheless remained in the field until the end of October.[46]

The Percy rebellion failed because the earl and his family misjudged the king's capacity for bold and decisive action in a crisis. They had risen for no other reason than that they judged Henry expendable and that they would be able to further their own self-advancement more effectively under another king. The one consistent thread in the career of the first earl of Northumberland had been family aggrandisement. Until 1403 he barely put a foot wrong.

Indeed, had the Percys successfully placed the earl of March on the throne under their protection, they would probably have made significant concessions to Glyn Dŵr in Wales and taken considerably more power for themselves in the north. In effect there would have been a dismemberment of the kingdom similar to one proposed two years later. Henry's victory thus preserved not only his dynasty, but also the integrity of the kingdom.

The battle of Shrewsbury was a defining moment both for the future of the Lancastrian dynasty and the kingdom of England. The regime was profoundly shaken by the defection of the family which had in effect put Henry IV on the throne. But there was now no shortage of others to take their place, especially royal kinsmen. Henry Beaufort, now bishop of Winchester, became Chancellor. John Beaufort, earl of Somerset, who had been captain of Calais since 1401, became Chamberlain of the Household. The earl of Westmorland took over the west march and became effective deputy of the king's fourteen-year-old son Prince John as warden of the east march. Sir John Stanley, who had been wounded fighting at the king's side at Shrewsbury, succeeded Hotspur to the principal offices in Chester. And there was new aristocratic blood coming to the fore, especially in the persons of Richard Beauchamp, earl of Warwick, Thomas Beaufort, later duke of Exeter and, above all, Prince Henry who had so distinguished himself during the battle. A stronger regime, more dependent on the king himself, emerged from the rebellion.

There were to be further rebellions and crises to be surmounted over the next three years, but after 1403 the Lancastrian dynasty was never to be as seriously at risk again until the later years of Henry VI. While Shrewsbury did not end the Welsh revolt, or completely eradicate the threat from the house of Percy, or finally lay the ghost of Richard II (the myth of whose survival the king's remaining enemies continued to propagate), the failure of the rebellion of 1403 left the king more secure on his throne and confirmed the outcome of the revolution of 1399. Yet that revolution proved not to be an endpoint. It was not the first time in the history of England since the conquest that a king had been deposed; but it was the first time for two hundred years that the direct line of descent had been broken. By usurping the throne, rather more than by being the agent of Richard II's deposition, Henry IV placed the right to the crown itself at the centre of political conflict. He, and more spectacularly his son, were sufficiently successful for their subjects to overlook the dubious legitimacy of his dynasty. But eventually, when the Lancastrian regime floundered under Henry VI, its originary flaw became once more a significant political factor. By virtue of the revolution of 1399 fifteenth-century English politics thus acquired a dynastic dimension which set them distinctly apart from the politics of earlier centuries.[47]

Notes and references

1   Goodman, *John of Gaunt*, 167–8. While the story is late, it might have had substance.

2   For the most recent discussion see Saul, *Richard II*, 397–404; Given-Wilson, 'Lancastrian Inheritance', passim; and *Chronicles of the Revolution*, 54–106.

3   For the suggestion that Richard had all along intended the destruction of the house of Lancaster see Given-Wilson, 'Lancastrian Inheritance'.

4   The account given in this and the following paragraphs draws particularly on Saul, *Richard II*, 405–17; Given-Wilson, *Chronicles*, 32–9, 119–61; Barron, 'The Deposition of Richard II', 132–49; Johnston, 'Richard II's Departure'; Sherborne, 'Perjury', 217–41. For a more positive interpretation of York's role in support of Henry see Biggs, 'Edmund of Langley', passim.

5   Tuck, 'Richard II and the Border Magnates', 22–39, and below pp. 38–9.

6   See, for instance Tuck, *Richard II and the English Nobility*, 187–225; Saul, *Richard II*, esp. 430–4 and 'Kingship', 55–6; Given-Wilson, *Chronicles*, 31–2. But note Barron, 'Deposition', 145, argues that 'it is doubtful whether Richard's government in the late 1390s was any more unpopular than most governments in the fourteenth and fifteenth centuries in England'.

7   See McNiven, 'Legend of Richard II's Survival', passim; Morgan, 'The Shadow of Richard II', passim; Strohm, *Empty Throne*,106–14. Note Adam Usk's parable about the greyhound which deserted Richard II to join Bolingbroke and would not leave his side during the campaign, but once he made himself king did not know him from any other man (*Chronicle*, 86–7).

8   Sherborne, 'Perjury', passim.

9   Given-Wilson, *Chronicles*, 192–7.

10 Ibid., 39–41, 153–61; Sherborne, 'Perjury', 228–40.

11 Sherborne, 'Perjury', 240–1 emphasises this interpretation.

12 *Rot Parl*, iii, 422–3; Given-Wilson, *Chronicles*, 41–6, 160–89, esp. 186; Saul, *Richard II*, 418–23.

13 Bennett, 'Edward III's Entail', passim; and Given-Wilson, *Chronicles*, 185–7.

14 McNiven, 'Legitimacy and Consent', 470–87; Pugh, *Southampton Plot*, 8; and Strohm, *Empty Throne*, passim.

15 Usk, *Chronicle*, 72–3.

16 Kirby, *Henry IV*, 75–9.

17 Ibid., 85.

18 Given-Wilson, *Chronicles*, 224–39; Crook, 'Central England', 403–10; McNiven, 'Cheshire Rising', 375–96.

19 Given-Wilson, *Chronicles*, 50–2, 240–5; Saul, *Richard II*, 425–6.

20 Given-Wilson, *Royal Household*, 188–99; Brown, 'Reign of Henry IV', and 'Commons and the Council', 7–8; Kirby, 'Council and Councillors', passim and *Henry IV*, 81–3. For biographies of leading retainers see the biographies in Roskell, *House of Commons*, ii, 549–52 (Cheyne), 790–2 (Doreward), iv, 189–93 (Rempton). For Erpingham, never recorded as an MP, see John, 'Sir Thomas Erpingham', 96–108, and Castor, 'Duchy of Lancaster', 55–69.

21 Cosgrove, *Medieval Ireland*, 543.

22 Kirby, 'Calais sous les Anglais', 19–21; Vale, *English Gascony*, 27–47.

23 Tuck, 'Henry IV and Europe', 107–12.

24 Ibid., 115–21.

25 Brown, 'English Campaign in Scotland', 40–54; Boardman, *Early Stewart Kings*, 226–9.

26 Boardman, *Early Stewart Kings*, 230–1; for Percy interests and ambitions in Scotland, especially their quarrel with the earls of Douglas for possession of Jedburgh, see Grant, 'Otterburn from the Scottish Point of View', 33–4 and McNiven, 'Scottish Policy', 505–7.

27 Davies, *Owain Glyn Dŵr*, 102–3.

28 Kirby, *Henry IV*, 110–16; Brown, 'Commons and the Council', 2–9; Rogers, 'Political Crisis', 85–96.

29 Ibid.

30 Bean, 'Henry IV and the Percies', 220–1; Brown, 'Commons and the Council', 7–9; Roskell, *House of Commons*, iv, 308.

31 McHardy, *'De Heretico Comburendo'*, 112–26; Strohm, *Empty Throne*, 32–62.

32 Ford, 'Piracy or Policy?', 63–78; Vale, *English Gascony*, 48–54; Vaughan, *Philip the Bold*, 51.

33 Davies, *Owain Glyn Dŵr*, 103–6. Conway was recovered in July.

34 Ibid., 182–3.

35 Ibid., 107–9, 179–81.

36 Ibid., 65–74; idem, *Conquest, Coercion and Change*, 431–43.

37 Davies, *Owain Glyn Dŵr*, 237–56.

38 Boardman, *Early Stewart Kings*, 246; Ford, 'Policy or Piracy?'.

39 Kirby, *Henry IV*, 146–51.

40   Bean, 'Henry IV and the Percies', 220–1; Harriss, *Cardinal Beaufort*, 19–21.

41   Bean, 'Henry IV and the Percies', 221–4.

42   Tuck, 'Richard II and the Border Magnates'.

43   McNiven, 'Scottish Policy', 267–71; Boardman, *Early Stewart Kings*, 267–71. It is puzzling, nevertheless that Douglas, whose lands had been regranted to the Percys, was prepared to fight for them at Shrewsbury. It is possible that, having decided to overthrow Henry IV, the Percys had indicated a willingness to drop their claim. It must also be remembered that the Douglas's rival, the Scottish earl of March, fought for Henry.

44   Morgan, *War and Society*, 213–18; Davies, *Owain Glyn Dŵr*, 184–5.

45   McNiven, 'Scottish Policy', 523–6.

46   Kirby, *Henry IV*, 155–60.

47   Strohm, *Empty Throne*, 196–214.

CHAPTER TWO

Henry IV, 1403–13

Continuing crisis, 1403–5

On the morrow of the battle of Shrewsbury, contemporaries were unlikely to predict that the beleaguered Henry IV would die peacefully in his bed ten years later, or that his dynasty would survive for a further fifty-eight years. Indeed nothing looked less likely. The king's other enemies were quick to take advantage of the disruption caused by the Percy revolt. Without formal declaration, the French abandoned the truce and reopened the war. As early as August one fleet raided and set fire to Plymouth; two months later it returned to help the Welsh besiege Kidwelly. And in November another made an attempt on Caernarvon. In France itself, the Count of St Pol, still pursuing his private war against Henry IV, prepared to invest Calais. Two fleets were raised in England to protect the northern and western approaches. The war at sea continued unabated and indiscriminately, causing losses to neutral Flemish, Hanseatic and Castilian shipping. The goods of English merchants in Flanders were seized in reprisal. As a result Anglo-Burgundian relations came under stress. Further south, the duke of Orleans mounted a full-scale blockade of Bordeaux in October 1403. Although his attack was beaten off, the pressure was maintained throughout 1404. Harlech and Aberystwyth fell to the rebels, who were in control of virtually the whole of Wales. Welsh parties were raiding the English border counties at will. In the spring, the Isle of Wight and Dartmouth were attacked by the French. On 14 July Glyn Dŵr concluded a formal alliance with the French and shortly afterwards a fleet was assembled at Harfleur to reinforce him. English naval defences were able to thwart this last threat, as well as to keep the Count of St Pol at bay off Calais and even to mount a raid on a Flemish island off Sluys. Fortunately the truce was restored and maintained with the

Scots, but nevertheless England was assailed on several fronts in the year after Shrewsbury. It is in this context that one should understand the proceedings in the two parliaments of 1404.[1]

Henry first called parliament for November 1403, but the date, as so often happened, was put back. When parliament met the king was in desperate financial straits and the commons highly critical. The notional gross annual income of the crown in the first years of the reign was approximately £100,000. Of this little over a third, an average of £36,000 came from customs and tunnage and poundage; about £35,000 came from crown lands (including the duchy of Lancaster), feudal casualties and other customary revenues; and some £32,000 from lay and clerical subsidies granted by parliament and convocation and paid in instalments. This was the notional sum. Collection and delivery, especially of landed income and taxation, probably fell short. In 1402 the council calculated that expenditure committed for that year came to £130,000. The defence of the realm consumed £56,000; annuities and grants of the Crown charged to the Exchequer took £24,000; the wardrobe was allocated £16,000 for the king's household; and £16,000 was needed to service loans. The remaining £8,000 was set aside for the cost of returning Queen Isabel to France. In fact, government financial records show that the total household costs of the king came to £42,000. The shortfall was made up by loans, and by delays in paying bills, whether the wages of military commanders (Somerset at Calais, Prince Thomas in Ireland and Rutland in Guyenne). Loans were repaid by assignments on future revenues, especially from customs and lay taxation. Often these assignments proved worthless because they were committed several times over. The Crown was deeply in debt, was suffering a chronic cash-flow problem, and was in danger of running out of credit.[2]

Crown finances were in such chaos by the end of 1403 for several reasons, some beyond its control. The defence of the realm, the cost of war in Wales, at sea and in France and of suppressing rebellion were unavoidable. War also reduced revenue, both in Wales where royal and Lancastrian estates were valueless, and at sea where the depredations of privateers and enemy shipping significantly reduced the volume of trade and thereby customs revenue, which fell in 1402–3 to £26,000. Customs revenue as well as income from land, had also fallen as a result of long-term economic trends. Rents and related landed income had stabilised in the first decade of the century, but customs revenue continued to decline as English merchants shipped less wool, upon which the most profitable customs dues were paid, and more finished cloth.

Yet some of the crisis was of Henry's own making. He maintained a lavish and costly household. He was on occasion exceptionally generous in the rewards he showered on his supporters. As a man, and a king, he was liberal and open-handed, uninterested in keeping account. His household finances, first under Thomas Tutbury and then Thomas More, were utterly mismanaged. Both keepers ran up huge debts and even then paid few of their bills. Henry lived well beyond his means. But one must be wary of accusing Henry of being totally irresponsible. His very high annuity expenditure had a hard-headed political purpose, and was arguably necessary. Through lavish patronage he secured the essential political commitment to his regime. He needed both to reward his own followers and to win over erstwhile supporters of Richard II. Moreover maintaining a lavish life-style was not mere waste. The prestige, reputation and authority of a king was enhanced by a magnificent court. Henry was extravagant and he was an incompetent financial manager; but these faults only exacerbated a financial crisis fundamentally beyond his control. The resources of the Crown were insufficient to meet all the demands placed on it early in his reign.

Contemporary critics did nevertheless blame the king. He had promised to live within his means and patently did not. To meet his uncontrollable household costs and to satisfy his innumerable annuitants and grantees, he did not hesitate to draw upon customs and taxation revenue which was voted by parliament for the defence of the realm. The failure to suppress the Welsh rising and safeguard shipping was blamed on the king for misuse of funds. In particular the mercantile community, which paid heavy taxes and advanced loans, had every justification in blaming the king for their losses, not only at the hands of privateers, but also because of the breakdown of the commercial treaty with Flanders. Even annuitants, whose fees and profits were delayed or left unpaid, would put up with so much and no more. And a new cause of unease had arisen following the king's marriage. Not only had Queen Joan been granted, at 10,000 marks, the largest dower ever settled on a queen, but also the presence of over forty Bretons, French and Spanish attendants fuelled resentment. Perhaps the most pervasive grievance, which touched most, was the abuse of purveyance for the royal household, which had the right to requisition supplies wherever it resided. When it descended on a neighbourhood (and Henry was constantly on the move in his early years), an army of purveyors would fan out, market to market, even house to house, to buy by compulsory purchase the necessary and substantial quantities of food and fodder. So expensive to run was the household and so short the ready cash that bills were rarely paid in full and frequently not at all. Suppliers, mostly unwilling purveyors by appointment to the Crown, great merchants and husbandmen alike, suffered directly as a result of the king's mismanagement.

It is not surprising, therefore, that when the commons gathered at Westminster in January 1404, both knights of the shires and burgesses quickly developed a head of steam about a king who had lost control of a significant part of his kingdom, had faced a major rebellion mounted by his principal supporters and was presiding over a bankrupt government. It is almost certain that Henry knew what he would face. A council meeting shortly before the opening of parliament, at which Sir Arnold Savage the soon-to-be elected speaker of the commons was present, probably discussed government strategy. It is almost certain that Savage was the royal nominee as speaker. He was well-qualified, having been speaker of the house in the previous parliament and likely to be trusted by the commons as well as by the king whose servant he was. While the speaker might be, and under Henry IV invariably was, a government nominee, he was elected for the duration of the parliament by the house. His role was to represent to the lords, and on occasion the king in person, the collective and agreed decisions and recommendations of the house. He was entitled to say no more and no less than that which the commons had agreed and authorised. He was answerable to them, not the king. By the early fifteenth century he had probably also assumed the duty of chairing their proceedings. In understanding what the speaker communicated to the lords and the king in parliament it is vital to understand that he spoke not for himself, but for the collective voice of the house, however that was reached (which is not known). He was but the spokesman. The king knew this, and allowed it. In so far as Savage, and other speakers of the commons during Henry's reign, were trusted councillors and confidants of the king, one might suppose that something of a charade was performed during these formal audiences. But not so; the speaker performed his part with conviction. For instance, when Savage informed Henry that the king was ill-served by the malicious advice of some of his councillors and promised to name names, he was doing his duty as speaker; it was not a personal attack by one councillor on his colleagues.[3]

The record of parliament merely sets out the statutes and notes the official communications of the commons. For the Hilary parliament of 1404 a rare surviving newsletter reveals that there was frank discussion, tempers were lost and the house stuck to a hard line during several weeks of confrontation.[4] Not only did they criticise the king for his improvidence, his excessive purveyance and extravagant grants to the queen's ladies, they also demanded that he should answer to them for the expenditure of any new grant they made. Furthermore, they asked that the earl of Northumberland be given the opportunity to explain his conduct to the Lords and, if found guilty of nothing worse than trespass, be restored. The king eventually gave way on all points and when on 20 March the commons did finally agree to vote a novel land tax, it was expressly on condition that it should not be repeated, that four treasurers of war should be appointed both to collect and to spend the revenue only on the defence of the realm, and that the continual council should be formally appointed and charged to attend to the good government of the kingdom.[5]

There was neither a desire to change the composition of the royal council nor to control it; rather an exhortation to councillors to do their duty. The most assiduous members were the Chancellor, Henry Beaufort and Thomas Langley, Keeper of the Privy Seal. The only new member was Thomas Neville, lord Furnival. In the event, while the political and military position continued to worsen during 1404, the new tax proved a failure. The treasurers found the task of collection beyond them. By the time another parliament was called to Coventry early in October, so desperate was the situation that both Crown and commons were more readily accommodating. After little more than a month the commons renewed customs and tunnage and poundage for two years from Michaelmas 1405 (when the preceding grant was due to expire), and voted a double tenth and fifteenth, the first immediately, and the second to be collected in two instalments in June and November 1405. The king conceded that he would set up a committee to look into resumption of crown lands; to suspend the payment of all annuities for a year from Easter 1404; and to accept that the new subsidies were to be used exclusively for immediate military expenditure. Two new war treasurers were appointed, Lord Furnival and Sir John Pelham, both councillors and prominent royal servants, who rather than collect the revenues, were to oversee their spending on their proper purpose and to answer themselves for them to the commons at the next parliament. Before parliament was dissolved on 14 November the lords undertook to make their own contribution of a land tax of 5 per cent; ten days later the convocation of Canterbury granted one and a half tenths; and the northern convocation followed suit.[6]

The generous supply voted at the end of 1404, although with strings tied, recognised the dangers facing the kingdom. It was sufficient to see the king through the coming year and to enable him, hopefully, to get a grip on affairs both at home and abroad. In Wales, royal forces made some headway early in 1405. The border garrisons had been strengthened during the winter of 1404-5. The taxation voted by parliament was used to reinforce the defences maintained by the marcher lords from their own resources with companies paid by the Exchequer. And on 27 April the prince of Wales's commission as king's lieutenant was renewed. But it was the prince's commanders, alert in their garrisons, who gained important victories at Grosmont in March and Usk in May which effectively checked further Welsh expansion in the south-eastern marches.[7]

But by May, Henry was faced by renewed baronial revolt. The continuing threat of dissent had been revealed in February when Constance, Lady Despenser, the sister of Edward, duke of York, attempted to kidnap the earl of March and his younger brother and to spirit them down to Wales. She and the boys were captured at Cheltenham, and her brother was implicated, arrested and imprisoned in Pevensey castle. This failed attempt to smuggle the Mortimer claimant to Wales was probably connected with the drawing up of the tripartite indenture at this time, by which the kingdom was to be divided between Glyn Dŵr ruling an enlarged Wales, Northumberland in the north and Sir Edmund Mortimer controlling the south. Northumberland, with the support of other peers and of Archbishop Scrope of York, rose in rebellion in May. Success depended on Northumberland first ambushing an unsuspecting earl of Westmorland at Witton castle on the Wear. But Westmorland, forewarned, raised loyal troops and alerted the king. Northumberland held back, but the unfortunate archbishop went ahead in Yorkshire. Westmorland confronted his ill-armed band of townsmen, peasants and clergy on Shipton Moor, which, after a three day 'stand-off', was allowed to disperse when its leaders, including the archbishop, surrendered to the earl. Scrope and his companions were taken in custody to Pontefract. On 3 June the king arrived; on the following day Sir Thomas Beaufort and the earl of Arundel held a military court under the law of arms, in which the archbishop was found guilty of treason. Despite a last minute plea to the king by Archbishop Arundel to honour his cloth, Scrope was executed as a traitor on 8 June. Wasting little time, Henry pressed north in pursuit of Northumberland, who fled to Scotland. Having secured the far north, he retraced his steps southwards to Worcester to confront the Welsh once more.[8]

The rebellion of 1405 was but a completion of business left unfinished in 1403. Henry IV had been magnanimous towards the earl of Northumberland in 1403. Although he had been stripped of his offices and imprisoned, the earl was pardoned for his trespass in February 1404 and restored to his estates. His castles had been taken into royal hands, not without difficulty and after stubborn resistance by his lieutenants. Indeed Northumberland's recalcitrance in refusing to surrender Berwick had called Henry back to the north in June 1404, where the earl, after ignoring several summonses, finally attended on the king at Pontefract and agreed to surrender the town and castle to him. Yet he was even restored to the captaincy of Berwick in November 1404.

Archbishop Scrope's involvement remains an enigma. He had no history of political involvement, no particular connection with the Percys; indeed he was a respected, saintly and politically somewhat naive cleric. The manifesto he put out in 1405 shows that his role, to which as a highly respected northern figure he was ideally suited, was to raise popular support behind Northumberland's essentially baronial movement. His criticisms of the court, complaints against ruinous taxation, the promise to make peace with the Welsh, and even grievances on behalf of the Church, had an obvious popular appeal. But tragically Scrope was abandoned by the earl. His execution, however, was hardly warranted. As Archbishop Arundel pointed out to the king, he himself, although condemned of treason by Richard II had been spared because of his cloth. The spontaneous and general response of horror to Scrope's martyrdom, as it was seen, revealed that Arundel's views were widely shared. It is equally puzzling that Henry, who was a man of known personal piety, authorised the execution. After all he had reacted with extreme moderation and leniency to the earlier treachery of the earl of Northumberland and to the continual dabblings of the duke of York in treason. Normally Henry was merciful. Whether it was the stirring of the commons, or the anticlerical prompting of courtiers, or the effect of stress, his usual sound judgement deserted him.

In the summer of 1405, Henry had no time for remorse. Owain Glyn Dŵr finally received the French assistance promised a year earlier. An expeditionary force landed at Milford Haven, seized Carmarthen, and with Welsh reinforcements marched west through Glamorgan and into England as far as the gates of Worcester. Henry and his army arrived at the town in late August in time to out-face them. No battle was fought and the Franco-Welsh army withdrew to Glamorgan, pursued by the English, who thereafter recovered that county.[9] Campaigning during 1405 was not restricted to Wales and the north. The war in the Channel had also intensified. A new fleet under the command of Prince Thomas had taken to the sea in May and had raided Sluys. In retaliation the new duke of Burgundy, John the Fearless, had attacked the Marck, one of the outposts of Calais, and the English fleet had cruised down the French coast raiding Picardy and Normandy. At the same time, in the south, the French had launched an assault on English-held fortresses in the Agenais and had further reduced the area under Lancastrian control in Guyenne. And even in Ireland, taking advantage of the distractions, Ard Mac Murchadha once more took to the field. In 1405 the level of warfare on all fronts rose to a new height. The subsidies granted at the end of 1404 were rapidly consumed or committed to new and desperate loans. By the end of the year the king had no choice but to call on parliament yet again.[10]

The parliament of 1406

At first, because of the continuing presence of French troops in Wales, Henry planned to meet his parliament on 15 February at Coventry. But the appearance of a French fleet off the mouth of the Thames caused the assembly to be called to Westminster two weeks later. The 'Long Parliament' met in an atmosphere of continuing military threat. As the year advanced Wales ceased to be the primary concern. In the royal letters issued on 9 February postponing parliament, the king expressed his confidence in the prince and his lieutenants. Although it is not clear that the prince himself, whose commission as lieutenant was extended for another year in April, ever took the field, his captains and their companies slowly extended the pacification of south Wales from Glamorgan into Gower and Carmarthenshire. In the autumn the reconquest of Anglesey was completed by troops from Ireland under Sir Stephen Scrope. By the end of the year Owain Glyn Dŵr had fallen back to central and northern Wales and was forced to defend himself on three fronts. The English were poised to recover the northern castles.[11]

But if the tide finally turned in Wales, and the threat from Scotland was virtually removed on 22 March, when just two weeks before his accession, the future James I of Scotland was captured off Flamborough Head, the situation in France became more worrying as the year progressed. The rival princes of France, John, duke of Burgundy and Louis, duke of Orleans, agreed to share government and to collaborate in a co-ordinated attack on the common enemy. Burgundy was to lead an assault on Calais, Orleans on Bordeaux. Henry IV, who was kept well-informed of developments in France, knew by mid-October that Burgundy was gathering troops at St Omer and that Orleans had already set off in strength towards Guyenne. Orleans' first objective was Bourg, which he beseiged on 31 October. Here, however, he made little progress. Burgundy tarried at St Omer until 17 November when he called off his campaign. But Henry took the threat to Calais seriously. On 20 October he ordered his retainers to stand by for an expedition to France that he intended to lead in person on 9 November. By 20 November, when the earl of Somerset, captain of Calais, took comand of a fleet to defend the Channel, the retainers had been stood down. Not until after Christmas, and after parliament had been dissolved, was it clear that the danger to the remaining possessions in France had passed.[12]

When the members of parliament gathered on 1 March 1406, they were as concerned about Wales and the keeping of the seas as they were about the defence of Guyenne and Calais. But they were also all too aware that, despite the generous grants at the end of 1404, Henry had still been unable to pacify the principality and had been faced by yet another rebellion that had threatened the dismemberment of the kingdom. And nothing appeared to have been done to put the household in order. Although their speaker, Sir John Tiptoft, was selected on the second day, it was three weeks before he was allowed to present himself to the lords to make his protestation and to ask for the customary liberties of the office. On this occasion he pointed out that despite the large grants already made, neither the Welsh nor the French threats had been mastered and voiced the concern of the commons for the provision of 'good and abundant governance'. When two weeks later, on 3 April, he reported the commons' resolutions, it was clear that they were still prepared to offer little in response to the request for supply. It is probable that at this time the speaker first, and unsuccessfully, asked for the nomination of councillors in parliament. He certainly asked that the prince of Wales should reside continuously in Wales, suggesting that the commons believed he had been neglecting his duty; that all aliens attending the queen be expelled; and that the defence of the seas should be put in the hands of two fleets raised by the merchants of the kingdom. The king agreed the last and a joint committee of the commons and the council was established to administer the raising and payment of the fleets. After five weeks of debate, when parliament adjourned for Easter, little had been achieved, except two stop-gap measures for Wales and the seas.[13]

Parliament was due to reconvene after a three-week recess on 26 April. However, during the recession Henry suffered either a stroke or a heart attack. Because of his malady, and his inability therefore to ride up to Westminster, the second session was postponed from day to day until 30 April, when it appears the two houses met without him. Henry recovered sufficiently to travel to London from Windsor by boat and he appeared in parliament soon after. Business hanging over from the previous session was completed when he agreed to the expulsion of forty named aliens. Then, after two weeks' debate, the speaker came once more before king and lords to ask that in order to secure good government the king would nominate his council in parliament. After negotiation, in which Archbishop Arundel led for the king, the request was finally conceded. The concession was so significant that the nominated councillors were reluctant to serve unless it were declared by the king that the agreement was made by his own free will. The terms of the bill show why. The council ('the wisest lords of the realm') would have supervision over all that would be done for the good of the government of the realm, encompassing both justice and finance. Most importantly the council took control of royal expenditure, the issue which had exercised successive parliaments since 1401. Henry still retained his freedom to exercise his grace to grant pardons, benefices and offices.

The council named in May was the existing council. It was not its composition, but its function which concerned the commons. It soon became clear that before the lower house would vote taxes it wanted evidence of reform and assurance that household expenditure would be controlled. It no longer trusted statements of intent. As debate dragged over the following month, complaints were made about the misappropriation of the wages of the Calais garrison, the continued failure of the prince of Wales to take up his command and the excessive cost of the administration in Ireland. Moreover, the commons insisted that, under the terms agreed in 1404, the treasurers of war could only be discharged after their accounts had been audited in parliament. When finally the speaker came before the lords on 19 June he secured the establishment of a parliamentary committee of audit, but no answer to his request that household expenses be cut and annuities reduced. The session ended in deadlock, with only a limited extension of customs granted to the crown.

The summer recess, which lasted four months, was quiet. The king enjoyed a leisurely tour of the midlands and for once did not take to the field. The third session did not open until 18 October, in the climate of renewed threats to Calais and Bordeaux. Even so it took a further two months for king and commons to come to agreement. The sticking point, as before, was the commons' insistence on specific guidelines for the council in its administration and control of the household and royal expenditure. The crown did not begin to give way until after 18 November. Intense negotiation led to the eventual enactment on 22 December of thirty-one articles, which regulated the proceedings of the council, enjoined that household regulations should be strictly enforced and set out in detail the ways and means to restrain the king's liberality and to ensure that he lived within his means. But the commons did not win all their points; in particular, they failed to secure a guarantee that the council would refund the grant of taxation should it be misspent. A new and more aristocratic council was nominated and a lay subsidy of a tenth and fifteenth granted before the dissolution.

What tipped the balance is hard to tell. Possibly the approach of Christmas as well as the Crown's needs made compromise more desirable; all parties were probably exhausted. Possibly too the intervention of the prince of Wales was decisive. He began to attend meetings of council regularly from 8 December. Thereafter he was a key figure in government. Indeed it appears that there was a change of government in or around 8 December. On that day the speaker, Sir John Tiptoft, was made treasurer of the household. The knights and esquires – Cheyne, Doreward, Pelham, Savage and Waterton – who had served on council since the accession of the king were removed. The new council which took the oath to observe the thirty-one articles was less closely identified with the household, of which only the treasurer and steward remained members. Its leader was Thomas Arundel, archbishop of Canterbury. For one who had been so prominent during the usurpation, he had until 1406 stayed in the political background. He emerged as a key figure in the negotiations between lords and commons in May and thereafter was at the forefront. On 30 January 1407 he became chancellor and presumably took the chair of the council.

The Long Parliament of 1406 was a turning point in the political history of Henry IV's reign. It ushered in a significant change in both the character of the regime and the practice of kingship. However difficult his relations with parliament had proved, he and courtiers (unlike Richard II) had never been the subject of personal attack. Indeed, in the summer of 1406 the commons went out of their way to commend his righthand man, Sir Thomas Erpingham.[14] And while his close companions stepped down from council during the year, none was hounded from court; all continued to enjoy favour and find honourable employment. Conflict between commons and Crown did not focus, as it had before, and would again, on the role of the king's corrupt favourites. Nor was the hostility of the commons co-ordinated and sustained by baronial opposition. After the fall of the Percys, Henry enjoyed the support of all the leading peers and the advance of the Beauforts as yet caused little resentment.

An analysis of the composition of the commons in 1406 further suggests that the king's interest was well represented among the ranks of its leading members, the knights of the shires, where he commanded a majority. While historians write collectively of the 'commons' in opposition to the Crown, in reality the lower house was itself divided between critics and supporters, and the course of the assembly was characterised by intense conflict and debate on the floor of the house.[15] The king's critics in the commons were not mounting a constitutional challenge to the Crown. They did not wish to control government. What they wanted, as they reiterated frequently in 1406, was for the king to provide good government and to manage his finances effectively.

Henry was not a man who stood on his dignity. He was willing to accept criticism. Early in his reign his confessor, Philip Repington, wrote bluntly to him warning of the consequence of the mismanagement of affairs and the collapse of law and order; this in no way hindered Repington's career. Sir Arnold Savage spoke bluntly to him as both speaker of the house of commons in 1404 and as a councillor.[16] While no doubt it annoyed him, similarly Henry did not resent parliamentary opposition as an unwarranted assault on his regality. Indeed it is reasonable to suppose that he still accepted, as a one-time Appellant, that the king was answerable to his subjects, and was thus prepared to argue and to negotiate, to wheel and to deal. Henry's kingship was a hands-on, highly political kingship.

Why, however, was Henry prepared, of his own free will, to relinquish the direct exercise of power in 1406? The answer lies in the collapse of his health. The malady he suffered at Easter left him disabled. It transformed the course of the parliament, already engaged on the familiar round of seeking to find a way of curbing the king's profligacy, and thereafter the course of the reign. It is possible that the heart condition he probably suffered, on occasions intensely, after 1406, was connected with the strange bout that struck him shortly after the execution of Archbishop Scrope in July 1405. A recent examination of the king's health has demonstrated that he suffered a second more serious heart attack in 1408 which left him permanently incapacitated. He was near to death early in 1409 and, although he recovered, by the spring of 1412 it was reported that he could no longer walk.[17] But even from Easter 1406 he was far less active and less closely involved in the affairs of state than he had been. Whilst no public reference was made to his health, it was in May 1406 that he made it known through Arundel that he wanted the council to have supervision over the government of the realm. Indeed, the articles recorded by the clerk of parliament on 24 May make it explicit that, 'considering the labour he must expend on the government' and 'because he cannot attend to them personally as much as he would wish' he asked the council to take over 'so that by their labours he personally may be better relieved of the work'.[18] This is not the wording devised to conceal a palace coup, it is a statement of the actual situation. It took another six months to agree the details because in the unprecedented circumstancese it was difficult to define arrangements which would satisfy king, court, council and commons respectively. Eventually, however, agreement was reached acceptable to all parties. Thereafter the reign was set on a new course, in which the government of the realm lay in the hands of the council.

Rule by council, 1406–13

Compared with the first seven years of Henry's reign, the remaining six were stable and conflict-free. They were years of consolidation in which the house of Lancaster established itself more firmly on the throne. The settlement of December 1406, which instituted a conciliar structure of government, survived until the end of the reign. The dominant political factor remained the king's ill health, which deteriorated remorselessly in stages throughout the rest of his life. Since he was never able again to attend to business for any sustained period, governments had of necessity to be in one form or another conciliar. While new tensions and stresses arose, especially those between the king's two elder sons, they were contained within that framework; rivalry between the prince of Wales and Prince Thomas, disruptive as it came to be, was of less significance than the fact that both parties pursued their rivalries within the pattern of politics established in 1406. Moreover, notwithstanding disagreement over policy and competition for their father's favour, the princes and their supporters shared one overriding aim in common: the survival of the dynasty. It is this fundamental unity more than the factionalism associated with the later years of the reign which is the key to understanding Henry IV's ultimate success.

Having exerted himself to plan a further expedition into Wales in the spring of 1407, Henry seems virtually to have retired for the rest of the year: the summer was spent in a long and leisurely tour of his kingdom while his council conducted affairs of state.[19] The king seems to have been happy to delegate authority to Archbishop Arundel who even spoke for him during the parliament held at Gloucester in the autumn. He was well served by the archbishop and his council, who restored solvency and maintained tight financial control over the household. From December 1406 nearly all warrants were issued with the assent of the council. New grants were virtually stopped, royal revenues were more effectively collected, spending was curtailed. As keeper, Sir John Tiptoft reduced wardrobe expenditure and balanced the books. The freedom to draw on all sources to fund the household, conceded by parliament in 1406 and subsequently implemented in the spring of 1407, greatly assisted the council. Careful financial planning by the council (it met almost continuously for this purpose for six weeks in the spring of 1408 and again in 1409), enabled it to control its public expenditure and keep it in line with income raised by loans and assignments on guaranteed revenue.[20] Arundel's firm control of the Gloucester parliament secured a vote of confidence in the release of the councillors from their oath and the grant of one and half tenths and fifteenths. And Tiptoft's personal contribution and abilities were recognised by his promotion to Treasurer in the summer of 1408.[21]

The government was helped by the easing of most of its foreign and domestic pressures. During 1407 and 1408 the pacification of Wales continued to make progress. In 1408 Aberystwyth was recaptured, in February 1409 Harlech. But even before these fortresses were recovered, the rebels had been pushed back to the northern mountains and English control (and revenue collection) restored to the rest of Wales. The assassination of the duke of Orleans on the orders of the duke of Burgundy in November 1407 plunged France into civil war and ended the threat from that quarter. Even before the assassination, an effective commercial truce with Flanders had been agreed, extended for three years in 1408, encompassing the security of the seas. Although piracy still posed a threat in the Channel, Anglo-Flemish trade (and customs revenue) recovered. There were new problems to be faced. In December 1406 the unpaid Calais garrision mutinied. During the early months of 1407 a new and more secure financial agreement was reached by which the company of the Staple held back three-quarters of the wool subsidy to pay the wages. And on 19 February, Sir Thomas Rokeby, the sheriff of Yorkshire, crushed a last desperate invasion by the exiled earl of Northumberland on Bramham Moor. In the skirmish Northumberland was killed and with him died the last remaining English resistance to the regime.[22]

During 1407 and 1408 Arundel's administration consolidated Lancastrian control of the kingdom. However, the unity of conciliar government began to disintegrate in 1409. Nothwithstanding the measures taken to restore solvency, the costs incurred by the government began again to outstrip its income. Household debts began again to rise; purveyance once more became an issue. Matters were not helped by the fact that Arundel and the council had accepted in 1407 a vote of taxation which would cease in the middle of 1409 while conceding that they would not ask for a further grant until the spring of 1410. Financial stringency inevitably intensified the competition for preference between interest groups. It is in this context of renewed financial strain that the emerging rivalry between the prince of Wales and his younger brother, Prince Thomas, is best understood.[23]

Prince Thomas had spent most of his political career as lieutenant of Ireland. However the news that his father was at death's door brought him back to England at the beginning of 1409. Once home, he was reluctant to return. He was also Henry IV's favourite son. In May he was granted an assignment of over £7,000 in payment of his arrears. At the same time only small allocations were made for Wales. Prince Henry, whose time and responsibilities had largely been taken up with Wales in 1407 and 1409, was already anxious to play a more central role in affairs. He had joined the council at the end of 1406. His presence and the support he then gave Arundel had helped resolve the crisis of that year, but it would appear that during 1409 resentment of the favour now being shown to his younger brother spurred him to challenge Arundel's leadership of the council. In August, supported by the Beauforts, he sought unsuccessfully to have Thomas relieved of his post in Ireland and removed from the royal household. In November he complained that Arundel and Tiptoft had failed to honour an agreement to increase expenditure on Wales. Within a month he had undermined the archbishop's position. On 11 December Tiptoft resigned; on 21 December Arundel. Parliament had been called to meet at Westminster on 27 January 1410. The principal offices of state remained vacant over Christmas. The new Treasurer, Lord Scrope of Masham, was appointed on 6 January, but it was not until 31 January that Sir Thomas Beaufort was made Chancellor. The appointments reveal that the prince of Wales had had his way, but the length of time it took to make them suggests a long-drawn-out conflict at court in which it is likely that the king had resisted the ministerial changes.[24]

Parliament when it met was in its most critical mood since 1406. The prince of Wales proposed to offer the commons a guarantee of good government in exchange for the vote of a regular annual subsidy to the end of the reign: an extension of the formula successfully adopted in 1406. But the commons were not prepared to abandon their one political lever. It also became apparent that there was a powerful anticlerical voice in the house. Indeed awareness of this may have been the reason why at the last moment

Sir Thomas Beaufort, rather than his brother, Henry, Bishop of Winchester, was appointed Chancellor. The commons proposed that the permanent endowment of the crown should be enhanced by £20,000 *per annum* (the annual cost of the household) by the disendowment of the Church. Debate over it, and the Crown's own request for taxation, probably explain why parliament was adjourned for Easter on 15 March until 7 April. A week after they reconvened, the commons finally submitted eighteen articles, reiterating in substance the articles of 1406 concerning good government and requested that a new council be named, and as before, sworn in parliament. The articles were accepted and the new council was ratified. In addition to the prince and the principal officers of state, it comprised Henry Beaufort, Nicholas Bubwith, Bishop of Bath and Wells and one-time Keeper of the Privy Seal, Henry Chichele, Bishop of St David's, the earls of Arundel and Warwick and Lord Burnell. It would probably also have included John Beaufort, Earl of Somerset, had he not died on 10 March. The earl of Westmorland and Thomas Langley, Bishop of Durham, were excused because of their duties in the north. These were the prince's men; it was his government. But Prince Henry was probably disappointed that he could in the end only squeeze out of the commons a grant of three half tenths and fifteenths, in addition to the renewal of customs, to be paid over three years.[25]

Having, after several months of wrangling, secured control of the government and the nomination of a council to his own liking, the prince of Wales pursued policies very much as before. Arundel might have been excluded, but his principles remained dominant: tight control of the budget and cost-cutting at home and peace abroad. In June and July the council determined the budget. Now that Wales was under control, Calais, to which the prince himself had succeeded the earl of Somerset as captain, and control of the sea took priority. Sir Thomas Beaufort was confirmed as admiral as well as Chancellor, and a squadron of twenty ships was raised to tackle once more the endemic problem of piracy in the Channel and the North Sea. Early in 1411 some success was gained with the capture of the most notorious English pirate, John Prendergast. The truces with France and Scotland were extended; and the government moved closer to an understanding with the duke of Burgundy, particularly through tighter enforcement of the mercantile truce with Flanders. But as yet it remained steadfastly neutral in respect of the rivalry between Burgundy and the Orleanists for control of France. Finance remained its principal concern. In November it sought to raise additional revenue by means of distraint of knighthood. However, by the spring of 1411 it was apparent that the administration was still running at a deficit. The allocation to Guyenne was drastically pruned and the payment of royal annuities was once more curtailed. For once the council held back from borrowing or anticipating the next instalment of the subsidy. The intention was to balance the books by rigorous restraint on spending.[26]

But Prince Henry was still vulnerable to court intrigue. The council had refused to repay Prince Thomas' debts as lieutenant of Ireland unless he returned to his post. Thomas chose to stay in England. He found compensation elsewhere. In August 1410 a papal mandate was issued granting a dispensation for him to marry Margaret Holland, an heiress and the widow of John Beaufort. The marriage enabled the king to endow his second son at no expense to the Crown, but it threatened the Beauforts who had emerged as the prince of Wales's principal supporters. Prince Henry was placed in a dilemma; he could hardly object to a scheme that gave his brother an income befitting his dignity that would cost the Crown nothing, yet the marriage weakened his own position at court.[27]

The immediate cause of the fall of the prince's government at the end of 1411 lay in foreign affairs. In the summer of 1411 the tenuous peace in France collapsed and full civil war broke out between the duke of Burgundy and the Orleanists. Both sides sought English aid. The English government's inclination was to support Burgundy, to whom it had been drawing closer in the preceding year. In August negotiations began for a full alliance and preparations in the king's name were set in train to mount an expedition to France in support of the duke. However, in September, against his son's wishes, the king vetoed the campaign. Prince Henry defied his father and sent his own private force, under the command of the earl of Arundel. And this expeditionary force played a significant part in enabling Burgundy to regain control of Paris in October/November.[28]

But the prince of Wales's defiance of his father in the field of foreign policy galvanised Henry IV, despite his ill-health, once more to assert his authority. Since the winter of 1410–11 he had allowed his son to have the conduct of affairs; now he intervened to remove him. Parliament, which had been summoned to Westminster on 3 November to vote taxes to pay for an expedition to France, now met to determine a change of ministry. Rumours abounded that the prince of Wales, so desperate was he to hold power, encouraged by Henry Beaufort, sought to secure support for his father's abdication. This came to nothing, but may lie behind the king's warning to parliament that he would accept no 'novelties'. The commons, whose speaker for the second successive time was Sir Thomas Chaucer, a servant and kinsman of Henry Beaufort, seem to have supported the prince and his council. But without the king's approval, the ministry was doomed. On 30 November, on the speakers request, the king, in parliament, thanked the outgoing council for its good and loyal service and discharged its members of their duty. No new councillors were nominated in parliament, the commons renewed customs and made a derisory grant of an income tax on the model of 1404, before parliament was dissolved on 19 December. Two days later Sir Thomas Beaufort and Lord Scrope were dismissed. They were replaced by Archbishop Arundel and Sir John Pelham as Chancellor and Treasurer respectively. The prince of Wales had discovered that he could not challenge his father's ultimate authority. Henry IV had been prepared to allow him to administer the kingdom on his behalf, but he would not tolerate any usurpation of his prerogative.[29]

The new ministry represented a victory for Prince Thomas as well as Archbishop Arundel. The question of France remained the principal political issue. While the prince of Wales had favoured and still favoured a closer alliance with Burgundy, Arundel and Prince Thomas perceived greater advantage in an Orleanist alignment. They were wooed by both sides, but in May, by the treaty of Bourges the government concluded an alliance with the dukes of Orleans, Bourbon and Berry and the counts of Armagnac and Albret which promised spectacular gains. In return for military assistance the Orleanists were prepared to concede the terms of the treaty of Bretigny, by which in 1360 Edward III had been granted Guyenne in full sovereignty, and to make restitution of captured territory. Prince Thomas, it was decided, would lead an expedition of 4,000 men to assist them, for which he indented on 8 June. His principal captains were the duke of York and Sir Thomas Beaufort. Before embarkation, on 9 July Thomas was appointed lieutenant of Aquitaine and created duke of Clarence and Beaufort earl of Dorset. There was more than opportunism to this reversal of alliances. Arundel had always tended to favour the Orleanists. There were also particular Lancastrian links with Guyenne derived from the grant of the duchy to John of Gaunt. Many other Englishmen had their own ties with the duchy. The securing of Guyenne under the terms of the treaty of Bretigny was thus both historically and strategically a valid alternative diplomatic objective.[30]

The turn of events nevertheless infuriated the prince of Wales. It is possible that he had been given to understand that the king himself would lead the expedition – although it is hard to credit that anyone believed the public announcement that a man who could hardly mount a horse would go in person. The prince claimed that he had wished himself to serve, but had been prevented from raising a royal company worthy of his dignity. Indeed, he declared in a manifesto issued on 17 June, he had begun privately to raise a force, but his intentions had been maliciously misinterpreted by 'evil-minded persons' who had slanderously put it about that he planned to raise rebellion and depose the king. With this public justification he marched at the head of a large following to London, where he lodged from 30 June to 11 July demanding an audience with his father. This was granted and a reconciliation achieved. It has been supposed that Henry's armed demonstration was an attempt to force himself back into power. But this is highly unlikely. To say the least, it would have been foolish to attempt this at precisely the time that a royal army was being recruited. More probably it was a reaction against enemies in Prince Thomas's circle who had indeed accused him of treason. The outcome of the reconciliation was the promise that his detractors would be tried at the next parliament. Two months later, he descended again on London in strength to clear himself of the charge that he had embezzled the wages of the Calais garrison. Impetuous and high-handed, the prince was a young man with an exalted opinion of his own abilities and importance who could not accept his exclusion from power. But this was something to which he had to adjust until his father's anticipated death.[31]

The duke of Clarence's expedition sailed to Cherbourg on 9 August. By the time the troops landed the treaty of Bourges had been revoked by the Orleanists and their differences with the duke of Burgundy once more patched up. Notwithstanding, the English army set off on an unopposed *chevauchée* through France, plundering and destroying as it passed through the Cotentin, Anjou and Poitou. At Buzançais, on 15 November, it was bought off. A ransom of some £40,000 was offered and six hostages, amongst whom was the count of Angoulême, brother of the duke of Orleans, were surrendered to guarantee payment. Thus loaded with booty and the promise of ransom, Clarence withdrew his army to Bordeaux for the winter. English contemporaries and subsequent historians have tended to be dismissive about this campaign. True the avowed objective never materialised. By the spring of 1413 Clarence in Guyenne was negotiating again with Armagnac and Berry for an alliance to defend the duchy, but no longer under the terms of the treaty of Bretigny. It is likely in fact that Arundel and the king had expected the terms of the treaty of Bourges to be unattainable. But they nevertheless had achieved worthwhile objectives. They had reinforced Guyenne in strength; they had recouped the cost of mounting the campaign; and they had demonstrated to the French (and proved to themselves) that once again the English were capable, as they had in the days of Edward III, of marching at will through France. Even though the prince of Wales had opposed the campaign, it proved to be a portent of what was to come.[32]

By the end of 1412, the king's health had further deteriorated to such a point that all believed that his end was near. A new parliament was called for 3 February, but it was never officially opened because the king was too unwell. The business of the government began to come to a halt. In the last six months the financial situation was as sound as it had ever been. Loans had been raised to pay for the initial cost of Clarence's expedition; latterly nothing needed to be paid because of his success. The prince of Wales, in his brother's absence, began once again to be consulted by the council. He was at hand to take over when the inevitable occurred on 20 March 1413.

Henry IV died, according to tradition, in the Jerusalem chamber of the abbot's lodging at Westminster Abbey, thus fulfilling a prophecy that he would die in Jerusalem.[33]

Evaluation

Henry IV died worn out by the stress and strain of kingship. As a young man he had been the flower of chivalry, the admired of all admirers. He had many of the qualities needed by a king, indeed many which his son and heir shared. But he had come to the throne by force and not by hereditary succession. Early commentators interpreted his illness, leprosy as they wrongly identified it, as a divine punishment, especially for the exececution of Archbishop Scrope.[34] Some historians have envisaged him wracked by guilt and remorse, of having lost faith in himself.[35] But in truth the evidence for this is far from overwhelming. There is no need to suppose that he was any more than a very sick man. Henry IV had reluctantly seized the throne and successfully held it. In his last years he was a king more in name than deed. What is remarkable is that, notwithstanding the collapse of the king's health and the emergence of faction at court, the regime was so firmly founded that its existence was not threatened.

There were several reasons for Lancastrian success. Some, such as the failure of the opponents of the regime effectively to co-ordinate their assaults in the early years of Henry's reign, were fortuitous. Others, such as Henry's early steadfastness and decisiveness in a crisis and the crucial role of Archbishop Arundel, who was constantly at Henry's side, either behind the scenes in the early years, or on front stage in the later years, were personal.[36] But the reasons for the successful establishment of a dynasty run deeper. Henry sustained his hold on the throne through the support of a large and loyal personal affinity, the cost of whose maintenance was such a headache throughout the reign. In essence this was the Lancastrian affinity brought into existence by his father, but it was strengthened and extended during the reign. It included not only leading magnates, such as the earl of Somerset and his brothers, the earl of Westmorland and latterly young men such as the earl of Warwick, but also his own personal companions and confidants such as Erpingham, Pelham, Tiptoft and Grey of Codnor. Equally important were the numerous knights and esquires of the body who came to court less frequently, acting as his agents in the provinces, turning out to fight for him when summoned, representing their shires in parliament and stiffening the bench of their counties. They were particularly strong in Yorkshire, Nottinghamshire and Derbyshire and their presence was perhaps the key to his success against the Percys.[37]

Unsurprisingly many royal retainers and annuitants took advantage of their favour to advance their own personal interests, especially in his last, enfeebled years. In some counties, for example Nottinghamshire in the case of Sir Richard Stanhope, the king virtually allowed them a free hand; in others, as in Staffordshire, he put the full weight of the judicial system behind his own men when their position was threatened; and in others, as in the quarrel between two of his own senior men, Lord Furnival and the earl of Arundel in Shropshire, he stood helplessly by. In one region in particular, the marches with Scotland, disorder and crime spread alarmingly from the beginning of the reign as the crown abandoned the system of cross-border tribunals which had been developed since the middle of Edward II's reign. Parliamentary complaints in 1410 and 1411 highlighted the chaos which had ensued.[38] But just as the spiralling cost of government, so also the growth of partial justice and disorder was judged a price worth paying for the greater good of political security within the kingdom.

On the whole, however, the king's men, especially the inner circle of his courtiers, did not abuse their power excessively. The reign of Henry IV is remarkably free from the scandals that troubled the last years of Edward III or the late minority of Richard II. Herein, perhaps, lies another reason for the Lancastrian success. There appears to have been a higher level of probity and a greater concern for the common weal than a generation earlier, or for that matter half a century later. This is neither to ignore that some contemporary critics, such as the author of *Mum and Sothsegger*, held a pretty low opinion of the motives of men in public affairs,[39] nor to deny that Henry's servants and retainers were seeking their own self-advancement. But in the England of Henry IV men could be dismissed from office without being hounded by their rivals. No impeachment proceedings were initiated in any of his parliaments. Moreover men could criticise the king and his government without necessarily being accused of disloyalty. There was a level of trust and openness within the Lancastrian regime which itself added to its strength.

The Lancastrian regime took its tone from the king himself. He remains an enigma, who has divided historians. To Stubbs he was a great constitutional monarch, who offered as an alternative to Richard II's absolutism an experiment in parliamentary monarchy before its time. While the idea of a constitutional experiment initated by the king can no longer be sustained, it is perhaps equally misleading to argue, as McFarlane did, that Henry was unprincipled and only forced into concession by hostile subjects.[40] The parliamentary history of Henry IV's reign is distinctive and is best understood if it is accepted that Henry was willing to listen to criticism, debate with his critics and make concessions. It is not enough to say that because of the weakness of his title and his chronic financial difficulties he had no choice but to give in to the storm of criticism his incompetence aroused.

Henry's own political education began with the Appellants. They in their turn looked back to a style of participatory kingship practised by Edward III.[41] Henry took the throne as the representative of this tradition. As king he did not give an inch more than he needed to on the prerogatives of the Crown, and the evidence indicates that he and his advisers did all they could to secure parliaments favourably inclined to him. Analysis of the membership of the house of commons in his early parliaments suggests that he tended to enjoy the support of a substantial body of 'king's friends' who were his retainers, annuitants and office-holders. The Speaker was invariably the king's man too. Yet vocal and sustained opposition there was, presumably from those knights of the shire who were not his men and the more prominent and outspoken burgesses. It was not the house of commons as a whole which criticised the king so persistently, but an opposition 'party' within it, commanding considerable numerical support. But it is a hallmark of Henry's kingship, consistent with his earlier political career as a critic of Richard II, that he tolerated this parliamentary opposition, not always with a good grace, and was, even if grudgingly, prepared to accept it as 'loyal'. Unlike Richard II he did not stand on the principle of his high prerogative; rather he used what now are called parliamentary tactics to see him through. The early parliaments of Henry IV were not unlike the later parliaments of Elizabeth I.

Henry IV was a king genuinely concerned to work with and through the co-operation of his subjects. He may have made mistakes, have been unprepared for the sheer weight and complexity of government and have been spectacularly incapable of sound financial management, but he was never a would-be tyrant. His retainers knew this and his subjects came to know it too; he may not have been loved, but he won respect and commanded loyalty. In this lies the key to the durability of his regime after 1406 when his health gave way. On the one hand he was willing, if reluctantly, to recognise the necessity to entrust the administration of his kingdom to a council approved by parliament in which others, both Arundel and the prince of Wales, made a better fist of government than him; on the other they and their supporters rewarded him with their loyalty. For six years England was ruled by a council under a king whose interventions were intermittent (and at the end of 1411 unsettling). In practice, in the later part of the reign, because of the enforced circumstances of the king's ill-health the government of the kingdom was conciliar: a kind of Hanoverian kingship. This was not a constitutional experiment, but it was a precedent for what was to follow in the reign of his grandson. While superficially it was a period of faction, like the minority of Henry VI, fundamentally it was a time of political stability. For this the dynasty had to thank its supporters. Henry IV was well-served by his followers; better served than later usurpers. The commitment and unity of his family and servants sustained the dynasty in the last years of his life; it was a commitment for which not only Henry V, but also the infant Henry VI would have cause to be grateful.

Notes and references

1 Davies, *Owain Glyn Dŵr*, 192–3; Ford, Piracy or Policy? 77; Harriss, *Cardinal Beaufort*, 23–4; Nichols, *Medieval Flanders*, 322; Vale, *English Gascony*, 48; Vaughan, *Philip the Bold*, 183–4, and *John the Fearless*, 120–1.

2 For this and the following paragraphs see Given-Wilson, *Royal Household*, 93, 107–10, 128–38, 140–1; Harriss, *Cardinal Beaufort*, 30–2; Kirby, *Henry IV*, 127–8, 166; Rogers, 'Commons and Taxation', 52–8; Wright, 'Recovery of Royal Finance', 65–7.

3 Brown, 'Commons and Council', 11; Roskell, *History of Parliament*, iv, 309. Brown suggests that Savage also spoke his own mind. There is no way of knowing whether this was indeed so.

4 The report is a newsletter sent to the Priory of Durham. See Fraser, 'Some Durham Documents', 192–9.

5 For the proceedings of the parliament see Brown, 'Commons and Council', 10–12; Kirby, *Henry IV*, 163–9; Rogers, 'Commons and Taxation', 60–6; Roskell, *History of Parliament*, i, 87–8.

6 Kirby, *Henry IV*, 173–6.

7 Davies, *Owain Glyn Dŵr*, 118–21.

8 For this and the following paragraph see ibid., 185–6; Kirby, *Henry IV*, 185–8; Harriss, *Cardinal Beaufort*, 28–30; McNiven, 'Betrayal of Archbishop Scrope', 173–213.

9 Davies, *Owain Glyn Dŵr*, 193–4.

10 Harriss, *Cardinal Beaufort*, 25; Vaughan, *John the Fearless*, 21–3; Vale, *English Gascony*, 50–2; Cosgrove, *Medieval Ireland*, 343–4.

11 Davies, *Owain Glyn Dŵr*, 121–4.

12 Brown, *James I*, 16–17; Vale, *English Gascony*, 53; Vaughan, *John the Fearless*, 23–4, 37–41.

13 For the course of the parliament discussed in this and the following paragraphs see Brown, 'Commons and Council', 12–25; Kirby, *Henry IV*, 191–207; and Roskell, *House of Commons*, i, 88–9.

14 *Rot Parl*, iii, 577.

15 Pollard, 'Lancastrian Constitutional Experiment', 103–21.

16 Usk *Chronicle*, 136–42 (Erpingham); Brown, 'Commons and Council', 11; and Roskell, *House of Commons*, iv, 309 (Savage).

17 McNiven, 'Henry IV's Health', 761–72.

18 *Rot Parl*, iii, 572. While the seriousness of the King's condition has always been recognised (e.g. Jacob, *Fifteenth Century*, 99–100, and McFarlane, *Lancastrian Kings*, 103–4), disagreement has existed as to its significance. Are we, as McNiven, has asked 'to treat Henry as basically competent, even though afflicted by occasional bouts of severe illness, or as a chronic invalid with spells of passable health' ('Henry IV's Health', 772)? While others have perceived him as 'basically competent' and to have been in political or constitutional conflict either with the prince of Wales (Jacob, *Fifteenth Century*, 100 ff) or with parliament (Brown, 'Commons and Council', 26–9; Roskell, *House of Commons*, i, 91–9, Ormrod, *Political Life*, 27, or McFarlane, *Lancastrian Kings*, 92–3, 102–13), I have followed the line that he was a 'chronic invalid' who had no choice but to surrender administration and even policy-making to others for most of the time (see Pollard, 'Parliament of 1406', 115–17.

19 Kirby, *Henry IV*, 214–15; Wright, 'Royal Finance', 79–80; McNiven, 'Henry IV's Health', 145.

20 Roskell, *House of Commons*, i, 91–3; Wright, 'Royal Finance', 71–81; Given-Wilson, *Royal Household*, 109, 130–1, 141; Kirby, *Henry IV*, 215–19; Harriss, *Cardinal Beaufort*, 44–5.

21 Harriss, *Cardinal Beaufort*, 39; Wright, 'Royal Finance', 81.

22 Davies, *Owain Glyn Dŵr*, 123–6; Vaughan, *John the Fearless*, 43–8; Kirby, *Henry IV*, 219; For Calais see Grummitt, 'Financial Administration of Calais', 289–92. Grummitt's suggested redating of the mutiny to December 1406 may provide the explanation as to why the deadlock in the commons was finally broken that month. See above p. 54.

23 Wright, 'Royal Finance', 78–9; Harriss, *Cardinal Beaufort*, 37–8, 48–9; Given-Wilson, *Royal Household*, 48–9.

24 McNiven, 'Prince Henry', 6–7; Harriss, *Cardinal Beaufort*, 49–50; Allmand, *Henry V*, 42–3. There was possibly a growing coolness between Archbishop Arundel and Henry Beaufort which helped shape the factionalism at court (see Harriss, *Cardinal Beaufort*, 42; McNiven, *Heresy and Politics*, 128–35). It has also been suggested that Arundel, whose relationship with the king had its moments of strain, lost royal favour in 1409 (see Allmand, *Henry V*, 42).

25 Roskell, *House of Commons*, i, 93–6; Allmand, *Henry V*, 44–5; Harriss, *Cardinal Beaufort*, 51–2.

26 Allmand, *Henry V*, 46–7; Harriss, *Cardinal Beaufort*, 52–3.

27 Allmand, *Henry V*, 53; Harriss, *Cardinal Beaufort*, 63–5.

28 Allmand, *Henry V*, 48–50; Harriss, *Cardinal Beaufort*, 55–7.

29 McNiven, 'Prince Henry', 2 (abdication); *Rot Parl*, iii, 648 (novelties); Roskell, *House of Commons*, i, 97–9; Allmand, *Henry V*, 50–3; Harriss, *Cardinal Beaufort*, 57–8. I have followed McNiven ('Prince Henry') in interpreting the king's insistence on his prerogative at the end of 1411 as a response to the ambitions of the prince of Wales rather than as resistance to a parliamentary attempt to limit his powers (for which see Roskell, *House of Commons*, i, 98–9).

30 Allmand, *Henry V*, 53–5; Harriss, *Cardinal Beaufort*, 59–60; McNiven, 'Prince Henry', 14–15; Vale, *English Gascony*, 58–68.

31 McNiven, 'Prince Henry', 7–14; Allmand, *Henry V*, 56–8; Harriss, *Cardinal Beaufort*, 60–1.

32 Allmand, *Henry V*, 55–6 accepts the traditional view that this expedition achieved little. I have followed Milner, 'English Enterprise', 80–101. See also Pugh, *Southampton Plot*, 55–6.

33 Kirby, *Henry IV*, 248.

34 McNiven, 'Henry IV's Health', 753–9.

35 E.g. McFarlane, *Lancastrian Kings*, 103–4, 112; Kirby, *Henry IV*, 257.

36 But see Allmand, *Henry V*, 42 who questions Arundel's closeness.

37 The role of the affinity is discussed in Brown, 'Reign of Henry IV'; Given-Wilson, *Royal Household*, 226–34, 251–4; and Pollard, 'Lancastrian Constitutional Experiment'.

38 Payling, *Political Society*, 125–6, 191–5; Powell, *Kingship, Law and Society*, 121–5, 208–11, 216–20; Neville, *Violence, Custom and Law*, 96–108. It is not clear why Henry IV's government reversed royal policy in this respect. Dr Neville suggests that it was linked with the revival of the claim to sovereignty in 1400. It might also be linked with Percy aggression in south-eastern Scotland and, after 1405, the earl of Northumberland's defection. Even so, this would still not explain why after 1408, in spite of the representations made by John of Lancaster, warden of the east march, march-days were not reinstated.

39 Gross, 'Langland's Rats', 288–301.

40 Stubbs, *Constitutional History*, iii, 8, 73, 255, 257, 259; McFarlane, *Lancastrian Kings*, 93, endorsed, in more guarded terms, by Brown, 'Commons and Council' and Kirby, *Henry IV*, 256–7.

41 For the Appellants and their programme of conciliar government see Goodman, *Loyal Conspiracy*, 16–54; Tuck, *Richard II and the English Nobility*, 87–138; Saul, *Richard II*, 176–204. For Edward III, see Ormrod, *Reign of Edward III*, 46–50, 74–7, 105–20, 197–203. For further discussion of the constitution see below pp. 232–5.

CHAPTER THREE

The reign of Henry V, 1413–22

The first years, 1413–15

'As soon as he was made king', wrote Thomas Walsingham 'he was suddenly changed into another man, zealous for honesty, modesty and gravity.'[1] From this remark grew the legend of the irresponsible Prince Hal being transformed into the virtuous Harry the Fifth. There is no reason to suppose that the hard-headed young politician of the last years of Henry IV's reign had in fact been the haunter of taverns and brothels. The change that did take place was of a more sombre kind. Immediately he was king, Henry V ceased to be a mere man and took on the mantle of the austere, aloof embodiment of kingship. From the moment he ascended the throne his subjects were presented with an icon, the personification of the ideal monarch: christian warrior, fount of justice and exemplar of chivalry.[2] The problem facing the historian of Henry V's brief but spectacular reign is to distinguish reality from myth, truth from propaganda, and substance from image.

Henry V certainly wasted no time in establishing his authority over his kingdom in the spring of 1413. An obscure conspiracy in the name of a phantom Richard II was quickly brushed aside and, although there were rumours of plots and disaffection, there was no significant challenge to his right as the true heir to the throne of England.[3] His appointments to high office, while promoting those who had been closely associated with him as prince of Wales, did not constitute a rejection of his father's regime. Henry Beaufort, bishop of Winchester, and Thomas, earl of Arundel, were immediately made Chancellor and Treasurer on the first day of the reign; and John Prophet, who had held the post since 1406, was retained as Keeper of the Privy Seal. Clearly, on the new king's accession, there ceased to be any need for a formally constituted council. Men close to Henry such as Henry

Chichele and Richard Beauchamp, Earl of Warwick, Henry, Lord Scrope of Masham and, on his return from Aquitaine in 1414, Thomas Beaufort, Earl of Dorset, formed the core of his trusted councillors.[4] Although Archbishop Arundel also continued to be in attendance until his death in February 1414, the new royal government was in essence that which had ruled England under the prince of Wales in 1410–11.

But the new king's disposition for his household revealed a deeper and more significant sense of continuity with his father's regime. Henry V's first steward was none other than Sir Thomas Erpingham, the most respected and trusted of his father's retainers. And the new chamberlain of the household was Henry, Lord FitzHugh. FitzHugh's appointment was the most unusual and most revealing of all. FitzHugh was over fifty, like Erpingham, a man of Henry IV's generation, but unlike Erpingham hitherto unassociated with the inner household. A Lancastrian retainer since 1399, FitzHugh had not been a courtier and had had no connection with Henry as prince of Wales. He had fought for the new dynasty against the Scots and Percys and had been employed on embassies, but he had for the most part been occupied in local affairs in the north where his estates lay. He was probably admired and respected by Henry as a crusader and a devout christian.[5] His appointment as the king's chamberlain was a clear indicator of the tone to be set at the new court; but it was also a demonstration that Henry V saw himself as inheriting the leadership of the Lancastrian affinity as well as the throne of England.

Henry's smooth accession opened the way for the reconciliation of the heirs of those who had opposed his father. John Mowbray, the young Earl Marshal, and Thomas Montagu, the young Earl of Salisbury, were restored to their titles and entailed estates. In time the earls of Northumberland and Huntingdon were also to be brought back into the fold. The new reign promised a new beginning; the drawing of the line under the old divisions being marked ceremonially and symbolically by the solemn reburial of Richard II, according to the terms of his Will, in St Edward's chapel in Westminster Abbey in December 1413.[6] Crowned on 9 April, Henry V set out his programme in his first parliament that met at Westminster on 15 May. Through the mouth of his Chancellor, Henry Beaufort, he expressed his determination to put right those things that had so troubled previous parliaments in his father's reign. If granted the resources, he would restore 'bone governance', secure sound financial management of his household, defend the realm, and enforce public order. A reassured house of commons quickly voted him a tenth and fifteenth and the wool subsidies for four years.[7]

Henry was as good as his word as far as financial management was concerned. He improved by a programme of rigorous administration the revenues of all the crown lands; he undertook a more thorough exploitation of feudal prerogatives and tightened up the collection of customs revenue. At the same time he transformed the exchequer control over spending by drastically curbing the use of assignment on revenues by tallies as a means of payment and by reducing significantly the level of bad debts. He also reduced the cost of his household and the cost of annuities. Having offered to parliament to make a cut of £10,000, a general review of annuities was instituted. Payment was halted and recipients had to sue the king for renewal. By this means not only were the excessive costs incurred by Henry IV controlled, but the king was also able to redistribute his patronage. Although it did not prove possible to make significant reductions in the costs of Calais, Gascony, Ireland and the Scotish marches, in the first year of his reign Henry V nevertheless took significant steps to restore the solvency of the Crown.[8]

The new king's record in the field of public order was more ambiguous. His first objectives were to complete the pacification of Wales and the marches and to assert his authority over his principal subjects and retainers. Henry reestablished control over Wales in the first year of his reign by a judicious combination of further investigation of treasons and punishment of convicted rebels tempered by pardons and restoration at a price, the levying of collective fines for acceptance of communities into his grace and a rooting out of corrupt officials. While there were later attempts to rekindle the embers, which continued to cause concern, Wales was effectively settled by the eve of the French campaign in July 1415 when Henry felt confident enough to offer Owain a pardon.[9]

Two cases involving his own leading English servants demanded the new king's attention in the early months of his reign. The first concerned a feud between the earl of Arundel and John Talbot, Lord Furnival, in Shropshire. Not only was Arundel his newly appointed Treasurer, but Talbot was a long-standing member of the king's household as prince of Wales. A king who was to enforce the law had first to put his own house in order. Henry arrested Talbot and imprisoned him in the Tower and at the same time placed heavy recognisances on all the parties to maintain the peace. While Talbot was sent to Ireland as lieutenant, his principal servants were indicted before the Shropshire commission of the peace. Later, in 1414, however, when the King's Bench descended on Shropshire, Arundel's men were also indicted. The point was effectively made not only that none could rely on immunity for the misdeeds of their men, but also that the king intended to be obeyed by all, great as well as small.[10]

A similar demonstration of royal authority was intended for Sir John Oldcastle, another like John Talbot who had been Henry's companion in arms in Wales. Oldcastle was a notorious Lollard, who like several other knights had enjoyed royal protection before 1413. Since 1408 he had, in right of his wife, Joan, Lady Cobham, been a substantial landowner in Kent and had been summoned to parliament since 1410 as Lord Cobham. He may well have sponsored the bill for disendowment of the Church that year, which had ruffled clerical feathers; his own letters to Bohemia at the same time demonstrate that he was an advocate of disendowment and reform by the state. It seems as though he had high hopes of Henry V, as a knight of Christ, in carrying out a similar programme of reformation in England. Why it is not clear, since Henry as prince of Wales had revealed himself to be more hostile towards Lollardy than his father had been. Moreover the appointment of the piously orthodox Lord FitzHugh as Chamberlain of the Household ought to have confirmed that the new king's faith followed the school of Rolle and Hilton rather than of Wycliffe and Hus.[11]

Henry called Oldcastle before him for a series of interviews in the summer of 1413. The king was not prepared to tolerate heresy in his own household and, it seems, sought to persuade Oldcastle to recant. For Henry, it was not just a question of faith; in so far as a challenge to the authority of the Church was by implication a threat to order in the state, it was additionally a question of royal authority every bit as significant as breaches of the king's peace committed by his retainers in Shropshire. In the face of Oldcastle's obduracy he finally handed him over to Archbishop Arundel for trial. On 25 September Oldcastle was condemned as an heretic and returned to the Crown for burning. The king deferred execution for forty days. On the night of 19 October Oldcastle escaped from the Tower, went into hiding in north London, and (it was later alleged) planned a rising to depose the king and bring in a Lollard reformation by force. Early in the new year Henry rounded up the principal suspects, with the exception of Oldcastle himself who slipped the net. Three days later, on 11 January, contingents of supporters coming up to London were scattered. Many were arrested, and within a few days over a hundred hanged for treason and seven burned for heresy. Commissions of enquiry were set up to unearth sympathisers in the cities of Bristol and London and twenty counties. Thus, in the aftermath of Oldcastle's obduracy, the Lollards were purged.[12]

The event was a turning point in the history of Lollardy; it was a reflection of the king's own desire for a christian renewal within his kingdom. The reign witnessed an intensification of liturgical reform designed to engage the laity more fully in the rituals of the Church. Henry himself seems to have been devoted to the new cult of the Name of Jesus; according to his chaplain, who was the author of the *Gesta Henrici Quinti*, he advanced at Agincourt first and foremost 'in the name of Jesus (to whom is bowed every knee of those in Heaven, on earth and under the earth)' before the names of the Virgin Mary and St George.[13] Henry's personal devotion is most clearly reflected in the twin foundations of the Charterhouse at Sheen and the

Brigittine House at Syon, both close by the royal palace at Sheen (modern Richmond on Thames); both orders with an empahsis on spirituality, contemplation and private prayer. Towards the end of the reign he encouraged the modest reform of the Benedictine order, which he considered had become too worldly. The king promoted his own response to the challenge of heresy.[14]

The Lollard purge also led to a more general effort to assert royal authority on the kingdom. The principal business before the second parliament of the reign, which met at Leicester on 30 April 1414, was to enact measures to root out Lollardy and to impose public order. The Statute of Lollards extended the role of the state in the persecution of heretics. All royal officials were empowered to investigate and to co-operate with the ecclesiastical authorities in prosecuting Lollards and Lollardy itself was made a felony, with all the attendant penalties. The Statute of Riots extended a statute of 1411 giving JPs and sheriffs summary powers to suppress riots and enabled rioters who failed to appear before the courts to be found guilty in their absence. Other acts endeavoured to close the loopholes in law enforcement provided by the existence of so many private areas of jurisdiction in the kingdom. But the acts of the parliament were not as significant as the despatch of the court of King's Bench on a superior eyre through Staffordshire and Shropshire, the establishment of a powerful commission of inquiry on behalf of King's Bench in Nottingham and Derbyshire during the early summer, and the subsequent establishment of a third inquiry in Devon. King's Bench carried out a thorough review of legal administration in the two counties it visited and also summoned juries to make presentments. As a result nearly 1,800 indictments were received. The king himself moved to Burton Abbey and maintained a regular correspondence with his justices. There was for a few months a formidable demonstration of royal intent to impose law and order.[15]

There were, however, several powerful constraints preventing the king from making anything more than a show of law enforcement. King's Bench could not cope with the flood of business generated by the superior eyre and commissions of enquiries in five counties. While the more accessible counties in which disorder had recently been most prevalent had been visited, the vast majority of the kingdom was left alone. Subsequent disturbances in and complaints from the counties of Sussex and Northumberland revealed that the king's actions in the summer of 1414 merely scratched the surface. In response to a petition from the community of Northumberland which blamed the inhabitants of Tyndale, Redesdale and Hexham for the disorder in the region, a statute was passed in 1414 subjecting the liberties to royal justice in the county. But the act was a dead letter. Indeed the situation was exacerbated by the implementation of the Statute of Truces, passed in the same parliament, which was designed to counter piracy, but which made the resolution of cross-border incidents more difficult, the rein-statement of regular march-days more unlikely, and the restoration of order more distant. There was, even for Henry, a political limit to what he could achieve in the attempt to enforce order and secure personal control.[16]

Moreover, there are signs that during the summer of 1414 Henry's mind was turning towards a grander ambition that was rapidly to become his all-consuming obsession: the invasion and conquest of northern France. Reconciliation rather than punishment became the king's policy as he began to plan seriously for war. On 8 December he offered a second general pardon, without restriction available to anyone for a fee of 13s. 4d. but on the understanding in many cases that those pardoned would serve abroad. Process against most of those indicted in the summer was abandoned. There was anyway much to be said for a policy of reconciliation in circumstances in which no king could fully enforce the law. It may also have entered Henry's mind that a successful campaign in France, by both removing the principal disturbers of the peace from the scene and offering the opportunity of profit and honour abroad, would prove a more effective way to restore order in the shires than the heavy hand of justice. Henry V may conceivably have had a grand plan from the moment he became king to heal wounds at home by making war on France, and it is possible too that it was always his intention in the administration of justice to seek reconciliation rather than enforcement,[17] but the pattern of Henry V's diplomacy and foreign policy in the first year of his reign suggests that the momentous decision to make a major intervention in France was not taken until after the middle of 1414, and that only thereafter were his domestic policies subordinated to that end.

In the first months of his reign Henry V pursued the same objectives in France as had his father. The rivalry between the Burgundians and Armagnacs was exploited to secure Aquitaine. While Thomas, duke of Clarence, returned to England, Thomas Beaufort, earl of Dorset, remained in Bordeaux and during the summer of 1413 conducted a successful campaign, consolidating the gains of the preceding year. Early in 1414 a truce was agreed for a year and Dorset himself returned to England in the following summer. In the meantime the Armagnacs had recovered power in France and the duke of Burgundy, once more expelled from Paris, took the field against his enemies, campaigning to the north-east of the capital.[18] At first Henry seems to have been content to exploit the anxiety of both sides to secure his support to make the best marriage alliance and gain the most substantial territorial concessions either would offer. But he seems soon to have realised that so deep was the animosity between the warring factions, so desperate the desire of Burgundy to regain control of Charles VI and Paris, that there now existed such an opportunity to make good English claims in France that could not be ignored. In July 1414 an embassy was despatched to France which first secured an undertaking for assistance from the duke of Burgundy. It moved on to Paris where it demanded the throne of France, a huge dower for the hand of Princess Catherine, and the concession of the full terms of the treaty of Bretigny with the addition of the restoration of Normandy, Anjou and Maine to the English Crown – in other words the Angevin empire held by Henry II. The demands were deliberately outrageous. Indeed the ambassadors were instructed to abate the claim to the Crown if necessary.[19]

Unfortunately for Henry, Burgundy and the Armagnacs came to terms in the treaty of Arras in September 1414. While this fragile and insincere truce lasted, England had less room for manouevre. But over the following year, through a series of negotiations as Henry prepared openly for war, the Armagnacs who still controlled Charles VI made concessions, ultimately offering on the eve of the invasion a substantial part of the dower, the implementation of Bretigny and the addition of the Limousin. Terms conceding more than the treaty of Bourges of 1412 and potentially enforceable were in Henry's grasp. They were rejected because Henry was committed to war and had correctly calculated that Burgundy would not fight against him.

It is not clear precisely when Henry determined to go to war or what initially his aims were. He began amassing military stores and equipment, especially artillery and seige engines, in the summer of 1414. He declared his intention to recover his rights in France in the third parliament of his reign which met at Westminster in November 1414. He was granted a double tenth and fifteenth, payable in two instalments in February 1415 and February 1416, but accepted the advice that a further attempt at reaching a peaceful solution should be made. It is highly unlikely that at this stage Henry intended to come to terms and the negotiations were conducted more for the benefit of public consumption and propaganda than to avoid war. As soon as this embassy returned from France at the end of March 1415 to report the refusal of the French to concede his demands, a great council affirmed the king's decision to start recruiting an army to muster at Southampton on 24 June and agreed the arrangements for the government of the kingdom in his absence. An army of some 10,000 men, two thirds of whom were mounted, predominantly of archers, was recruited largely by calling upon the king's own tenants (in the principalilty of Wales, duchy of Lancaster and county of Chester), his peers, and the knights and esquires of the body, to serve as they were bound with their own retinues. They were indented for six months' service: wages for the first quarter were paid from the first instalment of the lay subsidy granted in November; those for the second were met by extensive loans raised on the security of the second instalment and the pledging of the crown jewels. During the early summer the army, its stores and the fleet to carry it to France were brought together and converged on Southampton. An embassy sent from France, making the final concessions to the king's demand, could not stop the invasion, which although delayed was ready to sail by the end of July.[20] At the eleventh hour, however, a plot against the king was revealed.

On 31 July Edmund Mortimer, earl of March, informed the king, then at Porchester castle, that Richard, earl of Cambridge, with the apparent support of one as close to the king as Henry, Lord Scrope of Masham, planned to remove him to Wales, there to raise rebellion in his name as king and to bring back the heir of the earl of Northumberland to raise the north. It was a futile plot, endeavouring to repeat the failed rebellions of a decade earlier, organised by a discontented and unstable nobleman who had little sense of what was politically or militarily practical. The earl of Cambridge was the landless younger brother, but heir apparent, of Edmund, duke of York. He seems to have been fuelled by resentment that he had been granted a title a year earlier by the king, but without the means to support the dignity. Why Scrope became involved in the last ten days is hard to understand. It might be that he had initially taken it upon himself to dissuade the plotters without informing the king; a fatal mistake when March himself revealed the plot. The conspirators, excluding March who received a royal pardon, were tried for treason, found guilty and executed within three days. Technically the charges were trumped up, for they had not actually raised rebellion and the indictment of having plotted to kill the king and his brothers, while implicit, was not strictly true. And it is almost certain that Scrope was only guilty of misprision of treason; that is to say not telling the king what he knew. But Henry acted swiftly and ruthlesslessly, exaggerating the danger, so as to make an example of those who still dared to doubt his legitimacy on the eve of his expedition.[21]

War in France, 1415–22

The expedition set sail on 12 August. Henry had kept his plans close to his chest. Some of his indentures had allowed for an expedition to Bordeaux, and this option had been retained until the summer. The destination in August was the mouth of the Seine, and the first objective was the capture of Harfleur. It is likely that the initial intention thereafter was to march through France to Bordeaux. In many ways the strategy was traditional. In the late fourteenth century the English had held Cherbourg and Brest as well as Calais. Possession of a second port on the northern coast would provide a second entry point to France for future expeditions. Harfleur itself commanded the Channel between Calais and the Cotentin; it was the main French base for naval operations in the Channel and its capture would immeasurably improve the security of English shipping, a demand which the commons had continuously made since 1399. Harfleur would establish a bridgehead in Normandy to which Henry had laid claim and it would also open a direct route to Rouen and Paris. A subsequent *chevauchée* through France, as Clarence had shown three years earlier, would demonstrate to the people of France that the government of Charles VI was unable to defend them, or if a French army did stand in his way, he would have the opportunity to inflict a decisive defeat.

As always in war, things did not go to plan. The five-week siege of Harfleur took longer than anticipated, and dysentery seriously depleted Henry's troops. No French army tried to relieve the town. As expected the Armagnac forces held back, because they were threatened in the rear by the duke of Burgundy. But when Harfleur finally surrendered on 22 September, having garrisoned it, Henry decided in a show of bravado to march his depleted and weary army across northern France to Calais. At first shadowed by the French host which greatly outnumbered them, the king's army was forced to march many miles out of its planned route to cross the Somme before its way was finally blocked near Agincourt. Henry had no choice but to fight a relativley fresh army three times the size of his own. He was able first to choose his ground, a ploughed field forming a passage some 900 yards wide between woods. It rained all night before the battle, turning the field into a quagmire. His force, a narrow line across the front, was protected by archers interspersed in wedges and at either flank. The French, on a wider front, drew up in three great divisions in line of route, each to be thrown in succession at the enemy, most on foot. There was no single commander, but so confident were they of sweeping all before them that most of the French leaders placed themselves at the front of the first division. Henry himself made his position in the centre of his line highly visible by wearing a crown and displaying all his banners. After several hours of inaction, he ordered his line to advance to within shooting distance of the French. This, as intended, precipitated the assault. An initial cavalry charge was thrown back; the routed cavalry impeding the advancing infantry. The confusion, the hail of arrows and the effect of the narrowing front in squashing the advancing men-at-arms into one another greatly hampered the attack. Even the intitial impact of such a weight of men in pushing the centre back worked to the English advantage, for the French became partly enveloped and open to counter-attack from three sides. The advance of the second French division confounded confusion. In the end, crushed together, stuck in the mud, falling over one another, the French were massacred. Even so a spectacular number of valuable prisoners, including the duke of Orleans, were taken. English casualties were light, the only fatalities of note being the duke of York and earl of Suffolk.[22] On 25 October Henry won an astounding victory against all the odds. He was able to return to Calais and then to London in triumph. His aggressive foreign policy and determination to go to war had been vindicated.

It might have been that the successful campaign of 1415 would have inclined Henry to attempt to secure the implementation of the treaty of Bretigny now open to him. However, success and the urging of such as Bishop Beaufort to continue to prosecute his rights, to finish what he had begun and to seek a permanent peace seem only to have strengthened his determination to make war. In his fourth parliament held at Westminster in his absence early in November a grateful realm voted him the wool subsidies for life from Michaelmas 1416 and a further tenth and fifteenth from November.[23] The immediate military need was to hold and replenish Harfleur where the earl of Dorset had been left in command. The count of Armagnac, who had survived Agincourt and was now constable of France, was determined to retake the town. In March he discomforted a foraging expedition under Dorset's command which was lucky to escape back to Harfleur. He followed up with a full investment of the port by land and sea.[24] While Harfleur remained in English hands, the French were not prepared to come to terms.

At this point a fourth player entered the scene. Emperor Sigismund had taken the initiative in calling a general council of the Church in Constance with a view to ending the schism. Not only did he need to persuade the rival popes to resign, but also he had to persuade their backers to come to agreement. Peace between England and France would greatly advance his cause. The turn of events in France was not hopeful. The Dauphin Louis, who had begun to emerge as an independent force, had died in December 1415. The count of Armagnac had immediately strengthened his hold on the government. But Duke John of Burgundy had the new Dauphin, John, in his pocket; the teenage boy was married to Burgundy's neice, the daughter of his sister and William Count of Holland. The intention was to install the Dauphin in Paris by force. Sigismund thus had to broker a peace within France as well as between France and England. In the spring of 1416 he visited Paris hoping to persuade the Armagnac lords to come to terms with England. He landed in England on 1 May. He stayed for several months, at first endeavouring to act as a mediator. There was a flurry of diplomatic activity during the summer, involving not only the emperor, but also Count William of Holland on behalf of Burgundy and embassies going to and from the rival camps in France. The sticking point remained Harfleur, which neither Henry V nor the count of Armagnac would surrender. Ultimately, on 15 August, the same day that an English fleet under the king's younger brother John, duke of Bedford, broke the sea blockade of the town at the battle of the Seine and effectively lifted the siege, the emperor by the treaty of Canterbury abandoned his efforts of mediation and formed an alliance with England. Having won Sigismund to his cause, Henry then sought to secure the active commitment of the duke of Burgundy. He crossed to Calais in October and enagaged in intense, but secret negotiations with Duke John and the Emperor Sigismund, who had preceded him. The intention was to form a triple alliance against the Armagnac government. A list of English articles reveals that Henry wanted Burgundy to recognise his right in France. This was probably the stumbling block, for Burgundy's aim was to secure control of the government of Charles VI through his puppet Dauphin, not to replace him. The only declared outcome was the agreement for a six-month truce, although duke John may have secretly agreed to assist Henry.[25]

Having achieved the best he could in preparatory diplomacy, Henry returned to England to prepare for a second invasion. Parliament, called once more to Westminster in November, voted another double tenth and fifteenth. And as he had done a year earlier the Chancellor, Bishop Beaufort, coaxed another two tenths from the convocation of Canterbury. Early in the new year indentures were being sealed for service for a year in France. The army was of over 10,000 men and was equipped and provisioned for seige warfare, conquest and occupation. It was preceded by a navy, first under the earl of Huntingdon and then the earl of March, retained to 'skim' the sea and protect the landing which took place at Touques on 1 August, on the Norman coast opposite Harfleur just beyond the mouth of the Seine. There was little doubt as to the English strategy in 1417.[26]

It took two years for Henry V to conquer Normandy. His first objective was Caen, the capital of lower Normandy, which fell to his assault on 4 September. Because the town resisted, it was looted. The savage treatment also stood as a warning to other towns, which quickly surrendered with the exception of Falaise (16 February 1418) and Cherbourg at the tip of the Cotentin peninsula which held out until the following September. While Henry campaigned in lower Normandy, the duke of Burgundy launched his own assault on the Armagnacs in the Seine valley. He occupied Pontoise and several towns on the west and south of Paris. He was pursuing his own independent aim, the seizure of Paris and the person of Charles VI, made even more urgent following the death of the Dauphin John in April. He finally took the city in May 1418, and massacred his prominent enemies, including the count of Armagnac himself. There may or may not have been collusion between the two, agreed secretly at Calais, but Burgundy's campaign effectively protected Henry's flank and enabled him to fight over the winter without opposition.[27] In June 1418, having secured the southern and eastern frontiers of lower Normandy, and while Burgundy was preoccupied with Armagnac counter-attacks in the vicinity of Paris,

Henry struck at Pont del'Arche, gaining a bridgehead over the Seine and opening Rouen to siege from all sides in July. It took until 19 January 1419 for the capital of Normandy to fall, and the English lost several casualties in the taking of it. Within three months thereafter the whole of Normandy was in English hands.[28]

A new round of diplomacy began. Having secured control of the government, Burgundy now presented himself as the defender of France against the English invader. But he had not destroyed the Armagnacs. In particular, the sixteen-year-old Dauphin Charles had escaped from Paris in May 1418 and was leading their resistance. The two parties had endeavoured to come to terms in the short-lived treaty of St Maur des Fossées in September 1418, which had foundered on the Dauphin's refusal to place himself under Burgundy's protection. The two sides had continued to negotiate competitively with Henry. After the complete loss of Normandy, the Dauphinm again put out feelers, but it was to Burgundy that Henry turned for a peace conference at Meulan between 30 May and 30 June with the duke, Charles VI, his queen and their daughter Catherine present. Duke John proved to be no more willing to cede Normandy and confirm the terms of Bretigny than had the count of Armagnac. And indeed he was already negotiating for another rapprochement with the Dauphin. It was with the intention of strengthening this that the meeting was arranged on the bridge at Montereau on 10 September at which, in the Dauphin's presence, John the Fearless was assassinated in revenge for all the assassinations he himself had countenanced. The situation in France took a new turn.[29]

As soon as he heard the news Henry seized the initiative and began the negotiations with Philip, the new duke of Burgundy, that led to the treaty of Troyes, agreed in principle before the end of 1419, but not finally sealed until 21 May 1420. It seems as though Henry immediately determined to exploit the assassination of John the Fearless to secure Burgundian support for his adoption as the heir to France. Philip, the new duke, did not rush into agreement, but having weighed up his options was happy to agree. An important factor was that, unlike his father, he had no ambition to be the *de facto* ruler of France himself. He was therefore willing to accept the formula that Henry would be adopted as heir to Charles VI, marry Princess Catherine, assume the government of France as Regent and undertake to bring all the parts of France under the control of the Crown. At last Henry had secured the commitment of Burgundy, and, through the quite extraordinary circumstances of the assassination, had been able to secure acceptance of his claim to the throne of France on conditions that had some prospect of fulfilment.[30]

During and after the negotiations leading to the treaty, the process of conquest continued unabated. The English completed the occupation of Normandy with the taking of Gisors (September 1419) and Chateau Gaillard

(December). Joint operations were undertaken to secure the countryside between Paris and Troyes. The marriage to Catherine having been celebrated in the cathedral at Troyes on 2 June, Henry set off with an Anglo-Burgundian force to capture Montereau before the end of the month and lay siege to Melun, which did not surrender until November. Then and only then did Henry and Catherine ceremonially enter Paris, before returning to England via Rouen and Calais to be received in London on 21 February after an absence from England of three and half years. His stay was to be short. After the coronation of Queen Catherine he undertook a tour of his kingdom raising loans and troops for his intended return to France. Parliament, which met at Westminster in May, ratified the treaty of Troyes, but was not asked to vote further subsidies. News of the defeat and death of his brother Thomas, duke of Clarence, at Beauge having reached him in Yorkshire in April, he set off for Calais in June to repair the damage. In August and September 1421 he vainly sought to bring the Dauphin to battle by cam-paigning as far south as the banks of the Loire. Having failed in that objective he turned to recover Meaux, another of the towns in Dauphinist hands disrupting communications between Paris and the duchy of Burgundy. There followed a five-month winter siege in which dysentry caused many casualties in the English camp. One was Henry himself, who after the fall of the town on 2 May 1422 retired to Paris and then Senlis to recuperate. But his health deteriorated, and, despite his efforts to take to the field again to assist the duke of Burgundy, he withdrew to Vincennes where he died on 31 August.[31]

Henry V died two months before his father-in-law, Charles VI, and just before he would have inherited the French throne under the terms of the treaty of Troyes. He had spent all but four months of the last five years of his life campaigning in France. What had he achieved? He had come within a hair's breadth of making a reality of the Plantagenet claim to the throne of France. Whether this was always his ambition is impossible to tell. In all his negotiations from 1414 he reiterated his demand for the recovery of his right to that throne. But on most occasions he seems, like Edward III, to have been using it as a negotiating lever. As late as June 1419 at Meulan he appears to have been prepared to abandon the claim in return for territorial concessions. On the other hand his territorial demands were always so excessive as to make one wonder whether he would ever have been content with the implementation of the treaty of Bretigny. It is best to conclude that he kept his options open. And because of the rift in France he was able to do so.

It cannot be stressed too much that Henry ultimately owed his military success in 1417–19 to the civil war in France. He was able to occupy Normandy virtually unopposed. He was never in all the campaign threatened by a French army in the field. John the Fearless's ambition to control the government of France played into his hand. To some extent the depths of the divisions in France were too tempting. Henry allowed himself to be sucked into the vortex of French politics and made the mistake of becoming a French politician, and a party to its civil war. The very conditions which allowed him to enjoy such spectacular military and diplomatic success in playing one side off aginst the other in a civil war also made it impossible to conclude a definitive peace. Until the assassination of John the Fearless neither side could afford to countenance the dismemberment of France. But Henry seems not to have understood that unless he negotiated with a united France the final peace he claimed to be pursuing would remain unattainable. This was the fundamental flaw in the treaty of Troyes. However skilfully drafted for legal and propaganda purposes, it was in the last resort no more than an alliance made between two parties in a civil war designed to destroy a third. By turning the French civil war into a dynastic conflict between the houses of Lancaster and Valois, the treaty did more to continue it than to end it. It was all very well for Henry to claim for his English audience that by becoming heir to Charles VI he had ended the war between England and France. This was mere sophistry; in reality he committed his English subjects to participate in and be one side of a civil war overseas. He had not ended the war; he had changed its character and extended it. Perhaps Henry V, like John the Fearless, made the mistake of underestimating the Dauphin Charles. Did he assume that a sixteen-year-old youth would be incapable of standing up to the might of England and Burgundy? But one would have thought that the Dauphin had already revealed that he was of a different mettle to either of his elder brothers who had been used as pawns in the game of French royal politics since 1413. Or did he gamble on the third and last son of Charles VI also dying young, leaving Queen Catherine as his only surviving child and his male heir, the duke of Orleans, a prisoner in the Tower?[32]

Troyes was a major misjudgement. By making himself a party to the civil war in France (and compounding that by undertaking alone to bring the whole of France to the obedience of his father-in-law), Henry surrendered the advantage he had hitherto enjoyed and exploited so skilfully. It is not that he could have or should have insisted on different terms, such as for instance the implementation of Bretigny. These too would have been unenforceable on a divided France. Indeed it can be argued that the terms of Troyes, especially the dropping of the claim to be king by rightful descent in favour of the adoption as heir by Charles VI, gave the best possible hope of securing victory in a civil war. As far as we know, however, Henry never considered the alternative of offering himself as the mediator between the new duke of Burgundy and the Dauphin. It is revealing that he made no attempt to play the peacemaker, the conciliator bringing all the parties together in trying to create a settlement, including the granting of sufficient of his territorial demands which both the Dauphin and the new duke of Burgundy might have accepted. A treaty in 1420 between all the contending parties which encompassed the implementation of Bretigny might not have secured that will o' the wisp of a final peace, but it would have given respite from war for a decade or so. But it seems never to have been contemplated. Henry V as soldier and diplomat was a brilliant opportunist who, like other successful territorial aggressors in later centuries, lost sight of what was achievable. The partisan alliance at Troyes committed Henry and his successor to an unwinnable war for thirty more years. In the end he led his kingdom and his dynasty down a path which led to disaster.

The home front, 1415–22

There was a danger too that had he lived much longer Henry V would have lost the support of his subjects in England. Although in France almost continuously since 1417, Henry never neglected English affairs. A stream of letters, often dealing with quite minor matters, flowed from camp or saddle to his ministers at home. Although the king was out of the country, his will was ever present. His council in England, at first under the duke of Bedford and then under his youngest brother, Humphrey, Duke of Gloucester, maintained a strict supervision of the administration of justice in the shires. When Henry himself was in England in the spring of 1421, he confirmed his determination to maintain firm control by the despatch of a superior eyre to Northampton where there had been recent disturbances and by enforcing his own arbitration in the incipient dispute between the earl of Warwick and Lord Berkeley. There was no letting up. The successful limitation of the level of disorder and lawlessness during these years was no doubt helped by the sense of well-being created by the flow of victories abroad, and even more so by the employment of many potential troublemakers in those victories, but Henry did not leave the security of England to chance.[33]

Henry V had also to protect his kingdom against the possible revival of Welsh rebellion; disaffection in Ireland; and, most seriously, the threat from Scotland. The pacification of Wales was completed by 1415. The communes were able to buy pardons from English commissions, but at the price of substantial fines. The way was opened for the leaders of Welsh society to be reintegrated into the English regime, the first stretch of which was by service in the king's armies in France. In Ireland Henry instructed his lieutenant since 1414, John Talbot, Lord Furnival, to wage vigorous war against the gaelic clans. Talbot, who had served the king in Wales, was a ruthless commander and just the man for the job; as one Irish annalist commented, 'from the time of Herod, there came not anyone so wicked'. So effective was his campaigning in 1415 that he left that part of the colony in the hinterland of Dublin still in English hands secure for the rest of the reign. But military success was achieved at considerable political cost. When he was called to France in 1419 he left the finances of the lordship in chaos, widespread resentment among the English colonists and the legacy of a feud with the earl of Ormonde which was to split the colony for over twenty years.[34]

The Scottish threat was more serious. James I was still the king's prisoner. In 1415, however, Henry had been on the verge of exchanging Murdoch Stewart, the son and heir of the Scottish regent, the duke of Albany, for Henry Percy. The Southampton plot caused a delay, but in February the exchange was completed. Percy was restored to the earldom of Northumberland and eighteen months later appointed warden of the east march with the express purpose of strengthening the defence of the north. It was vital for the king to secure the northern front while he was campaigning in France, the danger of which had been brought home to him by raids in July 1415, on the eve of his departure to France. In so doing Henry was able to play the duke of Albany, who was in no hurry to see the release of his king, against his enemies who were. An agreement for the temporary release of James in 1417, designed to strengthen the truce, was met by a full-scale attack on Roxburgh and Berwick by Albany in August 1417. Albany, it was reported, attempted to recruit both the fugitive Sir John Oldcastle and Maredudd ab Owain, the son of Owain Glyn Dŵr, to his cause. No English or Welsh support was forthcoming and Albany was repulsed by troops raised by the dukes of Bedford and Exeter (the newly promoted Thomas Beaufort). The 'Foul Raid', as Albany's failed campaign was christened, was followed up for two years by almost continuous harassment of southern Scotland led by Sir Robert Umfraville. Albany retaliated by sending troops under his younger brother, the earl of Buchan, to support the Dauphin in France, which were reinforced in 1421. These troops played a significant part in the defeat and death of the duke of Clarence at Beaugé. By 1421 Henry had enticed James I, as part of an agreement which was intended to lead to his release, to campaign with him in France. To make the point that James was an ally of the king he was installed as a Knight of the Garter on 23 April 1421, and he subsequently fought against his own subjects at the sieges of Dreux and Meaux. While Henry undoubtedly sought to encourage divisions within Scotland, it is to be doubted whether he set out to divert the Anglo-Scotish war to the fields of France. While his policy successfully secured the northern border, it did so at the cost of strengthening the 'auld alliance'. In his dealings with Ireland and Scotland Henry confirmed that his preferred option was war not peace, leaving a more difficult legacy for his successor.[35]

The successful prosecution of the war in France required not only security on other fronts, but also a ready supply of money and men. Parliament, which was so expertly managed by his chancellors and successive speakers on the king's behalf, voted eight and one third lay subsidies without strings between November 1414 and November 1419, which provided a steady flow of income between February 1415 and 1420. On the security of this, Henry was able to raise substantial loans from prominent individuals, especially Bishop Beaufort, other churchmen, the city of London and his subjects in general. By this means his troops were kept continually in the field. The troops themselves, both the expedition of 1417 and reinforcements in later years, were raised largely through his household, his captains being his re- tainers fulfilling their obligation to serve him in the field.[36]

But Henry's subjects were not willing to pay for and serve in the wars perpetually. The treaty of Troyes was presented as the achievement of a permanent peace partly because Henry had justified his war to parliament and his taxpaying subjects as necessary to enable him to recover his right in France. The treaty of 1420 secured that objective, and thus the need for war ended too. No new taxation was granted after 1420, but of course the peace was a fiction and the war still had to be fought and funded, and English resources were still needed. Henry's return to England in 1421 was primarily determined by his need to raise more money and more troops. And he was only partially successful in both. It is probable that he sought to raise a tax in the parliament that met in May 1421; if so it was refused. During his progress that spring he managed to raise further loans, which Adam Usk described as extortion. Without a hefty contribution from Henry Beaufort he might not have raised the money needed to pay for his last expedition. In December another parliament finally relented and granted a further subsidy, but Henry's resources were being stretched to the limit. The Calais garrison's wages were deep in arrears and soldiers no longer confident of regular payment were less willing to serve in France.[37]

In these later years, as the need for resources to sustain the war grew ever more pressing, a rapacious and arbitrary streak in Henry's character became more apparent. He had already revealed an ungrateful meanness in his dilatoriness in settling his father's debts and in paying his executors for his goods and jewels. In October 1419 he ordered the arrest of his stepmother, Queen Joan, on trumped-up charges of sorcery so that he could deprive her of her dower and use the £6,000 it produced to help pay for the war. Similarly he exploited small transgressions and technical faults in law to seize the property of other defenceless widows such as Alice,

Countess of Oxford, Anne, Countess of Stafford and Beatrice, Lady Talbot. In these last years, although on his deathbed he sought to make amends to his stepmother, Henry revealed that his much publicised concern for justice had its limitations.[38]

Indeed one can detect in Henry an impatience with the constraints of the English constitution. Henry, it has been suggested, saw parliament as a tool of government. In his first parliaments he sought to make the speaker his own agent and amended statutes after they were enacted. Both were resisted by the commons. As prince of Wales he had proposed that the commons vote the Crown regular taxation in return for the promise to deliver the good government they so persistently demanded. It was probably his ambition as king to secure an annual direct subsidy free of parliamentary assent.[39] The best he could achieve from any of his parliaments was the grant of customs for life in the euphoria following Agincourt. Henry had little time for the constraints of the law of treason either. The trial of the earl of Cambridge and his associates in 1415 stretched it beyond its reaonable limits, especially in the case of Lord Scrope who was guilty of no more than misprision, under the law only a felony.[40] Towards the end of his reign, Henry's pursuit of the obscure Sir John Mortimer led him to declare that an escape from prison by someone indicted or suspected of treason was itself treason. In May 1422 a jury had the courage to acquit Mortimer on the grounds that the extension of treason lacked statutory authority.[41] It is not surprising, therefore, that the commons were distrustful of the terms of the treaty of Troyes and insisted before they ratified them that the king declared that he had no intention to introduce French laws and customs into England.

Henry V's quarrel with Bishop Beaufort in 1417 is perhaps best understood in the same light. Beaufort was sent to the council of Constance by the king with instructions to support the ending of the schism by the election of a new Pope before a commitment to reform was made. This he succesfully did, throwing the decisive weight of the English vote behind the election of Odo Colonna as Pope Martin V. His reward, probably acceptable to Henry, was his elevation to the cardinalate. It is almost certain that Henry had intended Beaufort to stay in the Curia and use his influence to secure Papal backing for his cause in France. But in fact Beaufort was created a legate *a latere* with the right to continue to hold the bishopric of Winchester and exemption from the jurisdiction of Canterbury. In other words he was granted control over the Church in England. Henry would not tolerate such an encroachment on his authority within his kingdom, particularly when the new Pope proceeded to campaign for the repeal of the Statute of Provisors. Beaufort himself was threatened with the full force of the statutes of *praemunire* and provisors if he published the bulls; that is to say if he accepted the cardinalate and legatine powers. After two years hesitation Beaufort submitted and was restored to favour. Henry V would no more brook a challenge to his *de facto* control of the Church in England than he would his absolute secular authority.[42]

Evaluation

The dispute with Beaufort further illustrates the extent to which Henry V insisted on subservience from even his closest and most trusted subjects. He was a king, the Burgundian Monstrelet commented, who would not allow them to look him full in the face when they addressed him.[43] Historians, unlike subjects, must. One thing they should not do is see Henry, as he wanted the world to see him, as the special beneficiary of divine providence. He was a master of propaganda. His first *Life*, commissioned in 1416 to justify the war in France, presented him as a chivalric and christian warrior, a paragon of contemporary virtue.[44] He dressed in the clothes of the ideal monarch which he saw in the Mirror of Princes genre. As one historian has commented, 'he set himself . . . to be the perfect king, the exemplar of kingship and the saviour of his realm and people.'[45] He did so with considerable success, too, for according to the obituary notice filed by his council he was, 'the most christian warrior of the Church, the sun of prudence, the exemplar of justice, the most invincible king, and the flower of chivalry'. This view was perpetuated in the years to follow.[46]

That Henry was able and successful is not to be denied. He was the master of his realm. He ruled his greatest subjects with firmness, and, through his comradeship in arms with a generation of young noblemen, he recreated, however fleetingly, the sense of unity and harmony in the political nation that had been absent since the high days of Edward III. He restored confidence and appeared to deliver his kingdom from the throes of a long crisis. He inspired his companions and servants who dedicated the rest of their lives to the fulfilment of his project and the succession of his only son to his inheritance. He was, in the late-twentieth-century sense of the word, charismatic. But he did not, as King of England, fulfil, 'to near perfection, the traditional role'.[47] His military ambitions, which ran out of control, left his successor and his councillors with an impossible legacy. Had he lived longer, had he continued to commit England to a war to make himself master of France, he would soon have faced a crisis at home. His high-handedness with the law, his purges of those whose loyalty he suspected, and the rapaciousness of his last years suggest that as his obsession with France grew, so his intolerance of criticism or dissent would have led to conflict. His impatience with some of the constraints imposed by parliament make it all too likely that he would have come into conflict with that body sooner or later.[48] He was fortunate to die before his fame was tarnished. Others, especially the leaders of the Lancastrian affinity which had loyally served both him and his father, were left to cope with the consequences of his brilliant but mistakenly directed rule.

Notes and references

1 Galbraith ed., *St Albans Chronicle*, 69; McFarlane, *Lancastrian Kings*, 123–4, and Strohm, *Empty Throne*, 211–13.

2 For the construction of this image see Allmand, *Henry V*, 367–8; Harriss, 'Introduction', *Henry V*, 1–29, esp. 26; Powell, *Kingship, Law and Society: Criminal Justice in the Reign of Henry V*, 125–34.

3 Allmand, *Henry V*, 136–9; Powell, *Kingship*, 136–9. His right was challenged in 1415 (see below, p. 76). It is difficult to determine how secure the dynasty was. For the view that this was not until after the victory at Agincourt see Keen, *Later Middle Ages*, 323–5, 353–60. Henry himself, like his father, seems never to have taken possession of the throne for granted. Strohm, *Empty Throne*, 65–78, 89–98, argues that paranoia concerning his legitimacy drove him to invent and persecute 'enemies within'.

4 Harriss, *Cardinal Beaufort*, 70; Catto, 'King's Servants', 85–6; Allmand, *Henry V*, 352–3.

5 Catto, 'King's Servants', 85–7.

6 Harriss, 'Magnates', 31–6; Saul, *Richard II*, 428. For the reburial as a rite of dynastic atonement see Strohm, *Empty Throne*, 111–18.

7 Harriss, 'Management of Parliament', 143–4; Powell, *Kingship*, 135–6; Roskell, *The House of Commons*, 100–1.

8 Harriss, 'Financial Policy', 159–79; Allmand, *Henry V*, 387–91.

9 Davies, *Owain Glyn Dŵr*, 300–4, 326–7. Owain, who never surrendered, was dead by 1416.

10 Powell, *Kingship*, 216–24.

11 For the most recent discussions of whether Henry once had Lollard sympathies see Allmand, *Henry V*, 287–305 and McNiven, *Heresy and Politics*. His zeal to correct Lollards after he became king may be the zeal of the recent convert; on the other hand there was a tradition of austere Lancastrian religiosity running back to his great-grandfather Henry in the mid-fourteenth century. Shakespeare's subversive character, Sir John Falstaff, the companion of Hal's unruly youth, was originally called Sir John Oldcastle (see Corbin and Sedge, *The Oldcastle Controversy*, 9–28).

12   Allmand, *Henry V*, 287–305; Powell, *Kingship*, 141–61 stresses the personal and political character of the revolt; Hudson, *Premature Reformation*, 115–17, sets it in the heretical context. For the suggestion that the plot was invented by the king to justify a proscription of Lollard sympathisers see Strohm, *Empty Throne*, 65–78.

13   Taylor and Roskell, eds, *Gesta Henrici Quinti*, 85.

14   Allmand, *Henry V*, 272–9; Catto, 'Religious Change', 105–11.

15   Allmand, *Henry V*, 323–9; Powell, *Kingship*, 161–2, 168–94.

16   Powell, *Kingship*, 229–40. For disorder in Northumberland, possibly linked to the continuing exile in Scotland of the heir to the earldom, see Allmand, *Henry V*, 311–12 and Neville, *Violence, Custom and Law*, 108–13.

17   Powell, *Kingship*, 232–40.

18   Harriss, *Cardinal Beaufort*, 68–9; Vale, *English Gascony*, 67–9; Vaughan, *John the Fearless*, 193–9.

19   For this and the following paragraphs see Allmand, *Henry V*, 67–74; Vaughan, *John the Fearless*, 193–205; Pugh, *Southampton Plot*, 58–62; Curry, *Hundred Years War*, 94–7.

20   Harriss, 'Parliament', 146; Pugh, *Southampton Plot*, 59; Allmand, *Henry V*, 78–9, 210.

21   The most up-to-date account is to be found in Pugh, *Southampton Plot*, 64–136. See also Strohm, *Empty Throne*, 89–98 for a likening to a show trial in which the confessions were manipulated to enhance the king's legitimacy and security.

22   Allmand, *Henry V*, 80–2 (Harfleur) and 83–96 (Agincourt) provides a vivid account of the campaign. He makes a spirited defence of Henry's controversial order to kill the prisoners, pointing out that it is unlikely that many were killed (93–5).

23   Harriss, *Cardinal Beaufort*, 83–6. For Henry's triumphal return see ibid., 85 and Allmand, *Henry V*, 97–9.

24   Allmand, 102–3; Harriss, *Cardinal Beaufort*, 81–3.

25   Allmand, *Henry V*, 104–12; Vaughan, *John the Fearless*, 213–15. See Vaughan's irresistible comment that there were together in Calais that October 'the three champion double-crossers of the age', 214.

26   Allmand, *Henry V*, 112–13, 274–5; Harriss, *Cardinal Beaufort*, 86–7.

27   Allmand, *Henry V*, 113–20; Vaughan, *John the Fearless*, 217–27; Keen, 'Diplomacy', 189–91.

28   Allmand, 121–7. For discussion of Henry's settlement of Normandy see ibid., 185–204 and below pp. 170–1.

29 Ibid., 131–5; Vaughan, *John the Fearless*, 267–86.

30 Allmand, *Henry V*, 136–45; Vaughan, *Philip the Good*, 1–6.

31 Allmand, *Henry V*, 151–74 and below p. 85. The future Henry VI was born at Windsor on 6 December 1421.

32 For other recent evaluations of the treaty, all critical of Henry, see Allmand, *Henry V*, 440–2; Curry, *Hundred Years War*, 103–10; and Keen, 'Diplomacy', 189–93.

33 Powell, *Kingship*, 247–67. A vivid picture of his direct and personal style of government can be seen in his signet letters cited by McFarlane, *Lancastrian Kings*, 107–9.

34 Davies, *Glyn Dŵr*, 303–9 (Wales), Cosgrove, *Medieval Ireland*, and Pollard, *John Talbot*, 8–9 (Ireland).

35 Harriss, 'Magnates', 38; Bean, *The Estates of the Percies* (Percys); Bradley, 'Henry V's Scottish Policy', 177–95; Nicholson, *Scotland*, 247–52; Neville, *Violence Custom and Law*, 113 (Scotland).

36 Allmand, *Henry V*, 391–8 (finance), 205–32 (army and navy); Harriss, 'Parliament', 148, 164–8.

37 Usk, *Chronicle*, 271; Allmand, *Henry V*, 376–7, 397–8; Harriss, *Henry V*, 148–51; idem, *Cardinal Beaufort*, 106–9; Goodman, 'Responses', 240–52. For the difficulties faced by Henry in financing the wars in Normandy see Allmand, *Henry V*, 399–403.

38 Pugh, *Southampton Plot*, 138–40. His short chapter, entitled 'The Place of Henry V in English History' (passim) is an important antidote to the customary eulogies.

39 Harriss, 'Parliament', *Henry V*, 145; idem, *Cardinal Beaufort*, 84. See also Powell's discussion of Henry's sense of divine mission (*Kingship*, 125–34).

40 See above, p. 76 and n. 21.

41 Powell, 'Sir John Mortimer', 85–8.

42 Harris, *Cardinal Beaufort*, 91–100; for his relations with the Church see also Allmand, *Henry V*, 257–79.

43 Monstrelet, *Chronique*, iv, 9–10.

44 Taylor and Roskell, *Gesta Henrici Quinti*, xviii–xxviii.

45 Harriss, 'Introduction', *Henry V*, 26.

46 *PPC*, iii, 3. Henry was fortunate in his early historians. Unusually among late-medieval kings of England he was beloved of clerical writers. The claim by the author of the *Gesta* that he was 'the true elect of God' (p. 3) might have been excessive, but informs Walsingham's view too. His younger brother

Humphrey idolised him and commissioned Tito Livio to write a Life in c. 1438 which reinforced the idealisation of him as a chivalric hero.

47   Harriss, 'Introduction', *Henry V*, 209. Note, alternatively, Pugh, *Southampton Plot*, 145, 'a man of limited vision and outlook'. McFarlane's much-quoted assessment that he was 'the greatest man that ever ruled England' (*Lancastrian Kings*, 133) depends for its force on what one makes of all the other men that have ruled England and begs a question about the women.

48   Allmand (*Henry V*, 441–2) argues that Henry's 'error of judgement' concerning the treaty of Troyes which so encumbered his successor is best separated from his domestic achievements in evaluating his reign. This is not really feasible. On the one hand his success in reuniting England and restoring a degree of order is inseparably bound up with his early triumphs in France. On the other, the longer-term consequence of his 'error of judgement' in France was the undoing of both his domestic achievement and, ultimately, his dynasty. Thus it could be argued that that which he most feared was brought about by his own success.

CHAPTER FOUR

The minority of Henry VI, 1422–37

Politics, 1422–9

Henry V's death at the height of his powers was a shock to the political nation. Nothing reveals more clearly the command which he held over his contemporaries than their reaction to the event. Their first concern was with the proper interment of his body. Having been disembowelled, embalmed and placed in a double coffin, the corpse was solemnly carried first to St Denis, and then to Rouen at which places it lay in state. The cortège left Rouen on 5 October, moved slowly to Calais and crossed to Dover on the last day of the month. It was not until 5 November that it arrived in London. After the last celebration of a requiem mass the body was finally buried in Westminster Abbey on 7 November, over two months after his death.[1]

There had been no delay in proclaiming his nine-month-old son king. Despite the fact that the dynasty had only held the throne for twenty-three years, the succession of this infant was unquestioned. But it took time to settle the government of the kingdom. It was not until 28 September that a meeting of council convened at Westminster confirmed the officers of state in post. A permanent settlement was not considered until after the funeral of the dead king and the declaration of his last Will. And then it took a month to thrash out. The problem was made more complex by the death of Charles VI, so that the government of two kingdoms had to established. Moreover, Henry V's deathbed wishes for the future government of his kingdom had to be taken into consideration. Henry's desire was that the elder of his two surviving brothers John, duke of Bedford (now heir to the throne), should become regent of France, while the younger, Humphrey, Duke of Gloucester, should be regent of England. There was no objection to Bedford's powers in France, but the council, responding to Bedford's opposition, refused to establish a regency in England. Gloucester, under-standably, argued that the dead king's deathbed testament should be honoured to the letter; the majority of the council argued that they could not be ruled from the grave and that precedent, as in the case of Richard II, established that royal authority could only be held in trust and exercised by a council acting in the king's name. In the event the conciliar view prevailed. Glouces-ter was accorded the title of Protector and defender of the realm and recognised as president of the council, but it was clearly set down that he had authority neither to govern the realm in his own right nor to exercise personal control over the child king. Moreover, whenever, his elder brother was in England he was to step down and accord him precedence as heir to the throne. The settlement was declared in the first parliament of the reign when it met in December. And on 9 Decemebr the first council was form-ally established and nominated in parliament.[2]

The council which took over the government of England at the end of 1422 was an impressive body of men. It included all still living who had held office since 1399 and the senior members of the royal household. Prominent among the bishops were Henry Beaufort, Archbishop Chichele and Thomas Langley, who continued to serve as Chancellor. The duke of Exeter became the new king's tutor, and the earls of Norfolk, Northumber-land, Warwick and Westmorland were the principal lay lords. They were joined by Lord FitzHugh, Sir Walter Hungerford, Sir John Tiptoft and Thomas Chaucer, key members of the Lancastrian establishment. The majority, in their persons or their families, had close links with the house of Lancaster which stretched back before 1399. Thus continuity was maintained not only with the previous reign but also with the old ducal affinity.

While there were tensions and differences of view from the very begin-ning (it could not have been otherwise), the single most important feature of the settlement was the remarkable degree of unity of purpose shown by the political elite in 1422. It took over three months to establish the minority government; throughout this tense and difficult period personal rivalries and factional ambitions were put aside. The one overriding objective of the Lancastrian establishment was to secure the peaceful and orderly succession of the infant heir, who they knew would not come of age for fifteen years. There were several reasons for this happy outcome. One is that there were two royal brothers whose ambitions and interests ensured that neither would seek to disrupt the direct line of succession. A second was that the Lancas-trian affinity was still a unified force. A third, and most apparent, was the inspiration of Henry V, the overriding obligation and duty owed to his memory. But a fourth reason, less tangible yet no less important, was a sense of public probity and responsibility shared by the first generation of Lancastrian servants. In sum, despite the jitteriness which led to the trial and execution for treason of Sir John Mortimer, an obscure relation of the earl of March, early in 1424, the unchallenged succession of Henry VI demonstrated that the kingdom was united and the dynasty secure on the throne.[3]

The new governments in both England and France shared one common and overriding objective: to complete Henry V's mission and to pass on to his heir his full inheritance in both kingdoms. The council in England, meeting regularly at Westminster palace, set about this task with determination. It first of all clarified its own procedures. It determined a quorum, decided to accept majority decision-making, required all members to act impartially, honestly and confidentially, and it appointed a clerk to keep minutes. Its determining principle was collective responsibility. As a body, it was to act as far as possible as if it were an individual with one mind. Thus, as Professor Griffiths has noted, in the first eighteen months, the councillors appear to have shown little partisanship and were able to maintain law and order. At the same time, backed by the renewal of the wool subsidy and tunnage and poundage in the first parliament of the reign, the council maintained a tight control over finance, whilst nevertheless honouring many obligations of the dead king, settling as much as it could of outstanding wages of war, especially the debts of the Calais garrison, and fitting out reinforcements for France in 1423. And in the same year it concluded a treaty with the captive James I of Scotland who was released in exchange for a ransom, a marriage treaty with Beaufort's niece and a seven-year truce.[4]

But it proved difficult to sustain this high level of commitment, unity and impartiality. Inevitably the interests of councillors themselves came to intrude on the common good. In reality the immediate future of England lay in the hands of a triumvirate: Bedford, Gloucester and Beaufort. Much was to depend on their relationships. Gloucester was volatile and touchy, highly conscious of his own royal dignity and status, devoted to the memory of his eldest brother, but frustrated by the limitations placed upon him. Beaufort was phenomenally rich, proud and fiercely ambitious for his family, but sensitive about his status as of the half-blood of the royal family. Bedford was less flamboyant than the other two, but as jealous of his royal blood and status as his brother, as well as being as competent an administrator and skilled a politician as the bishop, and as watchful of his own interests as both. These three dominated English politics until Bedford's death in 1435. But it soon became apparent that Bedford and Beaufort formed an effective alliance, while Beaufort and Gloucester became rivals. The ill-feeling between the two perhaps originated in Beaufort's articulation of the view of Bedford and the majority of the council in the autumn of 1422 which successfully blocked Duke Humphrey's ambition. Indeed it would appear that Beaufort and his allies, and many councillors who were either related or otherwise connected with him, quickly established their dominance. Beaufort's prominence is not surprising given the indebtedness of the Crown to him, which was continued when he advanced another loan to help pay for reinforcements sent to France in 1423, and in the light of the role his family had played at the heart of affairs for twenty years.[5]

Until 1422 Gloucester had lived largely in the shadow of his elder brothers. He had distinguished himself at Agincourt and on campaign in 1417–19, but only during the last years of his brother's reign had he been given political responsibility in England. It was perhaps in reaction to his rejection in 1422 that he married Jacqueline of Hainault (the validity of whose previous marriage to John of Brabant was still in dispute) in January 1423 and decided to make good her claims to the counties of Hainault, Holland and Zeeland, which titles he himself began to use. Both Beaufort and Bedford opposed this adventure because it detracted from the main military effort and threatened the alliance with Philip of Burgundy. But they were powerless to stop Gloucester. In June 1424 the Protector handed over the presidency of the council to Beaufort, who had recently become Chancellor; in November he sailed. In his absence, Beaufort consolidated his grip on the council, using his position for the advancement of his own interests and followers and to throw the weight of conciliar support firmly behind Bedford's campaigns in France. When Gloucester returned to England in April 1425, his expedition having been a shambles, the rivalry between the two flared into public conflict and armed confrontation.[6]

The conflict came to the surface so quickly because behind the personal rivalry lay deep differences of policy which stirred up popular opinion especially in London. Notwithstanding that Bedford and Beaufort regarded Gloucester's expedition as reckless folly, Londoners, who since the treaty of Troyes believed that their commercial interests in the Low Countries had been sacrificed for dynastic advantage, enthusiastically supported a policy which promised to capture and secure a safe market for their goods, especially wool and cloth. Gloucester's early success in occupying Hainault led to anti-Fleming agitation which Beaufort suppressed. To increase the security of London he placed Sir Richard Woodville and a strong garrison in the Tower. When Gloucester returned, Woodville, with Beaufort's authority, refused him admittance. Gloucester was incensed by this affront to his dignity and challenge to his position as Protector of the realm. Throughout the summer tensions ran high both in parliament and on the streets. Finally on 30 October an armed confrontation took place. Beaufort fortified the Southwark end of London Bridge, and Gloucester called out the Londoners to defend their city from the bishop's aggression. Archbishop Chichele was hastily brought in to pacify the warring parties, but Beaufort, not confident of the outcome, appealed to Bedford to come to England to resolve the dispute.[7]

Immediately on landing at the end of the year, Bedford assumed the role of Protector and president of the council. A parliament was summoned to Leicester, away from the highly charged atmosphere of London, which met on 18 February. Even so tension ran high; all attending were required to go unarmed. Because some nevertheless tried to smuggle clubs and staves into the chamber, it became known as the 'Parliament of Bats'. It proved difficult to persuade Gloucester, who had taken umbrage at being just a peer among peers, to attend. After lengthy negotiation both parties agreed to submit to the arbitration of a committee of the council. The award was highly favourable to Gloucester. Beaufort was required to make a public apology to the effect that he had never intended an affront to Gloucester's dignity. His denial of treason was accepted. Gloucester for his part graciously accepted the bishop's apology and received him back into his friendship. The whole procedure amounted to a public humiliation for Beaufort, who immediately resigned the chancellorship.

Superficially the dignity and superiority of the royal house was reinforced. Even though Beaufort had appealed to Bedford, it was Gloucester whom Bedford publicly supported. But at a deeper level one suspects that Beaufort accepted the rebuff because he knew that Gloucester was more concerned with the trappings and show of status than the reality of power. Moreover, it is likely that Bedford had already assured Beaufort that he would remove the royal veto on his promotion to cardinal; on 26 March he was duly elevated by Pope Martin V. The price of a red hat was to grovel to Gloucester. But above all it reveals that the lords of the council, and Gloucester and Beaufort themselves, had neither lost sight of the imperative of unity, nor lost the will to sustain it. It is not the fact that Gloucester and Beaufort almost came to blows that is remarkable, but that they were able compose their differences.

Bedford proceeded to a clean sweep of the administration and a renewal of confidence in the kingdom. Not only was Beaufort replaced by Archbishop Kemp of York as Chancellor, but also Bishop Stafford was replaced by Lord Hungerford as Treasurer. In May the the four-year-old king was knighted; he then proceeded to dub a selection of young aristocrats and distinguished soldiers. Bedford remained in England for the whole of 1426, ensuring that the council, which Beaufort now rarely attended, was working to his satisfaction: that is to say that it supported and gave full backing to his policy in France. But he could not stay for ever. In the spring of 1427 he took reinforcements back to France. Before he left he and Gloucester formally endorsed the principle that the authority to rule in the king's name rested not in 'one singular person', but in all the lords of the council together.[8] A new council was sworn in, which still retained the core of old Lancastrian servants. Cardinal Beaufort, formally invested on landing at

Calais, sailed with him to lead an international crusade against the Hussites in Bohemia.

Gloucester resumed his role as protector, free of Beaufort and Bedford, but still curtailed by council. His remaining ambitions in the Low Countries were extinguished in January 1428, when a long-awaited papal verdict dissolved his disputed marriage to Jacqueline of Hainault. Rather than contest the judgement, he promptly married his mistress, Eleanor Cobham. Gloucester had also begun, somewhat belatedly, to build up his own following in England and in council, amongst whom were John Mowbray, restored to the duchy of Norfolk with his backing, John Lord Scrope of Masham, John, earl of Huntingdon and Thomas Montagu, earl of Salisbury, who was in dispute with Bedford over the county of Perche in France. In 1428 the council backed a new expedition to France, the largest since 1421, proposed by Gloucester and led by the earl. While the objectives and purpose of this campaign were not initially revealed, it was to be conducted independently in France. Salisbury was retained directly by the king and not by the regent; none of his recruits were to be landholders in France; and there was heavy investment in artillery. The expedition set sail in July.[9]

War, 1422–9

Under Bedford's command the conquest had been steadily expanded. In 1423, the triple alliance between England, Burgundy and Brittany having been reaffirmed, Le Crotoy at the mouth of the Somme had been taken, and the Champagne and Yonne valley had been occupied, the success of the campaign being assured by the earl of Salisbury's victory at Cravant. By the end of the year English and Burgundian troops controlled the whole of north-eastern France. For the 1424 campaigning season attention was turned to the southern borders of Normandy which were still not secure. Following up an initial French advance, an Anglo-Burgundian army under Bedford's command met and defeated the Dauphinists in the field at Verneuil. This victory, second only in importance to Agincourt, not only secured Normandy, but also opened up Maine to the south which was invaded and occupied in 1426. Thereafter, however, the advance began to falter. Repeated attempts to take Mont St Michel failed. In 1426 Brittany repudiated the alliance and Breton forces seized Pontorson which had to be recovered in 1427. The major English campaign of 1427, the siege of Montargis, failed; and at the end of the year parts of Maine rose in rebellion. John, Lord Talbot, recovered Maine in the spring of 1428, in the process immediately establishing his reputation for boldness and terror. By the summer of 1428 it was apparent that new life had to be injected into the war effort.[10]

The earl of Salisbury and his army arrived in Paris in June 1428. There the earl was able to insist that the major thrust should be towards Orleans rather than into Anjou as Bedford preferred. At first all went well. Bridge-heads were established over the Loire both upstream and downstream of the city and the assault began on 7 October. However, two weeks later Salisbury was shot and killed as he inspected progress. For a while operations were suspended, but Bedford decided to renew the campaign in November and moved up reinforcements under a triple command of the earl of Suffolk and Lords Talbot and Scales. But the besieging force was too small and too far advanced to maintain a full investment of the city. In April, the attackers were further weakened by the withdrawal of the Burgundian troops. At the end of the month Joan of Arc led the first relief. A few days later she returned with a larger army to begin the counter-attack; on 8 May the siege was lifted. Worse was to follow. On 17 June the major part of the English army was caught and routed at Patay. In the weeks that followed the triumphant French carried town after town until they came to the gates of Paris and the borders of Normandy itself.[11]

Orleans was a bridgehead too far. There had been some justification in striking towards the Dauphin's headquarters at Bourges south of the Loire; and it is arguable that the steady piecemeal conquest of France north of the river was proceeding too slowly without undermining resistance. Bedford's cautious strategy had nevertheless been achieved within the resources of England and Normandy. Gloucester's adventure in Hainault had had little adverse effect and in 1428 the council was happy to authorise Bishop Beaufort to recruit an army to join the revived crusade against the Hussites. The mistake was not to make the attempt on Orleans, but to denude the garrisons of Normandy to mount the second campaign. As a result the *pays de conquête* was vulnerable to counter-attack. Inspired by Joan of Arc the Dauphinists pressed home the advantage. The initiative won in 1415 was lost in 1429. Henceforward the English rather than the French were to be on the defensive. The fate of the Lancastrian project in France, and ultimately the dynasty itself was determined before Orleans.

Of course the full significance of the defeat was not immediately apparent. Indeed the council had been concerned about the progress of the siege of Orleans before it was abandoned. In April it agreed to send reinforcements which were to be financed by borrowing from the feoffees of the duchy of Lancaster. After news of the defeat at Patay, Beaufort agreed to the diversion of his crusaders for the defence of France and their arrival helped stabilise the front. Bedford had already proposed that the time was approaching for Henry VI to be crowned in both England and France. After the loss of so much of the conquest and the coronation of Charles VII as king of France at Rheims in July, it was now urgent.

Politics and war, 1429–37

Henry VI was crowned king of England on 6 November 1429. The coronation was the prelude to a major expedition to France in the name of the eight-year-old king designed to revive the impetus of the English conquest and to secure his title to the throne of France by his coronation. But before the expedition could be launched the resources of the kingdom had to be mobilised and the government of the kingdom re-ordered. The sixth parliament of the reign had assembled on 22 September. But it was not until December that it voted two whole lay subsidies, the most generous grant since 1416, for collection by November 1430. At the same time convocation granted its own financial support and subsequently the wool subsidy was renewed for three years. The wages of the garrison of Calais, which had once more fallen into arrears, were secured. During the early months of 1430 the largest expeditionary force since 1417 was recruited, led by no fewer than nineteen peers. Payment of wages could be met only by borrowing on the security of the subsidies, the principal creditor once more being Cardinal Beaufort, who leant over £8,000.[12]

Beaufort had returned to England before the coronation at which he officiated. Indispensable for his financial backing and diplomatic skills, he was formally readmitted to the council on 18 December. Gloucester had automatically stepped down as Protector once the king had been crowned, but was assured of his pre-eminence by his appointment as king's lieutenant. Before the royal expedition set sail, a revision of the government of the two kingdoms was instituted. Just as the protectorate had come to an end in England on Henry VI's coronation, so the regency would end in France the moment the king landed. The two kingdoms were now to be governed by the one council, even though it was split, with part staying in England, part travelling to France. Its collective responsibility was reasserted; it was ordained that no change to its membership or removal of officers could be carried out without the agreement of both parts; and Gloucester was sworn again to do all by the assent of the element in England. Finally, before the king crossed to Calais, Beaufort was able to renew the alliance with Philip of Burgundy, who on 12 February 1430 agreed to fight alongside the English in the coming campaign. The winter of 1429–30 witnessed an impressive show of common purpose. The crisis in France had rejuvenated the political community in England and had renewed its determination to retain Henry V's legacy.

But the hopes of 1430 were soon to be dashed. Instead of sweeping the French from Picardy and Champagne as a prelude to the capture of Rheims, in the face of determined resistance the Burgundian war effort petered out at the gates of Compiègne. And while the English managed to recover various places threatening the lines of communication between Calais, Rouen and Paris, by the end of the campaigning season no significant advance had been made. It was three months before Henry VI moved from Calais to Rouen, and his court remained in the Norman capital for more than a year. Beaufort returned to England at the end of 1430 to persuade parliament to raise yet more taxes to pay for yet more reinforcements. These helped clear the route to Paris. Only when this was achieved could Henry VI at last be escorted to Paris for his coronation, which he entered on 2 December. Even before he arrived Philip of Burgundy unilaterally agreed a truce with the French, quickly extended to six years. The coronation, a rushed and cut-price affair, was conducted by Beaufort on 16 December. Once it was done the king was hurriedly conveyed out of France and back to the safety of England on 9 February 1432. The expedition had achieved its political objective of the coronation of King Henry II of France, but it had been a military failure. The conquest had not been renewed; at best it had been stabilised around the borders left at the end of 1429, with the Lancastrians in command of Normandy and the Île de France and some of their marches in Maine, Perche, the Vexin and Picardy.[13]

The ten-year-old king returned to renewed political conflict at home. Gloucester was determined to maintain the supremacy he had enjoyed during the king's absence. On 6 November 1431 questions had been raised at council whether Beaufort should not have relinquished his see on becoming a cardinal, and whether in purchasing letters of papal exemption from the jurisdiction of Canterbury he was in breach of the statute of *praemunire* (which he was). Three weeks later the council authorised the sealing of writs against the cardinal, but it was decided to withold issuing them until the king returned to England. In the meantime Gloucester's position as chief councillor was confirmed and his salary increased, with the council agreeing to continue to pay it after the king's return. Beaufort, in the meantime, sought to remove his treasure from England, but his plan became known to Gloucester, who seized it. The writ against him was served immediately the king set foot at Dover. Before the end of the month Gloucester purged the council and royal household of long-serving supporters of both Beaufort and Bedford. Out went the Chancellor, John Kemp, the Treasurer, Sir Walter Hungerford, and the Privy Seal, William Alnwick; Ralph Cromwell and Lord Tiptoft were removed from their offices as Chamberlain and Steward of the Household. In came John Stafford, bishop of Bath and Wells as Chancellor, Lord Scrope as Treasurer and William Lyndwood as Privy Seal. Parliament having been summoned to assemble on 12 May 1432, Gloucester went one further and prepared a charge of treason against his rival. But Beaufort was cleared before the king and lords and his treasure returned. Nevertheless, while Gloucester had failed to ruin his rival, he successfully excluded him from power. And in the spring of 1433 the cardinal left to represent the English Church at the council of Basel.

Yet by then the duke of Bedford in France was becoming increasingly frustrated at the inability of the council in England effectively to support the stalled war effort. A special meeting of the whole council at Calais in the beginning of May attempted to open negotiations with the French and discussed future strategy. Unsatisfied with the outcome, and under pressure from the estates of Normandy to improve the security of the duchy, Bedford returned to England in June. He immediately replaced Gloucester as chief councillor and Beaufort, who had abandoned his mission to Basel, once more returned to the council table. His allies, Lord Cromwell and the earl of Suffolk, became Treasurer and Steward of the Household respectively.

Bedford's first step was to call parliament for 8 July, which gave him an immediate vote of confidence. Prorogued for the summer, when reconvened in the autumn, it pleaded with him to remain in England to take up the burden of government. His terms were the concession of greater authority than had ever been ceded to his younger brother. While the council and lords looked upon him as the only one who could provide 'full fructuous' rule,[14] he himself probably believed that only by asserting his personal authority could he sustain the fighting in France. By the spring of 1434, he was preparing to depart once more. But before he left, Gloucester, resenting his brother's domination and anxious to play his own independent role, once more criticised the way the war was being conducted, proposing a new expeditionary force funded by the confiscation of Beaufort's wealth under a charge of *praemunire*. Bedford took the criticism as a personal slight on his honour. The matter was put before the boy king who, in what was probably his first individual political initiative, successfully appealed to his uncles to become friends again. Bedford's demands were now met: the defence of Calais would be subordinated to the overall strategy in France under him as its captain and he would be supplied with a permanent field squadron of 800 men as well as 10,000 marks a year to help pay the garrisons.

Gloucester was left in England yet again as the chief councillor, but with little freedom of action. With Beaufort also departed on pilgrimage to Compostella, he seems to have absented himself for most of the succeeding year. In France the front was edged further from the borders of Normandy in the Vexin, Picardy and Maine, but the initiative could not be wrested from the French. Indeed in early 1435, further setbacks were suffered leading to the loss of Le Crotoy, the defeat and death of the earl of Arundel at Gerberoy as he sought its relief, and finally the loss of St Denis. Paris was once more under threat.[15]

This was the military context in which Bedford and the council began to look seriously for a truce. Peace feelers had been put out already. Both Pope Eugenius IV and the council of Basel made themselves available as mediators. In 1432 English negotiators had been authorised to start discussions with papal envoys and several meetings had taken place with Cardinal Albergati as go-between. In May 1433 the English had been prepared to negotiate directly with the French at Calais, but no delegation appeared. At the same time it was becoming increasingly difficult to sustain the Burgundian and Breton alliances. Although Duke Philip had agreed a truce with Charles VII at the end of 1431, he had in fact taken up arms with the English in both 1433 and 1434, as a result, in part, of the pressure of the Anglophile group at his court, the link with his sister Anne, Duchess of Bedford, and the hard work of Cardinal Beaufort. However, in February 1435 the Franco-Burgundian truce was renewed at Nevers and the essentials of a lasting treaty agreed. Already in the summer of 1434, the Emporer Sigismund and the duke of Brittany had made truces. By early 1435 the English were diplomatically isolated.[16]

Bedford and the council accepted the invitation to attend the general peace congress which, through Papal mediation and with enthusiastic Burgundian support, was convened at Arras on 5 August. Archbishop Kemp led an impressive English delegation, while Beaufort remained in Calais to conduct bi-lateral talks with both France and Burgundy, but particularly to save the Anglo-Burgundian alliance. The main congress rapidly deteriorated into a slanging match between the French and English delegations who refused to meet in the same room and conducted their argument through Albergati and his fellow mediating cardinal. The furthest the English would go was to agree to ransom the duke of Orleans, accept a marriage between Henry VI and a daughter of Charles VII and concede the right to all lands then held by the French – in other words to partition the kingdom. The French would accept nothing less than the renunciation of the treaty of Troyes and the title to the throne. At best they would accept that the king of England could continue to hold the lands he occupied as a suzerain. There was no meeting of minds. Henry VI having been crowned as Henry II of France, it was impossible for the English delegation to make any concession on his title. What had been justified in the short term, to reinvigorate the Lancastrian cause in France, was now revealed to be an impediment to the making of peace with honour. Only Henry VI could uncrown himself. The best they could hope for, and indeed were probably seeking, was a truce until Henry came of age. Even this was out of the question. On 6 September the English delegation withdrew.[17]

Immediately after the collapse of the congress, and despite Beaufort's efforts to prevent it, Charles VII and Duke Philip moved rapidly to finalise a treaty between them which was sealed on 21 September. Under its terms Charles apologised and made amends for the murder at Montereau and promised to cede to Burgundy a number of towns on the Somme and other lands of which the duke was then in possession. In return, Philip renounced his allegiance to Henry II, recognised Charles VII as king of France and entered a pact to make war on the English. The treaty of Arras undermined the treaty of Troyes and the legal justification for the English cause in France. Moreover the civil war which Henry V had so effectively exploited was now ended. Never again, after 1435, did the Burgundians assist the Lancastrians in making war on the king of France. And given its diplomatic isolation and virtual bankruptcy, unless the house of Lancaster was prepared to cede the throne in order to make peace, it would only be a matter of time before the English were finally defeated.[18]

To make matters worse for the government of Henry VI, the duke of Bedford died in Rouen, two weeks after the treaty was signed. The council was plunged into a crisis worse than that faced in 1429. A popular rising in the pays de Caux enabled the French to recover all of northern Normandy between and including Harfleur and Dieppe; Paris was cut off and fell in April 1436; and by the summer Rouen was threatened on three sides. The loss of Normandy seemed imminent. Moreover, Philip of Burgundy, having declared war on England, moved on Calais in the summer. Yet once again the council in England held firm, Gloucester and Beaufort sank their differences in the common cause and another Herculean effort was mounted to retain what remained of the conquest in northern France.

On Bedford's death, Gloucester, who succeeded his brother as captain of Calais on 1 November, became heir to the throne and chief councillor responsible for the conduct of affairs in both England and France, Beaufort, returning from Arras, took up his place on the council. No changes were made to the membership or the offices of state. All minds were bent to the purpose of saving Normandy and Calais. Yet another parliament, the tenth of the reign, assembled at Westminster on 10 October. In resposnse to the need for reinforcements to be sent to Normandy as soon as possible a tenth and fifteenth was granted, supplemented by a graded income tax which it was estimated would yield a further £9,000. Convocation matched the commons with the grant of a tenth and a half. It was initially intended to send to Normandy an army of 11,000 men, mainly archers, under the command of the twenty-five-year-old duke of York by the end of January. But the size was substantially reduced to 4,500 and a second force under Edmund Beaufort, Count of Mortain (Beaufort's young nephew) was commissioned to serve in Maine. Mortain's force was recruited more speedily, but diverted to reinforce Calais in March. The sailing of the main army was much delayed and it did not land until June, too late to save Paris, but in time to secure Rouen and begin the recovery of the pays de Caux. In the meantime Calais came under threat from Philip of Burgundy who laid siege in July. However, after three weeks, on hearing of the imminent arrival of the duke of Gloucester and a large relieving force, Burgundy struck camp. Gloucester followed up with a punitive raid into Flanders and returned to England laden with spoils within a month. Calais had been saved, as much due to the tenacious defence of Edmund Beaufort as to the relief brought by Gloucester. But Duke Humphrey, who had long emphasised the strategic importance of Calais, received the credit and glory; his stock was never higher and his victory, though in the event easily gained, was a much-needed boost to morale. In parliament in the following March he received the thanks of a grateful realm.[19]

But there could be no relaxation. York's term of office came to an end on 30 April 1437. He was eventually relieved by the ageing earl of Warwick with an army of over 5,000 men. In the meantime the burden of recovering the pays de Caux and securing the borders of Normandy fell on the broad shoulders of Lord Talbot, now marshal of France, who emerged as the most able and decisive of the English commanders. It was he who had organised the defence of Rouen in the winter of 1436; who recovered Tancarville downstream from Rouen on 8 November, the day that Warwick sailed into the mouth of the Seine; and who took Pontoise by surprise in the depth of the following winter.[20]

From 1429 Lancastrian military effort had been concentrated on northern France. But Normandy and Calais were not the only calls on the Crown. In France there was Gascony to defend as well. Throughout the minority of Henry VI, as indeed during most of the reign of Henry V, the needs of Gascony were given low priority. There was little pressure from the Dauphinists, themselves fully engaged in the north. Defence was competently managed by Sir John Radcliffe, steward of the duchy from March 1423, despite the fact that he was starved of men and resources. It was not possible for him to take the offensive, but truces agreed with the counts of Foix and Armagnac and the seigneur d'Albret ensured that there was no loss of territory. In 1433 these lords formally recognised Charles VI, but their desertion did not immediately lead to active war. Radcliffe, however, who had fought a running battle with the council for the payment of the arrears of his wages, was relieved in 1436. The government of the duchy was left in the hands of leading Gascons who continued to hold the fort. Because of the concentration by both parties on the war in the north, the minority of Henry VI was for Gascons a rare period of relative peace and prosperity.[21]

The council had to give more attention to Scotland. At the beginning of the minority it enjoyed the advantage of holding the king of Scots, James I, in captivity. Even so borderers on both sides were wont to disturb the peace. The council endeavoured to make a more lasting peace through the terms for James's release. A marriage treaty was sealed between the king and Joan Beaufort, daughter of the earl of Somerset, in 1424. Before James was released and the couple returned to Scotland, terms were agreed for the payment of a ransom, the renewal of the truce and the handing over of hostages to England. In the event, little of the ransom was paid; and in 1428 the Auld Alliance was renewed through the marriage of James's daughter Margaret to the Dauphin Louis and a commitment to military asistance. James initially used the treaty as a lever in his negotiations with England, renewing the truce in 1430 on terms more favourable to him. In 1433 Gloucester even sought, unsuccessfully, to negotiate a more lasting peace on the basis of the restoration of Berwick and Roxburgh. But neither English nor Scottish marcher lords were interested in peace. The English Warden of the East March, the earl of Northumberland, in league with the Scottish earl of March, organised an attack on Dunbar castle which was defeated at Piperdean in September. For his part, King James took the opportunity of the treaty of Arras to confirm the French alliance, despatch Margaret to France for her wedding and, in August 1436, launch an assault on Roxburgh. However, the campaign ended ignominiously after only two weeks. The English government was only spared further trouble on the northern border by the assassination of the high-handed James at Perth on the night of 20/21 February 1437 and the confusion in Scotland that ensued.[22]

The council could give even less attention to the problems of Ireland than it could to the Scottish march and Gascony. An attempt to provide more decisive government in Ireland, both to end the internal feud between the Talbot and Butler families and to reassert control over the Gael, was initially made by the appointment in March 1423 of Edmund Mortimer, earl of March as the king's lieutenant. He died of the plague in January 1425. James Butler, earl of Ormonde succeeded him, but for most of the minority Ireland was placed in the hands of a succession of lesser English peers, receiving only limited financial backing. The Irish resources were scarcely sufficient to sustain the administration, and, undermined from within by the continuing rivalry between the Talbot and Butler factions, the *de facto* English colony shrank by the mid-1530s to the area in the hinterland of Dublin later formalised as the Pale. Enough was done to hold on to the Irish lordship, but in the eyes of the author of the *Libelle of Englyssche Polycie*, composed about 1437,

> our ground there is a little corner
> to all Ireland in true comparison.[23]

The end of the minority

When *The Libelle* was written the time was approaching for Henry VI at last to enter his majority. The upbringing of a king, not just an heir to the throne but a reigning monarch, was a matter of great importance. His first years were spent in the care of women; his mother, Queen Catherine, aided by a nurse, Joan Astley, who was succeeded by a governess, Alice Butler, licensed, in the time-honoured traditions of the upper classes, to chastise him when the case required. When he was seven, by which time he was 'grown in person, wit and inderstanding', it was time to move into the world of men. On 1 June 1428 Richard Beauchamp, Earl of Warwick, the most renowned man of chivalry of the day, was appointed his tutor, to train him in moral virtues, literacy, languages, discipline and courtesy. The royal household in which he grew up was staffed by the most trusted Lancastrian servants, Lord FitzHugh (until his death in 1425), Lord Tiptoft and Sir Walter Hungerford. In it too, making it a kind of aristocratic boarding school, came to be lodged the principal wards of the Crown, most notably after 1425, Richard, Duke of York. From what little is known of the king's formal education it is apparent that it was conventional. By March 1427 he was familiar with the Primer; and he soon had two 'little coat armours' and a sword with which 'to learn to play in his tender age'. By 1432 Warwick was beginning to find his charge a handful. The eleven-year-old was by then 'in conceit and knowledge of his high and royal authority'. Warwick needed the authority of the council to impose discipline on the king and keep him to his studies.[24]

The child king made public appearances from an early date. In November 1423, when he was only two, he was brought at the commons' request to sit and occupy the throne; a ritual which was repeated at most if not all subsequent parliaments. When he was four, in April 1425, he was paraded through London in a ceremonial ride designed to demonstrate that he himself was not threatened by the violent dispute between Gloucester and Beaufort then at its height. By the the time of his coronations in 1429 and 1431, therefore, he was accustomed to the rituals of public display. It is not entirely clear when he first participated in public affairs. In February 1433 the council drew up a list of matters on which he should be kept informed; eight months later he was briefed by a delegation returning from the council of Basel. He successfully intervened, whether on his own initiative or on appeal is not clear, in the spring of 1434 to beg his two uncles to settle their differences. In the late summer of 1434, following the prompting of the duke of Gloucester it would appear, the twelve-year-old began to intervene more directly. This brought a swift response from the council, which hurriedly sent a deputation down to Cirencester to impress upon him that he was not yet of an age to make decisions and, while recognising his remarkable understanding, urged him to accept that he had not reached the age when he could assume the responsibility for the kingdom.[25]

The ending of a minority was inevitably a delicate matter. A king was expected to take some responsibility at sixteen, maybe fourteen, but in a transitional adolescence the support and guidance of a formal council was still considered necessary. It is difficult to state categorically when Henry's minority ended, precisely because it happened in stages. From the very beginning of the reign it was recognised that royal authority rested in his person even though, because he was too young, the council exercised it on his behalf. This principle was reaffirmed in November 1435. But towards the end of the year, after Bedford's death and the treaty of Arras and following his fourteenth birthday on 6 December, the young king began to attend council and some letters began to be issued by the king with the advice of the council. A major step was taken in the July 1436 on the eve of the departure of Gloucester's expedition to Calais; now for the first time the king began to make grants in his own name alone, in the first instance for the benefit of Gloucester and Beaufort personally. Over the next year Henry exercised his prerogative with ever increasing frequency in matters both large and small. However, in matters of policy, as opposed to grace, the council remained in control. As the king's sixteenth birthday approached a great council was summoned to meet at Merton Priory to regularise the relationship between king and council in the government of the realm. On 13 November a declaration on the matter was made.[26]

The declaration of 13 November 1437 has long been a matter of controversy. At one time it was thought to have led to conflict between king and council over control of the kingdom; and more recently to have been interpreted as imposing constraints on the king. While it is now accepted that the declaration was part of the normal process by which the minority was ended, differences of opinion still exist as to whether it marked the definitive end of the minority or was but a clarification of the *status quo* before the minority withered away in the succeeding years. The declaration was based on the terms agreed between Henry IV and parliament in December 1406 for the establishment of a council to take over significant responsibilities in the government of the realm. It is significant, no doubt, that two of the senior councillors in 1437, Cardinal Beaufort and Lord Tiptoft, had both been at the centre of debate and instrumental in forging the agreement of 1406.

Now, in 1437, the situation was different; the king was leaving childhood, rather than suffering debilitating illness. But the precedent appealed because in both cases a *modus vivendi* was being established whereby king and council shared responsibility for the time being, in particular in which a council was to assist an adult king in the exercise of his authority. As in 1406, it was declared that there was no limit on the exercise of the king's prerogative or grace. Indeed in 1437 the king was given greater freedom, for the requirement that the king's grants should be submitted to the approval of the council was not repeated. Yet it is clear that the council was to continue, as it did in 1406, to exercise responsibility in matters of state. Only if the council was divided or if there were matters (vaguely expressed) 'of great weight and charge' was it bound to refer to the king. And in these circumstances councillors were to seek his 'advis', implying that the final decision still lay with the council.

It is hard to see that this declaration restored the normality of rule by an adult monarch. Rather, as its use of the precedence of 1406 demonstrates, it established a formal, and thus abnormal, sharing of power between a monarch and a constituted standing council. However, as such, it could only have been a transitional arrangement. The way was open for the king in future to ignore the formally constituted council and to turn anywhere for counsel; and for him to resume full control over the making of policy and the exercise of royal authority. Because of the king's personality and the absence of conflict it is hard to determine precisely when that stage was reached. But in the long transition that marks the end of the minority in the late 1430s the declaration of November 1437, coming as it did shortly before his sixteenth birthday, marks the moment when the government of the realm passed from being in the hands of a council acting on behalf of a child monarch to being in the hands of an adult monarch acting through a council. In these terms the minority can be said to have ended in 1437.[27]

The conciliar achievement

The minority of Henry VI was the longest in English history. It has tended to receive a bad press from historians. Using the text, 'woe unto thee o land that is ruled by a child', the minority has been perceived as the genesis of later troubles. In particular the feud between Beaufort and Gloucester has been identified as the principal cause of failure. Yet despite bitter rivalry between the two, Beaufort's relentless pursuit of family aggrandisement and Gloucester's prickly pride, time after time in moments of crisis both men were willing to work together for the common cause. Their rivalry has been often stressed, their willingness to compromise in the king's interest less frequently. And this was still the case in 1437 when Henry VI came of age. The triumvirate of Bedford, Gloucester and Beaufort, despite the strains, tensions and rivalries between all three, effectively held the kingdom together.

There is undoubtedly much that can be found at fault in the conduct of the lords and magnates of the realm during the minority. They did not resist the opportunity to feather their own nests at the expense of the common good. Yet the record of the disposition of patronage in church and state – preferments to high ecclesiastical office, appointments to crown offices, and the disposal of wardships – suggests that consideration of needs of the realm was never completely neglected. Beaufort was the most zealous and successful of the councillors in pursuing the interests of his family and his friends. In 1424–5 he shamelessly exploited his position as chancellor for his own partisan interests. He was subsequently reined in, and although the large and widespread Beaufort network continued to benefit, even during those years when the cardinal himself was out of favour or absent from the kingdom, after 1425 the distribution of patronage was balanced. It is noticeable that, unlike Beaufort, neither Bedford nor Gloucester sought to exploit their periods of dominance to their own excessive benefit. They secured some rewards, but Gloucester in particular seems in those years when he held the springs of patronage to have been unwilling, or unable, to use them to strengthen his position.[28]

The fruits of office tended to be shared between councillors. Collective responsibility extended to collective benefit. This is revealed most clearly in the distribution and management of feudal casualties, especially the windfall of wardships. Apart from 1424–7, the council was generally vigilant in the assertion of royal rights: little was successfully concealed. The wardships tended to fall into the hands of councillors and their associates. Often only one-off payments were required and the terms were generous enough for the recipient to expect to make a reasonable profit. The respected earl of Warwick himself, royal councillor and the king's guardian from 1 June 1428, did not hesitate to use his position for his own advantage. He secured a favourable settlement of his long-standing claim to the Berkeley inheritance in 1424 and pursued a relentless course of aggrandisement in the midlands. But against this it must be borne in mind that councillors and servants of the regime came to be owed substantial sums in arrears of wages. Sir John Radcliffe, the long-serving and long-suffering steward of Gascony, received settlement of some of his wages by grants of wardships, culminating in the heiress of Walter, Lord FitzWalter who he married to his own son and heir. And the greater part of the biggest prizes, such as the custody of the estates of the duke of Norfolk and the duke of Bedford after their deaths, were reserved to the Crown and exploited for its benefit.[29]

The council also carried the heavy burden of maintaining law and order. There can be little doubt that lawlessness and disorder increased over the fifteen years. In 1431 the government faced a major social and religious rising in southern England, decisively crushed by Humphrey of Gloucester.

But the greatest threat came from aristocratic disorder, especially if it involved councillors themselves. It is not surprising that the growing tensions and rifts in the council in the 1420s, especially the quarrel between Gloucester and Beaufort, had a generally deleterious effect. It proved impossible to maintain complete impartiality or the rigorous enforcement of public order. Even an adult king had difficulty administering the law; the odds against a council acting collectively in the name of an under-age king achieving the same degree of success as Henry V were long. Several aristocratic disputes troubled the council in these years. Henry, Lord FitzHugh, and after his death his son, became embroiled in violent disorder in Yorkshire over possession of estates confiscated from Lord Scrope of Masham in 1415. The elder FitzHugh was a councillor; there was little the council could do to restrain him other than by exhortation. John, lord Talbot, not himself a councillor, but from 1424 the earl of Warwick's son-in-law, was a persistent irritant. Already a fierce rival with the earl of Ormonde for dominance in Ireland, in 1423 he went on the rampage in Herefordshire in pursuit of a quarrel with his one-time servant, Sir John Abrahall. By 1425 he was attacking Joan Beauchamp, Lady Bergavenny, the earl of Ormonde's mother-in-law in pursuit of one of the earl of Warwick's quarrels. The Talbot problem was resolved by sending him to France in 1427.[30]

Yet, the council was fully aware of its responsibilty to set a good example. A sustained effort was made to control and contain disputes. Besides general exhortation, twice, in 1424 and 1430, it was agreed that disputes between councillors would be brought before them and settled in council. The Warwick–Mowbray dispute over precedence and ownership of land was settled in parliament in 1425. In 1430 the duke of Norfolk and earls of Huntingdon and Warwick were made to swear that they would take any quarrels involving them to the council for settlement. The principal means deployed for resolving disputes and easing tension was arbitration, as in the case of the quarrel between Gloucester and Beaufort itself. It was arbitration that settled both the Beauchamp–Berkeley dispute and the Beauchamp–Talbot–Bergavenny feud in 1426. It is important not to lose sight of the fact that the council did all in its powers to contain and control aristocratic violence and that while the level of lawlessness, perhaps inevitably, increased, it did not threaten a general breakdown of political order.[31]

After 1429, perhaps because some of the more unruly lords such as Talbot were in France and perhaps because the gravity of the crisis led them to shelve their differences, the number of disputes seems to have decreased. The commons kept up the pressure. In 1433, in response to parliamentary concern about the rising general level of disorder, all the lords undertook to swear an oath to preserve the peace and not to maintain criminals. Moreover the oath-taking was extended during 1434 to the substantial gentry in all the shires and liberties of the kingdom. The level of lawlessness does indeed appear to have subsided for a while after this extraordinary act of collective self-policing. In one area, furthermore, the council enjoyed significant success. As part of the treaty with Scotland in 1424 border tribunals were restored. The procedures and remedies for dealing with cross-border breaches of the truce at regular march-days were elaborated in the following years, especially in an argeement drawn up in 1429. It has been suggested that the foundations of border law which survived until the unification of the kingdoms were laid during these years. And certainly the evidence suggests that the borders were less disturbed during times of truce during the minority than they had been either in the reigns of Henry IV or Henry VI.[32]

Despite all the council's efforts, however, there were ominous signs that by 1437 lawlessness was once more increasing. It is easy to disparage the self-regulatory policies pursued by the council and the tendency to seek arbitration, composition and promises of good behaviour rather than en-forcement of the full rigour of the law. But it is hard to see what else could have been done. As it was, the worst excesses of violence and lawlessness were controlled and an acceptable level of order was maintained. Neverthe-less, determined as the council was to rule impartially and effectively, there was unavoidably a tendency for dominant councillors to exploit their posi-tion at the centre to enhance and build up their power in the localities. Thus the earl of Warwick was able to consolidate his hegemony in the west midlands, at the expense of rivals such as the duke of Norfolk or Joan, Lady Bergavenny; Beaufort was in a position to promote his nephew, Richard Neville, earl of Salisbury as the successor to his father the earl of Westmorland in both the north-west and the north-east; and William de la Pole, Earl of Suffolk, took the opportunity to step into the shoes of Sir Thomas Erpingham at the head of the duchy of Lancaster interest in East Anglia. Stability was maintained, but at the expense of central authority.[33]

The council enjoyed similar success in its financial management. Until 1428 the commons, mindful of the assurances given by Henry V following the treaty of Troyes that the burden of the war in France would fall on his French taxpayers, and despite the endeavours on occasion by both Beaufort and Bedford to coax them, steadfastly declined to vote any lay taxes. They were happy to continue the subsidies on wool and tunnage and poundage, but this was the extent of their generosity. At first, by tight financial control, the council was able to meet all expenses, including the despatch of rein-forcements to France in 1423, from within regular resources. After 1424 by resort to loans, by exploiting feudal revenues, by novel taxation and by cutting other expenditure, the council was able to balance the budget. In 1429, under the rigorous management of the treasurer, Lord Hungerford, the war effort was once more being sustained by regular income without recourse to substantial loans or large-scale extraordinary taxation.[34]

The crisis of 1429–30 undermined this sound house-keeping. Following the coronation expedition, despite the renewed generosity of the commons, the government ran increasingly into debt as it borrowed more and more on the security of taxation. By 1433 the Exchequer had exhausted its credit. The income from all taxation voted and to be paid in the next two years was assigned; the accumulated debt was £168,000, more than two and a half times the annual income; and arrears of wages due to captains in France, the lieutenants of Ireland and Gascony and the wardens of the marches were accumulating at an alarming rate. The situation was made worse by a decline in revenue from customs and the inability after 1429 to raise sufficient taxes in Normandy and the *pays de conquête* to continue to carry the entire burden of supporting the garrison. Lord Cromwell's budget, presented to parliament in the autumn of 1433, revealed an annual deficit on regular and domestic income and expenditure alone of over £21,000. Cromwell insisted on a programme of expenditure cuts, including the reduction of salaries and cancellation of debts (especially to captains of war) starting with Bedford and Gloucester at the top. Household costs were saved by giving the monastery of Bury St Edmunds the privilege of accommodating the king at its own charge for four months.

Having instituted a thorough retrenchment, the Treasurer turned to parliament for supply. But the commons were prepared to vote only one tenth and fifteenth, and that reduced by £4,000 in relief of impoverished communities, to be paid over two years. Convocation was even less willing than parliament, and, similarly pleading poverty, granted only a further three-quarter subsidy. The Crown, therefore, had no choice but to resort to further borrowing to finance its planned offensive in France. In the two financial years 1433–5, it borrowed over £55,000. A general loan raised very little, so yet again the principal creditors were the city of London, the feoffees of the duchy of Lancaster and above all Cardinal Beaufort, whose loans now stood at over £20,000.[35] Matters became worse after 1435 because of the cost of saving Normandy and Calais in 1435–7. A further £75,000 had to be borrowed over the two years. By 1437, revenue was being anticipated at least two years in advance. And credit was becoming even tighter, as income from customs slumped as a result of the collapse of exports to Flanders. But the Crown was still solvent, if only just.[36]

The achievement of the minority council was substantial. It controlled and contained the potentially explosive divisions within itself, it held doggedly onto a significant part of the conquest in France, it kept the finances of the kingdom, stretched to the limit as they were, under control; it maintained stability and, with difficulty, the administration of justice in the kingdom as a whole; and finally, at the end, it orchestrated an orderly and peaceful transition of power to Henry VI when he attained his majority. Compared with the sleaze that characterised the declining years of Edward III or was soon to overtake the personal rule of Henry VI himself, the aristocratic oligarchy which ruled England between 1422 and 1437 demonstrated an impressive degree of purposefulness, probity and integrity. This need not occasion surprise. These men were the heirs to the Lancastrian establishment that had come into power in 1399. With their unflinching commitment to the dynasty they had helped put on the throne and their long experience in government (including conciliar government under the first Lancastrian), they were well equipped to shoulder the burden of ruling the kingdom. They demonstrated that conciliar government answerable to parliament could work. Their mission, largely achieved, was to pass on the authority exercised by Henry V. Indeed it was the inspiration of Henry V that sustained them over fifteen long and difficult years. It was for him that they crowned Henry VI in Paris and fought unrelentingly to hold as much of the conquest in France as they possibly could; and it was for him that they delivered the kingdom of England, secure and still solvent, into his son's hands. After 1437 it was up to Henry VI to build on the foundations provided by his father's men.

Notes and references

1   Allmand, *Henry V*, 174–81.

2   Griffiths, *Henry VI*, 11–27 for this and the following paragraph. My debt to Part One of this work and to Harriss, *Cardinal Beaufort* for what follows will be apparent. Together they provide the fullest and most detailed account of the minority and are essential works of reference to the primary sources.

3   Powell, 'Sir John Mortimer', 83–98.

4   Brown, *James I*, 24–33.

5   There are no biographies of Bedford and Gloucester other than Williams, *My Lord of Bedford*, and Vickers, *Humphrey, Duke of Gloucester*. Stratford, *The Bedford Inventories*, provides in its general information a recent overview of Duke John's career. Harriss, *Cardinal Beaufort*, deals sympathetically with Duke Humphrey.

6   Vaughan, *Philip the Good*, 31–9.

7   For this and the following paragraphs see Griffiths, *Henry VI*, 36–7, 73–83; Harriss, *Cardinal Beaufort*, 136–44, 151–9, 165–6.

8   *PPC*, iii, 231–42.

9   Harriss, *Cardinal Beaufort*, 168–72.

10   Allmand, *Lancastrian Normandy*, 24–32; Griffiths, *Henry VI*, 184–8; Pollard, *John Talbot*, 12–13.

11   Pollard, *John Talbot*, 13–17.

12   Griffiths, *Henry VI*, 189–94; Harriss, *Cardinal Beaufort*, 191–213; Wolffe, *Henry VI*, 48–64 for this and the following paragraphs.

13   Griffiths, *Henry VI*, 38–44, 94–100; Harriss, *Cardinal Beaufort*, 214–26, 229–38 for this and the following paragraphs.

14   *Rot Parl*, iv, 423.

15   Griffiths, *Henry VI*, 194–9; Pollard, *John Talbot*, 18–21.

16   Harriss, *Cardinal Beaufort*, 226–7, 240–2, 247–51; Vaughan, *Philip the Good*, 67–71.

17   Dickinson, *The Congress of Arras, 1435* passim; Harriss, *Cardinal Beaufort*, 247–51. The wider diplomatic context is discussed in Palmer, 'The War Aims of the Protagonists' and Allmand, *Lancastrian Normandy*, 273–8.

18   Allmand, *Lancastrian Normandy*, 39–40 and Vaughan, *Philip the Good*, 107, however, see the treaty as being less of a turning point.

19   Griffiths, *Henry VI*, 45, 200–4; Harriss, *Cardinal Beaufort*, 253–64; Pollard, *John Talbot*, 21–5.

20   Pollard, *John Talbot*, 45–9.

21   Griffiths, *Henry VI*, 182–4, 205–6; Vale, *English Gascony*, 98–105.

22   Brown, *James I*, 109–10, 151–5, 160–4 (and for a graphic account of the assassination, 172–81); Griffiths, *Henry VI*, 154–62; McGladdery, *James II*, 5–14.

23   Warner, ed., *The Libelle*, 37; Cosgrove, *Medieval Ireland*, 525–84; Griffiths, *Henry VI*, 162–7, 411–12.

24   *PPC*, iv, 133; Griffiths, *Henry VI*, 52–7, 59; Wolffe, *Henry VI*, 35–8, 45–7, 69.

25   Griffiths, *Henry VI*, 231–7; Harriss, *Cardinal Beaufort*, 231; Wolffe, *Henry VI*, 39, 41, 76, 79–80; For a discussion of the constitutional niceties involved see Watts, *Henry VI*, 111–22.

26   Watts, *Henry VI*, 128–33; Wolffe, *Henry VI*, 87–92.

27   Griffiths, *Henry VI*, 275–7, Watts, *Henry VI*, 133–40 and 'Minority', 127–31; Wolffe, *Henry VI*, 87–92 and 'Personal Rule', 45–6; and above, pp. 000–00.

28   Griffiths, *Henry VI*, 94–5; Harriss, *Cardinal Beaufort*, 109–11, 145–6, 160–5, 267–71.

29   Griffiths, *Henry VI*, 83–8, 94–6.

30 Aston, 'Lollardy and Sedition', 27–28 and Griffiths, *Henry VI*, 139–40 (Perkins' Revolt); Pugh, *Southampton Plot*, 119 and Watts, *Henry VI*, 203 (Fitzhugh/ Scrope); Carpenter, *Locality and Polity*, 378–80, Cosgrove, *Medieval Ireland*, 546–51 and Pollard, *John Talbot*, 10–11 (Talbot); Griffiths, *Henry VI*, 128–38.

31 *PPC*, iii, 148–52 and iv, 35–41; Archer, 'Parliamentary Restoration', passim; Griffiths, *Henry VI*, 135–8, 572; Carpenter, *Locality and Polity*, 380.

32 Griffiths, *Henry VI*, 141–5; Neville, *Violence, Custom and Law*, 115–17, 125–37, esp. 129.

33 Carpenter, *Locality and Polity*, 372–93 (Beauchamp); Harriss, *Cardinal Beaufort*, 267–8 and Pollard, *North-Eastern England*, 249–50 and 'Crown and the County Palatine', 73–6 (Neville); Castor, 'Rule of East Anglia', 74–7 (Suffolk).

34 Harriss, *Cardinal Beaufort*, 138–9, 146–8, 152–3, 158, 170–2.

35 Ibid., 232–3, 235–6; Griffiths, *Henry VI*, 108, 115–16, 118–22. I have followed Harriss's higher estimate of the deficit.

36 Harriss, *Cardinal Beaufort*, 264, 284–6.

CHAPTER FIVE

The majority of Henry VI, 1437–53

The king

There is no knowing when it dawned on his subjects that Henry VI was not the man his father had been. It is quite likely, however, that those closest to him knew well before he was sixteen that, despite all the effort to educate him for the role he was to assume, the young man was neither by inclination nor by character fitted to be king. This is suggested not only by the rash of advice books and exemplars, such as an edition of the *Mirror for Princes* and Tito Livio's life of Henry V, commissioned in the late 1430s, but also by the drawn-out and tentative transition of power itself. From the beginning Henry himself seems to have been personally satisfied with the arrangement that left him *carte blanche* in matters of grace (the distribution of patronage) but delegated effective decision-making to the council. And unlike the troubled transition to personal rule of Richard II, there is no evidence of conflict between him and any of his subjects over the nature and extent of his power. The personality of Henry VI in fact presents an almost insoluble problem for his historians. On the one hand there is a view that second childhood followed the first without the usual interval. In this interpretation Henry was 'inane', a simpleton who was quite incapable of exercising his will, who did not initiate policies or make decisions in any aspect of government, all of which, perforce, was left to those about him. At the other extreme lies the image of a king who did assert himself capriciously and sometimes vindictively but was quite incapable of providing a consistent and authoritative lead to his subjects.[1]

Attempts to understand the precise character of Henry VI's inadequate kingship between 1437 and 1453 are handicapped by the limitations of the evidence. Much of our image of the man is formed by reports of him written after the onset of his mental illness in 1453 from which he never completely recovered. Both hostile Yorkist propaganda which portrayed him as a puppet whose strings were pulled by his courtiers, and the sympathetic presentation of him in the image of a Carthusian monk by his confessor, John Blacman, drew upon the man he became after his illness, not the man he was before. The general burden of earlier evidence, provided by charges of seditious speech made in the 1440s, was that he was childish, not a real man.[2]

Furthermore, since all decisions before 1453 were formally recorded as made by the king, it is impossible to determine the extent to which in any one instance it was entirely his own, or taken on the prompting of others, or, even, taken entirely by others in his name. It is this which has enabled recent historians to draw quite contradictory views as to his personal role. In a question of such importance for our undersanding of the middle part of his reign, in which there can be no certainty, it becomes a matter of individual judgement. In the account which follows the judgement is made that, while Henry was largely indifferent to the affairs of state, he was capable of influencing policy and did so from time to time; that he willed the attempt to make peace with France, and, even late in his reign, he wished to see his leading subjects reconciled.[3]

Writing to the archbishop of Florence in November 1437 Piero da Monte, the Papal tax collector in England, drew attention to the adolescent king's intelligence, piety and royal bearing. The young man did not shun the necessary display and pomp of court. He seems to have insisted on all due deference being shown to him, not surprisingly perhaps since he had no experience of being other than king. But he has been justifiably described as a priest's king. His mysogyny, stressed by da Monte as early as 1437, and prurience, attested many years later by John Blacman who reported his horror at witnessing naked bathers at Bath in 1449, and his disapproval of licentious behaviour behind the scenes at his court, suggest a man who would have been more at home in a monastery than a palace. His principal interest, in which he became absorbed before he was twenty, to found great centres for the education of priests at Eton and King's College, Cambridge, suggest one more fitted to be a pastor than a prince. In 1450 he was described by a foreign visitor as 'very young and inexperienced and watched over as a Carthusian': in a nutshell, he was unworldly. There is no reason to suppose that, before 1453, Henry was other than a normal, healthy human being; unfortunately for his kingdom he was utterly uninterested in statecraft. Above all he was totally antipathetic towards everything to do with war. This would have created difficulties for any king in his relationships with his nobles who were imbued with the cult of chivalry; as the successor to Henry V in the midst of a long and costly struggle in France it was disastrous.[4]

The twentieth-century reader might have some sympathy with Henry's rejection of chivalry and all its works and might be tempted to offer a psychological explanation of such a comprehensive reaction against both his father and his mother, whose young widowhood had, it was rumoured, not been chaste. For Henry's subjects his indifference to matters of state was compounded by vacillation when he did have to make decisions and his fecklessness in matters of grace. From the very first, he was irresponsible, indiscriminate and unthinking in his largesse. He gave what he was asked to give, heedless of whether such gifts were personally, financially or politically wise. Offices were wantonly granted for life, on occasion within weeks to different petitioners.[5] Pardons were freely issued with little regard to the impact on the administration of the law. The king, it became rapidly known, was a soft touch. Royal profligacy had serious repercussions for the government of the realm. It undermined the policy of tight financial control maintained during the minority and wasted the royal demesne; it made it more difficult for the council to control and determine policy; and it encouraged factionalism as rival groups sought to control access to the king for their own benefit. But deeper still Henry's very disinclination to rule while he was apparently quite capable of doing so left a vacuum at the very centre of affairs.

It says much for the underlying unity of purpose and corporate strength of the council that it took some time for factionalism to overrun the government of the kingdom. Council continued to be responsible for the determination of policy until the end of 1443. It met formally in Westminster in sessions of four to six weeks, four to five times a year. During these sessions the king was invariably at hand in one of his nearby palaces and occasionally in attendance. At the same time the process can be observed whereby more and more of government business came to be exercised by courtiers and leading household servants, frequently acting in the king's name.[6] The immediate beneficiary of the king's coming of age was Cardinal Beaufort, who might be described as the king's chief minister until the early 1440s. His experience and wealth continued to make him indispensable; his network of kinsmen and associates in the council ensured his domination of it; and his commitment to the search for peace commended him to the young king. Gloucester, although overshadowed, still had his place on the council and was not excluded from favour.

From conciliar to personal rule, 1437–43

Henry VI's coming of age made no difference to the immediate need to defend his possessions in France. In Normandy little more than a holding operation was required in 1438 and 1439. While control of Montargis, an isolated outpost beyond Paris, was finally lost, Le Crotoy was rescued. An attempt to recover Harfleur in the summer of 1438 failed. But Normandy was not under pressure because in 1438 Charles VII launched a major invasion of Gascony that took his armies up to the gates of Bordeaux. Gascony held out, but the area under English control was much reduced and the need to send reinforcements to the south suddenly became pressing. Early in 1439 John Holland, Earl of Huntingdon, indented with the Crown as lieutenant of Guyenne for six years and a force of 2,300 men was raised to sail with him to Bordeaux. At the same time more reinforcements were despatched to Normandy. Military costs were not reduced. But no new subsidies were granted by parliament and income from customs had fallen to an all-time low. Security for continuing dependence on loans from Beaufort, the feoffess of the duchy of Lancaster and the city was hard to find; so difficult in fact that the Crown resorted for the first time to the sale of lands: Chirk and some properties in the west country were sold to Beaufort so as to honour its debts.[7]

In the circumstances, financial strain as well as the king's personal inclination led to a new search for peace. Early in 1438, responding to an initiative made by the duke of Brittany, an abortive attempt was made to set up negotiations using the captive duke of Orleans as an intermediary. At the same time contacts were resumed with Philip of Burgundy out of which developed negotiations not just to end the war between the duke and England, but also to seek a more general peace. Preliminary negotiations between Beaufort and the duchess Isabel took place at Calais in January and agreement was reached to hold a peace conference in the summer to which Charles VII would be invited. These negotiations began near Gravelines outside Calais on 10 July. The English delegation, led by Archbishop Kemp was impressive. As at Arras, Beaufort was to act as a roving intermediary, especially in association with the Duchess Isabel. The royal instructions permitted the negotiators to settle for partition of the kingdom, but Beaufort, it transpired, had been granted privately by the king freedom to include the king's title. The French, however, soon made it clear that they were in no mood to compromise, the most that they were prepared to concede being to allow the English to continue to hold their possessions in France in homage. Negotiations rapidly stalled. Beaufort concocted a revised proposal by which the English would suspend the use of the title for a period of time during a truce. The French appeared to accept this as worthy of further consideration, and discussions were halted while Kemp returned to England for further instructions. After intense debate in the council, at which the duke of Gloucester was vocal in his opposition, it was decided that the king could not compromise his title in France. By the time his reply had reached his embassy, the French had anyway packed their bags.[8]

The futile negotiations at Gravelines confirmed that no peace treaty between France and England was feasible. The English compromise would have raised as many problems as it resolved. Indeed as the English council rightly perceived, it would have in effect meant an orderly surrender and withdrawal from Normandy. Beaufort may well have believed that this was now advisable, but it was a step that English opinion, forcefully articulated by Gloucester, was as yet unwilling to countenance. However, the negotiations did yield a truce with Burgundy and the reopening of trade with Flanders, which led to a rapid recovery in customs revenue for the Crown. And as far as France was concerned, they left open the possibility that the duke of Orleans could in future be employed as an intermediary. But for the time being the war still had to be fought.[9]

Despite the setback at Gravelines, Beaufort had little trouble in resuming his dominant position in council on his return to England in September 1439. A parliament met at Westminster in November, which, in its second session after Christmas, voted one and a half lay subsidies to be paid up to Michaelmas 1441 and renewed the wool subsidies, tunnage and poundage for three. But parliament seems also to have provided the forum for a third attack on Beaufort by the duke of Gloucester. He presented an impressive catalogue of Beaufort's mismanagement and corruption since the reign of Henry V, bringing in all the old charges. Nothing in the event seems to have come of this last attempt to discredit the cardinal, who remained for the time being unruffled, and which was probably related to the concurrent intense politicking over the appointment of a new commander in Normandy. The earl of Warwick had died in office in April 1439. It was no doubt already apparent that the king would not go to France in person; the question was who would deputise. Beaufort had been assiduously building up the claims of his nephews John, duke of Somerset, released from captivity in 1438, and Edmund, earl of Dorset. In 1438 Dorset had been made governor of Maine for seven years and granted extensive properties in Normandy. Somerset, promoted commander in chief in Normandy after Warwick's death, was being groomed to succeeed him. Gloucester, it later became apparent, had his own eyes set on the command in Normandy. In the end a compromise candidate was found in Richard, duke of York, who was commissioned in June 1440.

At the same time Gloucester was at the centre of another dispute over the proposed release of the duke of Orleans to further the cause of peace. Humphrey himself lodged his objections in writing, claiming that Orleans could not be trusted, his release was likely to strengthen the French and that it was a betrayal of all those who had given their lives and goods for the cause. It was to no avail: Orleans was released at the end of the year. A public justification issued in the king's name ('of himself and of his own advice and courage'), and in terms which might have reflected his own views, stressed the strain of war on England and Normandy, his desire to bring to an end 'the war that long hath continued and endured that is to say an hundred years and more', and the expectation of Orleans as an honest broker.[10] The deliverance of the duke of Orleans did in the end prove to be abortive; but there was more to the initiative than mere pious hope. Orleans was a great prince of the realm of France. Charles VII had begun to face opposition from some of his greater subjects in the rebellion of 1440 known as the Praguerie. The return of Orleans, it could be hoped, would further destabilise French politics to the possible advantage of England.

Gloucester's opposition to the peace initiative in 1440 and his failure to secure the command in Normandy left him politically vulnerable. His credibility with the king was finally destroyed in the summer of 1441 by the humiliation of his duchess, Eleanor Cobham. Eleanor dabbled in the occult, employing astrologers and magicians, as she admitted, to help her have a child by Gloucester. In June her associates were accused of having conspired to bring about the king's death by necromancy. They implicated her. She was found guilty of treasonable witchcraft by both ecclesiastical and lay courts. Forced to do public penance for three successive days in London, she was then committed to life imprisonment, but not before she had been divorced from the duke. The scandal and humiliation involving the wife of the heir to the throne brought Gloucester's active political career to an end. It is highly likely that Eleanor's indiscretion gave others a golden oportunity to discredit him in the eyes of the gullible king himself, who was horrified by the work of the devil. Who was behind it, however, Beaufort or others at court, has never been apparent.[11]

Richard of York, after considerable delay, had arrived in Normandy in the summer of 1441. He landed in time to reinforce the campaign to save Pontoise which Charles VII was besieging in person. Despite the Herculean efforts of Lord Talbot, Pontoise eventually fell, but Charles had been persuaded that Normandy was still being effectively defended. In fact the garrisons were exhausted and the resources of Normandy were wasted. The English could not recover Louviers and Conches in which the French had been lodged since 1440; and in 1442–3 an English army, reinforced from England by Talbot, newly created earl of Shrewsbury, failed to recover Dieppe. It was perhaps fortunate for Richard of York in Normandy that Charles VII turned to Gascony on which he descended in 1442. By the end of the year the English were left holding little more than Bordeaux, Bayonne and their environs.[12]

In 1443, therefore, the council determined to mount one more major campaign. It was divided as to whether to relieve York in Normandy, or Huntingdon in Gascony. Beaufort agreed to finance it; and his terms included the commissioning of his nephew, John, newly created duke of Somerset, to lead it. While the plan undoubtedly represented yet another attempt by the cardinal to establish his nephew in France, the strategy finally agreed nevertheless had much to commend it. Somerset was, it seems, to lead an old-style *chevauchée*, passing through eastern Normandy, Maine and into France beyond the Loire, presumably to Guyenne, of which he was made lieutenant, as well as all other parts of France beyond Normandy that he could conquer. Conquest was hopeful, but a march through France to reinforce Gascony which drew the fire from elsewhere and lined the pockets of his troops was feasible. Unfortunately the expedition proved a disaster. Somerset advanced no further than Maine, took two fortresses en route (one controversially within Brittany) and then retired back to Normandy where he disbanded his troops. He returned to England at the end of the year and died in disgrace the following year, perhaps by his own hand. Somerset's expedition was effectively the last campaign. The war petered out at the end of the year when Charles VII finally took the initiative for a truce sealed at Tours in May 1444.[13]

Suffolk's regime, 1443–50

By the end of 1443, too, political control in England had passed into new hands. While formally policy had continued to be determined in council, the real centre of power had been passing to those who dominated the king's household and court. Insidiously those about the king tightened their grip on access to his person, disbursement of his patronage and control of policy. They could do so without conflict because all was done properly in the king's name. At the head of this emerging faction stood William de la Pole, Earl of Suffolk and steward of the royal household. Suffolk, who had served in France in the 1420s and been taken prisoner in 1429, had been appointed steward as Bedford's nominee in 1433. He was a regular attender at council from 1435. Gradually a group took shape around him. In April 1439 Sir Roger Fiennes was appointed Treasurer of the Household, opening the way for his brother James, a knight of the body, later Lord Saye and Sele, who ultimately succeeded to the office of Chamberlain. In 1439 too, Sir Thomas Stanley was made Controller. And in 1441, Sir Ralph Butler, soon to be created Lord Sudeley, succeeded Lord Bardolf as Chamberlain. The most important ecclesiastics in Suffolk's circle were William Aiscough, the king's confessor and bishop of Salisbury from 1438, and Adam Moleyns, privy seal clerk in attendance at the household, clerk of the council from 1438, promoted to Chichester in 1445.

As Suffolk continued to tighten his control of council and the great offices of state fell into the hands of his allies, there was neither division nor conflict between courtiers and councillors; the emergent courtiers were also the principal councillors. Partly this was the result of age removing many of the old stalwarts. Tiptoft and Chichele died in 1443; Hungerford and Alnwick retired. Gloucester had been ruined in 1441 and Beaufort finally withdrew at the end of 1443. In their place came the new courtiers, to whose ranks were added John Sutton, Lord Dudley, and John, Lord Beaumont. Suffolk was to become Chamberlain of England, Beaumont Constable of England in 1445, Moleyns Keeper of the Privy Seal early in 1444 and Lord Sudeley replaced Cromwell as Treasurer in mid-1443. Only Cardinal Kemp and the long-serving Chancellor, John Stafford, promoted to Canterbury, remained of the leading councillors of the minority. The dissolution of the council as a formal body rapidly followed the transformation of its membership. By 1444 counsel was given informally and all decisions were taken by those close to the king at court.

It has conventionally been presumed that this transfer of power was managed by Cardinal Beaufort. But it is equally possible that the ageing Beaufort too was pushed aside. The parliament that met early in 1442 was the first of the reign not to be dominated by Beaufort and his associates. His last significant act was to complete a final truce with Burgundy in 1443 and his resources were still needed to fund his nephew's disastrous expedition in the same year. Also his kinsmen were still prominent, especially Richard Neville, Earl of Salisbury, and Edmund Beaufort, Earl of Dorset, promoted marquess, a councillor from 1444, who was generously endowed by the king. But neither was at the heart of the court. Power in fact slipped from Beaufort hands as much as it was denied the duke of Gloucester. A new generation had taken command.[14]

Suffolk and his associates, although they had the advantage of managing the household and dominating the court, still had difficulty in controlling the king's wayward generosity and feckless disposition of his grace. The costs of the household, the size of its establishment and the scale of grants and annuities soared between 1437 and 1440; partly as the household clique took advantage for themselves and their friends, but partly as the king did as he wished. By 1440 parliament was already concerned about household costs, and in response to criticism, measures were introduced to ensure more effective management. But expenditure continued to escalate and to outrun income; in 1442 the commons demanded further action. It was to try to bring some degree of order to the exercise of the king's grace, and as well as to extend courtier control over the distribution of royal patronage, that new ordinances were promulgated in 1444. Under these a committee was established to vet all petitions, advise the king on the contents, ensure that decisions taken were minuted, and to oversee the procedure for implementation. In the event this attempt to restrain the king failed, for as subsequent successful petitions show, many still passed through without conciliar approval.[15]

Anyone with access to the king, lesser members of his ever-expanding household such as yeomen and valets, could secure the endorsement of a petition, but the biggest benefits were reaped by the principal members of the household, their friends, allies and dependants. Suffolk was promoted to marquess in 1444 and duke in 1448. He took for himself the wardships of Lord Morley's daughter in 1442 and the infant Margaret Beaufort, the duke of Somerset's heiress, in 1444, whom he endeavoured to marry to his son. He was granted lands and offices throughout England and Wales, the lands invariably for life and rent free. Such largesse, on a marginally smaller scale was lavished on James Fiennes, Lord Saye and Sele, Viscount Beaumont, Sir Thomas Stanley and many lesser household knights and esquires.

The principal beneficiaries sought to create regional hegemonies for themselves, based on their own property, royal offices and lands, and whatever windfalls came their way. In particular the offices and estates of the duchy of Lancaster proved particularly lucrative. Suffolk was supreme in East Anglia; Fiennes in Kent and Sussex; Beaumont in Leicestershire and Lincolnshire; Stanley in Cheshire. Other friends of the court, such as the earl of Salisbury in north-eastern England, held sway elsewhere. In south Wales, Gruffyd ap Nicholas emerged as a ubiquitous deputy for royal justiciars and marcher lords, virtually securing personal control of the region for the advancement of his own ends. It was at this time, too, that in north Wales Sir Thomas Stanley began to create a similar hegemony. The royal household itself grew to an unprecedented size, as ambitious or well-connected gentry were recruited as knights and esquires of the body. The royal affinity, the same body as deployed so effectively by Henry IV and Henry V to ensure their control of the provinces, was by the end of the 1440s only nominally operating in the the interest of the Crown. It had been hijacked by courtiers.[16]

In the circumstances it is not surprising that the administration of royal justice suffered. It is difficult to establish whether the general level of lawlessness and disorder increased after Henry VI came of age. It is not necessarily the case that either petty crime or aristocratic violence was any greater in the 1440s than in the 1430s. The king himself seems to have been as indifferent to the administration of justice, as he was to the defence of the realm and the management of patronage. His willingness to pardon all offences encouraged his subjects to take the law into their own hands. But by the same token his indifference enabled his council, at least until 1444, to mitigate as best they could the worst consequences of his negligence, especially where it involved his own tenants and officers. It is noticeable that several potentially serious conflicts were succesfully defused and contained.

Much is known about the conflict between Lord Grey of Ruthin and Lord Fanhope for control of the commission of the peace in Bedfordshire in 1437–9, which reached its climax in the probably accidental crushing to death of a number of people in a crowded court room, precisely because the council instigated a full inquiry. While the riotous behaviour of the principals has been stressed, it has not often been noted that the issue was resolved by the council. Similarly the hard-worked councillors were successful in bringing the long-running Neville family feud to an end in 1443; in pacifying temporarlily in the same year the quarrel between Lord Bonville and the earl of Devon in the west country; in defusing the conflict over possession of Berkeley which flared into life again after the death of the earl of Warwick in 1439; and again in 1443 finding a compromise between the king's tenants of Knaresborough, supported by the earl of Northumberland, and Cardinal Kemp in a dispute over the payment of tolls in the archbishop's markets of Ripon and Otley. It is perhaps no coincidence that all these disputes flared up in the early years of the majority and noteworthy that it was the council which arbitrated compromises, rather than the king that enforced justice.[17]

From 1444 there were fewer major disturbances of the peace until near the end of the decade. This does not mean to say that the quality of justice improved. Far from it; it reflected only the tighter control of power exercised by Suffolk and his associates at court. And justice in the second half of the decade came to be perverted for partisan ends. The systematic abuse of power in the king's name, practised particularly in East Anglia, Kent and Sussex, where extortion, fraud, theft, violence and intimidation were used to crush all opposition, had not been witnessed on such a scale since the reign of Richard II. It may be that the vivid picture painted in the Paston Letters of the misdeeds of Daniel, Heydon and Tuddenham in East Anglia give a distorted view, since the Pastons were on the losing side and not themselves impartial. But the tale of similar abuse in Kent and Sussex, revealed by offical inquiries in 1450, suggest that the substance is correct. Although the worst abuse of power was confined to East Anglia and the Home Counties, the contagion spread elsewhere. In Lincolnshire, Sir William Tailboys was able to perpetrate a series of crimes because he benefited from the protection of Suffolk and Viscount Beaumont, who supported his challenge to the local influence of Lords Cromwell (himself no angel) and Willoughby. Henry VI stood aside; but his frequent progresses in East Anglia in the company of the steward of his household gave the impression that he endorsed the insolence of office.[18]

Not only was Henry VI unable to prevent the abuse of power by his courtiers, he also presided over the financial collapse of his government. The king inherited a heavy burden of debt incurred during his minority and finances that were already stretched. To this he seems to have been indifferent. The escalating costs of his household, the generous provision made for a dowerless queen in 1445, and the astronomical cost of her homecoming added significantly to the strain. The available resources from the royal demesne were themselves reduced by the endowment of Eton and King's Colleges from the duchy of Lancaster and the steady alienation of royal lands and properties, many for terms of life or lives. Attempts to reduce waste and control costs instituted by household ordinances in 1445, and the establishment of a committee of officers in 1447 to manage expenditure, were ineffective. In 1448 crown jewels were sold to meet immediate debts; resort was once again made to purveyance for the household without payment; and the wages of minor servants were left unpaid.

At the same time the level of lay and clerical taxation fell; on average the Crown received only half a lay subsidy a year and the yield was reduced in 1445 by further remission. Parliament only grudgingly voted a half subsidy in 1445; and none in 1447. Moreover, in 1445 it refused to authorise further loans. Income had long been anticipated; now the same sources, particularly anticipated customs revenue at the ports, were assigned several times over by useless tallies, often disguised as fictitious loans, to royal creditors. Preference in securing repayment was given to courtiers and the queen, leaving many others, especially captains of war, the wardens of the marches and the captain of Calais, with substantial unsettled arrears. Economic recession further reduced income. The late 1430s were years of agrarian crisis and recession, reflected not only in a further decline of landed revenue for the Crown itself, but also in the number of appeals to the Crown for reductions in fee farms and subsidies, not all without cause. And in the second half of the decade a trade embargo with Flanders imposed by the duke of Burgundy once again halved the income of customs and poundage.[19]

Financial collapse first threatened at the end of 1446 when the treasury found itself unable to meet its commitments. The appointment of Bishop Lumley in December 1446, who instituted a rigorous programme of retrenchment and placed a freeze on all debt repayments, gave the Crown a breathing space. But Lumley's reforms depended on a revival of customs revenue and above all the avoidance of war. The Crown's debts, the maintenance of the garrisons in Calais, Carlisle and Berwick, and the current costs of the household, by now running at £27,000 a year, could only be met if the truce with France held. But notwithstanding Lumley's tight control, the total crown debt rose to the staggering sum of £372,000 by 1449. And in the spring of that year the commons insisted that it would not make further provision of lay subsidies, unless the king first cancel all assignments made in anticipation. Peace with France ceased to be a policy option; it became a financial necessity.[20]

Anglo-French relations, 1444–50

Probably in response to the king's wish, from the very outset Suffolk's ministry was dedicated to the search for peace. By the end of 1443 Charles VII himself had concluded that a truce was in his own interest, and after the failure of Somerset's expedition, upon which so much had been banked, the English too were desperate for a respite. Early in 1444 Suffolk, and an embassy drawn almost exclusively from the household, set off for Tours where on 24 May Henry VI was betrothed to the duke of Anjou's fifteen-year-old daughter Margaret; and four days later a twelve-month truce was agreed pending further peace negotiations. At the end of the year Suffolk returned once more to France to escort the king's bride back to England. Brought to England in great state, the young queen made a spectacular entry into London in May 1445 in which the high hopes for peace were articulated. Two months later a French embassy arrived. However, the talks stumbled once again on the refusal of the English to concede the title to the throne and of the French to concede a partition of the kingdom. All that could be achieved was an extension of the truce and an agreement, which did not materialise, for the two kings to meet in person.

It later emerged that during the discussions, or shortly after, Henry himself undertook to cede Anjou and Maine to his father-in-law. The French may well have proposed during discussions at Tours in 1444 that Duke René was granted the counties in return for a twenty-four-year alliance with England. If so, it was rejected then and again in the summer of 1445. But by the end of the year, partly through the young queen's intercession, Henry personally committed himself secretly to the surrender of Maine. Whether Suffolk and those close to the king knew of this concession is impossible to tell. Suffolk's strenuous denial in parliament in 1445 that there had been a secret deal may not be believed. He knew soon enough and thereafter was fully implicated in the 'cover-up'.[21]

Unfortunately, Charles VII made the proposed personal meeting with Henry VI dependent on the fulfilment of the secret agreement over Maine. The issue could not therefore be avoided. But Suffolk was only too aware of the potential reaction from Gloucester (still heir to the throne) and of likely opposition in Maine itself, where there was considerable English vested interest, as well as in Normandy and England. Matters were brought to a head by the financial crisis of December 1446 and the realisation that peace had to be secured at almost any price. The government could prevaricate no longer. First Edmund Beaufort, Marquess of Dorset and the major investor in Maine, was compensated with the vacant office of lieutenant general of Normandy, which Richard of York had expected to resume. It is likely that charges of York's maladministration, brought forward by Moleyns, were made at this time to justify his removal. York himself was compensated with Ireland. Secondly, it was determined that Gloucester should be removed. Arriving in February 1447 at Bury St Edmunds, for a meeting of parliament called in the heart of Suffolk's own country, the duke was arrested, thrown into prison and accused of treason. Three days later he was dead. It soon came to be believed that he was murdered. Whilst the charges of treason against some of his servants was at first pursued, six months later they were dropped. There are grounds for supposing that the intention was to neutralise Gloucester politically not to kill him. His death, however, provided a windfall for the Crown, from which the duke of York as well as the courtiers benefited.

With Gloucester removed, albeit perhaps more decisively than originally envisaged, the way was open for the public declaration of the cession of Maine in June 1447 and the appointment of commissioners to oversee its delivery. But this did not speed matters. The commissioners, Mathew Gough and Fulk Eyton, in collusion with Dorset and his captains, deliberately obstructed the process. Yet another date passed by. It was not until March 1448, when Charles VII drew up a powerful army and invested Le Mans, that the English finally accepted terms of compensation and withdrew. By this time the whole peace process, which had been launched with such optimism four years earlier, was thoroughly soured and compromised.[22]

In his ceaseless efforts to put pressure on Henry VI to honour his commitment to cede Maine, Charles VII also played on the military ambitions of the young James II of Scotland who came of age in the mid-1440s. A series of Franco-Scottish marriage treaties, culminating in the marriage of James himself to Mary of Guelders in 1449, tied Scotland into alliances with France, Brittany and Burgundy and led to renewal of war with England in 1448 and a victory over an English raiding party on the river Sark in October. In 1449 the truce was patched up, but in 1448 reverses on the Scottish border served further to discredit Suffolk's failing administration.[23]

In a desparate attempt to save face and recover the initiative, the government now launched on what proved to be an even more disastrous course of action. In 1443 Duke John of Brittany, who had maintained a largely neutral profile, was succeeded by his francophile son, Francis. By 1445 Francis had formally abandoned the English alliance; in 1446 he gave homage to Charles VII. Henry VI refused to recognise or accept this fact. Instead he promoted the cause of the duke's younger brother Gilles, a staunch anglophile, who had spent some of his youth in England in his own company. Gilles, not surprisingly (and perhaps justifiably) was arrested on the charge of plotting with the English to depose his brother. Relationships were made more tense by the occupation of a demilitarised border zone between Britanny and Normandy by troops ejected from Maine, which Duke Francis, as a subject of Charles VII claimed, was an infringement of the truce, but which the English claimed was entirely a matter between him and them. In 1449 the English decided to force the issue by seizing Fougères. But Duke Francis immediately appealed to his overlord, Charles VII, for assistance and in July French armies launched a full-scale invasion of Normandy. The seizure of Fougères, compounding the folly of the bungled cession of Maine, gave Charles VII the justification he needed to renew a war for which Henry VI was completely ill-prepared in either England or France.[24]

The demoralised and weakened English garrisons were no match for the French armies, which had been reorganised and strengthened during the truce. Edmund Beaufort, now raised to the title of duke of Somerset, had taken over the administration of Normandy in 1448 and had endeavoured to reform the administration and find money with which to pay the garrisons, but the steps he had taken had only succeeded in alienating Norman opinion. Eastern Normandy fell with scarcely a blow being struck; garrison after garrison, outnumbered, outgunned and isolated, quickly surrendered and the French armies were allowed to operate unchallenged in the field. Not until September did the government in England become aware of the seriousness of the situation. By then it was too late to save Rouen and the rest of upper Normandy which was evacuated as part of the terms of surrender. Re-inforcements were raised in England, but the relief army was cut to pieces at Formigny in April. By 12 August 1450 the English were completely expelled from Normandy.[25]

The loss of Normandy in 1449–50 was a rout even more spectacular than its conquest by Henry V thirty years earlier. The catastrophe was the immediate result of diplomatic and military folly, but it was rooted in the bankruptcy, exhaustion and demoralisation which had already been apparent at the beginning of the decade. The truce had merely served to undermine the will to resist even further. It is perhaps more remarkable that the English successfully held Normandy as long as they did, and a testimony to the dedication of its defenders and the tenacity with which they held on to their vested interest in the duchy after 1435, than that it fell so rapidly and tamely at the end.

Some sympathy could perhaps be extended to Suffolk in his efforts to find an honourable peace on behalf of such a supine and vacillating master. A negotiated settlement was never to be found unless Henry VI were pre-pared to surrender his crown of France: a concession he could never make. Suffolk and his fellow councillors were never alone in exercising influence or making policy. They found that the king's own unilateral action in sur-rendering Maine compromised them; and it could even be that the deluded

Breton policy was the king's wish. Paradoxically, Perhaps, Suffolk and his principal associates suffered from not being able to exercise enough control. The king was always accessible to others and, as we have seen, his capacity to make grants or issue pardons without thought or reference to his principal advisers made government more difficult. It is possible that some of the abuses of the regime were the consequence of lack of, rather than excess, of power. It is plausible too that, until the foreign policy began to unravel, the majority of the political nation was happy to accept a regime which, by the very fact of the king's open-handedness, did not create too many powerful enemies. Only when things began to go wrong did they turn against Suffolk, who was then blamed for the complete failure of policy.[26]

Crisis and revolt, 1450

The storm broke in the second session of the parliament of 1449–50, which opened at Westminster on 22 January 1450. Already indications of what was to come had been apparent in earlier meetings. Parliament called in February 1449 had voted a half subsidy in the first session, and a further half in the second session called to Wincherster in June, but the commons had shown their concern about the government's financial management by provisos which annulled grants made on the anticipated revenue. Criticism of Suffolk surfaced in the second session. It was fiercer in the opening session of the next parliament which met in November 1449, for already news had arrived of the fall of Rouen. But it was the murder of Adam Moleyns by mutinous soldiers at Portsmouth on 9 January which led directly to his downfall. Rumours that Moleyns had attempted to save his life by accusing Suffolk of treason, led the duke to volunteer to answer any charges and submit himself to the king's judgement. However, on the insistence of the commons, he was placed in the Tower and impeachment proceedings were begun. The lords were not minded to save him, particularly following the assault by his client, Sir William Tailboys, on Lord Cromwell within the precinct of the palace of Westminster the previous November. On 12 February he was impeached on the grounds that he had plotted with the French against Henry VI and planned to make his son king. The charges, to which were added accusations of his misrule and extortion at home, were for the most part unsustainable, but Suffolk had clearly been marked out as the scapegoat for the utter failure of royal policy. Not until 7 March did the Lords declare that he should be brought to answer. Ten days later, before the lords reached judgement, the king dismissed the charges concerning treason, found him guilty on the lesser and banished him for five years.

Suffolk set sail for the Netherlands on 30 March. But his flotilla was intercepted by a privateer, the *Nicholas of the Tower*, and on 2 May he was beheaded on the gunwale of the ship's boat. His headless body was thrown on Dover beach.[27]

Suffolk's murder, and the proclamation that it was an act of justice in the name of the common weal, as well as the rumour that the king would lay Kent waste in revenge, triggered a massive popular uprising, first in Kent, but spreading to Essex, East Anglia, Sussex, Hampshire, Wiltshire, Dorset, Somerset and Gloucestershire. Cade's Revolt, as the rebellion soon became known after the Kentish leader, Jack Cade, shook the regime to its foundations. Kent rose in mid-May, the rebel host eventually marching on London and establishing itself on Blackheath by 11 June. The king, who had been in Leicester for the third session of parliament, moved rapidly and in strength with most of his lords back to London. A delegation led by the archbishops was sent down to treat with the rebels. They received a list of complaints, focusing on conventional demands for reform (resumption of royal grants, removal of evil ministers, restoration of the old nobility to council, and the end of the abuse of power). The king's answer was to lead his army across the Thames to confront the rebels. But on his approach they withdrew, leaving the royal host to occupy Blackheath. Raiding parties were sent to harrass the retreating rebels. But some of the king's retainers at Blackheath sympathised with the rebels and threatened to join them unless certain prominent household men (including Lord Saye and Bishop Aiscough) were dismissed. At this the king's nerve failed, he acceded to the arrest of Lord Saye, withdrew to London and on 25 June abandoned the capital. On 29 June, the rising having now spread through several southern counties, Aiscough was captured and murdered in Wiltshire and Kentish rebels returned to Blackheath.[28]

Now the rebels were determined to enter London. They first occupied Southwark and on 3 July gained control of London Bridge and poured across the Thames into the city. For three days the city was pillaged. On 4 July Saye was taken from the Tower, 'tried' at the Guildhall, and executed. Each night the rebels withdrew to Southwark. On the night of 5/6 July Lord Scales and Mathew Gough, rallying the London authorities, sallied from the Tower and attacked the bridge. After an all-night battle, and at the cost of many lives including Gough, the London end was secured and access to the city once more denied the rebels. Cade now entered into negotiation with the archbishops of Canterbury and York and bishop of Winchester, who, unlike their king, had courageously remained in the capital. No doubt a promise was made to institute the reforms demanded by the rebels and a general pardon was agreed for all crimes committed before 8 July. Most of the rebels, satisfied with this, returned to their homes;

but Cade himself and other diehards determined to resist. They were pursued through Kent by Alexander Iden, the new sheriff; Cade himself was captured on 12 July and died of his wounds before he could stand trial.

The withdrawal of the rebels from London, and the death of Cade, did not mark the end of the uprising. While a commission of enquiry into the allegations of the rebels perambulated Kent between 20 August and 22 October hearing indictments against members of the old regime, disturbances and unrest, fuelled in part by returning discharged soldiers from France, continued in all the south-eastern counties and London; a new leader, William Parmynter, emerged in Kent. Parmynter's rising was in its turn subdued, but new leaders took his place. Not until February 1451 did the king, at the head of a powerful commission, ride down into Kent to visit retribution on them. Some thirty men were executed, and their heads subsequently exhibited on London Bridge. Yet in April a new rising occurred in the Weald, led by Henry Hasilden, which brought another tribunal into Kent and Sussex at the end of June and July. And this was not an end. Further risings took place in May 1452; disturbances continued sporadically through 1453 and 1454. South-eastern England was in a state of turmoil long after the suppression of the revolt.

It is as well to see political developments at court after the fall of Suffolk in the light of this continuing unrest. At first, a vacuum was left at the centre. It seems that many expected Richard, Duke of York, heir presumptive to the throne and the leading representative of 'the old nobility of the realm', would emerge as the principal councillor. He certainly did so himself; so did the clutch of prominent and discredited household men who, having failed to prevent it, rushed to present themselves to him when he returned from Ireland in September 1450; and so too did the common people. But his cause was not helped by Jack Cade, adopted the name of John Mortimer, claiming kinship with the duke; or others like the Yorkshire shipman who confronted Henry VI in April, declaring that York would deal with the traitors when he returned from Ireland.[29]

One reason that this did not come about is that York himself was indecisive and timid. Until 1450 he had not been an opponent of the regime. He had willingly gone to Ireland. He had not opposed the destruction of Gloucester. He could not have been unaware of the use being made of his name (the possibility that his agents were encouraging it cannot be discounted) and the delicate position in which this placed him, but he probably hoped, as the new heir presumptive, to be called upon as one above the fray. But for reasons which still puzzle his historians, he delayed his return from Ireland until September, and when he returned found that Edmund Beaufort, Duke of Somerset, was already ensconced at court. He made his way to Westminster from North Wales, sending letters ahead, first protesting against false accusations of treason, then presenting himself as the champion of reform. Having visited East Anglia, where in alliance with the duke of Norfolk he mobilised the support of those who had suffered under Suffolk, he went up to the newly elected parliament which met in November.

York's retainer, Sir William Oldhall, having been elected speaker, the duke himself made his entry to London at the head of a large retinue on 23 November. A week later a mass demonstration was organised outside parliament calling for action against Somerset for the loss of Normandy, followed by an attack on the duke himself and his principal associates in London. Somerset escaped to the security of the Tower, helped according to one account by York himself. The rioting was subsequently put down by York, who organised a display of royal authority in the city and arrested the ring leaders. What part York, or his lieutenants, played in orchestrating the commotion is not clear; it has been suggested that he had planned to arrest Somerset, but the attempt having failed, he promptly presented himself as the defender of king and his servants. Yet despite the bluster and high profile he gave himself, the duke was unable to make any impression on the court. He remained an outsider; while Somerset, leaving the Tower before Christmas, remained high in favour. In January York, having failed, withdrew once more from the scene.

One cannot be certain as to the extent to which in 1450 York held Somerset to blame for the loss of Normandy. It has been argued that his quarrel with Edmund Beaufort, who after all had not been closely associated with Suffolk's regime either, began as a matter of chivalric honour because of the manner in which Somerset had surrendered Rouen and other properties held by York. But equally, the sense of chivalric outrage which York later emphasised in his tirades against his enemy, may have been of less importance in the autumn of 1450 than the discovery that Somerset had already won the king's confidence and that he himself was already excluded from favour. He soon discovered that manipulating parliament to his ends was no substitute. He made matters worse for himself when, perhaps in desparation, at the end of May 1451 he allowed one of his men in the commons, Thomas Young, to promote a bill for his formal recognition as heir presumptive. Young was promptly arrested and sent to the Tower, and parliament was instantly dissolved.

The incident is revealing on two counts; first it suggests that York believed that recognition of his high birth would in itself secure him a place in office, and secondly it confirms what had become apparent since 1450, that he was politicaly inept. In 1450–1 York also presented himself as the champion of the common weal promising reform and renewal. A frequent view is that it was but a cynical parade of principle to exploit the circumstances and popular opinion. It may be, however, that consciousness of his position as heir presumptive, and even behind that of his latent claim to the throne in his own right, propelled him into an explicit espousal of the common good as a political platform. It is clear, however, that the majority of the lords did not share his outlook, that they themselves were suspicious of his intentions, and that he soon found himself isolated.[30]

Recovery, 1451–3

Edmund Beaufort, on the other hand, flourished. While successfully with-standing York's challenge at court and rallying the majority of the peers behind him, he also effectively stole his rival's reformist clothes in parliament. The question of resumption first arose in 1449. By 1450 the commons were unwilling to vote supply until the king had restored his domestic finances by resuming the grants of lands, offices and pensions which he had made so recklessly. In May, just before Cade's Revolt broke, the king accepted a bill which cancelled all grants since his reign began; but he immediately recog-nised 186 claims of exemption which largely invalidated the act. York took up the cause in the autumn, but it was not until the spring of 1451 that a second act was passed which, although it contained general provisos to protect interests such as the queen's, was not subsequently undermined. All grants were cancelled and new ones negotiated, leading to tighter control over patronage and the recovery of revenue. Income received from the royal demesne increased by some £7,000 *per annum* and the finances of the royal household were restored to a sound basis.[31]

A more difficult problem was posed by the personnel of the household. The worst offenders in Kent were brought to book by the commission of enquiry following the rebellion. But this did not prevent York sponsoring a bill to remove others, including Somerset, from the household. This, apart from the dismissal of Sir Thomas Stanley as the Controller, the king resisted. However, at the end of the parliament in summer of 1451 the concession was made of banishing some of the named men from the household for a year. It is the case, however, that several of the more notorious of Suffolk's associates such as Thomas Daniel, John Heydon, John Trevilian and Thomas Tuddenham suffered no serious hindrance to their careers. The household was reconstituted very much as it was before.[32]

The new regime was determined to impose its authority on the kingdom. During the summer of 1451, the king himself made judicial progresses, accompanied by his leading nobles, Somerset, the duke of Buckingham, the earl of Shrewsbury and others into Kent, then Surrey, Sussex, Hampshire and Wiltshire. But it was Richard of York, as chairman of the bench in the county, who intervened in Somerset in September to impose order on the earl of Devon besieging Lord Bonville in Taunton Castle. This was no impartial act. Devon was York's ally; he was in effect intervening on his behalf. Indeed the king, at Coventry, reprimanded the duke for exceeding his authority and commanded him, in vain, to appear before him, while taking his own steps to punish the principal participants. At the same time suspicion fell on Sir William Oldhall, York's chamberlain, who fled to sanctuary rather than face charges. By the end of the year York was moving into a position of outright opposition to the court.

In January 1452 York mobilised his retainers, tenants and allies (the earl of Devon and Lord Cobham) to make an armed demonstration in strength against the duke of Somerset. His articles and proclamations insisted that he was acting for the good of the realm to remove evil ministers from the court. Somerset was charged with responsibility for the loss of Normandy and Gascony, accused of being unfit to hold Calais, and of plotting to ruin him. Having failed to persuade Reginald Boulers, Bishop of Hereford, and the earl of Shrewsbury to act as intermediaries, he raised his men and moved from Ludlow up to London. Crossing the Thames at Kingston, he advanced to his manor of Dartford, hoping no doubt to raise Kent in his cause. Kent, however, did not stir. Confronted at Dartford by a powerful royal army, with almost all the nobles of the realm ranged against him, early in March he entered into negotiations and agreed to submit himself and his complaints to the king. He found, however, that he was taken into custody, his complaints ignored and himself forced publicly to make a declaration of loyalty and to accept arbitration by a panel of peers of the issues between him and his rival. Dartford ended in humiliating failure for the duke. Thereafter he was virtually confined to house arrest on his own estates, Oldhall was relentlessly pursued for treason, commisions of oyer and terminer were despatched to deal with those who had turned out for him, and Somerset was left supreme at court.[33]

One of the accusations levelled against Somerset was that he had presided over the loss of Gascony as well as Normandy. And this is so, for in the summer of 1451 Charles VII had turned his armies south. In the autumn of 1450 reinforcements under Lord Rivers had been commissioned, but without a grant of taxation to pay for the expedition, it had proved impossible to mount. The garrisons and towns of Guyenne fell with as little resistance as had those of Normandy. Bordeaux was surrendered on 30 June; Bayonne fell on 21 August. Next, it was rumoured, Charles would turn on Calais. Reinforcements were sent in the winter of 1451–2; immediately after the field of Dartford measures were taken to raise a fleet to sail for the protection of the town; and even the king declared an intention to visit it. But the threat receded. Instead the opportunity arose later in the year to recover

Bordeaux. The earl of Shrewsbury was commissioned in the summer to raise troops for an unspecified naval operation, perhaps a raid on Normandy, but a deputation from Bordeaux revealed that a group of the citizens would open the city to the English if they but came. Thus in September Shrewsbury was appointed lieutenant of Guyenne and he set sail with an army of 5,000 men. On 23 October 1452 Bordeaux opened its gates and rapidly the Bordelais, Libourne, Fronsac and Castillon were retaken.[34]

By the beginning of 1453 Henry VI, now thirty years old, seemed finally to have grown into his kingship. He had put the crisis of 1450 behind him; he had outfaced the challenge of the duke of York; he had shown a new decisiveness and determination in the enforcement of his authority over his subjects; he had taken a tighter grip on management of his household; he had successfully won back some ground in France; and, moreover, he had taken steps to strengthen the royal family. In November 1452 he ennobled his half-brothers, Edmund and Jasper Tudor, who were promoted to the earldoms of Richmond and Pembroke and endowed with lands from the royal demesne; in the following March Edmund Beaufort's niece, Margaret, was married to Edmund Tudor, thus tieing the duke more closely to the king. And, finally, as later became apparent, over the Christmas festivities, Henry finally begot an heir.

This new beginning owed much, if not all, to the duke of Somerset and Cardinal Kemp. Edmund Beaufort was a man of ability, politically more astute than York, and more circumspect than Suffolk. John Kemp, who had succeeded John Stafford as Chancellor on 31 January 1450 and as archbishop of Canterbury on 21 July 1452, was a veteran from the days of Henry V whose Keeper of the Privy Seal he had been in 1418–21, a councillor since the beginning of the reign, a protégé and ally of Cardinal Beaufort, who had served once before as Chancellor in 1426–32. Somerset and Kemp, the heirs of Cardinal Beaufort, not only brought a new sense of direction to his government, but seem to have been able to persuade Henry himself to play a more consistent and responsible role in affairs.[35] This was not, however, an impartial regime. The earl of Shrewsbury, Somerset's brother-in-law, was allowed to take the law into his own hands in 1451–2 in the long-standing dispute of his countess with Lord Berkeley, from which Somerset himself stood to gain. After Dartford, Lord Bonville was given a free hand in Devon. And as Lord Cromwell slipped from favour, a blind eye was turned to the seizure of his manor of Ampthill in Berkshire by the young and largely landless duke of Exeter. But as long as the regime was secure, such blatant partiality was of little significance.[36]

The extent of the success of the new ministry in restoring confidence was revealed in the parliament that met at Reading on 6 March 1453. The parliament was well-disposed towards the king, partly because of the success in Gascony and, perhaps, partly because of the high number of household men returned to the commons. A compliant house enrolled a formal condemnation of all criticisms that had been made of the court in 1450–1, Oldhall was attainted, tonnage and poundage were granted for life, as they had been to Henry V after Agincourt, and at increased rates, and a full fifteenth and tenth was voted. And above all the commons granted the king the provision to raise a force of 20,000 archers for the defence of the realm at four months' notice at any time in the future; a provision probably for a hoped-for expedition abroad rather than crushing rebellion at home. The king declined to take up the offer immediately and so instead a further half lay subsidy was voted to pay for reinforcements in Gascony. It would appear that in their longer-term grants the commons were endeavouring to provide a more permanent endowment of the Crown on the basis of which it could manage its finances more effectively.[37]

By the summer of 1453, therefore, Henry VI seemed at last to have begun to rule as well as to reign. New baronial disputes, it is true, had arisen: in Yorkshire the hot-headed young Thomas Percy, lord Egremont, was causing disturbance and in Glamorgan the earl of Warwick was refusing to hand over the castles of Cardiff and Cowbridge to the duke of Somerset to whom the king had recently granted them. But these matters seemed well in hand. On 16 July a commission of oyer and terminer had been appointed to bring Egremont to heal, and on 21 July Warwick was ordered to surrender the disputed lordships to Lord Dudley. The king himself set out on progress to the west country and was at Clarendon in Wiltshire early in August. It was at about this time that he heard of the defeat and death on 17 July of the earl of Shrewsbury at Castillon, who had foolishly attacked a well-entrenched gun park in his attempt to relieve the town.[38] Whether the news itself, or something else, was a trigger, the king suffered a total mental collapse. He fell into a coma, in which he could neither talk, nor walk, nor eat unaided, nor respond, and in which prostrate condition he was to remain for almost eighteen months. The whole course of the reign and future of the dynasty was transformed on that August day in Savernake Forest.

Notes and references

1   McFarlane, *Nobility*, 284; Watts, *Henry VI*, 104, who vividly describes Henry in 1445 'standing about in a variety of opulent costumes, grinning broadly and crying "Saint Jehan, grant mercis!" when Charles VII's name was mentioned'. For the view of Henry as vindictive and wilful, see Wolffe, *Henry VI*, 132–3 and 'Personal Rule', 42–3. For a kinder assessment of a well-intentioned Henry see Griffiths, *The Reign of King Henry VI*, 253.

2   Storey, *House of Lancaster*, 34–5; Watts, *Henry VI*, 103–4. See also below pp. 159–60 for later propaganda and hagiography.

3   See Watts' distinction (*Henry VI*, 105–11) between the king's private and public selves and his emphasis solely on the public exercise of royal will. It seems to me that while the public exercise of royal will is all that matters in the implementation and impact of declared policy, in the formulation of that policy the king's private wishes *are* as important as his capacity for implementing them. If, as Watts's argues, the nobility and councillors looked to the king to determine policy, it follows that they would strive to follow his wishes, however inchoate and vaguely expressed they were. Indeed, there is *prima facie* reason, on these grounds, for supposing that the policy followed *was* an attempt to make a reality of what the king wanted. The historian's problem, and it is fundamentally an unresolvable problem, remains in determining precisely where the king's initiative ended and his councillors' began. In the account that follows I have concluded that Henry did make known views of his own.

4   Griffiths, *Henry VI*, 235, 249–50, 254 (Henry's character) and 242–8 (the foundations); Wolffe, *Henry VI*, 135–45; But see Watts's alternative interpretation that the foundations were initiated by the council to make Henry look more like his father and to bind his household together (*Henry VI*, 167–71).

5   Griffiths, *Henry VI*, 365; Wolffe, *Henry VI*, 109.

6   Watts argues that in the autumn of 1441 there was a revival of formal conciliar government which lasted for at least two years (*Henry VI*, 145–51); Harriss, *Cardinal Beaufort*, 320–1, 349, noting the pattern of formal council meetings from 1439 until the winter of 1443–4, sees no such decline and revival. There is agreement, however, that the council as a formal governing body ceased to exist during 1444. See also Griffiths, *Henry VI*, 278–84.

7   Pollard, *John Talbot*, 50–1; Harriss, *Cardinal Beaufort*, 281–91; Vale, *English Gascony*, 110–12.

8   Allmand, 'Anglo-French Negotiations', 1–33; Griffiths, *Henry VI*, 446–50; Harriss, *Cardinal Beaufort*, 295–305.

9   Harriss, *Cardinal Beaufort*, 308–15; Griffiths, *Henry VI*, 457–61; Pollard, *John Talbot*, 52–4.

10 Stevenson, *Wars of the English*, ii, 451–60; Griffiths, *Henry VI*, 451–4; Harriss, *Cardinal Beaufort*, 315–17; Watts, *Henry VI*, 186–9. Harriss argues that the sentiments were not those of Beaufort and could only have been those of the king himself. Griffiths takes the view that it was Henry's personal opinion that tipped the scales against Gloucester's opposition. Watts suggests that the decision was made on the advice of his councillors and the declaration worded in the way it was so as to make it appear that the king was personally committed to peace.

11 Carey, *Courting Disaster*, 138–53; Griffiths, 'Eleanor Cobham', 381–99. It is likely that Eleanor was guilty of no more than commissioning a forecast of the king's death from two eminent astrologers, one of whom was himself executed.

12 Griffiths, *Henry VI*, 459–64; Pollard, *John Talbot*, 52–60.

13 Harriss, *Cardinal Beaufort*, 232–44. Jones, 'The French Expedition of 1443', 79–102.

14 Griffiths, *Henry VI*, 301–4, 333–67; Harriss, *Cardinal Beaufort*, 330–1. Watts, *Henry VI*, 158–66, 190–5, on the other hand, places Suffolk's rise to prominence earlier, and interprets the revival of conciliar authority in 1441 as linked to an attempt to thwart him. Note, too, Wolfe's judgement (*Henry VI*, 104) that he was already the king's most important minister in 1437.

15 *PPC*, vi, 316–20; Griffiths, *Henry VI*, 282–4; Watts, *Henry VI*, 213–15 and Wolffe, *Henry VI*, 113–15.

16 The process is fully documented in Griffiths, *Henry VI*, 333–67 and Wolffe, *Henry VI*, 109–16. Watts, *Henry VI*, 205–41 passim puts a more generous gloss on these developments, viewing the duke and his associates as altruistically filling the vacuum created by the king's indifference and creating an 'artificial power structure' which substituted for the king's will.

17 Griffiths, *Henry VI*, 570–9; Maddern, *Violence and Social Order*, 206–25.

18 Griffiths, *Henry VI*, 580–1, 584–8; Wolffe, *Henry VI*, 121–5. Watts, *Henry VI*, 216–21, argues that the worst abuses of power only occurred as the regime began to lose control and that the disorders in East Anglia, resulted from Suffolk's lack of control over the king's men.

19 Griffiths, *Henry VI*, 376–401; Harriss, 'Marmaduke Lumley', 143–9. For the economic circumstances see Hatcher, 'Great Slump', passim and Britnell, 'Economic Context', passim.

20 Harriss, 'Marmaduke Lumley', 150–74.

21 Griffiths, *Henry VI*, 482–94; Wolffe, *Henry VI*, 169–88; Watts, *Henry VI*, 222–6.

22 Griffiths, *Henry VI*, 295, 504; Wolffe, *Henry VI*, 191–200.

23 Griffiths, *Henry VI*, 408–10; Pollard, *North-Eastern England*, 221–2.

24 Keen and Daniel, 'English Diplomacy and the Sack of Fougères', passim; Griffiths, *Henry VI*, 508–14.

25 Ibid., 515–22.

26 For a recent defence of Sufolk's regime see Watts, *Henry VI*, 205–59, passim.

27 Griffiths, *Henry VI*, 286–8, 380, 388, 676–84; Wolffe, *Henry VI*, 215–29; Virgoe, 'William Tailboys and Lord Cromwell', passim and 'Death of William de la Pole', passim.

28 For this and the following paragraphs see Griffiths, *Henry VI*, 610–66; Harvey, *Cade's Rebellion*, passim; Mates, 'Sussex in 1450–51', 661–76.

29 For this and the following paragraphs see Griffiths, 'Duke Richard of York's Intentions', passim; and *Henry VI*, 686–92; Wolfe, *Henry VI*, 239–45; Johnson, *Duke Richard of York*, 78–100; Jones, 'Somerset, York and the Wars of the Roses', 285–307. For York's early career see also Pugh, 'Richard Plantagenet', passim.

30 Pugh, 'Richard Plantagenet', 107–9 (York's historians); and Watts, 'Polemic and Politics', passim (for the political thinking and rhetoric deployed by York and his opponents throughout the decade). As Watts points out, those who are sympathetic to York tend to follow the Yorkist propaganda; those who are not, the Lancastrian. See also his *Henry VI*, 266–71.

31 Griffiths, *Henry VI*, 387–90; Wolffe, *Henry VI*, 245–8; Watts, *Henry VI*, 282–90.

32 Griffiths, *Henry VI*, 573, 576–7; Wolffe, *Henry VI*, 248, 251–3. For the disharmony within the royal household resulting from the king's 'inner emigration' see Morgan, 'The House of Policy', 40–55.

33 Griffiths, *Henry VI*, 693–8; Wolffe, *Henry VI*, 253–6, 260–1; Johnson, *Duke Richard*, 100–24. Cherry, 'Mid-Fifteenth-Century Devonshire', 131–3; Storey, *House of Lancaster*, 84–104.

34 Griffiths, *Henry VI*, 522–31; Vale, 'English Gascony', 119–38.

35 Griffiths, *Henry VI*, 698–90; Wolffe, *Henry VI*, 261–2. Once more the problem arises as to the extent to which this new firmness of purpose was the result of the king becoming more assertive, or of Somerset providing more effective direction. Watts (*Henry VI*, 282–98) gives credit to Somerset for the manner in which he 'made use of the royal person' (293) to restore authority. Griffiths and Wolffe see the king himself playing a greater role. Note too that both Watts, *Henry VI*, 302 and Johnson, *Duke Richard*, 122–3 draw attention to evidence suggesting that Somerset's dominance was already under threat before the king collapsed.

36 Pollard, *John Talbot*, 130–3; Payling, 'Ampthill Dispute', 884–92; Cherry, 'Mid-Fifteenth-Century Devonshire', 133–5.

37 Griffiths, *Henry VI*, 699–700; Wolffe, *Henry VI*, 263–6.

38 Griffiths, 'Local Rivalries', 589 ff; Pollard, *North-Eastern England*, 255–7; Storey, *House of Lancaster*, 231–41; Hicks, *Warwick*, 84–5; Pollard, *John Talbot*, 136–8.

CHAPTER SIX

The fall of Henry VI, 1453–61

York's first protectorate, 1453–5

Until his collapse at the beginning of August 1453, whatever his failures and faults as a king, and they were many, Henry VI's title to the throne of England was not seriously in dispute. Eight years later he was overthrown and his dynasty replaced. In the confusion and uncertainty created by his sudden and complete mental and physical collapse decisions were taken, commitments were made and alliances were formed which proved irreversible and set the kingdom on a course that led to civil war and deposition. Nothing that had gone before pointed towards this outcome; events thereafter inexorably led to this end.

For seven months between August 1453 and March 1454 the government of the kingdom was paralysed. No one knew what was wrong with the king, or how long he would remain in his pitiful state.[1] For several months, in the hope and expectation that he would soon recover, nothing was done. Queen Margaret gave birth to a son and heir to the throne, christened Edward, on 13 October. Shortly afterwards, as the king showed no signs of improvement, it was decided first to call a Great Council to review the situation and secondly to prorogue parliament which had been due to reassemble on 12 November. At first it had been intended, no doubt by the duke of Somerset, to exclude the duke of York and his friends; but less partisan counsel prevailed and, since he was no longer heir presumptive to the throne, in the hope of reconciliation he was summoned. The council met on 21 November. However, the duke of Norfolk, acting on York's behalf, immediately presented charges of treason against Edmund Beaufort, demanding his removal to the Tower to await trial. York, embittered it would seem by his exclusion from court and office, thus gave the impression that he was more concerned with revenge than reconciliation in the greater interest of the kingdom. And no councillor, not even Cardinal Kemp, now seems to have had the stature, courage or the independence to persuade the council to resist his demand. On the 23 November Somerset was sent to the Tower.[2]

There followed, over the next four months, a period of intense political manoeuvring, of which the record has left only imperfect glimpses. The leading councillors sought to find an effective form of government for as long as the king was ill, while at the same time protecting their own interests, both for the present and for the future, if and when the king recovered. On 30 November, at a second Great Council, at which all the officers of state and chief household officals were present, an oath was taken to uphold the law and to act against anyone, of whatever estate, who flouted the king's and council's authority. York's restoration, as the nearest adult in blood to the king, even on his partisan terms, seems to have been accepted, with what enthusiasm we cannot tell. A few days later a smaller group agreed to take responsibility for the practical government of the kingdom during the king's infirmity. By mid-January the queen, now recovered from her confinement, threw her hat into the ring, and, according to one report, proposed the establishment of a regency with full royal powers being granted to her.[3] This, it seems, was rejected by the council. In mounting tension, the deadlock remained unresolved. The reassembly of parliament, having been postponed until 14 February, could not be postponed yet again. On the day before it convened the council confirmed York's supremacy by appointing him the king's lieutenant in its deliberations.

It would appear that all this time Cardinal Kemp, who as Chancellor could conduct the routine administration of the realm, succesfully prevaricated in the hope that the king would recover. But on 22 March the octogenarian cardinal died and the conciliar hand was forced. Not even the routine administration of the kingdom could be maintained without a Chancellor; and only the king, or his constitutionally appointed deputy, could select a successor. A delegation went to the king to seek his mind, only to find him completely uncomprehending and uncommunicative. Having failed once more to elucidate the king's will, the council proceeded to establish a protectorate on the exact model of the protectorate of 1422; on 28 March, with the suitable show of reluctance, York agreed to take up the burden; and on 3 April he was formally appointed by act of parliament. On the same day the personnel of a continual council of some twenty-four persons was nominated, after a great show of reluctance and special pleading of incapacity or incompetence by those present. The council included all the household officers and was not in itself outwardly partisan. The new protectorate was a caretaker administration with severely limited powers which could come to an end with the king's recovery at any moment. It nevertheless represented a fortuitous political opportunity which York grasped with both hands.[4]

York faced some daunting problems in the spring of 1454. He took over the captaincy of Calais from Somerset and entered into negotiations with the staplers and the garrison to repay debts and to secure the settlement of arrears of wages. These he brought to a successful conclusion, but he was never able to secure actual control. He was more successful in Ireland, where he was able to enforce his patent as lieutenant against the earl of Wiltshire. And he fitted out a navy to protect the southern coast of England and merchants from the privateers who had returned in strength since the loss of Normandy. But his major problem was the violence and disorder in Cumberland, Yorkshire, Derbyshire, Bedfordshire and Devon, which had escalated to a dangerous level since the king's collapse. In May 1454 immediate attention had to be given to the insurrection of the duke of Exeter and Lord Egremont in Yorkshire, which challenged his very authority as Protector.[5]

During the winter of 1453–4 York had formed an alliance with the Nevilles (Richard, Earl of Salisbury, and his son Richard, Earl of Warwick) which was to prove the most far-reaching political consequence of the crisis. It is likely that he already had an understanding with them when the council accepted his demand on 21 November 1454 that Somerset be charged with treason. Salisbury was at the heart of conciliar discussions thereafter and emerged as the successor to Kemp as Chancellor on 2 April. He was the first lay Chancellor for almost fifty years. Presumably he wanted the post. It is a measure of the importance of his support for York in the preceding months that he got it. Yet it is surprising that Salisbury, of all men, emerged as York's righthand man in 1454. It is true that he was his brother-in-law, York being married to his youngest sister, Cecily. In earlier times he had served under York in France. Salisbury may have been something of a mentor to the duke in his youth. But he had always been close to the court. Cardinal Beaufort's nephew, he had benefited spectacularly from his uncle's patronage. He had secured the greater share of the Neville inheritance in northern England, a virtual right to the wardenship of the west march, and control of the greater part of the duchy of Lancaster in Yorkshire. An assiduous courtier and councillor, he had by 1450 established a virtually unassailable dominance of northern England. Unscathed by the collapse of Suffolk's regime, he was a natural ally of his cousin, Edmund Beaufort, duke of Somerset. Throughout 1451 and 1452 he stayed close to the court and the household, calling up his retainers to support the king in strength against York in September 1451 and February 1452. His two younger sons, Thomas and John, had been knighted on 5 January 1453, and he was still attending council a month before the king collapsed.

Why he abandoned this favoured position, and threw in his lot with a man whom he might have judged would lose his authority as soon as the king recovered, still remains something of a mystery. There were some straws in the wind after 1450 that Salisbury's position at court was not quite as favoured as it had been before. The fee farm of Carlisle had been resumed by the Crown and granted to Lord Poynings, the heir to the earldom of Northumberland; William Percy, a son of the earl of Northumberland, had been provided to the diocese of Carlisle; and some manors in Richmondshire had been granted to Edmund Tudor when he had been elevated to the earldom of Richmond. But none of these grants and promotions seriously threatened his dominance in the region, or represented a major loss of influence at court. A man of his power could take such minor set-backs in his stride.[6]

Salisbury's relationships with the court were complicated after 1449 by the dispute between his eldest son and the duke of Somerset over the Warwick inheritance. Richard Neville succeeded to the earldom of Warwick and the greater part of the estates in right of his wife, Anne, full sister of Henry Beauchamp, Duke of Warwick. His inheritance to several of the estates, and even the title, were contested by his countess' half-sisters, Eleanor, Duchess of Somerset, and Margaret, Countess of Shrewsbury. These matters were still unresolved in July 1453; but far more explosive was the conflict between Warwick and Somerset himself over custody of the half of the Despenser lordships in Glamorgan which had passed to Warwick's uncle Edward Neville and his son, a minor, George. Warwick had initially been granted the custody of these lands; but on 15 June 1453 the king regranted their custody to Somerset, possibly after they had been resumed into royal hands. Within a month, just before Henry's collapse, Warwick was said to be holding Cardiff and Cowbridge castles by force in defiance of Somerset and he was ordered by the king to surrender them to Lord Dudley pending a resolution of the dispute. Warwick certainly had cause to side with York against Somerset.[7]

But Glamorgan was not the only county being disturbed by members of the Neville family in July 1453. The Nevilles and Percys had been uneasy neighbours in northern England for many decades. Although they had together supported the usurpation of Henry IV, in 1403 tensions came to a head during and after Hotspur's revolt. Following the disgrace of the Percys, the first earl of Westmorland and his favoured son by his second marriage, the future earl of Salisbury, had dominated Yorkshire and Cumbria without challenge. After the restoration of Henry, 2nd Earl of Northumberland in 1416 the two families had co-operated, if not necessarily closely, until 1449. It is not the case, as is so often assumed, that enmity between Neville and Percy was long-standing and deep-rooted; conflict broke out quite suddenly in 1453. Relationships had become more strained because of rivalry over precedence and the capture of Lord Poynings, the earl of Northumberland's heir, when raiding Dumfriesshire on Salisbury's behalf in 1448. The Percys too had begun to receive more favour, some of it at Neville expense. Much more visible was the emergence of the unruly Thomas Percy, Lord Egremont, Northumberland's younger son. Salisbury had held part of the barony of Egremont, in western Cumberland, and this he was required to surrender (with due compensation) to support the endowment of the new baron. But there is no direct evidence of even Egremont attacking Nevilles or their associates before 1453.

Violence between Nevilles and Percys, in the first instance perpetrated by the younger sons on both sides, did not erupt until after it became known in May 1453 that the earl of Salisbury had concluded a marriage agreement with Ralph, Lord Cromwell, for his second son, Sir Thomas, to marry Cromwell's neice and joint-heiress Maud Stanhope, the royal licence for which was issued on 1 May. Cromwell held the castle of Wressle in Yorkshire, and three other one-time Percy properties in fee simple by grant of the king. Wressle, it now seemed possible, would pass into Neville hands and not be restored to a Percy. Disorder occurred in both Cumberland and Yorkshire. Even before the king collapsed, the government was unable to bring either county under control, trusting initially to the earls themselves to discipline their sons and retainers. In August, after the Neville/Stanhope marriage was celebrated at Tattershall in Lincolnshire, the wedding party making its return to Sheriff Hutton was attacked by Egremont and his brother Sir Richard Percy at Heworth outside York. This brought the earls themselves into the fray. On 20 October their two forces, at full strength and supported by their principal allies, faced each other at Sand Hutton near York. A battle was averted by the intervention of the archbishop of York, the bishop of Durham and the earl of Westmorland. A month later, Salisbury gave his backing to York against Somerset; Northumberland pointedly absented himself from council. It is not inconceivable that Somerset, because of his dispute with Warwick in Glamorgan, had earlier given succour to the Percys. Immediate political calculation might explain Salisbury's decision to throw in his lot with York.[8]

Another dispute, that between Lord Cromwell and Henry Holland, Duke of Exeter, became entangled with the Neville/Percy quarrel. The feckless duke, York's son-in-law, had seized Ampthill in 1452. Before the king collapsed, Cromwell had been engaged in expensive litigation in the court of common pleas to recover the estate. Not surprisingly Exeter did all he could to obstruct the course of justice, leading to an armed brawl between supporters of both sides in the court itself at Westminster Hall on 4 July 1453. The marriage treaty with Salisbury had been made just so that Cromwell could secure himself backing at court. By 19 January 1454, Exeter had responded by allying himself with Lord Egremont. He pointedly did not support York's appointment as protector and soon laid claim to the office himself. Not surprisingly Cromwell sought the support of York in expediting his case. He presented a petition to parliament for the restoration of Ampthill which was granted. By the time that the sheriff of Bedfordshire was ordered to enforce the restoration on 12 May, Exeter and Egremont were up in arms in Yorkshire.[9]

Thus, when York marched north as Protector of the Realm to suppress the treason of the duke of Exeter and Lord Egremont he did so not only to enforce his constituted authority, but also as a *quid pro quo* for the support of two of his principal backers. The rebels soon dispersed: Exeter fled back to Westminster where he sought the safety of sanctuary and Egremont remained at large. In June, judicial proceedings at York, chaired by Duke Richard, received indictments roundly condemning the Percys. But at the beginning of August they were halted and no judgement was reached. A few weeks later Egremont and his brother, Sir Richard Percy, were defeated and taken prisoner in a skirmish at Stamford Bridge by Sir Thomas and Sir John Neville. The brothers were subsequently condemned for trespass, required to pay damages and in default of payment committed to Newgate. Exeter had already been taken from sanctuary and incarcerated in Pontefract in the charge of the earl of Salisbury. Peace was restored in Yorkshire on Neville terms, endorsed by the Protector.[10]

Yorkshire was not the only county in upheaval in 1454. A quarrel between Derbyshire gentry families led to the sack of Walter Blount's manor of Elvaston. None of the participants were at this time connected with Duke Richard. In an effort to demonstrate that as Protector of the realm he was determined to impose impartial justice on all, the duke left York and rode down to Derby to hear indictments. But Blount's enemies refused to appear and the proceedings proved abortive. From Derby the Protector rode on to Montgomery castle, to attempt, unsuccessfully, to discipline Gruffyd ap Nicholas, who had been disrupting western and central Wales and had survived all changes of regime. In Devon, where the earl of Devon took advantage of the protectorate to renew his attacks on Lord Bonville and to disrupt the rule of the county, York was totally powerless. He seems to have done nothing, not even to have given his backing to his erstwhile ally the earl. Preoccupied as he was in the north, the Protector ignored the disturbances in the West Country.[11] Yorkist propaganda was later to make much of the manner in which Duke Richard rigorously enforced the law as Protector, but he was able to do little more than make gestures. His hold on power was too tenuous and uncertain; the scale of the disorders in different parts of the country too great; and he was so beholden to the Nevilles and Cromwell that most of his energies were devoted to assisting them defeat their enemies. He may have wished to have made a bigger impact, but the task was beyond him.[12]

In the autumn of 1454, having returned to Westminster, York summoned another Great Council at which he proposed to proceed with the trial of the duke of Somerset. But the council prevaricated. The only outcome was a reform of the royal household which in fact marginally increased its size. By this time, it would seem the king was at last beginning to show signs of recovery. Shortly after Christmas he had fully regained his senses and was able to resume the powers of kingship. Early in the new year York surrendered his powers as Protector and Somerset was released from the Tower. For a month or two there was an uneasy lull. Sureties were given that Somerset would stay away from court until he had answered the charges against him. But at a council meeting at Greenwich on 4 March, over which the king personally presided, these constraints were removed and Somerset was absolved. He was restored to the captaincy of Calais and the king announced that the dispute between the dukes would be put to arbitration. Three days later Salisbury resigned as Chancellor; a week later the duke of Exeter was released and on 15 March the earl of Wiltshire, Somerset's close ally, was appointed Treasurer. When the king summoned a Great Council to meet at Leicester on 21 May, the Yorkist lords withdrew from court. It is almost certain that the intention was to condemn York and the Nevilles; they, justifiably considering their actions against Somerset, Exeter and the Percys, feared for their liberty, and in the light of the fate of Humphrey of Gloucester in 1447, perhaps for their lives. They determined, therefore, to use force to prevent the council meeting.[13]

St Albans and the second protectorate, 1455–6

The speed with which York and his allies raised troops, especially the Nevilles in the north, took the court by surprise. It was not until 18 May, when the king was about to set out for Leicester, that it realised what was afoot. Mediators were despatched (they were detained by the Yorkists), reinforcements hastily called, and the royal party began, cautiously, the journey north. On the morning of 22 May it entered St Albans with the Yorkist forces gathering outside the town. The king appointed the duke of Buckingham constable, in charge of his forces, and instructed him to negotiate. But York, remembering Dartford, was unwilling to compromise. Hardly had the attempted negotiations finished than the Yorkists launched their attack, led by the earl of Warwick. The king, wounded in the neck, took shelter; in the mêlée in the market square the duke of Somerset, the earl of Northumberland

and Lord Clifford were slain. After the fighting ended, York presented himself to the king. Four months after surrendering the protectorate, the duke was once again in power; but now by force not consent.

In the two years following Henry VI's collapse the English political world had been transformed. The king, even though he had recovered his wits, was a physically broken man, incapable of giving any but cursory and intermittent attention to affairs of state and even less able to assert his authority than he had been before August 1453. It would be wrong to assume, however, that he was necessarily, even then, the puppet that Yorkist propaganda made him out to be in 1460–1. York, on the other hand, because of his alliance with the Nevilles, was no longer isolated. He proved at St Albans that he commanded military strength that could not be ignored. Yet the politics of the kingdom had not become completely polarised. By killing their enemies York and the Nevilles had created a vendetta between themselves and the sons of their victims; a vendetta which the the new duke of Somerset in particular seems to have pursued remorselessly, as much against the Nevilles as York, once he came of age. But the nobility as a whole, especially the majority of the lords, had not taken either Somerset's or York's side; they still wished to find a way to heal the rift.

Immediately after the battle, the victorious Yorkists escorted the king back to Westminster. On 25 May, in a demonstration of his loyalty mounted for public consumption, York himself placed the crown on the king's head in a crown-wearing ceremony at St Paul's. The following day parliament was summoned to meet on 9 July. Somerset and his immediate servants were made to take the entire blame for what had happened and, while Lord Dudley and the duke of Exeter were arrested, very little victimisation followed. York became Constable of England and succeeded Somerset as constable of the Welsh castles of Aberystwyth and Carmarthen; Warwick was made captain of Calais. A new treasurer, Henry, Viscount Bourgchier, was installed; but there was no great redistribution of offices in favour of the victors and the royal household was left undisturbed.[14]

Some effort was made to return a favourable house of commons, but when parliament assembled, it soon showed itself independently minded. Its speaker was Sir John Wenlock, until recently Queen Margaret's chamberlain. It quickly introduced a bill of resumption. The lords, of whom many attended, established a series of committees, balanced in their composition, to deal with the major problems of defence and finance facing the kingdom. There seemed, for the time being, to be a collective effort by the lords to put the past behind them and restore unity. Nevertheless the most important business of the first session was the passage of an act pardoning and exculpating the Yorkist lords. It would appear that the king, who had been fit enough to open parliament in July, suffered some kind of relapse during the recess. As a result York was commissioned to act as his lieutenant during the second session which began on 9 November; and early in the proceedings a bill was brought forward for his reappointment as Protector for a second term. He was to serve until such time as the king relieved him of office in parliament, and the kingdom was to be governed by a council in the king's name.

The particular justification of the protectorate was the disorder in Devon, which York was commissioned to suppress. During the autumn of 1455 the conflict betwen the earl of Devon and Lord Bonville had intensifed. The cold-blooded and premeditated murder of Bonville's councillor, and locally respected lawyer, Nicholas Radford on 23 October had been particularly shocking. Matters came to a head in a pitched battle at Clyst St Mary, near Exeter, in which there were several fatalities. Despite his powers, York himself was in a delicate situation. The Bonvilles had formed an alliance with the Nevilles, who had insisted on the provision of the young George Neville, the brother of the earl of Warwick, to the bishopric of Exeter. Only after Clyst did York ride down to the West Country and then it was to receive the submission of the earl, his erstwhile ally, who was placed in custody. While order was restored to the west, it was on Bonville/Neville terms. Henceforth the earl of Devon was to be a friend of York's enemies.[15]

The second protectorate came to an end in February 1456, shortly before parliament was dissolved. The occasion was the failure of the bill of resumption in the house of lords; the reason was that the king's health had recovered sufficiently for him to relieve the duke of his office. But York remained for the time being the king's chief councillor, engaged in defending the north against the Scots. James II of Scotland had taken advantage of the divisions in England in the summer of 1455 to make an attempt on Berwick. He had failed, but in May 1456 formally renounced his truce with England. He moved against Roxburgh and raided Northumberland. York, based at Sandal for most of the summer, moved as far north as Durham, but made no counter-attack.[16]

It is difficult to gauge York's year of dominance and favour following St Albans. His short-lived position as Protector for a second term was not itself enforced on the king; he had willingly surrendered office in February and subsequently continued to act in the defence of the realm. The king, although in ill-health, seems to have been able to sanction his appointment as well as to end it. It seems as though the Yorkists themselves had endeavoured to form a government based on general aristocratic support. Attendance of the lords at parliament had been high; the commons had been associated with the establishment of the second protectorate; financial reform through resumption had been attempted. If any precedent were being followed for the rule after St Albans it was yet again that of the later years of Henry IV, when, because of the king's health, a conciliar form of government had been practised. There was, however, one fundamental difference between the arrangements established in 1406 and the experiment attempted in 1455–6. Henry IV had endorsed conciliar government arrived at by consensus; Henry VI had had to accept a settlement enforced upon him arising out of conflict. However much the Yorkists presented themselves as a legitimate reforming government of the king's natural councillors, the fact remained that they held power by might. Tensions ran high throughout the meeting of parliament; the Yorkists protecting themselves with bodyguards. The real precedent was 1386–8 when the Appellants, after victory in the field, had enforced themselves on Richard II. Such a government, however wide it made its appeal, could not have a long life. In the event, the only lasting advantage that the Yorkists made from St Albans was the installation of Warwick as captain of Calais, in which he had busied himself during the summer.

The emergence of Queen Margaret, 1456–9

Political developments between 1456 and 1459 are probably the most obscure and difficult to interpret in the whole of the fifteeenth century. This is partly due to the paucity and opacity of the evidence; partly to the colouring given later by accounts written after 1461; and partly to the very confusion at the time. It is particularly difficult to understand the attitudes, expectations and hopes of the lords as a whole and to perceive the alignments among them. There was no unity of purpose, no reassertion of the conciliar authority which had served the dynasty so well in the later years of Henry IV or the minority of Henry VI himself.

It is in these years too that the king's role is most enigmatic. One suspects that his wishes and opinion still carried some weight. It is still possible that he enjoyed phases of lucidity, interest and assertiveness and that, accordingly, those who remained closest to his own person exercised influence in his name. This group would seem to have included Bishop Waynflete of Winchester, the duke of Buckingham, the earl of Shrewsbury and Lords Beaumont and Dudley. It is noticeable that the personnel of the royal household remained largely unchanged throughout. Through all the upheavals, the king kept the same men about his person; esquires such as Thomas Daniel, John Trevilian and Thomas Tuddenham. Notwithstanding the storm of protest in 1450, these men were still at his side at the end of the decade. The household remained essentially untouched, one may guess, because the king made it clear that he wished to retain these men and that even York, with whom in 1456 the king was said to have no quarrel, respected that wish. Thus for a while there may have been two groups at court: those close to the person of the king who sought to articulate his will; and those, especially the heirs of the victims of St Albans and other enemies of the Yorkists, who gravitated to Queen Margaret. She created an independent source of power in her son's name based on the principality of Wales. Not until 1459 did the court groupings fully merge; only then, on the eve of civil war, did politics become clearly polarised between Yorkists and Lancastrians.[17]

Queen Margaret emerged as an independent political force in 1456. In February it was reported that 'she spareth noo peyne to sue hire thinges to an intent and conclusion of hir power'. By the end of 1457 several observers had commented on her influence at court.[18] What her aims were at this stage are harder to discern. Shakespeare's image of her as the she-wolf of France is derived almost entirely from hostile propaganda. Until 1453 she played the conventional role of queen consort. Only after the birth of her son and the elimination of Edmund Beaufort did she assert herself politically. Concern for her son's future was certainly one motive, and may have lain behind the bid to be regent in 1453–4. A kinder interpretation is that she extended her traditional role as supporter of the king to include exercising his authority on his behalf. The kindest is that she did not initially seek to destroy York as a threat to her son's inheritance, but to act as a mediator.[19]

The queen's first political intervention was in Wales in the late summer of 1456. Conflict had arisen in the southern counties of the principality from the attempt made by the duke of York to take possession of the castles of Carmarthen and Aberystwyth from Gruffydd ap Nicholas. Margaret encouraged Edmund Tudor, Earl of Richmond, to occupy them as lieutenant of the prince of Wales. But in August 1456 York's lieutenants (the duke being still in the north), Sir William Herbert and Sir Walter Devereux, with a force of York's tenants and retainers, retook Carmarthen and imprisoned Tudor. The court moved to Coventry, so as to be nearer the scene. A Great Council was summoned there early in October at which Herbert and Devereux submitted. York finally compounded with the crown in April 1457 to surrender Carmarthen and Aberystwyth to Jasper Tudor, Earl of Pembroke (who had suceeded his deceased brother in the service of the queen). Margaret's control was fully secured later in the year by coming to terms with Gruffyd ap Nicholas.[20]

Margaret also aimed to establish her influence in the central government of the kingdom. On 24 September 1456 her chancellor, Lawrence Booth, was appointed Keeper of the Privy Seal. Then, in October, York's kinsmen Thomas Bourgchier, Archbishop of Canterbury, and Henry Bourgchier, Earl of Essex, were removed from the offices of Chancellor and Treasurer. An opportunity also arose to weaken the hold of the Nevilles on the north when Robert, bishop of Durham, died on 8 July 1457; his replacement, provided on 22 August, was Lawrence Booth. Yet the queen did not at first exercise exclusive influence over the king. In October 1456 it had been reported that the duke of Buckingham's opinion was contrary to the queen's intent and that he had in fact protected York, who was still on good terms with the king. The new Chancellor and Treasurer appointed in the autumn of 1456, Bishop Waynflete and the earl of Shrewsbury, were not at that time her men. And it may be that compensation granted to York for the loss of the Welsh castles, as well as the renewal of his commission as lieutenant of Ireland, were due to the influence on the king of these lords. Nevertheless the sons of those killed at St Albans were favoured at court and promoted by the queen. A series of marriages sponsored by her, most prominently the matches between her cousin, Marie of Maine, and the young Thomas Courtenay, heir to the earl of Devon, and between the child widow of Edmund Tudor, Margaret Beaufort, and Henry Stafford, the second son of the duke of Buckingham, brought the greater court aristocracy closer to her. Slowly she strengthened her position.[21]

The queen's growing prominence was marked also by a shift of the centre of government to the midlands. The court began to spend longer periods there, exploiting the estates of the duchy of Lancaster and the county of Chester as well as the patrimony of the prince of Wales. It consolidated its political and military strength in the region and began to finance itself directly from Crown estates and other revenues; there was a distinct fall in the level of correspondence and administration passing through the chancery as the king's secretary began to play a more prominent role. Westminster was not visited for a year, and London, shaken during 1457 by a series of anti-alien riots, was largely abandoned. Financial support for the garrison of Calais was cut, leading the earl of Warwick to take to piracy in the Channel to sustain himself. In September 1457 Sandwich, which Warwick used as a base on the northern shore of the straits of Dover, was raided and sacked by a retaliatory French force under Pierre de Brèze. Piracy, on a scale unknown since the early years of Henry IV, once more rendered the Channel unsafe for shipping.[22]

It is in the context of growing disorder on the seas and the continuing enmity between the sons of those killed at St Albans and the Nevilles that we should perhaps interpret the last sustained effort at peacemaking under-taken during the winter of 1457–8. The court returned to Westminster from its long perambulation of the midlands in October 1457. A Great Council was summoned for November in which the king, or those speaking for him, having raised for the first time the force of archers authorised for the defence of the realm by the parliament of 1453, endeavoured to persuade the Yorkists and the duke of Somerset, the earl of Northumberland and Lord Clifford, now attached to the queen, to come to terms. The autumn meeting was fruitless, but the effort continued. In January and early February all the parties descended on London, accompanied in strength by armed retinues. The Yorkists lodged in the city; the Lancastrians outside its gates to the west. So great was the tension that the city maintained its watch on constant alert. Protracted negotiations over four weeks resulted in the announcement of an arbitration award by the king on 24 March. The Yorkists agreed to pay compensation to the sons of the fallen for the deaths of their fathers; to endow a chantry at St Albans; and (the Nevilles) to forgo the fines imposed on Lord Egremont in 1454. Egremont, who had escaped from the Fleet in 1456, agreed to go on pilgrimage and put up a bond for good behaviour. On 25 March a solemn Love-Day was celebrated in St Paul's. The Yorkists had atoned for their taking of blood, and peace was restored. A round of celebration, feasting and jousting followed until mid-May.[23]

It is hard to determine whose initiative the Love-Day was. It might have come from those closest to the king, putting into practice his desire for peace and reconciliation. Alternatively, it has been variously suggested, the inspiration may have come from the queen, in her traditional role as mediator, or even from the earl of Warwick. If the second were the case, it is puzzling that it was she, not the duke of Somerset, who joined hands with York in the ritual at St Paul's.[24] But whoever lay behind it, the St Paul's Love-Day proved to be but a shallow and short-lived reconciliation. By the autumn of 1458 Queen Margaret seems finally to have established her unchallenged authority at court. In October, the earl of Wiltshire replaced the earl of Shrewsbury as Treasurer and Thomas Tuddenham became Treasurer of the Household, as the queen tightened her grip on financial control. Matters came to a head at a Great Council in November.

By virtue of his precedence, his greater wealth and above all his more forceful personality, the earl of Warwick had emerged as the dominant member of his family. He was rapidly gaining renown and popularity by his exploits as captain of Calais, most recently an attack on the Hanseatic Bay fleet. He was a man less restrained than his father by residual loyalty to the house of Lancaster, more willing than York to enflame popular dissent for political ends, and more ready to use the sword to settle his differences than either. He appeared at the November council meeting to answer for his conduct and to plead for financial support. But while he was at Westminster a brawl broke out between his servants and those of the king. He and his men later claimed that an attempt had been made on his life. In the same month his father called his council together at Middleham and there resolved, it was later recorded, 'to take full part with the full noble prince, the Duke of York', which implies a military commitment, made presumably in answer to a request from the duke. The renewal of civil war was now but a question of time.[25]

Civil war, 1459–61

Both sides actively prepared for war over the winter of 1458–9. Warwick withdrew once more to Calais to plan an invasion; and the queen herself began to arm and gather her strength in the midlands, to which the court once more withdrew in the spring of 1459. Members of the royal household were ordered to attend the king at Leicester on 10 May, armed for two months' service. A Great Council was then summoned to meet at Coventry in late June. The Yorkist lords, who did not attend, or were not invited, were thereupon indicted on unspecified charges. They were already mobilising their own forces.[26]

The Yorkists took the initiative. Their plan was to rendezvous at Ludlow and from there advance to confront the king. Warwick crossed from Calais with a section of the Calais garrison; Salisbury set out from Middleham with a substantial army drawn from the northern marches. The court endeavoured to intercept both forces. Warwick managed to evade one detachment of the royal host south of Coventry. But another, much more powerful, royal army under Lords Audley and Dudley intercepted Salisbury at Blore Heath, near Newcastle-under-Lyme, on 23 September. Although outnumbererd, Salisbury won a bloody and pyrrhic victory, and was able to pass on, with a much depleted force, eventually to join Warwick and York at Worcester. Here the lords solemnly declared their loyalty to Henry and sent emissaries to the king calling upon him to dismiss his evil ministers and to reform the government of the kingdom. Their appeal was rejected and, the king himself taking the field in arms, the royal host advanced on Worcester. The Yorkists withdrew to Ludlow and drew up their forces at Ludford, below the town. There on 12 October the two armies finally came face to face. Heavily outnumbered, and deserted by elements of the Calais garrison under Sir Andrew Trollope, York, his sons Edward, Earl of March, and Edmund, Earl of Rutland, Salisbury and Warwick, stole away during the night. York and Rutland made it to Ireland; the other three eventually reached Calais. The rebellion had ended in ignominious failure.[27]

Queen Margaret wasted no time in pressing home her advantage. A parliament had already been summoned to Coventry before the rout at Ludford. The assembly, which met on 20 November, was packed with royal supporters and had but one purpose: to condemn York and his associates. The process of attainder was adopted; a committee of lawyers preparing the bill with great care. At the same time the royalist position was justified in the *Somnium Vigilantis* which set out to demonstrate that no cause justified the raising of arms against the king, not even the cause of reform. It took a month to pass the act of attainder which stripped twenty-seven rebels and their heirs of noble status and confiscated their estates. The threat of wide-spread proscription and the parallel requirement that all the lords present should undertake an oath of loyalty to the king, brought many men sympathetic to the Yorkists to heel. Before the act was passed the king issued pardons to several of those who had marched with them, including prominent retainers of the duke of York himself such as Sir Walter Devereux, Sir William Herbert and William Hastings. And lords such as Fitzhugh, closely associated with the Nevilles, found it prudent to take the oath.[28]

It would seem as if the forfeitures were intended to be permanent. The Crown quickly appointed its own administrators and arranged for the income to be paid directly into the coffers of the household; very few estates were granted as rewards to loyal supporters of the Crown. The revenues of the Yorkshire estates of the the earl of Salisbury, for instance, were set aside to pay the arrears of the earl of Northumberland as warden of the east march; a few months later he was granted a lease of the estates. The forfeitures were to be used to strengthen and renew the Crown not to reward its followers and perpetuate division.[29]

But the government still needed to secure control of these estates, win over Yorkist followers and sympathisers and, above all, destroy the Yorkist lords, safe in their sanctuaries of Dublin and Calais. Jasper Tudor, Earl of Pembroke, was given the task of taking possession of the Yorkist castles in Wales. But he did not reduce Denbigh until March 1460, and the southern castles were still in Yorkist hands in the summer. A commission of oyer and terminer was appointed in February to enquire into disturbances throughout Wales; and a month later the commissioners were empowered to offer pardons to all rebels not attainted at Coventry. In the north, Lord Clifford and the earl of Northumberland had little difficulty in taking possession of the Neville estates, but the earl of Salisbury's affinity, many of whose members purchased pardons, remained intact. By the summer they were beginning to disturb Yorkshire. In both Wales and the north, notwithstanding later Yorkist propaganda to the contrary, the government was too hesitant and insufficiently ruthless in the proscription of its enemies.

The duke of York was relatively safe in Dublin. He took the opportunity of his exile to call an Irish parliament and, by making concessions to the Anglo-Irish establishment, gain support among its ranks. Warwick in Calais was more vulnerable and the Crown concentrated its military effort over the winter of 1459–60 on dislodging him. Somerset was re-appointed captain of the town. Late in October he crossed the Channel and seized the castles of Guisnes and Hammes, from which he endeavoured to harass the garrison in Calais itself. But he was defeated in a skirmish at Newham Bridge. In the meantime, on 15 January, Warwick raided Sandwich, seized the ships riding in the harbour and took Lord Rivers, the Lancastrian commander, prisoner. So confident was Warwick in his command of the seas that in the spring he sailed to Dublin to consult with York. Following his return at the end of June, Lord Fauconberg led a second raid on Sandwich, captured reinforcements being prepared for the relief of Somerset at Guisnes, and held the port in readiness for the main landing by Salisbury, Warwick and March a few days later.

Gathering support in Kent, the Yorkists quickly moved on London, which opened its gates to them on 2 July. Three days later, having left Salisbury to deal with Lord Scales who was defending the Tower, Warwick, March and Fauconberg advanced north to Northampton, where on 10 July they met the royal army led by the duke of Buckingham and the earl of Shrewsbury. After a short encounter, in which the Yorkists had issued instructions to spare the common soldiers, decided by a timely switch of allegiance by Lord Grey of Ruthin, they routed their enemies. Buckingham, Shrewsbury and Lord Egremont were killed; the king was taken prisoner. The queen and the prince of Wales, who had prudently remained in Coventry, escaped. The king was escorted back to London on 16 July. Lord Scales, who had turned his cannon with devastating effect on the city, was still holding out in the Tower. However, in attempting to escape in disguise three days later, he was recognised on the river by some watermen and summarily executed.[30]

The victory at Northampton put the Yorkist lords back into the same position as after St Albans five years earlier. The propaganda issued by them had emphasised yet again the corruption of the king's government and the need for reform, while stressing their loyalty to the king himself. Once more, the chief officers of state were replaced, George Neville, Bishop of Exeter, becoming Chancellor and Viscount Bourgchier, Treasurer. But now, for the first time, a purge of the king's own household was initiated, with Salisbury making himself chamberlain. And a parliament was summoned to meet at Westminster on 7 October whose first business would be to repeal the acts of attainder passed a year earlier. In the meantime the duke of York's return from Ireland was awaited. He landed in the Wirral on 8 September and began a leisurely progress via his border estates to London. By the time he reached Abingdon, it was apparent that he had adopted the style of king. When he reached Westminster he went straight to the palace, which he entered as if it were his own. Three days after the opening of parliament, on 10 October, he strode into the lords' chamber as if to sit in the chair of state. Only when challenged by Archbishop Bourgchier did he hesitate. No one could doubt that he was claiming the throne for himself.

The lords went immediately into secret conclave at Blackfriars to debate York's claim. They could come to no resolution. On 16 October York's councillors submitted a a formal petition to the commons, laying claim to the throne by right of birth, which was passed to the lords. The lords then passed the issue to the judges, who themselves concluded that it was beyond their competence to decide. The deadlock was not broken until 22 October when the Chancellor reported that the king had instructed the lords to come to a decision. By the end of the month they came up with a compromise based on the treaty of Troyes, which was that York's right would be recognised, but that Henry VI would continue to hold the throne until his death, adopting York as his heir and the Protector of his realm. This accord, agreed by the king himself, was enacted in parliament and marked by a solemn crown-wearing by Henry VI at St Paul's on 1 November.[31]

It is not clear whether York made his bid for the throne in October 1460 with the knowledge and support of Salisbury, Warwick and March. According to the account given by Jean de Waurin from a version of events which Warwick's associates subsequently gave him, the Neville lords were both surprised and deeply opposed. Even Edward IV, then earl of March, he was told, opposed his father. The account is barely plausible, and all too easily explained by Warwick's circumstances when the story was told ten years later. York had taken a month to come up to London; he had been in Westminster several days before he came into parliament. His actions had been so public, his intention so obviously signalled, that it is impossible that Salisbury, Warwick and March did not know. Warwick and York may well have agreed this course of action six months earlier in Dublin. Perhaps the elder Neville had been kept in the dark. One has to wonder how enthusiastically the earl of Salisbury, who owed everything to the dynasty, would have supported the deposition of Henry VI. It is even conceivable that the Yorkist lords put on an elaborate charade of reluctance so as to make the final accord appear an honourable compromise.[32]

Whatever misgivings (if misgivings there had been) about the claim to the throne, there could have been no doubt in the minds of the Yorkist lords that Queen Margaret and her allies would reject the Westminster accord and that it would have to be enforced by the sword. Henry VI might have accepted the disinheritance of his son; no other Lancastrian did. Even while parliament sat, the Lancastrians were gathering their forces for the counter-attack. Although the Yorkists had gained control of London and the south-east in the summer of 1460, they were powerless in the south-west, Wales and the north. The queen herself first retreated to Wales, held by the earl of Pembroke, and then took ship to Scotland. In October, the duke of Somerset returned from Dieppe to the West Country, linked up with the earl of Devon and marched across England to join the earls of Northumberland and Westmorland and other Lancastrian lords in the north, all of whose forces had mustered at Hull. Penrith, Pontefract and Wressle remained in Lancastrian control and no amount of cajoling from Westminster could induce their surrender.

At the same time Queen Margaret in Scotland was endeavouring to form an alliance with the regent, Mary of Guelders. In the summer, James II, taking advantage of the battle of Northampton, had laid seige to and recovered Roxburgh, though the campaign had cost him his life. Queen Margaret could entertain reasonable hope that the Scots would be willing to support her cause. Immediately after parliament was prorogued, York and Salisbury set off to counter the threat, armed with a commission to restore order in Yorkshire. Finding, probably to their surprise, that a Lancastrian army, far larger than their own, controlled the county, they sought refuge in the duke's castle of Sandal. On 30 December, when out foraging for supplies, or even seeking to break out, York's army was caught near Wakefield and cut to pieces. York, the earl of Rutland and Sir Thomas Neville were killed; Salisbury was taken alive, removed to Pontefract and was there lynched by the mob. The heads of the dead were mockingly displayed on the gates of York, Duke Richard's adorned with a paper crown.[33]

As soon as she knew of the victory at Wakefield, Queen Margaret hurried from Scotland. At a council of war held in York it was determined to march south. A large force advanced to St Albans via Grantham and Stamford, reportedly pillaging and looting on its way and creating panic ahead of it. Warwick, having rapidly gathered reinforcements, marched out to meet it on 17 March. Here he too was defeated, though he escaped from the field; the king was reunited with his queen; and London lay open to attack. Fortunately for Warwick and the Yorkist cause, Edward, Earl of March, now the duke of York, had proved more successful in the Welsh marches. Having been sent there to raise reinforcements and to prevent the earl of Pembroke from joining the main Lancastrian army, he had defeated Pembroke at the battle of Mortimer's Cross on 2 February. Marching up to London from the borders, Edward met Warwick in the Cotswolds, rallied him and pressed on to London.

In the meantime the queen fatefully hesitated. Holding her army at St Albans, she demanded the submission of the city a day's march away. The citizens, fearful of the reputation of her troops, sought assurances of their safety. On 22 February a delegation of aldermen was prevented from leaving the city by some citizens. Five days later Edward and Warwick were admitted and welcomed. Without any further ado, claiming that Henry VI by joining with his queen at St Albans had broken his side of the Westminster accord, on 4 March Edward IV took possession of the crown in right of his title recognised in the last parliament, 'elected' by an unrepresentative assembly of favourably inclined prelates and lords. He then immediately set about raising new forces to pursue and defeat the Lancastrians who had retreated north.

Lord Fauconberg set out with the advance guard on 11 March; Edward two days later. By 27 March the main part of the army had reached Pontefract and made contact with the enemy on the further bank of the Aire. On 28 March a crossing of the river was forced at Castleford and on the following day, 29 March, the main armies met on the field of Towton. The battle, fought in snow showers, was long and hard. Only at the end of the day, when the Yorkists were reinforced by the arrival of the duke of Norfolk, did the Lancastrians break and flee, leaving hundreds dead on the field, killed in flight or executed after the battle. The dead in two days fighting included Lords Dacre, Clifford and Neville, and the earls of Devon, Northumberland and Wiltshire. The dukes of Exeter and Somerset escaped with the king, queen and prince of Wales who had remained in York.[34]

Towton was the decisive battle of a civil war that had been fought for eighteen months since the Ludford campaign of September 1459. It did not bring the war to an end; the deposed King Henry VI and his heir were still at large and fighting was to continue in Wales until the end of 1461 and in Northumberland, sporadically, until 1464. But, although he was not crowned until 28 June, Towton confirmed Edward IV on the throne he had occupied on 4 March. And while the battle did not finally seal the fate of the dynasty, it brought both the reign of Henry VI and the rule of the Lancastrian dynasty to an end.

Conclusion

The dominant image of Henry VI as a nonentity, uninterested in the affairs of state, the puppet in the hands of rival factions, drably dressed, and more a monk than a monarch, derives from the last six years of his reign, after the recovery from his madness, but when he was probably an invalid. It was this stage of his life which was portrayed by his chaplain John Blacman. This portrait needs to be treated with care; it was composed as part of the campaign for the canonisation of the king twenty five years later. Blacman looked for and highlighted christian, specificaly Carthusian, virtues. The portrait deliberately played down what small part he played in politics. Nevertheless it encapsulates two truths about the last years of his reign. One was that his subjects came to admire his very unworldliness and that for the most part they did not wish to see him deposed. The cult that later developed around his person was popular in character; and it pictured him as a saintly man who sought reconciliation and social peace. The other is that his very indifference to power and politics created circumstances with which with it was difficult for his leading subjects to cope. It was easier for the queen, close to his person and able to call upon her role as supporter of the Crown; it was harder for the Yorkists who never ruled with royal assent freely given. But there was a vacuum at the centre and a lack of collective will or capacity among the lords as a whole to fill it.[35]

Deposition was not entered into lightly. It took several years of continuous crisis to reach that moment. It is difficult to know whether York harboured a long-standing ambition for the throne, or only advanced his claim out of desperation. Proudly conscious of his descent and his status as a royal duke, he would not accept a secondary role in the affairs of the kingdom, especially as heir presumptive between 1447 and 1453. One reason, among others, for his hostility to Edmund Beaufort may have been the fear that Beaufort would seek to remove the bar imposed in 1407 on the sucession of his line to the throne. All, the king and queen not least, were fully aware that he was the heir to an alternative title to the Crown which had remained dormant since 1415. The potential had always existed for York to claim the throne and had been alluded to since 1450 at the latest. His own reluctance to advance the claim until 1460, by which time he had little alternative left, reveals as much about the depth of the roots put down by the Lancastrians, as it conceals about his deeper thoughts. The possibility of deposition was ever present in the flawed Lancastrian title, but it was never made explicit until the eleventh hour.[36]

Throughout these final years the majority of the political nation was loyal to the dynasty. Most of the sources, however, because they were composed after 1461 or by Yorkist sympathisers (or both), give a misleading view of the unpopularity of the queen and the Lancastrian regime. The much quoted judgement of the 'Davies' chronicle that the realm was out of all good governance because the king was simple and easily led and that the queen and her adherents did what they liked, is repetition of the propaganda put out by York and his associates in 1459–60. The queen, in particular, has been harshly treated because of this. By 1461 the Yorkists had gained some sympathy in Kent and London; but there was even less revulsion against the dynasty or the king than there had been in 1399.

One should not forget that the Lancastrians came near to winning the war in the spring of 1461. The Yorkists were victorious because their political weakness was offset by their wealth and military power, on land and sea. They had in Edward IV a more decisive leader and gifted general, released from the restraints of residual loyalty to the house of Lancaster by the breakdown of the Westminster accord. And in Warwick they had a man who used naval power to decisive advantage in 1459–60. In the event Edward IV and Warwick tipped the balance militarily in favour of the house of York.[37]

In the last resort the house of Lancaster fell because it lost the war, not because it was illegitimate (which it arguably was) and not because it was unpopular (which it was not). The unfortunate Henry VI inevitably carries a heavy burden of responsibility for the crisis which consumed him. Whether one sympathises with the man or not, the fact remains that he was a woefully inadequate king in a political system that hinged on the personal exercise of power and authority by the monarch. As we have seen, there are some indications that by 1453, at the age of thirty, he was coming to be a more effective, or rather less ineffective ruler than he had been in his early majority. The collapse of his mental and physical health transformed the political scene. It is clear that although he recovered sufficiently from his coma at the end of 1454 to play once again a role in public affairs, he was never thereafter fit enough or engaged enough to exercise the powers of the monarchy effectively. Only after Northampton was he reduced to the status of a mere puppet of a king that Bishop George Neville described in 1461. Herein lay the real tragedy, for if Henry had remained comatose, a properly constituted protectorate could have been established to manage the affairs of the kingdom: and there was substantial experience of conciliar govern-ment upon which to draw. But the circumstances after 1455 provided the worst of all worlds; a king who was a sane adult with his own will, but who was incapable of exercising it effectively.

However, the crisis of the 1450s did not derive entirely from the genetic accident of Henry VI's personality. In part, too, it derived from his father's inheritance and the burden of the war in France, the ultimate outcome of which was always likely to be defeat. Indeed it can be argued that the staving off of that defeat for a decade or more was in itself a remarkable achievement. Although compounded by errors of policy and the king's own folly, the war bankrupted the Crown and the shame of defeat undermined the standing of the dynasty. But there were other elements that were beyond the control of any government. Economic recession in the mid-fifteenth century, at the same time that royal finances were under strain, reduced the revenues available to the Crown even further and, moreover, intensified the pressure on the king's government to find remedies for the benefit of his subjects. Any king, any government, would have found the 1450s a difficult decade.

These circumstances, however difficult they were, need not necessarily have led to civil war. The Lancastrian dynasty had faced a similar problem in the later years of Henry IV's reign. Then, even though there were political rivalries and conflicts, the court and royal affinity were held together by their shared loyalty to the king and commitment to his cause. By the 1450s this was noticeably lacking. One can find several reasons for the change. One was the inheritance of half a century of Lancastrian rule, and especially the strains and tensions of Henry's reign itself. A regime that lacked purpose, that had presided over military disaster, was virtually bankrupt and seemed incapable of maintaining order, hardly inspired confidence. After half a century the Lancastrian affinity itself, that massive buttress to the dynasty in its first twenty-five years, had crumbled and disintegrated. The personal links and commitments that had tied the first generation of companions and servants of the dynasty to its first kings had disappeared; a new generation had a more impersonal and distant relationship with a king who failed to inspire or command them.

Even so, none of this in itself explains the disruptive impact of Richard of York. Duke Richard remains an enigma. He was not possessed of subtle political understanding or innate skill. It will probably always be impossile to tell whether he was driven more by personal ambition and pride than by a concern for the good of the common weal; and, as has been pointed out, in the circumstances the fact of his espousing the cause of the common good as a political platform is probably more important than the depth of his commitment to it. His conduct in 1453–4 is particularly revealing. Even though he did his best to present himself as the just ruler for the common good, he used the powers of the protectorate for partisan ends. He himself single-mindedly sought the destruction of the duke of Somerset, an objective achieved in 1455. Unlike Humphrey of Gloucester or Cardinal Beaufort, he was unable to rise above his personal animosities in the name of the common weal which he claimed to represent.[38]

Notwithstanding the necessary rhetoric to the effect, the political leaders of the 1450s showed little of the wider concern for the good of the kingdom that their predecessors had shown either in the reign of Henry IV or the minority of Henry VI himself. This was a new, more self-serving generation. Yet these men too were victims of the complex and seemingly irresolvable crisis that engulfed the kingdom in mid-century. Better to understand that crisis and to explore the process of recovery under successive dynasties in the later part of the fifteenth century, one can turn now from a political narrative to consider the wider context of the realm of England itself: the people of England; social and economic change; the church, religion and culture; and the constitution, government and administrative structures of the kingdom in the fifteenth century.

Notes and references

1   For discussion of the king's condition see Griffiths, *Henry VI*, 715–16; Rawcliffe, 'Insanity of Henry VI', 8–12; Wolffe, *Henry VI*, 271.

2   Griffiths, *Henry VI*, 719–25; Johnson, *Duke Richard*, 125–31; Watts, *Henry VI*, 302–8.

3   Gairdner, *Paston Letters*, ii, 297.

4   Griffiths, *Henry VI*, 725–6; Watts, *Henry VI*, 307–10; Wolffe, *Henry VI*, 278–81.

5   Harriss, 'Struggle for Calais', 30–53; Griffiths, *Henry VI*, 726–35; Johnson, *Duke Richard*, 142–4.

6   Pollard, *North-Eastern England*, 245–55; Storey, *House of Lancaster*, 105–23; Watts, *Henry VI*, 173, 201, 203–4, 258–9.

7   Wolffe, *Henry VI*, 268–9; Carpenter, *Locality and Polity*, 439–46; Storey, *House of Lancaster*, 134–5; Hicks, 'Cement or Solvent?', 43.

8   Griffiths, 'Local Rivalries'; Pollard, *North-Eastern England*, 255–9; Storey, *House of Lancaster*, 124–32.

9   Payling, 'Ampthill Dispute', passim.

10 Griffiths, 'Local Rivalries', 612–34; Pugh, 'Richard, Duke of York', 248–61; Storey, *House of Lancaster*, 142–9.

11 Castor, 'The Sack of Elvaston, 21–39, esp. 32–3; Griffiths, 'Gruffyd ap Nicholas', 205–9; Cherry, 'Struggle for Mid-Fifteenth-Century Devonshire', passim.

12 Harriss and Harriss, 'John Benet's Chronicle'. Modern assessments of York's achievement vary. Griffiths (*Henry VI*, 735) concluded that his primary concern was to consolidate his own position and to advance the interests of his supporters; Johnson (*Duke Richard*, 140–51), while recognising the pursuit of personal interest, suggested that he endeavoured to provide effective government; Pugh ('Richard, Duke of York', 260) judged that 'he had the vigour, firmness and resolution that qualified him to rule', a view endorsed by Watts (*Henry VI*, 311), 'he sought to uphold effective agencies of rule while attempting to reconcile their opponents'. For other aspects of York's government in 1454 see Griffiths, *Henry VI*, 726–35.

13 For this and the following paragraph see Armstrong, 'Battle of St Albans', passim.

14 For this and the following paragraph see Griffiths, *Henry VI*, 744–57; Johnson, *Duke Richard*, 158–73; Lander, ' Second Protectorate', passim; Watts, *Henry VI*, 317–23.

15 Cherry, 'Struggle for Power', 133–4.

16 McGladdery, *James II*, 98–9; Johnson, *Duke Richard*, 174; Griffiths, *Henry VI*, 808, 811–12; Harriss, 'Struggle for Calais', 43–7; Hicks, *Warwick*, 140–4; Watts, *Henry VI*, 333–5. Here and elsewhere (327–8 and 345) Watts argues that between 1456 and 1458 the Nevilles and York 'went their separate ways', because the Nevilles 'opted for noble unity and the council of lords in preference to the duke's adventures' (see also note 17, below). This interpretation is based ultimately on Jean de Waurin, whose account of these years owes much to a self-justificatory version of events supplied to him a decade later by Warwick, or by those close to him.

17 Watts (*Henry VI*, 323–31) has proposed that the lords as a whole collectively wished to establish a 'government of noble unity', which was undermined both by a sense that such a step would be unconstitutional and by a general reluctance to include York. It is not clear what a government of noble unity, or 'the rule of the lords', means other than the formalisation of conciliar government answerable to parliament which had respectable constitutional precedents, and could have been attempted had the will and unity of purpose really been present. For further discussion of the constitutional dimension see below pp. 232–4.

18 Gairdner, *Paston Letters*, iii, 75; Johnson, *Duke Richard*, 173, followed by Gross, *Lancastrian Kingship*, 49, argues that this referred to her determination to preserve her own livelihood in the face of resumption, not her desire to increase her political power. By the end of 1457, however, several observers had commented on her burgeoning influence at court and assertive political role. See, e.g., Gairdner, *Historical Collections*, 209; Harriss, 'John Benet's Chronicle', 217; Gascoigne, *Loci e Libro Veritatum*, 203–6.

19 For the most recent discussion see Gross, *Lancastrian Kingship*, 46–69, in which it is suggested that the initiative and drive came not from the queen herself, but from a group of royal advisers and officials, who feared for their futures after the fall of Edmund Beaufort (51–69). I would like to record my gratitude to Bonita Cron and Helen Maurer for sharing their thoughts on her career with me.

20 Griffiths, *Henry VI*, 779–80; Johnson, *Duke Richard*, 176–9.

21 Ibid., 772–5, 802–3; Gairdner, *Paston Letters*, iii, 108–9.

22 Griffiths, *Henry VI*, 777–8, 781–90, 801–2; Hicks *Warwick*, 144,146–8; Watts, *Henry VI*, 337–42. For the disturbances in London see Griffiths, *Henry VI*, 790–7.

23 Ibid., 804–5; Johnson, *Duke Richard*, 180–5; Watts, *Henry VI*, 343–4; Wolffe, *Henry VI*, 311–12.

24 Griffiths, *Henry VI*, 805, 'an olive branch, whose naivety and theatricality most likely sprang from the king himself'; Johnson, *Duke Richard*, 180, 'Henry himself seems to have believed it possible to produce a negotiated settlement between the various hostile families'. Hicks, *Warwick*, 133–6 also emphasises the king's personal role, but argues that Warwick forced the pace in seeking a settlement. But Watts, *Henry VI*, 343, argues 'It was surely the work of this council (a council of the lords), rather than the whimsy of the king'. One contemporary, John Whethamstede, abbot of St Albans, attributed a central role to the queen (Riley ed., *Registrum*, 301).

25 Watts, *Henry VI*, 346–50 suggests that the government had been dominated by York and his allies since the Love-Day and it was they who initially called the council. For the brawl in November see Davies, ed., *English Chronicle*, 78 and for references to other reported attempts to detain or attack Warwick in 1457–8, in Griffiths, *Henry VI*, 809; Hicks, *Warwick*, 132,152. For Salisbury's

decision see Pollard, *North-Eastern England*, 269–70. However, Watts, *Henry VI*, 328 interprets this as meaning 'almost certainly with the intention of restoring a workable authority of the lords', and Hicks, *Warwick*, 155–9 assigns it to an earlier year, dating the final breach after the Coventry council of June/July 1459.

26 Griffiths, *Henry VI*, 816–17; Johnson, *Duke Richard*, 185–6; Wolffe, *Henry VI*, 316–17.

27 Griffiths, *Henry VI*, 817–23; Pollard, *North-Eastern England*, 271–2.

28 Griffiths, *Henry VI*, 823–5; Johnson, *Duke Richard*, 189–2. For the *Somnium Vigilantis* see Kekewich, 'Attainder of the Yorkists', 25–34; Watts, 'Ideas, Principles and Politics', 128–9.

29 For this and the following paragraph see Griffiths, *Henry VI*, 825–9; Pollard, *North-Eastern England*, 272–8.

30 Watts, *Henry VI*, 354–7; Griffiths, *Henry VI*, 854–63.

31 Griffiths, *Henry VI*, 859–69; Johnson, *Duke Richard*, 196–218.

32 Waurin *Receuil des Croniques*, v, 315–18. Griffiths, *Henry VI*, 856–7, Hicks, *Warwick*, 187–90, Johnson, *Duke Richard*, 205, 216–17; and Watts, *Henry VI*, 357–9 all consider it a possibility that Henry's dethronement was discussed and agreed by York and Warwick in Dublin. Griffiths suggests that the Nevilles changed their minds after Northampton; Johnson proposes that Archbishop Bourgchier, who made it clear he would not crown York, was the stumbling block; Watts argues that the Nevilles had to resist him once they discovered that the majority of the lords were opposed and Hicks suggests that Warwick, responding to widespread opposition, brokered the compromise. The most recent discussion of the evidence and argument that York and Warwick did conspire to depose the king is to be found in Jones, 'Yorkist Claim'. Ross *Edward IV* (1974), 28 accepted that the claim was 'unexpected and unwelcome, apparently even to his closest allies'. See also the suggestion by Watts, 'Polemic and Politics', 32, that the claim to the throne was the only route open to York after the *Somnium Vigilantis* had undermined his justification for representing the common weal in opposition to the king.

33 Griffiths, *Henry VI*, 869–71; Johnson, *Duke Richard*, 218–23; Pollard, *North-Eastern England*, 279–82.

34 Griffiths, *Henry VI*, 871–5; Ross, *Edward IV*, 29–38.

35 Lovatt, 'John Blacman Revisited', passim.

36 For modern discussion of the issue see Griffiths, 'Sense of Dynasty', 13–37; Bennett, 'Edward III's entail', 580–609; Watts, 'Polemic and Politics', 32–6. Pugh, *Southampton Plot*, 134; Strohm, *Empty Throne*, 99–100.

37 Hicks, *Warwick*, 143–8, 174–5; Richmond, 'Naval Dimension', 1–17, esp. 14 and n. 70.

38 See above n. 12 for other interpretations.

PART TWO

THE REALM

CHAPTER SEVEN

The realm and its peoples

The realm

In 1461 the realm of England, that is to say the territories owing allegiance to the king of England, comprised the kingdom of England, the principality of Wales, the marcher lordships of Wales, the lordship of Ireland, the Isle of Man, the Channel Islands and the town of Calais in northern France. Until its final loss in 1453, for three centuries it had also included the duchy of Gascony in south-western France. Additionally, for twenty-eight years until 1450, the king of England had ruled Normandy and for a shorter time extensive neighbouring districts as king of France. The dominions of the king of England contained many different peoples, speaking several languages in different lands (even within the kingdom of England, for Cornish was still spoken in the far south-west), with different laws, customs and cultures. There were some two million English, the great majority living in England, but some as colonists settled in Wales, Ireland and Calais (perhaps 50,000 in all); approximately 200,000 Welsh, most living in Wales, but some settled in England; and probably no more than 400,000 Irish. Until 1453 there were a further 150,000 Gascon subjects of the king of England; thereafter the only remaining French subjects were the inhabitants of Calais. This gives approximately two and three quarter million subjects of the king of England, scattered over several lands and islands, of whom some 75 per cent were English. The realm of England was geographically, racially and culturally diverse.[1]

Calais and its march, the only remaining part of France under the rule of the king of England after 1453, was a company town, its government delegated to the Staplers, London merchants who were assigned the monopoly of wool export to continental Europe through their hands. But it was also a fort, or more correctly a string of forts, protecting a vital gateway into continental Europe, not only for merchants, but also for armies. Moreover possession of Calais secured English control of the straits of Dover for English shipping. Calais was of vital strategic interest to England – a barbican across the moat – not only defended by a permanent royal garrison, but also frequently victualled from England. Calais, despite the sea crossing, and it being within France, was to all intents and purposes a part of England.[2]

Lancastrian Gascony, the most distant English dominion lost in mid-fifteenth century, was in one respect similar to Calais, but in others quite different. Although nominally a great duchy, with borders defined by the treaty of Bretigny (1360) which encompassed a huge area of south-western France, in its last decades the *de facto* English lordship was little more than greater Bordeaux; to the wine trade, what Calais was to the wool. Bordeaux was ruled by a French oligarchy under the supervision of the king's seneschal, not an English trading company. Rule extended to a shrinking hinterland in the Bordelais and the Landes, encompassing the smaller towns of Bayonne, Dax and St Sever. Beyond this coastal strip there lay a broad march, over which the English and French fought for dominance, and in which towns and lordships switched allegiances to advantage. Briefly between 1360 and 1369, English Gascony extended far inland to encompass the pays de Quercy, where the Black Prince established a household at Montauban. But the little hill towns of Quercy never recognised English lordship and by the fifteenth century were effectively absorbed once more into the kingdom of France.[3]

The short-lived Lancastrian duchy of Normandy had a far more enigmatic status than Gascony. Conquered first by Henry V as king of England, it soon after became the cornerstone of his son's possessions in France as king of France. But the claim that the duchy under Lancastrian rule was part of France, not England, never quite carried conviction. Certainly French law was maintained, Norman administrators were employed, and taxes were paid by the traditional system to support the Lancastrian king's just cause in recovering his right. But Normandy, like Gascony, had once been a province in the possession of the kings of England; Henry V at first appealed to Norman separatism to support his regime in the duchy and in its last years the duchy was ruled, like Gascony, as an English dependency from Westminster. Moreover a considerable English settlement was encouraged, both as a new Anglo-Norman landed nobility and in the towns of Rouen, Harfleur and Caen. On the other hand, a significant number of Normans refused to accept English rule and the administration was plagued throughout its existence by brigands who claimed to be resisting a foreign occupation. Had English arms and diplomacy proved successful after 1435, admittedly an unlikely event, Normandy would unequivocally have become a dominion of the

English crown, not unlike Ireland, rather than the province of the Lancastrian France Henry V sought in the last years of his life.[4]

It is not surprising that the kings of England, who had such vaunting but unfulfilled ambitions in France, also laid claim to sovereignty throughout the British Isles. They had failed to make good their claim to Scotland. Indeed it has been suggested that the (temporary) recovery of Berwick, the last corner of Scotland in English hands, by the government of James III in 1461 marked the final end to the Wars of Scottish Independence. While Anglo-Scottish warfare was to continue for another century, the English Crown no longer seriously pursued the claim of sovereignty and treaties between the two kings began to look forward to a time when 'Great Britain', the whole island, would be at peace.[5]

English control over the island of Ireland was tenuous. The Crown had long recognised that its lordship there was severely limited. Most of the island was in the hands of the *Gaelidh*, the Gaelic Irish who had survived and successfully resisted the twelfth-century Anglo-Norman conquest. The population was mixed. On the one hand in the far north, west and south the 'wild Irish', or the 'Irish enemies', as they were called by the English, were quite outside the English lordship. Some parts had never been conquered or colonised. Among their number were descendants of early settlers who had gone native, 'English rebels', or 'degenerate English' who were by the mid-fifteenth century virtually indistinguishable in culture and conduct from the *Gaelidh*. In the south-eastern lowlands and midlands, however, where the lordship had once been more fully established, there were still many settlers and an Anglo-Irish nobility, notably the Butler earls of Ormond and the FitzGerald earls of Desmond, who acknowledged allegiance to the Crown, but had become more integrated into Gaelic society. There remained several ports, Limerick, Cork and Wexford which were also English, but the heart of the lordship was concentrated in the four counties of Dublin, Meath, Kildare and Louth, an area known as the English Ground, inhabited by English colonists under direct rule of the Crown, standing in opposition to everything that was Gaelic.

The English lordship in Ireland had shrunk and changed nature since 1300. In the face of the Gaelic resurgence, or English retreat as some would prefer to put it, attempts were made to draw the racial line between Gaelic and English more sharply. The Statute of Kilkenny of 1366 sought to 'throw a cordon around the colonial area to prevent further cultural infection'. For all who wished to continue to enjoy English privileges, it forbad intermarriage, all sexual relationships and fostering, the use of the Irish language, Irish dress, hairstyle and riding method. *Apartheid* failed. As late as 1447 a further statute was enacted in the Dublin parliament requiring the English males not to grow moustaches so that their racial identity would be clearly visible.

Opinions were divided as how best to preserve the lordship. Those with significant interests further away from Dublin and the English Ground, especially the members of the great Anglo-Irish families, advocated an open policy, engaging with and in the Gaelic world. Those who sheltered behind the military defences that protected the English Ground, calling upon financial and military support from England, were determined not to compromise. The deciding factors were, on the one hand, the inability of the Crown throughout the century to give any but cursory attention or minimal financial support to the colonists and, on the other, the fragmentation of Gaelic society which prevented the Irish chieftains from ever mounting an effective, combined assault on the remnant of the lordship. The result was the stabilisation of the Pale, as the English Ground came to be called, as the *de facto* lordship, with an ill-defined border zone between it and the Gaelic world beyond.[6]

English lordship was altogether more powerful and successful in Wales, which sharing a land border, was both easier to enforce and more dangerous to neglect. The Glyn Dŵr rebellion had shaken English control of Wales to its roots. For two or three years the whole of the country had been in rebel hands; the reconquest as well as the rebellion itself had caused widespread destruction. The revolt had demonstrated that a large number of the Welsh people had not come to terms with English rule; and although thereafter Wales once again was subdued, there is no reason to believe that the English were any more loved in the fifteenth century than in the fourteenth. English government was older in the marcher lordships which lay closer to England itself, more recent in the principality created at the end of the twelfth century in the north and west. But whether in marcher lordship or principality, the English ruled as a foreign power, supported by colonial settlements in the north-east, in the vale of Glamorgan, and in a string of new boroughs established in the principality after the conquest. As in Ireland, racial discrimination overlaid the class distinction between lord and tenant. The 'Saxain' enjoyed privileges denied to the 'Cymry'. English criminal law had been imposed by the Statute of Rhuddlan of 1384 (but Welsh land law had been allowed to stand). The Welsh themselves were a subject people. A penal code, similar in intent to the Statute of Kilkenny in Ireland, was imposed in 1401–2 at the height of the revolt. Confirmed periodically during the following century, it forbade any Welshman from acquiring property in England or in the English boroughs in Wales, holding major office in Wales, bearing arms, or fortifying their home. It also laid down that any Englishman who married a Welshwoman would lose his privileged status.

Yet during the fifteenth century, despite the reimposition of the conquest, the distinction between an English ruling elite and a subject Welsh people softened. First of all the process of Welsh invasion of the boroughs, begun during the fourteenth century, continued unabated; intermarriage was unaffected; and the Welsh resettled much of the vale of Glamorgan as English settlers ruined by the revolt withdrew. Secondly, during the century an anglicised Welsh gentry, already emerging before the revolt (and the minority who remained loyal to the English Crown is not to be overlooked), continued to grow. Armed with letters of naturalisation, they took on the local administration of principality and marcher lordship as deputies of absentee English officials and lords. The sense of Welsh identity was kept alive in the flourishing bardic culture, patronised by this same gentry, which celebrated the ancient independence of Wales and looked forward to a better future. One suspects that literary nationalism became a substitute for the political nationalism which was quietly being abandoned by a people which was coming to terms with the permanence of English domination.[7]

Racialism, in the sense that the late-medieval English believed themselves to be separate from and superior by birth to the Celtic peoples of Ireland and Wales, was ingrained. It followed that Irish and Welsh, who migrated to England as merchants, craftsmen, clerics, lawyers, students and mere vagabonds, were discriminated against as aliens in England itself. As aliens they were not entitled to own property (including benefices), become members of craft guilds or engage in any form of trade, or sue or plead in the common law courts. The richer tradesmen and professionals, however, could and did take out letters of denizenship which enabled them to enjoy the privileges of English subjects of the Crown. Several settled and prospered.

Scots migrants, of whom there were also many, were, like the French, 'enemy' as opposed to 'friendly' aliens. When open war erupted between the kingdoms there was usually a surge of applications for denizenship from men seeking to avoid deportation. There were fewer French migrants, but Gascons who wished to settle needed letters of protection and after the loss of Normandy there was a spate of denizenship offered to Normans who had worked closely with the Lancastrian government. The Crown even made life difficult for the foreign-born widows of its subjects who had failed to take out letters of denizenship before their husbands died.

What the attitude of the English people, as opposed to the government, was to British aliens is hard to determine. They were from time to time at the centre of riots and disturbances notably in the early 1430s, in London, Bristol, the universities and, in the case of the Welsh, in the border English counties. The city records of York reveal in the later part of the century that a number of men trading in the city suspected of being Scots had to prove their English birth. It is not clear, however, whether these men were the victims of xenophobic prejudice or unscrupulous rivals.[8]

Less ambiguous is the attitude to the foreign merchants. Significant numbers of Italian, German and Flemish merchants resided in English ports, especially London, forming distinctive communities. The Hanse had their own privileged trading posts, especially the Steelyard in London, an enclosed self-governing community. Others were supervised under the hosting system. The Italians (some 50–60 Venetian, Genoese, Florentine, Milanese and Lucchese) were the resident representatives of the leading international trading and financing corporations of Europe, importing precious goods from the Mediterranean and providing sophisticated financial services. They were resented not only because of their wealth, but also because they were believed to be taking bullion out of England. In fact, company records reveal that they bought more in England for export than they sold as imports, leaving a favourable balance of payments. Nevertheless, alien merchants were required to pay a higher rate of customs and subsidies than English merchants, and from 1440 were subject to a further tax on residence. The record reveals that there were no more than 2,500 aliens living in greater London. Between 1456 and 1458, however, at a time of deepening commercial recession and political crisis, there was a wave of rioting against them, especially the Italians, which led to a brief withdrawal to Southampton. It is not surprising that the Venetian author of the *Italian Relation* commented at the end of the century that the English hated foreigners and believed that they were trying to take all their goods. The fifteenth-century English were deeply xenophobic as well as fundamentally racist.[9]

There were, however, marked differences within England too. Cornwall was almost a world apart: inhabited by a Celtic people who still spoke their own language, and kept alive their own culture with enduring links with Britanny and were supported by an economy and independence of mind based on the ancient rights of tin-mining, fishing and piracy. Although held by the Crown, the duchy of Cornwall was a remote and separate corner of the kingdom. Kent, however, could not have been closer to the centre. Yet it too had a distinctive identity, stemming partly from its inheritance customs, the absence of great feudal lords, and its position straddling the high road from London to the Continent. Its inhabitants were more cosmopolitan and more assertive than those of most other parts of England.[10]

But perhaps the most distinctive corner of England, renowned too for the independence and assertiveness of its inhabitants, was the border with Scotland. In the wake of the Wars of Independence the borders had become, like central Ireland and south-western France, a volatile frontier zone with a distinctive economic, social and political character. They were not, however, as barbarous as has been imagined. First, there were two types of border area. In the west at Carlisle and in its vicinity in the Eden valley, and in the east in North Durham, there remained throughout the later middle ages a settled, manorialised, agricultural society. Carlisle itself, and Berwick on the Scottish side of the border but in English hands for most of the century, were the centres of cross-border trade. In times of truce, which was most of the time, farming and trading life carried on as normal; and recovery from the disruptions of war was rapid. Carlisle and Berwick were garrison towns, and the borders were therefore militarised in the sense that there were a small number of soldiers parmanently stationed there. But in times of truce these troops helped to maintain the peace rather more than to disrupt it.

The highland thieves, who struck such terror into the hearts of those that lived further away from the border, came from North Tynedale, Redesdale and Coquetdale on the English side. Here manorial organisation had collapsed and the clans were a law unto themselves. It was in this country that the future Pope Pius II spent an uncomfortable night and from which he was relieved to escape down to Newcastle. The borderers were licensed to raid into Scotland in time of war, but tended to have an unsure sense of direction once the truce was renewed. But the border dales of Cumberland and Northumberland were restricted as well as remote; and the elaborate and well-established system of march laws and march-days was usually capable of containing and controlling the worst disorders before they caused renewal of Anglo-Scottish war, or led to the descent of border gangs further afield than Hexham or Morpeth.[11]

Yet the northern borders exerted a powerful influence on contemporary imagination. They helped validate the notion, borne out by historical literature and endorsed by biblical text, that northerners as a whole were unruly and violent; and have enhanced the notion that England was a realm divided. There was a sense of difference between north and south. Northern and southern accents were picked out more clearly than other dialect differences. Chaucer joked about the northern accent; in the Wakefield second shepherd's play a character puts on, without fooling anyone, a southern pattern of speech. Administration (royal, ecclesiastical and baronial) was divided between north and south, usually along the line of the Trent/Humber. But the sense of where north ended and south began was uncertain and depended as much on where one lived. A high-ranking ecclesiastical arbitration panel led by the prior of Durham preserved the peace by banishing to the 'south' a member of the Manners family of Etal, close to the Tweed, stipulating that he could reside no closer than York. Students at the university of Oxford were organised for disciplinary purposes into northern and southern 'nations'. All who lived north of the Nene in Northamptonshire were deemed to be northerners. And the northern nation included the Scots.

The north of England was, apart from the precise ecclesiastical meaning, only in the loosest possible sense a province. There was in the counties of Nottinghamshire, Derby and further north a shared responsibility to raise troops in an emergency for the defence of the realm against the Scots. And this responsibility was treated seriously because of the still-remembered experience of invasion and destruction in the early fourteenth century. In the face of the Scots, particularly the Scots in arms, the northern counties were as one. But apart from the common enemy, there was much that divided northerners. Not only was there the division between borderers and the rest, but also there was a distinction of wealth and life-style between upland and lowland; the more scattered settlements of the pastoral-based economies of the Pennines, the North York Moors and the Lakeland fells on the one hand, and the more densely settled, nuclear villages of the arable-based economies of the vale of York and the East Riding on the other. And the large and rich county of Yorkshire arguably had more in common with midland England than with its more northerly neighbours.

Furthermore there was ready and constant communication between the north and all other parts of the kingdom, in all walks of life, throughout the fifteenth century. Whether it is merchants or lawyers, ecclesiastics or estate administrators, soldiers or pilgrims, cattle drovers or highwaymen, people were on the road between Newcastle and Oxford, Carlisle and London in all manner of business legitimate and illegal. Young people seeking education and training went up to the universities, the inns of court and apprenticehips in London (46 per cent of the Skinners' and Taylors' apprentices in the last two decades of the century were from the north); and some returned to practise in their home countries. The north, a large and diverse region, was not a separate province.[12]

The midland and southern counties, closer to Westminster and more densely populated, as recognised in the distribution of parliamentary seats, were similarly diverse. Communications were slow, allowing local and regional identities to flourish. In truth, England as whole, north and south, from Cornwall to Kent to the Scottish borders, was a network of interlocking and overlapping 'countries', to use the contemporary word. In a recent attempt to map these, no fewer than fourteen 'cultural provinces', have been identified, each with its own focus and different characterstics, shaped by geography, economy and history running back to early settlements, ethnic origins and past political organisations. The shadows of these ancient differences were still visible in the fifteenth century. Contemporaries like the Pastons in Norfolk were proudly conscious of the special identities of their own countries, but they nonetheless recognised that they were all English subjects of the one king, members of the same body politic and linked together in one economy.[13]

Economic change

Significant changes were taking place in the English economy during the later midddle ages; the single most important element of which being the dramatic and traumatic reduction in population by at least one third, and possibly up to a half, between the middle of the fourteenth century and beginning of the fifteenth. The scale and impact of this decline, which took place over the course of little more than two generations, is hard to comprehend in an era accustomed to population stability. Its cause was primarily the scourge of epidemic disease, predominantly bubonic plague and its connected pneumonic and septicemic forms. The population of the British Isles, like that of Europe as a whole, had grown to a point of density which in the early fourteenth century was accompanied by widespread famine. It is possible that it had at this point reached a level at which no further growth could be sustained and around which, without external intervention or technological development, it would have stabilised. But the coming of the plague from Asia to England in 1348, not so much in its first terrible visitation (the Black Death), but more critically in four subsequent pandemics (1361, 1369, 1374–9 and 1390–3), effectively culled the population by removing the capacity for regeneration after the first outbreak. Contemporaries noted the manner in which the subsequent outbreaks, especially the second and fifth, caused particularly high mortality among the young replacement generations (commemorated in the story of the Pied Piper of Hamelin), which would have prevented quick recovery.[14]

After 1400, death rates remained high, often reaching severe epidemic proportions locally, but more generally in 1433–5, 1438–9, 1463–4 and 1478–9. Local studies in the south-east, especially in the closed communities of the monasteries of Westminster and Christ Church Canterbury, as well as the crowded tenements of Westminster itself, have shown a persistently high death rate even beyond the end of the century. In Yorkshire, however, death rates might have begun to decline before 1500. Evidence of birth rates is hard to come by, and it remains uncertain as to whether they were low or high. Even if high, they were outmatched by the persistently high death rates. Thus the overall population of England probably continued to fall during the first half of the century (by perhaps a further 10 per cent), might have begun to stabilise in mid-century, and is unlikely to have started to rise again until the very end of the century at the earliest. It is probably the case that the total population in 1525 was still lower than it had been in 1377, when decline had already been well under way. The fundamental economic condition of late-medieval England was demographic decline and under-population created by the ravages of epidemic and endemic diseases.[15]

There may also have been a general cooling of the climate, reducing arable productivity on higher ground and intensifying coastal erosion on the eastern seaboard. A further recessionary force was the shrinking of the money supply. It has been calculated that the quantity of coinage in circulation in the first half of the fifteeenth century was but three fifths of the coinage in the early fourteenth century. Without a compensatory growth in credit facility, already highly developed, and in consequence of the reluctance of the kings of England, unlike the dukes of Burgundy, to devalue the coinage, money was scarce. Although *per capita* money supply may barely have altered, the total impact on economic activity was deflationary. The price of coal, lead and tin, mined in the north-east, the Pennines and Cornwall, fell to such a level that production virtually ceased in the middle of the century and did not revive until the last decade.[16]

Moreover the economy was vulnerable to harvest fluctuations, trade cycles and international crises. Trade was from time to time seriously disrupted by war and government policy. In the 1430s it virtually came to a halt between England and Flanders as a consequence of the attempt by the Bullion Ordinances to insist on cash-down payments for wool exported through the Staple. Although the Ordinances were revoked in 1442, they were imposed again in 1445, provoking another ban on English cloth in all the lands of the duke of Burgundy and causing a severe fall in exports, which lasted for at least twenty years. And after the loss of Bordeaux in 1453 the wine trade with Gascony was also dislocated, and remained much reduced for two decades. These disruptions contributed to two overlapping depressions in the mid-fifteenth century: one led by harvest failure and agrarian crisis, which was particularly severe in the north in the later 1430s and 1440s; the second occasioned by a general recession in European trade from the late 1440s until the 1460s, which had a greater impact on the south. The English economy in 1461 was in the depths of a slump.[17]

Late-medieval demographic, climatic, monetary and commercial trends had a profound impact on the structure of the economy, standards of living and, ultimately, the social order itself. The fall of population, and therefore the size of the productive labour force, had an immediate impact on agriculture. There was a general reduction of land under the plough (especially the more marginal), a widespread fall in grain production, and the desertion of less favourably placed villages. As rural populations shrank they became concentrated in fewer, more viable settlements. Landlords, especially the great estate owners, who in earlier centuries had exploited their demesnes by direct labour, now gave up their own agricultural enterprises and resorted to leases. At the same time there was a significant shift towards pastoral farming, which required less labour and for the products of which – wool, milk and meat – demand remained more buoyant except in the worst slumps. The upland areas of northern England, which had always concentrated on rearing sheep and cattle, enjoyed a brief boom in the early decades of the century. In the midlands, in the wake of contracting arable farming and abandoned holdings, sheep and cattle rearing began to to be practised on a large scale, both by tenant farmers and lesser landlords. Village desertions, especially in the midlands, were followed, and in some instances hastened, by enclosure of open fields and conversion to pasture.[18]

It followed from the contraction of agricultural production that small market towns, of which there were large numbers, some barely distinguishable from villages, suffered; indeed it has been calculated that the number of local markets was reduced by two thirds. Country markets responded directly to agrarian fluctuations and trends; larger towns with regional, national or international hinterlands were affected more indirectly. Some towns, such as Colchester and York, enjoyed a resurgence in the late-fourteenth century, before plunging into longer-term decline in the fifteenth. The question of whether there was urban decay in the post-plague era has vexed historians in recent years. Some of the difficulties arise from definitional problems, some from conceptual confusion. The aggregate wealth of a fifteenth-century town, measured by such indicators as tax yield or petitions for reduction of fee-farms, fell significantly. On the other hand *per capita* wealth, indicated by the prosperity of individual townspeople, may have increasd. By the end of the fifteenth century some townspeople, if fewer of them, were as wealthy as their predecessors in towns which were less prosperous than they had been. Moreover towns were business corporations in competition with one another. The growth of one was often achieved at the expense of a near neighbour. Thus, for instance, Lowestoft prospered at the expense of Great Yarmouth; Glastonbury, in Somerset, grew to the detriment of Wells and Taunton eclipsed its rival Bridgwater.[19]

Behind the cycle of urban growth and decline, and local redistribution, two trends stand out. One is the relocation of some manufacturing, especially the rapidly expanding cloth manufacturing, to the country, where costs were lower; the fifteenth century saw the rapid expansion of the West Riding, East Anglian and Cotswold manufacturing districts. The other is the shift of urban wealth southwards and westwards in response to trends in overseas trade, especially the greater concentration of exports through southern ports. Overall this led to a sustained decline of the wealth of towns along and behind the northern and central eastern seaboard, such as York, Grimsby, Boston and King's Lynn, while towns in the south-east and south-west, such as Exeter, Southampton and above all, London, barely suffered and indeed prospered.[20]

In the middle of the fourteenth century England had been a large-scale exporter of raw materials, especially wool and tin, to continental manufacturers;

by the end of the fifteenth century she exported mainly finished and semi-finished manufactured goods, predominantly cloth to continental markets. In the century from 1350 to 1450 wool exports fell by over 75 per cent from an annual average of over 40,000 sacks to 8–9,000 at which level they remained for the rest of the century. Cloth export, on the other hand, increased from under 10,000 to 60,000 broadcloths *per annum* in the same period. While the levels fell during the mid-century recession, they recovered after 1470 and had reached 70,000 by the end of the century. In terms of value to foreign earnings, cloth was worth considerably more than the wool from which it was produced. It has been calculated that between the end of the thirteenth century and the middle of the fifteenth the combined value of wool and cloth exports declined by about 10 per cent. But when one takes into account the scale of the contraction of the total economy, this represents a significant increase in real foreign earnings, even allowing for the mid-fifteenth century slump.

Throughout the century, English merchants carried only some 60 per cent of overseas trade. Of the rest approximately half was carried by the Hanseatic League, and half by the Italians. The overall consistency of the pattern conceals the conflicts and changes that occurred. English shippers waged a constant but losing struggle to gain access to the Baltic, which culminated in a trade war between 1468 and 1474. Defeat by the Hanse had important consequences not only for the merchants themselves, but also for the volume of trade handled by North Sea ports, for the Hanse thereafter concentrated its trade through the Steelyard in London. In the second half of the century too, as a result of upheavals in Italian politics, the numbers of Italians trading in London declined, leaving the Venetians as virtually the only significant group by 1500. English merchants were not, as yet, able to penetrate the Mediterranean. Within the English merchant community, the Staplers, who held the monopoly of wool exports, lost their dominance. They were replaced by the companies of merchant adventurers, especially the Londoners, cartels of general traders who dominated the export of cloth and the import of general merchandise. The trade carried by them concentrated particularly on the cross-Channel route from London to Flanders. By the end of the century English merchants were even more dependent on their control of the Channel than they had been at its beginning.[21]

All the structural changes in the fifteenth century enhanced the dominance of London as the focal point of the English economy. London was the only English city that could match the great European cities of Italy, the Low Countries or even France. Constantly replenished by immigration, its population barely fell below 40,000 throughout the century, leaving it by its end at least four times as large as the principal provincial cities of Bristol, Norwich and York. With London prospered its suburbs of Westminster and

Southwark and its outlying villages such as Tottenham or Havering, supplying the voracious appetite of the metropolis with perishable food and livestock pasture. The tentacles of London merchants stretched throughout the kingdom to ensure supplies of grain, meat and fuel. London merchants had dominated the Cotswold and East Anglian cloth trade from its beginning; by the end of the century, by dint of the superior credit terms they could offer, they had a stranglehold on the new West Riding manufacturing district, grasped from their competitors in York and Hull. London merchants similarly displaced their rivals abroad. York merchants, denied access to the Baltic in the last quarter of the century, sought royal protection for an independent share of the trade in the Netherlands. But by 1500 they had lost the struggle; the London merchant adventurers dictated terms.

London's gain was York's loss. At the beginning of the century York had been a great international trading city at the centre of an autonomous northern economy, enjoying direct trade not only across the North Sea and into the Baltic, but also as far afield as Bordeaux. By the end of the century this trade had collapsed; the city had shrunk and its role was little more than a regional market town. The once autonomous economy of York and its hinterland was subordinated into a national economy dominated by London. The creation of London's hegemony was perhaps the most important structural change in the fifteenth century with far-reaching consequences for the future development of the English economy.[22]

Standards of living

The fifteenth century was an age of recession; yet paradoxically, as the evidence of both the value of combined wool and cloth exports and the differential between population and price falls reveal, real wealth grew. While the total size of the economy fell, output fell less sharply and productivity increased. At the same time, there was a discernible downward redistribution of wealth resulting from a shortage in the supply of labour. The fifteenth century witnessed a decline in incomes dependent on the fixed asset of land and the employment of labour and a rise in the standards of living of those who lived by their own hands or had labour to sell.

The incomes of great landowners fell in approximate proportion to the decline of population and the contraction of arable husbandry. Some compensation was possible through realising capital assets, such as the sale of timber, by diversification into pastoral husbandry, by exploiting new industrial developments, and by investment in trade, but none of these could compensate for the reduction of the numbers of rent-paying tenants, the fall in the levels of rent and the contraction in the domestic market for grain. Lesser landlords, with small, compact estates under close family supervision, better placed to take advantage of new opportunites and to minimalise the cost of labour, did not perhaps, suffer as severely. Nevertheless, it is not to be imagined that landlords as a class faced financial collapse. Land remained a rock-solid asset; estates were for the most part efficiently managed by professional accountants who minimalised losses; and the incomes generated, although much reduced compared with earlier times, were still more than ample to sustain social distinctions.[23]

Yet what was the landlord's loss was the tenant's and labourer's gain. Market forces determined that rents fell. Tenants were in demand, and could and did move, especially in the first half of the century, from tenancy to tenancy seeking the best land and the best terms. On several estates rebates were offered to tenants in order to induce them to stay. Small-holding arable husbandry, employing low-cost family and seasonal labour, could, in all but the worst years, prosper. But livestock farming, even on a large scale could be even more productive. Labourers' wages, especially the wages of skilled labour, in country as well as town, rose, despite early legislative attempts to keep them down. Not only wage rates, but on the whole earnings rose.[24]

Thus during the fifteenth century there was a general rise in disposable income of husbandmen, artisans and skilled labourers. There was an increase in the consumption of meat, dairy products, ale and wine; more substantial houses with more rooms were built; more and better cloth was used for clothing; sheets, wall hangings, brass and pewter vessels were acquired; horse ownership grew; and more time was spent at leisure, in the newly opening ale-houses as well as at home. All this, in turn, further stimulated an increase in livestock production and textile, leather and metallurgical manufacturing. The greatest benificiaries of this virtuous circle, especially in the later decades of the century, were the middling sorts – yeomen, substantial husbandmen, self-employed craftsmen, brokers and factors, some of whom, especially those linked with the various stages of cloth manufacturing, were able to amass significant fortunes.

But one should not imagine too rosy a picture of the quality of life of middle England in the fifteenth century. The lack of technological development, the shortage of money in circulation and economically conservative attitudes ensured that there was no significant capital formation or investment. There was a ceiling to prosperity. Employment, earnings and income were far from secure. Harvest failure and trade stoppages were frequent and an ever present possibility, and in the mid-fifteenth century combined to produce periods of real hardship for all. Moreover, rising standards of living and real wealth did not abolish poverty. There were still many men and women, in town and country, deserving and undeserving, who could barely make ends meet and were dependent on the charity of the more prosperous. But, above all, there was little that could be done to improve health, immunity from disease and low life expectancy. It was a paradox of the fifteenth century with its high mortality, that those whom death spared, especially among the middling sorts, enjoyed a higher standard of living than did their ancestors or descendants in less disease-ridden eras. But even for the most favoured groups in society, prosperity was fragile and uncertain.

The decline of serfdom

The economic changes in late medieval England had important social and cultural consequences. On the one hand they extended freedom, stimulated social advance and encouraged wider political participation; on the other they prompted a determined and partially successful reaction from above, in defence of the social order and privilege.

Probably the most important social transformation in the later middle ages was the collapse of serfdom. Serfdom, which had intensified in the era of population increase and pressure on resources in the twelfth and thirteenth centuries, was a social institution that provided forced labour on the land for the benefit of lords. There were in essence two types of serfdom. One, the more ancient, was serfdom by blood. Certain persons, concentrated in some localities, even some villages, rather than evenly distributed, were unfree by birth and were possibly descendants of one-time slaves. While partially freed, in the sense that they held their own small-holdings, in strict law they could not own possessions, were required to labour for their lords, and were not allowed to marry, leave the manor, or to enter a holding without permission. And permission meant a payment (merchet, chevage or gressum). The whole edifice of these incidents of feudalism, including the payment of a death duty (heriot), was designed initially for the very practical purpose of maintaining a register of serfs, who could not be readily identified by dress, or colour of skin. Serfs by blood were often identified by the description of neif (or *nativus*, in Latin). A second, and more numerous category of serfdom was created in the twelfth century – serfdom by tenure. By deeming unfree all forms of tenure which involved a substantial part of the payment of rent by labour, the law subjected tenants who were not unfree by birth to the same conditions as neifs. It is to this category of serf by tenure to which the word villein commonly applies.

The sharp decline of population in the later fourteenth century, the reduction in the demand for grain, the growing shortage of labour and the abandonment of direct exploitation of demesne lands undermined serfdom.

Labour services were commuted to cash payments, the system of manorial control over movement of labour collapsed, and the incidents of feudalism reduced or abandoned. Copyhold, a new system of more secure tenure registered by formal record in the manorial court, was developed in many parts of the kingdom. Copyhold came, in time, to create a virtual freehold of tenure. Thus the reality of serfdom by tenure was swept away by the reversal of the economic forces which had created the conditions for its development three centuries earlier.[25]

Serfdom by blood was slower to die. No act of abolition was passed. Manumission, the buying of freedom, was possible, but not many could afford it. One who could, but did not, was the cloth manufacturer William Heyne of Castle Combe whose widow and son were persecuted by the lord of the manor, Sir John Fastolf. Serfs who had fled the manor could be tracked down; the dukes of Norfolk never abandoned the effort to pursue their fugitives from their manor of Forcett. A descendant of a fugitive serf who had prospered was always a tempting target for a bounty hunter who could expect a worthwhile commission on the fine levied by the fortunate lord whose rights could be traced. Serfdom by blood did, however, eventually die out by natural causes, if not until the sixteenth century. With commendable logic, the disability of serfdom, like the privilege of nobility, could only be passed on by the male blood; serfdom, too, was but seminal fluid. Where, as in the administration of the priory of Durham, periodic censuses were made of neifs, their number can be seen to have dwindled steadily over the fifteenth century, until it became no longer worthwhile to keep a record.[26]

The decline of serfdom during the later middle ages was of profound importance in several respects. As the inflammatory preaching attributed to John Ball during the Peasants' Revolt suggests, freedom of status was itself deeply desired. To call someone a villein, churl or rustic was enough to provoke a violent reaction. Freedom from the heavy financial burdens of serfdom also brought an increase in material prosperity, and was thus another element in a higher standard of living, as well as an intangible improvement in the quality of life. Finally these benefits were not limited to the poorest in village society. Serfdom, of either kind, had not prevented individuals from prospering in the countryside, as witness William Heyne. Attempts at its continuing enforcement were a particularly sharp grievance for many of those husbandmen, yeomen and tradesmen who were the principal beneficiaries of the economic changes of the era and a source of conflict between them and their betters.[27]

The beneficiaries of economic and social changes were not passive recipients of economic trends. The decline of serfdom, the reduction of rents and the increase in earnings were achieved because people, collectively and individually, asserted themselves. The later fourteenth century was a time of intense social upheaval, which culminated in the Peasants' Revolt. The memory of that revolt hangs over the fifteenth century. The threat of popular rebellion, rent strikes and other forms of direct action were ever present, and from time to time carried out. In 1426, as the culmination of growing conflict between them, twelve serfs of the manor of Farcombe in Hampshire turned on and murdered the lord of their manor. When the commons rioted, not just in 1450, but more locally as in Warwickshire in 1407 or 1485, the leaders took the names of Jack Straw or Master Mendall to draw upon the tradition of resistance and direct action. Whether or not one would describe this as class conflict, change came about because tenants and labourers took advantage of favourable economic circumstances to force concessions from landholders.[28]

Social mobility

Economic change encouraged social promotion and diversity. This is not to say that it created social mobility. England was already by 1400 a partially open society. It was not impossible for men to move upwards, or for that matter downwards. Upward social movement followed financial and political success. The routes to preferment through service, war, commerce and the professions for the talented but humble-born were already well established. The ultimate goal was the acquisition of land, title and lordship and entry into the ranks of the gentry. Only a few, such as the de la Poles who rose from trade in Hull to royal bankers to great earls of the realm, or the Pastons from serfdom through the law to county gentry, rose rapidly in a generation or two. Downward mobility was more systemic. There were some of high birth who through their folly ruined themselves and their families, but more pervasive was the custom of impartible inheritance which ensured that eldest sons received all. Younger sons were invariably granted a life-interest sufficient to maintain themselves as gentlemen, but unless they themselves were fortunate enough to win the lottery of an heiress or talented enough to prosper in the law, commerce or on the field of battle, their own children and grandchildren would sink into obscurity. During the fifteenth century England became more socially mobile, upwardly and downwardly. But above all, there was the widespread evidence that the commons were wealthier, more assertive and, it appeared from above, less deferential.

Writing in mid-fifteenth century, Peter Idley bemoaned the fact that nowadays 'a man shall not know a knave from a knight, for all be alike in clothyng and array'.[29] His comment falls in a long tradition of castigating the presumption of the lower orders. No one knew their place any more. In these circumstances it seemed both private virtue and social order were under threat. It was in an attempt to shore up the social hierarchy that a whole series of statutes were enacted in parliament. The Statute of Labourers of 1351 sought to control wages and employment. The sumptuary legislation, first introduced in 1363, against the wearing of 'outrageous and excessive apparel', sought to restrict the quantity and quality of cloth to be used by each clearly defined status group in society. Thereby all would be known and held in place by their appearance. Even prostitutes, by an ordinance of 1439, were to wear distinguishing clothing. Educational opportunity was restricted by statute in 1391 and 1406.

Concern that ordinary people were enjoying too much leisure, and spending it in riotous activities like football or games more appropriate to their betters like tennis or bowls, was expressed in statutes passed from 1388 seeking to encourage military training. The game law of 1390, by limiting the possession of greyhounds to those with an income from land of at least forty shillings a year, further restricted the rights of hunting to a privileged few. In its preamble it expressed concern that artificers and labourers, even on Sundays when they should have been at church, were confederating together under the guise of hunting to plot against the authorities; as probably they were, since the rights to game were a highly contentious issue. An act of 1414 required that in all actions at law the status or occupation of the parties should be given. And a whole series of statutes in the early fifteenth century, most famously the forty shilling freeholder electoral legislation of 1429, defined and restricted the politically enfranchised.[30]

On the surface this programme of social reaction was ineffectual. After a more rigorous attempt at enforcement in the 1370s, the Statute of Labourers was only occasionally evoked. The need to re-enact the sumptuary legislation every generation reveals that it was more honoured in its breach than its observance. Even the game laws had to be revived in 1485. And because parliamentary elections were held at public hustings it is difficult to see how, in the shires in particular, it was possible to enforce the franchise to the letter. Social mobility could not be stopped. Yet, on the other hand, the sheer persistence of the legislation might effectively have shored up the social structure and prevented matters, as far as the likes of Peter Idley were concerned, from getting worse. The social order was in its inegalitarian essentials maintained; nobility retained its privileges and preeminence and in some respects sharpened its distinctiveness.

Nobility

It was in this era that the concept of gentleman was developed and the distinction between gentility and lack of gentility (nobility and gentility were synonymous) articulated. The distinction was characteristically drawn not according to any rigid legal definitiion, but according to appearances. A gentleman was one who did not need to work with his hands and was generally to be recognised because of his life-style. In the fifteenth century an income of perhaps as low as 10 marks ($£6$ 6s. 4d.), the lowest sum conventionally set aside by fathers to support younger sons, could support one in the appropriate style. As Idley was so anxiously aware, the social boundaries remained flexible, between yeomanry and mere gentlemen, between urban and rural, and, one suspects, according to different social contexts. Herein lay the peculiar openness of English society. But openness had its limits. The College of Arms, which during the century began to play its modern role of providing coats of arms for the newly arrived, expected an income of $£10$ per annum before it would recognise undoubted gentility. And in mid-fifteenth century there were probably no more than 4,000 heads of families with such incomes, an elite comprising little more than 2 per cent of the population.[31]

There were distinct ranks of nobility or gentility, rising from the mere gentleman at the foot through squires and knights to barons, earls and dukes. In England not only was nobility open to the successful (and loss of nobility the fate of many younger sons), but also an unusual constitutional line had emerged between the lesser and greater nobles. The emergence of the parliamentary peerage, a group of some sixty families with the hereditary right on royal grant to a seat in the house of lords, left the lesser nobility to be represented in the house of commons. And within the lords, too, differentiation of rank, the elaboration of ceremonial and the obsession with precedence became more marked during the fifteenth century. Paradoxically, however, whereas the gentry may have been commoners by parliamentary definition, many individual knights were richer and locally more influential than some of the lesser peers.[32]

But true nobility was more than a minimal income, a leisured life-style, or a rank; it was also a set of values acquired by nature and nurture. On the one hand it was determined by blood and revealed in the lineage, frequently displayed and, when necessary, invented; on the other hand it was demonstrated by courtesy (a rigid code of correct conduct), generosity (openness of mind and ostentatious display) and honour (the word of an officer and a gentleman was his bond). Above all a gentleman was known from an ungentleman on horseback, engaged in hunting or at war. Hunting, particularly the pursuit of deer in forest or park, and hawking, was the sport of noblemen. The rights to game were jealously guarded; and the beasts were pursued according to elaborate rules and codes. Some great nobles enjoyed the privilege of forest hunting; but as red deer declined in number, park hunting became more common. Hunting was also perceived as a training for war, not least because it taught a man to ride and made him fit and hardy.[33]

The other noble sport – jousting – derived more directly from military training. It was war itself that was perceived as the true occupation of a nobleman. In the first half of the fifteenth century the English nobility had plenty of opportunity to practise the profession of arms. Yet it would appear that even at the height of Henry V's reign only a minority took up the option. In reality, although many of the trappings of a gentleman's life-style were created in the images of chivalry, war itself was too costly and too uncertain for all but the greater nobility (who served out of a sense of duty and obligation to the Crown), the fortune-seekers and those who simply enjoyed fighting. During the fifteenth century a more civil concept of nobility emerged. Political and administrative service were considered as proper as military; the gentleman bureaucrat, especially the lawyer and accountant, became an accepted figure. In some reactionary circles in the later part of the century these changes were seen as not only undermining true nobility, but also as lying at the root of social malaise. Chivalry was perceived to be in decline and calls were made for a revival. Critics like Caxton and Worcester need not have been concerned. Chivalry had never been what it used to be; and it was to be many centuries before its cult and the profession of arms lost their appeal to the English nobility. In truth, Peter Idley had no difficulty in knowing a knave from a knight.[34]

Townspeople and the 'middling sort'

In urban society reaction to social mobility and fragmentation was no less successful than in noble society. Whereas it was not unknown for the more successful burgesses to invest their fortunes in land and to establish themselves as gentlemen, the later middle ages also witnessed the successful closing of ranks within the greater towns by dynasties of richer merchants against the pretensions of artisans and craftsmen. Everywhere the attempts to open up town governments were defeated; control of civic life passed more firmly into the hands of more narrowly constituted oligarchies. Moreover towns and townspeople were becoming gentrified. Not only were these ruling oligarchs aping gentry habits, and in time the leading citizens of London and other cities being knighted, but also an urban gentry, in the sense of gentry taking up residence in towns, emerged.

Towns, in which there was a high turnover of inhabitants and the social order was more volatile, were perhaps more difficult to control than the countryside. Certain changes in the later middle ages, such as the development of craft guilds which enforced trade regulations, the emergence of the feast of Corpus Christi as an annual ritual celebration of the corporate identity, and the growth of civic pride expressed in public buildings, town histories, and aspirations for county status can all be interpreted both as aspects of a successful response to the perceived threats to hierarchy and homogeneity and as a result of the social pretensions of leading townsmen.[35]

The fifteenth century also witnessed in town and country the emergence of a distinctive middling sort, the *mediocres*, as they were identified in some towns, with their own culture and values. The symbolic rank of this middling sort is the yeoman. The word originally applied to a household rank lower than esquire, often associated with forest administration; but by the fifteenth century it had become a description of the social status of a countryman who held some sixty acres of land, freehold or customary, employing one or two farm hands, and enjoying a sufficient income to make him and his family comfortable and independent. They were sometimes still called franklins. Yeomen were less than gentlemen: they worked. They were more than husbandmen, because they were more prosperous. Yet they rubbed shoulders with husbandmen, artisans and traders in small town and country, many of whom combined small-scale husbandry with business and who, under the terms of the Statute of Additions, could with commendable flexibility be styled yeoman, *alias* chapman, *alias* mercer. In larger towns and cities their equivalent were the artisans and master craftsmen in the lesser trades who found themselves excluded from or only on the periphery of city government.

In parish, guild and manor, local officals were drawn from the ranks of this middling sort. They were churchwardens, wardens of parish guilds, tithingmen, jurors and constables. They also served the Crown as jurors at quarter sessions or on inquisitions. They supplied the lowest band of local administration. Possessing their own weapons, they were a key element of the local levies raised for defence of the realm (and in time many county militias were to be called the yeomanry). They were also the principal taxpayers, contributing the greater part of the subsidies on moveable goods levied every time parliament voted a tenth and fifteenth; and through them was articulated and represented the views of the communities which they led. If the house of commons was generous in its financial support of the Crown, as it largely was in the the reign of Henry V, or deeply reluctant as it was by the end of Henry VI's reign, this was partly because its members knew the mood of the taxpayer. Expectations that justice should be done and be seen to be done, and that the Crown should fulfil its role were readily articulated by men such as these. It is to this group above any other that the duke of York appealed in his critique of Henry VI's government and his call for reform. And, *in extremis*, it was this group, as the subsequent prosecutions and pardons show, who led popular rebellion against the Crown.[36]

The middling sort also formed the respectable local elite (*probes homini*) who framed the manorial by-laws regulating behaviour, dominated the parish guilds, organised church ales, and sponsored the parish rituals and games which became such a visible feature of village life in the fifteenth century. As employers and guardians of morality they ensured the passage of local ordinances (by common assent) banning football, and sought as jurors to regulate the opening hours of ale-houses, ban gambling and to prevent the running of brothels. Not, for the most part, wealthy enough individually to establish their own chantries, or to make substantial charitable bequests, they ensured that prayers were said for the salvation of their souls through parish guilds restricted to a respectable membership. They set up hardship funds to see them through personal misfortune, they founded schools for the education of their children, and they celebrated their identity in annual communal feasts. As churchwardens they saw to it that the fabric of the church and its furnishings were maintained and embellished collectively. The fifteenth-century *mediocres* not only dominated local societies, but also left a lasting mark on the English landscape and perceptions of Englishness.[37]

The poor

Rising standards of living and social promotion did not rid the world of the poor. They may have become fewer in number, both proportionally as well as absolutely, but there can be no doubt that fifteenth-century England was still populated with the unemployed, the disabled, the sick and the old, unable to fend for themselves. The received idea was that the poor, who would always be with us, would be rewarded in the kingdom to come. There was a spiritual duty, if not advantage, in the rich giving generously and indiscriminately of their surplus to the poor. There were many institutions established for their relief. Distribution of alms was one of the functions of monasteries. Hospitals had been founded not only for lepers (by the fifteenth century in decline), but also for care of the old and indigent. New foundations were still being made by wealthy benefactors, especially of almshouses, either permanent or temporary (*maisons dieu*).

Indiscriminate alms-giving, including the customary distribution of doles at funerals, continued, but attitudes were changing. The distinction between the deserving and undeserving poor began to shape the provision of charity. The able unemployed who resorted to begging (sturdy beggars), were seen by some to be work-shy, and their poverty the product of sloth. Vagabonds and the wandering poor were increasingly viewed as a threat to order, condemned by moralists, penalised by statute and passed on from settlement to settlement. The deserving poor, however, the disabled, the wounded veteran, the old and sick, the respectable who had by no fault of their own fallen on hard times were still to be supported. It was for these that the new almshouses and *maisons dieu* were established by wealthy benefactors, often specifying the kind of deserving poor to be supported. By the end of the century bequests in some wills had begun to move away from the distribution of largesse on the day of the funeral, to more specific philanthropic causes, often parochially focused.

Parishes too began to take up the burden. Under statutes of 1391 and 1403 incumbents were required to set aside a 'convenient' sum for the relief of the poor. The parochial laity also bore their share; hock-tide and other collections were devoted to the poor, parish guilds were managing funds for their relief; and parishes themselves began to establish almshouses for them. In Saffron Walden, for instance, a parish almshouse for thirteen poor people, the decrepit, blind and the lame, was managed by a board composed of twenty-four of the most 'worshipful' parishioners and supported by voluntary contributions from the more able residents. The same house distributed out-door relief to the bed-ridden poor within a radius of fifteen miles. In the Saffron Walden almshouse one sees the shape of the future: the distinction between deserving and undeserving, the criminalising of the undeserving and the assumption of more of the burden for the deserving on the shoulders of the parish. It is not that the numbers of the poor increased, or that they became more of a threat to order; it is rather that attitudes towards them changed, particularly in tune with the outlook of respectable, hard-working, 'worshipful' *mediocres*, who rejected indiscriminate charity in favour of targeted philanthropy.[38]

Women

One feature of fifteenth-century testimonial bequests is the provision by wealthy widows of *maisons dieu* for deserving poor women. Perhaps the most marginalised, the most powerless person in the fifteenth century, as in most ages, was the poor, single, old woman. But then women in general were unprivileged. The fundamental patriarchal nature of society was never questioned. Women were defined ambiguously by men as in the mould of either the Virgin Mary or of Eve. The Virgin Mary was woman as the sum of all virtues – chastity, modesty, submissiveness, silence. But she was also woman on a pedestal, a goddess, and as the mother of man, exercising special power over him. Eve was woman as the temptress, the lecherous harlot ever ready to lead him into the deep pit. To make sure that they conformed to one model rather than the other, women were subject to men, either their fathers or husbands. A woman's marriage was determined by her father. Her role as wife was as helper; one who shared in her husband's life and supported it, but who was subordinate to him. She ran the household, she cooked, she looked after the dairy, she spun, she brewed, she shopped, or if she were rich, presided over all these activities. But, while married, she had no independent voice, no individual right at law, and, if respectable, she went nowhere alone.

There is no reason to doubt that most women accepted their state as the second sex. Education and upbringing, the wisdom of their mothers and grandmothers, made sure that they knew their role. But they were not without some control over their lives. No marriage could be made without the consent of both parties. In respectable circles, within the conventions of an arranged marriage, courtship customs allowed the would-be couple to get to know and like each other, and indeed allow either party to refuse. And brave women could assert their right even against their parents. Marjorie Paston famously withstood the ire of her mother to marry the family bailiff, a marriage which the bishop of Norwich declared valid because he was convinced that it was entered into voluntarily. And, conversely, Christiane Harrington was able to secure a divorce after three years of refusing to consummate what she successfully demonstrated was a forced marriage. But once married a woman was expected to accept the authority of her husband.

Many marriages, as expected, turned out to be companionable partnerships, but some were not. A husband was expected to control his wife and had a right to chastise her with reasonable force. A shrew needed to be tamed. However, a wife terrorised by persistent abuse, could, as in the case of Cecilia Wyvell of York in 1410, secure a divorce, especially if she had a reputation for virtue and her husband was a notorious adulterer. But normally she had no redress. If, on the other hand, a husband was unable to curb his wife, or public disturbance was caused by her, she could be charged with the one gender-specific misdemeanour to which women were subject under by-laws: scolding. A Hereford law of 1486 laid down that scolds, who caused disturbances of the peace, discord between neighbours and confrontation with the town authorities, should be publicly humiliated in a ducking stool, imprisoned and fined. Most authorities were happy with a fine. Scolding – slander, malicious gossip and public quarrelling – was, it seems, considered subversive because of its public nature as a challenge to male authority and to due order. It is noticeable that it was the violence of the female tongue that was perceived as threatening to male domination; and that it was physical violence by men that ultimately enforced it.[39]

Some change in women's state took place during the later middle ages, especially in relationship to employment before marriage. The general shortage of labour in the late-fourteenth and early-fifteenth centuries extended the range of female occupations, especially for single girls. There is evidence to suggest that in a city like York girls could find their own employment, and not only in service, and were able to save money, to delay marriages, and to make their own choices of partner. In the countryside, too, girls are found in far greater numbers working as servants in husbandry at heavier labour traditionally reserved for men. But these developments heralded no permanent change. They were not universal. In Sussex, for instance, little evidence can be found for such a trend. By the end of the fifteenth century, if not earlier, when demand again more closely matched the supply of male labour, these opportunities had disappeared. Moreover, it is not proven that women, especially young women, preferred to work as low-paid wage servants rather than to marry and work traditionally as their husband's helper, or more independently as day labourers. Above all it seems unlikely that fifteenth-century women ever enjoyed the freedom of choice in such matters.

Unmarried women, not in service, who lived on their own, were 'ungoverned' and ran the risk of condemnation as prostitutes. A Coventry ordinance in 1492 forbade single women under the age of fifty to live on their own. That prostitution flourished, and that there were brothels to be found even in small market towns, cannot be denied. And maybe prostitutes were able to control their own lives. The problem is that so strong was the disapproval of independent women, so transparent the fear that men had of them, that their lives, unless they were represented as examples of the male norms of chastity, obedience and submissiveness, are invariably recorded unsympathetically.[40]

A small minority of women, by espousing chastity, were able to control their own lives more completely with male approval. For an exceptional few the legal state of *femme sole* allowed a woman, almost invariably a widow, the full legal rights of a man. These were usually the widows of merchants and artisans, who in these circumstances carried on their late husbands' businesses. The most eminent of all was Margaret Beaufort, the mother of Henry VII, who was granted this favour even when she was married to her third husband, Lord Stanley. Widows enjoyed, for the duration of their widowhood, especially if they were rich, a power over their lives that was normally denied to women. Several took vows of chastity, by which they declared themselves independent for life. One exceptionally independently-minded woman, Marjory Kempe, did so while married, with the agreement of her husband. And finally there were nunneries. Nunneries were small communities of women, not normally of more than a dozen, who managed their own affairs and made their own decisons within the rules of their order. But nuns, like all other women who from time to time controlled their own lives, only did so under licence from and under the supervision of men.[41]

National identity

While the status of women in relationship to men remained fundamentally unaltered throughout the later middle ages, the sense that they were, of whatever social status, nevertheless *English* women became more marked. The fifteenth century witnessed important developments in the formation of a national culture which was completed in the sixteenth. At the heart of this lay the emergence of English as both an official and a literary language. English had been used in place of the international clerical or courtly languages of Latin or French in the later fourteenth cnetury. As early as 1363 the proceedings of the opening of parliament had been recorded in English, but this did not become commonplace. The biggest boost to English, in terms of its use, and perhaps its development, during the last two decades of the fourteenth century was Lollardy. At the heart of the Lollard programme, so as to make Christianity directly accessible to the faithful, was the translation of the scriptures into English and the writing of English works of instruction. To judge by the surprisingly large number of surviving works, which were roundly condemned and banned, it would appear that there was already a wide potential readership and audience. But Lollardy was a heresy, its literature an underground literature. Indeed as long as Lollardy was perceived as a real threat to state and church, English was unlikely to be promoted officially.

All this was changed by Henry V. Even before he was king, Henry had shown himself inclined to encourage the use of English. In 1417, coinciding with his second invasion of France, he began its systematic promotion. From then until the end of his reign his informal letters were written in English. On one level the move was political; it was part of his effort to mobilise English patriotism against France. At a deeper level it might have been personal; an identification with what English represented, his subjects as a whole and not just the clerical and noble elites, which according to John Lydgate he had in mind in 1412 when he commissioned the poet to translate Collone's *History of the Destruction of Troy*:[42]

> *By cause he wolde that to highe and lowe*
> *The noble story openly were knowe*
> *In oure tonge, aboute in every age*
> *And y-writen as wel in oure langage*
> *As in latyn and in frensche it is*
> *That of the story the trouth we may not mys*
> *No more than doth eche other nacioun*
> *This was the fyn of his entencioun.*

It has even been suggested that Henry's own personal English style helped shape the style subsequently adopted in chancery and which became the basis of standard English. Be that as it may, Henry V's promotion of the language was a watershed. Thereafter English was adopted, and rapidly for informal written communication by institutions and individuals, throughout the land. In 1422 the Brewers Guild of London noted their decision from henceforth to record their minutes in English 'because our mother tongue hath in modern days begun to be honourably enlarged and adorned', and especially because it was used by the king. English did not sweep all before it: Latin and French remained for many decades the language of formal legal and financial documents. But the existence of English as a language of record and communication was established. Moreover, emulating their king, several of Henry V's nobles themselves commissioned translations of key works of European literature so that their stories were openly known, and thereby made available the canon of advice books, romances and treatises to a new readership. Lydgate in his dedication of the *Fall of Troy* did not hesitate to equate the promotion of the English language with the identity of the English nation, as did Henry V. Agincourt was presented as a triumph not just of the king, but also of the nation, even likened on several occasions in the *Gesta Henrici Quinti* of 1416 to God's elect nation. Under Henry's auspices St George took on his full identity as its special patron and protector.[43]

What was understood to be the English nation was spelt out in a submission to the council of Constance in 1417 to justify its continuing recognition alongside the French, Italians and Germans. The task was not easy. Nation was still a loose concept applied to any grouping by birth. At Constance each 'nation' was a *natio principalis*, as distinct from a *natio particularis* (a kingdom). The German nation, into which it was first proposed the English should be incorporated, comprised all Scandinavia and eastern Christendom. A common language did not necessarily identify a nation. Indeed Polton, in his submission that England was a *natio principalis*, while arguing that there were different kingdoms, particularly the Scottish, within the English nation, also had to concede that five languages were spoken. Although, he argued, a common language was the surest proof of being a nation, the dominance of English within the British Isles proved the existence of the nation. It is an argument, suspiciously imperialist in the modern sense of the word, which is entirely at one with the reality of the English realm in the early fifteenth century. The English nation encompassed more than the English-speaking peoples.

The sharpening sense of English national identity in the early fifteenth century, closely linked as it was with Henry V's military ambitions in France, was reflected in the development of what have been called national chivalries. Before the Hundred Years' War, chivalry was an international culture, even in some minds an international order. The winning of renown through deeds of arms was independent of kings and kingdoms; so too had been the destruction caused by knights errant. As part of a general move to curb, control and discipline the worst excesses of chivalry in the later fourteenth century and to channel it into the dedicated service of kings in pursuit of their dynastic ends, chivalry had been 'nationalised'. The development of a national orders such as the Garter symbolised the manner in which by the fifteenth century chivalry became subordinated to the needs and ends of rulers. The greatest honour was to be found in royal service, in pursuit of the king's ambitions. Thus Henry V's war in France was England's war, not only the war of the king of England, but also the war of the chivalry of England. A chivalric hero like John Talbot won fame and renown because he died for England.[44]

The development of a national chivalry is significant also because it points to the manner in which the nobility of England, by tradition and culture part of an international ruling class, became more English in outlook. They still purchased most of their most treasured possessions from French and Flemish craftsmen, richly illuminated manuscripts, panel-painted portraits and altarpieces and finely woven tapestries, the subject matter of which was cosmopolitan. The fashion for court etiquette and entertainment was still set in France, especially by the last Valois dukes of Burgundy. But, whereas the late-fourtenth-century exemplars of nobility (John of Gaunt and Bolingbroke), were European in outlook with European-wide reputations, their late-fifteenth-century counterparts were Anglocentric. Their principal language was English, not French; and they read works written in English, not French (albeit many in translation).

There were now English poets, most notably Chaucer, whom Caxton celebrated as England's poet laureate, as well as Gower, Lydgate and the Sir Gawain author. There was a tradition of English historical writing that specifically celebrated the glories of English history. And in 1470 Sir Thomas Malory completed his English-language version of the Arthurian tales, the *Morte D'Arthur*, which gave a specifically English context and twist to the received corpus of European romances. When Caxton published his translation of Ramon Lull's *Book of the Order of Chivalry* he made a particular appeal in his own epilogue for a revival of English chivalry: 'O, ye knyghtes of England, where is the custome and usage of noble chyvalry that was used in those (olden) days.' In addition to buying and reading his book he advocated a programme of reading English history, Arthurian legends and Gawain (all in or to be in his list).[45]

English noble culture was also eclectic. It was happy to adopt the popular outlaw balladry of Robin Hood. Sir John Paston retained a servant to entertain him with a play of Robin Hood as well as of St George. By the early reign of Henry VIII the tales of Robin Hood were considered fit material for court disguising. It is with Robin Hood that we come to a more clearly identifiable English culture. And it is suggestive that the ballads of Robin Hood, first written down in the fifteenth century, are linked with the new middling sorts. At the time they were fixed in a written form for a southern audience they celebrate a yeoman hero, an outlaw operating in the wild, free, northern forest where he rights injustice and restores social peace. The hero was remote from the normal, conventional, law-abiding and regulated life of the typical member of the audience, but he offered an imaginary better world.[46]

The Robin Hood tales were told by minstrels and performed by players. Play-making was another dynamic English cultural phenomenon of the fifteenth century. Minstrels and players of local nobles, gentry, towns and villages regularly entertained the monks of Fountains and Selby in the later part of the century. While associated particularly with the Corpus Christi festivals of the great boroughs such as London, York, Coventry and Chester, cycles of plays were performed throughout England in villages as well as towns in the early summer. While the plays were dramatisations of religious stories and themes, they were rendered in such a way as to be set in the daily experience of life. Plays too, like Robin Hood, crossed social boundaries. In noble households and at court they took the form of masques, pageants and disguisings. While, at all levels, drama was not isolated from Europe, especially Burgundian and Flemish, influences, it had independent roots in older English customs and developed into a distinctive English form.[47]

A distinctive English culture took root in the fifteenth century. It is a culture that in its shared language and shared national identity crossed social boundaries, but among the middling sort literacy and the demand for literature in the English language was increasing most rapidly. William Caxton, who established the first press and the first commercial publishing house in England in 1478, responded to this demand. Even before Caxton there was a surge in the output of books in English. The survival of so many manuscripts from the fifteenth century may only reflect the fact that the more recently a book was produced the more likely it is to have been preserved. But Caxton's very success as a businessman in devoting his press to popular works in English, as opposed to academic and religious texts in Latin as did the Oxford University Press founded two years later, suggests that he was responding to demand, not creating it. Good at marketing, he was always pleased to tell his customers that his text had belonged to this gentleman, or had been sponsored by that nobleman, or was aimed not at the rude and uncunning, but to clerks and gentlemen that understand gentleness and science. Nevertheless his publications, were they history or poetry or philosophy, were aimed at the new readership, those who could not read

Latin or French and would now be able to afford a much cheaper, printed book. And he made no secret of his appeal to their Englishness, as well as to their social aspirations.[48]

It would beg too many questions to claim that the fifteenth century witnessed the birth of the English middle class. Yet many of the changes which took place within the realm of England in the later middle ages sharpened the sense of Englishness. The dominance of the English peoples and their language over the other peoples of the British Isles, Scotland excepted, was confirmed and enhanced. All ranks of English people became more conscious of their Englishness; an Englishness summed up by a Venetian at the end of the century in these words:[49]

> The English are great lovers of themselves, and of everything belonging to them; they think that there are no other men than themselves, and no other world but England.

It was an Englishness in its xenophobic and racist aspects that might embarrass many, but certainly not all, at the end of the twentieth century. It was also an Englishness associated with those groups of prosperous, more independent men in town and country, who had most benefited from the economic trends. They created Merrie England, an England especially associated with parochial middle England in the fifteenth century, and which they were to help sweep away in the sixteenth. Some of them were acquiring wealth and putting it to work in ways that were to be called capitalist; some of their descendants would find protestantism attractive; and a good many wished to ape and, if possible, join their betters as gentlemen.

Notes and references

1   The population figures are based on Hatcher, *Plague*, 68–9; Williams, *Wales*, 90; and Nicholls, 'Gaelic Society and Economy', 409. The wide dominion of the kings of England and its implications are discussed by Griffiths in 'English Realm and Dominions', 83–105 and 'Provinces and the Dominions', 1–26. For the ambivalent status of the Isle of Man see Thornton, 'Scotland and the Isle of Man', 1–3.

2   A full history of Calais under the English is still awaited. But see the discussion in Griffiths, *Henry VI*, 524–9.

3   Vale, *English Gascony*, 1–26, 154–215; and Labarge, *Gascony*, 184–216.

4   Allmand, *Lancastrian Normandy*, chs 3 and 4; Curry, 'Lancastrian Normandy', passim; Jones, 'War on the Frontier', passim; Massey, 'Land Settlement', passim.

5   Pollard, *North-Eastern England*, 232; Grant, 'Richard III and Scotland', 118.

6   For Ireland in the fifteenth century see Cosgrove, *Medieval Ireland*, 525–660 and *Late Medieval Ireland*, passim; Ellis, *Tudor Ireland*, 53–84; Lydon, *Lordship of Ireland*, and 'Nation and Race', 103–24.

7   Davies, *Owain Glyn Dŵr*, 292–324; Williams, *Wales*, 31–164; Griffiths, 'Wales and the Marches', passim and *Conquerors and Conquered;* Britnell, *Closing of the Middle Ages?*, 134–8.

8   Pollard, *North-Eastern England*, 17–18; Neville, 'Local Sentiment', passim. See also below n. 10.

9   Sneyd (ed.), *Italian Relation*, 23–4; Lloyd, *England and the German Hanse*, 74–5, 130–2; Bolton, *Alien Communities*, 1–40; Dockray, 'Patriotism, Pride and Paranoia', passim and Du Boulay, *Age of Ambition*, 17–30.

10   Hatcher, *Rural Economy and Society*, passim; and Du Boulay, *Lordship of Canterbury*, passim; For other English regions see e.g. Dyer, *Bishopric of Worcester;* Poos, *Essex*, and Miller, *Agrarian History, III.*

11   Goodman, 'Anglo-Scottish Marches', passim; Ellis, *Tudor Frontiers*, 10–45 (comparing the Irish and English marches), 'Crown, Community and Government', and 'Civilizing Northumberland'; Lomas, *County of Conflict*, chs 2 and 3; Tuck and Goodman, *War and Border Societies*, passim; Neville, *Violence, Custom and Law*, passim; and Summerson, 'Carlisle and the West March', passim. See also above, p. 111.

12   For the debate over the north/south divide see Jewell, *North/South Divide*; Musgrove, *The North of England*; Dobson, 'Politics and the Church', 1–18 (8–11 for Manners); and Pollard, 'Characteristics of the Fifteenth-century North', passim. For London apprentices see Palliser, 'Urban Society', 136.

13   Phythian-Adams, *Societies, Culture and Kinship*, 13–18; Virgoe, 'Aspects of the County Community', passim.

14   Hatcher, *Plague*, and 'England after the Black Death', passim; Bolton, 'World Upside Down', 22–8; Horrox, *The Black Death*, 230–6 summarises recent estimates of the demographic impact. Herlihy, *Black Death*, 17–31 expresses doubt that the epidemic was bubonic plague, as did Twigg, *Black Death*. Twigg's tentative suggestion that the plague might have been anthrax diverted attention from the general argument that the disease was a viral infection no longer identifiable. Were Herlihy and Twigg to be correct, the contemporary practice of fleeing the plague would have been an entirely appropriate response. For discussion of the wider fourteenth-century context of demographic and economic change see Harvey, 'Crisis', 1–24.

15   Bailey, 'Demographic Decline', passim; Harvey, *Living and Dying*, 112, 124, 127; Hatcher, 'Mortality', passim. For discussion of whether the mechanism of decline was provided by high death rates or low birth rates see Bailey,

'Demographic Decline'. Evidence of a fall in death rates in the diocese of York at the end of the century is to be found in Goldberg, 'Mortality'. The irreconcilable views on whether population continued to decline or began to rise after 1471 are discussed in Britnell, *Closing of the Middle Ages?*, 244–7.

16   Bailey, 'Natural Disaster and Economic Decline', 185–9, 205–8; Lamb, *Climate*, 82, 93, 186–90; but note Bolton's word of caution 'World Upside Down', 44 (Climate). Britnell, *Commercialisation*, 179–85; Day, *The Medieval Market Economy*, 40–8, 59, 63, 94–7; Nightingale, 'Monetary Contraction', 560–75; Kermode, 'Money and Credit', passim; Mayhew, 'Velocity of Circulation'; and Bolton, 'World Upside Down', 41–2.

17   Britnell, 'Economic Context', 44–5; Bolton, *Medieval English Economy*, ch. 9 and 'World Upside Down', 40–5; Fryde, *Peasants and Landlords*, ch. 10; Hatcher, 'Great Slump', 240–592; Pollard, 'Agrarian Crisis', passim; Munro, *Wool, Cloth and Gold*, passim; Power and Postan, *Studies in Fifteenth-Century Trade* remains the standard survey.

18   Dyer, 'Deserted Medieval Villages', and 'Lost Villages', xii–xviii; Fryde, *Peasants and Landlords*, ch. 12; Pollard, *North-Eastern England*, 56–9. Debate still exists as to the extent to which enclosure and conversion to pasture before the early sixteenth century was the reaction to the voluntary abandonment of villages or the motive for evictions. Fryde cites several cases in the midlands where apparently viable villages were cleared by landlords wishing to increase rents by conversion to pasture. But Hatcher, 'Great Slump', 248–52 points out that wool prices between 1440 and 1480 were frequently so low as to make sheep rearing also unprofitable. It is to be noted too that most of the evidence for forcible eviction comes from after 1480. As well as enclosing for pastoral farming (cattle as well as sheep) landlords also enclosed parks, and some forcible evictions were carried out to satisfy the lust for hunting (see Pollard, *North-Eastern England*, 203, for some Yorkshire examples).

19   Hatcher, 'Great Slump', passim; Palliser, 'Urban Decay Revisited', passim; Shaw, *Wells*, 62–3; Holt and Rosser, *The Medieval Town: a Reader in English Urban History, 1200–1540*, and Reynolds, *An Introduction to the History of English Medieval Towns*. Goldberg, *Women, Work and Life Cycle*, 39–81 and Kermode, *Medieval Merchants*, 270–5, 314–18, provide recent discussion of the decline of York and further references.

20   Pollard, *North-Eastern England*, 78–9 and references therein. Note, however, Hatcher's comment ('Great Slump', 267) that few if any towns escaped the 'worst storms of the fifteenth century'.

21   Bolton, *Medieval Economy*, 290–4, 299–301, 317–19; Lloyd, *England and the Hanse*, 130–217; Kermode, *Medieval Merchants*, 248–51, 312.

22   Nightingale, 'Growth of London', passim; Palliser, 'Crisis in English Towns'; Pollard, *North-Eastern England*, 71–80; Kermode, *Medieval Merchants*, 252–3, 308–10.

23 Hatcher, 'Great Slump', 255–9; Britnell, *Commercialisation*, 193–4, and references cited therein. But see the evidence that the Greys of Ruthin were able to sustain the level of their income from their estates between 1392 and 1467 in Fryde, *Peasants and Landlords*, 250–3.

24 Hatcher, 'Great Slump', 259–63; Britnell, 'Economic Context', 55–8; Bolton, 'World Upside Down', 50–8. Dyer, *Standards of Living*, passim; Pollard, *North-Eastern England*, 48–52, 62–70.

25 Serfdom and its decline have been the focus of much debate. See Hilton, *Decline of Serfdom*, and *Transition*, Introduction; Ashton and Philipps, *Brenner Debate;* Martin, *Feudalism to Capitalism;* Rigby, *English Society*, 17–59 and, for a different perspective, McFarlane, *English Individualism*, 131–64.

26 Lomas, *North-East England*, 178–9; Hare, 'Lords and Tenants', 19–25; Fryde, *Peasants and Landlords*, 218–19, 248–9.

27 Kettle, 'City and Close', 159; Hare, 'Lords and Tenants', 21.

28 Harvey, 'Was there Popular Politics?', passim, and *Cade's Rebellion;* Dyer, 'Redistribution of Incomes'; Hare, 'Lords and Tenants', 24–5.

29 Evelyn, ed., *Idley's Instructions*, 160.

30 *English Historical Documents, IV*, 461,465, 993–5, 911, 1004, 1153–4.

31 Morgan, 'English Gentleman', passim; Gray, 'Incomes from Land'; In 1486 John Harrington, the common clerk of the city of York, was described by Sir John Aske of nearby Aughton as being the son of a poor gentleman, 'though he (the father) were never taken here but for a yeoman' (Pollard, *North-Eastern England*, 88).

32 Rigby, *English Society*, 181–203; Given-Wilson, *The English Nobility*, 29–83.

33 Keen, *Chivalry* (nobility); Cummins, *The Hound and the Hawk*, passim; Almond, 'Medieval Hunting', passim; Orme, 'Medieval Hunting', passim; Pollard, *North-Eastern England*, 198–207.

34 Keen, *Chivalry*, 41; Morgan, 'English Gentleman', 17–19; Goodman, 'Responses to Requests'; Griffiths, 'Public and Private Bureaucracies'; Storey, 'Gentlemen Bureaucrats'.

35 Rigby, *English Society*, 165–76 and 'Urban "Oligarchy"', 62–86; Horrox, 'Urban Gentry'; Palliser, 'Urban Society'; Kermode, *Medieval Merchants*, 60–8. Shaw, *Wells*, 167–76 for a small town.

36 Kumin, *Shaping of a Community*, passim and Carnwath, 'Thame'; De Windt, 'Local Government', passim (jurors); Goheen, 'Peasant Politics?' passim; Dyer, 'Medieval Rural Community', passim; and 'Taxation and Communities', passim; and McIntosh, 'Local Change and Community Control'. A useful case study of a small town and its vicinity is provided by Newman, *Late-Medieval Northallerton*. For the contemporary use of the word *mediocres* see Rigby, *English*

Society, 171–2. The term 'middling sorts' was a sixteenth-century coinage, but there can be little doubt that those it described existed in the fifteenth. The judgement that 'in jury service, in manorial courts and above all in parish the rural middling sort governed the poor and in rotation each other' is as true of the earlier century as the later. See Barry and Brooks, ed., *The Middling Sort*, 20. See also Wrightson, 'Sorts of People', passim.

37 Kumin, *Shaping of a Community*, passim; Burgess and Kumin, 'Penitential Bequests', passim; Burgess, *Bristol Records*, xi–xliv; Rosser, 'Communities of Parish and Guild', passim and, 'Going to the Fraternity Feast', passim; Barron, 'Parish Fraternities', passim; Bailey, 'Rural Society', passim; Hutton, *Merry England*, 5–68.

38 Cullum, 'Pore People Harberles', 36–554; Harvey, *Living and Dying*, ch. 1; Orme and Webster, *English Hospital*, 127–46; Rubin, 'The Poor', passim and *Charity and Community*, 289–99; Bennett, 'Conviviality and Charity', 19–41 and Shaw, *Wells*, 228–48 (for provision in a particular place). For the alternative view that changing attitudes were linked to economic growth and pressures on resources in certain parts of England in the later decades of the fifteenth century, see McIntosh, 'Local Change', 227–30 and *Controlling Misbehaviour*, 15–62, 172–8. The growing chorus of complaint against idleness, the disapproval of ale houses and the condemnation of most sports may indicate that men and women enjoyed more leisure, but they also reveal a highly moralistic outlook among the middling sort. 'The work ethic in England long preceded the Protestantism with which it is conventionally associated' (Harper-Bill, 'English Religion', 116).

39 See Further Reading for the substantial literature on late-medieval women. For the story of Christiana Harrington see Habberjam, 'A Fifteenth-Century Divorce Case', 50–60; and of Cecilia Wyvell, Macrae-Spencer, 'Putting Women in their Place', 186–7.

40 For the debate over women and work see Goldberg, *Women, Work, and Life Cycle* (passim); Mate, *Daughters, Wives and Widows*, esp. 21–72; Bailey, 'Demographic Decline', 5–11. For the more general proposition that the fifteenth century witnessed a 'golden age' for women see Barron, 'Golden Age', passim and the riposte by Bennett, 'Medieval Women, Modern Women', passim. For the Coventry ordinance see Goldberg, 'Women', 120. Books for, about and by late-medieval women contain many layers of ambiguity, but it may well be that they reveal more equal personal relationships between men and women than either legal status or clerical mysogony recognised (see, for an introduction to this issue, Coss, *The Lady*, ch. 6).

41 Barron and Sutton, *Medieval London Widows*, xxvi–xxvii; Jones and Underwood, *The King's Mother*, 187–8; Cullum, 'Vowesses and Female Piety', passim. For nunneries see Further Reading.

42 Bergen, ed., *Lydgate's Troy Book*, i, 4, 11.111–18; Allmand, *Henry V*, 410, 420–2; Britnell, *Closing of the Middle Ages?*, 127–47. For Lollardy see below, pp. 212–16.

43   Crowder, *Unity, Heresy and Reform*, 111–26; Genet, 'English Nationalism', passim.

44   Wright, 'The *Tree of Battles*'; Pollard, *John Talbot*, 122–30; Keen, *Chivalry*, 179–99, 219–49.

45   Caxton, *Order of Chivalry*, 124–5; McKendick, 'Tapestries from the Low Countries', and Vale, 'Anglo-Burgundian Nobleman', passim; Richmond, 'Visual Culture', passim and the references cited therein.

46   Dobson and Taylor, *Rymes of Robyn Hood*, and Holt, *Robin Hood* which emphasises the aristocratic milieu, are the best starting points for the fifteenth-century ballads. See also Coss, 'Aspects of Cultural Diffusion' and Richmond, 'An Outlaw and Some Peasants'.

47   Wickham, *Early English Stages*, i, passim; Holt, *Robin Hood*, 137–8; Johnston, 'Traders and Playmakers', passim. See also the publications of the Records of Early English Drama Society.

48   Blake, *England's First Publisher, Caxton and His World* and *William Caxton*. For the spread of literacy, in English see Cressy, *Literacy and the Social Order*. Note too the establishment of lending libraries (*EHD*, 496–7, 835–6). See also below pp. 389–90.

49   Sneyd (ed.), *Italian Relation*, 20–1.

CHAPTER EIGHT

The Church and religion

England and Rome

One group of Englishmen stood apart from their fellow countrymen because they were members of a separate order which was itself part of an international organisation – the clergy. The Church was responsible for the spiritual well-being of all persons, for enforcing the moral code and for the salvation of souls. All male, celibate, educated in Latin, subject to separate law-courts and answerable to Rome, the 30–40,000 ordained clergy in England were in many respects a caste apart. Moreover, although less than 5 per cent of the population, the clergy collectively held some 25 per cent of the landed wealth in the kingdom and received in the form of tithes and other oblations a further significant share of the wealth produced by the laity. The Church was a privileged and substantially endowed institution, performing an essential function not only spiritual, but also judicial in cases of marriage, probate, breaches of faith and defamation.[1]

The *Ecclesia Anglicana* claimed to represent the whole of the British Isles at the council of Constance in 1417. In fact the Irish provinces of Armagh and Dublin were independent and, after a long struggle against the claims of York, the Scottish dioceses had been recognised as separate, although without an archbishop until the elevation of St Andrews in 1472. Of the two English provinces, Canterbury, which encompassed the Welsh dioceses, was considerably larger than York. Each enjoyed its own customs, its own system of courts, its separate convocation of clergy and its separate obligation to pay taxes to Papacy and Crown. There was a long history of competition for precedence between the two, settled in a compromise which enabled the archbishop of York to style himself primate of England and Canterbury primate of All England.

The clergy in these provinces looked to Rome, not only as the spiritual head of the universal church, but also as the focus of a steady stream of necessary routine business concerning dispensations, licences, promotions and court cases. The Papacy was the 'Well of Grace' for favours and patronage for both clergy and laity, and the Curia was the supreme court for all ecclesiastical jurisdiction. A permanent team of agents and proctors was kept busy there on behalf of English clients. Early in the sixteenth century, Cardinal Christopher Bainbridge of York became a permanent resident at the Papal Court charged with protecting English interests. Englishmen were thus constantly toing and froing between Rome and Canterbury and York, as were papal nuncios and tax collectors from Rome to England. Some specific matters were delegated to English bishops as legates, notably the two archbishops. Henry V prevented Henry Beaufort, bishop of Winchester, from receiving the powers of legate *a latere* (all Papal authority in England). Not until Cardinal Wolsey in the third decade of the sixteenth century did the Crown allow an English churchman to receive these powers; and shortly afterwards Henry VIII took them for himself.

The English Church was integrated into the Church universal by other means than ecclesiastical business and politics. Many religious houses in England were exempt from the authority of English bishops either because they were cells of European, usually French, houses (the alien priories), or because they belonged to orders, most notably the friars, the Cistercians and Premonstratensians who were answerable directly to their mother houses. Moreover there was a steady stream of provision of Italians and other continental churchmen to prebends, dignitaries and sees in England, often held *in absentia*; as well as Englishmen provided to benefices elsewhere. Furthermore the clergy and laity paid taxes, if only on a modest and strictly controlled level, to Rome. The English Church cannot be separated from the universal Church of which it was a part.[2]

Yet the Church in England had a strong sense of its Englishness. It had developed its own local customs in the application of the canon law, most notably in probate, and in liturgy. The great majority of the clergy were English by birth. And although some high-born clerics made spectacular careers for themselves, not always through their own innate ability, and many a rectory or prebend was found for the younger sons of the gentry, most of the clergy were in fact recruited from that middle stratum of society which was becoming more prominent during the century. The Church, above all, provided the best career opportunities for gifted sons of yeomen, artisans and traders who could afford the initial costs of schooling. Most of the bishops came from such backgrounds, not from the privileged circles of the aristocracy.[3]

But the Englishness of the Church was most apparent in the exercise of royal influence and the willingness of the hierarchy to serve the Crown. By the beginning of the fifteenth century the Crown had largely won the battle with the Papacy over provision to benefices, asserted in the late fourteenth century through the Statutes of Provisors and *Praemunire* which limited Papal freedom to appoint and forbade appeal to Rome on such matters. Despite the attempt of Martin V (1417–31) to recover the right of the curia to provide for lesser benefices, the Crown and lay patrons retained firm control. And even at the highest level, the election of bishops, the Crown exercised a virtually unchallenged right to nomination. The result was that for the most part the episcopacy and the cathedral chapters were composed of diplomats and administrators, pastors and intellectuals, who had been in royal service, or otherwise won royal favour. And at the lower prebendal and parochial levels, the nominees of senior clergy, influential laymen and the local gentry were generally provided. Indeed, the right of presentation (advowson) of a candidate for a benefice to the bishop for institution was a jealously guarded property-right.

Thus the domination of English patrons over provisions at all levels ensured that the the personnel of the Church was largely sympathetic to the interests of the political nation at large. This is not to imply that there was recurring conflict with the Papacy. Because it was in the best interests of the Crown to enjoy good relationships with Rome, it was usually willing to satisfy its reasonable requests for its nominees. By the early sixteenth century there was a particularly close rapport between England and Rome; a sign not of the weakness of the Crown, but of its confidence. Rome by then largely accepted that the controlling influences in the appointment of the clergy at all levels lay in English hands.

It is not surprising, therefore, that the Church in England identified with the needs of the realm. It was integrated into the administration and politics of the kingdom. Not only did the Church provide the Crown with civil servants, diplomats and councillors, it also paid heavy taxes through its convocations. It held many civil franchises, most prominently the great palatinate of Durham, but also the liberties of Ely, Bury St Edmunds and Hexhamshire and lesser hundredal rights. Ideologically, too, the Church was a buttress to the state. Popular rebellion against the Crown was condemned by the Church; and in its turn the state gave its support to the suppression of spiritual rebellion against the Church.

There were areas in which conflict and tension existed, particularly those in which the Church provided a haven from royal justice. But during the century, especially in its latter half, the Crown whittled away some of the rights of the lesser sanctuaries, which had only ever provided a temporary refuge for fugitives from justice, began to narrow down the benefits of clergy, and to assert, through the the the extension of *praemunire*, the right of the common law courts to hear a wider range of cases, especially those concerning disputes over tithes. This development did not pass unnoticed. There is evidence that Cardinal Morton (1486–1500) asserted the counter-claims of the diocesan rights of Canterbury and that later Cardinal Wolsey, as legate, sought to claw back ecclesiastical powers and privileges. But there was no great clash of principle between Church and state during the later middle ages. The trend towards greater royal influence and domination was in the last resort accepted. While the Church was not yet the established Church of England of the post-Reformation world, it was already part of the English establishment and its outlook had become rather less international and rather more national.[4]

The English clergy

The reputation of the English Church in the later middle ages is tarnished. Protestant propaganda, apparently confirmed by contemporay records, ensured that it was perceived for centuries as corrupt and its clergy negligent. The late-twentieth century has taken a more sympathetic view, tending to emphasise the sound health of the institution. The quality of the clergy, the attitude of the laity to them, and intensity of belief are important issues of current debate.[5]

The Church was itself a complex organisation difficult to manage and open to abuse. The core pastoral and administrative units were the diocese; Canterbury containing eighteen, including four in Wales, and York three. The larger of the sees of England were themselves divided into archdeaconries; Lincoln had eight, York four. The archdeaconry of Richmondshire in York was administratively almost a separate diocese; that of Chester in Lichfield and Coventry was the remnant of an earlier diocese encompassing the county of Chester and southern Lancashire. All sees were subdivided into deaneries, groups of parishes which dealt with minor ecclesiastical matters. At the base lay the parishes, some 8,800, each with its incumbent or deputy who provided the essential cure of souls.

A simplified description of the ecclesiastical hierarchy hides the actual complexity. First it ignores the religious houses of which there were some 900, including hospitals. The Benedictines, the richest and most powerful order, were subject to episcopal control and visitation, but a number of religious houses in each diocese were exempt from external discipline. Secondly every diocese was fragmented by peculiar jurisdictions which undermined administrative efficiency. These peculiars ranged from the exempt jurisdiction held by a great Benedictine Abbey such as St Albans or Bury St Edmunds, through prebendal peculiarities such as Masham in York, to collegiate and chapel foundations. They even crossed episcopal boundaries. Thus the archbishops of York held Hexham as a peculiar within the diocese of Durham, while the bishops of Durham held peculiar jurisdiction in Northallerton and Howden in York. Thirdly the bishoprics were divided between monastic and secular sees. Nine cathedrals were staffed by monasteries (all Benedictine but one, Carlisle, which was an Augustinian house); in two, the double sees of Bath and Wells and Coventry and Lichfield, duties were shared between a monastery and a dean and chapter; and the remaining were governed by chapters of secular canons and prebendaries. Fourthly, at the other end of the scale, approximately 40 per cent of parishes were appropriated to monasteries and university colleges; that is to say the rectory was endowed in the institution and the parochial duties were carried out by a vicar, who was appointed by the corporation. The Church was a complex kaleidoscope of rights and privileges which made it exceptionally difficult to administer.[6]

The ambitions of career clerics, the competing demands of administration and cure of souls, and the desire of the Crown to deploy benefices as rewards for its servants created additional pressures. Pluralism and absenteeism were built into the system. A benefice, whether a see, prebend, parish or perpetual chantry chaplaincy, was a freehold property for life; beneficed clergy had tenure. A benefice was therefore the first aim of most ordained clergy; but it was also the principal means of rewarding service and talent. Successful clergymen, especially those in royal service, accumulated benefices. Few were as notorious as Bishop Whickham in the late fourteenth century, or even as well rewarded as Alexander Lee, Edward IV's almoner, who in the later fifteenth century accumulated six prebends, two rectories and the mastership of a hospital and was said to draw an income of 800 marks from them. More typical was Bishop John Russell of Lincoln, who never held more than four benefices at any one time, and only two (neither with cure of souls) other than his see as a bishop. Holding more than one benefice with cure of souls was forbidden by canon law, a prohibition only rarely breached, as in the case of Alexander Lee. It was even more exceptional for more than one senior post to be held by one man. Prior Richard Bell of Durham unsuccessfully sought to continue to hold his monastic post after he was elected bishop of Carlisle. One of the reasons why contemporaries condemned Cardinal Wolsey was that he was allowed to hold a succession of bishoprics as well as the abbey of St Albans *in commendam* while he was archbishop of York.[7]

However, pluralism, if normally on a modest scale, was tolerated in the Church. It inevitably led to absenteeism. It is impossible to conceive that John Russell, much engaged in royal diplomacy and administration, could have devoted much time to his pastoral duties as rector of Towcester between

1471 and 1476. On a more mundane level parochial clergy were licensed to be absent from their cures to attend university, or serve a patron, or go on pilgrimage. The effective operation of the Church thus depended at all levels on the employment of deputies and stipendiary priests. At the highest level of episcopal administration, bishops depended on teams of officials such as sequestrators and vicars-general, often holding suffragan titles. In York only a handful of the canons, the cathedral dignitaries of Dean, Treasurer and Precentor were required to be resident. The others were absentee, and the services they were required to provide daily in the choir were conducted by vicars choral. And in the parishes pastoral care was often entrusted to stipendiaries on short-term temporary or part-time contracts. There was available a large pool of unbeneficed clergy who depended for their livelihood on such insecure employment in parishes, or as chaplains in aristocratic households, serving parochial guilds or picking up fixed-term chantry posts.[8]

With fewer benefices than there were qualified candidates, and given the prevailing culture of pluralism, there was inevitably a scramble for preferment, in which patronage was vital. Thus patrons promised future preferment. The Papacy issued letters *in forma pauperum* granting a reservation for future provision when a benefice became vacant; the Crown granted its own offices in reversion; holders of advowsons granted the right of future presentation, or nomination, to their clients. A profitable way to exploit benefices was to resign a living in favour of a pension paid from it for life by the next and future incumbents. This came close to trafficking in ecclesiastical office and thus the sin of simony. Fees were customarliy paid at all stages of ordination and induction. It was difficult to determine when such a fee for administration crossed the line into the purchase of a living. For those without the backing of an influential patron to lobby on their behalf, sweeteners could help secure preferment.[9]

Even though the Church operated as a spoils system for the benefit of its more fortunate, ambitious or unscrupulous members, its effectiveness depended on the quality and dedication of the clergy in post at both parochial and diocesan level. Training was lengthy and costly, especially if a candidate sought a university education. In the early fifteenth century there seems to have have been a significant fall in new ordinations, lower even than the fall in population, and the prospects of university-educated clergy were reduced. Understaffed by mid-century, it is possible that the quality of recruits, as well as the number had fallen. The trend was reversed and by the end of the century rates of ordination had returned to their pre-plague levels. At the same time, perhaps inspired by the lead taken by Henry VI in his great educational foundations of Eton College and King's College, Cambridge, a wave of school and college endowments throughout the kingdom was directed towards improving clerical education. By 1500 there were more, and arguably better educated, clergy chasing the same restricted number of benefices and swelling the ranks of the short-term and temporarily employed.[10]

How well the beneficed clergy carried out their duties is hard to determine. Records of episcopal visitation reveal that the authorities and parishioners were more concerned about behaviour than theological competence. Neglect of property, failure to conduct services, unlicensed absenteeism and especially sexual lapses seem to have loomed largest. Celibacy was difficult to maintain. On the whole the authorities and parishioners seem to have been tolerant of sexual liaisons as long as they were discreet. On the other hand, the archdeacon of London would not tolerate a brothel specialising in the provision of clerical needs. Keeping up appearances seem to have been more important than the rigorous enforcement of discipline.[11]

On the whole the quality of the episcopal bench during the fifteenth century was high. At the beginning of the century the Crown tended to promote administrators and diplomats, able clerical politicians such as Thomas Langley of Durham or Philip Morgan of Ely, in preference to scholars or pastors. Henry VI, however, showed a marked preference for those who shared his educational and pious concerns, men such as William Wayneflete or John Carpenter. Under the Yorkists and Henry VII there was a return to the more traditional administrator, such as John Russell (who was also a scholar) or Richard Fox. There were always a handful of sons of aristocrats promoted for political reasons to heights well beyond their abilities, none more so than Robert Neville, bishop of Durham (1437–57); but other aristocratic bishops such as Henry Beaufort of Winchester, or George Neville of York were men of outstanding talent. For the most part the bishops were men of ability and personal probity.[12]

A third of the clergy was in religious orders. The great Benedictine houses such as Durham or Westminster housed seventy or more brethren, but houses of less well-endowed orders, such as the Premonstratensians were as small as a dozen or so. Overall the numbers of monks and friars remained stable, picking up slightly to over 10,000 by 1500, of which 3,000 were friars. Much has been made of the occasional scandal and general laxity that characterised so many monasteries in their later centuries. Sexual transgressions, in both male and female houses, were generally rare. Some abbeys were notoriously unruled, as Dorchester was revealed to have been in mid-century, but for the most part the faults revealed in visitations were minor misdemeanours such as running in the cloister, gossiping and guffawing during divine service, or singing out of tune or, in nunneries, wearing silk or keeping pets. Few monasteries exhibited that spiritual zeal that had accompanied their foundations. Meat was now eaten more regularly; personal possessions were now tolerated; and a great cosmopolitan Benedictine house like that of Westminster, where the cloister was hardly cut off from the world, had more of the air of a well-endowed university college than of a place of contemplative retreat. The larger houses were more preoccupied with the effective management of their estates, their relationships with their influential neighbours, and the exercise of local political power, than with spiritual zeal.

The cause for greatest contemporary concern lay at the opposite extreme, the very small houses which were insufficiently endowed to maintain their function. From time to time such houses were dissolved. On the other hand, some new houses were established and there were pockets of renewed zeal. Two orders were buoyant: the Bridgettine Order founded recently by St Bridget of Sweden received influential backing and the sponsorship of none other than Henry V in the foundation of Syon Abbey; and the Carthusian houses, collective hermitages committed more determinedly than most other orders to the contemplative ideal, were noted for their high spiritual reputation. Monasticism was not entirely a spent force.[13]

The Church was a cumbersome, multi-faceted and deep-rooted institution. Like many complex organisations, the management of its own affairs took up a good deal of its energies. Its bureaucracy tended to serve the needs of its own members as much as the needs of those it served. Considering its size and fragmentation, it was effectively administered. But no one would claim that all was as it should have been. It had its own internal critics. From the author of *Dives and Pauper* in the first decade of the century, through Thomas Gascoigne in the 1450s to John Colet early in the sixteenth century there was maintained a steady flow of criticism of ecclesiastical abuses – the pursuit of riches, the neglect of pastoral duties, the failure to preach – most of it by clergymen themselves and much of it representing a frank endeavour to confront their shortcomings. Some of the criticisms stemmed from internal rivalries and jealousies, especially between the mendicant orders and the secular clergy. There was a particularly strong vein of satire concerning friars, the mendicants whose rule entitled them to beg for alms, but who also by the fifteenth century had accumulated substantial property. Awareness of faults in some quarters, and the desire of the university of Oxford to do something about them through the councils of Pisa and Constance, show that the Church was not completely complacent. Moreover, the maintenance of the practice of parochial and monastic visitation reveals that it was concerned to maintain standards of clerical behaviour. Nevertheless, calls for reform of ecclesiastical practice and the disciplining of individual offenders had but superficial effect. The authorities were concerned more with appearances than substance. It is notable that although sexual laxity received considerable attention, ecclesiastical courts were reluctant to probe too deeply into financial irregularities and the sleaze surrounding clerical careers. The late-medieval Church was never prepared to address the problem of simony.

However, that flaw was probably less damaging than its narrowing doctrinal orthodoxy, which led to the hounding of Reginald Peacock, Bishop of Chichester (1450–9), for daring to debate with the Lollards.[14]

Anticlericalism and heresy

For the most part the laity accepted the Church for what it was. It is hard to find evidence of sustained anticlericalism that does not carry implications of heresy. Personal quarrels, sometimes leading to assault, flared between individual clergy and their neighbours, but incumbents tended to fall foul of their parishioners as a result of their individual failings. Tithes were sometimes a matter of dispute not because, for the most part, parishioners objected in principle, but because an incumbent had sought to abuse his right, or where the exact rights were themselves uncertain. The church courts were kept busy by suitors in matters of debt, defamation, marriage and probate. It does not seem to have been the laity in general, but the Crown in particular that objected to them as an alternative source of law. If one were to follow the literary sources one would conclude that the mendicant orders were particularly unpopular. Yet the evidence of Wills shows that testators continued to hold them in high regard, adding to the property they already held. It is possible that among the gentry and nobility a certain disdain for the clergy had crept in; but it is hard to identify a general resentment of the clergy simply because they were members of a privileged and wealthy caste. Most people, at almost all levels of society, had relations who were clergy; fathers continued to educate sons for clerical careers, perhaps in the hope of later advantage; parochial incumbents, stipendiary priests and chantry chaplains provided many services for their communities, especially as schoolmasters and wardens of hospitals, over and above their spiritual care. There seems to have been little popular objection to clergymen taking mistresses. The clergy were in many respects fully integrated into society. And this, as much as any other aspect, gave the Church a particularly English character.[15]

There was, however, one strand of opinion that was truly anticlerical (or anti-sacerdotal as it ought to be styled): Lollardy, the first English heresy. It arose out of a complex set of influences. One was an old academic tradition, which took the Pauline comments on predestination to their logical conclusion and was expounded by the Oxford theologian, John Wycliffe, who died in 1384. Wycliffite ideas would have been restricted to high intellectual circles had not circumstances in the fourteenth century been particularly propitious for their dissemination. The psychological impact of the recurring and devastating plague epidemics, interpreted as God's punishment on sinful mankind, the disaster of the Schism (1378–1417) which undermined the authority of the Papacy and by extension the clergy as a whole, and the general climate of more open religious debate and criticism of the failings of the Church in England in the later fourteenth century encouraged and enabled them to spread beyond the university. Wycliffe's speculation thus inspired an heretical movement.[16]

Beginning with the doctrine of predestination, that some souls are destined for salvation and others for damnation, Wycliffe argued that Christians could do little to influence their own fate and that the celebration of the mass whereby Christians could earn salvation was therefore pointless. Thus the Eucharist did not witness the actual transubstantiation of bread and wine into the body and blood of Christ, but was only a symbolic representation of the same. Similarly he challenged the sacrament of confession, arguing that God alone could forgive sin. In all this there was no role for a mediating priesthood or an established Church. The true Church was the body of those predestined for salvation, true Christians. It followed that Wycliffe rejected the Papacy, advocated the disendowment of the Church and the dissolution of the monasteries. Authority lay in the bible, which should be translated into English and made available to all. In scripture lay the revealed word of God.[17]

Wycliffe was an evangelical, who anticipated the principal doctrines of protestantism. In the quarter century following his death, his ideas were developed and promoted by a dedicated group of followers, themselves priests and academics. At the heart of their project was the translation of the bible, over which great scholarly care was taken, and the provision of a collection of teaching manuals, sermons and commentaries. Some 250 copies of the Lollard bible, identified by its heretical prologue, and some 294 separate sermons and commentaries, all in English, have survived. These are the remnants of the output of Lollard scriptoria which tirelessly produced them all by hand. Put into the hands of cells, they became the focus of prayer, reading and discussion, sustained and inspired by peripatetic ministers.

Perhaps the most significant aspect of early Lollardy is not that the heresy arose, but that it was able to establish itself. In the climate of late-fourteenth-century religious turmoil, all manner of religious ideas were expressed in English. Walter Hilton and Nicholas Love were writing at the same time about personal piety. *Piers Plowman* was a more radical work than it was later perceived to be. The friars, also in English, preached scathingly about the shortcomings of the secular clergy, up and down the country. It was not always easy to identify the Lollard text.

Lollards also enjoyed protection in high places. Wycliffe himself had been employed by John of Gaunt. Gaunt may subsequently have distanced himself from his protégé and become strictly orthodox in his own views, but a group of highly-placed courtiers, known as the Lollard knights, and perhaps other sympathisers, seem to have delayed intensive persecution during Richard II's reign. It might be no coincidence that, as long as Gaunt lived, there was no sustained attack on the Lollards. And in the localities several Lollard priests are known to have been protected by sympathetic patrons. Even under Henry IV, when the state threw its weight more decisively behind the efforts of Archbishop Arundel to expunge the heresy, Lollards were not heavily pressed. The first sustained move to root out Lollardy at source was Arundel's 'Constitutions' of 1409 followed by the publication of a comprehensive index of proscribed texts in 1411. Preaching in English was restricted, licensing of book publication was introduced and academic freedom in the universities was curtailed. Lollardy was cut from its intellectual roots. The final steps were taken by Henry V following Oldcastle's rebellion, in which the full authority of the Crown, locally as well as centrally, was put at the disposal of the Church in seeking out and handing over suspects.[18]

Wycliffe and his disciples had pinned their hopes on the Crown taking the lead in reformation; after all it was already in conflict with the Papacy over provisions and *praemunire*. If not the Crown, then it was hoped parliament would take the initiative. That there was some sympathy in parliamentary circles is revealed by the fact that in Henry IV's reign a carefully planned and thought-out bill for the disendowment of the Church was introduced in the Commons. Henry V, on whose shoulders perhaps fantastical hopes had been placed, made it clear once and for all that reform would not come from above. In his long interviews with the king before he was condemned, Oldcastle possibly discovered that the man who he thought was sympathetic, was firmly set against the Lollard programme. His defiance enabled Henry to crack down on known groups. Lollard disturbances later in the century, most notably in 1431, were an admission that the movement had failed in its wider ambition of persuading the Crown to take the lead in reforming the Church. Once Lollardy was associated with sedition against the Crown it was bound to be crushed. By working to end the Schism, by seeking to reform the monastic orders, and by promoting in his new foundations an orthodox spirituality, Henry V emphatically placed the power of the Crown against doctrinal change. At the same time, Arundel's successor at Canterbury, Henry Chichele, developed a positive liturgical response to heresy. In so far as Henry V answered Wycliffe's call for the state to assert itself in religion, he did so to counter his ideas rather than to advance them.[19]

After 1414 Lollardy was driven underground. Yet it survived. The nature and strength of later Lollardy is, however, difficult to determine. One problem lies in the definition of Lollardy itself. One perception is that there was a clear line of development between Wycliffe's teaching, the work of his followers in Oxford, and the establishment of a coherent Lollard movement among the laity. Another is that Wycliffite ideas mixed with other more popular heresies and complaints without the same theological rigour to form a heterogeneous and incoherent body of views conveniently lumped together by the authorities as Lollardy. Was the man who ostentatiously turned his back on the raised Host a Lollard, or an atheist? Surviving trial records, and John Foxe's reading in the sixteenth century of the record of processes now lost, show a range of views, many of which were not Wycliffite. Once the persecution of heresy was established all manner of heterodox views were unearthed, revealing scepticism on the one hand and a range of eschatological views on the other, which were not strictly Wycliffite.[20]

Another problem lies in the very nature of the process. Those accused of Lollardy were presented with a statement of their supposed views which they were required to abjure. Most did so. Did heretics easily recant and return to the fold; or did they, as they considered an oath made to a clergyman to be worthless, merely go through the motion. Only recidivists were executed; only then, when charged for a second time, was the faith tested. Moreover, persecution was sporadic. Bishop Alnwick undertook a rigorous drive against East Anglian groups in 1428–31. The bishops of Lincoln were concerned throughout the century by heretics in the southern parts of the diocese, but there is no evidence of sustained pressure. One is left uncertain as to whether persecution was sporadic because the heresy was generally dormant, or because it was only of concern to the occasional bishop.[21]

There were persistent Lollard sects in specific locations in the Thames valley and midland towns, especially the Chilterns and the Cotswolds (even in particular parishes such as Amersham and Burford), Bristol, Coventry, Northampton and London. Time after time, generation after generation, heretical cells were revealed in these places. Persecution did not eradicate them. Moreover groups were known to each other and maintained supportive links, such as safe houses in time of trouble. They may have been connected by the arteries of trade; on the other hand they also radiate out from Oxford. It is possible that they were the successors to groups founded by the first Wycliffite missionaries. It was normally the leaders of these groups who attracted the attention of the authorities and were brought before the courts; they were often men, and women, of local substance, of the middling sort. Since they outwardly conformed, some even serving as churchwardens in their parishes, they were extremely difficult to dislodge. In this way pockets of heresy survived until the Reformation.[22]

However, Lollardy, to which never more than a minority was attracted even in its heyday, was sustained by only a tiny number in its later years. It was not the numbers of Lollards who were of significance, but the strength of their conviction and ability to survive, which ensured that the authorities remained alert to the threat. The Church took them seriously, knowing that, unlike the more individualistic expressions of scepticism or atheism which also came to its attention, they represented a fundamental threat, root and branch, to its existence. Persecution may have failed to eradicate heresy; but it successfully contained it. Most of the laity remained uncontaminated.

Chantries and cults

Lollards, one can suppose, were committedly Christian. But what of the rest? In the eyes of protestant reformers in the sixteenth century and generations of subsequent historians (the heirs of the Lollards), the benighted majority were credulously superstitious and in the grip of a morbid fear of death. As the age has been approached more sympathetically in the later twentieth century, so both these received notions have been challenged. The roles of relics and icons, the intercessionary powers of saints, and prayers for the dead are now perceived as integral elements of a widely-shared and positive religious conviction. Yet late-medieval lay spirituality remains in many respects elusive. While its distinctive characteristics are well documented, and the scale of lay participation in religious life apparent, the depth of commitment and motivation remains problematic.[23]

Of the difficulties facing the historian seeking to understand the religious temper of the age, the question of evidence is foremost. There survives considerably more, and in increasing quantity, both written and visual, concerning the religion of the laity. The growing quantity itself poses a problem since one cannot be sure whether it reveals intensifying devotion or merely provides fuller information about long-standing practices and beliefs. Wills, for instance, which have been much used in recent years, become far more numerous in the later fifteenth century. Is it safe to assume that the concerns of testators on the scale revealed for the end of the century are applicable to earlier, less well-documented generations? Printing too led to the publishing of the principal handbooks of spirituality in great number. This suggests the existence of a buoyant demand, but was the market, as well as the technology, new? Moreover, while it is possible to note that such books were published, it is not possible to be certain how widely they were read or how comprehended.

The character of the evidence, too, is deceptive. The greater part is financial; that is to say, as in the case of churchwardens' accounts or instructions to executors, it is concerned with expenditure and intended provision, not with the reasons for spending. It is not easy to tell whether it was a reflection of piety, a response to clerical advice, or conventional practice and social conformity.[24] Furthermore, the evidence is heavily slanted towards the more privileged and wealthier. Printed devotional works, although cheaper than even the most unadorned hand-copied texts, were still expensive and could only be afforded by men and women of substance. And while in some places the establishment of parochial lending libraries made these works more widely accessible, their access was restricted to the better-off and content open only to those who could read and understand them.[25] Will-makers were, by definition, those with goods to dispose and the means to make provision. The richer the testator, the more lavish the intended provision could be. But even at the more modest level of craftsmen and husbandmen, whose wills contain small donations to parish church or fraternity, the evidence still concerns those who were of standing in their local communities. The evidence rarely extends to the propertyless.

However, the ends for which money was spent are well documented: the rituals of death and the transition of the soul from this world to the next. It was important that men and women made a good death by receiving, in the proper frame of mind, final absolution and remission of their sins, for which a handbook, *The Book of the Craft of Dying*, was available. It was also vital that they had made provision for prayers to be said, in as great a number as possible, to ease and shorten the passage of their souls through the terrible pains of purgatory. The doctrine of purgatory was essentially a feature of the later middle ages. Originally the Church had held out little hope of redemption after death. Christians were faced with the prospect of eternal damnation if they had not done full penance before they died. Purgatory, albeit that its pains were stressed, offered the hope of atonement thereafter. Thus, although it was still necessary to receive final absolution and to make a good death, there was added the prospect that, through provision of prayers thereafter, it was still not too late for the soul to be fully purged of its sins. Far from the predestination believed in by Wycliffe and his followers, the orthodox view in the later middle ages extended the opportunities for salvation.[26]

The doctrine of purgatory thus stimulated significant expenditure on chantries, prayers and other good works after death as well as in life. The scale varied in proportion to wealth. Royal and very wealthy founders established collegiate chantries. The most famous was Edward III's foundation of St George's, Windsor, completed by Edward IV and Henry VII. Henry V's project to establish a monastic complex near his palace at Sheen, and Henry VI's twin foundations of Eton and King's College, though in different form, were similarly inspired. Lesser figures, such as the dukes of York at Fotheringhay, created smaller colleges. Others continued to patronise the monasteries of which their ancestors had been founders; some, including modest gentry families, turned parish churches into family mausolea. But most frequent was the establishment of a perpetual chantry attached to a cathedral or parish church.

All perpetual chantries required the diversion of significant resources. Since the continued endowment could not be guaranteed (as indeed events in Edward VI's reign were to prove), there was much to be said for enhancing existing foundations. An even less expensive option was to commission monks to sing prayers for a limited period, or to fund a trental (a set of thirty masses), months minds or annual obits for a term of years. Benefactions of schools, almshouses, the creation of *maisons dieu* and other provisions for the poor, if only by means of doles at the funeral, all had behind them the purpose of securing the prayers of the beneficiaries for the benefactor.[27] Prayers for the dead were not restricted to the lords and gentry who could afford individual provision, perpetual or temporary. At the parochial level fraternities and guilds provided the same service on a collective basis. Membership of guilds, commonly for an entrance fee of 6*s.* 8*d.* and subscription of 1*s. per annum* and restricted to men and women of good reputation, secured, among other things, the service of a chaplain who celebrated masses for the deceased members, past and future.[28]

Many guilds were dedicated to Corpus Christi. The feast of Corpus Christi, celebrated on the Thursday after Trinity Sunday, like the doctrine of purgatory, was a late-medieval development. At the heart of this cult lay the veneration of the Eucharist, the consecrated host, itself, as the actual body of Christ. While lay people did not themselves fully participate in the celebration of the mystery of the mass, observation of and identification with the central miracle (the transformation of the bread and wine into the body and blood of Christ) was itself one of the most important of the good works that could help secure salvation. Associated with Corpus Christi were two other cults which grew in popularity in the later middle ages. One was the mass of St Gregory and the devotion of the Five Wounds, based on the supposed vision of the Pope, who while celebrating mass saw Christ standing on his tomb displaying his wounds and the implements of the passion. The devotion of the Five Wounds was for the blood of Christ what Corpus Christi was for the body: the other half of the veneration of the mass. Indulgences could be earned by the carrying of images of the wounds or the implements. And closely related to both cults of Corpus Christi and the Five Wounds was that of the Holy Name of Jesus, promoted by Henry V, in which simply the name itself was venerated.[29]

The developments of Corpus Christi, the Five Wounds and the Name of Jesus are all aspects of the manner in which religious belief became more Christo-centric in the later middle ages; that salvation was to be found through the direct intercession of Christ. This is not to say that the general company of saints was demoted. Indeed the cult of the Virgin Mary also grew in importance, witnessing the development of the belief in her own immaculate conception and the related promotion of her mother St Anne. Mary, as the mother of Christ, grew in stature as did the entirely mythical St Catherine of Alexandria as the so-called bride of Christ. These saints and all the others were perceived as intermediaries, intercessors with Christ on behalf of those who adopted them. They were yet another channel through which both forgiveness of sins and protection could be sought. Many were popular because it was believed that they could intercede in the event of sudden death without benefit of the last rites. St Catherine would do so, so too would St Barbara and St Christopher. But they were also protectors against misfortune in life. St Margaret of Antioch assisted women in childbirth; St Agatha offered protection against breast cancer; St Edmund, an English equivalent to St Sebastian, protection from the plague. Guilds were formed in honour of saints, altars were dedicated to them, their images provided focuses of prayer. The relics of Christ and the saints, such as the Holy Blood of Hailes, were centres of pilgrimage, as were the burial places of others (St Thomas at Canterbury, or St Cuthbert at Durham, for instance) and sites at which the Virgin Mary had made an appearance, most notably Walsingham. All pilgrimages earned remission of sins, especially if a particularly arduous journey were undertaken, either to the shrine of St James at Santiago or, above all, to Jerusalem itself.[30]

Superstition and magic

It is hard to draw a line between veneration of the saints and superstition. There was much in the late medieval religion that was superstitious in the sense that worshippers believed that the saints, the Virgin Mary and indeed Christ himself possessed magical powers. Objects when venerated, even words when incanted, could work miracles and effect cures. It was the practice, for instance, after the paschal candle had been extinguished on Ascension Day, for the wax to be re-used, shaped into wafers, stamped with the image of the crucifiction (the lamb and flag), then blessed and sold as mementos of the passion and Corpus Christi. These were carried about the person and were believed to have certain magical protective powers, including for women a further protection against the dangers of childbirth. Many religious houses possessed holy girdles, much mocked during the dissolution of the monasteries, which local women could touch to secure further protection. An annual ritual such as the Rogation Day procession was closely linked to beneficial magic to make the earth fertile. There was widespread popular belief in the power of magic associated with holy places, wayside shrines, charms and spells, many, but not all of which, the Church approved.[31]

Some of the ramifications of this can be illustrated by reference to the Middleham Jewel, which, because it almost certainly belonged to an aristocratic lady, reveals that the superstitious dimension to late-medieval religion was not restricted to the poor and uneducated. The Jewel is a gold container for a paschal disc, made in the third quarter of the fifteenth century. It is engraved on both sides. On the side worn facing the body is a nativity, depicted as witnessed by St Bridget, and the badge of the lamb and flag. Around the rim are etched fifteen saints, including Sts Anne, Barbara, Catherine and Margaret. On the face presented to the world is set a large sapphire, the Trinity is depicted in the conventional Throne of God form, and etched around the rim are the words 'Ecce Agnus Dei qui tollis peccati mundi', 'Misere Nobis' and the words 'Tetragrammaton Ananizapta'. On one level the iconography reflects the main trends of the fifteenth century. The person for whom the jewel was made was familiar with the Visions of St Bridget, had her own intercessory saints, and had a particular veneration for the Virgin Mary and Corpus Christi. The sapphire had its own iconography; its colour blue was the symbol of purity, and by extension the Virgin Mary, but it was also believed to have medical properties, especially helping problems with the eyes, and was supposed to offer protection from treachery. Much more revealing are the cabalistic words Tetragrammaton and Ananizapta. The first means, literally four-letter word and stands for the name of God (Jveh) which cannot be spoken; the second is a magic incantation of Greek root carrying the meaning of recovering one's senses or being renewed, and in some texts associated with a 'cure' for epilepsy. It might be suggested that together they mean 'Arise in the name of God'. Taken with the other elements the jewel would seem to have a particular purpose to protect the wearer against sudden, unshriven death. But it was a multi-faceted talisman providing both through christian imagery and magical spells an all-embracing protection for body and soul in this world and the next.[32]

The same mixture of the devout and the credulous is revealed in the commonplace book of Robert Reynes (d.1474), churchwarden of Acle in Norfolk. The greater part of this book of miscellaneous jottings concerns his responsibilities as warden and his own selected devotional passages. They include: a verse life of Saint Anne, a selection of instructional and moralistic material on the sacraments, the ten commandments and the works of mercy; a legend associated with the devotion of St Bridget; a devotion on the drops of Christ's blood, and an apocryphal Papal indulgence for those who carried nails of the length used at the crucifixion and worshipped them daily with five Pater Nosters, five Aves and a psalm (both linked to the devotion of the Five Wounds); and invocations against fever and toothache, astrological prognostications, and a formula for conjuring angels.[33]

Conjuring of spirits, even angels, was not entirely to the Church's liking. Throughout the middle ages it had difficulty in drawing the line between beneficent and malignant magic. At one extreme was the miracle of the mass which lay at the centre of its rituals; at the other lay sorcery and the conjuring of devils. The Devil was believed to be working incessantly to subvert Christians. Indeed this belief strengthened during the century. While witch persecution was still a thing of the future, the *Malleus Mallificarum* of 1480 spelt out the manner in which the Devil operated. The incantation of virtuous names and prayers, often of an extremely cryptic kind, were deployed for protection against the enemy of mankind. The Holy Name of Jesus itself was one such incantation. Magic was integral to belief.

The Church was less sure of the occult sciences. During the fourteenth century astrology had been developed, especially by a succession of scholars at Merton College, into a highly refined technical skill. Astrology, which might be defined as applied astronomy, explained the nature of the world and the universe. The belief that the heavenly bodies exerted a predictable influence on earthly matter was elaborated into a complex mathematical model which was used to explain and predict not only natural events, including the workings of the human body, but also human behaviour and political happenings. Academic astrologers, who set themselves up as expert advisers and forecasters to rulers, were intially kept at arm's length in England, especially by the royal court where there tended to be considerable scepticism. Astrologers who dabbled in high politics, especially those who advised Eleanour Cobham in 1442, also gave their science a bad name. Indeed they were condemned, wrongly, as sorcerers. But notwithstanding official disapproval, astrology, simplified in almanacs and expounded in English, began to find a wide audience, especially for its medical applications. Alchemy, the art of turning base metal into gold, was, however, forbidden, not so much because the process was magical, but because if successful it would have undermined political control and because many rogues used the cover of alchemy for counterfeiting. Nevertheless there was a lingering belief in the possibility of it working; and in 1456 a group of alchemists successfully petitioned Henry VI to allow them to practice, not only in the vain hope that they might rescue the kingdom from its bankruptcy, but also because it was believed that there would be a beneficial medical spin-off for the ailing king.[34]

All the occult sciences were detailed in the widely owned *Secretum Secretorum*, a compilation reputed to be Aristotelian in origin, which was both an advice book for princes and an introduction to secret knowledge of a magical kind. Belief in magic and the occult was widespread because there was so little human control over the natural world, particularly over physical health. In such circumstances it is not surprising that magical explanations and protections were sought. Christianity was part of this wider culture. Contemporaries themselves had doubts about some of its magical practices; indeed by the early sixteenth century christian humanists like Erasmus poured scorn on the more implausible elements. It is not surprising, therefore, that to the modern mind much of the outward show of late medieval religion appears superficial, superstitious and credulous.

Lay piety

While the forms of outward show are apparent, far more difficult to gauge is the depth of inner conviction. However, many of the new cults of the later middle ages, and the whole doctrine of purgatory, developed hand in hand with, and indeed tended to depend on, a new level of direct lay participation and understanding. Stemming, it has been argued, from the pastoral reforms of Archbishop John Thoresby of York (1352–73) and drawing upon the example of hermits and recluses in his diocese, and especially the teachings of Richard Rolle of Hampole (d.1349) and Walter Hilton (d.1396) a programme of personal devotion was promoted. Rolle's *Meditations on the Passion* and Hilton's *Scale of Perfection* and *Epistle on Mixed Life* became widely circulated as did the parallel texts of the anonymous *Cloud of Unknowing* and the translation in 1410 by Nicholas Love, prior of Mountgrace Priory, of Bonaventura's *Meditatione de Vitae Christi* into *The Mirror of the Blessed Lyfe of Christ*. These works all advocated and offered guidance on contemplation, especially on the passion of Christ and the miracle of the mass, so as to induce a mystical state in which the Christian could reach a state of detachment, inner peace and oneness with God. The contemplative experience of the hermit and anchorite was made available to others.

Initially composed for the use of the religious, this body of mystical literature was taken up and adapted for use by the laity because of the patronage of certain influential nobles and gentry, because Thoresby and his followers made it the centrepiece of their programme of Christian renewal, and because it offered an orthodox alternative to Lollardy. The principal lay sponsors, such as Henry, Lord FitzHugh of Ravensworth, and Henry, Lord Scrope of Masham, were also sponsors of the new religious orders – the Carthusians and the Bridgettines – which were also inspired by the same eremetic ideals. But the crucial development was the promotion by the clergy of the idea that such mysticism, in moderation, could and should be practised by the laity. Thus was evolved the concept of the mixed life – combining the active and the contemplative – whose most famous practitioner was to be Sir Thomas More. The laity were encouraged through their own devotions, through their own prayer, and their own contemplation on the passion of Christ, to develop their own inner religious life which was entirely compatible with the busy life of their wordly affairs. To the modern mind such personal religion perhaps seems unexceptional; but in the later middle ages it was a novel departure for a society which had tended to leave religious experience and devotion strictly to the clergy.[35]

What happened in England, developing especially in the diocese of York, was not unique. Franciscan influences, especially via the writings of Bonaventure, were strong. In the Netherlands the *Devotio Moderna*, which produced the most renowned of the contemplative texts, Thomas à Kempis's *Imitation of Christ*, fulfilled the same need. But it developed a distinct English identity. Its practice among the gentry and peerage is well attested. Many English nobles and even gentry acquired copies of the principal devotional guides. Roger Thornton of East Newton (Yorks) copied Hilton's *Epistle* into his commonplace book for his own personal use. Prominent women, notably the two mothers of kings, Cecily Neville, Duchess of York and Margaret Beaufort, Countess of Richmond, became exemplars of the practice, Margaret herself sponsoring the first translation into English of *The Imitation of Christ*.[36]

Linked to personal piety was the use of Books of Hours, each a collection of prayers, psalms and the offices of the day, centred on the Mass of Our Lady. For the wealthy lavishly illustrated, these were the principal focus of personal devotion and contemplation, often in a specially created oratory. The trend towards personal devotion and more private religion can be seen also in the greater use of household chapels, in the practice of giving licence for masses to be celebrated in the seclusion of oratories in times of illness or bereavement, in the acquisition of the privilege of participating in mass in the chancel rather than hearing it from the nave and, after death, in being buried there; and, of course, in the establishment of chantry chapels.[37]

But the mixed life was not restricted to the upper classes. All the laity were encouraged to know and understand their religion. To this end, clergy were exhorted to ensure that their parishioners were familiar with the basic liturgy and at least knew the Creed, the Pater Noster, the Ave Maria and, in time, the Ten Commandments. While tighter controls had been placed on preaching in response to the Lollard threat, the parochial clergy were encouraged to instruct the faithful through sermons. The parish priest was provided with texts of sermons, especially copies of John Mirk's *Festial*, which was composed possibly as early as 1380 to counter Wycliffe's teachings. Basic points of doctrine were elaborated in wall and glass painting, especially in the great doom painting that was usually created above the rood screen, and in plays such as the York Pater Noster Play, performed by a guild for the instruction of the laity. Printing seems to have advanced this process further at the end of the century. Parochial lending libraries were soon established in many places to make the more complex, and more expensive, works of devotional literature available to parishioners who would not themselves have been able to afford their own copies. New works such as the *Kalender of Shepherdes*, translated from the French, were printed and circulated to aid the instruction of simple men. Parishioners were expected to understand, to reflect on, and to interiorise the meaning of the rituals which they witnessed and in which they participated.[38]

Lay participation

One might question the sophistication of doctrinal understanding and depth of spiritual engagement achieved by most parishioners, but there can be no doubt that they were fully involved in the organisation and management of parochial affairs. Responsibility for the maintenance of the fabric of the parish church, excluding the chancel, and for the provision and maintenance of service books, vestments, altarpieces and other ornaments and utensils lay collectively with the parishioners. Income was usually available, either from property (purchased or donated), or from livestock kept by the parish. But rarely was this enough. The coffers were replenished by a stream of donations and bequests; there were regular annual collections, associated with the ritual activities of the year such as Plough Monday, Hock Tide, Rogation and Corpus Christi. For exceptional fund-raising needs entertainments and Church Ales, the progenitor of the Church fete, were also held, and in some parishes a Church house built in which to hold them. To manage the accounts and to be responsible for the raising and spending of money churchwardens were appointed, assisted in large parishes by assistant keepers, responsible for lights and altars, a sexton, summoner, and organ-keeper.

While guilds were separate voluntary bodies from the parish, relationships between the two were close. The parish church housed the guild altars and chapels; leading parishioners, from whose ranks churchwardens and keepers were drawn (and frequently the incumbent), were themselves members of the guilds; and many guilds played a key part in raising parochial funds. The line between guild and parish is sometimes difficult to discern, especially in the West Country where it was customary for clubs to be formed based on peer groups, occupations or activities, such as the Young Men, Maidens, Weavers, and Archers at Croscombe in Somerset, which maintained their own lights and undertook their own fund-raising activities.

Perhaps the most striking aspect of fifteenth-century parochial activity is the extent to which it extended beyond the necessary. The stream of bequests, from the humble as well as wealthy parishioner, ensured that many churches had substantial collections of plate, vestments and books. But more visible is the constant improvement and addition to the fabric and furnishing of the building. Nearly one half of the churches of England were substantially rebuilt or extended in the perpendicular style in the later middle ages, especially in the later fifteenth century and early sixteenth century by the raising of bell-towers (notably in East Anglia and the West Country), which often involved considerable local effort and dedicated fund-raising. But it was not only towers and their bells that were added; in the same period great rood screens were erected, new organs provided, pulpits and lecterns installed and pews fitted. The perception of a medieval parish church at the end of the twentieth century is essentially that of the building created during the fifteenth.[39]

The impressive evidence of the active involvement of parishioners in the adornment and enlargement of their churches, and their willingness to pay heavily for it, suggests a genuine religious commitment. Yet we should not necessarily conclude that this was a golden age of popular Christianity in England. We know how the laity were expected to respond, but not that they did. Complaint continued that parishioners did not attend mass as frequently as they should; now also because men would sooner resort to the new ale-house. If not drinking, they would be trading: in 1449 a statute was enacted banning fairs on Sundays and feast days. When at church men and women gossipped, or joked, or conducted business. And are we to believe that every parishioner attended the Church Ale because he or she was fired by zeal for a new rood screen, or felt a deep obligation to contribute to rebuilding the tower? The growing perception of a need to preach, and the continuing demand from the clergy for printed instructional works and aids to catechism to the end of the century and beyond, suggest that the ploughman had still not learnt his Pater Noster.[40]

In particular one wonders how far down the social scale religious zeal penetrated. The evidence identifies those who were to some extent literate and had surplus disposable incomes. Churchwardens and keepers, unpaid but carrying great responsibility, were drawn from the local elites, who were jurors, manorial or borough office-holders, and tax collectors. Only men and women of good repute who could afford the admission fee and the annual subscription were members of the parish guilds. They are, once more, the representatives of the middling sort. But what of the poor and needy who materialised in significant numbers to receive doles at funerals;

or those at Pott Shigley in Cheshire who, after 1495 under the terms of the bequest of the wealthy Geoffrey Downes of London, could have the loan of a cow in return for their prayers for his soul; or those who in their old age accepted places in almshouses and *maisons dieu*, a gown and pin money in exchange for daily attendance at requiem masses and the reciting of prayers for their founder's soul? Were they truly grateful, to both God and benefactor, for what they had received?[41]

Since religion is a social activity as well as a spiritual experience, there was a significant element of secular motivation involved in the manifestation of lay piety in the later middle ages. Convention and conformity were powerful motivators. One cannot always tell, at this distance, and through the formal language of wardens' accounts, Wills and conveyances, whether an act was the expression of deep piety, or the doing of the done thing, or keeping up with one's neighbours. To be a warden, to be seen to be a benefactor, to be a patron of the Church, to possess the full panoply of a private chapel were other means by which wordly status, worship and honour could be displayed.[42]

It has been suggested that during the fifteenth century the upper classes began to distance themselves from the communities of their parishes, either in their private chapels, or in personal pews, or by sitting in the chancel. The privilege of possessing copies of the bible in English, suitably approved by the bishop, was restricted to the better sort. It was to such men of wealth and standing, too, that the concept of the mixed life was specifically addressed. Walter Hilton in the *Epistle* recommended that the mixed life should be restricted 'to *some* secular *men* who have authority with *considerable* ownership of wordly goods and who also have a lordship of other men to govern and sustain them'. Moreover, well-informed and opinionated patrons and founders tended to assert financial, moral and even spiritual control, not only over those who were the beneficiaries of their charity, but also over the clergy who were employed by them to execute it. It is possible that the elaborate celebration of Corpus Christi in towns was fostered by urban oligarchs not only to hold the urban communities together but also to reinforce their own control. Similarly guilds and fraternities functioned to display the exclusiveness of their members and to define communal identities in their own reflection. Religious practices gave expression to social distinctions and attitudes.[43]

There was too a gender as well as a class dimension to late-medieval religious practices. It has often been supposed that the particular form of late-medieval contemplative piety was more feminine. The two most celebrated English mystics of the fifteenth century, whose writings have been used most frequently to define the spirit of the age, were women: Margery Kempe and Julian of Norwich. Margery, however, whose public weepings and disturbances made the authorites jittery, fitted uneasily in the English preference for respectable, understated, interiorised religious devotion. Her fame, like that of Julian whose orthodoxy was also at one time doubted, rests upon the fact that she was exceptional and not typical. Men felt far safer with the piety of upper-class widows, not just the famous aristocrats such as Cecily Neville, Margaret Beaufort or Margaret Hungerford, but also of countless others of all ranks who took vows of chastity. The *Abbey of Holy Grace*, with its specific feminine imagery and analogy, addressed propertied women of all ranks, who wished to practice the contemplative life and follow the well-promoted models of aristocratic widows as paragons of proper female behaviour. The role of devout Christian, in the pattern of the silent and submissive Virgin Mary, distanced widows from the exercise of family power which their status potentially gave them.[44]

The religion of late-medieval men and women is thus elusive and ambivalent. But the characteristics of the christianity they were expected to practise, and many did, are clear. It was Christo-centric, focused on the miracle of the Eucharist and the passion of Christ; it was superstitious and credulous; it encouraged personal commitment and understanding; it demanded practical participation; and it allowed a more interiorised devotion. By empowering personal lay participation, it blurred the distinction between clergy and laity. It was for the most part a restrained, undemonstrative religion. It was, perhaps, complacent. And it was the religion of the privileged and propertied who were expected to set a good example.

Above all it was an English religion.[45] Orthodox christianity became in the fifteenth century widely and directly accessible to the English people through the vernacular. The common characteristic of the late-medieval devotional literature was that it was in English, whether as translation of the French or Latin, or as new composition. Sermons were preached in English; prayers were recited in English; the catechism was conducted in English. It was in the fifteenth century that the Pater Noster became the Lord's Prayer. The introduction of printing, and its commercial exploitation by Caxton and his successors, confirmed that there was a significant demand for devotional and instructional works in English, both for the laity to use in their private meditation and for the clergy to use in their pastoral duties. To some extent the Church responded to the Lollard challenge for a religion more accessible to the laity. The use of the vernacular, the expanded involvement of prominent parishioners in its affairs, integration into the fabric of state and society and the greater subordination to the Crown, had made the Church more English at the end of the fifteenth century than it had been at its beginning. By the early sixteenth century the *Ecclesia Anglicana* had become more discernably a Church *of* England as well as the Church *in* England.

Notes and references

1   See Further Reading for recent studies of the late medieval Church.

2   See Further Reading and, for Henry V and Beaufort, Harriss, *Cardinal Beaufort*, 91–114.

3   Swanson, *Church and Society*, 30–9; Davies, 'Episcopate', passim and 'Wars of the Roses', 138–40. For individual bishops see Storey, *Thomas Langley*; Harriss, *Cardinal Beaufort*; Davis, *William Waynflete*.

4   Swanson, *Church and Society*, 89–139, 149–521, 82–90; Harper-Bill, *Pre-Reformation Church*, 30–2; Kaufman, 'Henry VII and Sancturary', passim.

5   Heath, 'Between Reform and Reformation', passim. The more glowing modern assessments are to be found in Duffy, *Stripping of the Altars*; Harper-Bill, *Pre-Reformation Church* and 'English Religion', passim; and Rosser, 'Communities of Parish and Guild', passim.

6   Swanson, *Church and Society*, 1–6, 16–26; Kettle 'City and Close', passim; Dobson, 'Cathedral Chapters', passim. See also Further Reading.

7   Swanson, *Church and Society*, 53 (Lee); Emden, *Oxford*, 1609–11 (Russell): Dobson, 'Richard Bell', 209–11.

8   Swanson, *Church and Society*, 46–50, 60, 66, 78–9; Heath, *English Parish Clergy*, passim; Dobson, 'Later Middle Ages', passim and 'Residentiary Canons', passim; Storey, *Diocesan Administration*.

9   Swanson, *Church and Society*, 40–81.

10 See Further Reading for recent work on recruitment and education.

11 Swanson, *Church and Society*, 60–2; Heath, *English Parish Clergy*, 104–8.

12 See above n. 3 and Pollard, 'Crown and County Palatine', 67–88.

13 Catto, 'Religious Change', 109–11 (Syon), *EHD*, iv, 769–801 and Gasquet, *Collectanea Anglo-Premonstratensia* (visitation records). For the religious orders in general see Further Reading.

14 Barnum, *Dives and Pauper*; Pronger, 'Thomas Gascoigne', passim; Gascoigne, *Loci et Libro Veritatem*, 29–30; Harper-Bill, 'Dean Colet's Convocation Sermon'. For Peacock see Swanson, *Church and Society*, 323–5 and Catto, 'Fall of Peacock', passim.

15 For the modern debate over anti-clericalism on the eve of the Reformation see Haigh, 'Anti-Clericalism' and Dickens, 'Shaping of Anticlericalism'. See also Swanson, *Church and Society*, 189–90, 259–60; Harper-Bill, *Pre-Reformation Church*, 77–8. For bequests to friaries see Goldthorpe, 'Franciscans and Dominicans in Yorkshire'.

16 For the context of late-fourteenth-century heresy see Harper-Bill, 'English Religion', passim.

17 Leff, *Heresy*, ii, 494–558; Hudson, *Premature Reformation*, 278–13; and Wilks, 'Predestination, Poverty and Power', passim.

18 Hudson, *Premature Reformation*, passim and *Lollards and their Books*; Goodman, *John of Gaunt*, 241–4, 265; McFarlane, *John Wycliffe*, passim, and *Lancastrian Kings and Lollard Knights*, 137–226; Aston and Richmond, *Lollardy and the Gentry*, esp introduction, and chs 1, 5, 6 and 7; McNiven, *Heresy and Politics*, passim.

19 Aston, 'Lollardy and Sedition', 1–44; Catto, 'Religious Change', 98–102, 111–15; and Powell, 'Restoration of Law and Order', 61–3; McNiven, *Heresy and Politics*, passim.

20 Thomson, *Later Lollards*, passim; Hudson, *Premature Reformation*, 446–507.

21 For later trials see Tanner, *Heresy Trials*, *Kent Heresy Proceedings* and 'Kentish Lollards', passim.

22 Davies, 'Lollardy and Locality', passim; Hudson, *Premature Reformation*, 446–507; Davis, 'Lollard Survival', passim, and *Heresy and Reformation*; Plumb, 'Rural Lollardy', passim; Lutton, 'Lollards, Townsfolk and Gentry', passim; and Hope, 'Lady and the Bailiff', passim.

23 The theme of death is explored in Binsky, *Medieval Death*; and Aston, 'Death', passim.

24 See Further Reading for Wills and their use.

25 *EHD*, iv, 835–6, 496–7; Barron, 'Expansion of Education', 239–43.

26 Bossy, *Christianity in the West*, 30–144; Burgess, 'Vain Thing Vainly Invented', passim; Duffy, *Stripping of the Altars*, 338–48.

27 See above n. 25 and Further Reading.

28 Bainbridge, *Gilds in the Medieval Countryside*; Barron, 'Parish Fraternities', passim; Rosser, 'Communities of Parish and Guild', passim; Scarisbrick, *Reformation and the English People*, ch 1.

29 Rubin, 'Corpus Christi Fraternities', passim, and *Corpus Christi*, passim; Duffy, *Stripping of the Altars*, 43–4.

30 Duffy, *Stripping of the Altars*, 113–16, 155–205, 238–56; Finacune, *Miracles and Pilgrims*; and for the continuing vitality of pilgrimage up to the Reformation, Bernard, 'Vitality and Vulnerability', 201–18. The Holy Blood of Hailes, as also the Rood of Grace at Boxley Abbey (Kent) which miraculously moved, were shown to be hoaxes in 1538 (ibid., 227–8).

31 Duffy, *Stripping of the Altars*, 266–98; Bernard, 'Vitality and Vulnerability', 219–30.

32 Cherry, *Middleham Jewel and Ring*, 16–31.

33 Linnell, 'Commonplace Book of Robert Reynes', 111–27; Duffy, *Stripping of the Altars*, 71–3; Harper-Bill, *Pre-Reformation Church*, 89.

34 Carey, *Courting Disaster*, chs 7–9; Kieckhefer, *Magic in the Middle Ages*, 120–39, 151–75; Gross, *Lancastrian Kingship*, 18–25. For the importance of astrology in the practice of medicine see Rawcliffe, *Medicine and Society*, 82–103 and Jones, 'Information and Science', passim.

35 Swanson, *Catholic England*, 8–24, 96–149; Hughes, *Pastors and Visionaries*, 64–297 passim; Carey, 'Devout Literate Laypeople', passim; Lovatt, 'Imitation of Christ', passim. Hughes stresses the influence of the Thoresby circle; Swanson and Harper-Bill ('English Religion'), following Lovatt, see a more general diffusion of ideas into England from continental influences.

36 Armstrong, 'Piety of Cecily, Duchess of York'; Jones and Underwood, *King's Mother*, 180–201, esp. 184–5 and 197–8.

37 Pollard, *North-Eastern England*, 182–8; Backhouse, *Books of Hours*; and Harthan, *Books of Hours*, 11–41; Duffy, *Stripping of the Altars*, 210–22, 26–65.

38 Duffy, *Stripping of the Altars*, 53–87, 81–5, 131–54.

39 See Further Reading for references to recent works on parochial lay participation.

40 Bossy, *Christianity in the West*, 66–70. Two years after the 1449 act men from Cowpen Bewley in Country Durham were brought before an ecclesiastical court for attending Ripon Market on Sundays in Lent (Pollard, *North-Eastern England*, 12).

41 See the sceptical comments of Richmond, 'Religion and the English Gentleman', passim and also Rubin, 'The Poor', passim; Pollard, *North-Eastern England*, 175–82. For the growth of lay involvement see Swanson, *Church and Society*, 255–60.

42 Pollard, *North Eastern England*, 175–82.

43 Richmond, 'Religion and the English Gentleman', 198–9 and 'English Gentry and Religion', 121–6, 138–40, 143–50, esp. 121–6 for the elaborate instructions left by Geofrey Downes for his chapel at Pott Shrigley, Cheshire, which included the establishment of a herd of 100 cows to be let to the poor of the village, the only payment being their prayers; cf. the strict code of behaviour laid down for both the poor recipients of his benefaction and the conduct of the warden by the regulations drawn up for Hosyer's Charity in Ludlow in 1486 (Swanson, *Catholic England*, 234–41), as well as the tight control Thomas, Lord Burgh, sought to exert over the chantry and hospital he wished to establish by the terms of his Will in 1496 (Richmond, 'Religion', 198–200). See also Swanson, *Catholic England*, 108 (Hilton); McCree, 'Religious Guilds', passim; Rosser, 'At the Faternity Feast'; and James, 'Ritual, Drama and Social Body', passim.

44   Richmond, 'English Gentry and Religion', 140–2; Meech and Allen, *The Booke of Marjory Kempe*, Hirsh, *The Revelation of Margery Kempe*; Beckwith, *Christ's Body*, esp. ch. 4 and Goodman, 'Piety of John Brunham's Daughter' (Margery Kempe); Cullum, 'Vowesses and Female Piety', passim and 'Charitable Giving', passim; Swanson, *Catholic England*, 96–104 (Holy Grace); Jones and Underwood, *The King's Mother*, 1–8, 193–201, 238–9; Hicks, 'Piety of Margaret Hungerford (d.1478)'; see also Riddy, 'Women Talking', passim, and for the role of women in Lollardy, McSheffrey, *Gender and Heresy*.

45   For Wales see Williams, *Welsh Church* and *Wales and the Reformation*, esp. chs 1 and 2, and the comment that 'it is difficult to escape the conclusion that most of them [the Welsh] were no more than superficially christianised' (27). The first book in Welsh, a primer, was not published until 1546 (34). For Ireland see Watt, *Church in Medieval Ireland* and for the distinctive religion of the borders with Scotland see Goodman, 'Religion and Warfare', passim.

CHAPTER NINE

Government and politics

Monarchy

One important role of the Church in public affairs was to sanctify the authority of the monarch by the ritual of coronation. During the fifteenth century the importance of such validation increased in proportion to the uncertainty of the claim to the throne of the individual monarch. Henry IV was the first to be anointed by the holy oil of St Thomas Becket, which had been 'discovered' by Edward II in 1318, and rediscovered by Richard II shortly before his deposition. Changes in the order of the ceremony for the coronation of Henry VI in 1429, which gave greater prominence to the presentation of the new king by the clergy over his 'election' by the people, enhanced the theocratic nature of the office. Edward IV added the lauds of majesty to the ceremony to the same end. The ritual of coronation as it was shaped during the fifteenth century removed all doubt that the king was the Lord's anointed, presented on behalf of God by his priests, to rule over his subjects. Although the king of England was not, as was the king of France, ordained a priest by coronation, he nevertheless acquired a quasi-sacred status set apart from and above his subjects. He was, thereby, invested with unlimited power, answerable only to God; his subjects were bound not only by the laws of the land, but also by their duty as Christians to obey him.[1]

Yet the coronation also imposed obligations towards his subjects on the king. By his solemn coronation oath he bound himself to defend the realm, to administer justice and to preserve the well-being of all his subjects. Moreover, as all the advice books for rulers reiterated, the king was expected to take advice before he exercised his God-given authority. There thus existed an underlying ambiguity. The monarch was both given to the people by God to rule by divine right and at the same time he entered, implicitly, into a contract with them to perform certain duties on their behalf and to do so with their assent. In theory, and usually in practice, there was no conflict, if the king was perceived as ruling of his free will for the common good and in accordance with the wishes of his subjects. But what were subjects to do if the king ruled unjustly and solely for his own ends without concern for their good, or, at the other extreme, neglected his obligations entirely? Could they force the king to rule for their good? Could they impose counsel on him? Could they depose him if he refused? These were fundamental issues which exercised political thinkers throughout the middle ages. The answer given by theocratic theorists was that resistance was wrong. Since the king was answerable in the last resort to God, God alone could punish him. It was the duty of subjects to show fortitude and to await God's judgement. Yet, in England subjects did rebel; subjects did seek to impose their counsel on their king in the name of the common good; and they did depose their kings. Henry IV justified the deposition of Richard II on the grounds of his tyranny; the deposition of Henry VI was justified on the double grounds of his illegitimacy – as the descendant of Henry IV who had usurped the throne – and his negligence. In practice, an English king could be removed by his subjects.[2]

The English monarchy was described by Sir Thomas Fortescue, the most celebrated constitutional commentator of the fifteenth century, as a mixed monarchy, combining in itself both *dominium regale* and *dominium politicum*. This meant both unrestrained rule and rule bound by political practicalities, rendered in modern terms as both absolute and limited. Fortescue's commentary stressed that it was both. Herein lies the source of debate about the nature of the English constitution in the later middle ages. Fortescue was a polemicist and career politician, not a political philosopher, who wrote his treatises (*The Governance of England* and *De Laudibus Legem Anglie*) to instruct a prince of Wales in exile in the 1460s. They contain both his description of the English constitution and his advice to the prince as to how he should govern once he becomes king. They are the product of specific political circumstances. His analysis and advice are moreover those of a common lawyer, imbued with the procedures of the law, the process of parliament and the centrality of statute.[3]

Recent commentators have been at pains to stress that his perception of a mixed monarchy was not a prescription for constitutional limitations, or for anything less than total sovereignty. He was, it is argued, merely reflecting received ideas from the Mirror of Princes genre on the need for the king to seek counsel and abide by the procedures of the law. To rule politically was to rule wisely; but there were no legitimate restrictions to kingship. The kingdom was part of the king; the king was the head of the body politic which was the kingdom. Without the head there was no living body. Thus the *dominium politicum et regale* was 'the ploy of a clever and well educated lawyer rather than the ideal of a believer in constitututional checks and balances'.[4]

It is, however, possible that Fortescue's perception was also shaped by his experience as a servant of the Lancastrian monarchy. The formulation of a mixed monarchy encompassses an inherited view of the constitution which shaped Henry IV's thinking and had guided the opponents to Richard II. The concept of *dominium politicum* harks back to the conflicts of the late-fourteenth century, continued into early Lancastrian practice, that monarchs should not change the law at will, or tax without assent. It stood then in opposition to Richard II's pereption of *dominium regale* alone. Arguably Fortescue's formulation has a specific historical context, as a merging of two conflicting perceptions of kingship in late medieval England, one which stressed the absolute unrestrained authority of the king, the other the exist-ence of legitimate checks. One emphasised the indivisibility of the king and the kingdom; the other recognised a distinction between king and subjects.[5]

The powers of the Crown, the proper balance between regality and limitation, were matters of uncertainty and change in late-medieval England. Controversy arose, for instance, in the context of Richard of York's challenge to Henry VI. York claimed that the king, led astray by evil counsellors, having failed to defend the kingdom and to administer justice, and having neglected the common good, could be forced to change his ways; that, in short, imposing counsel on the king was justified by the fact that the king was negligent in carrying out his coronation oath. The crown retaliated in 1459 in the *Somnium Vigilantis* that nothing justified rebellion, not even the claim that it was in the interest of the common good; only through absolute obedience to the king could the common weal be served. The effectiveness of this argument, it is suggested, led York to abandon his stance as the leader of the king's loyal opposition in favour of his claim to be the legitimate king himself. The fact that Edward IV made good this claim to the throne, and thus adopted the same royalist view, might have had a bearing on future perceptions that the common weal was best served by a strong monarchy. This same outlook lay behind the statement of Bishop Russell in 1483 that God had ordained who should be king and that the body politic must needs accept His ordination. It was encapsulated by Edmund Dudley in 1509, who stated in his *Tree of Commonwealth* that God had made the prince for His service and the weal of His people; that the prince was to protect the people and they were to obey the prince. In this way, during the later decades of the century, the perception of the status and power of the monarchy seems to have shifted back towards the concept of *dominium regale*.[6]

For the most part, however, fifteenth-century English men did not debate the fine points of the constitution. Far more important for their daily lives than the theoretical nature of the English monarchy was the impact of the king's power in practice. There are two dimensions to this. One lies in the institutions and conventions of government which had evolved, some to give expression to royal power, others to curtail it; the other lies in the severe restrictions placed upon the actual exercise of royal power by the social and political structure of late-medieval England.

Government

By 1399 England was the most uniformly governed kingdom in Europe. Greatly assisted by the compact size of the kingdom and the absence of great feudal liberties, earlier kings had established an administrative machine at Westminster whose tentacles reached out to every corner of the realm. There were three permanant departments of state (Chancery, Privy Seal and Exchequer) together employing some 250 staff clustered in and around the royal palace. Chancery, under the Chancellor, was the principal executive office, from which flowed a stream of royal letters and commands to other departments and officials, to royal officials throughout the kingdom and to subjects, all under the authorisation of the Great Seal of the kingdom. Chancery was supported by the office of the Privy Seal, which had migrated a hundred years earlier from the royal household itself, which acted as a conduit for orders and commands from the king and his council to the Chancellor, but also on occasion giving direct orders itself.

The Exchequer, under the Treasurer, divided into two offices, the upper exchequer of account and the lower exchequer of receipt and issue, was the central financial office of the kingdom. It collected the king's revenues from lands, feudal dues, customs and taxation and spent them on his behalf, or supplied other spending departments. The Wardrobe, which like the Privy Seal had once been part of the royal household, had become the principal war office. In practice the Exchequer did not actually collect all its revenues. It had evolved a system of assignment, whereby royal creditors were given tallies to find settlement at source from a sheriff, customs officer or tax collector; a system which could become particularly complex if the same revenue at source was committed to more than one recipient.[7]

All these offices had evolved elaborate procedures and bureaucracies. In the Exchequer, complex systems had been developed to check and double check the books. Both Chancery and Exchequer kept full and meticulous records in great rolls. The personnel were clerical, but by the fifteenth century laymen were beginning to invade the civil service, as it would now be styled. While the Chancellor was usually a cleric, the first lay Treasurer was appointed by Edward III, and from the reign of Henry IV it became usual for the Treasurer to be a layman. Clerical or lay, the chief offices were political appointments; and it is to be doubted that they played much part in the routine of their work. By 1399 both offices had become slow and cumbersome bureaucracies and their staff jealously guarded their jobs and working practices. Because a peripatetic king, often far distant from Westminster, frequently needed to send out orders quickly and to collect and spend money rapidly, royal government could never be conducted entirely from Westminster. The king's secretary, constantly in his company, and using his signet as his authority, sent orders directly to his subjects as well as his officers in Westminster; the financial officers of the chamber of his household did not rely solely on subventions from the Exchequer, but could and did collect money directly.

The resort to systematic household government by Edward II and Richard II, frustrated by their bureaucracies and the attempts to restrict their freedom of action through control of the offices of state, had led to conflict. In the late 1450s, in response to political crisis, Margaret of Anjou once again endeavoured to govern the kingdom through the household. Edward IV, as the leader of the victorious faction in 1461, followed the same path. Subsequently under the Yorkists and Henry VII the role of the household in government, based on the signet and the chamber, became dominant over the Chancery and Exchequer. In the later fifteenth century, however, this was no longer controversial and was accepted as an expedient and necessary response to crisis. Yet the chamber later became subservient once more to a reformed Exchequer in the mid-sixteenth century, while the office of secretary (controlling the signet) eventually followed the Privy Seal into becoming a department of state. The structure of government in late-medieval England was flexible, changing in response to political circumstances and to the tensions between a cumbersome bureaucracy and the need for a flexible executive.[8]

These conditions are reflected in the role of the king's council. Whereas the routine administration of the kingdom through the great departments of state is well-documented, the role of the council, which did not normally keep regular minutes, is less clear. That all kings employed a standing, or as it was later styled, privy council, is without doubt. The council comprised the chief officers of state – the Chancellor, Treasurer and Keeper of the Privy Seal, senior clerics, great noblemen and close associates of the king. It normally met in Westminster, under the presidency of the Chancellor except when the king attended. The council co-ordinated the government of the kingdom on the king's behalf. It advised the king, made some decisions as delegated to it, implemented others made by the king personally, and supervised routine conduct of legal and fiscal administration. It was always more than an executive body. Thus when a king was unfit or under age, the council was charged with collective responsibility in the king's name, most notably during the minority of Henry VI; but even under a fit and authoritative king such as Henry V or Edward IV the council took initiatives. Henry VII attended council more frequently than his predecessors, often taking it as the council attendant on his travels. Under him, too, began the practice of establishing permanent sub-committees, the board of surveyors of Crown lands and the council learned, to oversee chamber finance and the exploitation of feudal rights respectively. In addition Edward IV and Richard III established regional councils – in Wales and the north – which were charged, initially under the colour of being the councils of the heir to the throne, with the supervision of government in those parts. Conciliar government was elaborated and extended towards the end of the fifteenth century, but the essential functions remained unchanged.

Kings seeking advice on great matters of state, especially in times of crisis, sometimes called Great Councils. These comprised all the peers of the realm and nominated representatives from the shires. Their role was entirely consultative, but they could be used, as they were in the first and last years of the Lancastrian regime, to rally support and give weight to potentially divisive decisions. They lapsed under the Yorkists and, although revived by Henry VII, by mid-sixteenth century they were a thing of the past.[9]

Great Councils were a half-way house between the standing council and parliament, which was also a consultative assembly. Parliament, fully established by 1399, was a representative assembly of the realm with established powers, precedents and procedures. It consisted of two houses of the lords, in which approximately 60 peers and 45 bishops and senior abbots assembled by summons, and of the commons, in which 74 representatives of the shires and approximately 180 representatives of the boroughs were elected to attend. By the end of the fourteenth century it was established that the lower clergy were not represented in the commons. They met separately in the lower house of the two convocations, and voted taxation (generously in the fifteenth century) to the Crown independently. They were, however, still represented by proctors in the commons and when parliament met at Westminster the southern convocation was usually in close communication. Parliament was called, prorogued and dissolved entirely at the king's discretion. Its meetings were short, a session rarely extended beyond six weeks, and there was normally only one session. Under the Lancastrians, because of demand for taxation, meetings were frequent; after 1461 when war was less frequent, parliament met less often.[10]

Royal writs of summons to the house of lords became hereditary during the fourteenth century. The peerage, defined as the upper rank of the nobility in terms of this hereditary privilege, was a parliamentary body.

Earls and dukes had always been summoned to parliament as lords. By the end of the fourteenth century a further category of hereditary barons had been created, separated from leading knights only by their hereditary right to a summons. Inevitably, however, some lines died out; thus the process of creating new peerages by writ, usually as a reward for loyal service to the Crown, developed in the mid-fifteenth century. The attendance of the lords, especially the temporal lords, was not usually very high. The core was always provided by royal councillors. Indeed the sessions of the lords, called as they were to advise the monarch as well as to receive bills from the commons, were in essence meetings of an extended council.

The commons played a more complex role. Procedures for election in county or borough court were well established. The most important development in the fifteenth century was the restriction of the county franchise in 1429 to the forty-shilling freeholder, which, since there was no register and ballot was by public show of hands, encompassed men of modest means well below the rank of gentleman. At the beginning of the fifteenth century all but a handful of boroughs were represented by their residents or men associated with them. After 1422, however, the invasion of boroughs by outsiders gathered pace so that by the end of the century there was a significantly greater proportion of county gentry sitting in the house than at its beginning. Even so MPs ranged from royal councillors and knights of the shire wealthy enough to be peers, to obscure and humble shipmen, port-reeves, tailors and hackneymen. The knights of the shire dominated the house, but it was a heterogeneous body combining lesser nobilty, lawyers, wealthy merchants, artisans and craftsmen, together representing the third estate of the realm. Sessions were chaired by its speaker (a role that had emerged in 1376), his election being the first business. More often than not the speaker was a royal nominee. Little is known about debates because the commons did not keep a record. What is known has largely to be derived from the formally enrolled record of decisions of parliament.[11]

Parliament was important because of the established principles that the king could neither tax his subjects nor amend his law without the consent of the commons. The voting of taxes by the commons was the principal business of most parliaments and the fundamental reason why parliament existed. Most opened with a request for supply; the terms and the amount were negotiated; and the session ended after the bill voting a subsidy had been passed. The commons occasionally haggled, sometimes refused. While, as in 1406, supply could be delayed until the Crown responded to complaints and criticism of the conduct of government, the principle of no supply without redress of grievances had not yet been established. Taxation was specifically for the defence of the realm and not for the general financial needs of the Crown. It came in two forms: indirect taxation – the customs

Effigy of Henry IV
(1367–1413) on his
Tomb in Canterbury
Cathedral, Kent,
UK/Bridgeman Art
Library.

Choosing the Red and
White Roses in the
Temple Garden, 1910
by Henry A. Payne
(Harry) (1868–1940).
Houses of Parliament,
Westminster, London,
UK/Bridgeman Art
Library.

Court of the King's Bench, Westminster Hall, from 'The Microcosm of London', engraved by J. Black (fl.1791–1831), pub. By R. Ackermann (1764–1834) 1808 (aquatint) by T. Rowlandson (1756–1827) and Pugin, A. C. (1762–1832). Private Collection/The Stapleton Collection/Bridgeman Art Library.

Ms 265 f.IV Edward IV, with Elizabeth Woodville, Edward V and Richard, Duke of Gloucester, later Richard III, English. Dictes of the Philosophers, (c. 1477). Lambeth Palace Library, London, UK/Bridgeman Art Library.

Knight's Yeoman/Robin Hood, G. 11588. The British Library.

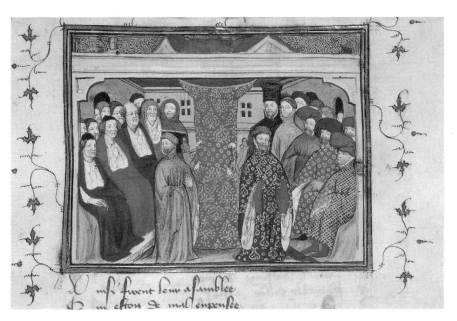

The Empty Throne, ms Harley 1319, f.57. The British Library.

John Talbot and Henry VI, ms Royal 15 E VI, f.405. The British Library.

Mount Grace Priory, view of the Priory Church from the South West. English Heritage Photographic Library.

The Virgin and Child with Saints and Donors (The Donne Triptych) by Hans Memlinc. The National Gallery Company Ltd.

Thomas Paycocke's House, Coggeshall, Essex. National Monuments Record.

A Scolding Wife (Henry VII Chapel, Westminster Abbey). National Monuments Record.

Henry V by an unknown artist. National Portrait Gallery.

Henry VII by an unknown artist.
National Portrait Gallery.

Henry VI by an unknown artist,
RCIN 403442, OM 8 WC. Royal
Collection Enterprises.

Richard III. The Society of
Antiquaries of London.

Edward IV. The Society of
Antiquaries of London.

on wool exports and the subsidies on the import and export of other goods (tunnage and poundage); and direct taxation – usually the lay subsidy raised on the movable goods of the king's subjects at the rate of a tenth for townsmen and a fifteenth for countrymen. Customs were by the fifteenth century invariably renewed at each meeting of parliament. In 1415 Henry V was voted them for life, a privilege repeated for Henry VI in 1453 and Richard III in his first parliament. Thereafter it was customary for the king to be voted customs revenue in his first parliament.

Since 1334 there was a fixed quota of the tenths and fifteenths on every vill, so that the commons voted the lump sum and it was up to individual communities to determine who actually paid. In time, especially after the late-fourteenth-century population decline, this sum bore little relationship to the actual level and distribution of taxable wealth. Reductions were secured in 1446 for impoverished vills which had suffered severe decline. Conversely, by the end of the fifteenth century, there were many centres of growth which were under-taxed. The commons, however, were reluctant to allow a general overhaul of the system. Experiments were conducted in other forms of taxation, income tax, parish tax, land tax and (most notoriously) poll tax, but none provided a politically acceptable alternative with a high enough yield. Moreover the commons would only vote fifteenths and tenths for limited periods (no more than three years) and insisted that they should be used only for the purpose of the defence of the realm; occasionally, as in 1406, it was willing to agree that the revenue could be spent on the king's domestic costs, but only under strict terms. The king was expected to live of his own, that is to say from the income from his estates, feudal rights and incidental sources such as the mint, to meet his personal needs. Occasionally a king sought to raise money by a forced loan or free gift (benevolence). But these, too, offended the commons; and in 1483 Richard III passed a statute outlawing benevolences (it did not however prevent Henry VII from raising a 'loving contribution' and Henry VIII an 'amicable grant'). Lack of a substantial independent endowment, as Fortescue saw it, and the subsequent need to turn to parliament with cap in hand, was one reason the Crown found it difficult to establish an unrestrained *dominium regale*.

The principle that laws could not be changed without the assent of parliament lay behind the parliamentary control of taxation; a finance act needed to be passed. All legislation was initiated in the form of bills or petitions, presented by the Crown (as in the finance bill), or by individual members, or by local communities. Some were adopted by the house as a whole, became common petitions and were presented to the lords in its name. The procedure for three readings of bills was refined during the fifteenth century, as was the passage of amended bills between the two houses. After a final reading, bills went to the lords for approval and the royal assent, at which point they became statutes, amending all previous law. All manner of business passed through the house, from private bills seeking privileges and benefits for individual members to major alterations to the law of the land – such as the treason law. Much was concerned with adjusting and fine tuning the common law, especially the procedures of the legal system, land law and commercial law, reflecting the interests of the members of the house among whom lawyers, landowners and merchants were dominant. Parliament was the supreme court of the land. It was thus also the forum for treason trials either by impeachment, in which the commons were the accusers, appeal in which lords were accusers, or attainder in which the Crown was the accuser.[12]

The law

Parliament's role as the supreme court was an elaboration of the simplest form of royal law-giving by the answering of a petition for justice. Beneath parliament lay a network of courts which administered law. England, including the great liberties of Chester and Durham, was under one uniform, or common, royal law. The two principal courts which sat in Westminster Hall were the Court of Common Pleas and the Court of King's Bench. Like all branches of royal administration originally housed in the king's court, they had become established in Westminster in the thirteenth century. Common Pleas, the busier, on which bench sat five or six justices, dealt with cases between free subjects over the possession of land and debt. King's Bench, which nominally sat in the king's presence, was staffed by four or five justices and dealt with breaches of the king's peace, felonies (serious crime) and trespasses. Both were courts to which more important cases were removed from lower local courts.[13]

Until the early-fourteenth century justice in the localities had been administered by general eyres in which royal justices came down from Westminster. These were abandoned and replaced by a compound system involving twice yearly assizes, conducted by justices on six regular circuits and the quarter sessions of the county justices of the peace. These were supplemented by special commissions of oyer and terminer (to hear and to determine) to deal with major disruption of the peace and, until 1414, occasional tours of King's Bench (on eyre). Local landowners, untrained in the law, served as justices of the peace. Over the fifteenth century the number of justices increased; the peers, and even senior clergy, began to sit on numerous county benches as a matter of course; it became customary on changes of regime to purge the bench to ensure the presence of reliable men, especially men retained by the king; membership was manipulated by the Crown as a means of exercising control. But assize justices, invariably nominated to the quorum, always sat on every bench; and in practice, as the claims for expenses show, only a minority of the nominated JPs ever attended. The justice dispensed was largely determined by the trained lawyers, the assize judges, in their number. All serious cases, and many involving the gentry themselves, were removed to King's Bench.

The twice-yearly sheriff's tourn, in many places absorbed into liberty and borough courts, still operated. In these, minor offences, petty debts and petty squabbles, as well as the assizes of bread and ale, were handled. At the lowest level lay the manorial courts administering local, customary, law dealing with registration of landholding, local regulation (by law) and minor misdemeanors. Customary law, varied from locality to locality, and the administration belonged to the lords of manors (the holding of the right defined lordship of a manor), but it was supervised by the higher courts. Finally, separate from the system of common law, lay the ecclesiastical courts, administered by the bishops and their officials, which handled matters of probate, defamation, slander and matrimony.[14]

Although there existed a co-ordinated system of courts which on paper offered both immediate justice and the recourse to higher appeal, there were, inevitably, many shortcomings. In criminal cases there was no public prosecution. Cases were by indictments drawn up by a jury of presentment sworn to present accusations. The indictments could be drawn up by the jury itself from its own knowledge, or could be an endorsement of a private accusation. An alternative was appeal by a wronged individual in the name of the Crown, or by an approver, in which an accused felon turned king's evidence. The procedures were complex and slow. It could take up to eighteen months to bring the defendant to the court; and often the defendant could avoid appearance by being declared an outlaw and subsequently receiving a pardon. Once the defendant was in court, all the tricks and procedures of the law could be used to delay. Trial juries, as well as sheriffs who empanelled them, and judges, were open to the pressures of labouring (lobbying outside the court), embracery (labouring to pervert the course of justice) and maintenance, often by means of threats and bribes, by which the more influential sought, as was expected of them, to protect their servants and followers. Even where the course of justice ran smoothly, juries frequently lessened the severity of the crime, or gave an outright acquittal, to avoid imposing the death penalty. The rate of conviction was low; and pardons were readily available.[15]

It is not easy, therefore, to evaluate the quality of justice administered by the king's courts. Generally the fifteenth century has been associated with the failure of justice, lawlessness and disorder, and especially upper-class violent disorder. Before making a judgement, several factors have to be borne in mind. The first is that contemporary comment bewailing the lawlessness of the age might have derived from rising expectations rather than worsening circumstances. The second is that there is more surviving detailed evidence of alleged disorder, especially violent disorder, than for earlier centuries. The records of King's Bench have survived in impressive numbers. Much of this evidence, however, is of indictments only: the record of relatively few final judgements has survived. It is not the level of actual crime that increased so dramatically in the fifteenth century, but the level of recorded alleged crime. Moreover, because violent disorder involving the gentry was considered more serious and was more difficult to settle at quarter sessions, it was more frequently referred to the upper court. Thus the lawlessness of the upper classes enjoys a higher profile in the surviving evidence. Furthermore, not all violence was necessarily what it at first sight appeared to be. Because the processes through the civil courts over property rights could be so tortuous, a breach of the peace, *in vi et armis*, was often committed so as to transfer a case to the speedier King's Bench. The pulling down of a fence, or the forcible entry to a property, was sometimes a ritual act, occasionally collusive.[16]

Nevertheless much real violent crime was committed, and often by those people who, as justices of the peace, were expected to keep order. Yet even here we need to understand the social context. The law could only be enforced by the local elites themselves and it is hardly surprising that they resorted readily to violence in the pursuit of their own disputes. Indeed, it has been argued, the use of violence in the pursuit of claims and in the enforcement of justice itself was taken for granted in a society which saw war as the expression of the highest lay ideals. The notion of trial by battle still underlay the procedures and principles of the common law. If Henry V could wage a just war to recover his right in France, so too could Lord Moleyns to recover his right in Gresham. And we need to draw a distinction between what contemporaries accepted as a reasonable level of violence in pursuit of rights and justice and the complete collapse of order. Most of the worst cases upon which the low reputation of the fifteenth century is based occurred when the Crown failed to fulfil its duty to provide justice, either in the latter years of Henry VI, or during periods of outright civil war.[17]

Contemporaries were fully aware of the shortcomings of the law and its administration. One response was the development of chancery and conciliar courts as a source of equitable justice, using procedures and principles drawn from the ecclesiastical civil law. Chancery developed as an equity court in the fifteenth century, particularly to enforce contracts, to uphold enfeoffments to use (trusts), and, by the end of the century, to settle property disputes.

These actions, and the later establishment of the court of Star Chamber, providing a speedy and final settlement of disputes which involved breach of the peace, eventually enabled the Crown to offer more effective remedies.[18]

A more informal, and often satisfactory, response to legal dispute was the resort to arbitration. Rather than take a case through the costly and time-consuming processes of law, in which the outcome could only be a winner and a loser, parties sought the arbitration of a third party, often a local lord, whose council heard the evidence and negotiated an award that was acceptable to both parties. Such arbitrations did not always hold, but they usually did, to the great advantage of all; the parties who saved face and money, the arbitrator who gained authority and prestige, and the local community as a whole for whom social peace was preserved. The recourse to arbitration was particularly marked in the mid-fifteenth century when the Crown's authority was especially frail. It used to be seen as a symptom of the collapse of the legal system, but by promoting reconciliation, it was an important antidote to the divisive and confrontational impact of the common law. Perhaps it was resented by the common lawyers themselves because it denied them profitable business, but the frequency to which it was successfully resorted is another reason why we should not take too gloomy a view of the fifteenth-century attitude to law and order.[19]

Court and household

It is apparent, however, that while the kingdom of England possessed highly centralised institutions, a sophisticated system of royal government and a uniform legal system, all of which were perhaps the envy of fellow monarchs, the actual power of the Crown was nevertheless severely limited. The reasons are not hard to find. Communications were slow; it took five days for an urgent letter from Westminster to reach York and another five for a reply to arrive. The holders of feudal liberties, especially in the parts more distant from Westminster, where the king's sheriff was excluded, jealously guarded their administrative independence. The coercive power of the state was feeble. It lacked a standing army, except for three small border garrisons in Berwick, Carlisle and Calais; in time of emergency it relied on calling out a militia by means of commissions of array. It had no police force; it had no full-time, paid civil service in the provinces. The state barely existed. Government was therefore a delicately balanced two-way process, resting on the in-grained obedience, willing consent, and co-operation of the king's subjects. The king's will could only be mediated through them, specifically the local landed elites who filled the offices of sheriff, coroner and escheator, sat on the commissions of peace and array, and represented their communities in parliament. At the same time all those who served the Crown, sat in parliament or frequented the law courts sought to use royal influence for their own profit and advantage. Rule rested on a partnership between Crown and subject, each needing the other. The king ruled, but in Fortescue's term, it was political rule.[20]

The focus of politics was the royal court; and the locus of the court was the royal household. The distinction between the two is fine, but real. The household was the collective body which accompanied the king. It was highly structured, being divided between the *domus providencie* and the *domus magnificencie*. The *domus providencie*, downstairs, over which the Steward presided, supplied the material needs and administrative support. Already the principal domestic offices, such as the Butler or Carver were sinecures granted to courtiers. The *domus magnificencie*, upstairs, over which the Chamberlain presided, was attendant from the most personal to the most ceremonial on the king, including the chapel. Here the court gathered. It had its own ceremonial and rituals, linked to life cycles (births, marriages and deaths), to the great festivals and saints' days (especially St George), to moments of state such as the welcoming of ambassadors, and to the king's self-indulgence in feasting to excess (Edward IV), hunting obsessively (Henry VII) and promoting tournaments (both). The more magnificent a court kept by the king, the more prestige he enjoyed. The Yorkists made much of Henry VI's failure on this count, although the criticism was disingenuous, since after 1453 the king was in no fit state himself to keep court in the accustomed manner. Nevertheless Edward IV and his successors did their utmost to ensure full publicity for the splendour of their establishments.

Courtiers, great noblemen, councillors and boon companions of the king alike provided the point of contact between subject and monarch. Nothing could be achieved, no place secured or favour granted, as the corespondence of the Paston and Plumpton families reveal, unless it was expedited by one's connections at court; and the better the connections, the closer to the person of the king, the greater the chance of success, the more in demand a courtier was. It is not surprising, therefore, that during the century the literary genre which bemoaned the corruption of the court and the sycophancy of courtiers (the caterpillars of the commonwealth), in contrast to the purity of life in the country, revived.[21]

The royal household provided another link between Crown and subject through the knights and esquires of the body, the king's retainers, in receipt of his fee and livery. The royal household still retained its military function; the knights and esquires provided through their own companies the core of the king's army at war. Henry IV called upon his household to raise his army to invade Scotland in 1400 and to defend his throne in 1403 and 1405; Henry V called upon them again to lead the invasion of France. Henry VI's councillors mobilised the knights and esquires of the young king's household to accompany him on his coronation expedition to France in 1430. Edward IV did the same in 1475. Henry VII raised his household, like Henry IV, for war against Scotland in 1496, to defend his throne in 1486 and 1487 and to suppress revolt in 1489 and 1497. The household, through the knights and esquires of the body, was a military establishment, enabling the king to raise troops rapidly in an emergency.[22]

But by the fifteenth century the knights and esquires of the body had also acquired a political role. They were the eyes and ears of the king in the country. The establishment of some forty knights and eighty esquires was drawn as far as possible from all the parts of the realm and the knights and esquires themselves served on a shift rota at court. They held royal offices in their counties, sat on the commission of the peace and were elected, if possible, to parliament. They were the king's men in the provinces, proudly wearing his collar and badge (the Lancastrian SS; the Yorkist suns and roses with the lion of March for Edward IV and the white boar for Richard III; and the SS with the union rose for the early Tudors), and equally proudly portrayed as such in their funerary effigies.[23]

The king might seek to retain a permanent presence and direct influence through his men, but he did not attempt to displace the local landed elites, especially the great landed families. In the summer of 1483, Bishop Russell intended to remind the lords in what was to have been the first parliament of Edward V that, 'the politic rule of every region well-ordained standeth in the nobles'. His appeal for the lords to stand firm, like rocks in a stormy sea, was particularly apposite for the circumstances of a minority, but his basic point applied to all occasions. The peers, especially the earls and dukes, had the wealth and resources to wield power with some degree of autonomy in the provinces. They could not be ignored. But equally part of a magnate's strength derived from royal favour and the effective exercise of royal authority in their countries. Good rule depended on partnership between Crown and lords.[24]

Bastard feudalism

Like the king, the great lords too maintained their own retinues. Bastard feudalism has probably been the most debated aspect of late-medieval political structure. It was given this tag in the nineteenth century because it was believed that the legitimate feudalism of the earlier middle ages had been debased by the substitution of money fees for personal fealty. At its feet was laid the blame for the principal woes of the fifteenth century: aristocratic disorder, the abuse of power and the blight of the overmighty subject. After a sustained historiographical onslaught, little now remains of this view. Indeed, some would argue that the term itself should be discarded. At the heart of what is meant by bastard feudalism is the practice of retaining by indenture for life – the arrangement whereby a lord entered in to a solemn contract (indenture) with a retainer in which the lord promised to pay a fee in exchange for service in war and peace for life. The practice, which had ancient antecedents, developed in the early fourteenth century as a means for raising royal armies by sub-contract. The king contracted his great lords to provide so many soldiers; they in their turn entered into long-term con-tracts with their dependents to provide the necessary numbers whenever they were called. The arrangement was similar to that of the royal house-hold itself. Richard II was the first to resort to imitating aristocratic practice by adopting and distributing his own badge of the White Hart.[25]

Several points need to be made about indentured retinues. It has long been established that retaining did not necessarily secure the exclusive life-long attachment that the wording of the standard contract implied; some men, whose services were much in demand, entered into contracts with several different lords. It has been suggested that, cynically pursuing their own self-interest, such retainers rarely thought twice about turning their coats. However, instances of time-serving tend to come from districts where, and times when, magnate affinities were in flux and futures uncertain. Loyalty was in normal times more deeply ingrained. Similarly the idea that lords surrounded themselves with hordes of retainers was misplaced. Num-bers were generally small. At any one time there were only ever a handful of retinues that contained as many as eighty feed men. This was partly because of cost, but it was partly because of the context in which lords retained. The largest and best documented of all, that created by John of Gaunt in the late fourteenth century, existed to support the international military ambitions of an English royal duke who campaigned incessantly in France and also pursued a claim to the throne of Castile. Richard of York, another royal duke, was the king's deputy in France and then Ireland. The Nevilles and Percy, as wardens of the marches, were licensed to retain the reserves in defence of the borders against Scotland. Humphrey, Duke of Buckingham, was the king's captain of Calais in the 1440s when he retained a significant number of men. The common factor is that the well-documented large retinues, with the exception of that recruited by Lord Hastings under Edward IV (who retained on the king's behalf as the cham-berlain of his household and his steward of Tutbury), is that they belonged to generals. Most lords, especially the mere barons, as the income tax returns for 1436 revealed, retained on only a very modest scale, and then usually to meet their own household, legal and estate needs.[26]

Probably the fourteenth century saw indentured retaining at its most widespread and its abuse most prominent. Legislation was introduced in 1390 to restrict the right to retain non-resident household servants other than lawyers to lords of the realm, who were entitled only to engage such men of the rank of esquire and above for life. The act was reinforced in 1406 and 1429. In 1468 Edward IV banned retaining for life, permitting only household service. His legislation was re-enacted by Henry VII in 1504. The Yorkist and early Tudor acts were designed not to eliminate retaining, but to enable the Crown to license it. The real problem in the fifteenth century was illegal retaining; that is to say the hiring of gangs and the distribution of livery for a week or two for an attack on a rival, as for example did Thomas Percy, Lord Egremont, in 1454, or the earl of Shrewsbury and Lord Grey of Codnor in 1468. Its resurgence in mid-century was a consequence of the breakdown of royal authority, not a cause. In 1468 Shrewsbury and Grey took advantage of Edward IV's differences with Warwick to pursue their own quarrel. But then they were quickly prosecuted. If retaining ran out of hand, the fault lay not with the practice, but with the Crown's inability to enforce the law.[27]

Retaining was in fact but the most formalised element of 'good lordship'. The principal cement in the hierarchy of society was lordship and its reciprocal, service. Everyone was defined in relationship to others, either by lordship over their inferiors, or by service to their superiors. Social values were focused on the proper performance of either lordship or service. All lords were the centres of fluctuating circles of dependents, employees, tenants, neighbours and hangers-on, 'well-wishers' who expected to benefit from their generosity or influence, and in return were willing to undertake tasks for them. It was taken for granted that those with wealth, authority and connections in high places would use their influence for the benefit of others. In an exchange of reciprocal obligations, favours were done in return for services rendered. The surviving correspondence of the Pastons, Plumptons and Stonors reveal how ingrained these attitudes were. A lord's reputation, or 'worship', depended in part on the effectiveness with which he exercised his influence to the benefit of those who looked to him. The more effective he was, the more men he attracted to his service. Effectiveness itself depended on his own standing with greater lords and the king in particular. Thus favour at court, or good connections with those close to the king, was essential for those who wished to carry political weight. Loss of favour, by the same token, diminished the capacity to offer 'good lordship' and thus led those who provided service to turn towards others perceived to be more beneficially placed.[28]

The tortuous and delicate nature of these relationships is revealed in an incident in the career of Sir William Plumpton in the mid-1470s. Plumpton was a feed retainer of the earl of Northumberland, aggrieved because the office of deputy steward of Knaresborough (Northumberland was steward) had been granted by the earl to his neighbour and rival, William Gascoigne, and because he had been removed from the commission of the peace for the West Riding in 1475. He wished to be restored to both. In November 1475 he bombarded Godfrey Green, his agent in Westminster, with instructions to lobby various courtiers, including the duke of Gloucester and Lord Hastings, to approach the earl or even the king on his behalf. Green acted more circumspectly. His contacts told him that since Northumberland was fully at liberty to 'have no deputy such as shall please him, and can thank him for the gift thereof', such approaches over the deputy stewardship would do more harm than good. Moreover, he refused to complain to the same lords about Gascoigne personally since, he explained, this would be interpreted as malice, and would be seen as a disworship to Northumberland. Hastings was approached in the matter of the bench, only for Green to be accused of seeking to make a 'jelosie' between the two lords. Plumpton was not the most tactful of men. The king instructed the earl to put his 'meynie' (following) in order; two years later he did so. The affair, exceptional perhaps because it centred on rivalry within a lord's affinity, nevertheless reveals the interrelationship of lordship and politics, both locally and at court.[29]

Locality

The dispute between Plumpton and Gascoigne touches on a further aspect of political society; the importance of locality. Godfrey Green was busy in Westminster lobbying courtiers on matters concerning the politics of the West Riding of Yorkshire. Historians have only recently begun to consider in depth the framework within which this local politics worked. If looked at from the point of view of royal administration, the county and borough are central. Each had its sheriff or mayors and lesser royal officers, its justices of the peace, and each elected its representatives to parliament. Local politics can be analysed in terms of the local magisterial elites who held office and represented the community of the shire or borough in parliament. On the other hand, viewed from the perspective of lordship, through which provincial rule was exercised, the relationship of sheriffs, justices of the peace and MPs to lords is critical. Late-twentieth century local studies of the landed elite (as distinct from the urban oligarchies) have either focused on counties or on baronial families. Those which have focused on counties, the units of royal administration, have stressed the role of the gentry, the strength of the county community to which they belonged, and the horizontal bonds that drew them collectively together. Those that have focused on baronial families have stressed the power of lords, retaining and vertical ties.[30]

To a large extent, however, the late-medieval county community as an independent political body is an illusion. Contemporaries had a sense of belonging to the body of the shire, most clearly articulated through elections to parliament, when the knights were required to represent the community in a gathering of the communities of the realm. Constitutional practice, the very frequency of parliaments, and the opportunities that those parliaments offered for groups within the counties to voice their concerns and lobby the Crown, made something of a reality out of the convention. And the custom of addressing complaints in the name of the community reveals that it was a meaningful concept to contemporaries. But the community represented by the county was rarely much wider than the self-interest of those who dominated its society. This is suggested, for instance, in the late fourteenth century parliamentary protests against retaining and the distribution of liveries which were dressed up as a defence of the liberties of the county community. But the complaints were those of unfeed substantial gentry, and one source of resentment was exclusion from the advantages of receiving a fee. Similarly, one can observe how those in the Paston circle, excluded from Suffolk's patronage in East Anglia, expressed their hostility to his regime in terms of the well-being of the community of the shire. The concept of the communal interest was a useful ideal to cite, but it tended to be cited when personal interest was at stake.[31]

The shire gentry, unlike urban elites, did not form organised bodies acting corporately. The true force in local politics was that of the baronial affinity, of lordship. And lordship both went beyond and was subsumed within county boundaries. The tentacles of power of some great lords, like an earl of Warwick in the midlands, stretched over several counties; yet within the same counties there were other lesser lords, such as Lord Ferrers, of whose interest he needed to take account. On the other hand, no single lord dominated Yorkshire. In the north of the county the Nevilles of Middleham dominated Richmondshire, the Percys dominated the lordship of Knaresborough as well as the East Riding, and the Talbot earls of Shrewsbury were the lords of Sheffield. The illusion of an independent county community was created in some parts of England from time to time. The county palatinate of Chester was dominated by gentry families; but the earl of Chester was the king, and royal dominance in Chester, until it fell into the hands of the Stanleys later in the fifteenth century, was unquestioned. Nottinghamshire until 1460 had no dominant lord; but there were lesser affinities dominating different parts of the county. In the central south-west (Dorset and Wiltshire), too, there were no resident great lords, and local power was exercised by the leading and extremely wealthy gentry families, some of whom rose to lesser peerages. The failure of Henry VI to assert the local power of the Crown and the duchy of Lancaster led to a vacuum in several localities, and here, if great lords did not step in, as they did in Yorkshire or East Anglia, lesser lords emerged as did Viscount Beaumont through the honour of Leicester.[32]

Unlike counties, lordship was fluid. The power of lords waxed and waned. In the south-west of England the Courtenay earls of Devon built up an hegemony in the late-fourteenth century which fell apart in the mid-fifteenth century. In the midlands, the earls of Warwick exercised a hegemony which itself came under threat after 1446, as an incomer, Richard Neville, sought to sustain it in the face of rivals. After the collapse of the duke of Suffolk's ascendancy in East Anglia in 1450, the dukes of Norfolk and earls of Oxford sought to take his place. Percy dominance of the north, built up by the first earl of Northumberland in the reign of Richard II, was shattered by rebellion in the reign of Henry IV, never to recover. In its place, the hegemony enjoyed by the Nevilles of Middleham grew and grew until it reached its apogee under its inheritor, Richard of Gloucester, in the 1470s, by his accession to the throne in 1483 to be absorbed into the Crown.[33]

Local politics was also a two-way process. Just as Bishop Russell declared that the political rule of every region well ordained stood in the lords, so it might be said that the rule of every district well-ordained stood in the local gentry. The gentry, especially the more substantial, knightly gentry who formed the official and representative elite in the counties, were not at the beck and call of the lords. They too were the heads of households, the lords of manors, the lords of tenants and centres of local power. Perhaps the best way to see local political structure is as a web of interlocking networks, both vertical and horizontal, partly determined by lordship, partly by kinship, partly by geography, themselves changing, rising and falling. Attempts have been made to delineate these networks. The Plumptons were members of just such a one which had as its focal point the duchy of Lancaster honour of Knaresborough. They were one of a dozen or so leading gentry families within the honour who tended, after 1399, to look to the Percys who were themselves the leading tenants of the duchy. Sir William and Sir Robert were linked by ties of marriage to most of the other leading gentry families; they called upon them, and were in their turn called, to act as witnesses to title deeds, to act as feoffees and to be arbitrators for their neighbours. They were called upon by their tenants and well-wishers to advance their causes, just as they turned, usually, to the earl of Northumberland, to advance their own. Such networks were replicated throughout the kingdom. They did not necessarily stop at county or honorial boundaries. Richard Clervaux of

Croft, on the Yorkshire bank of the Tees, moved in a circle which straddled the boundary with Durham which ran along the river.[34]

Like the politics of the realm too, local politics was the focus of both conflict and co-operation. The apparent contradiction between a local political society seething with rivalry on the one hand, and living harmoniously together on the other, derives from the nature of the principal evidence available. Legal records, especially the indictments before King's Bench, lead one to suppose that lords and gentry were for ever in dispute, often resorting to violence and ceaselessly seeking to advance themselves at the expense of their neighbours. Property conveyances and related documents, however, suggest that they collaborated to protect property rights and to foster ties of mutual support. In fact most property was securely held, and disputed property has attracted disproportionate attention. Moreover, for every dispute that went the full course of law, another was successfully settled by arbitration. Finally, the evidence, including much private correspondence, by focusing on property, its acquisition, management and protection, distorts our perception of provincial political and social life.[35]

Patronage and principle

Godfrey Green's letter to Sir Robert Plumpton was about patronage: the patronage of the king, who, as duke of Lancaster, had made Northumberland the steward of his lordship; the patronage of the earl of Northumberland, as steward of Knaresborough, as far as the post of his deputy was concerned; and the patronage potentially available to the deputy steward. Plumpton's lobbying reveals the importance of office. It reinforces a sceptical view of political behaviour that has dominated accounts of the fifteenth century in the later twentieth century. Cynical about the motivation of politicians in general, recent historians have tended to perceive fifteenth-century politics as devoid of principle and dominated by self-interest. But were politics only about 'patronage'? Did not ideology and principles play a part too?[36]

In fact, fifteenth-century politics has never been seen solely in terms of the pursuit of self-interest. It has always been recognised that foreign policy tended to divide opinion in the fifteenth century. One of the principal reasons for the emergence of faction at court in the later years of Henry IV was the issue of whether England should ally itself with the Burgundians or the Armagnacs in the civil war in France, and whether English policy should concentrate on interests in Acquitaine or the Low Countries. In the early years of Henry VI's majority, passions ran high as to whether the war should be pursued to the bitter end, or an accommodation should be sought with France. And one of the reasons for the quarrel between Edward IV and Warwick after 1464 was the question of whether England should ally itself with Burgundy or France. In all these cases, in the politics of 1409–13, 1437–44, 1464–9, one can also point to conflict at the highest level over office and influence at court, but there has never been any doubt that the leading politicians, the prince of Wales and his brother Clarence, Gloucester and Beaufort, Edward IV and Warwick, also took their stands on conviction.[37]

Closely related to foreign policy is the matter of chivalry and honour. The English upper class was imbued with the culture of chivalry. It was important to many that they should have the opportunity to go to war and to win renown on the field of battle. War, above all successful war, was not merely an opportunity to profit through loot and ransom, it was also the occasion to live out the highest ideals of their culture. Chivalry, it was believed by some, could heal the wounds that divided the realm in mid-century. On a personal level, too, honour was often at stake. Thus Richard of York challenged the duke of Somerset after 1450 for dishonourably surrendering his garrisons in France. Questions of precedence at court or in parliament, in which the honour and standing of individuals were at stake, were likewise matters of profound importance.[38]

Moreover lordship, itself at the very heart of patronage, was founded on a code of moral and ethical behaviour. Good lordship required respect for the law and the principle of equity; it did not countenance the perversion of the law for personal gain. It demanded loyalty and condemned treachery. Not everyone lived up to these ideals, but loyalty was a deeper force in political society than has generally been recognised. Richard III's actions in 1483 were controversial then precisely because of the questions they raised about respect for the law, loyalty and duty. One reason why the earl of Northumberland promoted and favoured William Gascoigne over Sir William Plumpton after his restoration in 1470 was that Gascoigne had been notably more loyal to his house than had Plumpton in the preceding decade. Good lordship too contributed towards the overall goal of main-taining social peace; that 'love and amity' between neighbours which it was the conventionally expressed aim of arbitration awards to restore through the intervention of good lords themselves. Politics *were* personal relationships. Contemporaries did not perceive that the world would be made better by social or political change. It would only improve if individuals behaved better and dutifully fulfilled their responsibilities according to their station, even though, the world after the Fall being as it was, most of the time, most people (even lords who should have known better), behaved badly.[39]

Little distinction was drawn between private and public spheres; standards of private behaviour were also standards of public behaviour. The common weal was best served when lords lived up to the highest ideals. But above all the king, as the supreme lord, was by his coronation oath pledged to maintain justice for the common good. The maintenance of justice was itself a public issue of concern to all. Many matters which concerned parliament, and were the source of long-running dispute between the king and his subjects, were just such questions of conflicting principle. The king claimed, for instance, by ancient prerogative the right to purvey for his household; to buy at fair prices supplies for his entourage within a set radius wherever he lay. While the concept of a fair price was accepted, abuse frequently occurred, not only through individual corruption, but also through inability of the Crown to pay immediately in cash. Such abuse was most frequent with a highly peripatetic court under a profligate king. Purveyance thus was a reiterated complaint under Henry IV and again during the early majority of Henry VI. It was one aspect of a general criticism of these kings for their failure to live within their means, which led parliaments to seek to impose constraints. This in its turn raised the fundamental issue of the competence of subjects to impose limitations.

Real constitutional issues were from time to time at stake; Royal councils worried over the niceties of the establishment and ending of minorities in 1422, 1436 and 1483, and when Henry VI was incapacitated in 1454. In 1422, 1436, the 1450s and 1483 the ambitions of the magnates, the pursuit of power, and the pressure of their followers for reward and advancement were all at work; but so too were fundamental matters concerning the government of the realm. In truth, and not surprisingly, politics in the fifteenth century was a mixture in varying proportions of the pursuit of self-interest and a concern for the proper government of the realm.[40]

Popular participation

Fifteenth-century politics are, nevertheless, assumed to be the preserve of the landed and urban elites. This was far from the case. Contemporary propertied elites were most in fear of direct popular action by means of demonstrations, riots and armed uprisings. Popular disturbance was never far from the surface. Local riots, especially over economic and social grievances, sometimes orchestrated by disgruntled gentry, were frequent. Some, the 'Perkins Revolt' of 1431 for instance, were fuelled by religious dissent. More feared, because of the association with the Great Revolt of 1381, were tax protests, such as the Yorkshire rising of 1489. Most feared was a general rising against the whole regime as experienced in 1450. In many revolts, especially those that occurred in the later 1450s and later 1460s, it is possible to discern the hand of dissident noblemen fomenting trouble for their own ends. But the commonalty would not rise and risk loss of life and property without undue cause. A York or a Warwick skilfully appealed to popular grievances, but he would not have done so with such success had there not been simmering resentment ready to be exploited.[41]

However, an undue emphasis on direct action can hide other, and argu-ably more significant, manifestations of continuous indirect popular parti-cipation in politics. Governments were continuously on their guard against subversive speech, especially in pubs. Informers were paid for reporting tittle tattle. A stream of disparaging remarks about the competence of Henry VI came to the notice of the government. Incautious critical comments about Richard of Gloucester in a York tavern were reported to the civic authorities. They were sensitive because political discussion itself was clearly commonplace. And not just talk. The first popular manifestos (in the ver-nacular) were produced by the Lollards, notably the twelve conclusions of 1395 which were posted in London. Three different versions of manifestos drawn up by the rebels in 1450 have survived. In the following twenty years the publication of a manifesto was a regular feature of aristocratic mobilisa-tion of popular support. Its production and circulation implies an informed and literate audience. Governments replied with their own propaganda, visual as well as verbal, in 'joyous entries', in genealogies, in proclamations and from the pulpit. After 1450, public opinion was considered important enough to be routinely wooed and won.[42]

Moreover the notion that the house of commons represented the com-mons as a whole in parliament was not entirely fictional. The county and borough franchises were for the most part open enough to involve participa-tion in elections well below the level of the gentry and burgesses. A forty-shilling freeholder was a husbandman with forty acres or more. Could returning officers always know whether an elector was a freeholder worth forty shillings? In practice elections were determined by the quality rather than the quantity of the votes received, but in law MPs, once elected, represented all their constituents. And during the early part of the century many small-scale tradesmen and craftsmen actually sat in the house as representatives of lesser boroughs. When they voted for a tenth and a fifteenth, MPs com-mitted ordinary men to pay taxes; and subsequently they, or their like, had to collect them. The fears and concerns of the taxpayer were ignored at their peril. It is likely that reluctance to vote supply, criticism of waste at court, resentment at failure to use taxes effectively, as well as the promotion of bills to reform abuses or change the law reflected, indirectly at least, the interests of constituents as a whole. It is likely too that the cynical view of parliament-arians and their motives expressed in *Richard the Redeless* in the first decade of the century was by no means restricted to the urban and rural elite.[43]

In particular there was one group, the enfranchised middling sort, who carried considerable weight. Often literate, usually well-informed yeomen, substantial husbandmen and prosperous artisans and traders bore the burden of paying taxes. As jurors, constables, sheriff's bailiffs and churchwardens they shouldered the petty administration of the kingdom. They were the targets of government propaganda; they admired Henry V as a king who made England powerful, and Richard of York and the earl of Warwick later appealed to them when his successors failed. They provided the local leadership which articulated popular grievances in the name of the common weal to their representatives in parliament. And, when this proved fruitless, they led local contingents in revolt. There was thus a substantial popular involvement in politics, articulated by village and small town elites, which had a continuous influence on the course of events. Sir John Fortescue wrote from exile in praise of their kind, in comparison with the downtrodden French, in the 1460s. He may have been somewhat nostalgic about their virtues, but he knew that they played a significant, if indirect, part in his *dominium politicum*.[44]

Crisis and change

The English political system was not static during the later middle ages. Is it possible to discern broad trends at work during the fifteenth century? The most sweeping hypothesis is that between mid-fourteenth and mid-fifteenth centuries the Crown lost power in relationship to its subjects; between 1461 and 1540 it recovered it. In order to win support for his wars in France, it has been argued, Edward III made a range of concessions to his landed subjects which had the cumulative effect of weakening the Crown and strengthening its greater subjects. The principal elements of this shift were: a softening in the law of treason; the partial withdrawal of the Crown from the direct administration of justice in the provinces; the development of devices to enable tenants-in-chief to escape the heavier burdens of feudalism; the development of indentured retaining as a mechanism for raising troops; and the strengthening of parliament in order to secure financial backing for the war in France. Edward III's policy of marrying his children into the ranks of the English aristocracy, while initially helping to bind the political nation more closely together, led to disputed successions to the throne. So emerged the overmighty subject.[45]

The counter-argument is that Edward III engaged in a fruitful and constructive partnership with his landed subjects which, far from weakening the Crown, strengthened it. Society was widening, especially as the gentry grew in numbers and significance; the scope of the state was growing and royal intervention was expanding; kings had to bring the nobility and gentry into government more fully, because there was much more to govern. If the state became less centralised, it was because the scope of the partnership between Crown and subject was extended. Medieval monarchy, however, was always intensely personal not institutional; and success still depended ultimately on the personal ability of the king, something of a lottery in an hereditary monarchy. Henry V had no more difficulty commanding the early fifteenth-century kingdom than did Edward I the late thirteenth. If crisis overwhelmed the kingdom in mid-century, it was only the personal incapacity of Henry VI which led to catastrophe. As K. B. McFarlane put it: 'only an undermighty ruler had anything to fear from overmighty subjects; and if he were undermighty his personal lack of fitness was the cause, not the weakness of his office and its resources'.[46]

Discussion of this fundamental issue focuses on the unfortunate Henry VI, who undoubtedly failed as a king. In considering whether he was entirely to blame, several points can be borne in mind. First, whether one sees the process since mid-fourteenth century as the widening of political society and the extension of government as a partnership between Crown and subject, or as concession to subjects, in both scenarios the pressure on the personal qualities of the king and his skills of management intensified as a result. Secondly, it is arguable that during the early-fifteenth century the late-medieval English dominions grew to such a size and complexity that they were becoming more difficult to rule with the resources, human and material, available to the Crown. In particular, by taking on the conquest of France, Henry V left for his son a legacy of military and political commitments which any king, however fit for the office, would have found difficult to sustain. Thirdly, the great slump of the mid-fifteenth century, which cut back income from Crown land, reduced customs revenue and made it harder to raise taxes significantly impoverished the Crown. And finally, the foundation of Henry VI's regime came to be undermined by the manner in which his grandfather had become king. As the reign regressed from disaster to disaster, the question of the legitimacy of his dynasty arose once again, and confidence in the sacral quality of his kingship was eroded.[47]

Thus, to some extent, the office of the Crown and its resources were under greater strain in the middle of the century than they had been at its beginning. The difficulty of weighing the personal incompetence of Henry VI against the declining strength of his office is raised particularly in consideration of the peripheries of the kingdom in mid-century. The king had greater difficulty ruling those parts of the realm furthest from Westminster. Wales and the marches, the far north and Ireland. To some extent circumstances were beyond his control. The marcher lordships in Wales enjoyed a level of independence uncommon in England. There was a greater concentration of more extensive liberties in the north of England than in the south. The need to defend the borders against Scotland led to the development of wardenries entrusted to the Nevilles and Percys, who alone had the resources to fill them, and who could turn their power against the Crown.[48]

Yet the Crown had little alternative but to delegate military command on the borders of Scotland and in Ireland to local lords. Given the lack of royal resources and the inability to maintain an army, the use of the power, local roots and standing of the great lords had much to commend it. While the stability and defence of the marches was the priority for the English in Ireland, the dominant Anglo-Irish families provided the best solution. The Fitzgeralds effectively represented the Crown in Yorkist and early Tudor Ireland. In Wales and the far north the Crown always had the potential to assert its authority. The substantial endowment of the prince of Wales, the county of Chester, and the royal castles provided a local base for royal government, which, after the defeat of Owain Glyn Dŵr, Henry V effectively deployed. In northern England the addition of the duchy of Lancaster gave the Crown a more effective presence after 1399. Moreover, since the Crown nominated its prince bishop, the county palatinate of Durham was effectively in its control. From mid-fourteenth century a succession of trusted confidantes and councillors of the king acted as *de facto* regents in the palatinate. The early Lancastrians had no difficulty in ruling the north, especially under the duumvirate of Bishop Langley and the earl of Westmorland between 1406 and 1425. But in 1437, by appointing Robert Neville as bishop of Durham, the government of Henry VI virtually surrendered the palatinate to the Neville family. For twenty years Richard Neville, Earl of Salisbury, took advantage of Henry VI's indifference to build up his own hegemony in the region. In so far as the north of England became an arbiter of the king's fate during the Wars of the Roses, it did so because of particular political actions, not because the region became intrinsically ungovernable.[49]

The recovery of the Royal Authority

Explanation of the recovery of royal authority after 1461 involves a similar balance between changing circumstance and royal effectiveness. Haltingly the Crown recovered under the Yorkists and early Tudors. Fortescue's programme, set out for the exiled Lancastrian prince of Wales, of making the Crown financially less dependent on its subjects and developing conciliar government as a counter-weight to noble power, was followed under Edward IV and Henry VII. Edward IV began the process of the resumption of royal lands. Always having to balance the competing claims of rewarding supporters and replenishing the royal coffers, he and his successors slowly rebuilt the crown estate. Edward himself added the duchy of York; after the destruction of his brother, George, Duke of Clarence in 1477, he resumed the midland estates of the earldom of Warwick. Richard III brought with him the Neville of Middleham estates in the north; Henry VII the earldom of Richmond. The Crown became thereby better endowed. The twists and turns of civil war provided further windfalls of forfeited lands, not all of which were restored to their families.

The land so acquired was better managed and the revenues increased through the development of chamber finance; and eventually income rose further through economic recovery. Revival of overseas trade also boosted income from customs and excise from 1470, and especially after 1490. Thus by a combination of policy and good fortune the regular annual income of the Crown recovered to over £110,000 by 1509, not far short of its level at the beginning of Richard II's reign. Financial recovery was underwritten by the absence of foreign war. It is not at all clear whether this was entirely by intent until after 1492. The level of parliamentary taxation fell, but so too did the burden of royal indebtedness incurred by war, which had so crippled the government of Henry VI.[50]

As important as the financial benefits of the extension of the royal demesne and the avoidance of war were the political consequences. Crown lands and royal offices provided the foundation for the re-establishment of an effective royal affinity in the provinces. Once more a process begun by Edward IV was completed by Henry VII. Successive kings were assisted by the collapse and failure of the Beauchamp/Neville hegemonies and the assimilation of their estates. Assimilation was reinforced by restrictions on retaining, which Henry VII completed by enforcing exclusive service to himself.[51]

The extension of the king's affinity, sustained by the expanded royal demesne and the collapse of magnate hegemonies, accounts for the rise to greater prominence in politics and government of the wealthier knightly families after the 1470s. It would be wrong to suppose, however, that the gentry took the place of a disappearing peerage. When the Crown absorbed the Beauchamp and Neville inheritances in 1478 and 1485 it extended its direct interest in the south-west, midlands and north. Those who had been officers and retainers of dukes and earls became servants of the Crown. The 'independence' of these gentry was an illusion: they were now the king's men, receiving his fee, filling his offices which earlier had been in the gift and possession of magnates.[52]

From this shifting political circumstance flowed certain administrative changes such as the creation by Henry VII of conciliar sub-committees to oversee the royal demesne and to exploit royal rights, as well as the development of new councils in Wales and the north. The provincial councils were, in their genesis, political. The council of the prince of Wales established at Ludlow in 1473 under the presidency of Earl Rivers was a device to extend royal supervision to an unsettled region. Richard III initially intended to follow the same precedent with a council for his own prince of Wales, based in the north. But after his son's premature death he established the first formal Council of the North, with both judicial and political functions as a means of retaining his personal control over the region now that he was king. Chamber finance and household government were the means by which kings insecure on the throne, and initially ruling only with factional support, could be certain of controlling their kingdoms. Only slowly, by trial and error, did this become a system of government.[53]

Kings between 1461 and 1509 were at bottom more concerned with survival than with government. On one level the frequency with which the throne changed hands by force (five times between 1461 and 1485) further undermined the sacral authority of the Crown. Yet monarchy itself was never questioned. Paradoxically, the claims of successive usurpers to be *the* legitimate king and the recycled propaganda that they would restore unity, reestablish the rule of law and foster the common weal, tended to strengthen the Crown. The perception gained ground that only through authoritative monarchy and through unquestioning obedience to the king, whoever he was, could the ills afflicting the kingdom be overcome.

Successive monarchs were also served by a succession of able councillors and civil servants, who seem to have shared Fortescue's view of what should be done. They carried through a programme of royal revival at times, it would seem, almost in spite of the king himself. It was the Crown, the kingdom of England they served, and they saw the project through thick and thin under Edward IV, Edward V, Richard III, Henry VII and Henry VIII. The government of England was sustained in the later fifteenth century by a body of largely clerical civil servants who were, if anything, more monarchical than the monarchs. It might well be for this reason that the kingdom did not collapse into anarchy and that even when the king himself was weak, the Crown remained strong. This 'new foundation of the Crown' helped tilt the balance of the constitution away from the *dominium politicum* back towards the *dominium regale* and took further the process by which king and kingdom, Crown and state came to be separable. It was a development which only became apparent with hindsight and in the wake of the ultimate political success of Henry Tudor. In the spring of 1461, on the morrow of his victory at Towton, these possible developments over the next half century were no doubt a long way from the mind of the untried eighteen-year-old who had just become Edward IV.[54]

Notes and References

1   Armstrong, 'Inauguration Ceremonies', passim; McKenna, 'Coronation Oil', 102–4; and above ch. 2.

2   The most recent discussion of royal authority is Watts, *Henry VI*, 16–38. See also Gross, 'Fallibilities of the English Kings', 54–6. For the deposition articles of Richard II see Barron, 'The Tyranny of Richard II', and above pp. 22–5, 64–6.

3   Fortescue, *On the Laws and Governance of England*, ed. Lockwood; and *De Laudibus Legem Anglie*, ed. Chrimes. For the context of the composition of these works see Kekewich, *John Vale's Book*, 53–66; Gross, *Lancastrian Kingship*, 61–90; and Lockwood, *Laws and Governance*, xv–xxxix. Gunn, *Early Tudor Government*, 15 draws attention to the legal dimension.

4   For discussion of the meaning of *dominium politicum et regale* see Chrimes, 'Theory of Dominium', and *English Constitutional Ideas*; Burns, *Lordship, Kingship and Empire*, 58–70; and Lockwood, *Laws and Governance*, xxix–xxxiv. The idea of total sovereignty is stressed by Kekewich, *John Vale's Book*, 64–6 (from whom the quotation comes, 64) and Gross, *Lancastrian Kingship*, 7–8, 63–4. The traditional, 'whig' view of the concept is expressed most forcefully in Wilkinson, *Constitutional History of England*, 199–204. For discussion of Fortescue's advice for strengthening the monarchy see below pp. 257–8, 378.

5   For Edward III's Kingship see Ormrod, *Edward III* and Waugh, *Edward III*. See also Ormrod, *Political Life*, ch. 4 and Gillingham, 'Crisis or Continuity?' 59–80. The constitutional conflicts of Richard II's reign can be approached through Jones, *Royal Policy*, Saul, *Richard II* and Tuck, *Richard II*. Richard II's perception of kingship has been explored by Saul, 'Vocabulary of Kingship' and 'Kingship', and by Walker, 'Views on Kingship', passim. The differences in perception are also reflected in the approaches of modern historians. Whereas Watts stresses the indivisibility of king and kingdom, Harriss, 'Political Society', passim and 'The King and his Subjects', passim stresses the distinction between crown and political society. The two are not necessarily incompatible; one expresses the theory from the monarchical point of view, the other the practice as experienced by the subject.

6   Watts, 'Ideas, Principles and Politics', passim, and 'Polemic and Politics in the 1450s', passim; Chrimes, *English Constitutional Ideas*, 168–91 (Russell); Dudley, *Tree of Commonwealth*, 31. For the suggestion that the term 'commonweal' first emerged in the 1450s see Starkey, 'Which Age of Reform?', 13–27.

7   Brown, *Governance* provides the most comprehensive description of the structure of late medieval government outlined in this and the following paragraphs.

8   Gunn, *Early Tudor Government*, 144–52.

9   Ibid., 48–50; Harriss, 'Political Society', 37–8; Brown, 'The King's Councillors', passim and *Governance*, 30–42; Lander, 'Yorkist Council and Administration' and 'Council, Administration and Councillors', passim; Holmes, 'Great Council', 840–62. See also above pp. 151–4.

10 Roskell, *House of Commons*, vol. i, 6–23. For convocation see Swanson, *Church and Society*, 108–10 and for clerical taxation, ibid., 110–18 and McHardy, 'Clerical Taxation', passim. The role of proctor of the clergy in parliament is discussed by Davies and Denton, *English Parliament*, 100–6.

11 For the lords and composition of the commons see Powell and Wallis, *House of Lords*; Brown, *Governance*, 177–207; Roskell, *House of Commons*, i, 24–54; Harriss, 'Political Society', 40–6 and *King, Parliament and Public Finance*.

12 Taxation and the legislative procedures of the house are discussed in Gunn, *Early Tudor Government*, 122, 131–3, 136–7; Brown, *Governance*, 207–37; Roskell, *House of Commons*, i, 69–142; and Davies and Denton, *English Parliament*, 109–84.

13 Brown, *Governance*, 100–40; and works cited in Further Reading; Powell, 'Law and Justice', passim. Note, however, that at the lowest level customary law, which varied from locality to locality, was administered.

14 Musson and Ormrod, *English Justice*, 42–74 and Powell, *Kingship, Law and Society*, 48–114. For further references see Further Reading.

15 Powell, 'Law and Justice'; Maddern, *Violence and Social Order*, 114–34.

16 Post, 'Crime in Later Medieval England', passim; Powell, 'Law and Justice'; Maddern, *Violence and Social Order*, 22–59.

17 Maddern, *Violence and Social Order*, ch. 3. For Moleyns and Gresham see Richmond, *Paston Family: First Phase*, 47–60; for other examples of violent crime see, idem, 'Murder of Thomas Dennis', passim; and Payling, 'Murder, Motive and Punishment', passim, which also reasserts the view that it was a weakness of the Crown in the fifteenth century to fail to punish violence among the landed classes. For the particular circumstances of the Scottish borders see Neville, 'Keeping the Peace', passim and for the development, especially after 1424, of the procedure of march-days for dealing with cross-border incidents during the time of truce see idem, *Violence, Custom and Law*, 125ff.

18 Avery, 'Equitable Jurisdiction', passim: Pronay, 'Chancellor, the Chancery and the Council'; Guy, 'Equitable Jurisdictions'; Gunn, *Early Tudor Government*, 81–3.

19 Powell, 'Arbitration and the Law', passim; and 'Settlement of Disputes by Arbitration', passim; Rawcliffe, 'The Great Lord as Peacekeeper', passim; Rowney, 'Arbitration in Gentry Disputes'; Pollard, *North-Eastern England*, 116–19.

20 Harriss, 'Political Society'; and, 'Dimensions of Politics', 2–7; Ormrod, *Political Life*, 56–77; Carpenter, *Wars of the Roses*, 27–46. For the debate as to whether

later medieval developments strengthened or weakened the monarchy see below, pp. 255–7.

21 For recent literature on household and court see Further Reading.

22 See above pp. 31, 40–1, 50, 75, 99 and below pp. 302–4, 356, 358, 363–4.

23 Morgan, 'King's Affinity' and 'House of Policy'; Horrox, *Richard III*, 226–72. For the antecedents see Given-Wilson, *Royal Household* and 'King and Gentry', passim.

24 Chrimes, *Constitutional Ideas*, 172; Harriss, 'Dimensions', 2–10 and 'King and his Subjects', 14–21.

25 Hicks, *Bastard Feudalism*, 1–68 and 'Bastard Feudalism', passim; Coss, 'Bastard Feudalism Revised'; Walker, *Lancastrian Affinity*; and Jones and Walker, 'Private Indentures'. For Richard II see Given-Wilson, *Royal Household*, 212ff. Care has to be used in handling the phrase 'Bastard Feudalism': its use varies from the description of the practice of indentured retaining to the characterisation of the whole of late-medieval society.

26 Walker, *Lancastrian Affinity*, passim; Pollard, *North-Eastern England*, 122–31, and 'Northern Retainers'; Hicks, 'Fourth Earl of Northumberland', and 'Lord Hastings' Indentured Retainers?', passim; Bean, *Estates of the Percy Family*, 85–97, 130–5; Johnson, *Duke Richard of York*, 15–21; Rawcliffe, *Staffords*, 72–7; Pugh, 'The Magnates, Knights and Gentry', 101–3. This is not to imply that such lords only retained for military purposes. Note too the stress in Hicks, *Bastard Feudalism* on forms of association other than formal indenture.

27 Cameron, 'Livery and Retaining', passim; Hicks, '1468 Statute', passim; Jones and Walker, 'Private Indentures', 31–2; Saul, 'Abolition of Badges', passim; and Given-Wilson, *King's Affinity*, 236–43. For the political context of the 1468 act see below p. 281.

28 Horrox, 'Service', passim and 'Personality and Politics', passim.

29 Kirby (ed.) *The Plumpton Letters*, 52–3; Pollard, *North-Eastern England*, 139–41.

30 Carpenter, 'Gentry and Community', passim; Coss, 'Bastard Feudalism', 54–8, Harriss, 'Dimensions'; Pollard, 'Society, Politics and the Wars of the Roses', 8–9; Lander, *Justices of the Peace* and the particular studies listed in Further Reading.

31 Maddicott, 'County Community' and 'Parliament and the Constituencies'; Pollard, *North-Eastern England*, 153–4. For a trenchant critique of the concept see Carpenter, 'Gentry and Community', 340–56. For different perceptions of the protests against Gaunt's retainers see Saul, 'Abolition of Badges' and Walker, *Lancastrian Affinity*, 253–60 and for East Anglia see Virgoe, 'County Community', passim and Richmond, *Paston Family*, 53–63.

32 Carpenter, 'Gentry and Community', 356–65 and Pollard, *North-Eastern England*, 125–31; Castor, 'Rule of East Anglia', passim.

33 Carpenter, *Locality and Polity*, 399–486, but see Hicks, *Warwick*, 51–2 and 'Between Majorities'; Griffiths, *Henry VI*, 584–92; Richmond, *Paston Family: Fastolff's Will*, 165–216 (East Anglia in the 1460s); Cherry, 'Courtenay Earls of Devon', passim; Pollard, *North-Eastern England*, 141–2.

34 Pollard, *North-Eastern England*, 108–20, 126–7, and 'Richard Clervaux'; *Plumpton Letters*, 3–13, 301–41. See also Maddern, 'Friends of the Dead'; Carpenter, 'Stonor Circle', passim, *Locality and Polity*, 281–346 and 'Gentry and Community', 366–74; and Richmond, *John Hopton*.

35 Carpenter, *Locality and Polity*, Part I, passim; Harriss, 'Dimensions', 2–7.

36 Carpenter, 'Political and Constitutional History', passim and *Wars of the Roses*, 43–4, 63–4; Powell, *Kingship, Law and Society*, 1–6 and 'After "After McFarlane"', 1–16. Who you know, of course, has never ceased to be of importance in the advancement of careers in politics, the Church and the professions.

37 See above pp. 60–2, 119–21 and below pp. 277–9.

38 Hicks, 'Idealism', passim and Mercer, 'Lancastrian Loyalism', 23–37; Pollard, 'Society, Politics and the Wars of the Roses', 14–15; Jones, 'Somerset, York and the Wars of the Roses', passim; Harriss, 'Dimensions', 7–8; Gunn, 'Chivalry and Politics'; Archer, 'Parliamentary Restoration', passim.

39 Horrox, 'Personalities and Politics'; Arthurson, 'Question of Loyalty'. Hicks, 'Lancastrian Loyalism' and Mercer, 'Lancastrian Loyalism'.

40 Given-Wilson, *King's Affinity*, 41–8, 98–101, 111–13; Griffiths, *Henry VI*, 320–2; Gunn, *Early Tudor Government*, 130–1. See also above pp. 92–3, 107–8, 141–3 and below pp. 324–5.

41 Arthurson, 'Rising of 1497', passim; Harvey, *Cade's Rebellion* and 'Popular Politics?', passim; Hicks, 'Yorkshire Rebellion'; and above pp. 109, 132, 156, 160 and below pp. 281–3, 291–2.

42 Storey, *House of Lancaster*, 34–5; Attreed, *York House Books*, 696; Hudson, *English Wycliffite Writings*, 24–9, 150–5; Hicks, *Warwick*, 191–210, 271–5. For propaganda and its use see Allan, 'Royal Propaganda'; Doig, 'Political Propaganda'; Richmond, 'Hand and Mouth'; Ross, 'Rumour, Propaganda and Public Opinion'. Political manifestos first appeared during Cade's Revolt.

43 Dyer, 'Taxation and Communities', passim; Pollard, 'Lancastrian Constitutional Experiment', 103–9; Gross, 'Langland's Rats', passim; Harriss, 'Dimensions', 10–14.

44 Goheen, 'Peasant Politics?', 43–62; Kumin, *Shaping of a Community*, 103–25, 125–47; De Windt, 'Local Government', passim. Harvey, *Cade's Rebellion*, 73–111. See also above, ch. 7, pp. 188–90.

45 Keen, *Later Middle Ages*, 143–65; Prestwich, *Three Edwards*, 165–244; Kaeuper, *War, Justice and Public Order*, 62, 132, 181, 383–90; Lander, *Limitations*, passim;

Coss, 'Bastard Feudalism Revised', 52 also identifies a subversion of royal authority, but at an earlier date.

46 Carpenter, *Wars of the Roses*, 24–3, 41–3, drawing on Harriss, 'Political Society', esp. 56; Gillingham, 'Crisis or Continuity?'; Ormrod, *Edward III*, esp. 200–2; Musson and Ormrod, *English Justice*, 158.

47 Bennett, 'Edward III's Entail', 600–4; Britnell, 'Economic Context', 58–64; Griffiths, 'Provinces and the Dominions', 4–12; Gross, 'Fallibilities', 65 ff; Harriss, 'Political Society', 57; Ormrod, *Political Society*, esp. 130–7; Strohm, *Empty Throne*, esp. 196–212. But see Gillingham, 'Crisis or Continuity?', 61–4, denying the existence of a financial crisis.

48 For Wales and Ireland see above pp. 171–3; for Northern England, Pollard, *North-Eastern England*, 400–5.

49 Ellis, S., *Tudor Frontiers*, 3–45 and 'English Territories', 187–204 and Pollard, 'Crown and the County Palatine', passim. I have changed my view on this issue since the publication of *North-Eastern England*.

50 See below, pp. 310–11, 371–2.

51 See below, pp. 311–12, 366–71.

52 For the idea of an independent gentry see Carpenter, *Locality and Polity*, 61–44; Harriss, 'Political Society', 56; Richmond, 'After McFarlane', 46–60; and Walker, *Lancastrian Affinity*, 250–61. A distinction needs to be drawn between the growing importance of the gentry in political society and the extent to which the gentry in any county exercised independent power. For the recovery and expansion of the royal affinity under the Yorkists and early Tudors see Gunn, *Early Tudor Government*, 24–42; Morgan, 'King's Affinity' and 'House of Policy' and Starkey, 'Age of the Household', passim.

53 See below pp. 300, 311, 340, 366–7, 372–3, 378.

54 For discussion of Fortescue's proposed remedies and their implementation see Griffiths, 'Provinces and Dominions', 20–1; Gross, *Dissolution*, 8–13; and Watts, '*New Ffundation*'. For the emergence of a civil service see Guth, 'Sir Reynold Bray', 47–54.

PART THREE

YORK AND TUDOR

CHAPTER TEN

The first reign of Edward IV, 1461–71

Securing the throne, 1461–4

Decisive as it subsequently proved to be, Towton did not immediately bring civil war to an end. With fluctuating intensity, open conflict continued for a further three years. There was sustained Lancastrian resistance in Northumberland and North Wales; there were Lancastrian plots; there was Scottish and French intervention, in particular war with Scotland until 1464; and there was recession and unrest with which to contend. The initial survival of the new regime was touch and go. And although Edward IV had snuffed out almost all resistance by June 1464, the regime still remained fragile thereafter. The last stronghold in Wales, Harlech, was not taken until 1468. The deposed king was still at large until 1465, and thereafter his son, Edward, prince of Wales, remained in exile in France awaiting the opportunity to recover his right. As long as there was a king over the water, Edward IV could never be entirely secure on the throne. Moreover, he came to the throne with a far narrower power base than Henry IV had enjoyed and less support among the political nation. As a consequence Edward IV was more dependent on the support of the Nevilles than ever Henry had been on the Percys and faced a more pressing need to offer reconciliation and find new support than had the earlier usurper.

In the aftermath of his victory at Towton, the new king secured control of Yorkshire and Durham, receiving the submission of Bishop Booth on 22 April. It may have been news of the surrender of Berwick to the Scots by Margaret of Anjou that prompted him to move further north to Newcastle, which he reached by 1 May. Here some fugitives of Towton were brought to him, the most prominent of whom, the earl of Wiltshire, was forthwith beheaded. But Edward did not advance beyond the Tyne. It was important for him to be crowned as soon as possible. Accordingly he left Lord Fauconberg as captain of Newcastle, while he began his journey back to Westminster, via Lancashire, Cheshire and the midlands. The Nevilles – Warwick and Montagu as well as Fauconberg – were left in command of the north.[1]

The coronation took place on 28 June. Among the knights of the Bath, traditionally dubbed on its eve, were the new king's brothers, George and Richard; on its morrow the elder, George, was created duke of Clarence. The following day Edward's principal followers were ennobled: Viscount Bourgchier was created earl of Essex and Lord Fauconberg, earl of Kent. The leading Yorkist retainers were created barons: Sir Walter Devereux (as Lord Ferrers), Sir William Hastings, Sir William Herbert, and Sir Humphrey Stafford of Southwick prominent among them. But the celebrations were short-lived and the first parliament was postponed until the autumn; the kingdom still had to be subdued. Henry VI, Queen Margaret and their son had escaped to Scotland; their supporters held Northumberland and North Wales; rebellion was being fostered in the south-west and rumours abounded that Charles VII of France was about to launch an invasion.[2]

A joint Lancastrian-Scottish invasion of northern England in late May and June, in which Carlisle had been besieged for six weeks and the county palatine of Durham had been raided in support of a Lancastrian rising, was defeated by the Neville brothers and Bishop Booth. The king was free to turn his attention to Wales where Lancastrian supporters still held out. Having made a thanksgiving pilgrimage to Canterbury, he himself moved to Bristol, but in the event left it to Herbert and Ferrers to attempt to chase their old enemy, Jasper Tudor, Earl of Pembroke out of the principality, while Edward himself remained in Ludlow to establish control of the central marches. Pembroke castle fell to Herbert on 30 September. A counter-attack by the earl was defeated outside Caernarvon a few weeks later and Denbigh was secured early in January. But Jasper Tudor managed to retain Harlech. While the whole of Wales was never brought under effective Yorkist control until that castle was recovered seven years later, the danger was at least contained. In the summer of 1461, too, the death of Charles VII and the succession of his estranged son as Louis XI brought a respite from the fear of French intervention. In the far north the castles of Alnwick and Dunstanburgh were secured and Lord Ogle, also ennobled after the coronation, concluded a truce with the Scots, thus isolating the remaining Lancastrian pockets of resistance in Naworth under Lord Dacre and Bamburgh under Sir Ralph Percy. And finally, with the recovery of the out-lying fortress of Hammes in October, the new regime secured full control of Calais.[3]

By the time parliament finally assembled on 4 November, Edward IV could feel reasonably secure. The main business was the formal enactment and declaration of his legitimate title to the throne, and an act of attainder punishing some 130 traitors for meticulously identified acts of treason from the killing of the heir to the throne (the duke of York at Wakefield) in December 1460 to the Lancastrian rising in Durham in June 1461. Most of those attainted, whose estates were confiscated, including fourteen lay peers, were either dead or still actively in arms against the king. Many opponents, such as Lord Rivers and his son Lord Scales, had already received pardons; others were encouraged to come to terms in the succeeding years. An act of resumption was passed, but its impact was much reduced by the many exemptions allowed by the king, and various statutes which had lapsed on the change of dynasty were renewed. The king did not ask for a grant of taxation, but before the assembly was prorogued on 21 December he did thank the commons for their support and promised that he would be as good and gracious a sovereign as ever there had been.[4]

But the king and his advisers had no cause to be complacent. In the early months of 1462 further steps were taken to secure the north. Naworth was taken and an agreement was reached to support dissident Scottish nobles, which led to the extension and strengthening of the truce with the regency government of Scotland under Mary of Guelders. But a plot focusing on the earl of Oxford, uncovered in February, and a rash of popular disturbances, in one case in Wells in Somerset with distinctly treasonable overtones, revealed that the king's control was only superficial. Disorder, in the wake of civil war, was widespread. Thus in the spring Edward set out on a long judicial progress through the midlands, which took him from Coventry to Lincoln and eventually Leicester in July.[5]

In the meantime, Margaret of Anjou, having lost Scottish support, set off for France to make a personal appeal to her kinsman Louis XI. And Louis, taking up his father's policy, gave her a lavish welcome and, in a formal agreement reached on 28 June, committed himself to aid an invasion of England in exchange for the cession of Calais. By August Edward IV, fully aware of the new threat, had fitted out a navy under the earl of Kent which eventually raided the coasts of Brittany and western France. Whether the raids convinced Louis that Edward was well prepared to meet an invasion, or whether he merely changed his mind, by the time Margaret and her band of exiles finally set off in October it was with only nominal French military aid and her destination was the far north of Northumberland. She landed at Bamburgh; Alnwick and Dunstanburgh fell into her hands; and the Scottish government renounced the truce. Edward IV reacted immediately. He called his household together and marched rapidly north. But, not long after his arrival in Durham late in November, he was struck down with measles and his army moved on without him to reinforce the earl of Warwick, who had already laid siege to the castles. The main royal fear was that the Scots would invade in strength to support the Lancastrians. It was probably because of this fear, doubts about Bishop Booth's loyalty and the overriding need to keep possession of Norham, which belonged to the bishop of Durham, that on 7 December the king ordered the sequestration of the bishop's temporalities and sent the bishop himself into internal exile at Pembroke College, Cambridge. Despite the Scottish threat, Warwick was able to invest all three castles without challenge; the garrisons at Bamburgh and Dunstanburgh negotiated to surrender on Christmas Eve; Alnwick followed early in January.[6]

It is in the context of the fear of a major Scottish invasion that we should understand the king's decision to offer terms to the Lancastrian rebels at the end of 1462. He needed the Northumbrian castles intact and in English hands. Thus it was that the duke of Somerset, Sir Ralph Percy and their allies were pardoned, received back in his grace and restored to their estates. Percy was even given command of Bamburgh and Dunstanburgh on behalf of the king as soon as they were handed over. Edward IV has been criticised for his foolish generosity to his enemies; but there was method in his madness. He could hope that Sir Ralph Percy, the head of his family during the minority of the fourth earl, would put the defence of Northumberland against the Scots before his hatred of the Nevilles. Moreover, the county could not be defended unless the castles in the far north were defensible and in the hands of captains who could call upon the loyalty of the local inhabitants. At the same time there was something to be said for a policy of conciliation towards the personal enemies of the houses of York and Neville. If they could be won over, especially in the context of war against one of England's traditional enemies, Margaret of Anjou could be isolated and further resistance by Lancastrian loyalists brought to an end. In the event the policy failed, but in the context it was understandable.[7]

Having, as he believed, settled the north on a more lasting basis, in January 1463 Edward himself returned south, stopping at Fotheringhay to celebrate a month's mind for his late father and in order to prepare for his second parliament which was to meet at Westminster on 29 April. Edward was welcomed to London, with Somerset at his side, in triumph on 24 February. The confidence that the Yorkist establishment shared that the far north was now secured is shown by the fact that Warwick and his brother John, Lord Montagu, also returned south to convey the bodies of their father, the earl of Salisbury and brother Sir Thomas Neville to formal interment in the family mausoleum at Bisham on 15 February. Parliament when it met proceded to reverse the attainders of Somerset and his brother-in-law Sir Henry Lewis. Its principal other business was the enactment of a series of measures to protect English agriculture, trade and industry from external competition in the face of worsening recession. Outside parliament much public display was made of the new rapprochement between the king and the duke of Somerset with jousting at Westminster and hunting at Windsor, the duke even, it was reported, being given the honour of sharing the king's bedchamber. At the same time an embassy from the duke of Burgundy was lavishly entertained, the outcome of which was a plan for the representatives of the kings of England and France and the duke to meet at St Omer to consider a general truce.[8]

However the euphoria was brought to an abrupt end by the news that northern Northumberland had once more fallen into Lancastrian hands. In March Sir Ralph Percy had admitted Margaret of Anjou into Bamburgh and Dunstanburgh. His treachery seems to have been contained until in mid-May Alnwick was also turned over to the Lancastrians by Sir Ralph Grey, hitherto a reliable Yorkist lieutenant in the county. The king's first action, on hearing of Grey's treachery, was to send Montagu, who had just been created warden of the east march, to the north, with Warwick to follow as soon as possible. In the meantime the king persuaded parliament to vote its first taxation in response to a promise to lead an army against the Scots; a variation on a fifteenth and tenth which was styled an aid and was to be paid in two instalments in August and November. Parliament was prorogued on 17 June. Having secured a further grant from convocation, and fitted out a fleet to support his operations along the coast, the king set off for the north himself. At Northampton a riot occurred against the duke of Somerset whom Edward sent, according to one source, to North Wales for his own protection.[9]

In the meantime the Scots had laid siege to Norham. Warwick rapidly gathering reinforcements in the north moved quickly to the garrison's aid. After fifteen days the siege was lifted, the Scottish army retreated and Warwick followed with a raid into Scotland. Edward, still declaring his intention to lead an invasion of Scotland, summoned troops to meet him at Newcastle on 13 September. Before resuming his journey north, however, he went down to Dover to instruct his ambassadors to France, led by the Chancellor, George Neville, for the forthcoming negotiations at Hesdin. He did not travel north again until the end of November, his intention by then being not to invade Scotland, but to conclude a truce, agreed to run from 16 December until October 1464. No action whatsoever was taken against the Northumbrian castles; the Lancastrian garrisons, strengthened by the duke of Somerset and another recalcitrant rebel, Sir Humphrey Neville, being allowed the free run of Northumberland. Edward's strategy now was to isolate the Lancastrian diehards diplomatically, before moving in for the kill.[10]

Although Edward's attention was deflected by renewed popular agitation in Lancashire, Cheshire, Gloucestershire and Cambridgeshire, to which he turned, the momentum of negotiations with the French and the Scots was maintained. Warwick was called south to extend the truce with France to cover the sea as well as land – an agreement reached on 12 April 1464. It was while marching north to Norham to meet and escort the Scottish envoys to York for further negotiations that on Hedgely Moor in late April 1464, Lord Montagu ran into and defeated a Lancastrian force under the command of the duke of Somerset and Sir Ralph Percy. Percy was killed on the field. The king returned north in May. By the time he arrived in York, Montagu, soon to be rewarded with the earldom of Northumberland, had achieved another, and more decisive victory over Somerset at Hexham on 15 May. Somerset was captured on the field and executed four days later; Lords Roos and Hungerford were taken in flight and later executed at Newcastle. The truce with Scotland having been renewed for a further fifteen years on 1 June, the new earl was free to move on the three Northumbrian castles. Alnwick and Dunstanburgh, which had been granted to him, yielded without resistance on 23 June; Bamburgh, a royal castle held by Grey and Neville, surrendered after a brief but destructive bombardment. While Neville escaped with his life, Grey was handed over to the king, tried before the constable of the realm, the earl of Worcester, and executed at Doncaster on 10 July. Margaret of Anjou and her son had earlier slipped back to France, leaving Henry VI in the care of his loyal followers. After Hexham he was taken into hiding in northern England, but was ultimately betrayed in July 1465 and brought to London to be held a captive in the Tower. Only Harlech, which successfully resisted yet another siege in the autumn of 1464, remained in Lancastrian hands.[11]

The new regime

One reason why it took three years to secure the peripheries of the kingdom was that the regime enjoyed little committed support. The number of Yorkist peers, other than those ennobled by Edward IV, was low; a quarter had continued to oppose him after Towton. Henry Bourgchier, Earl of Essex, his brothers William (Lord FitzWaurin) and John (Lord Berners) and younger son Humphrey (Lord Cromwell) were his kinsmen. John Tiptoft, Earl of Worcester, Thomas, Lord Stanley and the lesser peers Rivers, Audley, Dinham, Greystoke, FitzHugh, the newly promoted Ogle and Scrope of Bolton were the only significant figures early in the reign not associated with his father, and the last four of these were Neville associates. It is not surprising, therefore, that he continued to rely so heavily on the Nevilles – Warwick, his uncle Fauconberg until his death in 1463, Montagu and George, Bishop of Exeter, promoted to York in 1465.[12]

The weakness of committed support explains, in part, the policy of conciliation followed by the regime from the beginning. The very public reconciliation with Henry Beaufort, Duke of Somerset, at the end of 1462 was not an isolated phenomenon; it was at one with general policy and given such prominence to encourage the others. Edward was generous to the brothers and sons of those that had fought against him and were still opposing him; Thomas Hungerford, Henry Courtenay and John de Vere, Earl of Oxford, who was allowed to succeed to his title and lands in 1464 only two years after the execution of his father. Such generosity extended to many below the ranks of the peerage, such as Sir William Plumpton and Thomas Tresham, and even to such partisan household servants of Henry VI as Thomas Tuddenham. It caused resentment in some quarters and was clearly a risky policy. Indeed it largely failed. Not only Somerset, but also Hungerford, Courtenay and De Vere subsequently rebelled. Nevertheless it could be argued that the policy of reconciliation helped the new regime to survive its first fragile years.[13]

The new regime also lacked resources. England was in the trough of a recession in agriculture, industry and trade. Revenue from customs, voted to the king for life in 1465, were at an all-time low. The royal demesne had been enlarged by the addition of the duchy of York, but the revenue from these lands, forfeited estates and those in royal hands by reason of wardship was initially lower than it might have been because of agrarian difficulties, the redistribution of forfeited estates to reward followers and the disruption of civil war. Not until 1463 did Edward dare to ask parliament for a subsidy. Yet the costs of defending the kingdom were high: the east march alone consumed £6,000 in the year 1463–4. The precise state of the royal finances in these first years is not known, but they were precarious. It is conceivable that the reason Edward did not press ahead with the promised invasion of Scotland, and the recovery of the Northumbrian castles after their loss in 1463, was that the parliamentary grant was already consumed.[14]

Thirdly, the new regime was faced by the determination of Margaret of Anjou, who had in her company both the deposed Henry VI and his heir, to continue to fight. As long as the head of the house of Lancaster was at liberty, the Yorkists could never be confident of their hold on the throne. There was always an alternative king to whom dissidents could turn with a clear conscience. And in the first years of the reign France, Scotland and, to a degree, Burgundy exploited this circumstance to the full. There was much to be said in favour of a diplomatic offensive in 1463 to isolate the Lancastrians, before once again dislodging them from the far north. So weak and short of resources was the regime in its early years that it had little alternative but to follow the course of action it did.

Finally, Edward IV was young and inexperienced. He was still only eighteen when his father died and he seized the throne. To Scottish and

French observers in 1464 he appeared to be under the domination of the earl of Warwick. The wordly-wise Bishop Kennedy of St Andrews wrote that Warwick was 'the governor of England under King Edward'. 'They have but two rulers,' joked the governor of Abbeville about England in a letter of March to Louis XI, 'M. de Warwick, and another whose name I have forgotten.' It was once argued, largely on the basis of comments such as these, that Warwick was the real ruler of England in the early 1460s and Edward but a puppet. It is now appreciated that there was more to the young Edward than this. But it might be going too far to argue that Edward was fully in command of the earl, directing affairs from the centre. It is not possible to determine who ultimately was the author of policy. There is no reason to suppose, for instance, that Warwick, while he may have been more sceptical of its likely success, disagreed with the policy of conciliation. Indeed he matched the king's reconciliation with his personal enemy the duke of Somerset, by his own reconciliation with Sir Ralph Percy and Sir Humphrey Neville, the leading active adult members of the two families with whom he had been at daggers drawn. Together, in these years of crisis, the king and earl formed a formidable partnership.[15]

Yet well-informed contemporaries were perhaps correct to note that there was something unusual in the relationship between the powerful subject and the inexperienced king. Warwick was licensed from the beginning to take the initiative in negotiations with the Scots, as Kennedy knew from the other side, and by the end of 1463 he was beginning to engage almost independently in diplomacy with France. He corresponded directly with Louis XI, using the Scottish agent, William Moneypenny, as his intermediary. At no point does it seem that he went beyond what Edward authorised, but the impression is given, and clearly was given then, that he, and his brother George as Chancellor, had an independent authority. The earl's wealth, the stretch of his estates, and the scale of his hospitality greatly impressed contemporaries and suggest that, like Cardinal Wolsey in a later reign, he behaved from the beginning as more than a mere subject of his king. And this is not surprising given his power, his formative political experience in the 1450s, Edward IV's youth and the king's dependence on him.[16]

Certainly Edward was exceeedingly generous to the earl and his family. It was not simply that Warwick was lavishly rewarded with offices and lands on an unprecedented scale, but that he and his kinsmen were given almost unhindered control of both Calais and the straits of Dover as constable of Dover and warden of the Cinque Ports, but also a free hand in northern England. In Yorkshire, in addition to his own inherited estates, he was confirmed by the king as steward of all the duchy of Lancashire lordships, allowed to take possession of the honour of Richmond, and granted all the Percy estates in the North Riding and Craven, as well as the custody of the estates of his insane uncle, Lord Latimer. In Cumberland and Westmorland he was granted the forfeited Clifford and (in 1465) Percy estates as well as the hereditary shrievalty of Westmorland. In Lancashire he received the stewardships of all the duchy lordships. The removal of Bishop Booth in 1462 enabled him, in the king's name, to dominate the administration of the palatinate – a domination continued after Booth's restoration in 1464 by the presence of his brother John as chief steward. Northumberland, in 1464, came under control of John Neville, promoted to the earldom. To cap it all, in 1465 George Neville became archbishop of York, annexing not only spiritual authority, but also extensive temporal power to the family's hegemony. With land went men. While Edward retained a handful of men there, the earl was at liberty to recruit followers throughout the region, within the duchy of Lancaster as freely as elsewhere. It is true that Warwick and Monatagu were expected to, and did, find the men and resources successfully to defend the region in the early years; but it was folly to allow such a concentration of power into the hands of one family, even though perhaps it was the price demanded for their support, and it betokens a relationship between king and subject heavily weighted towards the subject. It is not surprising that Louis XI came to believe that Warwick was the key to power in England.[17]

The king's marriage

The extent to which Edward IV was in awe of Warwick is revealed by the manner of his secret marriage to Elizabeth Woodville on 1 May 1464. Elizabeth was the daughter of Richard, Lord Rivers, whom the king had pardoned in 1461, and who had been a royal councillor since March 1463. She was the widow of John Grey, Lord Ferrers of Groby, and the mother of two sons. Although her mother, Jacquetta of Luxembourg, was of aristocratic stock, as a widow and the daughter of a lesser English peer she would not have been considered entirely the appropriate choice for a king. It can only be the case that he married Elizabeth, in the face of convention and in preference to the expected diplomatic match, because he was in love.

Matters were made worse by the king's deception. He knew that his marriage was the most important counter he possessed in international diplomacy. He had already rejected a proposal that he should marry Isabella of Castile. Since the autumn of 1463, as England and France grew closer, the idea for a marriage between Edward and Louis XI's sister, Bona of Savoy, had gathered pace. At the negotiations in London in April 1464 between Warwick and Louis' ambassador, the idea seems to have been advanced further; Warwick despatched a letter to Louis which encouraged him to think that Edward was willing and further negotiations between the two kingdoms were scheduled to continue at St Omer in May. These were postponed and Warwick's commissioned was renewed. At no point does it appear that the earl was instructed by Edward to negotiate a marriage, but he was encouraged to continue discussions even though the king was already married. The fact that Edward made his marriage to Elizabeth in secret, and did not announce it until the end of September, reveals that he knew he would face the disapproval of Warwick, as well as other councillors. It was the manner of the marriage, as much as its fact, which shows Edward's lack of confidence and judgement.[18]

Much has been made of Elizabeth Woodville's unsuitability, the rapaciousness of her family and the destabilising effect it had on the Yorkist regime, much of it based on propaganda generated later by Warwick. The queen herself has been much maligned. In so far as one can tell, she had only very modest material demands, her household was never extravagant, she played virtually no part in politics until after Edward IV's death and was content to play the conventional supportive role of queen and mother. There was no great windfall of estates showered on her kinsmen. The marriages, in the following two years, of her five sisters into the ranks of the established peerage (the duke of Buckingham, and the heirs of the earls of Arundel, Essex, Kent and of Lord Herbert), of her eldest son, Thomas Grey, to the Holland heiress, and especially of her brother to the sixty-five-year-old dowager duchess of Norfolk raised a few eyebrows; but these connections with the queen and the the court were as much sought by the families of the spouses as they were by the queen herself, and were at the king's instance. The greatest political beneficiary was her father, promoted Earl Rivers and made Treasurer of England in 1466. He became the dominant figure at court, the centre of a faction of 'New Yorkists', using his somewhat naive daughter's household as the basis of his influence and for the promotion of his connections.[19]

The breach with Warwick

Rumour later circulated in Europe that the marriage marked the beginning of the quarrel between the king and his most powerful subject. But publicly, at least, Warwick showed his full support and acceptance. He was one of those who escorted Elizabeth to Reading Abbey on Michaelmas Day 1464 for her formal introduction to the world as queen of England. He presumably gave his assent to the marriage of his aunt, the duchess of Norfolk, to the queen's young brother. He still continued to receive grants and favours from the king, even as late as November 1467 being granted the valuable wardship of Francis, Lord Lovell. His brother George, too, was promoted to the archbishopric of York in 1465. Both remained high in the confidence and council of the king. Yet the political world changed after 1464. Edward IV was no longer as beholden to Warwick as he had been. The change is apparent in developments at court. The queen's coronation on 26 May 1465 was the focus for glittering court ceremonial, including a great tournament at Westminster on the following day in which Lord Stanley excelled. Edward's highly chivalric court style was forged in the years of relaxation following his marriage. In April Lord Scales had accepted the commission of the ladies of the court to perform a feat of arms with a figure worthy of his status. And so was set in motion the plans for the great tournament between him and the Bastard of Burgundy which, after much delay, finally took place at Smithfield in 1467. From this new, youthful, courtly world Warwick seems to have been distant.[20]

The occasion of the open estrangement between Warwick and Edward was disagreement over foreign policy. By 1465 the king found himself being courted not only by Louis XI, but also by the great princes of France, including the dukes of Burgundy and Brittany, who rebelled against their king in the summer. While the existing truces with France, Burgundy and Brittany were all regularly renewed, the choice facing England was between an alliance with Louis or with the dukes. National sentiment and tradition clearly favoured a triple alliance against France; but there were reasons for considering a break with tradition. England had become engaged in a damaging trade war with the duke of Burgundy. Commercial relationships between the Netherlands and England had deteriorated as a result of the steps taken to protect English trade in the spring of 1463. Matters had been made worse for the Low Countries by the devaluation of the English currency ordered by Edward IV in September 1464. A devaluation of 20 per cent was triply rewarding: it brought an inflow of revenue from the clipping of the coinage; it made English goods, especially woollens, more competitively priced abroad; and by increasing the money supply gave a much needed boost to demand in the sluggish economy at home. However, it led immediately to a Burgundian ban on the sale of all English cloth in the duke's territories. The government responded with its own ban on the import of all goods from Burgundy.[21]

During 1465 negotiations held fire as France was engulfed by the brief War of the Common Weal. England cautiously remained neutral. Although defeated on the field of battle, Louis was able to make sufficient concessions to his enemies to restore peace. But the treaty of Conflans in October, by restoring the Somme towns to Burgundy, had made the duke stronger, and the death of Isabella, countess of Charolais, in August freed Charles of Charolais, the heir to Philip the Good, for an advantageous marriage alliance. In the spring of 1466 Edward IV commissioned a further embassy under Warwick's leadership to treat with both France and Burgundy in order to discover what was on offer. The meeting held between Warwick and Charles in April to discuss further the count's proposal to marry Edward's sister Margaret was not a success, the two apparently taking an instant dislike for each other. Negotiations with the French, the following month, were more amicable, but led only to a renewal of the truce and the proposal that a marriage should be concluded between Margaret of York and a prince of France.

Throughout 1466 a stream of envoys passed to and fro between the courts of England, France, Brittany and Burgundy. It soon became apparent that Warwick, with Lord Wenlock, his deputy in Calais constantly at his side, was advocating and actively pursuing a French alliance; Rivers, whose links through his countess were with the Burgundians, led in the negotiations with Charles of Charolais standing in for his ageing father. By October, Charles and Edward IV had put their signatures to a secret non-aggression pact and agreed to further negotiations concerning a marriage alliance and commercial relationships early in the new year. These made little headway because Duke Philip was reluctant to revoke his edict. At the same time a French legation arrived in London and parallel negotiations were conducted with them. The outcome was that Edward IV empowered one English embassy to travel to Bruges to discuss an alliance with Burgundy and another under Warwick to go to France in May 1467. Warwick and his embassy were lavishly entertained by Louis XI, who treated Warwick with almost regal dignity. During the course of these negotiations in both London and Rouen, Louis offered a marriage alliance, a pension of 4,000 crowns, extensive commercial privileges in France to compensate for the loss of Flemish markets, and a willingness to go to arbitration over English claims to Normandy and Gascony in exchange for an offensive alliance against Burgundy.

As Warwick was being feted in France, the Bastard of Burgundy arrived in London for the long-awaited tournament with Lord Scales in Westminster on 11–15 June. Before then, however, on 8 June, and five days after a new parliament had opened, George Neville was dismissed as Chancellor, the king himself riding with prominent members of his court to receive the seal from the archbishop in his house at The More. The tournament itself, which made a deep impression on contemporaries, was brought to a sudden end by the death of Philip of Burgundy. The same news cut short Warwick's stay in France; on 24 June he landed in Dover in the company of a French embassy. But the French were virtually ignored by the king. After three fruitless weeks the legation left empty-handed. In the meantime, even while the French embassy was in London, Edward brought to a successful conclusion long-standing negotiations with Castile. And on 15 July, the day after the French departed, he announced that he had renewed his non-aggression pact with the new duke of Burgundy.

By mid-July, if not earlier, it was apparent to Warwick that he had lost the argument. On 28 September the way was cleared for a full Burgundian alliance with the lifting of the trade embargo; two days later Margaret of York came before the council formally to declare her willingness to marry Duke Charles. On 20 November a new trade treaty with Burgundy was signed. By the time the marriage treaty was ratified in February 1468, the breach between king and earl was common knowledge.[22]

It cannot have been the case that the earl had been deceived by Edward. The king had openly played Burgundy against France so as to secure the best possible terms. But in effect he had also played Rivers against Warwick, the two not only advocating rival foreign policies, but also competing for dominance at court. Warwick was probably unwise to have become so committed to a Francophile policy, and he might not have realised until later how much the odds had been stacked against him. Howewer, his anger at having lost the argument, his realisation of the extent to which he had lost influence with the king (which was forcefully brought home by the dismissal of his brother), and the humiliation of his loss of face in France led him to withdraw from court. He retreated to his estates in the north of England in July 1467, where he remained until the following spring. As the well-informed John Warkworth commented, after the dismissal of George Neville, Edward and Warwick 'were accorded diverse times, but they never loved together'.[23]

Warwick, indeed, had several grievances against the king by the autumn of 1467. Not only had he lost his position of pre-eminence at court and been humiliated over foreign policy, but he had also been thwarted by the king in his hopes that his elder daughter Isabel might marry the duke of Clarence. He was embarrassed by the revelation that he had been secretly negotiating with the Papacy for a dispensation. More damagingly, a captured messenger sent from Margaret of Anjou to her supporters in Harlech reported that it was widely said in France that the earl's sympathies were now with the Lancastrians. Summoned to London to answer for himself, he proudly refused to go. In the end, Edward IV was willing to allow Warwick to deny the allegation from Yorkshire.

Yet it was true that there was talk at the French court of a rapprochement between Warwick and Margaret of Anjou. The letters of the Milanese ambassador were full of gossip that the earl was contemplating rebellion. The source may have been the reports of the Scottish agent, William Moneypenny, through whom Warwick communicated with Louis XI.

Moneypenny encouraged the king to believe that none loved him as much as Warwick and that England loved none as much as Warwick. But there is no hard evidence that the earl was planning rebellion over the winter of 1467–8. It is likely, however, that as Warkworth later recorded, he 'took to him in fee many knights, squires and gentlemen as he might'.[24]

Edward IV was well aware of the danger of driving his mighty, and apparently popular, subject into revolt. In November he granted him the wardship of Lord Lovell. He accepted Warwick's word that he had not been engaged in treasonable correspondence. He left his younger brother Richard, Duke of Gloucester, in the earl's charge. In January, through the mediation of the more flexible George Neville, Warwick accepted the invitation to attend a council meeting at Coventry, where he was reconciled with Lords Herbert and Stafford, although not with Rivers and his son Scales. From February he was attending council again more regularly. In July 1468 he played his part in the ceremonial departure of Margaret of York to her new life as duchess of Burgundy, by escorting her to Dover. In the same month the decision to take a more aggressive approach to the Hanseatic League, with disastrous consequences in the subsequent war at sea, might have been a sop to him. As late as October he was still considered an influential figure at court by one of the Paston agents who lobbied him for royal favour. Throughout 1468 king and earl appeared to be reconciled.[25]

The king himself seems to have determined to reunite the rival factions at court by the traditional means of war against France. He had opened the first session of his third parliament on 3 June 1467 by declaring that he intended to live upon his own resources and charge his subjects with taxes only in great need and urgent causes concerning the well-being and defence of the realm. That declaration was a prelude to a further act of resumption, which provided more of an opportunity to review patronage than to increase royal income. A year later, when he opened the second session of parliament at Westminster on 12 May 1468, he announced that he had just completed a treaty with the duke of Brittany and having come to terms with Scotland, Castile, Denmark, Naples and above all Burgundy, he now intended to invade France. Parliament willingly voted two fifteenths and tenths; and both convocations further aid. But little came of these grand intentions. The grants of taxation were used in part to underwrite his sister's dowry, and some was used to fit out a fleet and recruit a small force under Lord Mountjoy to assist the duke of Brittany.[26]

Louis XI, however, was quick to respond to the threat. He came to terms with both Burgundy and Brittany and gave instant support to Margaret of Anjou's intrigues within England. He sponsored a landing in Wales by Jasper Tudor, Earl of Pembroke, designed to reinforce Harlech and raise

Wales. But Tudor was defeated by Lord Herbert (created earl of Pembroke himself for his services) and, in the aftermath of that defeat, the demoralised garrison of Harlech finally surrendered. In July, the confessions of a captured Lancastrian agent called Cornelius revealed a trail of traitors going up to Lord Wenlock and, by implication, Warwick. The lesser men were rounded up; Sir Thomas Cook, a prominent and wealthy citizen of London, was lucky to escape with a heavy fine for the lesser conviction of misprision of treason. In November, a more serious plot was unearthed involving Hugh Courtenay, Thomas Hungerford and ultimately the earl of Oxford. Oxford turned king's evidence and escaped with a pardon, but the others were executed as traitors in January 1469. Edward's declaration of his intention to invade France only served to open old wounds.[27]

From the end of 1467 disorder and lawlessness seem to have increased again. There were riots in Kent against the rule of Earl Rivers early in 1468. In Yorkshire some of the East and West Riding gentry, one-time Percy retainers, refused to pay the ancient rent of 'Petercorn' to St Leonard's Hospital in York in a protest which was clearly political in purpose. A major feud erupted between Lord Grey of Codnor and Henry Vernon in Derbyshire, which led to the setting up of a commission of oyer and terminer to deal with the 'great riots and oppressions' in six midland counties. Already in parliament there had been complaints voiced against the heavy lordship of Edward IV's principal courtiers. The statute restricting retaining passed in the second session of parliament in May/June 1468 may well have been a response to these disturbances and pressures for action.

By the end of 1468, the general level of disillusion and dissatisfaction with Edward IV's regime was becoming apparent. The king had not, John Warkworth commented, brought the promised peace and prosperity, rather there had been continued unrest, further taxation and disruption of trade. The principal complaint about taxation was that the two grants of 1463 and 1468 had not been used for their avowed purposes – war against Scotland and France. It is not clear whether the trade embargo on Burgundy itself in 1464, or its lifting in 1467, was considered the more hurtful; either way the king was blamed for the effects of the recession. It is apparent too that Edward was believed to have allowed certain courtiers, especially Earl Rivers, to abuse their power. The court jester offended the king but won sympathy by his quip that the rivers of the kingdom were so swollen that they had become impassable. By the end of the decade Edward IV was beginning to appear only marginally better than Henry VI. This in itself would not have mattered were it not for the fact that Henry VI was still alive and his cause being promoted by the king of France; and that there existed in the disgruntled earl of Warwick a powerful figure prepared to exploit the opportunity.[28]

Warwick's rebellion

Warwick's plans were meticulously laid. They involved the suborning of George, duke of Clarence, the securing of the Papal dispensation for his marriage with Isabel Neville and the organisation of a rising in the north. The path had been made easier by the recall of the young Richard of Gloucester to court at the beginning of 1469. All depended on the maintenance of absolute secrecy and dissembling. Warwick himself continued until the last moment to maintain the pretence of his reconciliation with the king. In the spring of 1469 he was commissioned to command a fleet for the safe-keeping of the sea, perhaps against the Hanseatic League, although when his ships put to sea they were reported to have harrassed the west coast of France. In April he crossed to Calais and represented his king in a meeting with Duke Charles and the Emperor at St Omer. In May he attended the ceremony at Windsor in which Charles was invested in the Order of the Garter. So unaware was Edward that he and his court set out in early June on pilgrimage to Walsingham. It was then that Warwick sprang his trap.[29]

There had already been trouble in the north. In April 1469 a popular rising under a captain who took the name of Robin of Redesdale had been put down by John Neville, earl of Northumberland. This was immediately followed by the rising led by Robert Hillyard, who took the name of Robin of Holderness, demanding both the abolition of Petercorn and the restoration of the earl of Percy. This too was promptly suppressed by John Neville. But thirdly, in early June, another Robin of Redesdale appeared stirring up popular discontent. But he was no peasant leader, rather a member of the Conyers family of Hornby, whose head, Sir John, was Warwick's steward in Richmondshire. This rising was instigated by Warwick's officers, and although it gathered substantial popular support as it moved south, it was in essence a mobilisation of the powerful Neville affinity against the king.[30]

Warwick himself rode to Sandwich early in June to launch his new ship, *The Trinity*. With his daughter Isabel and Clarence, and attended by Archbishop Neville and the earl of Oxford, he then crossed to Calais on 6 July. By this time, Edward had discovered that 'Robin of Redesdale' was marching south, proclaiming his intention of removing the king's evil ministers. He called up troops from Wales and the West Country under the earls of Pembroke and Devon, recruited what men he could locally and sent the Woodvilles away for their own protection. On 9 July he wrote to Warwick and Clarence calling upon them to deny rumours about their actions. Two days later Clarence and Isabel were married and on 12 July Warwick published a manifesto condemning the covetous rule of those about the king, likened Edward IV to previous kings who had been deposed, announced that he would lay his plans for remedy and reformation before the king, and summoned supporters to Canterbury on 16 July. After gathering followers in Kent, Warwick and his company marched to London where they received further, but more guarded support, and set off towards Coventry.[31]

However, the king had already been defeated. The troops brought up by Pembroke and Devon were overwhelmed at Edgecote, near Banbury, on 26 July. William Herbert and his brother were captured, taken to Northampton and executed on Warwick's orders. Humphrey Stafford fled, but was seized by a mob in Bridgwater and lynched. A few days later Earl Rivers and his son Sir John Woodville were hunted down in the Forest of Dean and murdered. Meanwhile the king, with only a small escort, was intercepted by Archbishop Neville at Olney. He was imprisoned first in Warwick Castle and, from mid-August, in Middleham.

Warwick's intentions are not clear. One of his first actions was to summon a parliament to York for 22 September. The Milanese ambassador to France reported the rumour that he intended to depose Edward and replace him by Clarence. Certainly the earl, who remembered all too well how it had proved impossible to rule in the name of the feeble Henry VI, could not have expected to rule for any length of time in the name of the vigorous Edward IV. Indeed, he discovered that he could not govern the kingdom with Edward as a prisoner even until September. There were riots in London, the duke of Norfolk besieged Sir John Paston in Caister castle and, for Warwick most threateningly, at the end of August Sir Humphrey Neville raised the borders in the Lancastrian cause. The meeting of parliament was cancelled and the king was released from house arrest to authorise the raising of troops to defeat Neville. Neville and his brother were captured and executed at York on 29 September. Some form of agreement with Warwick, the terms of which remain unknown, was reached, for the king was able to summon his lords and councillors to York and then in state return to London in October. Sir John Paston reported that 'the king himself hath good language of the Lords of Clarence, of Warwick and of my lords of York and Oxford, saying they be his best friends; his household men have other language.' In so far as he had destroyed his enemies at court, Warwick had been successful; but otherwise his actions had solved little.[32]

It is possible that the series of meetings of an enlarged council held between November and February 1470 to patch up the differences between Warwick, Clarence and the king and his supporters was part of the agreement reached between Edward and the earl. The appointment of William Grey, bishop of Ely, to replace Rivers as Treasurer was probably acceptable to both sides. The earl might well have accepted too the promotion of his erstwhile charge, the young duke of Gloucester, to the constableship of England, though less willingly accepted the surrender of the justiciarship of South Wales to which he had promoted himself in August. He would not have welcomed the release of the young Henry Percy from the Tower on 27 October. The Percy restoration was a delicate matter, since John Neville, earl of Northumberland, had remained stalwartly loyal to the king. In compensation, Edward's eldest daughter, Elizabeth, was betrothed to Neville's heir, George, who was created duke of Bedford in January 1470; and a month later John himself was granted estates in Devon from the Courtenay inheritance that were worth approximately the same as the Percy estates in Northumberland. Only then was Henry Percy restored to all his lands on 1 March.[33]

However, by March 1470 Warwick and Clarence were already plotting further rebellion. Disorder had not abated. Carmarthen and Cardigan were in the hands of Warwick's followers, who refused to hand them to Richard of Gloucester; in Gloucestershire the ancient feud between the Berkeleys and Talbots was settled in a pitched battle on Nibley Green; in Lancashire Edward Stanley, the son of Lord Stanley, took up arms to recover Hornby from Sir James Harrington; and in Lincolnshire Richard, Lord Welles, his son Sir Robert and his sons-in-law attacked Sir Thomas Burgh in his manor house at Gainsborough. The king could not intervene directly in all of these disputes. He chose to assert his authority in Lincolnshire because the victim, Sir Thomas Burgh, was Master of the Horse and a senior member of his own household. Lord Welles and Sir Richard Dymmock obeyed a summons to appear before him. However, on 4 March Sir Robert Welles, exploiting fears that the king intended to wreak vengeance on those that had joined Robin of Redesdale's rebellion, raised a general insurrection. By 12 March Edward had learnt that Warwick and Clarence were behind the insurrection.[34]

Sir Robert Welles was instructed to lure the king north, while Warwick and Clarence brought up men from the midlands. The king however demanded Welles submit on pain of his father's life. He rashly attempted a rescue. His small and poorly equipped force was routed near Empingham in an engagement that quickly became known as 'Lose-coat Field', for the speed with which the rebels shed their armour. Seized in the rout, Sir Robert confessed to the involvement of Warwick and Clarence, and further evidence was found in the baggage which detailed the rebel plan to depose Edward and replace him by his brother. Edward IV, his army ever growing in size, marched northwards to confront the Richmondshire rebels under Lord Scrope of Bolton; John Neville, loyal to his king, raised the northern marches; and Warwick and Clarence shadowed the king. When Edward threatened them, they crossed towards Manchester hoping to find the support of Lord Stanley and the earl of Shrewsbury. Whereupon Edward continued his journey north to York where he received the submission of Scrope, Sir John Conyers and their fellows. Now confident that his rear was secure, on 24 March he proclaimed Warwick and Clarence traitors, restored Henry Percy to his title while promoting John Neville to the higher rank of Marquess Montagu. However, by the time Edward marched out of York on 27 March, Warwick and Clarence had broken camp and fled south-wards. The king chased them to Devon, but was unable to prevent their escape from Dartmouth.

Warwick, his countess, daughters and Clarence took ship first for South-ampton, where they were beaten off by Anthony, Earl Rivers, and then Calais where they were denied entrance, despite the sympathy of Lord Wenlock. But they were reinforced by a squadron of ships under the com-mand of Thomas Neville, the Bastard of Fauconberg, who deserted the fleet which had been commissioned to defend the seas against the Hanse. For a while they kept their station in the Straits of Dover, seizing a convoy of Flemish merchantmen. But eventually they turned down Channel and put in at Honfleur on 1 May where they sought asylum from Louis XI.

Edward IV, meanwhile, rounded up those suspected of complicity in the rising, and commanded the earl of Worcester, acting as constable, to make an example of those seized in the abortive attempt on Southampton. It was his adding the punishment of impalement to the other barbarities of draw-ing and quartering to which traitors were conventionally subjected which earned for him the soubriquet of the 'Butcher of England'. But most of those arrested were pardoned, while the earl of Oxford escaped to join Warwick in France. Some steps were taken to strengthen the defences. Sir John Howard, now Lord Howard, was sent to take command of Calais; Dover and the Cinque Ports were handed over to Sir John Scott as deputy of the earl of Arundel. Richard of Gloucester replaced Warwick as warden of the west march, with Sir William Parr as his lieutenant; Warwick's estates were for the most part left alone. But, in June, the restored earl of Northumberland replaced Marquess Montagu as warden of the east march, a move which, although it was the logical end of the earl's restoration, proved to be a concession too far for the loyal John Neville to accept. Otherwise, however, Edward waited on events in France while maintain-ing, in league with the duke of Burgundy, a blockade of Warwick's fleet in the mouth of the Seine.[35]

Louis XI quickly took advantage of his good fortune. While reluctant to be drawn into a naval war with Burgundy, he was prepared to give refuge to the English rebels and seek to effect a reconciliation between Warwick and Margaret of Anjou. Louis secured the agreement of Warwick and Clarence at Amboise on 8 June. Queen Margaret proved more reluctant. She was escorted to Amboise at the end of the month, and after much pressure agreed to a marriage between Edward, prince of Wales, who was now seventeen, and Warwick's younger daughter Anne. But she insisted that Warwick and Clarence should depose Edward IV first, before she and her supporters would return to England. On 22 July Warwick, this time diplomatically accompanied by the Lancastrian Oxford, returned to Angers to be formally reconciled with Queen Margaret and to undertake to restore Henry VI to the throne.[36]

Warwick's plan, co-ordinated from France, was to organise yet another northern rising in Richmondshire and Cumberland while he beat the blockade. The rising duly took place early in August, this time led by Lord FitzHugh who had been his lieutenant on the west march. Edward, who now knew only too well what the danger was, yet again called up his household men and marched north. The rebels withdrew before him, submitted and sued for pardon which they were granted by the king at York on 10 September. Edward delayed in Yorkshire partly no doubt to ensure he had full control, and partly perhaps in case Warwick attempted a northern landing. Slipping the blockading fleet scattered by a storm, Warwick's flotilla, however, crossed to the Devon coast, where it landed on 13 September.[37]

The Readeption

Rapidly recruiting support, Warwick, Clarence, Pembroke and Oxford marched to the midlands where the earl of Shrewsbury and Lord Stanley joined them. At the same time the commons of Kent rose once more in rebellion. Edward, at Nottingham, called Montagu to his aid. But he threw in his lot with the rebels. Edward now found himself in the trap he had avoided in March; with only a few companions – most prominently Gloucester, Rivers and Hastings – he fled to King's Lynn where he boarded ship for the Netherlands on 2 October. Although chased by a Hanseatic squadron, the party succcessfully landed on the Dutch coast and were given shelter by Louis of Bruges, lord of Gruthuyse, who had several times been a Burgundian ambassador to England. London was in uproar; Queen Elizabeth took sanctuary in Westminster. On 3 October the Tower was handed over to the mayor and William Waynflete, Bishop of Winchester, took charge of the shaken and fragile Henry VI. On 6 October the earl of Warwick led his triumphant troops into the city and presented himself on bended knee to his sovereign. The Readeption of Henry VI, dated from 29 September, had begun.[38]

The contrast between the events of September 1470 and the preceding spring and autumn of 1469 is revealing. When Warwick's quarrel with Edward IV was but an internal dispute within the house of York, a matter essentially of court factionalism, the majority of the political nation stood aloof. The more widespread support Warwick received when he took up the cause of the House of Lancaster and the speed with which Edward's position crumbled revealed the extent of his failure. In September 1470 his regime collapsed.

Henry VI was now a pitiful figure, quite incapable of ruling. Accordingly Warwick assumed the title of Lieutenant of the Realm, pending the return of Margaret of Anjou and the prince of Wales, who it was expected, would become Protector. It was therefore an interim government which Warwick led. George Neville became Chancellor; John Langstrother, the prior of the Hospital of St John, Treasurer; and John Hales, Bishop of Coventry, Keeper of the Privy Seal. Otherwise the officers of government remained much the same. Several Yorkists in addition to the queen had fled to sanctuary, including the Chancellor, Robert Stillington, and Privy Seal, Thomas Rotherham. The earl of Worcester did not, was captured and executed. Otherwise leniency was shown. Yorkist lords such as Dinham and Dudley were able to make their peace; even Sir Richard Woodville, younger brother of the queen, was left unmolested. Few rewards were distributed. Warwick made himself chamberlain, admiral and captain of Calais again; Clarence, after a delay, became lieutenant of Ireland; Oxford was appointed constable (and had the pleasure of presiding over the trial of Worcester, who had condemned his father and brother); and Montagu was restored to the wardenship of the east march. Parliament was summoned to Westminster on 26 November. Although the records have not survived, it would appear that only Edward IV and Richard of Gloucester were attainted, while Clarence was declared duke of York. More permanent dispositions awaited the return of the exiles.

At Angers, the distrustful Margaret of Anjou was unwilling to commit herself until after she had received first-hand confirmation from a French embassy (not despatched until the end of November) that Henry was restored. Only then did she start her journey home, arriving at Rouen before the end of December. The terms of an alliance to which Warwick had committed himself were agreed by early February. Similar to that discussed by Warwick and Louis XI in 1467, they encompassed a ten-year truce; a trade agreement; the promise of Holland and Zeeland from a dismembered Burgundy for Warwick. But Louis XI could not wait for the alliance to be sealed. On 3 December he declared war on the duke of Burgundy; early in February he recovered St Quentin and Amiens, two of the Somme towns. Louis' impetuosity combined with Margaret's excessive caution were in the event to tip the scales against the Readeption.[39]

Charles the Bold had at first been circumspect in his welcome to Edward IV and his companions. His continued neutrality was pressed by the dukes of Somerset and Exeter still resident at his court. Thus for the first three months of their exile the Yorkist refugees were the private guests of Louis de Gruthuyse. However, once Louis XI declared war on Burgundy, and Charles heard that the English were likely to ally themselves with the French, he became more friendly. He received his brother-in-law on 2 January and agreed to support an expedition to recover his throne. At the same time Somerset and Exeter returned to England with assurances that Charles was still personally inclined to recognise the new English regime should war not be declared. On 13 January Edward moved to Bruges and began his preparations. Messsengers were sent to his supporters in England, including the duke of Norfolk and the earl of Northumberland. Direct aid from Burgundy, however, was limited to a few ships and some Flemish troops; Edward had to borrow also from English merchants in Flanders and to seek aid from the Hanse in return for the promise of concessions. It was only a very small force of just over 1,000 men in a handful of ships which gathered at Veere ready to sail to England by the end of February. Queen Margaret herself had still not sailed. Indeed the same contrary winds which prevented her departure from Honfleur in February delayed Edward IV as well. Warwick, however, who had taken defensive measures against a possible Yorkist invasion as early as December, and had commissioned the bastard of Fauconberg to patrol the Straits of Dover, was ready.[40]

Edward IV's recovery of the throne

The Yorkist expedition set sail on 11 March. The earl of Oxford having prevented a landing at Cromer, Edward and his small band stepped ashore at Ravenspur at the mouth of the Humber on 14 March. Here they found a cautious welcome. Edward, aping Henry IV who had landed at the same spot, claimed to have returned only to recover his duchy of York. This proved sufficient for the city of York to open its doors. But he soon passed on towards Wakefield in the hope of raising his tenants there. But here, *The Arrivall*, the official account of the campaign, candidly noted, he received little support, and so his vulnerable force took the road past Pontefract to Nottingham. Edward was not challenged in Yorkshire because of local politics. Henry Percy, the restored earl of Northumberland, who was favourably disposed to him, could not raise troops because his tenants and retainers in the East and West Ridings still remembered Towton. Montagu, who was based at Pontefract, could not raise the country either; they had even less love for him than for Edward IV. As *The Arrivall* commented, the earl of Northumberland's sitting still caused all the men in the north parts to sit still; those in the North Riding too.[41]

Within ten days Edward was clear of Yorkshire and into Nottinghamshire. At Nottingham he was joined by 600 men from the north-west led by Sir William Parr and Sir James Harrington. A force under the command of the duke of Exeter and earl of Oxford at Newark failed to intercept him. At Leicester, Lord Hastings called up to 3,000 men from the north and west midlands. The army, now some 5,000 strong, pressed on to confront Warwick at Coventry, himself awaiting reinforcements under the duke of Clarence from the West Country.

Warwick, ever a cautious general, had waited until he had maximised his strength. Clarence, however, had long been the target of his brother's blandishments. As early as the summer of 1470, while Warwick negotiated with Margaret of Anjou, Edward had sent an emissary to him. Since October, according to *The Arrivall*, he had been under pressure from his family to return to the fold. His position in the new regime was vulnerable. While indispensable to Warwick before the restoration of the Lancastrian government, his future was already looking uncertain. On 3 April, three miles out of Warwick on the Banbury road, Edward and Clarence joined forces.[42]

The brothers having been reconciled, their combined army challenged Warwick to battle. Understandably the earl declined, whereupon the Yorkists promptly marched to London. The city gates were opened to them on 11 April. Already Archbishop Neville had submitted to Edward. Now Henry VI, who had been paraded around the city in a last attempt to rally support on the preceding day, but whose lack of majesty had inspired more pity than awe, surrendered to his 'cousin of York', naively declaring that he knew he was safe in his hands. Then, having given thanks at both St Paul's and Westminster Abbey, Edward was reunited with his queen, who on 2 November last had given birth to their first son. There was no time for celebration. Lord Berners arrived with further reinforcements from Kent and then on Saturday the king marched out on the road to St Albans to face Warwick, who, having been joined by Montagu, Exeter and Oxford, was ready to give battle. That night Edward camped close to the enemy lines just north of Barnet.

The battle which was fought in thick mist on Easter Sunday, 14 April, was confused because the armies had not been aligned opposite each other. In the mêlée, friend mistook friend for enemy. The battle was decided when the earl of Oxford attacked Montagu's men thinking they were Edward's. Monatagu himself was killed and the Lancastrian army as a whole began to disintegrate. Oxford made good his escape; Exeter, left for dead on the field, later found his way to sanctuary in Westminster. The Yorkists suffered many casualties. Lords Cromwell and Say and the heirs of Lord Berners and Lord Mountjoy were killed; Rivers, Gloucester and possibly Clarence were all wounded.

Warwick was killed in flight. For fifteen years he had dominated English politics. To many commentators he has been seen as the archetypal overmighty subject, driven by insatiable ambition and lust for power. That is probably over-harsh. He was, for a nobleman not of the direct royal blood, unprecedentedly wealthy and powerful. His position and status, especially after the death of his father in 1460, placed him inevitably at the centre of affairs, and he was driven as much by self-preservation as self-advancement. Edward IV did not handle him with conspicuous skill, changing from excessive generosity to ill-disguised deceit. Certainly Warwick could not accept loss of influence and in his last few months seemed to be prepared to go to any lengths to regain power. More threatening to the political order was his wooing of the commons and readiness to call up the many-headed monster of popular revolt. In the end he was a rogue elephant, a danger not only to Edward IV, but also to his whole class. His body was taken, with that of his brother, to be laid out for public view, before burial, privately, beside their father in the family mausoleum at Bisham.[43]

After the battle the victorious Yorkists returned to London where a *Te Deum* was sung in St Paul's in thanksgiving, but there was no time for extended celebration. On the very same day as Barnet was fought, after yet further delays caused by contrary winds, Margaret of Anjou finally landed at Weymouth. Hearing of Warwick's overthrow, and having been joined by the duke of Somerset and the earl of Devon, she resolved to fight. Edward IV set out to intercept her army as she moved through Gloucestershire to cross the Severn and join the earl of Pembroke in the marches of Wales. He reached Cirencester on 29 April and finally caught up with his enemy outside Tewkesbury on 4 May. A barrage of arrow- and gun-fire provoked the duke of Somerset to attack. But the Yorkists held their ground and forced the Lancastrians back. They eventually broke. Wenlock, the earl of Devon and John Beaufort were killed in the mêlée; Edward, Prince of Wales, although accounts differ, was probably caught and killed in flight. Queen Margaret herself and the ladies of her household, including Anne Neville, escaped, but the duke of Somerset and others took sanctuary in the Abbey. Two days later Edward had them removed. Somerset, Hugh Courtenay, the brother of the dead earl of Devon, and Langstrother were tried before a constable's court, over which the duke of Gloucester presided, and were summarily executed. Other prisoners, including Sir John Fortescue, were spared. A few days later Margaret and her ladies surrendered.[44]

However, the war was not brought to a final end on the field of Tewkesbury. There was unfinished business. At the end of April the men of Richmondshire belatedly rose in arms. On 7 May, therefore, Edward set out again to return north. He was met by the earl of Northumberland at Coventry with news that the northerners had submitted to him at York.

Edward thus turned back towards London, which was now under attack from a force led by the Bastard of Fauconberg. Fauconberg had been at sea since the beginning of the year, patrolling the coasts on Warwick's behalf and preying on shipping. After Barnet he had put in to Calais, picked up 300 men from the garrison and crossed to Kent, where he stirred up rebellion. The mayor and aldermen refused to allow him to pass through the city. On 12 May he attacked the southern end of London Bridge. But London was well-defended by Earl Rivers, the earl of Essex and Lord Dudley, who prevented an attempt by Fauconberg to cross the river at Kingston the following day and beat off a concerted attack on both sides of the river (Fauconberg had brought up his ships) on 14 May. Four days later Fauconberg withdrew when Edward's vanguard of 1,500 men approached the city.[45]

In two campaigns in two months Edward had defeated both his enemies. He had the good fortune and advantage of facing divided armies which he could engage separately, and had been allowed, in the early days, too much freedom of manoeuvre. His speed of action had prevented either Warwick or Margaret from gathering all their forces. Had he delayed after Barnet, he would have found himself assailed by enemies joining forces from the West Country, Wales, the north and Kent. By his decisiveness, boldness and grasp of strategy he had regained a throne which six months earlier he seemed irrevocably to have lost.

When Edward IV entered London in triumph on 21 May, therefore, there remained but one piece of business: to dispose of Henry VI. On the very night of his arrival, according to John Warkworth, the earliest and most independent account, the harmless fifty-year-old, who believed that he was safe in the hands of his cousin of York, was put to death on his orders. The official story, circulated to Europe in *The Arrivall*, was that on hearing that his son was dead and wife a prisoner Henry was so stricken that 'of pure displeasure and melancholy he died'. It is conceivable that the news brought on a stroke, but few in England believed it. The brutal truth was that once his son and heir was dead, so too was the unfortunate Henry himself doomed. The body was given due respect, carried to St Paul's and there, the face exposed, it lay for a day before being transferred to Blackfriars for the funeral on 24 May, and was then taken upstream by barge for burial at Chertsey Abbey. The body was reported to have bled on the pavement at both St Paul's and Blackfriars; within a few years a flourishing cult grew around the figure of the innocent and saintly man who had had the misfortune to have been born a king.[46]

For the victorious Edward IV there was still some mopping up to be done. He went down to Kent to subdue the county. Subsequently in July both Kent and Essex were subjected to two judicial commissions. Most of the guilty were fined, only a few hanged; which led a London chronicler to comment that 'such as were rich were hanged by the purse, and the other that were needy were hanged by the neck'. So thorough was this visitation that Kent, which had been disturbed and rebellious for two decades, was finally pacified. The Bastard of Fauconberg had submitted to Richard of Glouceester at Sandwich on 27 May. He was pardoned and subsequently entered the duke's service. But he could not keep out of trouble, and having dabbled again in treason was executed in September. Calais was brought under control in July with the appointment of Lord Hastings as captain and a settlement of the garrison wages. Two Lancastrian earls remained at large. Jasper Tudor, Earl of Pembroke, who was in Wales, retreated to the west after Tewkesbury, taking his young nephew, Henry, Earl of Richmond, with him. An effort to dislodge him in July failed, but under increasing pressure from the Yorkists he took ship for Brittany in September. The earl of Oxford, with Viscount Beaumont, had fled to Scotland after Barnet. He soon sought refuge in France, from which base, sponsored by Louis XI, he endeavoured to continue the fight over the next two years.[47]

Notwithstanding that one or two of his enemies had escaped, in the summer of 1471 Edward IV was more securely in control of his kingdom than he had ever been before. There was now no longer a rival claimant to the throne to whom dissidents could turn; the Nevilles had been eradicated. During his first reign, while the Lancastrian cause survived and he was so beholden to Warwick, Edward had never had complete freedom of action. But he had also been young and inexperienced: his judgement of men and events had not always been sound, he had often been complacent and neglectful, and, more seriously, he had not been able to hold factionalism at court in check.[48] Only his decisiveness in a crisis and his military skill had saved him. Now he could start afresh, but the question still remained as to whether he would be able to reunite his kingdom, assert his authority effectively, and restore the peace and prosperity for which his subjects yearned after two decades of upheaval.

Notes and references

1   Scofield, *Edward the Fourth*, i, 174–8; Pollard, *North-Eastern England*, 285.

2   Scofield, *Edward the Fourth*, i, 181–8.

3   Pollard, *North-Eastern England*, 225, 286; Summerson, *Medieval Carlisle*, ii, 446–7; Ross, *Edward IV*, 48–9; Scofield, *Edward the Fourth*, i, 197–206.

4   *Rot Parl*, v, 462–8; Scofield, *Edward the Fourth*, i, 217–21.

5 Pollard, *North-Eastern England*, 225; Scofield, *Edward the Fourth*, i, 230–4, 245–9; Ross, *Edward IV*, 43; Storey, *House of Lancaster*, 196–7.

6 Scofield, *Edward the Fourth*, i, 250–67; Pollard, *North-Eastern England*, 294–7. See also Ross, *Edward IV*, 43–5 for fear of French invasion in the summer of 1462.

7 Scofield, *Edward the Fourth*, i, 273–4; Pollard, *North-Eastern England*, 292–4; Hicks, 'Lancastrian Loyalism', passim; Ross, *Edward IV*, 51–2 describes Edward's leniency as a blunder.

8 Scofield, *Edward the Fourth*, i, 268–9, 273, 277–89. For the reinterment of the Nevilles see Payne, 'Salisbury Roll', 187–93 and Hicks, *Warwick*, 228.

9 Pollard, *North-Eastern England*, 298–300. For contemporary comment see Gairdner (ed.), *Historical Collections*, 221–2. It is more likely that Somerset fled to Wales.

10 Scofield, *Edward the Fourth*, i, 293–4, 297–306, 308–15; Pollard, *North-Eastern England*, 226–7.

11 Scofield, *Edward the Fourth*, i, 318–20, 323–9, 332–9; Ross, *Edward IV*, 57–61; Pollard, *North-Eastern England*, 228.

12 Ross, *Edward IV*, 64–83.

13 Pollard, *North-Eastern England*, 292–3. For resentment at the generosity shown to Tuddenham see *PL*, iii, 292. Against the failures, set the success with Lord Rivers, who, if the informant of the duke of Milan is to be believed, was willing to declare as early as August 1461 that the cause of Henry VI was irretrievably lost (*CSPM*, i, 102).

14 For the recession in the early 1460s see Hatcher, 'Great Slump', 241–4; and Britnell, 'Economic Context', 41–64. For royal finances see Wolffe, *Royal Demesne*, 143–68 and Ross, *Edward IV*, 371–5.

15 Waurin, *Cronicques*, iii, 173–4, 184; Kendall, *Warwick the Kingmaker*, 97 for the older view and Ross, *Edward IV*, 63 for the revision. Hicks, *Warwick*, 255–7 stresses that Edward was always dominant. For the view that Edward's policy of conciliation was aimed, in part, at limiting Neville power see Carpenter, *Wars of the Roses*, 163, 168.

16 Scofield, *Edward the Fourth*, i, 441–9 provides a detailed summary of Moneypenny's role. For his letters see Morice, *Mémoires*, iii, 159–61, 169–71. See also below n. 22. For Warwick's generosity and magnanimity see Thomas and Thornley, *Great Chronicle*, 207.

17 The grants are detailed in Ross, *Edward IV*, 437–8. For the manner in which Warwick was allowed to consolidate his power in northern England see Pollard, *North-East England*, 285–300.

18 Scofield, *Edward the Fourth*, i, 320–9, 343–5; Ross, *Edward IV*, 84–92.

19   For the most recent revaluation of Queen Elizabeth's career see Sutton and Visser-Fuchs, 'Most Benevolent Queen', 214–45. For the manner in which she has become maligned by historians see also Pollard, 'Elizabeth Woodville and her Historians' (forthcoming). The political impact of the queen's family is discussed in Lander, 'Marriage and Politics', 119–52; Hicks, 'The Changing Role of the Wydevilles', 60–86; and Ross, *Edward IV*, 92–9.

20   Hicks, *Warwick*, 257–63 provides an overview of the developing breach. For early reports, and the view of the first continuator of the Croyland Chronicle see Lander, 'Marriage and Politics', in *Crown and Nobility*, 108–9. As early as February 1465 Margaret of Anjou, in France, had heard a report of a 'very great division' (*CSPM*, i, 115–16). In August 1469 the duke of Milan was informed, in a dispatch based on Warwick's briefing, that 'since her coronation she (the queen) has always exerted herself to aggrandise her relations . . . to such a pass they had the entire government of this realm' (ibid., 131). See also Scofield, *Edward the Fourth*, i, 354, 374–7; Ross, *Edward IV*, 91–2, 95.

21   Scofield, *Edward the Fourth*, i, 357–8, 360–3, 367; Ross, *Edward IV*, 359–65; Munro, *Wool, Cloth and Gold*, 159–61.

22   For the course of English diplomacy from 1465 to 1468 see Scofield, *Edward the Fourth*, i, 402–32; Ross, *Edward IV*, 104–12. For the Smithfield tournament see Anglo, 'Anglo-Burgundian Feats of Arms'.

23   Warkworth, *Chronicle*, 4. Hicks, *Warwick*, 263–71 discusses the relationship between King and Earl from 1467 to 1469.

24   Scofield, *Edward the Fourth*, i, 440–4; Ross, *Edward IV*, 115, 118, 125; *CSPM* i, 120, 122. Gross, *Lancastrian Kingship*, 76–81, suggests that Sir John Fortescue was strenuously lobbying Louis XI with a rapprochement in view and that the king deliberately fed these ideas to the Milanese ambassador knowing that they would be passed on to Edward. See Warkworth, *Chronicle*, 4 and Pollard, *North-Eastern England*, 301–3 for Warwick's retaining.

25   Scofield, *Edward the Fourth*, i, 456, 465–9; Ross, *Edward IV*, 118, 121; *PL*, v, 303–5.

26   Scofield, *Edward the Fourth*, i, 450–3; Ross, *Edward IV*, 111–13, 349.

27   Scofield, *Edward the Fourth*, i, 454–5, 458–62, 480–2; Ross, *Edward IV*, 99–101, 122–4. Edward IV also retook Jersey, which had been occupied by the French since 1461 (Scofield, 477–9; Ross, 113). Until recently, Sir Thomas Cook, whose case was reported in detail and sympathetically by his one-time apprentice, Robert Fabyan in the *Great Chronicle of London*, was judged to have been falsely accused and to have been the victim of Woodville rapaciousness (see, for instance, Ross, *Edward IV*, 99–101). However, further investigation has demonstrated that it is highly likely that he was guilty of treason. See Hicks, 'Sir Thomas Cook' and Sutton, 'Sir Thomas Cook', 85–108.

28 Warkworth, *Chronicle*, 11–12; Ross, *Edward IV*, 119–20, 124–5; Thomas and Thornley, *Great Chronicle*, 208 (the king's jester); Hicks, 'Statute of Livery'. It is posible that Warwick was largely responsible for disseminating the accusations of corruption and abuse of power against Rivers. They featured prominently in his manifesto in 1469, and found their way into Waurin's narrative, attributed to 1467, but almost certainly told to the author in 1469 (along with a possibly selective account of the events of late 1460). See Kekewich, *John Vale's Book*, 212–13; Waurin, *Cronicques*, ii, 346–9; and above n. 20.

29 Scofield, *Edward the Fourth*, i, 488–90.

30 Ross, *Edward IV*, 439–40; Pollard, *North-Eastern England*, 303–5.

31 For this and the following paragraph see Ross, *Edward IV*, 128–33 and Hicks, *Warwick*, 271–82.

32 CPM, i, 131; Ross, *Edward IV*, 133–6; *PL*, v, 63; Waurin also carried the report that Warwick intended to replace Edward by Clarence (*Cronicques*, i, 346–9).

33 Scofield, *Edward the Fourth*, i, 491–506; Ross, *Edward IV*, 136–7.

34 Hicks, *Warwick*, 282–6; Pollard, *Richard III*, 47; Smyth, *Lives of the Berkeleys*, ii, 111–12; Jones, 'Richard III and the Stanleys', 35; Storey, 'Lincolnshire and the Wars of the Roses', 64–82. The events of the spring of 1470 were recorded in the *Chronicle of the Rebellion in Lincolnshire*, an official version commissioned by Edward IV.

35 Scofield, *Edward the Fourth*, i, 509–23; Ross, *Edward IV*, 138–45; Pollard, *North-Eastern England*, 309–10.

36 Scofield, *Edward the Fourth*, i, 523–37; Ross, *Edward IV*, 146–7; Hicks, *Clarence*, 74–85 and *Warwick*, 292–5. The text of the agreement between Warwick and Margaret is printed in Kekewich, *John Vale's Book*, 215–18.

37 Pollard, 'Lord FitzHugh's Rising', 170–5.

38 Scofield, *Edward the Fourth*, i, 537–9; Ross, *Edward IV*, 147–52; Pollard, *North-Eastern England*, 311–12.

39 Ross, *Edward IV*, 155–60; Wolffe, *Henry VI*, 342–5; Hicks, *Clarence*, 86–96.

40 Ross, *Edward IV*, 159–60.

41 Bruce, *Arrivall*, 7; Pollard, *North-Eastern England*, 312–14.

42 Bruce, *Arrivall*, 10–11; Ross, *Edward IV*, 156–7; Hicks, *Clarence*, 96–100.

43 The fullest, most recent account of the battle is to be found in Hammond, *Barnet and Tewkesbury*, 66–80. Ross, *Edward IV*, iv, 137 sums up the traditional view of Warwick. Hicks, *Warwick*, 6, 311–12 offers a modern apology.

44 Ibid., 81–102 and for the death of the Prince of Wales, 123–6.

45 Ibid., 103–15; Pollard, *North-Eastern England*, 105; Richmond, 'Fauconberg's Kentish Rising'.

46 Warkworth, *Chronicle*, 21; Bruce, *Arrivall*, 38. For recent discussion of the evidence see Hammond, *Barnet and Tewkesbury*, 11–12 and Pollard, *Richard III*, 53–5. For Henry's posthumous cult see Bernard, 'Vitality and Vulnerability', 206–9; Lovatt, 'A Collector of Apocryphal Anecdotes'; McKenna, 'Piety and Propaganda: the Cult of Henry VI', 72–81; and Walker, 'Political Saints in Later Medieval England', 85–7, 95–8; and Wolffe, *Henry VI*, 351–8.

47 Thomas and Thornley, *Great Chronicle*, 220–1; Ross, *Edward IV*, 112–15; Hammond, *Barnet and Tewkesbury*, 112–15. Economic revival after 1471 might also have had some bearing on the pacification of Kent (see Hatcher, 'Great Slump', 270–2).

48 For a more enthusiastic assessment of Edward during his first reign see Carpenter, *Wars of the Roses*, 180–1.

CHAPTER ELEVEN

The second reign of Edward IV, 1471–83

Re-establishing the Yorkist regime

Sforza di Bettini reported to Galleazo Maria Sforza, Duke of Milan, on 17 June 1471 that Edward IV was now in full control of England without any obstacle whatsoever.[1] He was broadly correct. Yet Edward IV was still the leader of a faction recently victorious in a civil war, who had not eliminated all opposition. His first priority was to secure effective control of the kingdom in the hands of those he could trust. It is not surprising therefore that he still chose to rule through a small group of highly favoured relations and prominent retainers to whom local and regional power was entrusted.

The Yorkist regime as it was re-established in the summer of 1471 was founded on the same principles as before. The main difference was that the earl of Warwick was replaced by the king's brothers – the dukes of Clarence and Gloucester. Clarence, supported by the young earl of Shrewsbury, was quickly established in the midlands and the south-west, where he received grants of most of the Beauchamp inheritance, the honour of Tutbury and the forfeited Courtenay estates. Gloucester kept the wardenship of the west march and was granted the Kingmaker's estates in the north where he was expected to work alongside the restored earl of Northumberland and Lord Stanley, who came to dominate Lancashire and Cheshire. Royal influence was sustained in East Anglia by the dukes of Norfolk and Suffolk and the rising Lord Howard. Wales and the Marches were at first entrusted to William Herbert, second earl of Pembroke, confirmed on 27 August 1471 in the office of Justiciar of South Wales, which his father had been granted in tail male, and to the earl of Shrewsbury who was made Justiciar of North Wales. All were supported by the knights and esquires of the body whom the king had retained in most parts of the kingdom.[2]

Having recovered his kingdom so emphatically and secured power in the hands of those he could trust, Edward IV set out on the path of reconciliation. Throughout his first reign he had always been willing to pardon his enemies; after Barnet and Tewkesbury he could afford to be magnanimous. The lives of his surviving principal enemies who fell into his hands were spared: the duke of Exeter in 1471, the earl of Oxford in 1474. Now those who had devoted themselves to Henry VI were encouraged to make their peace and enter his service, most notably Sir John Fortescue and John Morton, soon to rise to high rank, Sir Richard Tunstall (Henry VI's last chamberlain) and, through the good offices of Lawrence Booth, Bishop of Durham, the heir to the Nevilles of Westmorland, Ralph, Lord Neville. None of the bishops who had supported the Readeption, including initially George Neville who had saved himself by surrendering Henry VI to King Edward, were subsequently victimised. Only thirteen persons, most of them dead, were attainted after the civil wars of 1459–71 (compared with 114 in 1461), and then not until 1475, the final session of the parliament which first assembled in the autumn of 1472. In contrast, twenty-five attainders were reversed in the same time.

But there was a second, not so statesmanlike reason for the low number of attainders. Neither Warwick nor Montagu were in the event attainted because the king's younger brothers had their eyes on their inheritance. It would appear that attainder was at first intended and the Neville estates were first treated as forfeit. As soon as he had recovered his throne Edward granted the larger part of Warwick's inheritance, concentrated in the midlands and the south-west, to George of Clarence and the remaining Neville portion, concentrated in the north, to Richard of Gloucester. But it soon became apparent that neither brother was to be content with the grant of these patrimonies on the conventional terms of the king's pleasure with the risk that they could be restored to the heirs. For while Warwick had had no son, his heir male for his paternal inheritance was his nephew George Neville, Montagu's son, and his daughters were heiresses to the remainder. Furthermore his widow, the countess Anne, not Warwick himself, as the heiress to Beauchamp, was the legal possessor of all the Beauchamp and Despenser estates; in strict law these could not be touched by the attainder of the earl. Had the law followed its natural course, the countess of Warwick would have remained in possession of the greater part of the Warwick inheritance, while George Neville would have inherited the Neville of Middleham patrimony. The king's brothers, whose demands on his gratitude, one for loyal service, the other for timely reconciliation, were great, soon made it apparent that they would be satisfied with nothing less than secure titles to elements of the dismembered Warwick inheritance. As a result Edward IV was faced with a complex legal and political tangle that in the event took three years to resolve and put attainder out of the question. And if Warwick were not to be attainted, then neither were his principal followers, especially his retainers from the north and elsewhere, who had so often rebelled over the preceding two years.

To make matters worse, ill-feeling soon developed between the dukes of Clarence and Gloucester over the division of the spoils. Clarence, it seemed, wished to retain control of the greater part of the inheritance through the future right of his duchess as if she were sole heiress, thereby denying not only his mother-in-law, but also his sister-in-law, Anne, the widow of Edward, Prince of Wales. Gloucester, understandably, felt that he should receive a greater share. To this end he first sought to marry Warwick's younger daughter, Anne. In the spring of 1472 Clarence was reported finally to have accepted that his brother would marry Anne, but he was said to have declared that he would part with none of his livelihood. Nevertheless he was persuaded to accept a partition in principle and was compensated with the titles of earl of Warwick and Salisbury as well as a handful of manors. However, he successfully prevaricated over the implementation of the agreement. By the summer of 1473 Gloucester seems to have lost patience and forced the issue, almost certainly with Edward IV's conniv- ance, by espousing the cause of his mother-in-law, Anne Beauchamp, the dowager countess of Warwick, who had remained in sanctuary at Beaulieu abbey for two years while her estates had been occupied by Clarence. In May she was allowed to leave the abbey and travel north to join Gloucester and his duchess. It was rumoured that the king had restored her to her inheritance and that she had granted it all to Gloucester. Perhaps this was threatened.[3]

By the autumn Gloucester and Clarence were reported to be about to come to blows. At length the king imposed a settlement, although it appears to have taken the threat of resumption in December 1473 to have forced Clarence to submit. The compromise that was finally reached in parliament by successive acts in 1474 and 1475 effectively divided the Warwick inher- itance between the brothers on a regional basis; Clarence took most of the south; Gloucester the north. It was indeed Clarence who made the greater concessions. He had to agree to Gloucester receiving Barnard Castle from the Beauchamp inheritance and to give up his claim to Richmond to his brother. The acts of parliament, by disinheriting both the countess of War- wick and the duke of Bedford, gave both brothers far greater security than that of a grant during the king's pleasure. Nevertheless the whole episode, the king's willingness to manipulate the law of inheritance to satisfy the ambitions of his brothers and their own bickering left a bad taste in the mouth of at least one well-placed contemporary and was an ominous re- minder of the fragility of Yorkist family unity.[4]

Edward did not only have to deal with conflict within his own family circle. Richard of Gloucester clashed with others beside his brother in his determination to establish himself as the dominant figure in the north. He quarrelled with Bishop Booth of Durham as well as Clarence over possession of Barnard Castle; and he competed with the earl of Northumberland for influence in Yorkshire; a rivalry which was calmed by the arbitration of the king himself in May 1473 and formally resolved in Gloucester's favour a year later when the earl was retained by the duke. While Gloucester was able to slip into Warwick's shoes in the north, win the confidence of his retainers and within four years establish his unchallenged command, Clarence in the midlands proved less able to establish his authority. By the summer of 1473 the midlands were so seriously disturbed that the king had to undertake an extended judicial progress in an attempt to restore order. At the end of the year he relieved Clarence of the stewardship of the duchy of Lancaster honour of Tutbury and appointed Lord Hastings in his place.

Disorder was considerably worse in Wales and the marches as parliament made clear to the king in 1472 and 1473. The earls of Pembroke and Shrewsbury proved ineffective. Accordingly in June 1473 the king called the marcher lords together at Shrewsbury where they agreed to co-operate in the enforcement of the law. But this also proved inadequate. A council had already been formed to administer the principality. In the winter of 1473–4 Earl Rivers, having been appointed the prince's tutor and Bishop John Alcock of Rochester the president of the council, the three-year-old prince and his entourage took up residence at Ludlow and began to assume the responsibility for governing Wales and the marches. Ireland too was disturbed. The Irish parliament asked for military support, but Edward was no longer willing to place royal troops in his elder brother's hands. Accordingly he appointed his own knight of the body, Sir Gilbert Debenham, as chancellor and in a revised indenture transferred all the responsibilities of the office of lieutenant to his new appointee. While keeping the title of lieutenant of Ireland, Clarence was thus effectively removed from that office too.[5]

It is possible as well that Edward suspected Clarence of dabbling in treason once again. The earl of Oxford remained in exile, receiving encouragement and occasional material aid from Louis XI. In the spring of 1472 he was raiding the marches of Calais from France. It was on the suspicion that he had been in communication with the earl that the archbishop of York was suddenly arrested on 25 April 1472 and imprisoned in Calais, where he remained for two and a half years. Oxford subsequently sought help in Scotland, but was back in France in early 1473. Loius XI fitted him out with a small fleet with which he descended first on the Essex coast and then on Cornwall, where he occupied St Michael's Mount for several months.

At the same time Thomas Clifford, brother of the fugitive Lord Clifford, attempted to raise rebellion in Hartlepool, the principal settlement in the family's Durham lordship of Hart. At one point, in the autumn, Edward was reported to have sent for the Great Seal from the Chancellor Lawrence Booth, 'as he did at the last field'. There is, however, no evidence that Clarence was caught up in these intrigues; his acceptance of his demotion and loss of lands in 1474 suggests that he realised that he had little option but to remain in the family fold.[6]

The French expedition, 1475

The early years of Edward's second reign were not as free from obstacles as had been reported. The king had his hands full restoring order and pacifying his own quarrelsome brothers. This gave more urgency to Edward's plan to reunite the kingdom by leading his subjects in war against France. More or less immediately after he recovered his throne, Edward set out to form an offensive alliance with Brittany and Burgundy. It would seem that he intended to place the fact of an alliance before parliament when it finally met at Westminster in October 1472. Edward did indeed seal an agreement with the duke of Brittany to invade France before 1 April 1473, but this deal, and the hoped-for support of Burgundy, evaporated in the autumn, even as parliament met to vote taxes.[7]

Nevertheless Edward persevered. In an address to parliament, he appealed through a spokesman for support for invasion of France to recover his rightful throne of France and the duchies of Normandy and Guyenne as the most effective way both to protect the kingdom from the threats of her enemies and to restore law and order within the kingdom. The appeal argued that an expedition abroad would occupy the multitudes of riotous malefactors still troubling the kingdom, and pressed the point that internal peace had never prevailed in any reign except when there had been outward war. It was an old argument, but none the less effective for that.[8] The lords and the commons, mindful of the precedent of 1453, voted taxation to support a force of 13,000 archers, but with novel strings attached. Rather than the conventional tenths and fifteenths, they voted an income tax of 10 per cent, which it was calculated would raise over £118,000 (nearly four times a single tenth and fifteenth). All was to be held in special repositories and not to be released until the king mustered his army, which he undertook to do by Michaelmas 1474. When it became clear, however, by the spring of 1473, that the yield would fall well short, parliament agreed to a conventional tenth and fifteenth to be paid by 24 June into the same repositories.[9]

While the commissioners set about the task of collecting these sums from grudging taxpayers (John Paston II had already written to his father Sir John, a member of the commons house, praying that they should not grant any more taxes), Edward IV began again to pick up the diplomatic pieces.[10] In January 1473 a new embassy to Burgundy made little headway because Duke Charles was preoccupied with a claim to the duchy of Guelders. Eventually, in August, it was possible to agree details of a projected joint invasion and dismemberment of France at Bruges. But once more Duke Charles's attention turned elsewhere and the plans were shelved.

In the meantime Edward did his best to secure the neutrality of other parties. He had been negotiating with the Hansards since 1472 to end the trade war which he had begun in 1468. These negotiations finally came to a head in a series of intense conferences in Bruges and Utrecht in the summer of 1473, leading to the treaty of Utrecht (February 1474), in which Edward virtually gave in to all the Hansard demands for the restoration of trading privileges.[11] Parallel negotiations were being conducted with James III of Scotland by the bishop of Durham. A preliminary agreement for a marriage between the infant heir to the Scottish throne and Edward's four-year-old daughter, Cecily, and for a truce between the two kingdoms to last for forty-five years was drawn up in July 1474 and formally sealed at Edinburgh in October. And finally, by the treaty of London on 25 July 1474, Duke Charles was at last persuaded to enter a formal alliance against France. According to the terms of the joint invasion plans drawn up by the two powers Edward agreed to land in France before I July 1475. Within a month he began to raise his army.[12]

The treaty of London was sealed some six weeks after the opening of the sixth session of parliament. It was soon discovered that little progress had been made in gathering the taxes voted over a year earlier. Since Edward would not have the cash in hand to meet the first instalments of his troops' wages, or to pay for ordnance and transport, he set out to discover what his subjects would be prepared 'to show by way of their good will and benevolence what sums it would please them to give the king to help his expedition'. By this, the first benevolence, Edward raised at least £20,000. Furthermore, when the extent of waste, fraud and theft in the collection and banking of the 1472 income tax was revealed to parliament in January 1475, the commons voted an additional one and one third subsidy in compensation. Even then, however, they were not willing to release the taxation until the king was ready to sail.[13]

By this stage military preparations for the invasion were well advanced. In the autumn of 1474 recruitment had begun for what was probably the largest army (over 20,000 including non-combatants) so far to set sail for France in the fifteenth century.[14] To carry the army across the Channel ships were impressed from all along the south and east coasts; and from early in 1475 naval patrols put to sea to secure the crossing. As the troops and transports converged on the downs and ports of south-east Kent in May and June, the last touches were put to the diplomatic groundwork. The neutrality of Denmark and Castile were secured, and to complete the isolation of France, the offensive alliance with Brittany was renewed. Preparations were finally completed on 20 June when the five-year-old prince of Wales was made titular head of state during the king's absence and the government of the kingdom vested in a council headed by Cardinal Bourgchier. After four years of planning, Edward IV was at last poised, with the support of a triple alliance, and the backing of a large army, well-provisioned and paid for six months, to descend on France and emulate the achievements of Henry V.

That all was not well was, however, already apparent to Edward. Duke Charles of Burgundy, whose full commitment and involvement was essential to the endeavour, was proving a fickle ally. In June 1474 he had turned his attention to the further extension of his power to the east by investing Neuss. What had been expected to be a quick expedition turned into a long, costly and exhausting winter campaign. Neuss had still not fallen by April and a stream of English envoys failed to persuade the duke to abandon the siege. Only when Louis XI conducted pre-emptive raids into Picardy and Burgundy itself did Charles give up. He did not return to Flanders with his weary army until the end of June. Even before the English army set sail, doubts about the capacity and willingness of Burgundy to fight alongside the English were growing. Louis XI for his part had already proposed that Edward should consider the advantages of a quick settlement.[15]

But there was no stopping the campaign at the eleventh hour. It took three weeks from 7 June to transship the English army to Calais. Edward joined his troops on 4 July. It was not until 14 July that Duke Charles came to join him; and he arrived without an army, only his personal guard. All that the duke now offered was a safe-conduct through his northern French territories to Peronne, from which he could advance to St Quentin, held by the friendly count of St Pol. Edward had little option but to follow this plan. He arrived at Peronne on 5 August, but the following day his vanguard found St Quentin closed to him. Duke Francis of Brittany, like Burgundy, also failed to take the field. Abandoned by his allies, and Louis XI bearing down with a powerful army, it did not take Edward long to decide to come to terms. On 14 August negotiations were begun. Edward demanded £15,000 immediately and £10,000 a year, a marriage alliance between the Dauphin and one of his daughters, and a trade agreement as the price for his withdrawal. Louis XI accepted all these terms. They were, he knew, substantially those that he had offered Warwick in 1467. The kings agreed to meet to ratify the treaty on a specially constructed bridge over the Somme at Picqigny. In the meantime Louis offered to entertain the English troops in Amiens, where they happily incapacitated themselves. Their commanders accepted rich presents and substantial pensions from the French king in recompense, some, such as the duke of Gloucester who was reported to have wished to fight, openly, others such as Lord Hastings, secretly. The two kings met as agreed on 29 August, with elaborate courtesy on a bridge parted by a grille to prevent any repetition of the murder of Montereau half a century earlier. A seven-year truce and all the other terms were thereupon formally agreed and immediately afterwards the English army began its withdrawal, arriving at Calais on 4 September to start the transshipment to England. Edward himself crossed on 18 September and arrived back in London on 28 September, three months after he had set out with such high hopes.[16]

The king's Great Enterprise ended ingloriously and tamely after such elaborate, time-consuming and costly preparation. Charles of Burgundy was reported to be furious at Edward IV's sudden *volte-face* – but having so comprehensively failed him, he should hardly have been surprised. Several contemporaries were sceptical of Edward's intention ever to fight, believing that his purpose all along was to seek terms similar to those gained. The scale and complexity of his preparations, the determination with which he pursued his diplomatic ends and the persistence he showed in persuading parliament to support his invasion suggest that this was unlikely. He had intended to make war against France. But his plan had depended on the alliance with Burgundy. It was perhaps always more hopeful than realistic to expect Charles the Bold to follow the course of Philip the Good after 1419. It is to be doubted, however, that Edward seriously expected to be able to win the crown of France or even to recover either Normandy or Guyenne. The appeal which Edward made to parliament when it opened in the autumn of 1472 probably reflected his actual motivation. He believed that war against France was the best means to restore peace in England and unite the kingdom behind him. The invasion of France was perceived as a policy to put the final seal on his recovery of the throne of England.[17]

Edward and his commanders consistently maintained that the outcome was a triumph – France had been forced to pay heavily for peace and the king had secured by negotiation more than he might in the end have gained by fighting – a view endorsed by the Crowland Chronicler. The French for their part skilfully put it out that the English were cowards. But there was something in the official English view, unheroic as it was. £85,000 was some return for the cost of the enterprise. The king's subjects, who had revealed their reluctance to support the campaign in the first place, could now be relieved of further taxation for the immediate future (and indeed the remaining, uncollected, tenths and fifteenths were remitted), the mercantile agreement would help economic recovery, and there was a serious prospect that England would be at peace for several years to come. Yet there was a rash of disorder caused by discharged soldiers. The principal disturbances centred on Hampshire which the king himself speedily pacified. It is possible, too, that lawlessness in Wales and the marches, which led to further enhancement of the supervisory powers of the prince's council, and riots in Yorkshire in the spring of 1476, which the duke of Gloucester and earl of Northumberland were ordered to quell, were linked to demobilisation.[18]

It has also been proposed that the disastrous events that followed Edward IV's death eight years later would have been avoided had Edward shown more valour than discretion; had he imitated Henry V and defied Louis's army. It is true that the circumstances were broadly similar to 1415 (the English army was alone facing a confident foe) and that, providing he avoided being drawn into the costly and futile defence of conquered territory, the dividends of another Agincourt could have been infinitely greater to Edward IV than the benefits of the treaty of Picquigny. Whether it follows, as is suggested, that the political nation would then, like the 1420s, have been united in its loyalty to the victor's heir, is a moot point. The Yorkist brothers had already revealed that they did not share the same family solidarity as the Lancastrians. The avoidance of war in the short term, by reuniting the royal family and peerage behind their king, was of benefit to Edward, his regime and his subjects; and was considered honourable by them.[19]

The fall of Clarence

The major event of 1476, emphasising the new-found dynastic solidarity, was the solemn re-interment in July of Richard, Duke of York, and Edmund, Earl of Rutland, in the family mausoleum at Fotheringhay. The bodies of the duke and his son, who had fallen at Wakefield, were exhumed at Pontefract on or shortly before 21 July. On 22 July a requiem mass was celebrated by Lawrence Booth, Bishop of Durham – shortly to be archbishop of York – and on the following day a magnificent cortège, led by Richard of Gloucester and including the earl of Northumberland, Lord Stanley and other northern lords, Lawrence Booth and other bishops and northern abbots, and including 400 poor bedesmen on foot, set off for Fotheringhay. It took seven days. The procession was met by the king, the queen, the duke of Clarence, other lords and prelates at Fotheringhay on 29 July. The burial and the celebration of another requiem mass, led by the Chancellor Thomas Rotherham, Bishop of Lincoln, took place on 30 July and was followed by a gargantuan banquet. Curiously there is no reference in the surviving accounts of the presence of the king's mother, the dowager duchess Cecily. While the reburial was in part a personal ritual, it was also an elaborately staged and publicised state event, displaying to the world the unity and power of the Yorkist monarchy, in retrospect to be revealed as somewhat hollow, but at the time intending to mark the final establishment of the dynasty.[20]

Nevertheless the distrust and suspicion between Edward and Clarence remained. Rumours never ceased to circulate the courts of Europe that Clarence was only waiting the opportunity to make himself king. The harmony of 1476 was brought to an end by the consquences of the death of Charles, Duke of Burgundy, at the battle of Nancy on 5 January 1477 and the immediate outbreak of a war of Burgundian succession, in which Louis XI invaded and took possession of Artois and Burgundy itself from the defenceless Mary, sole daughter and heiress of Charles. Edward IV's first reaction, having called an emergency Great Council of his lords to Westminster in February, was to order Lord Hastings to his post in Calais and to reinforce the garrison. At the same time a round of feverish diplomacy was inaugurated in northern Europe to find a husband, champion and ally for Mary of Burgundy. Early in this the widowed and childless Duchess Margaret proposed that her brother George of Clarence should marry her step-daughter. Clarence was fortuitously available since his twenty-five-year-old duchess Isabel had died in December 1476, two months after giving birth to her last child.

In many ways, despite the unseemly haste, Clarence was an ideal candidate for Mary's hand, but the match was immediately vetoed by Edward IV because it would have committed him not only to costly military aid and the abandonment of the treaty of Picquigny, but also because it would have placed the power of the Burgundian state at Clarence's disposal. The first opportunity to forge a dynastic link with the Low Countries since Edward III had failed to secure the county of Flanders for his younger son Edmund went begging. Insult was added to injury by Edward's own, half-hearted proposal, that Earl Rivers should be the English candidate for Mary of Burgundy. Clarence was deeply aggrieved. As the Crowland Continuator commented, 'each began to look upon the other with no fraternal eyes'. As the acrimony deepened Clarence determined to demonstrate, without resorting to rebellion, that he was a power not to be ignored.[21]

The means Clarence chose were bizarre. On 12 April he seized Ankarette Twynho, who had been a lady-in-waiting of Duchess Isabel, and her servant John Thursby. The two were taken to Warwick castle and there, on 15 April, found guilty of poisoning the duchess and her son and summarily executed on the same day. At the same time Clarence accused Sir Roger Tocotes of aiding and abetting the alleged murderers. The victims of this high-handed and illegal action were relatively obscure, but Tocotes was a man of considerable substance, a key member of the duke's affinity since 1468. The action, taking the law into his own hands, was a direct challenge to the king's authority. Tocotes almost certainly brought it to Edward's attention, who called in the trial records.

By then the king had found a means of demonstrating his even more formidable power to Clarence. He arrested the eminent Oxford astrologer Dr John Stacey, who confessed under torture that he had, with others, including Thomas Burdet of Arrow in Warwickshire, cast horoscopes which predicted the early deaths of both the king and the prince of Wales. They were found guilty before a special court comprising no fewer than five earls and twelve barons in a judgement, reminiscent of that found against Eleanor Cobham in 1443, of imagining and encompassing the king's death by necromancy. Stacey and Burdet were executed at Tyburn on 20 May. Clarence was not named; but just as in 1443 the condemnation of Eleanor Cobham had been designed to discredit Duke Humphrey, so this too was intended as a warning to the duke. Clarence, however, blundered on. He immediately confronted the king's council with a declaration of the innocence of the dead men read by Dr Goddard, who had expounded Henry VI's title to the throne at the beginning of the Readeption. Burdet, like Tocotes, was one of Clarence's principal followers. In so futilely (he was already dead) defending his man he seemed to protest too much an innocence which had never been questioned. He brought retribution on himself. Towards the end of June he was charged before the king at Westminster with violating the laws of the realm (almost certainly in the Twyno affair), arrested and committed to the Tower.[22]

Clarence remained in prison for six months while the king pondered what to do. In November 1477, it seems, it was finally determined to place charges of treason before a parliament summoned to meet on 16 January. The parliament itself was almost certainly packed. Clarence had few friends amongst the peers; any remaining kept silent. It has been calculated that there were at least fifty-six royal servants present, and influential lords, who had been present at the council meeting which decided to try Clarence for treason, secured the election of many more. Perhaps a half of the membership of the house of commons was primed. The day before parliament opened the king celebrated the marriage of his second son, Richard, Duke of York, to Anne Mowbray, heiress of the duchy of Norfolk. The wedding, the jousting, the banquet and the creation of twenty-four new Knights of the Bath thereafter were carefully stage-managed both to divert attention and to demonstrate the unity and harmony of the political nation as it prepared to destroy the king's brother once and for all.[23]

At the opening of parliament, the chancellor preached to the ominous text from St Paul: 'Not without cause does the king bear the sword.' There was but one piece of business, the trial by attainder. The king himself presented the charges; no one spoke in defence of the duke; he was declared guilty. The formal act of attainder offers both a justification for the duke's destruction and a list of his treasons. Notwithstanding the king's forebearance and mercy, Clarence had proved both ungrateful and incorrigible and the safety of the realm now demanded his removal. He had demonstrated his guilt by securing letters of exemplification of his nomination as heir of the house of Lancaster in 1470; he had spread the sedition that Edward was a bastard; he had encouraged Burdet to raise rebellion and plotted to send his heir to his sister the duchess of Burgundy; and he had usurped the authority of the king in the trial of Ankarette Twyno.

Whether the duke was actually guilty of any bar the last is hard to determine. It has been shown that an apparent corroboration of the charge concerning the exemplification of 1470 in Warkworth's chronicle was in all probability taken from the act of attainder itself. Moreover acquiring an exemplification (or copy) was not in itself treasonable. The rumour that Edward IV was illegitimate had surfaced before and was to surface again. It might be that the offence of Robert Stillington, who was arrested during the parliament, although shortly pardoned, for 'utterance prejudicial to the king', was to repeat this rumour. But again spreading the rumour was not treason. This is true of most of the charges. The case against Clarence was flimsy. On the other hand, he might, as rumour persistently held, have sailed dangerously close to treason on more than one occasion since 1471. The proceedings of the parliament were a show trial. It achieved its purpose, for reasons of state, of finally ridding the king of his incorrigible brother.[24]

The death sentence was passed on 7 February. Execution was delayed by the hesitant king for ten days. Finally, after prompting from the speaker of the house of commons, the duke was privately put to death in the Tower on 18 February, by means unknown (although the story rapidly emerged that he had been drowned in a butt of malmsey). He was still only twenty-eight, a young man who seems to have had little ability and less judgement to match his high birth and position. His body was taken to Tewkesbury and there buried beside his duchess on 25 February. Parliament was dissolved on the following day.

Much discussion has taken place over the responsibility for Clarence's destruction. It was neither, as the Shakespearean tradition maintains, the outcome of the duke of Gloucester's plotting, nor, as Duke Richard subsequently wished others to believe, against his wishes. He was well rewarded for his acquiescence, if not support, even before the trial began.[25] Five years later Dominic Mancini was told, possibly from sources close to the duke of Gloucester, that Clarence was the victim of the queen's envy and her family's greed. It is true that the queen's relations were increasingly influential at court; had played a prominent role in the wedding of the king's younger son Richard and Anne Mowbray, and helped to ensure the return of a docile parliament. The queen herself, however, was not an active or influential political figure at court.[26] If she spoke with the king, it is likely to have been on the prompting of her brother Earl Rivers, or her eldest son the marquess of Dorset, who had been much favoured by Edward since 1475. Of these two, Dorset gained modestly from Clarence's fall, for he was granted, only the day after Clarence's execution, the stewardships and related offices in Somerset, Devon and Cornwall which Clarence had held as well, later, as the wardship of his heir Edward, earl of Warwick. He was to grow in influence over the remaining years of Edward's reign. Rather than point to the Woodvilles in general, or the queen in particular, it might be more fruitful to think of Dorset, also accused by Mancini of causing Clarence's death, as one more likely to have influenced the king.[27]

But perhaps Edward needed no prompting, for all that he was reported to have suffered from remorse. Clarence's high-handed actions, coupled with his failure to wield effective authority on the king's behalf, might well explain why Edward first moved against him. But it does not explain the decision taken, some five months after his arrest on lesser charges, to proceed to treason. The tragedy for Clarence was not that he was incompetent and unpredictable, but that, as the king's own brother, he could seriously undermine the stability of the regime. In the end it seems to have been accepted by the Yorkist establishment that for reasons of state there was only one way that the Clarence problem was to be resolved; and the king himself implemented it.[28]

In truth the whole story of the destruction of Clarence does not reflect well on the king, his family and his regime. Afterwards, however, as the Crowland Chronicler commented, having demonstrated that not even his own brother could defy him, he could henceforth rule without fear of opposition. He was now able to enjoy the fruits of success to the full. As Commynes had observed, he was already beginning to go to seed when he met Louis XI on the bridge at Picquigny in 1475. By the time he died he was, as a result of 'the delight he took in his pleasures', 'very fat and gross'. It is the hallmark of the last five years of the reign that contemporary chroniclers commented little on domestic events. In these years the court was at its most splendid and impressive. They were the years which Thomas More recalled nostalgically as a golden age; and on them Edward IV's reputation for the successful restoration of royal authority is based.[29]

The regime, 1478–83

The precise character of Edward IV's rule in his last years is hard to ascertain. Professor Ross, drawing effectively on the evidence of the king's personal stamp on administration, argued that he took his duties most seriously. The Crowland Chronicler testified to the manner in which the king made sure that his estate officials kept him fully informed, and to his memory of the names and circumstances of the men of substance throughout his kingdom.[30] Edward made effective use of his council, to which he recruited a team of able and dedicated administrators, diplomats and lawyers, both clerical and lay. Prominent among them were Thomas Rotherham (the Chancellor), Henry Bourgchier, earl of Essex (the Treasurer), John Morton (the Master of the Rolls) and John Russell (the Keeper of the Privy Seal), as well as the leading household men, Lords Hastings, Howard and Dinham. These councillors worked tirelessly to increase revenue, pursuing royal rights (there was a marked increase in the enforcement of feudal dues) and to settle legal disputes. It was towards the end of Edward's reign that the council began to develop an identity and mission of its own in the enforcement of royal authority on behalf of the Crown a conciliar mission that was to be developed further under Henry VII.[31]

Although Edward IV kept a sharp eye on his finances, routine administration fell to his household servants and estate officials. The abundant surviving records of the chamber reveal how the royal demesne was systematically managed on the traditions of private estates and how thorough supervision yielded increased revenue from some, if not all, lordships. Similar attention was paid to improving the efficiency and honesty of customs collection. The king also benefited from an up-turn in the economy, rising rents and increasing trade. The result was that by the end of his reign he was receiving, directly into his coffers, some £65,000–£70,000 p.a.

It is important to keep this achievement in perspective. Total royal income still lagged behind what it had been as late as 1450; the significance of the switch to chamber finance lies more in the improvement of cash flow than in the increase in yield. Secondly, throughout his reign Edward continued to balance the need to make himself solvent against the requirement to reward servants. In the last resort financial management was subordinated to political ends. Nevertheless Edward gained a reputation for avarice, particularly abroad where it was widely believed that personal greed became the mainspring of his foreign policy in his last years. It is perhaps so, but he was no miser. He spent lavishly. Political calculation as well as personal indulgence lay behind a splendid court and a reputation for magnificence. On his death, there was not, as rumoured, a vast treasure salted away;

indeed the coffers were virtually empty. But he succesfully created the illusion of being wealthy. Thus while Edward did not achieve Fortescue's ideal of a financially independent monarchy, he successfully convinced his subjects that he had.[32]

While it is agreed that Edward IV did rule as he pleased in the last five years of his reign, his historians have never agreed in their assessment of the manner in which he was pleased to rule. On the one hand there is a tradition, stretching back to his French contemporary Commynes, that he was a shallow playboy, prone to tyrannical acts; a king lacking in political judgement or the capacity to sustain a coherent foreign policy, who was ultimately responsible for the failure of his dynasty to survive him for little more than two years. On the other hand, there is the view, its roots in the writings of another contemporary, the Crowland Chronicler, that Edward IV was a king with 'an iron will and great fixity of purpose', who was the very model of a medieval monarch, indeed 'one of the greatest of English kings', who was able to rescue the kingdom 'from what can best be described as a shambles and leave his dynasty secure on the throne'.[33] In making an assessment of Edward the man and his kingship in the last five years of his reign there are two aspects to be considered: the structure and character of the regime and the conduct of foreign policy.

There is not necessarily a contradiction between a man who gave himself over to frequent debauchery and a ruler who kept a firm grip of his subjects and his government. How firm a grip did Edward maintain and to what end? After 1478 he continued to delegate political control in the provinces to the leading members of his family, his court and household. Indeed in some respects the policy was extended and intensified. Two regions were ear-marked for his infant sons. Wales and the marches were by 1478 supervised by the prince's council based in Ludlow under Bishop Alcock of Worcester and Earl Rivers. Rivers was able through his position to build up a significant power in the region. The process of creating an appropriate landed endow-ment in the east midlands and East Anglia for the king's second son, Richard, Duke of York, was begun by the grant of lands formerly belonging to Lords Welles and Willoughby, the setting aside of Fotheringhay and other duchy of York estates in the region as his inheritance and, in 1478, his marriage to Anne Mowbray the heiress of the last Mowbray duke of Norfolk. Until the duke of York came of age, Edward called upon the services of Lord Howard and the duke of Suffolk to exercise royal authority in these districts. The promotion of the king's step-son, Thomas Grey, Marquess of Dorset, might best be seen in the same light. After 1478, the south-west was entrusted to him on the basis of the wardship of the young earl of Warwick and a string of his stewardships. In 1474 he had married Cecily Bonville, the heiress of both Bonville and Harrington, who, as the grand-daughter of Richard

Neville, Earl of Salisbury, was also the king's first cousin once removed. She brought with her a substantial estate in Somerset and Devon with which to endow his heir.[34]

In other parts of the kingdom senior members of the royal household were given extensive power. Its chamberlain, Lord Hastings, was already well-established in the north midlands, his authority based on his office as steward of the duchy of Lancaster, lordship of Tutbury and his own estates in Leicestershire. The steward of the household, Lord Stanley, was the principal office-holder in the county palatine of Lancaster and in the earldom of Chester, and acted on the king's behalf in those counties. And its comptroller, Sir William Parr, emerged to a lesser extent as the key figure in the far north-west. But Parr's interests in Cumberland dove-tailed into the most significant of the regional hegemonies, that in the north created for and by Richard, Duke of Gloucester. Gloucester, on the basis of his Neville and other estates, the offices of chief steward of the duchy of Lancaster in the north and warden of the west march, and an effective partnership with the northern lords, dominated the five most northerly counties of the kingdom. The king himself, through his lesser household men, retained a direct personal interest only in the south-eastern and west midland counties.[35]

Edward IV's rule was founded on regional hegemonies under his most trusted kinsmen and associates. It was the rule of a refashioned royal affinity, owing its loyalty to the king himself. The significance of this manner of kingship is difficult to assess. On one level Edward did little more than recreate the Lancastrian polity as originally established by Henry IV – the rule of the kingdom entrusted to his kinsmen and his own retainers. There was nothing novel either in the kingdom being ruled through the king's affinity or in the king building up the power and prestige of the royal family. Edward, however, went further than Henry IV in entrusting greater power in fewer hands. Moreover, there is every sign that even at the end of his reign he was adding to the regional power and wealth enjoyed by, and to be enjoyed by, members of his family. Thus in his last parliament acts were passed creating a county palatinate centred on Cumberland for Richard of Gloucester; transferring the Holland inheritance of the dukes of Exeter to the child heir of the marquess of Dorset, who was both the queen's grandson and the king's cousin; and settling the duchy of Norfolk on his younger son after the death of Anne Mowbray. Although the king's early death prevented the full implementation of these acts, it is unlikely that Edward would later have reversed them. There is no reason to suppose that the move towards the creation of appanages for the benefit of the king's immediate family, with its potential implications for the future unity of the kingdom, was but a short-term expedient.[36]

There is no doubt that after 1478 the regime was effective. The king expected each of his magnates to keep the peace and maintain order. Clarence's failure to impose his authority on the midlands after 1471 was a contributory factor to his fall. In 1476, it was reported, Edward expressed frustration that the earl of Northumberland could not keep the peace within his own meynie (following), as a result of which royal disapproval the earl quickly settled the quarrel between Sir Thomas Gascoigne and Sir William Plumpton. And where his own retainers fell into conflict the king acted firmly. Thus the bloody feud between the two knights of the body, Sir John Saville and Sir John Pilkington, for domination of the duchy of York lordship of Wakefield, which came to a head at precisely the same time as the conflict with Clarence was at its peak, was subject to a powerful commission of oyer and terminer under Richard of Gloucester. The king's lieutenants in the regions were expected to keep order and to hold things still. And this, after 1478, they largely achieved.[37]

It followed that the administration of justice in the regions was left largely in their hands. There were fewer complaints about lawlessness and disorder after 1478. This might have been because the principal forum for complaint, parliament, only met briefly once more in the last months of the reign. And evidence from the far south-west, Wales and Lancashire suggests that the regime did not succeed completely in imposing order. But there can be little doubt that lawlesness was reduced to manageable proportions. Moreover, the policy of locally brokered arbitration, whatever its long-term implication for the enforcement of justice, helped maintain harmony among the landed elites in parts of the kingdom. Broadly speaking, the courts were involved only if this brokerage broke down. Yet that justice could be partial. It was possible, as in the north under the duke of Gloucester, as long as his direct personal interest was not involved, for justice to have been administered fairly. And certainly the north benefited greatly from the ending of magnate feuds which the duke's hegemony entailed. But of other parts of the kingdom there is less known. It has yet to be discovered, for instance, whether the marquess of Dorset was a keen upholder of impartial justice in the West Country. It is possible, as has been suggested, that the loyalty of the political nation as a whole was won by the benefits of 'self-regulation reinforced by monarchical intervention' which engendered power-sharing with landed society. But the danger existed that the real beneficiaries would be the king's agents rather than the king himself; a danger revealed in 1483 when the political elite of the north rallied not once, but twice, in support of the king's brother against his son.[38]

Arguably, too, the regime shared too much power with men whose dependence on the king was total, but who themselves did not necessarily see eye to eye. There was no love lost between Hastings and Dorset, who were rivals for the captaincy of Calais and were said by Mancini, no doubt on the basis of malicious gossip, to have been in fierce competition over their mistresses. It was said that Richard of Gloucester distanced himself from the queen's relatives after 1478. Although he never withdrew from court, as did Warwick, the events of 1483 reveal that he was unrestrained by affection for Lord Rivers and ready to exploit the rivalry between Hastings and Dorset for his own advantage. As is revealed by his reported death-bed appeal to his leading courtiers to end their disagreements, Edward IV was aware of these rifts, but was incapable of ending them. While after 1478 he contained incipient rivalry, he neither eradicated nor resolved it.

Moreover, by concentrating power in the hands of a fractious few, Edward also ran the risk of alienating the excluded. Over the last five years of his reign a number of his greater subjects found cause for resentment. Henry Stafford, Duke of Buckingham, although a powerful landowner in the west midlands and south Wales and married to the queen's sister, was given little favour or employment. The earl of Pembroke, at first given wide powers and privileges in Wales in 1471, was systematically excluded from the government of Wales thereafter, as was the leading figure of south-west Wales, Sir Rhys ap Thomas. The acts of parliament transferring the Holland and Mowbray inheritances to Dorset's heir and the young duke of York, just like the acts of 1474 and 1475 in favour of Clarence and Gloucester, disinherited heiresses and materially damaged the prospects of Lord Neville, the heir to the earldom of Westmorland, Lord Berkeley and, most ungenerously of all given his loyal service to the king, Lord Howard. Not only did Edward promote a favoured few at the cost of others, but he also consistently put the self-interests of his immediate family before those of even his own loyal servants.[39]

One should not rule out the possibility that Edward IV was influenced in his manner of kingship by current chivalric ideas. It has been suggested that he was influenced by the model of the service nobility of Valois Burgundy, exemplified by Louis de Gruthuyse, whom he created earl of Winchester in 1472, and who had been his host in 1470–1. And there was possibly even an Arthurian colour to a regime which focused on the king and a band of trusted knights. It might not be too fanciful to suppose, in an era which saw a revival of Arthurian literature and chivalric enthusiasm, that the king and his court self-consciously saw themselves seated at the round table, even though they may have failed to notice that the Arthurian tales were of treachery, betrayal and failure.[40]

Finally the king left himself dangerously dependent, as he had at the beginning of his reign, on one man; this time his brother Richard, Duke of Gloucester. The king could not afford to offend Richard of Gloucester after 1478. Gloucester had always been loyal, but he had built up a hegemony in the north as powerful if not more powerful than that enjoyed by Warwick.

After 1475 he had deliberately concentrated his estates and offices there. And while the king had extracted a price for his generosity, and had carefully tied strings to the creation of a patrimony for his youngest brother in the region, such was Gloucester's power, standing and authority in the north by 1480 that Edward IV dare not cross him. The extent to which he was beholden to Gloucester was to have a damaging impact on the conduct of foreign policy in the last years of his life.[41]

Foreign affairs, 1478–83

Edward IV's shortcomings are apparent in his conduct of foreign affairs after the death of Duke Charles of Burgundy in January 1476. Difficulties in securing from Louis XI prompt and full implementation of the terms of the treaty of Picquigny, especially in delivering the annual pension and in completing the commercial treaty, had developed almost at once. After the death of Duke Charles, Louis immediately took advantage of his alliance with England to invade and seize Artois and the duchy of Burgundy itself from the defenceless young Mary of Burgundy. It was only the stubborn resistance of the Flemings that prevented him overrunning Flanders. Edward IV, who refused to allow Clarence to marry Duchess Anne, valued the terms of the treaty of Picquigny too highly to renounce it.

After Anne had married Maximilian of Austria, the king then began to play one side against the other. In 1477 and 1478 he demanded from Louis the extension of the truce beyond seven years, securities for the future payment of the pension, the full implementation of the commercial treaty and, above all, the immediate payment of his daughter Elizabeth's jointure as the future wife of the Dauphin. At the same time differences with Maximilian over commercial relationships with Flanders, outstanding since the trade war of the 1460s, were finally resolved. By the end of 1478 he went so far as to agree, secretly, to renew the articles of the Anglo-Burgundian treaty of 1474, if Maximilian would pay the annual pension. Maximilian's timely victory over the French at Guinegatte in 1480, which turned the tide of the war in the Netherlands, allowed Edward to put more pressure on Louis to accede to his demand to pay the jointure. However, the French king correctly judged that the continued payment of the pension was more important to Edward. When Edward sealed a marriage alliance between his daughter Anne and Maximilian's infant son, Philip, the heir to Burgundy (without a dower, but a pension from Maximilian) in August 1480, Louis XI promptly withheld the payment of the next instalment of his pension. Edward did not revoke Picquigny.[42]

The diplomatic scene was transformed by Edward IV's decision to invade Scotland. Since 1474 Edward and James III had carefully maintained the terms of the treaty of Edinburgh. The truce began to collapse in 1479 as a result of the actions of the two kings' brothers – Richard, Duke of Gloucester, and Alexander, Duke of Albany. Both had reluctantly agreed to the treaty of Edinburgh. Albany in particular seems to have first caused breaches of the peace on the border, perhaps secretly encouraged by Louis XI, to whose court he fled in May 1479. Early in 1480 Edward IV took an aggressive line, demanding reparation and threatening retaliation if his demands were not met. They were not and preparations for war were begun, the duke of Gloucester being appointed the king's lieutenant on 12 May 1480. After autumn raids and counter-raids, in the spring of 1481 Edward IV threw himself into intensive preparations for a full-scale invasion of Scotland, which he intented to lead in person. Yet, notwithstanding the effort, the expense and the solemn justification to the Pope of a war to recover his rights over Scotland, as in the 1460s, Edward did not take to the field. Instead in August, under Gloucester's command, an attempt was made to recover Berwick and border raiding was renewed.

In 1482 Edward was encouraged to revive his Scottish ambitions by the defection of Alexander of Albany who arrived in England in April. By the treaty of Fotheringhay on 11 June Edward recognised Albany as king of Scotland and undertook to assist him to recover his throne in exchange for homage, the return of Berwick and the cession of a significant stretch of south-west Scotland. The military command was immediately entrusted to Gloucester who led a substantial army to invest Berwick in mid-July. The town fell immediately. Leaving a force to invest the castle, Gloucester marched unopposed to Edinburgh to depose James III and install King Alexander. However, at the eleventh hour, Albany came to terms with his brother and the Scottish lords. Gloucester had little choice but to withdraw, but on his return secured the reduction of Berwick castle and the full restoration of Berwick to English control after twenty-one years of being reunited with Scotland.[43]

For all the cost and effort the English return for the invasion of Scotland was meagre. And Edward IV, although his first reaction to the recovery of Berwick was exultant, was later reported to be 'grieved' at how little the campaign had achieved.[44] Edward's grief may well have been prompted by the disastrous turn which occurred in his Franco-Burgundian diplomacy as a result. Throughout 1481 Edward had been under pressure from Maximilian of Austria to honour the treaty of 1480, revoke Picquigny and invade France. Towards this end he concluded in May a treaty with Duke Francis of Brittany for the marriage of the prince of Wales with the duke's sole daughter and heiress Anne. But an invasion of France in 1481 was clearly out of the question as Edward committed himself against Scotland. Nevertheless the possibility of the revival of the triple alliance was sufficient to induce Louis to pay the postponed 1480 instalment of the pension in exchange for a secret undertaking to continue to honour the truce between them. In January 1482 Maximilian renewed the pressure on Edward to honour his agreement to assist him by sending at least 5,000 troops. Edward prevaricated.[45]

The situation was transformed, however, by the death of Mary, Duchess of Burgundy, on 27 March following a riding accident. Flanders and Brabant, exhausted by the war, and no longer having reason to support Maximilian, opened independent negotiations with Louis. Louis, for his part, grasped the opportunity to come to terms with Maximilian now faced by rebellion in the Burgundian territories. On 23 December the king and duke came to terms at Arras. They agreed that the Dauphin would now marry Mary of Burgundy, the daughter of Maximilian and Mary, and that Artois and Burgundy would be ceded to Louis as her dower. England was totally excluded. Picquigny was revoked. Edward lost both the marriage of Elizabeth with the Dauphin and his pension. His French policy lay in ruins.

It is hard to understand Edward's conduct of foreign policy after 1475. In one respect the disastrous denouement was fortuitous and beyond his control; he could not have predicted the early death of Mary of Burgundy which led rapidly to the rapprochement between Burgundy and France. It is perhaps ironic that in the course of this complex diplomatic game conditions arose in 1481 which were far more propitious for a renewal of the Hundred Years' War than in 1475, and that on this occasion it was England itself which was diverted by an entanglement on its other border. Moreover, just as in 1475 Charles the Bold had been shut out of negotiations by Louis and Edward, so in 1482 Edward was shut out by Louis and Maximilian.

It is impossible to determine precisely what Edward's aims were in playing Burgundy against France. One explanation is that in all his dealings he was shamelessly opportunistic. Seeking to maximise the payments either side would make to him, and minimise the payments he would make himself, he became too greedy. Alternatively, it is possible that he was genuinely torn between a desire to maintain the treaty with France, the marriage of his daughter and the valuable pension, and a wish to revive traditional English foreign policy. He could not make up his mind, and his tortuous foreign policy reflected indecision rather than cunning. Whichever way one looks at it, however, his foreign policy after 1475 lacked coherence, for which Edward ultimately paid the price of isolation.

Equally puzzling is the Scottish entanglement which ultimately undermined the continental policy. It is conceiveable that he so deluded himself that he was in such command of international relations that he believed he could engage in a war against Scotland without damaging his continental interests. But the explanation probably lies elsewhere. The war with Scotland was not of Edward's choosing; he was dragged into it by Richard of Gloucester. There are many pointers towards Gloucester's enthusiasm for the war. He had taken an independently aggressive line towards Scotland before 1474, and he had had to be restrained then by his brother. War with Scotland, especially a war of successful border raiding, was to the liking of many of his northern retainers and tenants. The recovery of Berwick, albeit that the Westminster-influenced Crowland Chronicler could not see its advantages, was of major benefit to the inhabitants of the northernmost counties. As commander of the troops in the field, he was an influential voice in the determination of strategy. He benefited most from the treaty of Fotheringhay, for the lands ceded by Albany in south-west Scotland were granted to him as part of the county palatine created in January 1483. And he continued the war after he became king. The Scottish war was Gloucester's war, and Edward had little choice but to follow his brother. By 1479 Edward could not run the risk of alienating him. The examples of Warwick, Clarence and even Albany were all too apparent. Edward appeased his brother's ambitions as the price of his continuing loyalty, even though it effectively undermined his Franco-Burgundian policy. Thus Edward's domestic policy, his style of kingship, and the character of his regime also helped to throw his foreign policy into confusion.[46]

The end of the reign

A parliament, the first since 1478, had been summoned on 15 November, before the treaty of Arras, to meet at Westminster on 20 January 1483. The principal intended business was probably the passage of those acts of parliament designed to settle inheritances on the duke of York and the marquess of Dorset and to reward the duke of Gloucester. But the king was reported to be so incensed by the collapse of his foreign policy that he could talk of nothing but revenging himself on France. Parliament voted a subsidy for the hasty and necessary defence of the realm. If not against France, it might have been to support the continued war with Scotland, for Albany had once again turned to England and had confirmed the terms of the treaty of Fotheringhay on 12 February. Parliament was dissolved six days later. Which direction English policy was taking early in 1483 is impossible to determine, for the fickle Albany patched up his differences with his brother in March, and Edward IV began once more to make overtures to France. At the end of the month, however, 'about Easter-time', he took ill;

ten days later, on 9 April, he died. It is not clear what his fatal illness was, but it was probably related to the dissolute life he led. He was only forty-two and his heir was but twelve years old.[47]

Edward IV's reign ended with his foreign policy in disarray and the kingdom at war with Scotland, but there can be little doubt that the internal peace enjoyed by the kingdom and the evident recovery of prosperity in the southern counties reflected well on his reign. He was an open, affable, generally merciful man, whose private vices were not judged by his contemporaries to undermine his public virtues. In this, as with his reluctance to go on his travels again, he somewhat resembled Charles II. Yet no sooner had he died than his achievement in reuniting the kingdom after two decades of intermittent civil war disintegrated. In part this is accountable by the sheer misfortune of the timing of his death. Had he lived a further six years, even four years, his heir would have been old enough to have succeeded unchallenged to the throne (as twenty-six years later did Henry VIII). In part the collapse of the Yorkist dynasty was brought about by the unforeseeable actions of his trusted younger brother in the months following his death; a brother, whose character and motives Edward conspicuously failed to understand. But in part too the regime failed to survive because of its own internal contradictions and Edward IV's own failures.

The failures were political. Administrative reform and financial retrenchment, managed through the agency of the household, effectively and assiduously carried out by his able councillors and servants, began the process of restoring the authority of the monarchy. But administrative reform was not enough to establish a dynasty. Edward did not create a collective commitment to the future of his dynasty under his son and heir strong enough to survive a minority. A combination of his willingness to rule through mighty subjects, and his failure to defuse the tensions between them, left his regime vulnerable. He was no Henry V or Henry VIII; he did not command the same dread as other monarchs whose dynasties survived minorities. His interest in the affairs of state and the act of governing was neither intense nor sustained. His vision did not stretch beyond his origins. His rule stayed as it had begun, that of a faction victorious in two civil wars. Despite the overwhelming nature of his victory in 1471, the regime remained as it was refashioned, and as Edward continued to shape it until the eve of his death, essentially the rule of the Yorkist family and associates over a conquered kingdom. Edward IV, as his cavalier attitude to the rules of inheritance in order to benefit his own kin reveals, was, unlike Henry V, unable to transcend in the wider interests of the kingdom the partisan character of his dynasty's origins and his family's self-interest. Yet the house of York, unlike the house of Lancaster, had little sense of family solidarity. It should thus not occasion surprise that Edward IV's sons were quickly removed not from without by his family's enemies, but from within by one of its own members, the dead king's brother, Richard of Gloucester.

Notes and references

1   *CSPM*, i, 156.

2   For this and the following paragraphs Ross, *Edward IV*, 181–7; Hicks, *Clarence*, 111–27 and 'Warwick Inheritance'; Pollard, *North-Eastern England*, 316–22; Lander, 'Attainder and Forfeiture'; Morgan, 'The King's Affinity' and 'House of Policy', 64–7.

3   *PL*, v, 135–6; HMC, *11th Report*, Appendix VII, 95.

4   *Rot Parl*, vi, 100–1, 124–5; Pronay and Cox, *Crowland Continuations*, 132–3.

5   Pollard, 'St Cuthbert and the Hog', 111 (Booth); Hicks, 'Dynastic Change', 83–4 (Northumberland); Carpenter, *Locality and Polity*, 516–20 and 'Duke of Clarence', 23–48 (the midlands); Griffiths, 'Wales and the Marches', 159–61; Lowe, 'Patronage and Politics', 545–73; Ross, *Edward IV*, 193–8 (Wales); Quinn, 'Aristocratic Autonomy', 601–6 and Hicks, *Clarence*, 126–7 (Ireland).

6   Hicks, *Clarence*, 117–22; Scofield, *Edward the Fourth*, ii, 57–63; Pollard, 'St Cuthbert and the Hog', 124, n. 9.

7   For the course of diplomacy 1471–5, see Ross, *Edward IV*, 205–14 and the references therein.

8   The address is preserved in the registers of Canterbury Cathedral Priory and is printed in *Literae Cantuarienses* (Rolls Series, 1889), vol. 3, 274–8, summarised in Scofield, *Edward the Fourth*, ii, 42–4; and discussed in Lander, 'The Hundred Years' War', 228–30 and Gross, *Lancastrian Kingship*, 93–6, for which see the suggested link with the *Boke of Noblesse*.

9   Lander, 'Hundred Years' War', 231–4; Ross, *Edward IV*, 214–18.

10   *PL*, v, 161–2.

11   See above n. 7 and, for relationships with the Hanseatic League, Scofield, *Edward the Fourth*, ii, 67–84; Bolton, *Medieval Economy*, 306–11; Lloyd, *German Hanse*, 208–17.

12   Pollard, *North-Eastern England*, 231–3; Ross, *Edward IV*, 210–14.

13   Pronay and Cox, *Crowland Continuations*, 143–5; Scofield, *Edward the Fourth*, ii, 106. A correspondent of the duke of Milan was greatly impressed by the manner in which Edward 'plucked out the feathers of his magpies without making them cry out' (*CSPM*, i, 193). See also Ross, *Edward IV*, 216–18 and Lander, 'Hundred Years' War', 231–4.

14 For military preparations see Ross, *Edward IV*, 218–23; Lander, *Hundred Years War*, 243–9, 321; Commynes, *Memoirs*, 237.

15 Ross, *Edward IV*, 224–6.

16 Ibid., 226–34. Commynes, *Memoirs*, 238–65 provides a first-hand account of the events.

17 Ross, *Edward IV*, 223–6. See Lander, 'Hundred Years' War', 226–8 for the view that the invasion was a continuation of the war started in 1471 and fought on English soil and revenge on Louis XI for the aid given to Warwick then.

18 Pronay and Cox, *Crowland Continuations*, 136–7; Commynes, *Memoirs*, 265–6; Ross, *Edward IV*, 236–7; Scofield, *Edward the Fourth*, ii, 156, 163–4.

19 Richmond, '1485 and All That', 186–91 (on Edward's failure). But see Lander, 'Hundred Years' War', 220–5 for the alternative view that the English were generally not enthusiastic supporters of entanglement in France.

20 Sutton *et al.*, *Reburial of Richard Duke of York*, passim.

21 *CSPM*, i, 211 (rumours about Clarence), 175–7, 184–6; Ross, *Edward IV*, 239–40; Hicks, *Clarence*, 128–33.

22 Hicks, *Clarence*, 133–40; Carpenter, 'Duke of Clarence', 130; Lander, 'Treason and Death', 246–9.

23 For the composition of the house of commons see Hicks, *Clarence*, 147–58; for the wedding, ibid., 144–5 and Scofield, *Edward the Fourth*, ii, 203–6.

24 Pronay and Cox, *Crowland Continuations*, 136–7; Hicks, *Clarence*, 159–69; Ross, *Edward IV*, 242–3; Lander, 'Treason and Death', 252–66.

25 Hicks, *Clarence*, 142–3.

26 Ross, *Richard III*, 32–4; Pollard, *Richard III*, 83; Hicks, *Clarence*, 150–2.

27 Mancini, *Usurpation*, 62–3, 67–9; Hicks, *Clarence*, 144–6, 149–50. For the grants made to Dorset see *CPR, 1476–85*, 139, 212, 263, 283–4; Ross, *Edward IV*, 336 and Hicks, 'Wydevilles', 73–4. The king retained possession of the estates. As with Hastings in the midlands, the basis of Dorset's influence lay in office-holding.

28 Carpenter, 'Duke of Clarence', 40; Ross, *Edward IV*, 243–4.

29 Pronay and Cox, *Crowland Continuations*, 146–7; Commynes, *Memoirs*, 258, 414; Mancini, *Usurpation*, 66–7; More, *Richard III*, 4–5.

30 Pronay and Cox, *Crowland Continuations*, 146–7, 152–3; Ross, *Edward IV*, 301–7, 374–5.

31 Ross, *Edward IV*, 310–12; Lander, 'Yorkist Council', 27–46. See also Watts, '*A New Ffundation*', 31–53 and below, pp. 366–7, 378.

32 Ross, *Edward IV*, 371–87; Wolffe, *Crown Lands*, 51–65 and 'Royal Estates'; Horrox, 'Financial Memoranda', 210–13.

33 Green, *History*, V, 37–8; endorsed by Lander, 'Edward IV', 52 ('iron will'); Carpenter, *Wars of the Roses*, 194, 205 ('greatest of English kings'). For the historiographical tradition see Lander, 'Edward IV', passim.

34 See above, n. 2; Hicks, 'Wydevilles', 74–9; Lowe, 'Patronage and Politics', passim; Ives, 'Andrew Dymmock', 223–5; Ross, *Edward IV*, 335–6 (Richard of York's endowment).

35 For Hastings see Dunham, *Hastings' Indentured Retainers*; Hicks, 'Lord Hastings' Indentured Retainers?', passim; Rowney, 'The Hastings Affinity'. For Stanley see Jones, 'Richard III and the Stanleys', and Jones and Underwood, *The King's Mother*, 58–60. For Parr see Booth, 'Cumberland and Westmorland', 149ff. For Dorset see Hicks, 'Wydevilles', 73–4; Ross, *Edward IV*, 336–7. For Gloucester see Pollard, *North-Eastern England*, 322–41; Horrox, *Richard III*, 27–88 and *Richard III and the North*, passim; Hicks, *Richard III as Duke of Gloucester*; Carpenter, *Locality and Polity*, 525–47 and *Wars of the Roses*, 191–4.

36 *Rot Parl*, vi, 204–57, 215–18; Ross, *Edward IV*, 202–3, 248–9, 336–9; Summerson, 'Carlisle and the English West March in the Later Middle Ages', 99–101, makes the important point that the palatine powers were modelled on Durham, in which in practice the king retained ultimate control. Potentially, however, there was a significant difference between an episcopal palatinate in the King's 'gift' and an herediatary lay palatinate.

37 Pollard, *North-Eastern England*, 140–1; Hayes, 'Ancient Indictments', 37–44.

38 Ross, *Edward IV*, 407–12, Carpenter, *Wars of the Roses*, 194–6. To Ross 'England was not a noticeably more law-abiding country in 1483 than it had been in 1461' (412). To Carpenter, on the other hand, 'political control was . . . the key to the enforcement of order and it was [this] that Edward was able to achieve in this period' (196). For Gloucester in the north see Pollard, *North-Eastern England*, 335–7. For arbitration see above p. 243.

39 Mancini, *Usurpation*, 64–5, 68–9; Pollard, *Richard III*, 83–4; Thomas More, the reliability of whose information is questionable, was confident that Edward knew the court lords were at variance and tells how he sought on his deathbed to reconcile them, especially Dorset and Hastings (*History*, 5, 11–14). For the alienated lords see Rawcliffe, *The Staffords*, 28–9; Hicks, 'Wydevilles', 80–1; Griffiths, *Sir Rhys ap Thomas*, 34–6; and Pugh, 'Magnates, Knights and Gentry', 110–12.

40 Vale, 'Anglo-Burgundian Nobleman', 128; Pollard, 'Society, Politics and the Wars of the Roses', 14–15, drawing upon an unpublished paper by M. K. Jones.

41 Pollard, *North-Eastern England*, 322, 338–41, 242–3. There is no doubt that Edward IV first promoted his brother in the north, but compelling reason to suppose that by 1480 Gloucester had capitalised on the king's favour to his own advantage (ibid., 339 and notes).

42 For diplomacy and international relations from 1475 to 1480 see Scofield, *Edward the Fourth*, ii, 177–88, 191–202, 222–301 and Ross, *Edward IV*, 245–56. Edward IV allowed Margaret of Anjou to return to France in January 1476 in exchange for £10,000 and a renunciation of any title to the crown of England or to her dower lands. She, the unfortunate woman, was treated no more generously by Louis XI and died in virtual poverty in 1482, deserving more sympathy for her tragic life than has normally been accorded her (Scofield, *Edward the Fourth*, ii, 157–9).

43 Pollard, *North-Eastern England*, 233–41; Macdougall, *James III*, 128–9, 144–8, 152–5, 168–70; Ross, *Edward IV*, 278–83, 287–90, 292–3.

44 Pronay and Cox, *Crowland Continuations*, 149; Pollard, *North-Eastern England* 241–2.

45 For international relations from 1480 to the treaty of Arras in 1482 see Scofield, ii, *Edward the Fourth*, 306–14, 318–21, 324–33, 341–4, 350–7; Ross, *Edward IV*, 283–6, 290–2.

46 Pollard, *North-Eastern England*, 242–4.

47 For the last months of the reign see Scofield, *Edward the Fourth*, ii, 358–64; Ross, *Edward IV*, 292–5. For the king's illness, death and funeral see Ross, *Edward IV*, 414–18.

CHAPTER TWELVE

Edward V and Richard III, 1483–5

The accession of Edward V

Edward V, who came to the throne at the age of twelve, reigned but seventy-eight days. He was never crowned, and probably never saw his thirteenth birthday. His brief reign is dominated by his deposition on 24 June 1483. Very little is known of him or his personality. Plaudits concerning his precocious wisdom and kingly merits contained in a draft sermon written by his Chancellor, John Russell, Bishop of Lincoln, which was to have been delivered to his first parliament, and in the account of his deposition later written by Dominic Mancini cannot be taken at face value. Russell's words were the conventional stuff of politics; Mancini's testimony that 'in word and deed he gave so many proofs of his liberal education, of polite, nay rather scholarly attainments far beyond his age' needs to be read in the knowledge that it was deployed in his text to highlight a tragic tale.[1] Edward V may well have struck contemporaries as a youth of great promise, but by the very nature of things one can never know. As a twelve-year-old, by established precedent, during the first four years of his reign, his kingdom would be ruled by a council acting in his name. The first responsibility facing Edward IV's councillors and kinsmen was to establish a system of government during the minority that would preserve his inheritance. They failed totally to live up to the trust placed in them.

The council in Westminster met as soon as it could to determine the structure of the new government, possibly even before Edward IV's funeral on 20 April. Divisions of opinion were reported second-hand by one contemporary, Dominic Mancini, and cryptically by another, the second continuator of the Crowland Chronicle, who appears to have been present. Three inter-related issues were paramount: what constitutional form should be adopted, who should be the head of the minority government in the king's name, and who should control the king's person? It seems as if the queen, present because of her new status, and her son the marquess of Dorset made an immediate bid for power. A rift between them and Lord Hastings, who proposed that the duke of Gloucester, then in Yorkshire, should head the new government, quickly became apparent. Dorset, Earl Rivers's deputy lieutenant of the Tower, was reported to have boasted that his party was so powerful that 'even without the king's uncle (Gloucester) we can make and enforce decisions'. Hastings, whose antipathy towards Dorset was common knowledge, may have pushed the case for a protectorate under the duke. A rumour that he had been nominated protector by his brother before he died circulated in London. Crowland refers to a codicil to the king's will.[2] No actual documentation of Edward's supposed last wishes has survived.

Even if Edward had nominated his brother, as the precedent of Henry V showed, the council was not bound to follow the wishes of a dead king. It seems that the option was discussed and rejected. It was decided instead that Edward V should be crowned immediately, so obviating the need for a protectorate.[3] The precedent of Richard II, who was ten when he came to the throne, rather than of Henry VI who was nine months, was to be followed. Moreover, Henry VI's protectorate had ended when the king was crowned, aged seven, in 1429. The conciliar decision, therefore, to fix the coronation for 4 May and to dispense with a formal protectorate was constitutionally correct. But again, following the precedent of 1377, it was agreed that, as the king's paternal uncle, Gloucester should become the chief councillor.

This still left the question of who would be responsible for the king's tutelage and have control of his household. The Crowland Chronicler commented that 'the more foresighted members of the council' thought that the queen's relatives (her brothers, Rivers and Sir Edward Woodville, her sons Dorset and Sir Richard Grey) should be excluded.[4] It is not known whether these 'foresighted members' (the Chancellor Thomas Rotherham, the Keeper of the Privy Seal, John Russell, and the Master of the Rolls, John Morton?) carried the day. Hastings, who did not trust the Woodvilles to honour the agreement concerning the structure of government, feared perhaps that Earl Rivers would, when he arrived with the king in London, impose a Woodville regime. The most bitter dispute seems thus to have focused not on the constitutional arrangements but on the size of retinues brought up to Westminster for the coronation. Hastings even threatened to withdraw to Calais, of which he was captain, if the queen did not advise her son to bring only a modest retinue.[5] On this she gave way. But it would seem that the question of the control of the person of the king was left unresolved.

Events away from the council chamber were already taking a separate course. Gloucester heard the news of Edward IV's death on or about 15 April. He may have been forewarned, for a rumour of the death had already spread. The duke's first reported public act was to pledge his allegiance to his new king, Edward V, at York Minster. He also entered into correspondence with the two noblemen who were to be his allies in the immediate future: Henry Stafford, Duke of Buckingham, and William, Lord Hastings. There is no evidence of association between Buckingham and Richard before 1483. It is perhaps of significance, however, that Richard was so quickly in contact with one who had been so clearly out of favour in recent years and perhaps resented the favour shown to Rivers and Stanley in Wales and the marches. These three, Richard and Buckingham in the country and Hastings in London, quickly forged an alliance.

Gloucester and Buckingham joined forces, both accompanied only by modestly sized retinues, at Northampton on 29 April. There they entertained Earl Rivers and his principal officers who, with the king, had reached Stony Stratford on their road from Ludlow. Rivers assumed that on the morrow they would join together to accompany the king in state to London and his coronation five days later in Westminster Abbey. Like Duke Richard and Hastings, Rivers had shared exile with Edward IV in 1470–1. Like Richard, he enjoyed a reputation as a cultured, pious and chivalric man. But he was also a hard-headed politician who had used his position as governor of the prince of Wales to enhance his own power and influence. He was not the sort of man to take risks if he sensed danger. On the night of 29 April he believed that he, Gloucester and Buckingham were as one over the arrangements for the government of the realm and the care of the king. At dawn on 30 April, however, he was seized by the dukes' retainers and immediately taken the ten miles back to Stony Stratford. There the dukes arrested Sir Richard Grey and Sir Thomas Vaughan, the treasurer of the king's household, and dismissed the king's attendants. According to Mancini, Gloucester, 'who exhibited a mournful countenance',[6] told the king that Rivers and his family were morally unsuited to be his guardians, that they had conspired to kill him and that they had sought to deny him the protectorate promised by Edward IV. While Richard and Buckingham, now with Edward V in their charge, resumed their journey to London, Rivers, Grey and Vaughan were sent north to imprisonment at Middleham and Sheriff Hutton. News of this palace coup quickly reached London where the queen, having initially tried to raise the city on her behalf, fled to sanctuary in Westminster with her younger son, Richard of York, her daughters and Dorset. London was held for the dukes by Lord Hastings who welcomed them to the city a few days later.

It is impossible to be certain why Gloucester used force at Stony Stratford. Perhaps, given the speed with which events were unfolding and the slowness of communications, he did not know of the decisions reached by the council and decided to settle the issue by force. But, as events were quickly to demonstrate, he was determined to accept nothing less than a protectorate. And, if Mancini is to be believed, Hastings was urging the duke to take steps against the queen's kin. Moreover, the principal objective of the *coup d'état* was to secure control of the person of the king, without which his own position might have been vulnerable. Whatever the council at Westminster might propose, Gloucester was set on exercising complete power during the minority. Thus on 30 April he took the law into his own hand.

On 10 May, at a formal meeting of council, Richard was appointed protector, the coronation was postponed to 24 June (later altered to Sunday 22 June) and all the lords in London as well as the mayor and aldermen were required to swear an oath of fealty to the young king. This, and Gloucester's declaration of intent, reassured the city. Once Gloucester was established as protector, royal government carried on much as before. Rivers, Dorset and their closest associates were stripped of offices and grants; Buckingham was lavishly rewarded and established with almost vice-regal power in Wales. The triumvirate seemed to have achieved its objective of excluding the queen's family. While the council refused to support Gloucester's demand that Rivers should be tried for treason, preparations were nevertheless set in train for the coronation and the meeting of parliament that would follow immediately. Discussion was also initiated on the form of government after the king was crowned.

In the short term the seizure of power at Stony Stratford successfully secured control of the kingdom for Richard and his allies. In the longer term, even if Richard's thinking extended no further than the immediate present, it created as many problems as it solved. The coronation could not be postponed indefinitely. It would be difficult to hold it without the king's mother, brother, sisters, half-brothers and other uncles present. Yet by his action at Stony Stratford Gloucester had created implacable enemies in Rivers, Sir Richard Grey and the rest of their family who were either in captivity, sanctuary, hiding or exile. Whatever their relationship before 30 April, there can be no doubting the animosity between Richard and the Woodvilles thereafter. After the coronation the king's wishes could not be completely overlooked; and he is likely to have wanted his mother's family restored. One option open to Richard was to buy time by extending the protectorate, and therefore the government excluding the Woodvilles, after the coronation. It seems from the text of John Russell's draft sermon for the opening parliament of the reign that at one stage he was indeed planning to seek authority for both this and his continued tutelage of the king.[7] It is not known whether this course of action was proposed to the council and rejected.

It is hard to believe that Richard had seized power on 30 May only to be protector of the realm and guardian of the king for just two months, reverting to chief councillor and surrendering custody of Edward V after the postponed coronation. It may well be that Richard's intention from the start was to install himself in complete power until the king came of age.

The usurpation of Richard III

The apparent calm was shattered when on Friday 13 June, during a council meeting at the Tower, the protector suddenly accused Hastings, Lord Stanley, Archbishop Rotherham of York and Bishop Morton of Ely of treason. Hastings was seized, taken outside and beheaded without even the pretence of a trial. The other three were thrown into prison. It is now known that on 10 June Richard had sent letters north to the city of York and others, calling on them to raise troops to rescue him from the danger he and his men faced in London from the plots and sorcery of the queen and her adherents, who threatened 'the final distruction' of all who followed him.[8] On 13 June he justified his actions on the grounds of the same Woodville plot against him. Events moved rapidly. On Monday 16 June Richard surrounded the Westminster precinct with a large force, threatening to enter and seize the young duke of York. The archbishop of Canterbury, fearing more the desecration of sanctuary than the safety of a ten-year-old prince, persuaded Queen Elizabeth to surrender him. Writs were now issued cancelling parliament, and the coronation itself was postponed once more until November. By now all routine government business had come to a halt.

On Sunday 22 June, the day Edward V was to have been crowned, Ralph Shaw preached a sermon at St Paul's Cross in which Richard's claim to the throne as the only legitimate heir of York was first advanced. Two days later the duke of Buckingham repeated the claim before a gathering of the mayor and aldermen of London in the Guildhall. On 25 June, the day on which parliament was to have met, a group of lords, knights and gentlemen attended Richard at Baynard's Castle, his mother's London house, and petitioned him in the name of the three estates to take the throne. They did so again on the following day, 26 June, when he formally took possession and sat in the king's chair in the court of King's Bench in the Great Hall at Westminster. While these events were happening in London a substantial army was being gathered in the north. Troops were still mustering, when, on 25 June, on Richard's orders, Rivers, Grey and Vaughan were executed at Pontefract, like Hastings, without trial. The northern army, numbering some 4,000 men, finally arrived in London on 2 or 3 July in time to police the coronation which was held on 6 July.

Less than three months after his brother's death, Richard III made himself king. It is of course possible that Richard was, as he claimed, the legitimate heir to the throne of England, duly recovering his right after he had been informed of the fact of Edward V's illegitimacy by a troubled Bishop Stillington. It is possible, but highly implausible. The case finally put together concerning the bastardy of the princes, and enrolled in a parliamentary statute of January 1484, is theologically sound. It was that Edward IV had entered a pre-contract of marriage with Eleanor Butler before he had married Elizabeth Woodville and that this rendered his children by her illegitimate. Under canon law, had Edward IV entered a pre-contract of marriage with Eleanor Butler, all the children born of a later union, before or after Eleanor's death, even if Elizabeth Woodville had been ignorant of the previous liaison, would have been illegitimate. In this respect the fact that Edward IV and Elizabeth Woodville had married clandestinely made matters worse. Moreover, it was perfectly acceptable in law to raise objection on these grounds several years after the event. The pre-contract story, in its final form, presented a strong legal case.[9]

There are, however, several sound reasons for doubting its truth. While it is the case that parliament was a proper body to adjudicate on matters of inheritance that resulted from illegitimacy, in England in the later fifteenth century an ecclesiastical court should have heard the original charge. It did not. Moreover, even if it had been proved true, deposition was not the only course. Edward V, like Elizabeth I later, could have been declared legitimate and all doubts removed. The stain of illegitimacy could have been removed by the ritual of coronation. Above all, the revelation of the princes' bastardy was so timely and convenient as to leave little doubt in the minds of contemporaries that it was but the colour for an act of usurpation.

There is, too, a suspicious degree of confusion over the precise detail of the charge of illegitimacy as it was first advanced in June. Mancini's account of the sermons and speeches hints at a change in the story. At first the charge appeared to be that Edward IV himself was a bastard; two days later it seems that the princes were. Royal letters were issued immediately after Richard made himself king absolving his subjects of the oath of loyalty to Edward V in ignorance of Richard III's true title. That title, the letters declared, had been shown in a petition presented by the lords spiritual and temporal and the commons on 26 June. A copy was sent to Calais for publication. Unfortunately neither that, nor any other copy, has survived. The earliest surviving version is that transcribed as part of the parliamentary act settling the throne on Richard several months later. This purports to reproduce that petition verbatim, but doubts have been cast on its veracity.

It is possible that the final, official version had been subsequently amended. Even so, there is no reason to doubt that the substance of the original petition of 26 June was the same: namely that 'all the issue of the said King Edward been bastards'.[10]

What motivated the usurpation has been endlessly discussed. One explanation, much favoured in recent years, is that Richard III acted only in self-defence. It is true that on 13 June Hastings and the other arrested councillors were accused of plotting against him. The accusation was given substance many years later by Polydore Vergil who described how Hastings began to suspect Gloucester's intentions after the violent seizure of power at Stony Stratford. Unfortunately no independent contemporary evidence of the conspiracy exists. It is also inherently unlikely that Hastings would have plotted with the Woodvilles. On the other hand he, Stanley, Rotherham and Morton may have opposed a plan for the protectorate to be extended beyond the coronation. Even so, a conciliar caucus in opposition to the protector hardly constitutes a treasonable plot. Yet Richard himself had already, three days before he made his accusation, called for troops from the north to protect him, so he claimed, 'as it is now openly known' from a new plot by the queen to murder him.[11] It is difficult to see how the queen in sanctuary still represented a serious threat, and strange, if the plot were *openly* known on 10 July, that he had not dealt with the conspirators then. The only plausible explanation is that Richard invented this conspiracy to justify his actions and to preempt opposition before he made his own claim to the throne.

The most frequent defence in mitigation is that Richard III was forced into all his actions in 1483 to protect himself from Woodville malice. Throughout the late spring and early summer of 1483 Richard justified his actions at every stage by attacking the Woodvilles, whom he accused of ruining the kingdom as well as Edward IV's health and of plotting to destroy him and all the old nobility of the realm. This was effective propaganda because the favour shown to the queen's relatives had been resented in some quarters. The ease with which Richard disposed of them suggests, however, that they had not been a real threat. Moreover there is little evidence of animosity between Richard and the queen's family before 1483. We have only Richard's word for their plotting against him. Yet the Crowland Chronicler as well as Mancini believed that they initially sought to control Edward V and dominate his government, possibly at the duke's expense. Richard III did not entirely invent the Woodville scare.[12]

Richard may have nurtured deep-seated fears about his future if he once lost royal favour for another reason. Influence became critical to him after the death of George Neville on 4 May 1483. His title to the Neville estates was thereby reduced to a life interest. He had need to hold power so as at least to prevent others from undermining his position, and at most to amend legislation in his favour. Indeed he may well have known that George Neville was dying before he seized power on 30 April. Richard could not afford to take the chance of allowing others to rule because he stood to lose his hard-earned place as a great northern magnate. In this respect, therefore, not against the Woodvilles, but because of his own vulnerability, self-preservation may have been a powerful motive driving him on from one act to another in 1483.[13]

It is clear, however, that in 1483 the House of York was a house divided. Tensions, which had been held in check by Edward IV's personal mastery, burst instantly into the open on his death. The very speed with which conflict occurred is a telling indictment of Edward's regime. Henry V, be it remembered, had died abroad. Nothing was determined concerning the arrangements for the government of the kingdom during the minority of his son until after he had been buried two months after his death. Then the political nation had been as one. The contrast between 1422 and 1483 cannot be more marked. In 1483 the dead king was buried in indecent haste, before many of his magnates could attend; a faction of the council sought to hurry through the establishment of the new regime. While it is true that a short minority created more uncertainty and tension than a long one, what is distinctive about 1483 is not that there was a scramble for power, but the speed with which the leading members of an hitherto apparently harmonious establishment were at each others' throats. For this, Edward IV was partly responsible, although he could not have foreseen that his own brother would have been the agent of destruction.[14]

Personal ambition, awakened after Edward IV's death, is the one common strand that would make sense of all Richard's actions. He may well have been convinced that he alone had the ability and therefore the right to rule England. He may even have convinced himself that he was surrounded by enemies seeking to destroy him. It is no longer believed that he had long intended to take the throne for himself and had only been awaiting the opportunity, but Richard might have determined to take the throne soon after Edward IV's death, in which case the seizure of power at Stony Stratford was a step in that direction. Alternatively the fateful decision might have been taken only hesitatingly and reluctantly just before he became king because his plan legally to extend his protectorate after the coronation until the king came of age had been thwarted by Hastings and others.

Perhaps in retrospect what happened appears more controlled and more deliberate than was in fact the case. We like to see Richard III masterminding a brilliantly conceived and skilfully executed *coup d'état*, where perhaps there was only confusion, ignorance and fear.[15] Richard might have had a plan to take the throne by one means, but found that he had to change it as events developed. It is not clear why Richard called for northern troops on

10 June when in the event he did not need them. It might have been his initial intention to stage a parliamentary 'election'; a plan which was subsequently abandoned after 13 June. Was 13 June, therefore, unplanned? Was everything brought forward in a rush because Hastings and others had discovered that he had called for troops?

However we interpret his actions, it is clear that Richard III dictated events in 1483. He took his politically seasoned victims by surprise in their lodgings or in council chamber. He acted ruthlessly, liquidating without due trial those whom he saw to be standing in his way. And he did so to the utter amazement of his contemporaries. 'An insane lust for power', secretly nurtured and disguised, biding its time and awaiting its opportunity, seemed to some contemporaries to offer the only explanation of how the figure of probity which had been the duke of Gloucester became the figure of treachery which was Richard III.[16] Above all he deposed a boy of twelve, his nephew, who *on his own insistence* had been placed in his trust. The magnitude of what he did should not be played down. Edward V was not of an age to have caused personal political offence. He could not be accused of tyranny, like Richard II, or gross incompetence, like Henry VI. He had begun to reign, but he had not yet ruled. The usurpation of 1483 was of a fundamentally different order to those of 1399, 1461 or even 1485. Those, whether justifiable or not, were acts of the last resort. In 1483, uniquely, deposition was used as a weapon of first resort.[17]

The fate of the Princes in the Tower

It is likely that at some unknown date between 22 June and mid-September Edward V and his brother Richard were put to death; precisely when, by whom, by what means has never been, and is unlikely ever to be known. Rumours of their deaths quickly began to circulate. Dominic Mancini reported that even before he left London in mid-July they had disappeared, but when he wrote his account at the end of the year he admitted that he did not know whether they were dead or alive. By 1484 it was widely believed in both England and on the continent that they were dead. A list of the dates of kings compiled before 1485 confidently gave the death of Edward V as 26 June 1483. The Crowland Chronicler, writing in the spring of 1486, recalled that a rumour arose in September 1483 that they were dead. Speaking to the estates general at Tours in January 1484, the chancellor of France, Guillaume de Rochefort, reminded his audience, as they knew, that Edward IV's sons had been murdered. In the spring of 1484, Richard himself was forced to take steps to attempt to stop the spread of seditious rumour that almost certainly concerned the princes; as the author of the *Great Chronicle of London* noted many years later there was at this time 'much whispering . . . among the people that the king had put the children of King Edward to death'. There is an impressive array of evidence dating from before 1500, some very early, that reflects the universal belief that the boys met their deaths at Richard's hands before the middle of September 1483.[18]

But it remains the fact that Richard III's responsibility cannot be proved. The bones found in the Tower of London in the seventeenth century, exhumed and examined in 1933, even if they were proved to be the bones of the princes, cannot help date their deaths to a sufficient degree of accuracy to determine the issue. In the light of the inconclusiveness of the evidence it is not surprising that attempts have been made to pin the blame on others, especially Henry VII. After he took the throne in August 1485 Henry was equivocal about the question of the princes. The attainder of Richard, late duke of Gloucester, accused him of the shedding of infant's blood; but no inquiry or investigation was set in train. He left the matter unresolved because it was not in his immediate interest to encourage discussion of a question which would have drawn attention to the better claims of both Edward, Earl of Warwick, and Elizabeth of York. Even less credible is the notion that one, or even both of the princes survived. No one of political importance believed for one moment that Perkin Warbeck was indeed Richard of York – not even his backers. Recent theories concerning the survival of the children incognito into the reign of Henry VIII are even more implausible.

However much one tries to find alternative explanations, it remains most likely that contemporary opinion was correct in the assumption that Richard III murdered the princes, and did so early in his reign. The conduct of Richard III's enemies, from the moment they adopted Henry Tudor as their candidate for the throne in October 1483, points to a shared conviction that Edward V and his brother were dead. Elizabeth Woodville's actions for the next two years, erratic and self-defeating as they proved to be, are inexplicable except in the context of a belief that her sons by Edward IV were dead. Henry Tudor, after secret negotiation conducted on his behalf by the two mothers, would not have publicly declared in Rennes Cathedral on Christmas Day 1483 that he would marry Elizabeth of York as his queen unless he, she, his mother and her mother had not been confident that her brothers were dead.

But beyond this the belief that Richard had murdered the princes was as important as the truth of the matter itself; the perceived truth, not the actual truth was of political significance. The imputed crime of murdering the princes was all the worse for the fact that they were innocents. Albeit that a certain tolerance of political murder had developed in England since 1450, and albeit that contemporaries might even have been prepared to accept the summary executions of Hastings, Rivers, Grey and Vaughan in June 1483, the imputed murder of the princes was different. They were not worldly-wise politicians, but children, below the age of consent, in the care and under the protection of the uncle who it was believed killed them. There was in contemporary comment a powerful sense of outrage that innocent children had been so abused. It was believed that, in taking Edward V's throne and killing him and his brother, Richard III had stepped beyond the bounds of acceptable political behaviour. For this he was condemned. Such condemnation probably had a bearing on the unwillingness of many of his subjects to accept him as lawful king. Hostile rumour, protest and dissent characterised his brief reign and the conviction that he had murdered his nephews seriously handicapped Richard's efforts to secure himself on the throne.

Buckingham's rebellion

The coronation of King Richard III was a splendid occasion well attended by the lords spiritual and temporal and leading gentry of the kingdom. This does not necessarily mean that Richard's accession was rapturously received. For many, attendance was politic, especially as they had already come up to Westminster for another coronation. Of course there was a good turn-out of the king's own committed supporters, many of whom had recently arrived from the north. Prominent among those present were the duke of Buckingham; John Howard, Duke of Norfolk, Edward, Viscount Lisle and William, Viscount Berkeley, all three promoted in reward for their recent support; and the bishops of Durham, St David's, Lincoln and Bath and Wells. A crop of men, several lately members of Edward IV's household, created Knights of the Bath in the traditional pre-coronation ceremony, and many gentlemen and ladies in personal attendance on the new king and queen who had long served them, attended. But the unprecedented military presence, the ostentatious welcoming of Sir John Fogge out of sanctuary to grace the occasion and the very noticeable absence of the archbishop of Canterbury from the banquet following the ceremony revealed the underlying political reality.[19]

Richard was probably not deceived by the attendance of a number of his brother's erstwhile servants at his coronation. He knew that his usurpation had caught them by surprise and that they were still in disarray. He therefore sought to capitalise immediately on his advantage to win their more committed support. He could exploit the desire of men in royal service to stay in favour and could appeal as a crowned monarch to their allegiance, before God, to his office if not his person. Continuity was therefore his watchword. He presented himself as the true heir to Edward IV, politically as well as genetically, desiring only to govern as before. A few changes had to be made: Viscount Lovell became chamberlain of the household in place of Hastings; John Kendall became king's secretary and Thomas Metcalfe, chancellor of the duchy of Lancaster. But in general Richard's own close associates received few immediate rewards; and some, such as the installation of Sir John Conyers as a Knight of the Garter, cost little. The king hoped that the local ruling elites would be reassured to find that their lives would be little altered by his usurpation.[20]

Two weeks after the coronation the king set out, accompanied by a magnificent entourage which included five bishops and several lords, to show himself to his subjects. His route took him up the Thames valley, over to Gloucester, and then through Warwick, Coventry, Leicester and Nottingham to York, where he arrived on 29 August. It was, as intended, a triumphal progress. As a letter by John Kendall to the city of York reveals, the progress was a carefully orchestrated piece of propaganda, in which pageants and ceremonial entries designed to royal order were staged at every opportunity. York was to put on a particularly impressive show 'for there come many southern lords and men of worship with them, which will mark greatly your receiving their graces'.[21] The route taken enabled the king to consolidate support in the upper Thames valley where the new chamberlain of his household, Viscount Lovell, was influential, in the west midlands where he now controlled the estates of the earldom of Warwick (the young earl, Clarence's son, was also in the party); and the north-east midlands where Hastings had until recently managed the duchy of Lancaster interest on Edward IV's behalf. But the climax was the triumphal return to York. He stayed in the city for over three weeks. On 8 September his son and heir Edward was invested as prince of Wales. The only fly in the ointment was the unwillingness of the archbishop, Thomas Rotherham, now free again, to participate. But the city was rewarded for its enthusiastic backing by the concession of the long-desired reduction in its fee farm.

These three and a half weeks in York were to prove the high-water mark of the reign. Even as the king heard solemn mass in the great minster and feasted in the archbishop's palace, trouble was stirring in the south. Not long after he left London a plot to rescue the princes from the Tower had been discovered and thwarted. At the same time an attempt was made to smuggle their sisters out of sanctuary in Westminster to safety abroad. At the end of August, Buckingham, who had left the royal entourage at Gloucester to go on to his Welsh estates, was appointed to head a judicial commission to try treason in London and the Home Counties. By late September a conspiracy for risings throughout southern England aimed at the restoration of Edward V, in which Margaret Beaufort, Countess of Richmond and mother of Henry Tudor, was deeply involved, was well advanced. The king, who set out on a leisurely return from York on 20 September, seems to have known. In reaction to the rumour that both the princes were now dead, or probably following more certain intelligence, the conspirators turned instead to Henry Tudor, who, according to the Crowland Chronicler, they asked to marry Elizabeth of York, Edward IV's eldest daughter, and with her share the throne. At this late stage too, the duke of Buckingham threw in his lot with Richard's enemies, suborned it would seem by his prisoner, John Morton, Bishop of Ely, himself in the thick of it. According to Crowland too, the king also discovered Buckingham's planned treachery and kept a careful watch on him. He lingered at Pontefract until 8 October preparing to meet the uprising, but astutely waiting for the rebels to declare themselves.[22]

On or just before 10 October the rebellion finally broke. There were risings in Kent, spreading westward to Wiltshire by 23 October and the far south-west by early November. The risings were poorly co-ordinated and occurred as a series of chain reactions as the initial rebels in Kent, quickly dispersed by the duke of Norfolk, retreated westwards. The king himself marched via Nottingham and Oxford to Salisbury, where he arrived at the beginning of November, but sent troops to intercept Buckingham, who found that he could raise little support in Wales and that his crossing of the Severn was hindered by floods. He sought to flee, but was captured and brought to the king at Salisbury where he was promptly executed on 2 November. The king then pushed westward, reaching Exeter by 8 November. Henry Tudor arrived off Plymouth, but was too late to be of any assistance and so turned back to France. Many rebels submitted, but several managed to escape from west-country ports to join Tudor in exile. The rebels were scattered before they were able to bring their full force together. It is unlikely that they realised that the king had infiltrated their conspiracy. This would explain the speed and certainty with which Richard himself acted once the uprising began and its rapid collapse as he moved against it. It may even be that he deliberately dawdled in the north in September to entice the rebels into action.

The list of those ultimately attainted for treason in the parliament of January 1484 shows that, the duke of Buckingham and countess of Richmond apart, there were no peers involved. The leaders were men who had been prominent in Edward IV's household. Sir John Fogge, Sir John Cheyney, Sir Giles Daubeney, Sir Richard Guildford, Richard Haute and William Brandon whom Richard had endeavoured to bring round to his side. It was a rebellion of Edwardian Yorkists who had not been able to oppose the usurpation itself. Buckingham's participation is harder to fathom. Vergil, thirty years later, argued that it was because Richard had gone back on his promise to grant the duke his share of the Bohun inheritance. In this, however, he was wrong, for the process of transferring the title had already begun when Buckingham rebelled. Vergil himself discounted the popular view current in his day that the duke had his eye on the throne. Yet this is not impossible. He did have a remote claim, which in Henry VIII's reign contributed to his son's undoing. Alternatively he may have jumped too soon onto what he judged to be the winning side. It is curious that Thomas, Lord Stanley, rightly suspected because of the involvement of his wife, the countess of Richmond, came out for Richard. One explanation might be that he originally intended to raise the north-west on his son-in-law's behalf, but on hearing that Buckingham had rebelled, led the troops he had mustered to support Richard. There was no love lost between the two men; and Stanley was the principal beneficiary in North Wales from Buckingham's fall.[23]

The midlands stood by the king. To this extent the royal progress had proved to be a success. Rebellion was restricted to the southern counties from Essex to Cornwall. His enemies had declared their hand and had been routed. His victory confirmed the short-term success of the usurpation and the issue had been clarified: all he now had to do was to destroy the makeshift alliance of diehard Lancastrians and Edwardian Yorkists who had gathered around Henry Tudor. Once done, he would be secure.

Richard III's government, 1483–5

Richard III returned to London on 25 November 1483. His immediate priorities were to reformulate his regime so as to be secure of the dissident south and to convince still doubting subjects that he had a right to the throne. Both Henry IV and Edward IV before him had survived their difficult early years: so might he. Captains of the king's army which had suppressed the rising were immediately made sheriffs and constables of strategic castles in the southern counties. The same men headed the judicial enquiries which were established to indict the principal rebels. A considerable number submitted and threw themselves on the king's mercy. But nearly a hundred were finally attainted for treason. Before the formal process of enquiry, indictment and conviction was completed, royal officers began to confiscate and occupy the estates of the condemned and the king himself started to redistribute them to trusted followers. Thus was instituted, even before the act of attainder was passed, what the Crowland Chronicler writing in 1486 characterised as a tyrannical plantation of northerners in the south.[24]

The tyranny in mind was not so much the actual behaviour of the new 'lords', but the transgression of the notion that the local communities should be ruled by their own native elites. In the eighteen months following the October rebellion approximately three dozen northerners of Richard's household, a large number of them Yorkshiremen, were brought in to fill offices, sit on the commissions of the peace and array, and enjoy the lands of attainted rebels. However the scale and impact of the plantation must not be exaggerated. Not only northerners were involved. King's servants from the west midlands and East Anglia were also deployed. Several of those promoted in the southern counties, even among the northerners, had existing connections either by marriage or inheritance with the counties in which they subsequently played a prominent role. Moreover the incomers never formed more than a minority in local office. The king, who after all had just crushed a rebellion and had the capacity to reward generously, was able to retain the service of most of the lesser peers across southern England (Lords Dinham, Ferrers of Chartley and Zouche, for instance, were enthusiastic supporters) as well as many of the resident gentry who had not been implicated. A glance at the composition of the commissions of the peace or of array in 1484 or 1485 shows that many local gentlemen, if only through fear or prudence, were willing to collaborate with the new regime. Indeed several rebels soon made their peace and were welcomed back. After 22 August 1485 a veil was discreetly drawn; it was in nobody's interest then to challenge the myth that they had all resisted the regime.

Those planted had a specific role to play. They replaced Edward IV's one-time esquires and knights of the body as the representatives of the king's household in the region. They had to supervise the government of the counties in which they settled, prevent future rebellion and defend the coasts against anticipated invasion. It is unlikely that Richard considered the 'plantation' as anything but a temporary measure until Henry Tudor had been destroyed and the 'old lords' had made their peace. Nevertheless, all reservations made, the measures taken to secure the south still continued to cause resentment. There was a steady trickle of further defections to Henry Tudor and a recurrence of plots, such as that associated with William Collingbourne in July 1484 whose doggerel:

> *the cat, the rat and Lovell our dog,*
> *rule all England under a hog*

caught the popular mood.[25] Indeed such was the scale of continuing disaffection in the south that in November 1484 more of the newly appointed sheriffs were drawn from the ranks of northern household men than in the immediate aftermath of the rebellion. There was no disguising the fact that in the last resort Richard had to depend on outsiders to retain control. Even though small in number, they were a constant reminder to the majority of local gentry that Richard was a king who had imposed his rule on them.

Elsewhere in England it was easier for Richard to establish his authority. On the whole the peerage supported him. He relied particularly on the Howards, father and son – John, duke of Norfolk and Thomas, earl of Surrey – especially in East Anglia: his chamberlain Francis, Viscount Lovell, a magnate of substance whose role extended, like Lord Hastings under Edward IV, beyond that of mere courtier; his nephew, John de la Pole, Earl of Lincoln, heir to the elderly earl of Suffolk; William Herbert, Earl of Huntingdon, his son-in-law (he married Richard's illegitimate daughter, Katherine), who was promoted to high office in south Wales after Buckingham's defection; and, in the north, Lord Stanley, Ralph, Earl of Westmorland and the earl of Northumberland. Stanley presented a dilemma. He had supported Richard in October 1483, yet was clearly not to be trusted. Moreover there was a history of conflict between him and the king, his family and some of the king's retainers, which resurfaced towards the end of the reign. But Richard appreciated that he could not afford to drive him into open opposition. The magnates, political realists, were unwilling to take unnecessary risks, especially after what they had witnessed in the summer of 1483.[26]

The majority of the bishops behaved similarly. Some senior ecclesiastics were enthusiastic: Dudley of Durham (who died in November 1483) and his successor, John Shirwood, Langton of St David's, Redman of St Asaph's, Russell of Lincoln, and Stillington of Bath and Wells. The two archbishops – Bourgchier of Canterbury and Rotherham of York – stood pointedly aloof, but in Rotherham's case leaving his senior diocesan staff to work for the king. Only Courtenay of Exeter, Morton of Ely and Woodville of Salisbury declared for Tudor. The episcopal bench, as the amicable relationship between Langton and Morton representing the rival claimants in Rome in 1485 suggests, appears not to have put political partisanship before duty to mother Church.[27]

Richard III's own household, on which he primarily depended, was largely, though by no means exclusively, northern in character. Neither William Catesby nor Sir James Tyrell were northerners. But Sir Richard Ratcliffe, Sir Robert Brackenbury, Sir Marmaduke Constable and many other intimates were. Once he became king, Richard was determined to retain, through his household servants, his personal interest in and control of the region. At first, like Edward IV in the Welsh marches, he used the household of the prince of Wales, based at Middleham and Sheriff Hutton, as the body through which to rule. But in March 1484 the prince died.

Since Richard himself spent May, June and most of the July following in Yorkshire and Durham, he did not need to make alternative arrangements at once. But when the king returned south he left a newly constituted council, composed of his principal northern retainers and the peers of the region, under the presidency of his nephew, the earl of Lincoln, to represent his authority. The first Council of the North was established for political ends. The revenues of the king's ducal estates were immediately assigned not only to support its running costs, but also to reward with substantial annuities his new councillors.[28]

The establishment of the council may not have been anticipated by the earls of Northumberland and Westmorland (Ralph, Lord Neville, succeeded his great uncle to the title in November 1484). Northumberland in particular had probably expected that the new king would surrender much of his personal interest in the region and allow him to step into his shoes. Westmorland too could have hoped for promotion: in June 1483 the king had promised that his support would be the making of him. While both earls were generously rewarded in terms of land and annuities, neither received any addition to their power. Northumberland was overlooked as president of the new council; and although he was given a grand new title as warden-general of the marches, in practice he continued as before as warden only of the east march. The king kept the office of warden of the west march in his own hands, making Lord Dacre his deputy. Neville, who might even have hoped for that office himself, also found that in the long vacancy following the death of Bishop Dudley the government of the bishopric of Durham fell to an episcopal council of the king's men. While Richard avoided creating new mighty subjects in the north, his policy ran the risk of alienating the very magnates who had supported him in 1483, in part at least, in the very hope of becoming more mighty.[29]

While Richard III, with all the patronage and authority of the Crown at his disposal, was able to govern his kingdom, he still faced widespread scepticism about the validity of his title. His need to counter this underlay the first act of his first and only parliament. Parliament had been summoned to meet in November, but it had been cancelled because of the rebellion. It did not meet at Westminster until 23 January. The assembly was, understandably, pliant and subservient. The evidence has not survived with which to determine whether the house of commons was packed with the king's supporters; the election of William Catesby, the king's confidential servant, as speaker in the first parliament in which he had sat is nevertheless strongly suggestive. According to the Crowland Chronicler, the acts ratifying Richard's title to the throne (Titulus Regius) and attainting over 100 traitors, were passed without opposition 'on account of the great fear affecting the most steadfast'. Before the assembly was dissolved the king was granted tonnage and poundage for life by the pliant assembly; the first to be so honoured.[30]

The Titulus Regius was passed, as it states, for 'the quieting of men's minds' and for removing 'the occasion of all doubts and seditious language'. Its form is unusual, in that it repeats the purported words of the petition presented to the king in June 1483, giving it retrospectively the authority of statute. Its significance lies not only in setting out the definitive version of Richard's claim to be the only man to have the right to the throne by inheritance (by virtue of his nephews' bastardy), but also in doing so in explicitly propagandist terms. It contrasts, in lurid detail, the moral and political corruption of the previous regime with his own matchless virtues.[31] The king's anxiety about his title is underlined by two unusual steps taken during the session and immediately after parliament was dissolved on 22 February. Richard called nearly all the lords spiritual and temporal and the leading members of his household together to swear to uphold his son's right should anything happen to him. And he summoned the leading members of the London companies together at Westminster to brief them on the subject. Richard still had difficulty in convincing his subjects of his right to the throne.[32]

Polydore Vergil had little doubt, a generation later, that Richard also began to put on 'the show and countenance of a good man whereby he might be accounted more righteous, more mild, better affected to the commonalty and more liberal especially to the poor'. One cannot be certain whether the rest of the legislation of parliament and other reforms arose out of a concern for the common weal, or from a need to win support. As duke of Gloucester, Richard had been concerned to administer impartial justice before 1483. He made public proclamation several times during his reign of his desire to see justice maintained: 'the king's highness is fully determined to see due administration of justice throughout his realm,' he declared in November 1483. He referred on more than one occasion to the profession of justice made by him at his coronation. He encouraged the clerk of his council, John Harrington, to discriminate positively in favour of petitions from the poor in an initiative which is seen as the first step towards the establishment of a court of poor requests. Several articles of the Council of the North show a similar concern to maintain law and order. As late as the summer of 1485 he convened a conference of senior judges to discuss certain difficult points of law raised by three recent cases.[33]

In the light of this well-attested interest, the legislation of his parliament dealing with the administration of the law, allowing bail to prisoners and regulating juries, and with some of the finer points of land law might be seen to reflect a true concern for justice. But there was nothing necessarily exceptional about the statutes of the 1484 parliament. One act, the abolition of benevolences, although remembered later as a good act made in his time, might have been offered as a concession in return for customs for life. And it is difficult to see what interest the king had in the acts tidying up commercial law. Moreover one should neither assume that the legislation was introduced by the Crown, nor view it in isolation. Successive parliaments under Edward IV, Richard III and Henry VII dealt with inadequacies of the law concerning conveyance and inheritance of land, the regulation of commerce and the administration of justice. They did so because the members of the house of commons who introduced most bills were drawn from the ranks of landowners, merchants and lawyers. A meeting of parliament, whoever the king, whatever the political circumstance, was always an opportunity for routine amendment of the law.[34]

In the administration of finance Richard had even less room to make an impact than in the administration of justice. A king was expected to live within his means and not to tax his subjects excessively. Thomas More later castigated Richard for his profligacy: 'free was he called of dispense and somewhat above his power liberal; with large gifts he get him unsteadfast friendship, for which he was fain to pill and spoil in other places and get him steadfast hatred.' The condemnation is unfair. Richard did not inherit a full treasury; surviving records reveal that the protectorate had faced financial difficulties. Richard, once king, incurred heavy expenditure suppressing rebellion in 1483, fighting the Scots in 1484 and preparing to face invasion in 1485. There was little wanton liberality. In so far as he rewarded his friends generously this was largely out of the revenues of his ducal or confiscated estates. He paid close attention to the smooth running of the chamber system of finance inherited from his brother. But this had only marginal effect on his overall solvency. By 1485 he needed to resort to loans. Although the king's servants might have exerted pressure on potential lenders, these were not forced loans and a date in 1487 was set for repayment. Nevertheless the very resort to loans effectively counteracted whatever political advantage had been gained from the abolition of benevolences. By the end of his reign, Richard was finding it difficult to present himself to his subjects as a king who did not need to appeal to his subjects for aid.[35]

Richard's conduct of foreign policy came to be dominated by the need to neutralise the threat from Henry Tudor. However, when Richard came to the throne an indiscriminate and unofficial naval war was raging in the Channel, initiated it seems by Edward IV in his anger over the treaty of Arras. England was also at war with Scotland. From the beginning of the protectorate until the summer of 1484, Richard continued to pursue this aggressive foreign policy, perhaps in the hope of rallying the kingdom behind him. He intensified the war at sea against France, and extended it against Brittany, as well as Scotland. On 18 February 1484 he declared that by advice of parliament he was determined 'to address us in person with host royal' towards Scotland by land and by sea. Captains were summoned to muster at Newcastle by the end of May, but the death of the prince of Wales delayed his arrival in York until 1 May.[36]

It is possible that this blow, both personal and dynastic, contributed to the decision not to press ahead with the invasion. Although he toured Durham and Yorkshire for three months, the muster at Newcastle was cancelled. Instead he adopted the more modest strategy of victualling Dunbar (handed over to an English garrison by the duke of Albany in the preceding year) and sponsoring a raid by Albany and the earl of Douglas into the west march. Dunbar was successfully replenished, an English fleet defeating the Scots at sea off Scarborough. But the raid into south-west Scotland ended in disaster at Lochmaben on 22 July. Lack of resources, and the belated realisation that with foreign backing Henry Tudor represented a serious threat, caused a change of direction. On 18 June the king agreed a truce with Brittany, offered aid against France, and began to negotiate the delivery of Tudor. By the end of July he had accepted James III of Scotland's repeated overtures for peace. At Nottingham on 14 September, Richard himself leading the English team, a three-year truce was concluded and a marriage agreed between the heir to the Scottish throne and Richard's niece, Anne de la Pole.[37]

The truce with Scotland freed Richard, not before time, to devote all his diplomatic attention to Henry Tudor. In his efforts to persuade the Bretons to hand him over, Richard was not helped by the volatility of Breton and French politics. Duke Francis was a weak ruler, unable to master the factions at his court, one pushing for closer co-operation with France, the other, under Pierre Landais, pressing for an English alliance to resist French ambitions. France too, under the regency of Anne of Beaujeu, was divided. The duke of Orleans sought to engage the support of Brittany, Burgundy and England against the regent. By the autumn Brittany had agreed to arrest Henry Tudor. But he was warned, and fled to France, where his cause was taken up by the government of Anne of Beaujeu, fearful of an English intervention in support of the duke of Orleans. Henry Tudor was a far greater danger to Richard III in France than he ever had been in Brittany. The support of France inspired a resurgence of defections and disturbances in England in the autumn of 1484, and also helped undermine the loyalty of the Calais garrison, part of which deserted to him with their prisoner, the earl of Oxford, in November. As early as December 1484, when Richard issued commissions of array, he anticipated an invasion.[38]

Bosworth Field

Richard III did as much as he could to counter Henry Tudor's appeal in England. Queen Elizabeth Woodville and her daughters were persuaded to leave sanctuary in the summer of 1484 and they were feted by the king. The precedence given to Elizabeth of York at Christmas, who pointedly wore the same clothes as the queen, shocked some at court, who perhaps misinterpreted a display designed to demonstrate backing for Richard, not Henry Tudor. Some success was achieved in winning back Woodville associates and Richard almost carried off the major coup of bringing the marquess of Dorset back to court.[39]

Another ploy was the flamboyantly staged removal of the body of Henry VI from Chertsey Abbey to St George's chapel, Windsor in August 1484. Henry Tudor claimed to represent the Lancastrian line and later expended considerable time and money in seeking his predecessor's canonisation. Already in 1484 the last Lancastrian enjoyed a flourishing cult. Edward IV had sought to suppress it. Richard pointedly reversed his policy by having Henry VI reburied alongside his brother. He also began to patronise Henry's foundation at King's College, Cambridge. By so publicly sponsoring the cult of the now venerable king, Richard hoped to undermine Tudor's appeal as the heir to Lancaster.[40]

In other ways Richard sought to distance himself from his brother and to draw upon the reputation of the saintly Henry VI. He attacked the corruption of the previous regime. In the Titulus Regius he had emphasised the depravity of a court given over to lechery. He made a scapegoat of Edward IV's mistress, Jane Shore, who was forced to do public penance as a whore. In March 1484, in a circular to the bishops, he launched a campaign of moral rearmament, charging them to punish after their demerits all those that promoted vice. In the same vein, the king's proclamations against his enemies in the service of Henry Tudor stressed that 'many be known openly as murderers, adulterers and extortioners contrary to the pleasure of God'. These may have been the king's personal views, but he may have calculated that an advantage lay in presenting himself as a king from the same pious mould as Henry VI. His own court was not exactly dull: too much singing and dancing, according to the Crowland Chronicler.[41]

The climax to Richard's campaign to neutralise Henry Tudor's appeal in England was his plan to marry his niece, Elizabeth, himself. In March 1485, after a short illness, Queen Anne died. In the weeks before her death, Richard's apparent lack of concern, suggested by his unwillingness to visit her in her quarters, gave rise to the rumour that he had poisoned her. These were only intensified by the speed with which he made known after her death his intention to marry his niece. He was met, however, with the determined opposition of his closest associates, especially Ratcliffe and Catesby, who well understood that such a marriage would not only undermine Henry Tudor, but would also weaken them by the restoration of rebels whose lands they, and many other loyal household men, held. Their threat to rebel if he persisted forced him to climb down. And so, shortly before Easter (3 April), he appeared at St John's, Clerkenwell, and there denied before the mayor and aldermen, many lords and his household staff that there was any truth in the 'rumours'. Furthermore on 11 April letters were sent to many boroughs, including the city of York, ordering the corporations to do the same because, and the text is worth quoting in full:

> divers seditious and evil persons in London and elsewhere enforce themselves daily to sow seeds of noise and slander against our person . . . to abuse the multitude of our subjects and alter their minds from us, some by setting up bills, some by spreading false rumours.[42]

Richard's credibility, already strained by the widespread belief that he had murdered his nephews, was dealt a further blow by the humiliation of having to deny rumours that he had poisoned his wife and planned to marry his niece. His attempt to present himself as a righteous and God-fearing king set upon restoring morality to public life was compromised. And the episode left him a virtual prisoner of the support from which he had now revealed he wished to distance himself.

By the spring of 1485 all the strands, domestic and foreign, came together. The threat from France became more immediate when the duke of Orleans submitted in March 1485. In the summer of 1485 substantial resources were put at Henry Tudor's disposal: a fleet was fitted out at Harfleur and part of the French army stationed in Normandy, due to be disbanded, assigned to him. An eleventh-hour agreement to send archers to Brittany in the hope of a diversion came to nought when Landais fell from power and the pro-French faction in the duchy seized power.

As Henry busied himself in Normandy with his French backers organising the invasion of England, Richard himself prepared for the imminent battle. The south coast was well defended, commissions of array set the county militias on their toes. On 11 May he left Westminster for the last time. He journeyed restlessly between Kenilworth and Coventry, before making Nottingham his headquarters in June. Spies kept him informed of his enemy's preparations. As a precaution against treachery, he took Lord Stanley's son and heir, Lord Strange, into his entourage as a hostage. It was a long and anxious wait. But eventually, on the evening of 7 August, Henry landed in Milford Haven.[43]

Henry set off on a measured march up the Welsh coast and then westwards through central Wales into Shropshire. Richard had word of the landing on 11 August when he summoned several of his knights and esquires to him. The duke of Norfolk knew by 14 August and was calling his men to join him at Bury St Edmunds two days later. Although the city of York seems not to have received a summons, and sent themselves to the king to know how many men he might want, the earl of Northumberland was raising troops in Beverley. In the confusion and haste, it seems, not all the king's messages were delivered and not all his reinforcements raised. The king himself moved up from Nottingham to Leicester on 16 August, or a day or two later. Henry, meanwhile, had gathered strength in Shropshire and was moving towards London via Stafford and Lichfield. At the same time Lord Stanley and his brother Sir William were converging with separate forces. A meeting almost certainly took place between Tudor and one of the brothers who pledged support. Cheshire might have already been raised by them in his cause. On 21 August Richard moved out from Leicester to intercept Henry. The two armies engaged in the plain known as Redemore, south of Market Bosworth, on 22 August.

The exact location and course of what proved to be one of the most significant battles fought on English soil are the subject of controversy. Bosworth, for all its fame, is singularly poorly documented. On the morning of 22 August such was the confusion in the king's camp that the customary mass was not celebrated: an omission that was later interpreted as an ill omen. Battle was joined between troops under the duke of Norfolk, probably on the right flank of the king's line, and the vanguard of Tudor's army, led by the earl of Oxford. When Norfolk's men began to fall back, the king, seeing Henry Tudor standing a little way off, as he supposed exposed and vulnerable, suddenly led his own men in a charge designed to end the battle quickly. But Richard had overlooked the presence of Sir William Stanley, of whose treachery he was already aware, also standing to one side with his retinue. Once Richard was engaged in hand-to-hand combat, and the impact of his charge took him close to Henry, Stanley moved in for the kill. As soon as the news of his death spread, the rest of his army broke and fled.

Richard III lost a battle he should have won. The sources, meagre as they are, agree that he outnumbered his enemies and suggest that he probably had the advantage of the land. Knowing how many peers fought for him is impossible. Some have suggested that only six took his side and that at least three quarters of their number stayed away. On the other hand, it has been argued that at least twenty fought for him, almost half the adult and active number in 1485. Some, such as Lovell, Huntingdon, Audley and Dinham, could not get there; others like Scrope of Bolton, Scrope of Masham, FitzHugh and Greystoke from the north may well have been present but in Northumberland's battallion. He may have been deserted by some, but in his anxiety to engage Henry before he attracted more recruits, Richard may have faced him before all his own supporters had joined him. In the light of his own experience in 1471, this would have made sound sense.[44]

But the battle was lost on the field, not beforehand. The critical elements were his own fatal charge and the failure of the earl of Northumberland on his left wing to engage. Had Northumberland's northern levies fought, Richard would surely have carried the day. Yet as the Crowland Chronicler reported, 'in the place where the earl of Northumberland stood with a fairly large and well-equipped force, there was no contest against the enemy and no blows were given or received in battle'. And, he added, many northerners in whom he put such special trust fled before coming to blows. However, several, among his household who participated in the fatal charge, including Sir Richard Ratcliffe and Sir Robert Brackenbury, were killed. Nevertheless the notion that Northumberland betrayed him has gained ground. Four years later, when the earl himself was murdered during a tax revolt, it was suspected that his retainers, remembering the battle, were reluctant to defend him. And it was said that the commons of the north 'bore a deadly malice against him for the disappointing of King Richard at Bosworth Field'. There is even a suspicion that the earl was in communication with Henry before the battle. Certainly, as we have seen, disappointment at not being given a free hand in the north could have given a motive for his standing aside and awaiting the result. Yet immediately afterwards both he and the earl of Westmorland were taken into custody by the new king and only released at the end of November under strict conditions of good behaviour. This, in contrast to the generosity shown to the Stanleys, was no reward for masterly inactivity. A plausible alternative explanation, given by Polydore Vergil, is that the king charged impulsively before Northumberland's men could be brought into action. His own tactical blunder, rather than betrayal by the northern earls, may have cost Richard the battle, his throne and his life.[45]

Richard III's reign ended in disaster on 22 August. He had failed to win the confidence of his subjects. The means by which he made himself king, the belief that he had murdered his nephews, his over-reliance on his northern followers, his inability to stem further desertions to Henry Tudor and failure to discredit him meant that in the end all hung on the balance of this one battle. Yet had Richard won at Bosworth, lords and county gentry, practised in the art of survival and accustomed to accepting God's will, would probably have accepted the judgement of a decisive battle in his favour. Thus had it been Henry Tudor's body, not Richard's, taken from the field, stripped naked and flung over a horse, he might well have succeeded in establishing his own branch of the Yorkist dynasty on the throne. As it was, Richard's corpse was buried with little ceremony at the Franciscan friary in Leicester. He was still only thirty-two; and he was the only usurper of four to fail in the fifteenth century.

Richard III destroyed the house of York. Were there more positive achievements? His parliament reaffirmed the principle that taxes could not be raised without parliamentary assent. He pioneered the court of poor requests, which under the Tudors was to become an important avenue of legal redress for the less advantaged. More controversially it has been claimed, on the basis of a misreading of Titulus Regius, that parliament authorised his accession to the throne rather than ratified a *fait accompli*.[46] Richard III had little time to contribute to other developments. He tightened up the supervision of financial management in the chamber, but for the most part he was content just to follow where his brother had led. His only significant initiative in the government of the realm was the establishment of a council in the north as an extension of the royal council to rule a distant part of the realm. His primary purpose was political, to retain his own personal control of the region from which he came, not administrative or constitutional. Indeed the council did not survive his downfall. It was later re-established by Henry VII, but the connection with the Tudor Council of the North was tenuous and coincidental. Richard III's lasting achievement was less formal. By the very fact of becoming king Richard added a substantial northern estate to the Crown lands, completing the assimilation of the Warwick inheritance.

It is anyone's guess as to what might have happened had Richard succeeded. That he was a man of ability and energy is rarely denied. He was and remains controversial. It seems that he divided contemporary opinion as much as he has divided historians. Then, as now, he inspired the devotion of some, the revulsion of others. His virtues were the conventional virtues of his age. In many ways, paradoxically, he appeared to be not unlike Henry V; a pattern of chivalry, a benefactor of the Church, and enforcer of the law.[47] Had he come, like him, to the throne by normal succession he might have proved as successful a king. Yet he did not. And it is the fact that he did not, that he deposed his nephew who was a child in his trust so as to take the throne for himself, that defines him as a man who did not live up to the high ideals of christianity and chivalry he claimed to espouse. The difference between Henry V and Richard III is the measure of the difference between the houses of Lancaster and York as ruling dynasties of England during the fifteenth century.

Notes and references

1 Chrimes, *English Constitutional Ideas*, 176 ('his gentylle wite and rype under-stondynge, ferre passynge the nature of his youthe'); Mancini, *Usurpation*, 93.

2 Mancini, *Usurpation*, 75; Pronay and Cox, *Crowland Continuations*, 153; Ives, 'Andrew Dymmock', 225.

3 Pronay and Cox, *Crowland Continuations*, 153.

4 Ibid.

5 Ibid., 155.

6 Mancini, *Usurpation*, 77.

7 Chrimes, *Constitutional Ideas*, 177–8.

8 Attreed, *York House Books*, 2, 714.

9 Helmholz, 'Sons of Edward IV', provides an authoritative discussion.

10 Horrox and Hammond, *Harleian MS 433*, iii, 29; *Rot Parl*, vi, 241.

11 Mancini, *Usurpation*, 91; Attreed, *York House Books*, ii, 714.

12 Hicks, *Richard III*, 103, 99–100, 107–8; Pollard, 'Dominic Mancini's Narrative', 158–9.

13 Hicks, *Richard III as Duke of Gloucester*, 26–30.

14 Carpenter, *Wars of the Roses*, 206–7 and Horrox, *Richard III*, 89 stress the tensions created by the shortness of the expected minority. Ross, *Edward IV*, 423–6 finds Edward IV at fault, as does Richmond, '1485 and All That', 172–208. Horrox, *Richard III*, 128–35, concludes that he was partially to blame, but Carpenter, *Wars of the Roses*, dismisses such suggestions out of hand, focusing instead on the 'ineptness' (sic) of Richard III himself.

15 As advanced by Wood, *Richard III* and 'Friday the Thirteenth', 155–68.

16 Mancini, *Usurpation*, 91.

17 Horrox, *Richard III*, 328 ('weapon of first resort').

18 For this and the following paragraphs see Pollard, *Richard III*, 115–39 and the references given on 241–2, 250–1; and, for the Lewknor King List, Morgan, 'Death of Edward V', 229–32.

19 Sutton and Hammond, *Coronation of Richard III*, 29–46, 270–4.

20 Horrox, *Richard III*, 138–48.

21 Rous, *Historia Regum Angliae*, 121–2; Attreed, *York House Books*, ii, 713; Raine, *Fabric Rolls of York Minster*, 210–12; Ross, *Richard III*, 148–52; Tudor-Craig,

'Richard III's Triumphant Entry', 130–1; Dobson, 'Richard III and the Church of York', 145–7; Attreed, 'The King's Interest', 30.

22   Pronay and Cox, *Crowland Continuations*, 163. The most recent account of the rebellion is Gill, *Buckingham: Rebellion*. See also Horrox, *Richard III*, 149–77; Arthurson and Kingwell, 'The Proclamation of Henry Tudor as King of England'; Chrimes, *Henry VII*, 20–8; and Griffiths and Thomas, *Making of the Tudor Dynasty*, 95–6.

23   For Buckingham see Horrox, *Richard III*, 162–3 and Rawcliffe, *The Staffords*, 30–5. For Stanley and Margaret Beaufort see Jones and Underwood, *The King's Mother*, 63–4, Jones, 'Richard III and Lady Margaret Beaufort', 30–3, 'Richard III and the Stanleys', in *Richard III and the North*, 31–2, and 'Sir William Stanley of Holt', 18–19.

24   Pronay and Cox, *Crowland Continuations*, 171; Horrox, *Richard III*, 179–205; Pollard, *North-Eastern England*, 346–53.

25   Thomas and Thornley, *Great Chronicle*, 235; Horrox, *Richard III*, 276–90.

26   Ross, *Richard III*, 153–69; Horrox, *Richard III*, 208–11 (Wales), 218–21 (East Anglia); Griffiths, *Sir Rhys ap Thomas*, 35–8; and for the Stanleys above n. 23. For the West Midlands, where it is has been suggested Richard had difficulty in asserting his authority see Carpenter, *Locality and Politics*, 547–59. For Ireland, upon which Richard's reign had little impact, see Quinn, 'Aristocratic Autonomy', 608–11.

27   Ross, *Richard III*, 132–4; Pollard, 'St Cuthbert and the Hog', 120; Davies, 'Bishop John Morton'.

28   Horrox and Hammond, *Harleian MS 433*, iii, 107; Pollard, *North-Eastern England*, 353–8.

29   Pollard, *North-Eastern England*, 358–61 and 'St Cuthbert and the Hog', 121–3; Horrox, *Richard III*, 214–18; Summerson, 'Carlisle', 101–4.

30   Pronay and Cox, *Crowland Continuations*, 171; Ross, *Richard III*, 184–90; Roskell, *Commons and their Speakers*, 293–7.

31   *Rot Parl*, vi, 240–1.

32   Pronay and Cox, *Crowland Continuations*, 171; Sutton, 'Richard III's Tytylle and Right', 2.

33   Vergil, *Three Books*, 192; Horrox and Hammond, *Harleian MS 433*, ii, 48–9, iii, 107; Sutton, 'Administration of Justice', 4–15.

34   Hanbury, H. G., 'Legislation of Richard III'. For similar legislation in the preceding and succeeding parliaments see Ross, *Edward IV*, 341–50, 359–61 and Chrimes, *Henry VII*, 177–84, 220–3.

35   More, *Richard III*, 9; Horrox, 'Financial Memoranda' and *Richard III*, 299–308; Ross, *Richard III*, 299–308; Wolffe, *The Royal Demesne*, 188 ff.

36 More, *Richard III*, 9; Halliwell, ed., *Letters*, i, 157; Grant, 'Foreign Affairs', 117–22 and 'Richard III and Scotland', 115–48; Davies, 'Richard III, Brittany and Henry Tudor', passim.

37 Grant, 'Richard III and Scotland', 130–45.

38 Griffiths and Thomas, *Making of the Tudor Dynasty*, chs 8 and 9; Antonovics, 'Henry VII', 169–74; Horrox, *Richard III*, 290–3; Grant, 'Foreign Affairs', 124–6.

39 Pronay and Cox, *Crowland Continuations*, 173; Horrox, *Richard III*, 293–4.

40 Lovatt, 'John Blacman Revisited', 177–8; Walker, 'Political Saints', 85–6, 95–6; Bernard, 'Vitality and Vulnerability', 208–9.

41 Horrox and Hammond, *Harleian MS 433*, iii, 139; Gairdner, *Paston Letters*, vi, 81–4; Pronay and Cox, *Crowland Continuations*, 171. For the moralistic tone of Richard's propaganda see Ross, 'Rumour, Propaganda and Public Opinion'.

42 Pronay and Cox, *Crowland Continuations*, 175: Halliwell, *Letters*, i, 159.

43 Antonovics, 'Henry VII', 175–8; Davies, 'Richard III, Brittany and Henry Tudor', 113–16; Ross, *Richard III*, 203–9; Grant, 'Foreign Affairs', 126–8.

44 For the campaign see Ross, *Richard III*, 210–26 and for the battle itself, Foss, *Field of Redemore*. For discussion of Richard's support among the peerage at large see Pugh, 'The magnates, knights and gentry'; Ross, *Richard III*, 235–7; and Richmond, '1485 and All That', 173–7 (and Appendix 2, following 208); and Pollard, *North-Eastern England*, 363–5.

45 Pronay and Cox, *Crowland Continuations*, 181; Thomas and Thornley, *Great Chronicle*, 242; Vergil, *Three Books*, 224. Northumberland's inactivity and the behaviour of the king's northern retainers is discussed by Hicks, 'Dynastic Change'; Horrox, *Richard III*, 319–20; Richmond, '1485 and All That', 177–80 (all of whom agree that the earl deserted his king) and Ross, *Richard III*, 221–3 (who argued that this is 'a view which commands little credence') and Pollard, *North-Eastern England*, 361–5 (who is equivocal).

46 See Dunham and Wood, 'The Right to Rule' and McKenna, 'Myth of Parliamentary Sovereignty'.

47 For the king in person see Ross, *Richard III*, 127–46; Pollard, *Richard III*, 182–210; Sutton, 'Curious Searcher', 58–90; Jones, 'Richard III as a Soldier', 93–112; and, controversially, Hughes, *Religious Life of Richard III*.

CHAPTER THIRTEEN

The reign of Henry VII, 1485–1509

Politics and rebellion, 1485–8

Henry Tudor was proclaimed king as soon as the victory was won. Having arranged for the deposed king's body to be buried at Leicester, the new King Henry VII set off on a triumphal progress to London, where he arrived on 3 September, a splendid welcome by the citizens being orchestrated for him. He went straight to St Paul's where he gave thanks and laid up his banners – St George for England, the dragon of Cadwallader for Wales and a Dun Cow for his earldom of Richmond. While preparations were begun for his coronation, fixed for 30 October and writs were despatched summoning his first parliament for 9 November, the king himself travelled down to Surrey for an emotional reunion with his mother at Woking.[1]

The reins of government were promptly taken up. Henry's immediate concern was to impose his authority on the north. There were rumours that the earls of Northumberland and Westmorland, who had withdrawn from the battlefield without becoming engaged, were planning to promote the infant Edward, Earl of Warwick, as a rival to the throne. Henry quickly took possession of the boy and lodged him safely in the Tower of London. The northern earls submitted to the king and they too were taken into custody. Lords Clifford and FitzHugh were commissioned to offer pardons, receive followers of the late king into Henry's grace and, reinforced by Lord Stanley, to raise troops both to crush dissent and to defend the border against the Scots. By the coronation, the king was assured that his 'politic and mighty purveyance' had secured the north.[2]

Elsewhere in the kingdom, the king relied on the handful of men whom he knew and could trust. The earl of Oxford soon held sway in East Anglia;

Jasper Tudor, Earl of Pembroke, created Duke of Bedford, was entrusted with Wales. In the southern counties, where Henry's accession was welcomed, a group of returning exiles emerged as the king's principal servants: Edward Courtenay, promoted to the earldom of Devon; Sir Giles Daubeney, Sir John Cheyne, Sir Robert Willoughby, Sir Richard Guildford and Sir John Risley. Several were promoted to the peerage, and most came to hold high office in the king's household. These men, with Stanley, promoted Earl of Derby, Reginald Bray, a servant of the king's mother who became chancellor of the duchy of Lancaster, Thomas Lovell the Chancellor of the Exchequer and treasurer of the chamber, and John, Lord Dinham, the new Treasurer, were the principal laymen sworn to the king's council. The interim Chancellor was Thomas Rotherham, succeeded on 7 October by John Alcock. The most important cleric in Henry's service was John Morton, who succeeded Alcock as Chancellor in March 1487, soon after he returned to England, and was promoted to Canterbury later in the same year following the death of the long-serving Thomas Bourgchier. Peter Courtenay, Bishop of Exeter, was Keeper of the Privy Seal for two years, succeeded in diocese and office by Richard Fox, the king's secretary from the beginning of the reign.[3]

Henry was crowned on 30 October; his first parliament met on 7 November. Its speaker was the king's man, Sir Thomas Lovell. Its primary business was to ratify the title. The justices of the exchequer having determined in advance that by the fact of being king his attainder had been reversed, a bill was enacted which simply asserted that Henry was king. He himself bluntly told the commons that he was king by right (unamplified), confirmed by the judgement of God on the field of battle. Unlike all previous usurpers, he made little pretence that he was king other than by force. Moreover, he took the unprecedented step of dating his reign from the day before Bosworth so that he could attaint both Richard III and those who had fought for him. Having also reversed the previous attainders, parliament followed the precedent of 1483 and voted him tunnage and poundage for life, granted him £14,000 p.a. for the support of his household, and passed an act of resumption.

It would appear that voices were raised against this peremptory attitude, for some in the house had the temerity to raise the question of his marriage to Elizabeth of York, 'in whose person, it seemed to all, there could be found whatever appeared to be missing in the king's title elsewhere'. Indeed it was believed by some that Henry had promised at Rennes Cathedral on Christmas Day 1483 not only to marry Elizabeth of York, but also to 'take with her, at the same time, possession of the whole kingdom'. This, plainly, he had not done. As Henry and his advisers understood, any attempt to attach his title to the throne to that of the house of York would create more problems than it would solve. The matter of Elizabeth's legitimacy had to be clarified. The Titulus Regius of Richard III, in which the children of Edward IV had been declared illegitimate, was nullified. There was then the tricky question of whether Elizabeth, the elder daughter of Edward IV, or Edward, Earl of Warwick, his nearest surviving male relative, was his true heir. And behind this lay the uncertainty about the fate of Edward IV's missing sons, whom everyone presumed to be dead, but the precise circumstances of which were not known. It is not surprising, therefore, that the marriage was delayed. Only when the legislation of the parliament was complete and Henry's title to the throne on his own terms clearly enacted, did he announce on 10 December that he would indeed marry Elizabeth of York on 18 January next. It was to be two years before she was to be crowned as queen consort.[4]

Henry VII made much in his early propaganda of the claim that he had united the warring roses and thus pacified a kingdom that had long been scarred by civil war. The theme was stressed in the elaborate pageants produced on his orders by the city of York on the occasion of his first, politically sensitive visit in April 1486; it was dutifully repeated by Pope Innocent VIII in his bull of dispensation for the marriage when it was issued; and it was absorbed by contemporary commentators. Behind the propaganda, subsequently enshrined as truth, lay the fact that Henry VII, as he was all too aware, was yet another usurper, dependent on a narrow clique, and as yet with only a tenuous hold on power.[5]

The first rebellion occurred, perhaps predictably, in the north, in the spring of 1486. Henry had already discovered that it was difficult to rule the province without the support of the earls of Northumberland and Westmorland. They were released in December 1485 and Northumberland was restored, under close supervision, to the wardenship of the east march. But, even as Henry set out on his first progress to the north, he heard that there was a rising in the vicinity of Middleham led by the chamberlain of Richard III's erstwhile household, Viscount Lovell. This melted away in the face of the king's prompt reaction, and the public rallying of the earl of Northumberland to his cause. Henry was able to secure the region before returning south, via Worcester where a parallel rising led by Sir Humphrey Stafford of Grafton had also fizzled out. The north of England did not in the event prove to be a major centre of resistance and revolt. This was partly because the leading nobility and gentry, who had prospered under Richard III, had even longer memories and had learnt to ride with changing fortunes and to make themselves amenable to whoever held power. And it was partly because, from the start, he encouraged this outlook by binding potential dissidents in Yorkshire to his cause by the systematic use of recognisances for good behaviour.[6]

A greater threat came not from Richard III's heartland, but from remaining members of the house of York, especially the de la Pole family, first of all Edward IV's nephew John, Earl of Lincoln; Edward, Earl of Warwick; and Edward IV's sister Margaret, Dowager Duchess of Burgundy. A sequence of conspiracies were hatched in England, drawing in both obscure and unlikely confederates. A group in Oxfordshire, focused on the circle of Viscount Lovell (who fled to the Netherlands in 1486), and the abbot of Abingdon revealed themselves in 1487; other conspirators, including an inveterate plotter John Taylor, had their roots in the service of George, Duke of Clarence, and promoted the cause of his captive son, Edward, Earl of Warwick. Yet others, such as the more eminent Sir Robert Chamberlain who was seized at Hartlepool as he sought to flee abroad in 1491, were from the de la Pole circle in East Anglia. But behind most of the plotting lay Margaret of Burgundy, who Henry believed, according to Polydore Vergil, pursued him 'with insatiable hatred and fiery wrath'.[7]

The conspiracies against Henry VII drew their sustenance from abroad rather than domestic discord. Henry himself became king through French intervention, designed deliberately to destabilise and isolate the kingdom while France pursued its attempts to absorb Brittany and dismember the Burgundian state. Henry, conscious of his debt to the government of Charles VIII, sealed a truce with France for a year on 12 October 1485, extended for a further three years in January 1486. Given this neutrality, the French were able to make inroads into Brittany in 1486, and, partly by fomenting rebellion in Flanders, were able to prevent Maximilian of Habsburg, the regent of the Burgundian lands on behalf of his infant son Philip, from coming to their aid. There was, therefore, an incentive for Maximilian to aid a rebellion in England designed to overthrow Henry VII and place a Yorkist on the throne.

Margaret of Burgundy co-ordinated the plot. A young man, given the name of Lambert Simnel, perhaps the son of an Oxford organ-maker, was found to impersonate Edward, Earl of Warwick. He was shipped to Ireland where the king's deputy, Thomas Fitzgerald, Earl of Kildare, who had taken advantage of the recent turmoil in English politics to reinforce his own independent power, gave his backing. In February 1487 the imposter was 'crowned' King Edward in Dublin. Two months later, the earl of Lincoln, who for a year had attended court and shown every sign of supporting the new regime, fled himself to join Lovell in Flanders. There the English lords were given the backing of 2,000 troops who had recently been discharged from Maximilian's service, under the command of Martin Schwarz. The invasion fleet set sail at the end of the month for Dublin.[8]

Henry VII was fully on his guard. Even before the flight of the earl of Lincoln, he had persuaded his mother-in-law, Elizabeth Woodville, to surrender her estates and withdraw to Bermondsey convent and had taken the precautionary measure of placing her son, the Marquess of Dorset, in the Tower. What grounds he had is unclear, but he had trusted neither of them since their double-dealings in 1484–5. After Lincoln's flight he and the court had set off on progress to East Anglia, ostensibly it was said to taste Norfolk beer, but in reality to snuff out any de la Pole-inspired rising. But shortly after Easter, probably after receiving intelligence of the rebel plans, he suddenly set off for Kenilworth and Coventry, calling upon his household men to join him. Events were following a pattern uncannily similar to 1485.

The earl of Lincoln's army landed in Furness on 4 June. He made his way over to Wensleydale, hoping to raise support from ex-Ricardians on the way. He had after all been president of Richard III's council in the north, upon which several of the leading notables of the district had served. But the response was disappointing. Sir John Conyers, who commanded Middleham, stood aloof, and most of his neighbours followed his example. Only the Lords Scrope of Masham and Bolton came out for him. Nothing daunted, the rebels pressed on past York, held firmly by the earl of Northumberland and Lord Clifford, through Doncaster to arrive on the banks of the Trent near Newark on 15 June. Henry himself acted as swiftly. He moved forward to Leicester, on to Nottingham by 13 June, and then down the south bank of the Trent. The armies came to blows at Stoke, near Newark, on 16 June. As before Henry placed his van under the command of the earl of Oxford; and the battle was decided before noon in favour of Henry Tudor, as at Bosworth, by the clash of the vanguards. The bloodshed, however, was greater. Lincoln and Schwartz were both killed; Simnel was found alive, spared and in time given employment in Henry's household. Stoke confirmed the outcome of Bosworth and ensured that Henry VII, unlike Richard III, would not be a transient monarch.

Following the battle Henry pushed north, travelling as far as Newcastle on Tyne. Many who were suspected of involvement in the rising, or even of insufficiently enthusiastic opposition to it, submitted to the king, sued for pardons and were bound on recognisance for good behaviour. Even the lords Scrope, who had not actually fought against the king, were allowed to make their peace, though at a cost of their personal liberty and bonds of massive proportions. Thus in the aftermath of Lincoln's rebellion the screw was tightened on northern loyalty and obedience.[9]

The king returned to Westminster in good time for the meeting of parliament summoned for 9 November. Its principal business was to attaint twenty-eight rebels. A grateful commons also voted the king two tenths and fifteenths to offset the costs incurred in the defence of the realm. But perhaps the most important event was the coronation of Queen Elizabeth on 25 November, almost two years after she had married the king, and a year after the birth of an heir to the throne, Arthur. Having suppressed the first major challenge to his throne, and having established beyond all doubt that he was the ruler of England, Henry could now accord his consort this honour without fear that it would be taken as a recognition of any right she might have had to the throne in her own name.[10]

In the aftermath of the rebellion the king had also to turn his attention to Ireland and relationships with the Netherlands. Henry browbeat Kildare into submission; in June 1488 the earl took an oath of allegiance, administered by the king's ambassador, and entered into recognisances for his future conduct. On this basis Henry confirmed him as his lieutenant, but to encourge his loyalty he also sent Sir Richard Edgecombe to Dublin with 500 men. Henry also judged that the time had come to open meaningful negotiations with Maximilian of Austria. In January 1488 the commercial treaties between the Netherlands and England were renewed, but developing relationships with Maximilian of Austria were disrupted by further rebellion in Flanders against the regent's rule and his imprisonment by the Brugeois from the end of January to May.[11]

International relations, 1488–93

The continuing success of French involvement in both the Netherlands and Brittany in 1488 led Henry to review his relationship with his erstwhile sponsors. In the summer he allowed Edward Woodville, Lord Scales, to undertake a private expedition to assist the Bretons which ended in disaster, and Woodville's death on the field of St Aubin du Cormier on 28 July. In the wake of this crushing defeat, Duke Francis submitted to the French. On 9 September he died and Charles VIII claimed the wardship of his infant daughter and heiress, Anne. In response to a Breton appeal for help, Henry declared at a meeting of a specially convened Great Council in November 1488 that he would revive the triple alliance to protect the duchy against France.

The estates of Brittany, anxious for support, entered into the treaty of Redon on 10 February 1489, whereby England agreed, in traditional form, to provide military assistance in the shape of 6,000 archers. Four days later Henry came to terms with Maximilian, in effect renewing Edward IV's treaty of 1478 against France. Of equal importance to him were the negotiations with Ferdinand of Aragon, which had begun in England in the summer of 1488 and came to completion in Spain in the Treaty of Campo del Medino in March 1489. This fixed the terms of a marriage between Prince Arthur, and Catherine of Aragon, agreed terms of trade between the two kingdoms, bound both sides not to assist each other's rebels, and set down an undertaking to support each other against France. While the treaty was never in the event fully ratified, it set the pattern of Anglo-Spanish alliance for fifteen years. The diplomatic round was completed by treaties with Portugal and Denmark. Scotland could be ignored, for the assassination of James III in 1488 had thrown that kingdom into turmoil.[12]

To endorse his diplomatic offensive and to raise taxation to pay for the promised aid to Brittany, Henry called his third parliament to meet, again at Westminster, on 13 January 1489. While much routine legislation was passed concerning economic, social and legal policy, including the first act against enclosures, the principal business was the passing of a finance bill, voting £100,000 in a combination of income and property tax. Parliament was prorogued on 23 February, and troops were despatched in April both to Brittany and to Calais to support Maximilian. In Brittany the English expeditionary force took the town of Concarneau, but achieved little else. In Flanders, the reinforced Calais garrison, under the command of Lord Daubeney, rescued the town of Dixmude for Maximilian, who was yet again facing rebellion stirred up by the French.[13] The fruits of this diplomatic and military effort were meagre. In July Maximilian came to terms with France by the treaty of Frankfurt, which confirmed the terms of the 1482 treaty of Arras and by which he formally renounced the contract of marriage to the Duchess Anne, which he had made in 1486. The war fizzled out when in October Anne of Brittany accepted peace with France.

In the meantime Henry had been faced by yet another rising in the north. The taxpayers of northern Yorkshire resented the imposition of yet another subsidy to pay for war in Brittany. This was a popular protest, not a political rebellion. Northumberland faced the protestors near Thirsk on 27 April where, in mysterious circumstances, he was attacked and murdered. It was rumoured that some of his entourage had colluded 'for the disappointing of King Richard'. A more general rising followed. The king, fearing perhaps Scottish and foreign involvement, acted promptly. Once more he called out his household men. He sent the earl of Surrey, recently released from the Tower, ahead to restore order. Henry arrived in York in time to impose exemplary justice on the ringleaders. The earl of Surrey, who had passed his test, took Northumberland's place.[14]

Henry VII's revival of traditional English foreign policy had not met much success. Yet he continued to offer support to an independent duchy of Brittany. Renewed negotiations with both the Duchess Anne and Maximilian of Austria, now fully recognised in the Netherlands as regent, led to the reconstruction of the triple alliance. The alliance was sealed by the election of Maximilian to the Order of the Garter and the marriage, by proxy, of Maximilian and Anne in the autumn of 1490. All was set for the renewal of war against France in 1491. Yet once again the alliance collapsed. While Maximilian was diverted by a war in Hungary, Charles VIII sent support to Philippe de Clèves who had occupied Sluys for several years in opposition to Maximilian. He also encouraged Scottish action against England, and stirred up dissidents in England, most prominently Sir Robert Chamberlain who attempted to defect in January 1491. Brittany itself fell with little resistance to a full-scale French onslaught. Henry could provide only token assistance, raiding the Norman coast and sending 2,000 men under Lord Willoughby. With her duchy overrun and her treasury empty, the duchess came to terms with Charles VIII on 15 November. On 6 December she married Charles and her duchy was absorbed into the kingdom of France.[15]

Even now Henry refused to accept defeat. To the fourth parliament of the reign, summoned to Westminster on 17 October 1491, he declared his intention to invade France to recover his right and was granted two tenths and fifteenths, with the promise of a third should he remain abroad for more than eight months. The usual preparations of raising men, gathering transport and collecting provisions was set in train. The army was ready to sail from Portsmoth by early summer. Lord Willoughby was sent to raid Normandy in strength in June, and an attack was mounted on Sluys in August. It was not until the first week of October that the army estimated as 25,000 strong crossed from Dover to Calais. On 18 October it moved out to besiege Boulogne, while Henry's ambassadors reopened negotiations with King Charles. The parties came to terms on 8 November. The treaty of Étaples provided for peace between the two kingdoms, encompassed the regulation of customs duties, and included an agreement not to support each other's enemies or to condone piracy. Additionally Charles undertook to repay in instalments all Henry's recent costs in support of Brittany and the arrears from the treaty of Picquigny of 1475; which came to approximately £5,000 *per annum*. The peace was proclaimed with rejoicing in London on 9 November and Henry returned to his capital in triumph on 22 November.

For Charles VIII the treaty of Étaples was one piece of a diplomatic jigsaw being completed in preparation for his planned invasion of Italy. A further piece was fitted when by the treaty of Senlis on 23 May 1493 he came to lasting terms with Maximilian by returning Artois and the Franche Compté, in exchange for the abandonment of Burgundian claims to the Somme towns and the duchy itself. Thus within two years the diplomatic map which had dominated Anglo-French relations for a century or more was redrawn. For Henry VII the immediate gains of Étaples were straightforward. He had come through a period of confused and expensive international wrangling with his coffers replenished. It is possible that he had never intended to fight against France in 1492; that he had deliberately sought to exploit Charles VII's known desire to restore peace with England at the best possible price. Yet it is hard to believe that he had been as clear-sighted, or events were so fully under control. For four years England had been pursuing its traditional aggressive foreign policy in support of an independent Brittany. Henry could not afford to neglect the traditional role of the king of England in pursuit of his right in France. But there was a third consideration. A new pretender to the throne of England had appeared in Ireland in the autumn of 1491 and had been invited to France early in 1492 where he was welcomed and recognised by Charles VIII as King Richard IV. While it is stretching plausibility to suppose that the invasion of France was mounted with the intention of neutralising Perkin Warbeck, there can be no doubt that the removal of French support for Perkin Warbeck was one welcome outcome of the final settlement.

Perkin Warbeck

The origins of the Warbeck conspiracy are obscure. It is now known that he was born in Tournai in the early 1470s, and, after several short-lived apprenticeships in different Flemish towns, went to Portugal in 1487. There he joined the service of the Portuguese merchant Pregent Meno, and it was with him that he sailed to Ireland in 1491. In Cork he was taken up by a group of Yorkist exiles, including John Taylor, who persuaded him to take on the role, initially of the earl of Warwick, but ultimately of Richard, Duke of York, the younger son of Edward IV. He mastered the role and was sponsored by the earl of Desmond. Charles VIII showed the first interest and arranged for the would-be Richard IV and his court in exile to be escorted to France. Following the treaty of Étaples, and fearing that he would be surrendered to Henry VII, Warbeck fled to Malines. The Duchess Margaret there upon recognised him as her nephew, the son of Edward IV, and adopted him as her protégé. Whether Margaret was deluded, or was perfectly aware of the imposture, for the next three years she played her part in promoting his cause with conviction. He was proclaimed the true king of England and almost immediately messengers were sent out to make contact with the one-time Yorkist household servants then in positions of authority and trust under Henry VII.

An invasion was planned for the summer of 1493. Henry VII, whose spies had penetrated the conspiracy, tightened coastal defences, attempted to close Ireland as a launching point, and himself toured the midlands in readiness. At the same time he sent an embassy to Flanders to seek to convince the young Duke Philip, now of age, that Warbeck was an imposter.

The ambassadors secured an agreement not to give official backing, but failed to curtail his step-mother, the dowager duchess. Unsatisfied with this, in the autumn Henry imposed a trade embargo.[16] However, Maximilian, having been elected emperor, took Warbeck with him to Austria in 1493. The imperial party did not return to Flanders until August 1494, in time for Warbeck to participate in the Recognitions of Duke Philip in Louvain and Antwerp. In the parade at Louvain the 'Duke of York' rode with an escort of twenty in the Yorkist livery. In the early months of 1495 a force of 1,500 men, under the command of Rodrigue de Lalang, an esquire of Duke Philip's household, was recruited and a flotilla of fifteen ships fitted out at Flushing, largely at the expense of the duchess.

All this was known to Henry. Indeed the ease with which conspirators could enter England to recruit dissidents to their cause, and with which information could be gathered in Flanders, made this a very open conspiracy. Henry was helped particularly by Sir Robert Clifford, who, having defected to Warbeck's cause, on discovering that he had been deceived by an imposter, turned double agent. Henry countered the public display of the mountebank duke of York in Flanders with his own lavish ceremonial installation of his three-year-old son, Henry, as the real duke. And early in 1495 he called in Clifford and rounded up the principal conspirators, chief among them being the steward and chamberlain of his very own household – John Radcliffe and Sir William Stanley. A series of show trials came to a climax with the execution of Stanley on 16 February. The involvement of such senior members of the household revealed how deeply Warbeck's agents had penetrated the regime. It has been doubted whether Stanley was guilty and whether Clifford's testimony was reliable. But it seems that many, whether or not they really believed that Warbeck was genuine, were so uncertain of the long-term future of the regime, even after ten years, that they were prepared to hedge their bets. All it would take, they knew, was one decisive victory.[17]

Henry VII was ready for that battle should it come. In case of Scottish involvement he commissioned the earl of Surrey to array the northern counties for the defence of the border. But he was more concerned about his vulnerability to attack from Ireland. Irish politics were volatile and difficult to control from a distance and with inadequate resources. In 1494 he secured the submission of Desmond and he believed, after an extended visit to England, the backing of Kildare who, under heavy bonds, he had confirmed as deputy lieutenant. Yet in the summer of 1495 Desmond rebelled again. Henry removed Kildare from office, made his son Henry, Duke of York, the nominal lieutenant and sent Lord Poynings with a small force as deputy. Poynings was instructed to arrest Kildare and to bring the Irish chieftains to heel by whatever means necessary. But repression was no more effective than conciliation. By the spring of 1495 the rebellion had spread and Desmond was in contact with the alternative duke of York.[18]

The small invasion fleet set out from Flushing at the end of June. It first attempted to land on the Norfolk coast, but was repulsed. Moving south around the Thames estuary, the invaders put ashore at Deal on 3 July. But the advance party of some 300 men was overwhelmed by local levies. The remnant made their way to Ireland, landing at Waterford on 23 July to assist Desmond in a siege of the town. But the combined Irish-Fleming forced failed to break down its defences before it was relieved by Poynings. Warbeck's diminished band withdrew into central Ireland, making their way eventually to the north from whence they sailed to Scotland, presenting themselves to James IV at Stirling castle on 20 November.[19]

The Anglo-Scottish truce had been maintained, not without threats of war, since 1485. The young king of Scotland, James IV, had inherited the throne in shameful circumstances as a youth when rebellious nobles had defeated and killed his father at the battle of Sauchiburn in 1488. Almost exactly the same age as his new guest, he was anxious to make a name for himself in the old quarrel with England. Thus he took the opportunity, like the Emperor Maximilian before him, to treat Warbeck as a royal prince and to advance his cause. The two became almost inseparable; in January Warbeck married Katherine, a daughter of the earl of Huntley. By Easter 1496 James's intention to invade England was well known.[20]

Henry strengthened the border defences, which had become significantly run down, and set about isolating Scotland diplomatically. Negotiations with Duke Philip of Burgundy, which had begun almost immediately after Warbeck's flotilla had left port, concluded with the the treaty known as the *Magnus Intercursus* in February 1496. The treaty brought to an end the trade war which had been damaging to both sides for three years and paved the way for a more permanent rapprochement and the return to normal relations between England and the Netherlands. Henry was in the fortunate position of being courted by all sides. Spain and Maximilian because they wanted him to join the Holy League against France; France because she wanted him to stay out. Charles VIII, in particular, was in no position to revive the Auld Alliance. The Spanish monarchs, through their ambassadors Puebla in England and Ayala in Scotland, were especially anxious to avert an Anglo-Scotish war. Their aim was to fulfil the terms of the treaty of Campo del Medina of 1489, finalise the marriage between Arthur Tudor and Catherine of Aragon and tie Henry VII down to an alliance against France. They certainly did not wish to see Henry deposed. Thus through the summer of 1496 they worked tirelessly to make peace through a projected marriage between James IV and Henry's baby daughter Margaret. But James was determined on war. He mobilised in July and August and crossed the Tweed on 20 September, Warbeck publicly calling upon the people of the north to rise in support of their true king. The raid lasted four days before the Scots retreated in the face of an English army under Lord Latimer marching up from Newcastle.[21]

Henry declared war and set about planning a full-scale invasion. A Great Council authorised an immediate forced loan; parliament, which met on 16 January, voted the generous equivalent of four tenths and fifteenths. In the meantime, the earl of Surrey kept the pressure on the Scots by a winter raid into Teviotdale and the garrisons of Berwick and Norham were further strengthened. Once again Lord Willoughby de Broke was given command of a powerful navy which gathered at Portsmouth. Lord Daubeney, the victor of Dixmude, was given command of the army, raised predominantly by yet again calling up the king's household men. It was to number some 10,000. De Broke set out from Portsmouth on 16 May; Daubeney's army was to muster at Newcastle on 25 May.[22]

But as the contingents made their way north, and before Daubeney himself had set out, the West Country revolted against paying such heavy taxes to wage a war at the other end of the kingdom. Beginning in Cornwall in mid-May, the rising spread to Somerset where disgruntled gentry led by Lord Audley gave their backing. When they entered Wells at the beginning of June, the rebels publicly declared for the duke of York in Scotland. From Wells they made straight for London, taking up positions on Blackheath. The king rapidly mobilised noble retinues and the levies of central England. On 17 June the royal army under the command of the earl of Oxford fell upon the rebels and routed them. Audley and Michael Joseph an Gof, the Cornish leader, were executed. The survivors fled back to the West Country pursued by the king, whose forces nevertheless did not cross beyond the Tamar into Cornwall.[23]

The rebellion put paid to the projected invasion of Scotland. Willoughby carried out his part of the campaign, but Daubeney was diverted to Blackheath and many of the contingents marching north stopped in their tracks. Taking advantage of the English confusion, James IV launched his own assault on Norham on 1 August. He broke camp on the approach of the earl of Surrey, who marched into Scotland to threaten Ayton castle. On 20 August, however, a temporary truce was agreed, to be formally signed at Ayton on 20 September for seven years. By then Warbeck had left Scotland with his wife and thirty companions. His handful of ships sailed first to Ireland where he endeavoured unsuccessfully to raise support. It was only after further adventures at sea that he finally waded ashore near Land's End on 7 September.[24]

Warbeck hastily rallied the defeated Cornish and counter-attacked. On 17 September they assaulted and nearly took the city of Exeter in a two-day battle. Repulsed, and weakened, they moved on to Taunton. Henry had already raised his household yet again and, led by Daubeney, the royal army moved into Somerset. Faced by this overwhelming power the rebel army took to its heels, leaving Warbeck to save himself. He managed to reach Beaulieu, but there he was recognised, detained and handed over to Henry's men. Brought back to Taunton to face the king, he confessed on 5 October that he was indeed an imposter. With calculated clemency, Henry intended to allow Perkin to become a servant of his court. He was kept under close surveillance, but on 9 June 1498 he escaped his minders and fled Westminster Palace. Soon retaken, he was now incarcerated in the Tower with the earl of Warwick.

A year later a desparate plot was hatched for both to escape. This may have been part of a wider conspiracy involving the earl of Suffolk who fled from England to the court of Duke Philip at the same time. Suffolk was persuaded to return to the fold. But by this time, Henry had in his hands the two men who had promoted, planned and controlled Warbeck's conspircay from the beginning – John Taylor and John Attwood. In an effort to rid the kingdom once and for all of future conspiracies around the two prisoners in the Tower, the decision was made to bring them to trial for treason and, inevitably, execution. Warbeck, Taylor and Attwood were tried before a household court at Whitehall on 16 November 1499. The bit players were arraigned and condemned before a court of oyer and terminer at the Guildhall two days later. On 19 November the pitiful earl of Warwick, who probably had little idea as to what was happening, was tried by his peers before the earl of Oxford. Warbeck was hanged on 23 November; Warwick executed on 28 November. Puebla reported to his Spanish master that not a drop of doubtful royal blood remained in England. He was wrong, but as the new century approached Henry could hope at last for a little peace.[25]

Hopes for peace at home were encouraged by international developments. The intense diplomatic activity between Spain and England, notwithstanding the war of 1496–7, led first to the confirmation of the treaty of Medina del Campo. The terms of the marriage treaty were renegotiated and formally confirmed in July 1497. Catherine was to come to England in 1501, when Arthur became fourteen, bringing a dowry of 200,000 crowns. In August the couple were formally betrothed. After ratification in Spain, and the securing of papal dispensations, the young couple were married by proxy in May 1499. The bride landed at Plymouth on 2 October. The marriage was celebrated on 14 November, but within six months, Prince Arthur, who was still only fifteen, died. So anxious were Ferdinand and Isabella to retain the English alliance that negotiations almost immediately began for a rematch between Catherine and the new heir to the throne, Prince Henry.

Despite controversy over whether the marriage between Arthur and Catherine had been consummated, the treaty between Spain and England was renewed and Catherine and Henry were formally betrothed in June 1503.[26]

The year 1503 also witnesed the culmination of negotiations for a lasting peace between England and Scotland. The proposal that James IV should marry Margaret Tudor was first mooted in 1495. It was revived in September 1499, and eventually taken up in 1501. Negotiations were completed in January 1502. The treaty of London established a general and far-reaching peace between the two kingdoms and set out the terms of the marriage between James and Margaret, which was not to be celebrated until after 3 September 1503, two months before Margaret's fourteenth birthday. The treaty was duly ratified and eighteen months later the young princess travelled to Scotland, escorted by the the earl and countess of Surrey. With France, the empire and Spain embroiled once more in Italy, Henry embarked on a policy of neutrality and non-intervention, bringing to his subjects a brief respite from the convulsions of the preceding two decades.[27]

Henry VII's kingship

In the jubilee year of 1500 Henry had cause to feel more reasonably secure. It had taken him longer than either Henry IV or even Edward IV to rid himself of his enemies. It has sometimes been argued that since both Lambert Simnel and Perkin Warbeck were imposters, their conspiracies were thereby less threatening. But this is to misunderstand the circumstances. Henry VII had a weak title and had been an adventurer who owed his throne to an international conspiracy. His political roots in England were not deep; most of his subjects, including several in very high places, studiously kept their options open. Just as his predecessor had been overthrown by the chance of battle, so could he be. The Perkin Warbeck conspiracy was sustained for so long not in spite of its inherent implausibility, but precisely because even an implausible pretender to the throne stood a chance of toppling Henry Tudor. Thus the first fifteen years of Henry VII's reign, far from rescuing England from an anarchy that had supposedly plagued her, threw her into greater turmoil. England was mobilised twice for full-scale foreign war, paid for by the heaviest taxation since the reign of Henry VI, which triggered two popular revolts. Had all the forces of opposition come together in 1497 it is likely that Henry would then have been toppled. Yet he survived. By 1500 he was in control of his kingdom.

Henry VII was the candidate of an unforeseen coalition of diehard Lancastrians and displaced Yorkists. Before 1483 he could hardly have entertained realistic hopes of acceeding to the throne. A penniless and insecure exile, he had shortly before the death of Edward IV been prepared to negotiate his restoration. His early life shaped his attitudes and policies as king in several ways. Having been a conspirator, caught up in a world of subterfuge, he had learnt to trust few, to be resilient and to expect the unexpected. Having been an exile almost all his adult life he had no first-hand experience of English politics. And being dispossessed he had no personal following in England. Unlike the previous three usurpers he did not come to the throne as the leader of his own established retinue. He knew only those who had shared his exile with him, before and after 1483. He was an outsider in a way that neither Henry IV, nor Edward IV, nor Richard III had ever been.

Henry's circumstances largely explain why from the beginning of his reign he relied so heavily on his fellow exiles. The focal point was his court, as magnificent as Edward IV's. He himself was a compulsive huntsman, as well as a keen tennis and card player. He did not joust, but great moments of state, such as the creation of his younger son as duke of York in 1494, or the marriage of Prince Arthur in 1503, were marked by extended and elaborate tournaments. He both knew the political value of display and personally enjoyed the pleasure it gave. Proximity to the king at court, and on his progresses, which until his later years he made annually, was, as with all kings, vital to political favour and advancement. Key figures at court were Lord Daubeney, Lord Willoughby and Sir Charles Somerset, captain of the guard from 1486 and Daubeney's successor as chamberlain twenty years later. But perhaps the most important figure was the king's mother. Indeed there was none closer to the king than Margaret Beaufort, not even the queen, whose death in 1503 was a personal blow. She had played a significant role in paving his way to the throne, and continued to be close throughout the reign. After her death the image of Margaret as the model pious widow was carefully cultivated, but during her life she was deeply involved in public affairs.[28]

Courtiers were rarely solely courtiers. They were also councillors, administrators, ambassadors and military commanders. At the heart of the administration of the kingdom lay the council. The king himself was re-nowned for his attention to business. He frequently presided and his hand is to be found not only in the accounts of the treasurer of his chamber, but also on council minutes. When on progress, he took a small council attend-ant with him to deal with immediate matters. But customarily the council was based in Westminster, frequently meeting in the Star Chamber, chaired by the Chancellor, Archbishop Morton, from 1486 until his death in 1501. Other key councillors, not so frequently at court, were Bishop Richard Fox, the Keeper of the Privy Seal, and Reginald Bray, the chancellor of the duchy of Lancaster. Henry's council was an omnicompetent organisation, both offering policy advice and overseeing royal administration. Its range of responsibilities was continuously extended and its organisation refined. In 1487, by the so-called Star Chamber Act, it was empowered to meet specifically to deal with major cases of disorder and corruption. By the last decade of the reign it had established a group of sub-committees, including the court of audit, the court of poor requests, the council learned in the law to deal with the enforcement of Crown prerogatives, and the council of general surveyors to oversee the management of the Crown's estates. In the last years of his reign Henry re-established councils in Wales and the north, which were yet further off-shoots of the council in Westminster. Not all these bodies survived the reign, but they pointed the way to the future development of an established conciliar bureaucracy.[29]

While the supervision of government lay in the hands of a council whose tentacles stretched everywhere, the rule and defence of the kingdom depended on the knights and esquires of the king's household. However, Henry's household was not in origin his own. He reconstituted the household of Edward IV. Although the effective deployment of the household was essential to the survival of his regime, the greater part of it was not bound to him by personal or dynastic loyalty. In particular Henry had no choice but to employ those who had served Richard III as well as Edward IV and who, he rightly suspected, would be equally prepared to serve another. This political reality hastened the trend already in evidence under Richard III whereby the royal household itself was becoming institutionalised, serving the office of the Crown as much as the person of the king. There was, therefore, a different, more distant relationship between Henry and his household, than that enjoyed by his deceased father-in-law.[30]

Henry VII's awareness of the implications of his ambivalent relationship with his household, and his suspicion of some of its members, is apparent from the start in the formation of a bodyguard, the Yeomen of the Guard, from the veterans of his personal entourage at Bosworth, and in the extraordinary act of 1489 to provide for summary justice on those of all ranks within his own household who committed treason. He was already fostering and promoting the grooms and valets of his chamber such as Sir William Tyler, Sir Richard Chomeley and Sir William Smith long before the treason of the chamberlain and steward of the household revealed how unreliable it was even at its head. Thereafter, as has been stressed, the king retreated into his privy chamber (both literally by living more privately in his palaces, and metaphorically in the enhancement of the political roles of his more intimate servants), but the change was no sudden response to treason in 1495.[31]

Yet even after 1495 Henry needed the 150 or so knights and esquires of his body to administer his estates, supervise the administration of local justice and raise troops for him in emergencies. He thus developed means of control, enforced with ever tighter discipline as the reign progressed, to ensure their loyalty and service. One means was through the laws governing retaining. Henry no more sought to abolish retaining than had Edward IV; rather he sought to secure sole control over the power to raise troops through insisting on exclusive service to the Crown alone, and by licensing the right to retain. Any deviation was ruthlessly punished. Secondly he demanded exclusive service from all office-holders, whose responsibilities and duties were clearly specified and the performance of which was secured by bonds and recognisances. The king's retainers and office-holders were bound especially to supply military service. Thus, in all the crises of the reign, in 1486, 1487, 1489, 1495, as well as the two great military expeditions of 1492 and 1497, Henry had no difficulty in calling out his feed men. All the king's servants, the great as well as the humble, felt the force of the king's determination to enforce their loyalty. Thus Oxford, so Bacon tells, was reprimanded for illegal retaining; Daubeney was fined for embezzling the wages of the garrison of Calais. Two of his greatest captains, the one dominant in East Anglia, the other in Somerset, were firmly reminded that they were subordinate to the king. Henry was determined not to repeat Edward IV's mistake of allowing his greater subjects to build up their own power at his expense.[32]

Henry's approach to the peerage at large, those who traditionally supplied the armies of medieval kings and ruled the regions, was wary. Some peers were undoubtedly mistrusted. Thomas Grey, Marquess of Dorset, the queen's half-brother lost most of the estates he had secured under Edward IV and was regularly placed under close watch during crises. The de la Poles similarly were reduced in status. When Edmund succeeded his father in 1493 he was required to pay a substantial fine to enter his estates, diminished already by the attainder of his elder brother the earl of Lincoln, and was then constrained to accept demotion to an earldom on account of this diminished patrimony. Others who had been associated with the previous regime had to work their ticket. The fourth earl of Northumberland never recovered the captaincy of Berwick and was required to attend regularly at court where the king could keep an eye on him. His son, the fifth earl, when he came of age was not allowed to step even into these shortened shoes. Thomas Howard, Earl of Surrey, was held in prison until 1489. He was released when the fourth earl of Northumberland was killed and given the task of representing the king in the north in the next decade so that he could prove his loyalty – which he did. Other peers had less to prove. Lord Stanley, created earl of Derby, as the king's step-father was allowed a relatively free hand in Lancashire, Cheshire and North Wales. And the earls of Oxford and Pembroke (created duke of Bedford), as fellow exiles, were unquestionably committed to the regime. Henry did not wage a campaign against the nobility, but he treated many peers with caution and did not hesitate to make highly public examples of those who offended.[33]

Henry VII thus walked a tightrope between trust and enforcement. The balance varied in different parts of the kingdom according to local circumstances, as did the degree of success. He was probably more successful in the north of England than he dared hope. With the promotion of Richard Fox to the bishopric of Durham in 1494 he was able to restore the traditional policy of using the palatinate as an arm of royal government, a policy taken a stage further between 1502 and 1507 when the see was left vacant and the king administered the palatinate himself. He was helped too by his succession to the estates held by Richard III, of which there was no question that he would return to their rightful owners; Lord Latimer in the case of those once held by the earl of Salisbury, and the countess of Warwick in respect of Barnard Castle. Moreover as earl of Richmond he could claim to be recovering his own comital lordship in north-west Yorkshire. The local elite were his mesne tenants as well as his subjects. The experience of the veteran Sir John Conyers, a Knight of the Garter, was characteristic. Removed from his offices of steward and constable of Middleham and Richmond in 1487, he was one of the first to experience the full burden of recognisances and bonds. His grandson and heir, however, was restored to the same offices in 1490. Henry could not rule north-west Yorkshire without the service of the local elite; and the local elite valued royal favour too much to be too sentimental about the dynasty.[34]

In the administration of the borders Henry had to balance the imperative of enforcing his own authority with the needs of defence. In the west march, he followed the precedent of retaining the wardenship in his own hands and adopted the policy of divide and rule. Lord Dacre, his deputy, was denied the captaincy of Carlisle, required to share power with others, and starved of resources. He did become captain of Carlisle in 1501 but he was never given room to establish an independent power base. The result was probably detrimental to law and order in the borders, but as long as there was no extended warfare with Scotland, the consequences were not too damaging. In the east march, after the death of the fourth earl of Northumberland, the king used the resources of his Yorkshire estates to provide for the keeping of Berwick and to recruit the Northumberland gentry into his service for its defence in an emergency, and drew upon Bishop Fox to strengthen his castle of Norham – a policy which paid off in 1497. Thus while the north clearly was a source of unease in the first four years of his reign, in time it was effectively brought under control.

Some parts of the kingdom were effectively controlled throughout. Wales, under Stanley influence in the north and the the duke of Bedford in the south, with the assistance of Rhys ap Thomas in the far west, was effectively pacified. East Anglia, although there were tensions beneath the surface reflected in the rebellions of Lord Fitzwalter and the de la Poles, was held steady by the earl of Oxford. Kent was secure in the hands of the restored rebels of 1483, Sir Richard Guildford, the controller of the household, and the so-called Haute circle of gentry who had risen to prominence in Woodville service. And the east midlands, broadly the area which Edward IV had mapped out as a patrimony for his younger son Richard of York, came to be ruled after 1495 through Margaret Beaufort's own council based at her palace of Collyweston near Stamford.[35]

Henry was less successful in other parts of the kingdom where he began his reign in a strong position. In the north and west midlands, where he succeeded to the estates of the earldom of Warwick, he failed to master conflicts of interest, which led to serious disorder, linked to treason in the mid-1490s. Part of this stemmed from the long-running Mountford family quarrel. Henry's triumph in 1485 witnessed the restoration of Sir Edmund Mountford and the deprivation of his nephew Sir Simon who had prospered under the Yorkists. Simon eventually threw in his lot with Warbeck. The disorders also resulted in part from Henry's failure to build up an effective royal presence, even on the basis of the Warwick estates. And Henry Willoughby, whom he did promote in the north midlands, proved to be be more interested in using royal favour to pursue his own ends than the king's. It has been suggested that Henry failed in this region either to assert his personal authority or to delegate effectively. It was not until the end of the decade that, by extensive use of bonds and recognisances, the new regime began to exercise effective control of the midlands.[36]

In the south-west Henry may well have been guilty of complacency. Somerset, Dorset and Wiltshire had supplied a disproportionate number of the exiles of 1483. His victory was perhaps more enthusiastically welcomed in these counties than elsewhere. The local regime was founded on a small group of his intimates, prominent among them being Willoughby de Broke, John Cheyney and Lord Daubeney. It was probably a surprise to the king that many of the Somerset gentry, feeling that they had been neglected by the new regime, declared with Lord Audley for the Cornish rebels in 1497. Their rebellion was an embarrassment for Daubeney in particular, for he enjoyed close ties of kith and kin with many of them. His reluctance to challenge them directly possibly enabled the rebellion to reach such alarming proportions. His standing with the king may have been irreparably damaged thereafter, and there is a suspicion that his later fine was more a punishment for his political wavering than his financial impropriety.[37]

Henry's competence as king has been questioned in view of his compromises and failures in the far north-west, the midlands and the south-west. His ploy of divide and rule was frequently disruptive. But he did not hesitate to enforce his will when he wished. When the fifth earl of Northumberland and Archbishop Savage of York came to blows in Yorkshire in 1504, he imposed heavy penalties through the Star Chamber. Moreover the crisis of 1495-7 inspired Henry and his advisers to tighten their grip everywhere. The campaign to exploit feudal prerogatives and dues launched in 1495 was in part a means of bringing all the king's tenants in chief to heel. The more general and systematic use of bonds and recognisances, imposed on office-holders (especially in the first instance on constables of castles), debtors, evaders of the royal prerogative and disrupters of the king's peace, was similarly a response to that crisis. Henry undoubtedly made mistakes, but he rarely ignored their lessons or repeated them.[38]

The use of bonds and recognisances to enforce obedience was primarily political in intent, but it also, like the drive to enforce feudal prerogatives, had a financial dimension. Those who offended twice forfeited their bonds, and although the king usually compounded for a fine paid in instalments, the revenue generated was considerable. A well-endowed and wealthy Crown was, Henry knew, the longer-term guarantee of royal political success. Regular royal revenues rose by some 80 per cent to something in the order of £110,000. Revenues from Crown lands rose from some £25,000 to £40,000; customs from £34,000 to £48,000, to which was added nearly £10,000 from feudal revenues and fines and a further £10,000 p.a. from the French pension. To some extent Henry was the beneficiary of favourable economic trends. Although he exploited royal estates, forfeitures and minorities to the full, he benefited also from a general rise in the level of rents. Similarly with customs revenue, the Crown gained significantly by the revival of international trade, especially from the middle of the 1490s, and this despite the trade embargo with the Netherlands which was in force from 1493 to 1496.[39]

Nevertheless Henry's financial success owed as much to his own policies as to favourable circumstance. He did not allow himself to become entangled in extended wars. It is not that he did not go to war; until 1497, as we have seen, the expenses incurred in the defence of the realm were substantial. Yet Henry was able to raise well over £300,000 in subsidies and loans, including significant clerical taxation and the 'loving contribution' of 1492, in which Morton's famous fork played its part (those who spent little must have had savings tucked away, those that spent lavishly were obviously rich). Henry covered his military costs almost entirely through extraordinary revenue and without burdening the Crown with long-term debts. In the last decade of his reign, he avoided foreign entanglement; but even then he made 'loans' totalling a further £300,000 or more to support the Habsburgs in the last four years of the reign without in any way undermining his financial position. Henry VII's expenditure was high, far higher than either of the Yorkists, yet he retained a healthy balance, sustained by his regular income.

The thoroughness with which Henry VII exploited his sources of regular income and the efficiency of his administration were crucial to his financial success. He made estate management more systematic; he tightened the oversight of customs collection, and by the new book of rates introduced in London in 1502–3 he closed loopholes through which exporters and importers had avoided excise. The focal point of financial administration was the chamber, the financial office of the household, which after a brief interlude at the beginning of the reign, he developed almost into a separate office of state. The Exchequer, which remained the auditing department, did little more than collect taxes. In the last years of the reign, the scope of the chamber became ever greater and more complex. The king's personal supervision declined and its treasurer, John Heron, established his office at Westminster, where the court of general surveyors took over the general administration and co-ordination of all royal finance.

During the later middle ages various devices had developed whereby the king's tenants in chief could escape many of the financial burdens of feudalism. Previous kings had sought to limit the damage, but in the 1490s Henry VII launched a full-scale counter-attack, tracking down and bringing to book by special commissions those who entered or alienated lands without licence, or who sought to conceal wardships. Furthermore he revived prerogative wardship, the claim that the king had the prior right of wardship over all his subjects. Offenders were bound over, made to enter recognisances to fulfil their obligations and fined if they offended again. Until his death in 1405 Reginald Bray, his chancellor of the duchy of Lancaster, was the king's principal agent in this, although he found many willing hands at county level. After Bray's death, Richard Empson intensified the royal assault, made more systematic through the council learned in the law. Before the end of the reign the first master of wards and a surveyor of the king's prerogative were appointed. Nothing and no one was to escape the net.

The administration of justice, like sound financial management, was a matter of central political importance. Declarations made much of the king's determination to enforce the law, but the record of his reign suggests that the general level of law and order did not significantly improve. The king only took a personal interest in the settling of quarrels between his greater subjects, knowing that if these disputes were allowed to fester the throne would be threatened. His strategy was two-pronged. One, until his health began to fail, was himself to supervise, and on occasion intervene in, the course of law. The other was to develop and extend the judicial role of the conciliar courts, especially the council attendant and Star Chamber, to compensate for the short-comings of the common law courts. Using procedures of subpoena, deposition and examination of witnesses, these equity courts exercised speedy justice and sought to resolve disputes and enforce settlement rather than find for one party against the other. The Star Chamber Act set up a tribunal to hear cases of riot, retaining, bribery and corrupt administration of the law. It is not clear whether it was very active, but before 1509 it was already settling disputes over property in which token or even collusive violence had been deployed so as to get a hearing. The conciliar courts in time superseded both special commissions and informal baronial arbitration as a means of maintaining order. They had the advantage of being permanent and having full legal force.[40]

Henry's aggressive financial policies and the prominent role of common lawyers on his council led him also to adopt a more assertive policy towards the Church. His relationships with the Papacy and senior churchmen were close and cordial. He instituted the office of cardinal protector at the court of Rome in the person of Cardinal Bainbridge, Archbishop of York. He allowed the bishopric of Worcester to be filled by a succession of Italian bishops. And in the delegation of legatine powers to Cardinal Morton he permitted greater Papal involvement in the affairs of the Church than had Henry V. Yet during his reign the privileges of the Church within England came under threat. The clergy did not escape Henry's financial exaction, not only paying heavy taxation, but also being subject to fines for restorations of temporalities, or being forced to purchase pardons under *praemunire* proceedings. For political ends, the rights of sanctuary and the benefits of clergy were curtailed. Furthermore the common lawyers began to challenge the legislative preserves of Church courts. In 1507 Attorney-General Hobart went as far as to start *praemunire* proceedings against the bishop of Norwich, which proved a step too far, for in the storm that followed he was forced to resign.[41]

The last years, 1500–9

The historian may well be able to conclude that by 1500 Henry VII was secure on his throne. But there is no indication that either Henry or his subjects thought so. The king became less trusting and the regime harsher, more arbitrary and more rapacious the longer he lived. Polydore Vergil later commented that he had heard the king say that he wished to keep all Englishmen obedient through fear. And Edmund Dudley after the king's death confessed that 'he was much set to have many persons in danger at his pleasure', keeping, as John Heron noted in his account book, a list of names at hand. The intensified repression of the last years can be explained, if not necessarily justified, by the circumstances. Three deaths in the royal family between 1500 and 1503 left the king more vulnerable. His youngest son Edmund died in June 1500, Prince Arthur in April 1502 and Queen Elizabeth, after childbirth, in February 1503. From 1502 the future of the dynasty depended on the life of his second son Henry, still only ten years old when he became heir to the throne. The rebellion and flight of Edmund de la Pole in July 1501, after the execution of the earl of Warwick, thus took on more sinister significance. The deaths of some of Henry's most trusted servants, such as Cardinal Morton and Reginald Bray, also disrupted the regime. And above all Henry's own failing health created an atmosphere of anxiety. He suffered severe illness in 1504, in 1507 and again in 1508 when his life was despaired. It is in this context that one should set the report of the spy John Flamanck of a conversation that took place at the dinner table of the lieutenant of Calais, probably at the end of 1504. The company, Lord Daubeny's officers, speculated on who might succeed the sick king, should he die. Some reckoned the duke of Buckingham; others tipped Suffolk; but none had their money on the twelve-year-old prince of Wales. All agreed that they would lie low and wait on events. The shadow of 1483 still hung over the political world.[42]

It is not surprising, therefore, that Henry's foreign policy in the last years of the reign, over which he kept an ever-watchful eye, should remain essentially defensive. His aim was to maintain the neutrality of neighbouring states. He was aided by the continuing embroilment of France and Spain in Italy and their desire not to have England against them. And, after the death of Queen Elizabeth, he had at hand his own putative second marriage as a diplomatic counter, considering at one time or another the alternatives of marriage to Joanna of Naples as part of a Spanish alliance, Margaret of Angoulême in a projected French alliance in 1505, and perhaps more seriously a match with Margaret of Savoy, the daughter of Emperor Maximilian. None, however, came to anything.[43]

After the death of Prince Arthur the king was quick to renew the treaty with Spain by agreeing to the marriage of Prince Henry to Catherine of Aragon in February 1503. Ratification was delayed by the need to secure a bull of dispensation, and never took place because relations between the two kingdoms cooled after the death of Isabella of Castile in November 1504. Thereafter England moved closer to a revived Burgundian alliance. Since the *Magnus Intercursus* of 1496 there had been a series of conferences between representatives of England and Flanders in efforts to resolve outstanding differences over trade relations, including a meeting between Henry and Duke Philip at Calais in 1500. The flight of Edmund de la Pole to the court of the Emperor Maximilian, Philip's father, made Henry even more anxious to maintain good relations with the Habsburgs.

Isabella of Castile's heirs were two daughters, the elder, Joanna, being married to Philip of Burgundy. He claimed the throne of Castile in her name, while Ferdinand of Aragon took power as regent. After Ferdinand made peace with France in 1505 Henry VII abandoned his own projected Spanish match and halted negotiations concerning the marriage of Katherine to Prince Henry. He became more positively committed to Duke Philip as a consequence of the fortuitous landing of Philip in England in January 1506. Philip, on his way to Spain to make good his claim, sought refuge from a winter gale. Henry VII entertained his unexpected guest royally for three months, honouring him with the Garter and styling him King of Castile. In the treaty of friendship drawn up between the two in March 1506, Henry pledged his support in the recovery of Castile and undertook to marry Margaret of Savoy (she refused). In return Maximilian agreed to surrender Suffolk (which he did). The outstanding differences over the terms of trade between England and Flanders were resolved largely in England's favour. With financial backing, the would-be King Philip sailed on to Spain. There, a few months later, he died. His widow Joanna was removed to a monastery under the colour of her supposed madness and Ferdinand secured lasting control of Castile as regent in her name. Henry VII was able, however, to hold on to most of the advantages of the treaty of London by arranging with the Emperor Maximilian for the marriage of his daughter Mary to Duke Philip's infant heir, the future Emperor Charles V.

In the last year of his reign he continued to intrigue in the complex web of European alliances, but at the very end seems to have been outmanoeuvred and surprised by the alliance of Ferdinand and Louis XII further to dismember Italy by the treaty of Cambrai. By fortune as much as diplomatic skill, he achieved his aim of protecting himself from further outside intervention in English affairs, while, by means of the renewal of the traditional alliance with the rulers of the Netherlands, he had secured the conditions for commercial prosperity.

Henry kept as tight a grip on domestic as on foreign affairs. Because of his failing health, more of the exercise of power was entrusted to others and to the new prerogative councils. The last seven years of the reign were characterised by a sustained harassment of his subjects to ensure their continuing obedience. The principal vehicle was the council learned in the law which sought out and exploited the Crown's feudal prerogatives; the main tool was the imposition of bonds by which subjects were forced into crippling obligations; and the chief agents were Sir Richard Empson and Edmund Dudley. After the king's death Dudley listed eighty-four unjust exactions which he claimed had been made on the king's command. The victims ranged from the very great to the comparatively humble; from the fifth earl of Northumberland, to 'one Windial a poor man in Devonshire [who] lay long in prison and paid £100 upon a very small matter'. Technically legal in that he was reviving, extending and exploiting feudal prerogatives, many exactions were nevertheless unjust, arbitrary and, most important of all, deeply resented. But they were effective. Not only did they generate a significant income of several thousand pounds a year to help swell the royal coffers, but they also achieved the objective of binding through fear the obedience of his subjects.[44]

In his last years, Henry VII isolated himself from all but a few of his more intimate associates and councillors. Prominent among those close to him was his mother, whose influence had been recognised by Ayala in 1498. Her role became more pronounced as the king's illnesses became more frequent and his death appeared imminent. She was close at hand in April 1507, again in February 1508. She was also close to her grandson, the young prince of Wales, whose growth into adulthood was marked by the establishment of summer tournaments in which he performed, the first when he was just sixteen in 1507. And she was there, when on 21 April 1509 her son died at Richmond; and she was a leading player in the intrigue to withhold news of the death for thirty-six hours until the young Henry VIII was securely installed on the throne. She herself died two months later, but not until she had witnessed his marriage and coronation. Her dynasty had finally been established.[45]

The reign in perspective

Nothing became Henry VII's life like the leaving of it. His timing was impeccable. He had lived long enough to ensure that he was succeeded by an adult son, whose accession was joyfully welcomed by his subjects. He died soon enough to forestall the possibility of political crisis should an ambitious prince of Wales become the focal point of hostile reaction to his unjust and arbitrary rule. In the event the blame for that was taken by Empson and Dudley who, found guilty of constructive treason, were both executed. Their master was rapidly enshrined in the reputation of the English Vespasian. Polydore Vergil, who had begun collecting information from about 1506, completed his first version of his history of the reign in 1513. Drawing his inspiration from Suetonius' *Lives of the Caesars*, he modelled his account on the story of Vespasian, the military adventurer who in AD 69, had been the third emperor to usurp power in a year and whom no one expected to survive longer than his predecessors, yet who nevertheless rescued his country from anarchy and founded a dynasty which was to last for over a hundred years. The only fault that this great statesman had was his avarice.[46]

Polydore's assessment of Henry VII, so aptly founded on classical model and prophetic of the dynasty's future, nicely served the needs of the moment in the early years of Henry VIII in reinforcing the grip of the dynasty, while excusing the excesses of the later years. Thomas More in the first book of *Utopia*, written in the same decade, was rather more critical of a supposedly imaginary regime which had been characterised by the exploitation of 'old and moth-eaten laws' and 'indisputable royal prerogative' for the monarch's extortionate personal gain. It is highly likely that had the Tudor dynasty failed early in the sixteenth century, Henry VII, like Richard II, and with some justification, would have been condemned as a tyrant by the successor regime.[47]

That his regime was also venal, driven by the greed of the king himself, is evident too. Offices, not just those directly in the king's gift or at the lowest level, were sold. Sir Robert Reade paid 5,000 marks to become Chief Justice of Common Pleas. Justice itself was willingly sold; for £100 a case against the earl of Northumberland was dropped from the Star Chamber. Financial inducement for favours was commonplace and accepted. But Henry VII seems to have made selling of royal favour systemic. The willingness to accept payment to stop a case in Star Chamber leads one to doubt Henry's commitment to the enforcement of the law, even through his new agencies. Not surprisngly the servants followed the master to line their own pockets. That 'villein and caitiff of low-born birth', Reginald Bray, and others at the heart of government, made fortunes from the profits of office.[48]

Henry VII's lordship was heavy and unjust in its later years, in which he was neither the first nor last offender. It might be argued that the means justified the dynastic ends. It has long been assumed that, whatever else one might conclude, contemporaries were correct to observe that Henry was an able and astute politician. Recently, however, it has been suggested, largely on the basis of more detailed study of the provinces, that he never really understood the kingdom and how to rule it, and survived more by luck and determination than by political skill. In particular it was his failure to grasp the essentially consensual nature of the English polity, the need to establish a partnership between Crown and local elites, that led to endless plotting, disaffection and rebellion. In other words, it is suggested, Henry's despotic and arbitrary kingship, patterned perhaps on the French as Ayala suggested, was not only unwelcome but also self-defeating, for he came to the throne under more favourable circumstances than any other usurper in the fifteenth century. His problems were almost entirely of his own making.[49]

This assessment can be doubted on two counts. One is that it is not at all certain that Henry failed to rule in partnership with local elites. Whether in East Anglia, or Wales, or Somerset, or even Yorkshire he ruled as had kings before him, and kings after him, with and through the agency of local peers and gentlemen who were themselves his officers and part of his wider household. In some parts, most obviously Lancashire and East Anglia, he gave considerable authority to his trusted nobles, the earls of Derby and Oxford, who deployed their local power to royal ends. But, should any fail to meet his requirements he was quick to step in. He did not set out to undermine the nobility; he merely insisted, unlike Edward IV, that as Edmund Dudley put it, nobles should not presume to take office under the crown of their own authority. That Henry made mistakes, that in some counties there were outbursts of disorder and violence as well as disaffection, is not of itself surprising. No fifteenth-century king, particularly a usurper, was ever able completely to impose his authority and the king's peace throughout his realm. Moreover, as we have seen, Henry's priority was personal security, not the administration of impartial justice. The latter was sometimes sacrificed to the former.

It is also contentious to assert that Henry, as the inheritor of Edward IV's legacy, came to the throne in more favourable circumstances than any other usurper. Elizabeth of York was the Yorkist heir; failing her, Edward, Earl of Warwick. Henry always presented himself as the Lancastrian claimant; his badge was the red rose. He was an outsider to the Yorkist establishment, significant elements of which regarded him only as the least bad option. The partnership between him and the Yorkists who had opposed Richard III was never more than a matter of political expediency. Therein lay the seriousness of the threats to his regime presented by dissidents in his own ranks and by successive Yorkist pretenders. Henry's position in England was weak.

Since survival was the determining factor of Henry VII's kingship, to which all other considerations were subordinated, there remains the question of the extent to which he actively promoted the refoundation of the monarchy. His regime, as we have seen, was intensely conciliar. It has been argued that his councillors instituted a programme of monarchical renewal based on the reforms advocated by Sir John Fortescue and which began to separate the governing function of monarchy from the person of the king in whose name they functioned. In that can be seen the germ of the modern state. Those responsible were the councillors whom Henry attracted in exile, one of whom, John Morton, had shared exile with Fortescue in the 1460s. The initiative need not have come from the king, but he had the ability to select effective ministers and the insight to recognise that such develoment was in his political interest.[50]

The style of government pursued by Henry VII's councillors survived him. As of course did his dynasty. It was with the accession of Henry VIII that the Yorkist claim to the throne was finally undermined, for Henry VIII was indubitably the heir to Edward IV as well as to Henry VII. It is no coincidence that the Tudor Rose was his badge rather than his father's. And Edward Hall was correct at the end of his reign to comment, in the *History of the Illustrious Houses of Lancaster and York*, that although all other conflicts and disputes still flourished, the dynastic division, which in his view had been the fundamental reason why society had been earlier torn apart, had been healed in the accession of his master. Thus a central thread of English political history, dynastic legitimacy, which was broken in 1399 with the deposition of Richard II, was mended by the accession of Henry VIII in 1509.

Notes and references

1   Guth, 'Richard III, Henry VII and the City', 194–9; Pollard, *North-Eastern England*, 383 and n. 66; Jones and Underwood, *King's Mother*, 66.

2   Pollard, *North-Eastern England*, 368–9.

3   Condon, 'Ruling Elites', 109–42; Gunn, 'Courtiers', 23–49. Individual careers of some of these men are discussed in Condon, 'Reynold Bray', 137–68; Gunn, 'Sir Thomas Lovell', 117–53; Guth, 'Sir Reynold Bray', 47–61; and Luckett, 'Giles, Lord Daubeney', 578–95.

4   *Rot Parl*, vi, 267–384; Chrimes, *Henry VII*, 58–67; Pronay and Cox, *Crowland Continuations*, 162–3, 195.

5   Anglo, *Spectacle, Pageantry and Early Tudor Policy*, 8–108.

6   Cunningham, 'Henry VII and North-East England', 51–60; Pollard, *North-East England*, 370–5; Williams, 'Rebellion of Humphrey Stafford', 181–9.

7   Luckett, 'Thames Valley Conspiracies', 164–72; Arthurson, *Perkin Warbeck*, 15–18; Vergil, *Historia*, 16–17.

8   For this and the following paragraphs see Bennett, *Lambert Simnel*, passim and Weightman, *Margaret of York*, 155–61; Quinn, 'Aristocratic Autonomy', 611–13.

9   Cunningham, 'Henry VII and North-East England', 62–6; Pollard, *North-Eastern England*, 375–7.

10 *Rot Parl*, vi, 385–402; Chrimes, *Henry VII*, 78, 154–5.

11 Quinn, 'Aristocratic Autonomy', 613–14; Weightman, *Margaret of York*, 164–5.

12 Chrimes, *Henry VII*, 280–1; McKie, *Earlier Tudors*, 86–97; Currin, 'Henry VII and the Treaty of Redon', 343–58, and 'Persuasion to Peace', 882–904.

13 Chrimes, *Henry VII*, 198–9; Schofield, 'Taxation and the Political Limits', 227–56.

14 Hicks, 'Yorkshire Rebellion of 1489'; Hoyle, 'Resistance and Manipulation'; Bennett, 'Henry VII and the Northern Rising'; Pollard, *North-Eastern England*, 379–82.

15 For this and the following paragraph see Arthurson, *Perkin Warbeck*, 16–24; Chrimes, *Henry VII*, 280–1; McKie, *Earlier Tudors*, 97–108; and Currin, 'Treaty of Redon' and 'Persuasion to Peace'.

16 Arthurson, *Perkin Warbeck*, 42–68; Weightman, *Margaret of York*, 169–74. What follows is indebted to Dr Arthurson's detailed analysis of international relations in the mid-1490s.

17 Arthurson, *Perkin Warbeck*, 69–99; Jones, 'Sir William Stanley', 19–22; Cunningham, 'Establishment of the Tudor Regime', 192–5 (Fitzwalter); Carpenter, *Wars of the Roses*, 243 (doubts about guilt).

18 Arthurson, *Perkin Warbeck*, 103–16; Quinn, 'Earls of Kildare, 1494–1520', 638–43.

19 Arthurson, *Perkin Warbeck*, 117–25; Macdougall, *James IV*, 118–20.

20 Arthurson, *Perkin Warbeck*, 125–49; Summerson, *Medieval Carlisle*, 472–3; Macdougall, *James IV*, 122–3.

21 Macdougall, *James IV*, 125–33, who considers that James was reluctant to support Warbeck, but took advantage of the circumstances to mount what was from the Scots point of view a successful raid into England.

22 Arthurson, 'King's Voyage', 1–22.

23 Arthurson, *Perkin Warbeck*, 153–6, and 'Rising of 1497', 1–18; Luckett, 'Giles, Lord Daubeney', 583–92.

24 Macdougall, *James IV*, 133–41; Arthurson, *Perkin Warbeck*, 169–79.

25 Arthurson, *Perkin Warbeck*, 169–218; Cunningham, 'Establishment of the Tudor Regime', 214–15; Bergenroth, *CSP Spanish, 1, Henry VII*, 213.

26 Chrimes, *Henry VII*, 284–6, McKie, *Earlier Tudors*, 148–50.

27 Chrimes, *Henry VII*, 284; McKie, *Earlier Tudors*, 157–64; Macdougall, *James IV*, 248–51. The treaty did not remove all tensions from Anglo-Scottish relations.

28 Chrimes, *Henry VII*, 305–7; Gunn, 'Courtiers', 24–5, 28–31; Jones and Underwood, *Margaret Beaufort*, 66–92. For Henry's character see Polydore Vergil's portrait, *Historia*, 145–7; for his building works see Thurley, *Royal Palaces*, 25–37.

29 Condon, 'Ruling Elites', passim; Gunn, *Early Tudor Government*, 49, 81–3, 87, 126.

30 Horrox, *Richard III*, 268–72; Luckett, 'Crown Office and Licensed Retinues', 224–6.

31   Gunn, 'Courtiers', 31–3; Pollard, *North-Eastern England*, 387–8; Starkey, 'Rise of the Privy Chamber', 75.

32   Cameron, 'Livery and Retaining', 17–35; Luckett, 'Crown Office and Licensed Retinues', 226–38; Gunn, 'Courtiers', 30 and 'Sir Thomas Lovell', 139–49; Condon, 'Ruling Elites', 121–2.

33   Pugh, 'Henry VII and the English Nobility', 50–89 provides the fullest account of Henry's relationship with the peerage. See also Gunn, 'Courtiers', 28–30 and *Early Tudor Government*, 54–6. For the view that Henry worked against the peerage see Carpenter, *Wars of the Roses*, 223–8, 234–6, 240–1.

34   For this and the following paragraph see Cunningham, 'Henry VII and the North-East', passim; Ellis, 'Border Baron', 253–63; Pollard, *North-Eastern England*, 367–92; Summerson, *Carlisle*, 466–75 and 'Carlisle and the English West March', 105–13.

35   Griffiths, *Rhys ap Thomas* (Wales); Cunningham, 'Establishment of Tudor Regime', 184–225 (East Anglia), 235–93 (Kent); Jones and Underwood, *Margaret Beaufort*, 83–90.

36   Carpenter, *Locality and Politics*, 560–96 and *Wars of the Roses*, 243–5.

37   Arthurson, *Perkin Warbeck*, 163–5; Luckett, 'Giles, Lord Daubeney', 583–6 and 'Patronage, Violence and Revolt', 145–60.

38   Hoyle, 'The Affray at Fulford', 239–56; Gunn, *Early Tudor Government*, 124–6; Lander, 'Bonds, Coercion and Fear', 267–300. But see Cunningham, 'Henry VII and the North-East', 46–9 for evidence that bonds were used extensively from the beginning of the reign.

39   For this and the following paragraph see Gunn, *Early Tudor Government*, 114–18, 122–3, 125–7, 133, 137, 139–40, 144–9 and Chrimes, *Henry VII*, 119–34. For landed income see also Wolffe, *Crown Lands*, 66–75 and *Royal Demesne*, 195–225.

40   Gunn, *Early Tudor Government*, 81–3, 84, 99, 102–8; Chrimes, *Henry VII*, 147–93; Hoyle, 'Affray at Fulford', 254.

41   Harper-Bill, *Pre-Reformation Church*, 16–18.

42   Vergil, *Historia*, 177; Harrison, 'Petition', 86; Cunningham, 'Establishment of Tudor Regime', 217–29; Gairdner, *Letters and Papers*, i, 231–40.

43   For this and the following paragraphs see Chrimes, *Henry VII*, 284–97 and McKie, *Earlier Tudors*, 171–88.

44   Harrison, 'Petition', 82–99; Gunn, *Early Tudor Government*, 126.

45   Bergenroth, *CSP Spanish*, i, 178–9; Chrimes, *Henry VII*, 300–1; Gunn, 'The Accession of Henry VIII', 278–88; Jones and Underwood, *Margaret Beaufort*, 91–2, 255–6.

46   Vergil, *Historia*, and Suetonius, *Twelve Caesars*, 273–86.

47   More, *Utopia*, 43–6.

48   Condon, 'Reynold Bray', Gunn, 'Courtiers', 43–6, *Early Modern Government*, 126 and 'Sir Thomas Lovell', 136–9, 149–50. Later research has tended to bear out Cooper's view that Henry's reputation for rapacity was deserved. See Cooper, 'Henry VII's Last Years Reconsidered', 103–29.

49   Carpenter, *Wars of the Roses*, ch. 11, esp. 240 and 248 and 'Henry VII and the English Polity', passim.

50   Watts, 'New Ffundacione', 31–53 and Grummitt, 'Henry VII', 242–3 who stresses the novelty of the king merging public and private finances. See also the comment by Carpenter, *Wars of the Roses*, 246–8.

CHAPTER FOURTEEN

The end of the middle ages

Henry VIII's England

The unchallenged succession of Henry VIII, who combined in his person the claims of both the houses of Lancaster and York, represented a final resolution of dynastic conflict. Henry himself was not entirely confident of the fact. The destruction of Edward Stafford, Duke of Buckingham, in 1520 owed something to his being a descendant of Edward III; the shameful trial and execution in 1541 of Clarence's elderly daughter Margaret, Countess of Salisbury, had everything to do with the king's residual dynastic paranoia. So effectively did Henry pursue every remaining descendant of the old English royal family that, as Sir Thomas Craig put it towards the end of the reign of Elizabeth I, making use (as he said) of a scripture phrase, 'there was not one left to piss against the wall'.[1] The dynastic issue was indeed resolved once and for all. But what did it signify?

So successful was Tudor propaganda that by the end of the sixteenth century the perception that the dynasty had rescued the kingdom from anarchy became a deeply embedded historical 'truth' which survived until the twentieth century. Indeed on to this were grafted further notions of the development of a Tudor despotism, and of a new monarchy drawing upon and appealing to a new middle class. As the old feudal aristocracy destroyed itself in an orgy of bloodletting, a new progressive social force, promoted by the far-sighted Tudors, entered into its inheritance. The modern era had begun with the advent of the Tudors.[2]

Little of this tradition has survived the test of twentieth-century scholarship. A change of dynasty is no longer seen as carrying the same political, let alone social significance. A new era began with a new ruling family only in the realm of propaganda. It was long-term success and survival that gave the change of dynasty in 1485 its greater significance. In this way history was truly written by the victors. The idea of Tudor despotism, as a necessary period of firm rule to restore order, before the forces of progressive parliamentary democracy could take root, has also received short shrift. The notion of the rise of the middle class has been dismissed too. The nobility dominated both society and politics in sixteenth-century England every bit as much they had the fifteeenth and were to in the eighteenth. Only the notion of the new monarchy remains in dispute, representing the new style of royal government, the antecedents of which are nevertheless traced back to the reign of Edward IV. The middle ages did not end with the accession of Henry VII. Yet England in 1603, when his granddaughter died, was markedly different. A new era had by then begun, and medieval England may be said to have passed away. When did this happen? And by what criteria are we to judge its passing?[3]

The succession of the handsome, athletic, but untried Henry VIII in the spring of 1509 was welcomed as a new beginning. 'Oh my Erasmus,' wrote Lord Mountjoy to the renowned Dutch scholar, 'if you could see how all the world here is rejoicing in the possession of so great a prince.'[4] Such a panegyric was in line with the hopes of many after the tribulations of Henry VII's reign. But Henry VIII did not immediately turn England's face to a new world. For one, such optimism which greets a new regime is invariably dashed, and Henrician England was no exception. For another, in so far as Henry VIII did make a fresh start, it was by turning back, not moving forward; by seeking to revitalise the old 'medieval' traditions. Thus, having symbolically disposed of Empson and Dudley, the new regime became at once more open and aristocratic, welcoming the 'old nobility' to council and office. The young king, who had already shown his precocious skills as prince of Wales, threw himself into a round of tournaments and jousts. And Henry's councillors and diplomats were instructed to begin the preparations for a more aggressive foreign policy and a serious intervention in the affairs of Europe. Having honoured his father's agreement and married Catherine of Aragon as one of his first acts, he renewed the alliance with Spain. In 1511 England joined the Holy League against France; war followed in 1512. An expedition was sent to northern Castile for a would-be allied invasion of Gascony, but this came to nothing as King Ferdinand put his own priority of seizing Navarre first. At the same time, encouraged by the French, the Scots renewed border raiding. In 1513 Henry mounted a massive expedition to Calais and in alliance with the Emperor Maximilian defeated a French force at the battle of the Spurs, destroyed Therouanne and took possession of Tournai in Artois. In his absence James IV, keeping to his alliance with France, invaded northern England, but was routed and killed on Flodden Field. The following year, however, peace was made with

France, England retaining Tournai, sealed by the marriage of Henry's sister Mary to the elderly, and childless, Louis XII.[5]

The war of 1512–14 has been interpreted as Henry VIII's ambition to renew the Hundred Years' War. Certainly in his publicity campaign for the taxpayer he made much of his intention to recover his rights and of the earlier exploits of Henry V; an English translation of Livio's *Life* was published in 1513 on the eve of the king's departure; and the victorious cavalry skirmish during the siege of Therouanne was likened to another Agincourt. But perhaps, while the twenty-two-year-old monarch no doubt fancied the idea of himself as another Henry V, the reality, not only in terms of Henry VIII's martial abilities, was somewhat different. This was no turning back to 1415. Henry himself, probably as clearly as his councillors, knew that the circumstances and relative power of the combatants were quite different. In fact it was but a continuance of the more limited military ambitions of both Henry VII in 1492 and Edward IV in 1475. On all three occasions the English expeditions landed at Calais, and made but cautious entry into French territory with their rears protected by 'Burgundian' alliances; Henry VIII was even more cautious in 1513 by invading a French enclave within the 'Burgundian' county of Artois. In 1415, and again in 1417, Henry V had made the far bolder and ambitious descents directly on French soil. And like his grandfather and father, Henry VIII was quick to make an accommodating peace with France, part of the terms of which were the renewal of the pension first granted at Picquigny. The war aims were conventional, in line with the foreign policies of Edward IV and Henry VII; they were not an attempt to revive the war aims of Henry V.

Henry was to go to war against France twice more, in 1522–4 and the 1540s. What hindered him playing a major role in European rivalries was the ever-expanding cost of war as armies grew larger and firearms more central. The war of 1522–4 was effectively brought to an end by a tax boycott – the refusal to pay a benevolence, called an Amicable Grant to avoid the technicality of breaking the law. The war of 1543–6, which achieved an enlargement of the Calais pale by the capture of Boulogne in 1544, was funded largely from the proceeds of the monasteries. The loss of Calais in 1558, as well as the insurmountable cost, finally put an end to English ambitions in France.

Henry VIII, after his initial flirtation with an aristocratic revival, quickly returned to the style of government, albeit more formally constituted, developed by his father. The key men here were Sir Thomas Lovell, Treasurer of the Household, and Richard Fox, who remained Keeper of the Privy Seal until 1514. It was Fox who brought on Thomas Wolsey, the king's almoner responsible for the logistics of the 1513 expedition, who dominated the king's government for the next fifteen years. There could not be a more symbolically medieval figure than the great cardinal who co-ordinated the twists and turns of the king's foreign policy (including the Universal Peace of 1518 and the renewal of war against France but four years later) and oversaw the administration of government in England. Under Wolsey conciliar government in the king's name for the common good of the whole realm was pushed to a new level of intensity, especially through the court of Star Chamber. Under a king who was less inclined to pay attention to the detail of administration than Henry VII, the separation of king's government from the king's person was taken a stage further, almost tangibly in the existence of two circles of power around both the king and his great minister.[6]

It was also in the early years of Henry VIII that the institutionalisation of the old medieval royal household was completed. Under Henry, through the use of the ubiquitous livery chain of the Lancastrian collar of SS and the pendant Tudor Rose, exclusive retaining with the Crown was fully enforced. All were either directly or indirectly the king's retainers. Thus, in effect, the 'evils' of bastard feudalism were circumvented by the king becoming the exclusive bastard feudal lord. This did not mean that affinity, clientage and patronage came to end, or that conflict between king and greater subjects disappeared. They took other forms in other associations. At court a new inner household, the grooms and yeomen of the chamber, took full shape as the immediate political entourage of the king. Politics appear more intensely court-centred under Henry VIII than they had been before, both because of the weakening of old household ties of court and country, and because of the personality of the king himself. The peripheries of the kingdom, where the regime was unwilling to entrust power to great lords, but was unable to supply an effective alternative basis of government, remained unsettled. Border wars exacerbated a problem left unresolved by Henry VII.[7]

If one moves away from court into the country, Henry VIII's accession, no more than the accession of his father, made little difference to lives as they were led. The English economy, too, showed a remarkable continuity with the past throughout the first decades of the sixteenth century. All recent assessments agree that the total population of the kingdom remained little changed. In the early 1520s, when muster rolls and subsidy returns allow some degree of confident assessment of numbers, there were still probably fewer inhabitants in England than there had been in 1377. Growth was perhaps slowly happening, but it was not until after mid-century that it began to occur at a significantly discernible rate. London continued to expand at the expense of other cities, most notably York and Coventry. This was in part because the great Company of Merchant Adventurers, through its monopoly of the London–Antwerp axis, tightened its grip on cloth exports, the leading edge of the economy. But export-led growth was modest, amounting, it has recently been calculated, to little more than 0.1 per cent *per annum*. While cloth exports tripled between 1470 and 1540, they did so in three main surges in the 1470s, 1510s and 1530s. Over a seventy-year period this stimulated only a modest overall growth for the whole economy, unevenly distributed. International trade still flowed along traditional channels. Despite the early voyages of the Cabots, England took little or no interest in the New World. Its impact remained distant, indirect and seemingly irrelevant until the end of the century.[8]

Early Tudor commentators and legislators became vexed with certain economic problems, especially enclosures and vagrancy. 'Your sheep', Thomas More joked in his *Utopia* in 1517, 'do eat up men.' His comment reflected the reports of contemporary commissions of enquiry which found that much land had been converted from arable to pastoral. It is true that the number of sheep had grown, and was growing, in response to the lively demand for cloth and high wool prices, especially in the second decade of the century. And it is true that some landlords, looking for quick profit, had depopulated villages and enclosed the fields for pasture. Yet most conversion took place because arable land had been abandoned; cultivation contracted as a result of population decline. Sheep-rearing offered an alternative economic use. Indeed, the commissions of enquiry of 1517–18 revealed that landlords were as wont to remove villages and enclose fields to create deer parks as sheep runs. The concern over enclosures was provoked by the shortage of readily available manpower in the arable villages of England to be recruited into Henry VIII's armies. But the manpower was lacking not because of the greed of enclosers, but because of the absence of people.[9]

Vagrancy too was perceived as a problem for similar political reasons. There had always been a residuum of landless poor, often migrant labour seeking work from place to place. They were a headache for successive governments, especially in times of economic recession, because they were not settled and potentially disruptive. Thus there was a stream of legislation seeking to penalise vagrants and bring the undeserving poor firmly under control. But vagrants and the indigent apart, the disposable incomes and standards of living of most people in work in the early decades of Henry VIII continued to remain relatively high. Revenues contributed by parishioners, and entrusted to churchwardens for local expenditure, reached a peak in the 1520s. The chief beneficiaries of the late-medieval economic order were the new middling sorts – yeomen, husbandmen, independent artisans and small traders. Yet the social order remained firmly hierarchical and the dominance of the landed nobility unshaken.[10]

It was not until the fifth decade of the century that inflation and population growth, possibly interconnected, started to erode the accepted certainties of economic life. And even then their full impact was not to become apparent until the last decades of the century. While the transition from the medieval to the modern economy, from feudalism to capitalism in Marxist terms, was a long-drawn-out process, with its origins long before 1500 and its completion not until after 1800, the moment when the economy became modern in the sense of being driven by capitalism came long after the death of Henry VIII.

The Renaissance

So what was new? Wherein lay the sense of a new era? Some subjects of Henry VIII were proclaiming the end of the middle ages on his succession. We can return to Lord Mountjoy. In May 1509 he reported to Erasmus a conversation he had had with the new king. 'The other day he wished he were more learned. I said that is not what we expect of Your Grace, but that you will foster and encourage learned men. Yea, surely said he.'[11] By 'learned men', Mountjoy, Erasmus and the king understood men educated in the new learning, humanism. They were convinced that a new age was dawning at last in England, though one doubts that they really attributed it to Henry VIII. Indeed the very concept of the end of the middle ages and the beginning of the modern age was a humanist invention. It is commonplace to state that the men and women of the middle ages did not know that they were medieval. But it was so. The concept of the middle ages was the construct of renaissance scholars, the students of the new curriculum of the humanities, who proclaimed the dawn of a new age, the modern age, recovering the learning, literature and visual arts of the ancients, especially the Romans. The new age was the renaissance of the old. The regrettable millennium that fell between the two was, expressed neutrally, the middle ages; disparagingly, the dark ages.

The movement, for movement it was in both the sense of a process in motion and a programme of action, was gathering rapid momentum in England at the beginning of the sixteenth century. While the Renaissance effected a transformation in the style and, to a degree, content of the visual arts, it also transformed the educational practices of western Europe. The humanists, the educators, gave priority to the learning of a purified classical Latin and Greek (and the study of the great works of poetry, history and philosophy in those languages) over the use of Latin for studying theology, canon and civil laws which lay traditionally at the heart of the curriculum of the medieval universities. They also opened up university education for the laity and for lay purposes. The universities existed originally as centres of advanced vocational education for the clergy; now, the humanists claimed, the study of the humanities (or classics as we would say in the twentieth century) was equally applicable to the education of lay administrators, diplomats and governors.

Over a two-hundred-year period the humanists successfully persuaded European societies to adopt their educational programme. By the end of the sixteenth century the English elites, lay as well as clerical, were educated in the new manner. The process of adoption was slow and piecemeal. It began first at the level of cultural exchange. Medieval men of letters had never rejected the literature of the ancients, especially of the Romans. But they had been selective in the use of authors, had been careless over the transcription of the language, and had adapted and improved the content and meaning to suit their developing interests and preoccupations. Educated fifteenth-century Englishmen knew many of the classical works, but in a bowdlerised form. Thus visitors to and from Italy, of whom of course there was a steady stream of both English and Italian nationality on Papal business, began to make available new and improved texts of these standard authors. Humphrey, Duke of Gloucester, was one who became an enthusiastic collector, and even commissioned a humanist, Tito Livius, to write a panegyric of his revered brother Henry V. Others became aware of the new texts indirectly through contacts with France and the Low Countries. There were circles of learned laity, a group of Sir John Fastolff's servants in mid-fifteenth-century East Anglia and a group associated in Kent with the Hautes at the end of the century, for example, who promoted a new 'learned chivalry', in which the appropriate classical texts were given a new prominence. The new learning enjoyed something of a vogue in certain lay quarters, but it was still but a gloss on traditional forms.

Humanism was not interiorised, as it were, until English clergymen began to promote it. In the later fifteenth century, more enterprising young men such as Grocyn and Linacre went to Italy to learn the new languages and returned to teach them. New schools were founded to provide a linguistic grounding, notably Magdalen College school in Oxford in 1480 and John Colet's foundation of St Paul's early in the following century. The establishment of a new school itself was not a sign of the spread of humanist influences. Responding to the shortage of clergy in the first half of the century there was a gathering momentum of school foundations and educational provision of a more informal kind in the fifteenth century. It was the curriculum that mattered; and until the sixteenth century most schools taught 'vulgar' Latin. The foundation of a handful of schools specifically dedicated to the provision of the humanist curriculum was followed by the foundation of university colleges to do the same.[12]

The spread of humanism was boosted by printing. Printed books were in circulation in England by the late 1460s; the enterprising William Caxton set up his press in 1476; Oxford University its in 1478. The output of the early presses in England was highly traditional. Caxton, as a commercial publisher, produced translations of the most popular poetic, didactic and devotional works for the upper end of the lay market; the university press, the bible, commentaries and theological works in Latin for the academic market. It was not until the early sixteenth century that the presses in England began to publish in great numbers texts of a humanist nature and grammars for classical Latin. Printing made available a large number of correct editions of classical works and grammars at prices which scholars could afford. But so it did all books. Thus while contributing significantly to the spread of humanism, it contributed more to the general spread of literacy.[13]

There is no doubt that humanism was established in England by the first decade of Henry VIII's reign. But it still touched only a small minority, even though that minority was well-placed and influential, especially at court. Wolsey early in his career had been master of Magdalen College school, and he promoted humanists in his service as Chancellor; his successor was Sir Thomas More, the most accomplished scholar of his day. But humanism in the early sixteenth century remained deeply controversial. The universities, especially Oxford, were slow to be converted. Corpus Christi, Oxford, founded by Richard Fox in 1517, was the first college dedicated to humane studies.[14] The laity too were resistant. A curmudgeonly nobleman retorted to Richard Pace, the king's secretary and humanist, at dinner one day, 'I swear by God's body that I'd rather be hanged, than allow my son to study letters. For it becomes the sons of gentlemen to blow the horn nicely, to hunt skilfully, and elegantly carry and train a hawk.'[15] This in the 1520s was probably the general view of the landed elite. It was not until after mid-century that opinion had been swung over and that the study of letters came to be seen as one of the attributes of gentility itself.

The output of Henrician humanists was distinctive, if not voluminous. Sir Thomas More, in the second decade of the century, before a political career overtook him, wrote two works, one incomplete, which were self-consciously 'modern' versions of classical writings. His *Utopia* was an 'up-date' of Plato's *Republic* – a dialogue about the best state of the commonwealth, possibly drawing on reports he had heard of the newly revealed Mayan civilisation in the Yucatan. His *Richard III* was a Roman history, modelled on Tacitus and Suetonius. Both these works were written in Latin, although More himself also wrote an English version of his *Richard III*. More prosaic humanists such as Thomas Starkey and William Morrison less ambiguously devoted their pens in English to the service of the state in the 1530s. And at court Sir Thomas Wyatt and the young earl of Surrey developed a poetic style in English inspired by Petrarchian sonnets. These works, all by laymen, pointed to the future, but there were no immediate successors in mid-century.[16]

The same is true of the visual arts. Hans Holbein the younger came to England briefly in the late 1520s and then in 1532 to reside permanently until his death in 1543. On his first visit he constructed his More family portrait. His work represented the finest in northern European draftsmanship, creating representations of persons and objects in three-dimensional space, which amazed (and still amaze) for their likeness to life. But Holbein, a German, founded no school, and established no tradition of renaissance painting in England. Art and architecture remained largely untouched by Italian influences. In so far as there were English painters at work they were book illuminators, glass painters and heraldic decorators whose skills lay in miniature illustration. The late perpendicular style dominated architecture, both ecclesiastical and lay, throughout Henry VIII's reign. Italian craftsmen were invited to carry out special commissions in the new style such as the tombs of Henry VII and Elizabeth of York and the screen in King's College Chapel, Cambridge. Their influence is observable on the embellishment of buildings, such as the medallions on the central tower of Hampton Court, which were otherwise domesticated castles. Illustrations of the two lost early Tudor palaces of Richmond and Nonsuch suggest Netherlandish and northern French influences rather than Italian. The Renaissance touched England but superficially in the first half of the sixteenth century.[17]

Nevertheless there did emerge a distinctive humanist culture in Henrician England. What made it distinctive was its Christianity. Christian humanism was a particularly northern European phenomenon. It sought to marry the tradition of contemplative piety with the new linguistic and textual skills to generate a more profound and direct spirituality. Learning was to be dedicated to the service of God. Erasmus visited England twice, on the second occasion for an extended stay between 1509 and 1514. The primary concern of Erasmus, Colet and other clerics was to use their humanist skills on Christian texts, to produce, as had largely been done with the classics, authoritative editions. Erasmus own life's work was the provision of a modern Greek edition of the bible. Applying the same rigorous standards to the New Testament, they believed that, by recovering the original meaning, they could renew Christian belief in the same way as secular culture had been renewed. On one level the programme of the Christian humanists was an extension of the whole cult of late-medieval spirituality.

Even the criticism of the Church can, and perhaps should, be seen as the continuation of the time-honoured tradition of clergy berating clergy for failing to live up to the highest ideals of their order. Erasmus was particularly scathing about the scale of commercialisation, especially of indulgences and pilgrimage, as well as the superstitious nature of popular religious practice. Colet gained notoriety in 1511 for a sermon at St Paul's castigating the worldliness of the clergy. But neither man challenged doctrine or questioned the special status of the clergy. Indeed their intention was to renovate the Church and to restore a Christian priesthood living up to its high ideals. In this, as other clergy such as John Fisher and the devout layman Thomas More agreed, their desire was to renew and strengthen the Church as an institution clearly separate, distant and aloof from the laity.[18]

However, in two respects, Christian humanism was subversive. By castigating the commercialisation, superstition and occasional fraud practised in the name of religion, critics drew attention to much that was vulnerable in late-medieval spiritual practice. Moreover by editing the texts and recovering the original word of Gospel and Epistles, humanists were opening the way for others to make their own novel interpretations of doctrine. And this is what Martin Luther, himself a humanist scholar, did in the ninety-five theses which he pinned for public debate to the door of Wittenburg Cathedral in 1517. Humanist biblical scholarship, if inadvertently, encouraged the revival of heresy.

The Reformation

Undoubtedly the Reformation brought the most decisive, and divisive, break with the past to Henrician England. The Church in England on the eve of the Reformation can hardly be described as corrupt. Colet's criticisms notwithstanding, the shortcomings, institutional and individual, were longstanding and generally tolerated. There was no widespread anticlericalism. Criticism and complaint against individual clergy were usually directed at the incompetence or worse of the individual incumbent, not the order as a whole. Tithe disputes tended to occur not over the fundamental principle, but as a result of contested rights or personal animosities in particular places. They were more marked in urban parishes where the traditional means for supporting the parish priest were inappropriate. Richard Hunne, who was scandalously murdered in clerical custody in 1514, initially challenged the Church as a Lollard, and not simply because he resented paying a mortuary.[19]

Pockets of lay heresy still existed in early-sixteenth-century England. There was a marked increase in the numbers being detected and brought to trial after 1510, and it is clear from its later reuse that there was a considerable body of Wycliffite writing still in circulation. It is not clear, however, whether this was because Lollardy was reviving, or because certain bishops, notably Longland of Lincoln, were more zealous than their immediate predecessors in hunting it out. Lollardy was, by its very nature, an underground movement, sustained by small cells of the laity drawn from the middling ranks of society, especially in the urban centres of southern England. In themselves,

Lollards represented little threat to Church or state. Nevertheless, on the immediate eve of the Reformation they were once more perceived as a problem.[20]

The majority of parishioners remained orthodox Christians. There is no evidence to suggest that they were dissatisfied with the doctrine of the Church. Indeed continuing acceptance of the traditional order is indicated by the flourishing memberships of guilds and fraternities, the pulling power of popular shrines, and the contribution of sometimes considerable sums to new bell towers and rood screens. The massive yet complex demonstration of northern England against the Henrician regime in 1536 found its unity and strength in the notion of a pilgrimage in defence of the Church, using the eucharistic symbol of the five wounds of Christ as its badge. There are few signs that the English people as a whole wanted the Protestant Reformation.[21]

If the ground was being prepared for the cataclysm to follow, it is perhaps to be found in two, linked, late-medieval developments. One was the gradual extension of lay control, at all levels of society, over the Church. The Crown had since 1485 chipped away at certain privileges enjoyed by the clergy. Sanctuary rights had been redefined and restricted; benefit of clergy had been clarified and made more limited. And the common law courts had encroached steadily on the preserves of the ecclesiastical courts. Yet, on the other hand, both Henry VII and Henry VIII were more amenable to the Papacy, Henry VIII even allowing Wolsey to become legate *a latere* (that is to say the Pope's deputy in England with all his powers), which Henry V had point blank refused Henry Beaufort. Relationships between the Crown and the papacy had hardly been more cordial on the eve of the break with Rome; but paradoxically Wolsey's legation had shown that the government of the Church in England did not necessarily depend on the direct authority of the Pope.[22]

Further down the social scale the nobility and gentry revealed in the statutes of their foundations a desire to control the minutiae of religious conduct. This was happening too at parochial level where churchwardens on behalf of their parishioners were in many places providing and paying for supplementary clerical services, and even in some cases taking over the supervision of the incumbent. Such extension of lay participation in ecclesiastical administration ran parallel with an increase in liturgical and devotional knowledge. The later medieval Church, as we have seen, encouraged, by means of catechism, preaching and the publication of spiritual handbooks in English, lay knowledge of and ability to participate in divine service. It was but a short step to the provision of the bible itself in English. Colet and his fellow Christian humanists sought to reverse this trend. But they could make little impact. The clergy had lost, and were continuing to lose, some of their mystique as the sole possessors of arcane and powerful knowledge for the salvation of souls.[23]

Thus, it is arguable that the laity as a whole was becoming better informed and more involved in the affairs of the Church on the eve of the Reformation; that the gap between priest and parishioner was narrowing. But this is not to say that the Reformation was the consequence of such trends. It was caused by two specific developments: the spread of protestantism and the King's divorce. Lutheran doctrines reached England by 1520. They found their first foothold in Cambridge in a circle of young dons around Richard Barnes, the prior of the Dominican Priory. Because protestantism appealed to some sections of the clergy and the educated elite, it was perceived immediately as a serious threat. Indeed Henry VIII himself, no mean theologian, had already written and published his condemnation of Luther's doctrine, for which he had earned the title of Defender of the Faith from a grateful Pope. Repression, leading to persecution, began at once. Several protestants fled to the Netherlands from which John Tyndale published his first, Lutheran, English bible. By the end of the decade protestant heresy had become a serious problem; so serious that during his brief term of office as Chancellor (1529–32) Sir Thomas More became obsessed with its eradication. Assisted by the force of printing, which enabled the multiple reproduction of vernacular bibles, commentaries, digests and broadsheets on a scale and with a speed never available to the earlier heretical movement, the spread of heresy would have continued in England without other developments. But the King's Great Matter ensured that within thirty years England would become a protestant kingdom.[24]

Henry VIII became convinced in the late 1520s that his marriage with Catherine of Aragon was uncanonical. She had been married briefly to his brother Arthur, and it is indeed possible that the marriage had been consummated. What spurred his troubled conscience was the failure of the marriage to produce a male heir to the throne, and, as Catherine approached the menopause, his besottal with Anne Boleyn who refused to surrender herself to him as his mistress. Considering the good relationships enjoyed between Crown and Papacy, and especially the high standing of Cardinal Wolsey, an annulment ought to have been a matter of course. Previous European royal marriages had been annulled for less cause. But unfortunately Pope Clement VII was very much under the influence of the Emperor Charles V, Catherine's nephew, who viewed the proposed divorce as a family insult. For five years Henry endeavoured, first by diplomacy, then by threats, to secure his divorce. But nothing would move the Pope. In 1533, following the death of Archbishop Warham of Canterbury, Henry took the law into his own hands. Anne Boleyn succumbed and fell pregnant. The new archbishop of Canterbury, Thomas Cranmer, appointed because it was known that he would be compliant, authorised the divorce and conducted the marriage of King Henry and Queen Anne in time for their daughter, Elizabeth, to be born legitimate. To protect this action the king made a unilateral declaration of independence from Rome and nationalised the Church in England. By a series of statutes from 1532 to 1535, Henry broke with Rome and made himself the Supreme Head of the Church of England.

The consequences of this revolution from above were manyfold and profound. First it led directly to England becoming a protestant confessional state. To achieve his political end in the 1530s Henry needed the support of protestants, or as one might more accurately style them evangelists, of whom Cranmer was already one and the highly talented Thomas Cromwell, who succeeded More as the king's chief minister, was possibly another. Henry's own religious outlook was ambivalent. He seems to have remained fundamentally orthodox, but he had probably absorbed many of the ideas of the Christian humanists and thus countenanced the early assault on the cults of saints, relics and pilgrimages, many of which were now revealed to be frauds. He was also persuaded of the political advantage of making English the language of his Church of England, and thus authorised the first English bible as well as official articles of faith and books of instruction in the vernacular. And Henry agreed in 1536 to begin the dissolution of the monasteries, completed in 1540, possibly because he feared their potential as a Papal fifth column and probably because he could not resist the wealth they possessed.

Nevertheless, Henry and orthodox churchmen at court were able to insist in the six articles of 1538 and the King's Book of 1539 on the preservation of the fundamental doctrine of the eucharist, which had become the central point of differentiation between catholic and protestant beliefs. Protestants, like Wycliffe, denied transubstantiation and thereby any exalted role for the priesthood deriving from working the miracle. After Henry's death, in the six years of Edward VI's reign under Cranmer's skilled leadership, England was taken further down that road. Although stopped short by the young king's early death, and reversed under the catholic Queen Mary, a modified form of protestantism was eventually established as the religion of the established Church of England under Elizabeth I.

The majority of English people accepted this religious revolution. Resistance was sporadic and isolated. There was no popular counter-revolution. Some, of course, welcomed it; and their numbers grew, especially in the Church. The acceptance by the clergy as a whole is perhaps more remarkable than the acceptance by the laity. It seems that they collaborated in the destruction of their order for a variety of reasons. Some, like Cranmer, Latimer, Hooper and a clutch of new bishops and their followers, did so out of belief. Others, such as Gardiner and Tunstall, calculated that the greater danger was heresy, not the schism, and so initially accepted the break with Rome so as to work from within to fight the greater enemy; others, no doubt a considerable number, had no desire to jeopardise their careers and some saw the way to quick advancement; others perhaps thought it a storm in a teacup – the Church had been through worse crises and had survived. These last might have been proved right had Queen Mary lived longer. Those that resisted had their hands tied behind their backs. The frightening examples made of Saints Thomas More and John Fisher showed the consequences of individual, principled opposition. The Church international was quite unwilling, even if it had been able, to provide any kind of military assistance. And the die-hard theological traditionalists, after the martyrdom of St Thomas More, could not and would not resort to a public debate, let alone mount their own public campaign in the vernacular, for in so doing they believed they would concede part of the enemy's case. Thus the longer the schism lasted, the more deeply protestantism became entrenched.

While undoubtedly a minority of the laity, especially in the more urbanised south and east, quickly were converted to protestantism (and the existing Lollard cells provided isolated bases), there was no general welcome to the end of a thousand years of supposed subjection to an alien prelacy. As we have seen, the old order was not resented. But the depth of spiritual enthusiasm is unknowable. The lines between social convention, conformity and religious commitment are blurred. Moreover, the laity tended to follow where the clergy led. While the general level of doctrinal awareness was greater in the sixteenth century than it had been before, most lay people of any social status left the finer points of dogma to the experts. And since as a whole the clergy came to accept the changes, then who were they to argue against it. Parochial response depended much on the response of the incumbent. Behind this lay the considerable power of the state, both in compulsion and persuasion. To deny the Act of Supremacy was an act of treason. The loyal Pilgrims of Grace in 1536, despite the scale of their movement and the depth of their support, were unable to shift the regime by means less than open rebellion. Moreover there were substantial material inducements for the ruling elites – the nobility, gentry and burgesses, who were the magistracy in the provinces – to enforce the king's will. They shared in the plunder of the Church which went on apace from 1536.

It has occasioned some surprise that the old parochial, communal institutions, rituals and practices were swept away with such little resistance by reformers backed by the local magistracy. The infrastructure of Merry England, constructed, it has been argued, only after 1400, was being dismantled by 1600. There were to be no more cakes and ale, only a nostalgia for an imagined golden age that had passed.[25] But the new religious order had its compensatory social and spiritual attractions. The tendency for the demarcation between priest and layman to weaken, for the laity to participate more in their own religion, and to have a more prominent administrative role was hastened by the Henrician Reformation. Anglicisation of the liturgy widened access. In modern terms, parishioners were offered the opportunity to increase 'ownership' of their religion. In this, possibly, more than any particular doctrinal nicety, lay the positive appeal of the new order.[26]

The Henrician revolution, however, extended further than the Church. The constitutional, political and administrative consequences were as profound. Henry VIII claimed, in the preamble to the act for restraint of appeals, that England was an empire in that its king owed allegiance to no earthly power; it was a sovereign state. While in practice the kings of England in their relationship with the Papacy had asserted their independence from time to time, they had never before claimed it as a matter of principle. Henry VIII, by becoming the Supreme Head of the Church of England, asserted his answerability alone to God. The divine right of his monarchy was enhanced and the authority of his rule within his kingdom made more absolute.

On the other hand, the means that Henry used to authenticate and establish his new status bound him more tightly to the approval of his subjects. The break with Rome was at all stages a parliamentary process. It was the body of the whole realm, with the King in Parliament, which authenticated the establishment of England as an Imperial monarchy. Thus not only was parliament's role as the supreme law-making body enhanced, it was also extended as a partner in altering the constitution. Paradoxically the break with Rome both enhanced the Crown's authority and limited it. The Reformation Parliament set a precedent. Henceforth all religious change came to be authenticated by parliament: the further reformation under Edward VI, the catholic restoration under Mary, and the Elizabethan settlement. The Crown before the Reformation could not change the law or raise taxation without parliamentary assent; afterwards it could not change the religious settlement without assent either. However, since religion was so much more of a contentious issue after 1558 than even taxation, parliament became a forum for sustained ideological debate. In and outside parliament, a new dimension was added to political conflict, which extended, ultimately to issues of freedom of conscience and civil rights.

In the shorter term the new religious and constitutional issues were the concern of only the parliamentary class with fixed interests in the survival of the Church of England. The great redistribution of the landed wealth of the Church, not just that of the monasteries, but additionally a sizeable part of the secular property, effected a significant change in the social structure of the kingdom. Most of the wealth passed fairly quickly through royal hands. An opportunity to so endow the monarchy that it no longer had need of the financial support of its subjects was allowed to pass. The pressing needs of the time ensured a massive sale of property, first to the peerage, and then, by trickle-down effect, to lesser persons. The whole process was once known as 'the rise of the gentry', a singularly inappropriate phrase since the gentry had been in existence for centuries. If they became more important at the expense of another social group, it was not the peerage, who flourished also, but the clergy. The transfer of wealth, power and prestige was from clergy to laity, in religious, intellectual and academic spheres as well as the material and political.

The process of secularisation was particularly evident in the service of the state, where the laity in the sixteenth century rapidly displaced the clergy. While a class of lay administrators (gentlemen bureaucrats as they have been styled), had emerged in the fifteenth century, especially account-ants and lawyers in the service of greater subjects as well as the Crown, the reduction of the Church to an arm of the state in the sixteenth century opened the door for the creation of the secular civil service. Furthermore the very process of royal annexation of the Church added to the scale and scope of the royal administration in which to serve. The Crown now re-ceived all the clerical payments which had previously gone to Rome; for this the court of augmentations was established. Under the hands of Thomas Cromwell the machinery of government was further elaborated and the operation of royal government was separated a stage further from the royal person.

This process continued during the sixteenth century largely because of the accident of a minority being followed by two female rulers. Medieval English history had witnessed a recurring pattern of departments of state being forged out of, and separated from, the person of the monarch, only for a new intimate office to emerge. Thus the Chancery was established permanently at Westminster, but the Keeper of the Privy Seal stayed with the royal household. In time the keeper settled in Westminster and his role in the household was taken by the king's secretary. Thomas Cromwell was the last such secretary. His office was transformed into that of secretary of state, which subsequently became the office of the Crown's chief minister, but formally separate from the court. There was no further repetition of the cycle. The monarch's secretary, just as the keeper of the privy purse, became a private office, concerned only with the monarch's personal affairs. Here too Henry VIII's reign marked a decisive break with the past.

To ensure the security of the realm and protect the new order, the 1530s also witnessed a significant increase in centralisation. On a relatively minor scale the remaining palatinates of Chester and Durham were reformed and made full counties. The bishop of Durham still enjoyed a privileged status, but from 1536 it was the king's criminal law not the bishop's that was enforced between Tyne and Tees. Wales was abolished; or, to be more precise, the old marcher lordship and principality were replaced by a county system and the country fully incorporated into England. Possibly because the Crown feared Scotland (as yet unreformed) as a potential base for Papal counter-attack, in 1542 following the death of James V, Henry launched a six-year war to enforce, in vain, the union of the two kingdoms through the marriage of Edward, Prince of Wales and Mary, the child Queen of Scots. Ancient English ambitions were given added urgency by new circumstances. In the event, the possible danger was lessened by Scotland's own Reformation and the objective achieved by natural succession in 1603. Ireland, however, did become the launching point for catholic counter-attack, and thus in the later sixteenth century the process of full conquest and attempted assimilation into the English kingdom was once more renewed with determination. The foundations of the modern sovereign state, an English hegemony called the United Kingdom, were laid during the Reformation.

Finally, the Reformation was a further step in the creation of the sense of English nationhood. It was specifically an act of English assertiveness. The Church of England was established in defiance of a foreign authority; English rather than a foreign tongue became the language of religion. Given a grammatical structure, and shaped in the cadences of classical and biblical expression, English itself became a powerful and sophisticated vehicle of expression. A corpus of vernacular English literature was crafted in the late sixteenth and early seventeenth centuries which shaped an English identity which still had resonance at the end of the twentieth century. And England soon found herself, or chose to perceive herself, by the end of the sixteenth century as a nation alone, God's chosen people reborn, fighting against the Papal forces of darkness championed by the evil empire of Spain. England began, if not to turn its back on Europe, then to turn sideways on as it looked to the Atlantic, not only to fight the Spanish (and it is ironic that in the process England's pirates and privateers of whom governments in the fifteenth century had been somewhat ashamed, now became heroic sea-dogs), but also to find new markets and new wealth. Here indeed was a New World.

It is of course impossible to claim that there was either a sharp break with the past, or that there was a complete change during the sixteenth century.[27] Belief in the power of magic, in the malign exercise of witchcraft, in the potential of alchemy and the value of astrology remained strong until the later seventeenth century. Modern scientific thought was still a thing of the future. The old aristocratic values of chivalry and honour continued to be a powerful force. The Jacobean noble youth, albeit he was schooled in the new learnings of humanism and protestantism, still presented himself as a chivalric Englishman. Not until the seventeenth century was the full force of classicism felt in the visual arts. Elizabethan and Jacobean theatre was a hybrid forged out of the creative conjunction of the old parochial and courtly dramatic traditions, classical learning and the commercial opportunities of the thriving metropolis.

Likewise, many features which we associate with the modern age predate the sixteenth century. It is a paradox of the fifteenth century that while it was politically unsettled, it was socially stable. Rebellions and civil wars were common to centuries before and after the fifteenth. What set the century apart was the dynastic nature of the conflict which struck at the very heart of the political order. Yet the body politic as a whole did not suffer the dire consequences graphically described and endlessly repeated after 1461. Beneath the surface, changes were taking place which would have a profound impact on the future development of English society. English national identity and xenophobia were given sharper definition. The Church and the religious outlook of the laity became more English and less international. London emerged as the dominant metropolis of the whole kingdom and the focal point of an emerging national economy. And a self-consciously English middling sort in town and country became socially and politically more prominent. The origins of modern social structures are discernible amid the political upheavals of the century. The fifteenth century made a distinctive contribution to the long transition from medieval to modern society. Put in the terminology of previous generations it was a progressive century. Stubbs was wrong. In his terms, not all that was good and great was languishing; there were marked signs of returning health.

Periodisation is to place a pattern on the past which reveals more about the pattern-makers than the past being patterned. 'The Middle Ages' is no exception. They did not begin until humanists invented them. And they will not end until we cease to write and talk about them. But in so far as the term describes a particular stage in the evolution of English society, the relationships which it describes changed markedly between 1520 and 1620. And if one chain of events is to be identified as central to that process of change in England, it is that which unwound in the decade in which Henry VIII broke with Rome. To that extent one might justifiably claim that Medieval England ended in the 1530s.[28]

Notes and references

1   Cited by Aston, 'Richard II and the Wars of the Roses', 291, n. 22. See also above, pp. 354, 378–9.

2   See above, pp. 4–6.

3 For the middle class see Hexter, 'Myth of the Middle Class', passim; for 'New Monarchy' see Goodman, *New Monarchy* and Gunn, *Early Tudor Government*, 1–4; and for recent discussion of the historiography Watts, 'History, the Fifteenth Century and the Renaissance', 8–18.

4 Allen, *Erasmi Epistolae*, i, 450, cited by McKie, *Earlier Tudors*, 235.

5 For Henry VIII's policy towards France discussed in this and the following paragraphs see Gunn, 'The French Wars of Henry VIII', passim and Davies, 'Henry VIII and Henry V', passim, and references given on 235, n. 2.

6 For Wolsey see Gwynn, *The King's Cardinal*; Gunn and Lynley, *Cardinal Wolsey*; and Guy, *The Cardinal's Court*.

7 See Starkey, 'The Age of the Household'; Hicks, *Bastard Feudalism*, 201–17; Adams, 'Continuity and Change in the Noble Affinity', passim. For the peripheries see Ellis, *Tudor Frontiers*.

8 Britnell, *Closing of the Middle Ages?*, 105–13 and 'English Economy', 89–101; Andrews, *Trade, Plunder and Settlement*, 41–63.

9 More, *Utopia*, 24. More himself linked enclosure with the problem of vagrancy. One has, however, to be careful not necessarily to attribute these views to More himself. The structure of the text only makes it safe to conclude that he incorporated contemporary opinions with which he was familiar. See also Britnell, 'English Economy', 91 and *Closing of the Middle Ages?*, 203–4, 235–6, 253–6.

10 Britnell, 'English Economy', 105–7 and *Closing of the Middle Ages?*, 206, 222–5; Kumin, *Shaping of a Community*, 196–200.

11 McKie, *Earlier Tudors*, 235.

12 Weiss, *Humanism in England*; Hay, 'England and the Humanities in the Fifteenth Century'. For the fifteenth-century 'learned' laity see Fleming, 'The Hautes and their Circle' and Hughes, 'Stephen Scrope'; and for developments in the universities see Cobban, *Medieval English Universities*; Leader, *Cambridge*, vol. 1; McConica, *Oxford*, vol. 3.

13 For printing see Eisenstein, *Printing Press* and *Printing Revolution*; and Febrvre and Martin, *The Coming of the Book*. For Caxton see Blake, *England's First Publisher* and *Caxton and his World*.

14 Cobban, *Medieval English Universities*, 243–56, 313–14; McConica, *Oxford*, vol. 3, 66–8.

15 Furnivall, *Meals and Manners*, xiii.

16 See the introductory essays to More, *Richard III* and *Utopia*; Dowling, *Humanism*; Mayer, *Thomas Starkey and the Commonweal*; McConica, *English Humanists*; and Starkey, 'England', 146–63.

17   Rowlands, *Holbein* passim; Jardine, *Worldly Goods*, 302–6, 425–36; Thurley, *Royal Palaces*, passim.

18   Aston, 'Northern Renaissance', provides an excellent overview. For Erasmus see Nauert, *Humanism*, 146–62 and Jardine, *Erasmus*.

19   Haigh, 'Anti-Clericalism'; Dickens, 'Shaping of Anticlericalism'; Brigden, *London and the Reformation*, 43–68 and 98–103 (Hunne).

20   See above pp. 212–16.

21   See above, pp. 216–19, 222–7. See Bernard, 'Vitality and Vulnerability', 210–13 for the new cult of Elizabeth Barton, the Holy Maid of Kent, in the 1520s. There is a substantial literature on the Pilgrimage of Grace, the most recent being Bush, *Pilgrimage of Grace*.

22   For this and following paragraph, see above, pp. 222–6, 373.

23   See above, pp. 391–2.

24   See Further Reading for recent writings on the Reformation.

25   Hutton, *Merry England*, 69ff.

26   For this and the following paragraphs see in particular Elton, *Tudor Revolution in Government*; Starkey and Coleman, *Revolution Reassessed*; Fox and Guy, *Reassessing the Henrician Age*; Gunn, *Early Tudor Government*, and Stone, *The Crisis of the Aristocracy*.

27   Note the claim by Lawrence Stone that the years 1580–1620 were 'the real watershed between medieval and modern England' (*Crisis of Aristocracy*, 15).

28   As proposed also by Du Boulay, *Age of Ambition*, 16.

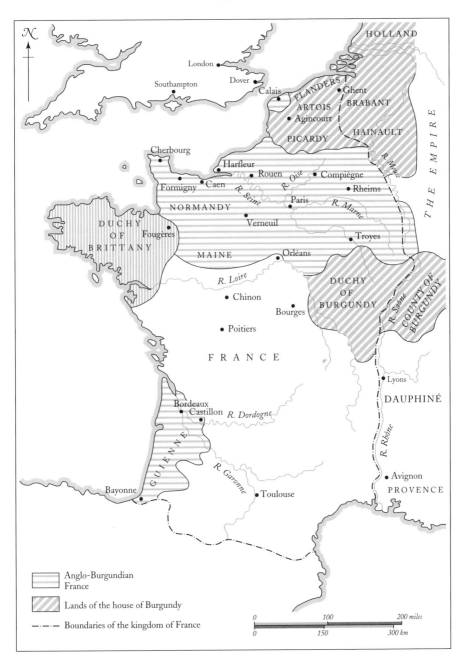

1   France, showing the furthest extent of Lancastrian possessions, *c.* 1429,
(after **M. H. Keen**, *England in the Later Middle Ages*)

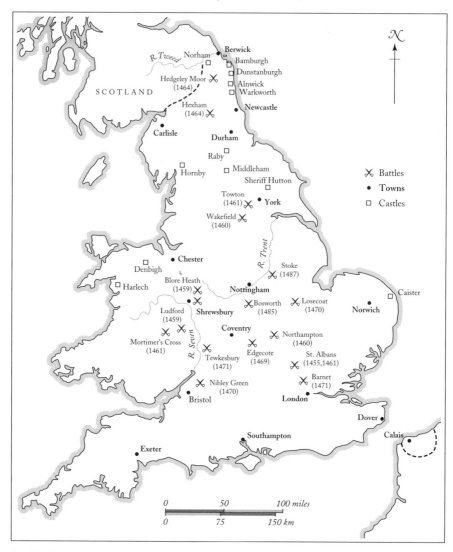

2   England during the Wars of the Roses (after A. J. Pollard, *The Wars of the Roses*)

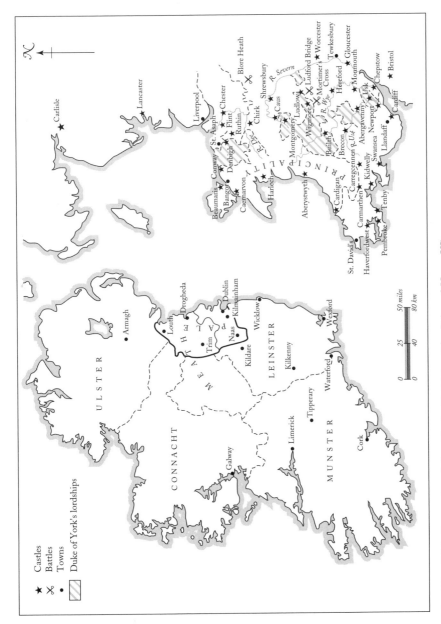

3   The Irish Sea region (after R. A. Griffiths, *The Reign of Henry VI*)

FURTHER READING

The suggestions for further reading which follow provide but an outline guide to selected, mainly recent, works on fifteenth-century English history. A full bibliography of works published before 1975 is to be found in E. B. Graves, *A Bibliography of English History to 1485* (Oxford, 1975), which can be supplemented by De Lloyd J. Guth, *England, 1377–1485* (Cambridge, 1976). The Royal Historical Society's *Annual Bibliography of British Irish History*, now also available in CDRom, gives a comprehensive running guide to publications. Where they are not given below, the full references are to be found in the Bibliography, which lists all the works cited in this book.

Sources

Jacob, *Fifteenth Century*, identifies the chronicle and record sources in its bibliography. Gransden, *Historical Writing*, is the best modern introduction to narrative sources and Hicks, 'Sources', discusses both narrative and institutional records. There are two editions of the Paston letters; Gairdner's contains additional materials and is ordered chronologically, making it easier to use than the two-volume, but more accurate, modern edition by Davis, for which an index is in preparation. The Cely and Plumpton letters have modern editions by Hanham and Kirby; Kingsford's edition of the Stonor letters is yet to replaced.

Extracts from the sources are to be found in many collections, but see e.g. Myers, *English Historical Documents*; Given-Wilson, *Chronicles of the Revolution*; K. Dockray, *Edward IV: a Source Book* (Stroud, 1999) and *Richard III: a Source Book* (Stroud, 1988); Goldberg, *Women in England*; Ward, *English Noblewoman*; Swanson, *Catholic England*.

General works

For a vivid introduction, see Lander, *Conflict and Stability* and for a fuller treatment Keen, *England in the Later Middle Ages*. Carpenter, *Wars of the Roses*, gives a recent, but controversial, view of the century. The essays in Horrox, *Fifteenth-Century Attitudes* are collectively a lively portrait of the age. The most recent, shorter accounts of Lancastrian and Yorkist England (by Walker and Horrox) are to be found in Allmand, *New Cambridge Medieval History*, which also provides a starting point for the European context. Thomson, *Transformation of Medieval England*, takes a 'long' fifteenth century, through from the late fourteenth century to the early sixteenth, and has an excellent compendium of information. J. R. Lander, *Government and Community: England 1450–1509* (1980) brings Yorkist and early Tudor England together as does Davies, *Peace, Print and Protestantism* and Guy, *Tudor England*. Curry, *Hundred Years War* provides an introduction to the principal focus of foreign affairs. The English possessions in France are considered by Allmand, *Lancastrian Normandy* and Vale, *English Gascony*. For Wales see Davies, *Conquest, Coercion and Change* and Williams, *Renewal and Reformation*; and for Ireland Cosgrove, *New History of Ireland*, vol. 2 and Ellis, *Ireland in the Age of the Tudors*. Scottish history can now be approached through the volumes in the Stewart dynasty series: Boardman, *Early Stewart Kings*; Brown, *James I*; McGladdery, *James II*; and Mcdougall *James III* and *James IV*.

Politics

The fullest narrative account of Henry IV's reign remains J. H. Wylie, *History of England under Henry the Fourth* (4 vols, 1884–9). A full modern history is still awaited. In the meantime McNiven's writings go some way towards supplying this and Kirby, *Henry IV* and McFarlane, *Lancastrian Kings* provide briefer narratives. Henry V is well served by Allmand, *Henry V* and Harriss, *Practice of Kingship*. Griffiths, *Reign of Henry VI*, is the fullest account of the politics of the reign, but should be supplemented by Watts, *Henry VI and the Politics of Kingship* and Wolffe, *Henry VI*. Scofield, *Edward the Fourth*, provides the full narrative of the reign of the first Yorkist, but should be read in conjunction with the more recent interpretation of Ross, *Edward IV* and Lander's essays reprinted in *Crown and Nobility*. For Richard III the most detailed modern studies are Horrox, *Richard III* and Ross, *Richard III*, but see also for shorter accounts Hicks, *Richard III* and Pollard, *Richard III*. The standard modern study of Henry VII's reign, Chrimes, *Henry VII*, has a heavy administrative emphasis, while R. L. Storey, *The Reign of Henry VII* (1968) gives the political history more emphasis. Recent research and debate has not yet been reflected in a comprehensive study of the reign. Three biographical studies, Harriss, *Cardinal Beaufort*, Hicks, *Warwick the Kingmaker* and Jones and Underwood, *The King's Mother*, supplement the principal reign-by-reign narratives.

Government and law

Watts, *Henry VI*, contains the most recent discussion of ideas of kingship, with which this work does not entirely concur. The role of the royal household is analysed in Given-Wilson, *Royal Household* and its role in politics elucidated by Morgan, 'King's Affinity' and 'House of Polity'. The court is visited in Griffiths, 'King's Court', and Horrox, 'Caterpillars of the Commonwealth'. For an introduction to the institutions of central government see Brown, *Governance of Medieval England* and, for their development after 1460, Gunn, *Early Tudor Government*. For parliament also see Davies and Denton, *English Parliament* and Roskell, *History of Parliament, 1381–1421*, vol. 1. The development of taxation is considered by Harriss, *King, Parliament and Public Finance*.

The informal political structure is discussed in Harriss, 'Political Society', 'Dimensions of Politics' and 'King and his Subjects', and in Ormrod, *Political Life*, Hicks, *Bastard Feudalism* and Carpenter, *Wars of the Roses*. Ellis, *Tudor Frontiers*, Jewell, *North–South Divide* and Neville, *Violence, Custom and Law* deal with the relationship between centre and peripheries. Carpenter, *Locality and Polity* (Warwickshire), Payling, *Political Society in Lancastrian England* (Nottinghamshire), Pollard, *North-Eastern England* and Wright, *Derbyshire Gentry* are examples of local and regional studies; Archer, 'Mowbrays', Rawcliffe, *Staffords* and Woodger, 'Henry Bourgchier' of baronial studies. The most recent history of the Paston family is Richmond, *The First Phase* and *Fastolff's Will*, with a third volume to come.

Popular involvement in politics, both violent and peaceful, can be approached through Hilton, *Bond Men Made Free*, Harvey, *Cade's Revolt* and 'Popular Politics?', Goheen, 'Peasant Politics' and Dyer, 'Taxation and Community'.

Musson and Ormrod, *English Justice* and Powell, *Kingship, Law and Society*, contain introductions to the common law. The central courts are studied in Blatcher, *King's Bench* and Hastings, *Common Pleas*. For justices of the peace see Arnold, 'Commission of the Peace', Putnam, *Proceedings*, Lander, *Justices of the Peace*, and Walker, 'Yorkshire Justices of the Peace'. Lawyers themselves are considered in Ives, *Common Lawyers* and Moreton, *Townshends*. Maddern, *Violence and Social Order*, provides a discussion of attitudes towards the law.

Economy and society

Bolton, *Medieval Economy* and Britnell, *Commercialisation* provide good starting points for the economy. Du Boulay, *Age of Ambition* makes graphic use of the literary sources for social institutions and relations and Rigby, *English Society* adds a sociological perspective. Dyer, *Standards of Living* is the essential starting point for that topic. The mid-fifteenth century recession is discussed by Britnell, 'Economic Context', Hatcher, 'Great Slump' and Pollard, 'Agrarian Crisis'. Agrarian history and social relations are considered comprehensively in Miller, *Agrarian History, III*, in Fryde, *Peasants and Landlords* and Hilton, *Decline of Serfdom* and particular regions are explored, e.g., in Dyer, *Lords and Peasants* and Poos, *Rural Society*. For towns, see Dyer, *Decline and Growth*, Holt and Rosser, *Medieval Town* and Thomson, *Towns and Townspeople*, and for individual places, Britnell, *Colchester*, Carlin, *Southwark*, Newman, *Northallerton*, Rosser, *Westminster*, Shaw, *Wells* and Summerson, *Carlisle*. A comprehensive history of late-medieval London is still to come.

For the nobility see Given-Wilson, *English Nobility*, Keen, *Chivalry*, McFarlane, *English Nobility* and Morgan, 'English Gentleman'. Trade and traders are to be encountered in Day, *Medieval Market Economy*, Power and Postan, *Fifteenth-Century Trade*, Lloyd, *England and the Hanse*, Kermode, *Medieval Merchants*. Parish and village are explored in Dyer, 'Medieval Rural Community', Kumin, *Shaping of a Community* and Hutton, *Merry England*. Cullum, 'Pore People Harberles', Rubin, 'The Poor' and *Charity and Community*, and McIntosh, *Controlling Misbehavior* put the poor, and attitudes towards them, in their place.

Leyser, *Medieval Women* and Coss, *The Lady* are recent introductions to the history of medieval women. Goldberg, *Women in England* and Ward, *English Noblewoman* provide extracts from the sources. Goldberg, *Women, Work and Life Cycle* and Mate, *Daughters, Wives and Widows* offer different views as to whether the condition of women improved during the century, for the broader context of which see also Bennett, 'Medieval Women, Modern Women'. Children are discussed in Attreed, '*Pearl Maiden*', Orme, 'Culture of Children' and Shahar, *Childhood*.

Church and religion

The fullest modern acount is Swanson, *Church and Society*, which is the best starting point for all aspects. Shorter accounts are to be found in Harper-Bill, *Pre-Reformation Church* and Heath, *Church and Realm*. For a comprehensive review of the historiography before 1990 see Heath, 'Between Reform and Reformation'. For relationships with the Papacy see Du Boulay, 'Fifteenth Century', Harvey, *England, Rome and Papacy* and Thomson, 'Well of Grace'. Cathedral chapters are discussed in Lepine, *Brotherhood of Canons*; Kettle and Johnson, *VCH Stafford* (Lichfield); Edwards, *VCH Wiltshire* (Salisbury); monastic cathedrals in Dobson, *Durham Priory* and 'Monks of Canterbury'.

Recruitment to the clergy is undertaken in Moran, 'Clerical Recruitment', Storey, 'Recruitment', Swanson, 'Universities, Graduates and Benefices'; clerical education in Moran, *Growth of English Schooling*, Davis, *William Waynflete*, Catto and Evans, *University of Oxford*, vol. 2; Leader, *University of Cambridge*, vol. 1, and Cobban, *Medieval English Universities*.

The standard work on the religious orders remains Knowles, *Religious Orders*, vols 2 and 3. For individual houses see Dobson, above, Harvey, *Living and Dying* (Westminster Abbey), Tillotson, *Monastery and Society* (Selby) and the theses by Rowntree, 'Studies in Carthusian History' and Gribbin, 'Premonstratensian Order'. Nunneries are not as well served as monasteries, but see Power, *Medieval English Nunneries*; Olva, *Convent and Community* and, for particular convents, Dobson and Donaghey, *Clementhorpe* and Tillotson, *Marrick Priory*. For hospitals see Orme and Webster, *Medieval Hospitals*, Rawcliffe, *Hospitals of Medieval Norwich* and Cullum, *Cremmetts and Corodies*.

A selection of texts concerning piety and beliefs is provided by Swanson, *Catholic England*. Bossy, *Christianity in the West*, offers a broad introduction and Duffy, *Stripping of the Altars* a detailed exploration of pre-Reformation religious beliefs. Rubin, *Corpus Christi* and Finacune, *Miracles and Pilgrims* examine particular manifestations. Local focus is to be found in Brown, *Popular Piety* (diocese of Salisbury), Heath, 'Urban Piety' (Hull), Fleming, 'Charity, Faith and the Gentry of Kent', N. P. Tanner, *The Church in late-Medieval Norwich, 1370–1532* (Toronto, 1984) and Vale, *Piety, Charity and Literacy* (Yorkshire). The quality of testamentary evidence, on which many local studies depend, is discussed in Burgess, 'Quick and Dead'.

The history of late-medieval chantries is to be found in Wood-Leigh, *Perpetual Chantries*; Kreider, *English Chantries*; Dobson, 'Foundation of Chantries' and Burgess, 'Increase of Divine Service'. Parochial foundations and organisations are discussed in Bainbridge, *Gilds in the Countryside*, Barron, 'Parish Fraternities', Rosser, 'Communities of Parish and Guild' and 'Going to the Fraternity Feast', Kumin, *Shaping of a Community*, Carnwath, 'Church Wardens' Accounts', and French, 'Parochial Fund-Raising'.

The standard work on Lollardy is Hudson, *Premature Reformation*, but see also McFarlane, *John Wycliffe and the Beginnings of English Nonconformity* (1952) for a succinct introduction and Thomson, *Later Lollards*, Aston, 'Lollardy and Sedition', Davies, 'Lollardy and Locality' and Tanner, *Heresy Trials*. Carey, *Courting Disaster* and Kieckhefer, *Magic*, dabble in the occult; and Rawcliffe, *Medicine and Society*, details one application.

BIBLIOGRAPHY

This bibliography is of works cited in the text. The place of publication is London, unless otherwise stated.

Acheson, A., *A Gentry Community: Leicestershire in the Fifteenth Century, c.1422–1485* (Cambridge, 1992).

Adams, S., 'Baronial Contexts? Continuity and Change in the Noble Affinity, 1400–1600', in Watts, ed., *End of the Middle Ages?*

Aers, D., ed., *Culture and History, 1350–1600* (1992).

Allan, A., 'Royal Propaganda and the Proclamations of Edward IV', *BIHR*, 59 (1986).

Allen, P. S., *et al.* eds, *Opus Epistolorum Desidarii Erasmis* (11 vols, 1906–47).

Allmand, C. T., 'The Anglo-French Negotiations, 1439', *BIHR*, 40 (1967).

Allmand, C. T., ed., *War, Literature and Politics in the Late Middle Ages* (Liverpool, 1976).

Allmand, C. T., *Lancastrian Normandy, 1415–1450: The History of a Medieval Occupation* (Oxford, 1983).

Allmand, C. T., *Henry V* (1992).

Allmand, C. T., ed., *The New Cambridge Medieval History, VII, c.1415–c.1500* (Cambridge, 1998).

Almond, R. L., 'Medieval Hunting: Ruling Classes and Commonalty', *Medieval History*, 3 (1993–4).

Andrews, K. R., *Trade, Plunder and Settlement: Maritime Enterprise and the Genesis of the British Empire, 1480–1630* (Cambridge, 1984).

Anglo, S., *Spectacle, Pageantry and Early Tudor Policy* (Oxford, 1969).

Anglo, S., ed., *Chivalry in the Renaissance* (Woodbridge, 1990).

Anglo, S., 'Anglo-Burgundian Feats of Arms', *Guildhall Miscellany*, 2, no. 7 (1995).

Antonovics, A., 'Henry VII, King of England "By Grace of Charles VII of France"', in Griffiths and Sherborne, *Kings and Nobles*.

Appleby, J. C. and Dalton, P., eds, *Government, Religion and Society in Northern England, 1000–1700* (Stroud, 1997).

Archer, R. E., 'The Mowbrays, Earls of Nottingham and Dukes of Norfolk, to 1432' (University of Oxford, D Phil, 1984).

Archer, R. E., 'Rich Old Ladies; the Problem of Late Medieval Dowagers', in Pollard, *Property and Politics*.

Archer, R. E., ed., *Crown, Government and People in the Fifteenth Century* (Stroud, 1995).

Archer, R. E., 'Parliamentary Restoration: John Mowbray and the Dukedom of Norfolk in 1425' in Archer and Walker, *Rulers and Ruled*.

Archer, R. E. and Walker, S., eds, *Rulers and Ruled in Late Medieval England* (1995).

Aries, P., *Centuries of Childhood* (1962).

Armstrong, C. A. J., 'The Piety of Cecily, Duchess of York', in Woodruff, *For Hilaire Belloc*.

Armstrong, C. A. J., 'The Inauguration Ceremonies of the Yorkist Kings and their Title to the Throne', *TRHS*, 4th ser., 5 (1948).

Armstrong, C. A. J., 'Politics and the Battle of St Albans, 1455', *BIHR*, 33 (1960).

Arnold, C, 'The Commission of the Peace for the West Riding of Yorkshire, 1437–1509', in Pollard, *Property and Politics*.

Arthurson, I., 'A Question of Loyalty', *The Ricardian*, 97 (1987).

Arthurson, I., 'The King's Voyage into Scotland: the war that never was', in Williams, *England in the Fifteenth Century*.

Arthurson, I., 'The Rising of 1497 – a Revolt of the peasantry', in Rosenthal and Richmond, *People, Politics and Community*.

Arthurson, I., *The Perkin Warbeck Conspiracy, 1491–1499* (Stroud, 1994).

Arthurson, L. and Kingwell, N., 'The Proclamation of Henry Tudor as King of England', *HR*, lxiii (1990).

Asch, R. A. and Birke, A. M., eds, *Princes, Patronage and the Nobility: the Court at the Beginning of the Modern Age, c.1450–1650* (1991).

Ashton, T. S. and Philipps, C. H., *The Brenner Debate: Agrarian Class Structure and Economic Development in Pre-Industrial Europe* (Cambridge, 1985).

Aston, M., 'Lollardy and Sedition, 1381–1431', *PP*, 17 (1960).

Aston, M., 'Richard II and the Wars of the Roses', in Du Boulay and Barron, *The Reign of Richard II* (1971).

Aston, M., *Faith and Fire: Popular and Unpopular Religion, 1350–1600* (1993).

Aston, M., 'The Northern Renaissance', in *Faith and Fire*.

Aston, M., 'Death', in Horrox, *Fifteenth-Century Attitudes*.

Aston, M. and Richmond, C., eds, *Lollardy and the Gentry in the Later Middle Ages* (Stroud, 1997).

Attreed, L. C., 'The King's Interest: York's Fee Farm and the Central Government, 1482–92', *NH*, 17 (1981).

Attreed, L. C., 'From *Pearl Maiden* to Tower Princes', *JMH*, 9, 1983.

Attreed, L. C., ed., *The York House Books, 1461–1490* (Stroud, 2 vols, 1991).

Ault, W. A., 'Manor Court and Parish Church in Fifteenth-Century England', *Speculum*, 42 (1966).

Avery, M. E., 'The History of Equitable Jurisdiction of Chancery before 1460', *BIHR*, 42 (1969).

Aylmer, G. E. and Cant, R., eds, *A History of York Minster* (Oxford, 1977).

Backhouse, J., *Books of Hours* (1985).

Bailey, M., '*Per impetum maris*; Natural Disaster and Economic Decline in Eastern England, 1275–1350', in Campbell, *Before the Black Death*.

Bailey, 'Rural Society', in Horrox, *Fifteenth-Century Attitudes*.

Bailey, M., 'Demographic Decline in Late Medieval England: Some Thoughts on Recent Research', *EHR*, 2nd ser., 49 (1996).

Bainbridge, V., *Gilds in the Medieval Countryside: Social and Religious Change in Cambridge* (Woodbridge, 1996).

Baker, D., ed., *Medieval Women* (Oxford, 1978).

Barnum, P. H., *Dives and Pauper* (EETS, os, i/i, 275, 1976; ii, 280, 1980).

Barron, C. M., 'The Tyranny of Richard II', *BIHR*, 41 (1968).

Barron, C. M., 'The Parish Fraternities of Medieval London', in Barron and Harper-Bill, *Church in Pre-Reformation Society*, (1985).

Barron, C. M., 'The "Golden Age" of Women in Medieval London', *Reading Medieval Studies*, 15 (1989).

Barron, C. M., 'The Deposition of Richard II', in Taylor and Childs, *Politics and Crisis*.

Barron, C. M., 'The Expansion of Education in Fifteenth-Century London', in Blair and Golding, *Cloister and World*.

Barron, C. M. and Harper-Bill, C., eds, *The Church in Pre-Reformation Society* (Woodbridge, 1985).

Barron, C. M. and Saul, N., eds, *England and the Low Countries in the Late Middle Ages* (Stroud, 1995).

Barron, C. M. and Sutton, A. F., *Medieval London Widows 1300–1500* (Woodbridge, 1994).

Barry, J. and Brooks, C., eds, *The Middling Sort of People: Culture, Society and Politics, 1550–1800* (1994).

Bartlett, R. and Mckay, A., eds, *Medieval Frontier Societies* (Oxford, 1989).

Bates, D. and Curry, A., eds, *England and Normandy in the Middle Ages* (1994).

Bean, J. M. W., *The Estates of the Percy Family, 1416–1537* (Oxford, 1958).

Bean, J. M. W., 'Henry IV and the Percies', *History*, 44 (1959).

Beckwith, S., *Christ's Body: Identity, Culture and Writing in Late Medieval Writings* (1993).

Bennett, J. M., 'Conviviality and Charity in Early Modern England', *PP*, 134 (1992).

Bennett, J. M., 'Medieval Women, Modern Women: Across the Great Divide', in Aers, *Culture and History*.

Bennett, M. J., 'A County Community: Social Cohesion Among the Cheshire Gentry, 1400–1425', *NH*, 8 (1973).

Bennett, M. J., *Community, Class and Careerism: Cheshire and Lancashire Society in the Age of Sir Gawain and the Green Knight* (Cambridge, 1983).

Bennett, M. J., *Lambert Simnel and the Battle of Stoke* (Gloucester, 1987).

Bennett, M. J., 'Henry VII and the Northern Rising of 1489', *EHR*, cv (1990).

Bennett, M. J., 'Edward III's Entail and the Succession to the Crown, 1376–1471', *EHR*, 113 (1998).

Beresford, W., *The Lost Villages of England* (reprint, Stroud, 1998).

Bergen, H., *Lydgate's Troy Book* (EETS, 1906).

Bergenroth, G. A., ed., *Calendar of State Papers, Spanish, 1, Henry VII* (1862).

Bernard, G. W., ed., *The Tudor Nobility* (Manchester, 1992).

Bernard, G. W., 'Vitality and Vulnerability in the Late Medieval Church: Pilgrimage on the Eve of the Break with Rome', in Watts, *End of the Middle Ages?*

Biggs, D., '"A wrong whom conscience and kindred bid me right": A Reasessment of Edmund of Langley, Duke of York and the Usurpation of Henry IV', *Albion*, 26 (1994).

Binsky, P., *Medieval Death: Ritual and Representation* (1996).

Black, J., ed., *The Origins of War in Early Modern Europe* (Edinburgh, 1987).

Black, R., 'Humanism', in Allmand, *The New Cambridge Medieval History*.

Blair, J. and Golding, B., eds, *The Cloister and the World* (Oxford, 1996).

Blake, N. F., *Caxton and His World* (1969).

Blake, N. F., *Caxton: England's First Publisher* (1976).

Blake, N. F., *William Caxton and English Literary Culture* (1991).

Blatcher, M., *The Court of King's Bench, 1450–1550* (1978).

Boardman, S. I., *The Early Stewart Kings: Robert II and Robert III, 1371–1406* (East Linton,1996).

Bolton, J. L., *The Medieval English Economy, 1150–1500* (1980).

Bolton, J. L., '"The World Upside Down": Plague as an Agent of Social and Economic Change', in Ormrod and Lindley, *Black Death in England*.

Bolton, J. L., *The Alien Communities of London in the Fifteenth Century: the Subsidy Rolls of 1440 and 1483–4* (Richard III & Yorkist History Trust: Stamford, 1998).

Bonney, M., *Lordship and the Urban Community: Durham and its Overlords, 1250–1540* (Cambridge, 1990).

Booth, P. W. N., 'Landed Society in Cumberland and Westmorland, 1440–1485' (University of Leicester PhD thesis, 1997).

Bossy, J., *Christianity in the West, 1400–1700* (Oxford, 1985).

Bradley, P. J., 'Henry V's Scottish Policy', in Hamilton and Bradley, *Documenting the Past*.

Brigden, S., *London and the Reformation* (Oxford, 1989).

Britnell, R. H., *Growth and Decline in Colchester, 1300–1525* (Cambridge, 1986).

Britnell, R. H., *The Commercialisation of English Society, 1000–1500* (Cambridge, 1993).

Britnell, R. H., 'The Economic Context', in Pollard, *Wars of the Roses*.

Britnell, R. H., *The Closing of the Middle Ages? England 1471–1529* (Oxford, 1997).

Britnell, R. H., 'The English Economy and the Government', in Watts, *End of the Middle Ages?*

Britnell, R. H. and Hatcher, J., eds, *Progress and Problems in Medieval England* (Cambridge, 1996).

Britnell, R. H. and Pollard, A. J., eds, *The McFarlane Legacy: Studies in Late Medieval Politics and Society* (Stroud, 1995).

Brown, A. D., *Popular Piety in Late Medieval England: the Diocese of Salisbury, 1250–1550* (Oxford, 1995).

Brown, A. L., 'The Commons and the Council in the Reign of Henry IV', *EHR*, 79 (1964).

Brown, A. L., 'The King's Councillors in Fifteenth-Century England', *TRHS*, 5th ser., 19 (1969).

Brown, A. L., 'The Reign of Henry IV', in Chrimes, *Fifteenth-Century England*.

Brown, A. L., 'The English Campaign in Scotland, 1400', in Hearder and Loyn, *British Government*.

Brown, A. L., *The Governance of Medieval England, 1272–1461* (1989).

Brown, M. H., *James I* (Edinburgh, 1994).

Bruce, J., ed., *Historie of the Arrivall of Edward IV in England* (Camden, old series, 1, 1838).

Burgess, C., '"For the Increase of Divine Service": Chantries in the Parish in Late-Medieval Bristol', *JEH*, 36 (1985).

Burgess, C., 'By Quick and By Dead: Wills and Pious Provision in Late-Medieval Bristol', *EHR*, 45 (1987).

Burgess, C., '"A Vain Thing Vainly Invented"; an Essay on Purgatory and Pious Motive in Late-Medieval England', in Wright, *Parish, Church and People*.

Burgess, C., 'Late Medieval Wills and Pious Convention: Testamentary Evidence Reconsidered', in Hicks, *Profit, Piety and the Professions*.

Burgess, C. and Kumin, B., 'Penitential Bequests and Parish Regimes in Late Medieval England', *JEH*, 44 (1993).

Burgess, C., ed., *The Pre-Reformation Records of All Saints Bristol* (Bristol RS, 46) Part 1 (1995).

Burns, J. H., *Lordship, Kingship and Empire: the Idea of Monarchy,1400–1525* (Oxford, 1992).

Bush, M. L., *The Pilgrimage of Grace: a Study of the Rebel Armies of October 1536* (Manchester, 1996).

Cameron, A., 'The Giving of Livery and Retaining in Henry VII's Reign', *Renaissance and Modern Studies*, 18 (1974).

Campbell, B. M. C., ed., *Before the Black Death: Studies in the Crisis of the Early-Fourteenth Century* (Manchester, 1991).

Carey, H., 'Devout Literate Laypeople and the Pursuit of the Mixed Life in Later Medieval England', *Journal of Religious History*, 14 (1987).

Carey, H. M., *Courting Disaster: Astrology at the English Court and Universities in the Late Middle Ages* (1992).

Carlin, M., *Medieval Southwark* (1996).

Carnwath, J., 'Church Wardens' Accounts of Thame, Oxfordshire, c.1443–1524', in Clayton, *Trade, Devotion and Governance*.

Carpenter, M. C., 'The Duke of Clarence and the Midlands', *Midland History*, 11 (1986).

Carpenter, M. C., *Locality and Polity: A Study of Warwickshire Landed Society, 1401–1499* (Cambridge, 1992).

Carpenter, M. C., 'Gentry and Community in Medieval England', *JBS*, 33 (1994).

Carpenter, M. C., 'Political and Constitutional History: Before and After McFarlane', in Britnell and Pollard, *The McFarlane Legacy*.

Carpenter, M. C., 'The Stonor Circle in the Fifteenth Century', in Archer and Walker, *Rulers and Ruled*.

Carpenter, M. C., 'Henry VII and the English Polity', in Thompson, *Reign of Henry VII*.

Carpenter, M. C., *The Wars of the Roses* (Cambridge, 1997).

Castor, H., '"Walter Blount was gone to serve Traytours": the Sack of Elvaston and the Politics of the North Midlands in 1454', *Midland History*, 19 (1994).

Castor, H. E., 'The Duchy of Lancaster and the Rule of East Anglia, 1399–1440', in Archer, *Crown, Government and People*.

Catto, J., 'Religious Change under Henry V', in Harriss, *Henry V.*

Catto, J., 'The King's Servants', in Harriss, *Henry V.*

Catto, J., 'The King's Government and the Fall of Peacock', in Archer and Walker, *Rulers and Ruled*.

Catto, J. I. and Evans, R., eds, *The History of the University of Oxford, II, Late Medieval Oxford* (Oxford, 1992).

Caxton, W., *The Book of the Order of Chivalry*, ed. Byles, A. J. P. (EETS 1926).

Cherry, J., *The Middleham Jewel and Ring* (York, 1994).

Cherry, M., 'The Courtenay Earls of Devon: the Formation and Disintegration of a Later Medieval Aristocratic Affinity', *Southern History*, 1 (1979).

Cherry, M., 'The Struggle for Power in Mid-Fifteenth-Century Devonshire', in Griffiths, *Patronage, Crown and Provinces*.

Chrimes, S. B., 'Sir John Fortescue's Theory of Dominium', *TRHS*, 4th ser., 17 (1934).

Chrimes, S. B., *English Constitutional Ideas in the Fifteenth Century* (Cambridge, 1936).

Chrimes, S. B., ed., *De Laudibus Legem Anglie* (Cambridge, 1942).

Chrimes, S. B. *et al.*, eds, *Fifteenth-Century England: Studies in Politics and Society* (Manchester, 1972).

Chrimes, S. B., *Henry VII*, (1972).

Clayton, D. J. *et al.*, eds, *Trade, Devotion and Governance: Papers in Later Medieval History* (Stroud, 1994).

Clough, C. H., ed., *Profession, Vocation and Culture in Late Medieval England* (Liverpool, 1982).

Cobban, A. B., *The Medieval English Universities: Oxford and Cambridge to c.1500* (Aldershot, 1988).

Coleman, C. and Starkey, D., eds, *Revolution Reassessed* (Oxford, 1986).

Collinson, P. *et al.*, eds, *A History of Canterbury Cathedral* (Oxford, 1995).

Commynes, Philippe de, *Memoirs: the Reign of Louis XI, 1461–83*, trans. Jones, Michael (Harmondsworth, 1972).

Condon, M., 'Ruling Elites in the Reign of Henry VII', in Ross, *Patronage, Pedigree and Power*.

Condon, M., 'From Caitiff and Villain to Pater Patriae: Reynold Bray and the Profits of Office', in Hicks, *Profit, Piety and the Professions*.

Cooper, J. P., 'Henry VII's Last Years Reconsidered', *HJ*, 2 (1959).

Cooper, J. P., 'Introduction' to McFarlane, *Nobility*.

Corbin, P. and Sedge, D., eds, *The Oldcastle Controversy* (Manchester 1991).

Cosgrove, A., *Late Medieval Ireland, 1370–1541* (Dublin, 1981).

Cosgrove, A., ed. *A New History of Ireland, II, Medieval Ireland, 1169–1534* (Oxford, 1987).

Coss, P. R., *The Lady in Medieval England, 1000–1500* (Stroud, 1980).

Coss, P. R., 'Aspects of Cultural Diffusion in Medieval England: the Early Romances, Local Society and Robin Hood', *PP*, 108 (1985).

Coss, P., 'Bastard Feudalism Revised', *PP*, 125 (1989).

Cressy, D., *Literacy and the Social Order: Reading and Writing in Tudor and Stuart England* (Cambridge, 1980).

Crook, D., 'Central England and the Revolt of the Earls, January 1400', *HR*, 64 (1991).

Cross, M. C., ed., *Law and Governance under the Tudors* (Cambridge, 1988).

Cross, M. C., 'The Religious Life of Women in Sixteenth-Century Yorkshire', *Women and the Church* (Studies in Church History, 27, 1991).

Crowder, C. M. D., *Unity, Heresy and Reform* (1977).

Cullum, P. H., *Cremmetts and Corodies: the Care of the Poor and Sick at St Leonard's Hospital York in the Middle Ages* (Borthwick Paper, 79, 1991).

Cullum, P. H., '"And His Name was Charite": Charitable Giving by and for Women in Late Medieval Yorkshire', in Goldberg, *Women is a Worthy Wight*.

Cullum, P. H., 'For Pore People Harberles' in Clayton, *Trade, Devotion and Governance*.

Cullum, P., 'Vowesses and Female Piety in the Province of York, 1300–1500', *NH*, 32 (1996).

Cummins, J., *The Hound and the Hawk: the Art of Medieval Hunting* (1988).

Cunningham, S., 'The Establishment of the Tudor Regime: Henry VII, Rebellion and the Financial Control of the Aristocracy, 1485–1509' (Unpublished University of Lancaster PhD thesis, 1995).

Cunningham, S., 'Henry VII and North-East England: Bonds of Allegiance and the Establishment of Tudor Authority', *NH*, 32 (1996).

Currin, J. M., 'Henry VII and the Treaty of Redon (1489)', *History*, 81 (1996).

Currin, J. M., 'Persuasion to Peace: the Luxembourg-Marigny-Gaguin Embassy and the State of Anglo-French Relations, 1489–90', *EHR* (1998).

Curry, A. E., *The Hundred Years War* (Macmillan, 1993).

Curry, A. E., 'Lancastrian Normandy: the Jewel in the Crown?', in Bates and Curry, *England and Normandy*.

Davies, C. S. L., *Peace, Print and Protestantism, 1450–1558* (1976).

Davies, C. S. L., 'Bishop John Morton, the Holy See, and the Accession of Henry VII', *EHR*, 102 (1987).

Davies, C. S. L., 'Richard III, Brittany and Henry Tudor', *Nottingham Medieval Studies*, 37 (1993).

Davies, C. S. L., 'Henry VIII and Henry V: the Wars in France', in Watts, *End of the Middle Ages?*

Davies, J. S., ed., *An English Chronicle of the Reigns of Richard II, Henry IV, Henry V and Henry VI* (Camden Soc., old ser., 64, 1856).

Davies, R. G., 'The Episcopate', in Clough, *Profession, Vocation and Culture*.

Davies, R. G., 'Lollardy and Locality', *TRHS*, 6th ser., 1 (1991).

Davies, R. G., 'The Church and the Wars of the Roses', in Pollard *Wars of the Roses*.

Davies, R. G. and Denton, J. H., eds, *The English Parliament in the Middle Ages* (Manchester, 1981).

Davies, R. R., *Conquest, Coercion and Change: Wales:1063–1415* (Oxford, 1987).

Davies, R. R., *The Revolt of Owain Glyn Dŵr* (Oxford, 1995).

Davis, J. F., 'Lollard Survival and the Textile Industry in the South-East of England', *Studies in Church History*, 3 (1966).

Davis, J. F., *Heresy and Reformation in the South-East of England*, (1983).

Davis, N., *Paston Letters and Papers*, 2 vols (Oxford, 1971–6).

Davis, V., 'William Waynflete and the Educational Revolution of the Fifteenth Century', in Rosenthal and Richmond, *People, Politics and Community*.

Davis, V., *William Waynflete* (Woodbridge, 1994).

Day, J., *The Medieval Market Economy* (Oxford, 1987).

Denton, W., *England in the Fifteenth Century* (1888).

D'Evelyn, C., ed., *Peter Idley's Instructions to his Son* (Oxford, 1935).

De Windt, A. R., 'Local Government in a Small Town', *Albion*, 23 (1991).

Dickens, A. G., *Late Monasticism and the English Reformation* (1994).

Dickens, A. G., *The English Reformation* (1st edn, 1964; 2nd edn, 1989).

Dickens, A. G., 'The Shaping of Anticlericalism', in *Late Monasticism*.

Dickinson, J. G., *The Congress of Arras, 1435* (Oxford, 1955).

Dobson, R. B., 'Richard Bell, Prior of Durham (1464–78) and Bishop of Carlisle (1478–95), *Transactions of the Cumberland and Westmorland Antiquarian and Archaeological Society*, new ser., 65 (1965).

Dobson, R. B., 'The Foundation of Perpetual Chantries by the Citizens of Late-Medieval York', *Studies in Church History*, 4 (1967).

Dobson, R. B., 'Cathedral Chapters and Cathedral Cities', *NH*, 19 (1973).

Dobson, R. B., 'The Later Middle Ages', in Aylmer and Cant, *History of York Minster*.

Dobson, R. B., 'The Residentiary Canons of York in the Fifteenth Century', *JEH*, 30 (1979).

Dobson, R. B., *Durham Priory, 1400–1450* (Cambridge, 1983).

Dobson, R. B., ed., *Church, Politics and Patronage in the Fifteenth Century* (Gloucester, 1984).

Dobson, R. B., 'Richard III and the Church of York', in Griffiths and Sherborne, *Kings and Nobles*.

Dobson, R. B., *Preserving the Perishable: Contrasting Communities in Medieval England* (Cambridge, 1991).

Dobson, R. B., 'Politics and the Church in the Fifteenth-Century North', in Pollard, *Age of Richard III*.

Dobson, R. B., 'The Monks of Canterbury in the Later Middle Ages', in Collinson, *Canterbury Cathedral*.

Dobson, R. B. and Donaghey, S., *The History of Clementhorpe Nunnery* (1984).

Dobson, R. B. and Taylor, J., *Rymes of Robyn Hood: an Introduction to the English Outlaw* (2nd edn, Stroud, 1997).

Dockray, K., 'Patriotism, Pride and Paranoia: England and the English in the Fifteenth Century', *The Ricardian*, 110 (1990).

Doig, J., 'Political Propaganda and Royal Proclamation in Late Medieval England', *HR*, 71 (1998).

Dowling, M., *Humanism in the Age of Henry VIII* (1986).

Du Boulay, F. R. H., 'The Fifteenth Century' in Lawrence, *English Church*.

Du Boulay, F. R. H., *The Lordship of Canterbury* (1966).

Du Boulay, F. R. H., *An Age of Ambition: English Society in the late Middle Ages* (1970).

Du Boulay, F. R. H. and Barron, C. M., eds, *The Reign of Richard II: Essays in Honour of May McKisack* (1971).

Dudley, E., *The Tree of Commonwealth*, ed. Brodie, D. M. (Cambridge, 1948).

Duffy, E., *The Stripping of the Altars: Traditional Religion in England, 1400–1580* (New Haven, 1992).

Dunham, W. H., *Lord Hastings' Indentured Retainers, 1461–83* (Connecticut Academy of Arts and Sciences, 39, 1955).

Dunham, W. H. and Wood, C. T., 'The Right to Rule in England: Depositions and the King's Authority, 1327–1485', *American Historical Review*, 81 (1976).

Dyer, A. D., *Decline and Growth in English Towns, 1400–1640* (1991).

Dyer, C. C., 'A Redistribution of Incomes in Fifteenth-Century England', *PP*, 39 (1965).

Dyer, C. C., *Lords and Peasants in a Changing Society: The Estates of the Bishopric of Worcester, 680–1540* (Cambridge, 1980).

Dyer, C. C., 'Deserted Medieval Villages in the West Midlands', *EcHR*, 2nd ser., 35 (1982).

Dyer, C. C., *Standards of Living in the Later Middle Ages* (Cambridge, 1989).

Dyer, C. C., 'The English Medieval Rural Community and its Decline', *JBS*, 33 (1994).

Dyer, C., 'Taxation and Communities in Late Medieval England', in Britnell and Hatcher, *Progress and Problems*.

Dyer, C. C., 'Lost Villages of England, 1954–1998', introduction to Beresford, *The Lost Villages* (1998).

Eales, R. and Sullivan, D., eds, *The Political Context of Law* (1987).

Edwards, K., *V C H Wiltshire*, 3 (1957).

Eisenstein, E. L., *The Printing Press as an Agent of Change. Communications and Cultural Transformations in Early-Modern Europe* (2 vols, Cambridge, 1979).

Eisenstein, E. L., *The Printing Revolution in Early Modern Europe* (Cambridge, 1983).

Ellis, S., *Tudor Ireland: Crown, Community and the Conflict of Cultures* (1985).

Ellis, S., 'Crown, Community and Government in the English Territories, 1450–1575', *History*, 71 (1986).

Ellis, S. G., 'A Border Baron and the Tudor State: the Rise and Fall of Lord Dacre of the North', *HJ*, 35 (1992).

Ellis, S. G., *Tudor Frontiers and Noble Power: the Making of the British State* (Oxford, 1995).

Ellis, S., *Ireland in the Age of the Tudors, 1447–1603* (1998).

Ellis, S. G., 'Civilizing Northumberland: Representation of the Tudor State', *Journal of Historical Sociology*, 12 (1999).

Elton, G. R., *The Tudor Revolution in Government: Administrative Changes in the Reign of Henry VIII* (Cambridge, 1953).

Emden, A. B., *A Biographical Register of the University of Oxford*, 3 (Oxford, 1959).

Evelyn, C. D., ed., *Peter Idley's Instructions to his Son* (Oxford, 1935).

Febrvre, L. and Martin, H. J., *The Coming of the Book: the Impact of Printing, 1450–1800* (1976).

Finacune, R., *Miracles and Pilgrims: Popular Beliefs in Medieval England* (1977, 2nd edn, 1995).

Fleming, P. W., 'Charity, Faith and the Gentry of Kent, 1422–1529, in Pollard, *Property and Politics*.

Fleming, P. W., 'The Hautes and their Circle: Culture and the English Gentry', in Williams, *England in the Fifteenth Century*.

Fletcher, A., *Tudor Rebellions* (3rd edn, Harlow, 1983).

Ford, C. J., 'Piracy or Policy? The Crisis in the Channel, 1400–1403', *TRHS*, 5th ser., 29 (1979).

Forde, S. *et al.*, *Concepts of National Identity in the Middle Ages* (Leeds, Texts and Monographs, NS 14, 1995).

Fortescue, J., *The Governance of England*, ed. Plummer, C. (Oxford, 1885).

Fortescue, J., *On the Laws and Governance of England*, ed. Lockwood, S. J. (Cambridge, 1997).

Foss, P. J., *The Field of Redemore: the Battle of Bosworth, 1485* (Leeds, 1990).

Fowler, K. A., ed., *The Hundred Years' War* (1971).

Fox, A. and Guy, J. A., *Reasssessing the Henrician Age: Humanism, Politics and Reform, 1500–1550* (Oxford, 1986).

Fraser, C. M., 'Some Durham Documents Relating to the Hilary Parliament of 1404', *BIHR*, 34 (1961).

French, K. L. *et al.*, eds, *The Parish in English Life, 1400–1600* (Manchester, 1997).

French, K. L., 'Parochial Fund-Raising in Late-Medieval Somerset', in French, *Parish in English Life*.

Fryde, E. B., *Peasants and Landlords in Later Medieval England* (Stroud, 1996).

Furnivall, F. J., ed., *Early English Meals and Manners* (EETS, 32, 1814).

Gairdner, J., ed., *Letters and Papers Illustrative of the Reigns of Richard III and Henry VII*, 2 vols, (RS, 1861–3).

Gairdner, J., ed., *The Historical Collections of a Citizen of London* (Camden Society, 2nd ser., xvii, 1876).

Gairdner, J. A., ed., *The Paston Letters, 1422–1509* (6 vols, 1904).

Galbraith, V. H., ed., *The St Albans Chronicle* (Oxford, 1937).

Gascoigne, T., *Loci e Libro Veritatum*, ed. Rogers, J. E. T. (Oxford, 1881).

Gasquet, E. A., *Collectanea Anglo-Premonstratensia* (Camden, 3rd ser., vi, i, 1904).

Genet, J. P., 'English Nationalism: Thomas Polton at the Council of Constance', *Nottingham Medieval Studies*, 28 (1984).

Gill, L., *Richard III and Buckingham's Rebellion* (Stroud, 1999).

Gillingham, J. B., 'Crisis or Continuity? The Structure of Royal Authority in England, 1369–1422', in Schneider's *Das Spätmittelalterliche Königtum*.

Gillingham, J. B., ed., *Richard III: a Medieval Kingship* (1993).

Given-Wilson, C., *The Royal Household and the King's Affinity: Service, Politics and Finance in England, 1360–1413* (New Haven, 1986).

Given-Wilson, C., 'The King and the Gentry in Fourteenth-Century England', *TRHS*, 5th ser., 37 (1987).

Given-Wilson, C., *The English Nobility in the Later Middle Ages* (1987).

Given-Wilson, C., *Chronicles of the Revolution 1397–1400* (Manchester, 1993).

Given-Wilson, C., 'Richard II, Edward II and the Lancastrian Inheritance', *EHR*, 109 (1994).

Given-Wilson, C., ed., *The Chronicle of Adam Usk, 1377–1421* (Oxford, 1997).

Goheen, R., 'Peasant Politics? Village Community and the Crown in Fifteenth-Century England', *AHR*, 96 (1991).

Goldberg, P. J. P., 'Mortality and Economic Decline in the Diocese of York, 1390–1514', *NH*, 24 (1988).

Goldberg, P. J. P., *Women, Work and Life Cycle in a Medieval Economy: Women and Work in York and Yorkshire, c.1300–1520* (Oxford, 1992).

Goldberg, P. J. P., ed., *Woman is a Worthy Wight: Women in English Society, c.1200–1500* (Stroud,1992).

Goldberg, P. J. P., 'Women', in Horrox, *Fifteenth-Century Attitudes.*

Goldberg, P. J. P., *Woman in England, c.1275–1525* (Manchester, 1995).

Goldthorpe, L. M., 'The Franciscans and Dominicans in Yorkshire', *YAJ*, 32 (1936).

Goodman, A. E., *The Loyal Conspiracy: The Lords Appellants under Richard II* (1971).

Goodman, A. E., 'The Piety of John Brunham's Daughter' in, Baker, *Medieval Women.*

Goodman, A. E., 'Responses to Requests in Yorkshire for Military Service under Henry V', *NH*, 17 (1981).

Goodman, A. E., 'The Anglo-Scottish Marches in the Fifteenth Century: a Frontier Society', in Mason, *Scotland and England.*

Goodman, A. E., *The New Monarchy: England 1471–1534* (Oxford, 1988).

Goodman, A. E., 'Religion and Warfare in the Anglo-Scottish Marches', in Bartlett and Mckay, *Medieval Frontier Societies.*

Goodman, A. E., *John of Gaunt: the Exercise of Princely Power in Fourteenth-Century Europe* (Longman, 1992).

Goodman, A. E. and Gillespie, J., eds, *Richard II: the Art of Kingship* (Oxford, 1999).

Gransden, A., *Historical Writing in England*, vol. II, *c.1307 to the Early Sixteenth Century* (1982).

Grant, A., 'Otterburn from the Scottish Point of View', in Tuck and Goodman, *War and Border Societies.*

Grant, A., 'Richard III and Scotland', in Pollard, *North of England.*

Grant, A., 'Foreign Affairs under Richard III', in Gillingham, *Medieval Kingship.*

Gray, H. L., 'Incomes from Land in England in 1436', *EHR*, 49 (1934).

Green, J. R., *A Short History of the English People*, 3rd edn (1916).

Gribbin, J. A., 'The Premonstratensian Order in Late Medieval England' (University of Cambridge, PhD thesis, 1998).

Griffiths, R. A., 'Local Rivalries and National Politics: the Percies, the Nevilles and the Duke of Exeter, 1452–55', *Speculum*, 43 (1968).

Griffiths, R. A., 'The Trial of Eleanor Cobham', *BJRL*, 51 (1968–9).

Griffiths, R. A., 'Wales and the Marches in the Fifteenth Century', in Chrimes, *Fifteenth-Century England*.

Griffiths, R. A., 'Duke Richard of York's Intentions in 1450 and the Origins of the Wars of the Roses', *JMH*, 1 (1975).

Griffiths, R. A., 'The Sense of Dynasty in the Reign of Henry VI' in Ross, *Patronage, Pedigree and Power*.

Griffiths, R. A., 'Public and Private Bureaucracies in England and Wales in the Fifteenth Century', *TRHS*, 5th ser., 30 (1980).

Griffiths, R. A., ed., *Patronage, the Crown and the Provinces in Later Medieval England* (Gloucester, 1981).

Griffiths, R. A., *The Reign of Henry VI: the Exercise of Royal Authority, 1422–1461* (1981).

Griffiths, R. A., 'The English Realm and Dominions and the King's Subjects in the Later Middles Ages', in Rowe, *Aspects of Government*.

Griffiths, R. A., *King and Country: England and Wales in the Fifteenth Century* (1991).

Griffiths, R. A., 'Gruffyd ap Nicholas and the Fall of the House of Lancaster', repr in Griffiths, *King and Country*.

Griffiths, R. A., 'The King's Court during the Wars of the Roses', in Asch and Birke, *Princes, Patronage and the Nobility*.

Griffiths, R. A., *Sir Rhys ap Thomas and his Family: a Study in the Wars of the Roses and Early Tudor Politics* (Cardiff, 1993).

Griffiths, R. A., *Conquerors and Conquered in Medieval Wales* (Stroud, 1994).

Griffiths, R. A., 'The Provinces and the Dominions in the Age of the Wars of the Roses', in Michalove and Reeves, eds, *Estrangement and Enterprise*.

Griffiths, R. A. and Sherborne, J. W., eds, *Kings and Nobles in the Later Middle Ages* (Gloucester, 1986).

Griffiths, R. A. and Thomas, R. H., *The Making of the Tudor Dynasty* (Gloucester, 1985).

Gross, A., 'Langland's Rats: a Moralist's View of Parliament', *Parliamentary History* 9: 2 (1990).

Gross, A., 'K. B. McFarlane and the Determinists: the Fallibilities of the English Kings, c.1399–c.1520', in Britnell and Pollard, *McFarlane Legacy* (1995).

Gross, A., *The Dissolution of the Lancastrian Kingship* (Stamford, 1996).

Grummitt, D., 'The Financial Administration of Calais during the Reign of Henry IV', *EHR*, 113 (1998).

Grummitt, D., 'Henry VII, Chamber Finance and the New Monarchy', *HR*, 72 (1999).

Gunn, S. J., 'The French Wars of Henry VIII', in Black, ed., *The Origins of War*.

Gunn, S. J., 'Chivalry and the Politics of Early Tudor England', in Anglo, ed., *Chivalry in the Renaissance*.

Gunn, S. J., 'The Accession of Henry VIII', *HR*, 64 (1991).

Gunn, S. J., 'The Courtiers of Henry VII', *EHR*, 108 (1993).

Gunn, S. J., *Early Tudor Government, 1485–1558* (1995).

Gunn, S. J., 'Sir Thomas Lovell (c.1449–1524): a New Man in a New Monarchy?', in Watts, *End of the Middle Ages?*

Gunn, S. J. and Lynley, P. G., eds, *Cardinal Wolsey: Church, State and Art* (Cambridge, 1991).

Guth, D. J., 'Richard III, Henry VII and the City: London Politics and the "Dun Cowe"', in Griffiths and Sherborne, *Kings and Nobles.*

Guth, D. J., 'Climbing the Civil Service Pole during Civil War: Sir Reynold Bray (c.1440–1503)', in Michalove and Reeves, *Estrangement, Enterprise and Education.*

Guy, J. A., *The Cardinal's Court: the Impact of Thomas Wolsey in Star Chamber* (Hassocks, 1977).

Guy, J. A., 'The Development of Equitable Jurisdictions, 1450–1550', in Ives and Manchester, *Legal Profession.*

Guy, J. A. and Beales, H. G., eds, *Law and Social Change in British History* (1984).

Gwynn, P., *The King's Cardinal: the Rise and Fall of Thomas Wolsey* (1990).

Habberjam, M., 'Harrington v Saville: a Fifteenth-Century Divorce Case', *The Ricardian*, 109 (1988).

Haigh, C., 'Anti-Clericalism and the English Reformation', *History*, 68 (1983).

Haigh, C., *The English Reformations: Religion, Politics and Society under the Tudors* (Oxford, 1993).

Hall, E., *The Union of the Two Illustre and Noble Houses of Lancastre and Yorke* (Merston, 1970).

Halliwell, J. O., ed., *Letters of the Kings of England*, vol. 1 (1848).

Hamilton Thompson, A., *The English Clergy and their Organisation in the Later Middle Ages* (Oxford, 1947).

Hamilton, J. S. and Bradley, P. J., eds, *Documenting the Past* (Woodbridge, 1989).

Hammond, P. W., ed., *Richard III: Lordship, Loyalty and Law* (Gloucester, 1986).

Hammond, P. W., *The Battles of Barnet and Tewkesbury* (Gloucester, 1990).

Hanawalt, B., ed., *Chaucer's England: Literature in Historical Context* (Medieval Studies at Minnesota, 4, 1992).

Hanawalt, B., *Growing up in Medieval London* (1993).

Hanbury, H. G., 'The Legislation of Richard III', *American Journal of Legal History*, 6 (1962).

Hanham, A., ed., *The Cely Letters, 1472–88* (EETS, 272, 1975).

Hanham, A., *Richard III and his Early Historians* (Oxford, 1975).

Harding, A., *The Law Courts of Medieval England* (1973).

Hare, J. N., 'The Lords and their Tenants: Conflict and Stability in Fifteenth-Century Wiltshire', in Stapleton, *Conflict and Community.*

Harper-Bill, C., 'Dean Colet's Convocation Sermon and the Pre-Reformation Church in England', *History*, 73 (1988).

Harper-Bill, C., *The Pre-Reformation Church in England, 1400–1530* (1989).

Harper-Bill, C., ed., *Religious Belief and Ecclesiastical Careers in Late Medieval England* (Woodbridge, 1991).

Harper-Bill, 'English Religion after the Black Death', in Ormrod and Lindley, *The Black Death.*

Harper-Bill, C. and Harvey, R., eds, *Medieval Knighthood IV: Papers from the 5th Strawberry Hill Conference* (Woodbridge, 1992).

Harrison, C. J., 'The Petition of Edmund Dudley', *EHR*, 87 (1972).

Harriss, G. L., 'The Struggle for Calais', *EHR*, 75 (1960).

Harriss, G. L., ed., *Henry V: the Practice of Kingship* (Oxford, 1985).

Harriss, G. L., 'Introduction', in Harriss, *Henry V.*

Harriss, G. L., 'The King and his Magnates', in Harriss, *Henry V.*

Harriss, G. L., 'The Management of Parliament', in Harriss *Henry V.*

Harriss, G. L., 'Financial Policy', in Harriss, *Henry V.*

Harriss, G. L., *Cardinal Beaufort: a Study of Lancastrian Ascendancy and Decline* (Oxford, 1988).

Harriss, G. L., 'Marmaduke Lumley and the Exchequer Crisis of 1446–9', in Rowe, *Aspects.*

Harriss, G. L., 'Political Society and the Growth of Government in Late-Medieval England', *Past and Present*, 138 (1993).

Harriss, G. L., 'The King and his Subjects', in Horrox, *Fifteenth-Century Attitudes.*

Harriss, G. L., *King, Parliament and Public Finance in Medieval England* (Oxford, 1995).

Harriss, G. L., 'The Dimensions of Politics', Britnell and Pollard, *McFarlane Legacy.*

Harriss, G. L. and M. A., eds, 'John Benet's Chronicle for the Years 1400–62', *Camden Miscellany xxiv* (Camden, 4th ser., 9, 1972).

Harthan, J., *Books of Hours* (1977).

Harvey, B. F., 'Introduction: the "Crisis" of the Early Fourteenth Century', in Campbell, *Before the Black Death.*

Harvey, B. F., *Living and Dying in England, 1100–1540: The Monastic Experience* (Oxford, 1993).

Harvey, I. M. W., *Cade's Rebellion of 1450* (Oxford, 1991).

Harvey, I. M. W., 'Was there Popular Politics in Fifteenth-Century England?', in Britnell and Pollard, *McFarlane Legacy* (1995).

Harvey, M., *England, Rome and the Papacy, 1417–64* (Manchester, 1993).

Hastings, M., *The Court of Common Pleas in Fifteenth Century England* (Ithaca, 1947).

Hatcher, J. A., *Rural Economy and Society in the Duchy of Cornwall, 1300–1500* (Cambridge, 1970).

Hatcher, J. A., *Plague, Population and the English Economy, 1348–1530* (1977).

Hatcher, J. A., 'Mortality in the Fifteeenth Century: Some New Evidence', *EcHR*, 2nd ser., 39 (1986).

Hatcher, J. A., 'England after the Black Death', *PP*, 144 (1994).

Hatcher, J. A., 'The Great Slump of the Mid-Fifteenth Century', in Britnell and Hatcher, *Progress and Problems.*

Hay, D., 'England and the Humanities in the Fifteenth Century', in Oberman and Brady, *Itinerarium Italicum.*

Hayes, R. C. E., '"Ancient Indictments" for the North of England, 1461–1509', in Pollard, *North of England.*

Hearder, H. and Loyn, H. R., eds, *British Government and Administration* (Cardiff, 1974).

Heath, P., *English Parish Clergy on the Eve of the Reformation* (1969).

Heath P, 'Urban Piety in the Later Middle Ages: the Evidence of Hull Wills', in Dobson, *Church, Politics and Patronage*.

Heath, P., *Church and Realm, 1272–1461* (1988).

Heath, P., 'Between Reform and Reformation: the English Church in the Fourteenth and Fifteenth Centuries', *JEH*, 41 (1990).

Helmholz, R. H., *Marriage Litigation in Medieval England* (Cambridge, 1974).

Helmholz, R. H., 'The Sons of Edward IV: a Canonical Assessment of the Claim that they were Illegitimate', in Hammond, *Lordship, Loyalty and Law*.

Herlihy, D., *The Black Death and the Transformation of the West* (Cambridge, Mass., 1997).

Hexter, J. H., *Reappraisals in History* (1961).

Hexter, J. H., 'The Myth of the Middle Class', in *Reappraisals in History*.

Hicks, M. A., 'The Case of Sir Thomas Cook', *EHR*, 90 (1978).

Hicks, M. A., 'Dynastic Change and Northern Society: the Career of the Fourth Earl of Northumberland, 1470–89', *Northern History*, 14 (1978).

Hicks, M. A., 'Descent, Partition and Inheritance: the Warwick Inheritance', *BIHR*, 52 (1979).

Hicks, M. A., 'The Changing Role of the Wydevilles in Yorkist Politics to 1483', in Ross, *Patronage, Politics and Power*.

Hicks, M. A., *False, Fleeting, Perjur'd Clarence* (Gloucester, 1980).

Hicks, M. A., 'Edward IV, the Duke of Somerset and Lancastrian Loyalism in the North', *Northern History*, 20 (1984).

Hicks, M. A., 'The Yorkshire Rebellion of 1489 Reconsidered', *NH*, 22 (1986).

Hicks, M. A., 'Chantries, Obits and Almshouses: the Hungerford Foundations, 1325–1478', in Barron and Harper-Bill, *Church in Pre-Reformation Society*.

Hicks, M. A., *Richard III as Duke of Gloucester: a Study in Character* (Borthwick Paper, 70, 1986).

Hicks, M. A., 'Piety of Margaret Hungerford (d.1478)', *JEH*, 28 (1987).

Hicks, M. A., ed., *Profit, Piety and the Professions in Later Medieval England* (Gloucester, 1990).

Hicks, M. A., 'The 1468 Statute of Livery', *HR*, 64 (1991).

Hicks, M. A., *Richard III: the Man Behind the Myth* (1991).

Hicks, M. A., *Richard III and His Rivals* (1991).

Hicks, M. A., 'Bastard Feudalism: Society and Politics in Fifteenth-Century England', in *Richard III and His Rivals*.

Hicks, M. A., 'Lord Hastings' Indentured Retainers?', in *Richard III and his Rivals*.

Hicks, M. A., 'Idealism in Late Medieval English Politics', in *Richard III and his Rivals*.

Hicks, M. A., 'The 1468 Statute of Livery', *HR*, lxi (1991).

Hicks, M. A., *Bastard Feudalism* (1995).

Hicks, M. A., 'The Sources', in Pollard, *Wars of the Roses*.

Hicks, M. A., *Warwick the Kingmaker* (Oxford, 1998).

Hicks, M. A., 'Between Majorities: the "Beauchamp Interregnum", 1439–49', *HR*, 72 (1999).

Hicks, M. A., 'Cement or Solvent? Kinship and Politics in Late Medieval England: the Case of the Nevilles', *History*, 83 (1998).

Hilton, R. H., *The Decline of Serfdom in Medieval England* (1969).

Hilton, R. H., *Bond Men Made Free: Medieval Peasant Movements and the English Rising of 1381* (Oxford, 1973).

Hilton, R. H., *The English Peasantry in the Later Middle Ages* (Oxford, 1975).

Hilton, R. H., *The Transition from Feudalism to Capitalism* (1976).

Hilton, R. H., 'Introduction', in *Transition*.

Hilton, R. H., *Class, Conflict and the Crisis of Feudalism*, 2nd edn (1990).

Hirsh, J. C., *The Revelation of Margery Kempe: Paramystical Practices in Late Medieval England* (Leiden, 1989).

Holmes, P. J., 'The Great Council in the Reign of Henry VII', *EHR*, 101 (1986).

Holt, J. C., *Robin Hood* (1982 and 1989).

Holt, R. and Rosser, G., eds, *The Medieval Town: a Reader in English Urban History, 1200–1540* (1990).

Hope, A., 'The Lady and the Bailiff: Lollardy and the Gentry in Yorkist and Early Tudor England', in Aston and Richmond, *Lollardy and the Gentry*.

Horrox, R. E., 'Financial Memoranda of the Reign of Edward V', in *Camden Miscellany*, 24 (Camden, 4th ser., 9, 1972).

Horrox, R. E., ed., *Richard III and the North* (Hull, 1986).

Horrox, R. E., *Richard III: a Study of Service* (Cambridge, 1989).

Horrox, R. E., 'Caterpillars of the Commonwealth: Courtiers in Late Medieval England', in Archer and Walker, *Rulers and Ruled*.

Horrox, R. E., 'The Urban Gentry in the Fifteenth Century', in Thomson, *Towns and Townspeople*.

Horrox, R., ed., *Fifteenth-Century Attitudes* (Cambridge, 1994).

Horrox, R., 'Service', in Horrox, *Fifteenth-Century Attitudes*.

Horrox, R., *The Black Death* (Manchester, 1994).

Horrox, R., 'Personalities and Politics', in Pollard, *Wars of the Roses*.

Horrox, R. E. and Hammond, P. W., eds, *British Museum Harleian Manuscript 433*, 4 vols (1979–83).

Hoyle, R., 'Resistance and Manipulation in Early Tudor Lay Subsidies: Some Evidence from the North', *Archives*, 90 (1993).

Hoyle, R. W., 'The Earl, the Archbishop and the Council: the Affray at Fulford, May 1504', in Archer and Walker, *Rulers and Ruled*.

Hudson, A., ed., *Selections from English Wycliffite Writings* (Cambridge, 1978).

Hudson, A., *Lollards and their Books* (1985).

Hudson, A., *The Premature Reformation: Wycliffite Texts and Lollard History* (Oxford, 1988).

Hughes, J., *Pastors and Visionaries: Religion and Secular Life in Late Medieval Yorkshire* (Woodbridge, 1988).

Hughes, J., 'Stephen Scrope and the Circle of Sir John Fastolf: Intellectual and Moral Outlooks', in Harper-Bill and Harvey, *Medieval Knighthood IV*.

Hughes, J., 'Northern Religious Life and Richard III', in Pollard, *North of England*.

Hughes, J., *The Religious Life of Richard III* (Stroud, 1997).

Hutton, R., *The Rise and Fall of Merry England. The Ritual Year, 1400–1700* (Oxford, 1994).

Ives, E. W., 'Andrew Dymmock and the Papers of Anthony, Earl Rivers, 1482–3', *BIHR*, 41 (1968).

Ives, E. W., 'The Common Lawyers', in Clough, *Profession, Vocation and Culture.*

Ives, E. W., *The Common Lawyers of Pre-Reformation England: Thomas Kebell, a Case Study* (Cambridge, 1983).

Ives, E. W. and Manchester, A. H., eds, *Law, Litigants and the Legal Profession* (1983).

Jacob, E. F., *The Fifteenth Century* (Oxford, 1971).

James, M. E., 'Ritual, Drama and Social Body in the Late-Medieval English Town', *PP*, 98 (1983).

Jardine, L., *Erasmus* (Princeton, 1993).

Jardine, L., *Worldly Goods* (1996).

Jewell, H. M., 'English Bishops and Educational Benefactors in the Later Fifteenth Century', in Dobson, *Church, Politics and Patronage.*

Jewell, H. M., *The North/South Divide: The Origins of Northern Consciousness in England* (Manchester, 1994).

John, T., 'Sir Thomas Erpingham, East Anglian Society and the Dynastic Revolution of 1399', *Norfolk Archaeology*, 35 (1973).

Johnson, P. A., *Duke Richard of York, 1411–1460* (Oxford, 1988).

Johnston, A. F., 'Traders and Playmakers: English Guildsmen and the Low Countries', in Barron and Saul, *England and the Low Countries.*

Johnston, D. B., 'Richard II's Departure from Ireland, July 1399', *EHR*, 98 (1983).

Jones, M. C. E., ed., *Gentry and Lesser Nobility in Later Medieval Europe* (Gloucester, 1986).

Jones, M. C. E. and Walker, S., 'Private Indentures for Life Service in Peace and War', in *Camden Miscellany, XXXII* (Camden, 5th ser., 3, 1994).

Jones, M. K., 'John Beaufort, Duke of Somerset and the French Expedition of 1443', in Griffiths, *Patronage, Crown and Provinces.*

Jones, M. K., 'Richard III and the Stanleys', in Horrox, ed., *Richard III and the North.*

Jones, M. K., 'Sir William Stanley of Holt: Politics and Family Allegiance in the Late Fifteenth Century', *Welsh History Review*, 14 (1988).

Jones, M. K., 'Somerset, York and the Wars of the Roses', *EHR*, 104 (1989).

Jones, M. K., 'War on the Frontier: the Lancastrian Land Settlement in Eastern Normandy, 1435–50', *Nottingham Medieval Studies*, 33 (1989).

Jones, M. K., 'Richard III as a Soldier', in Gillingham, ed., *Medieval Kingship.*

Jones, M. K., 'Edward IV, the Earl of Warwick, and the Yorkist Claim to the Throne', *HR*, 70 (1997).

Jones, M. K., 'Richard III and Lady Margaret Beaufort: a Reassessment', in Hammond *Loyalty, Lordship and Law.*

Jones, M. K. and Underwood, M. G., *The King's Mother: Lady Margaret Beaufort, Countess of Richmond and Derby* (Cambridge, 1992).

Jones, P. M., 'Information and Science' in, Horrox, ed., *Fifteenth-Century Attitudes*.

Jones, R. H., *The Royal Policy of Richard II: Absolutism in the Later Middle Ages* (Oxford, 1968).

Kaeuper, R. W., *War, Justice and Public Order: England and France in the Later Middle Ages* (Oxford, 1988).

Kaufman, P. I., 'Henry VII and Sanctuary', *Church History* (1984).

Keen, M. H., *England in the Later Middle Ages* (1977).

Keen, M. H., *Chivalry* (Newhaven, 1984).

Keen, M. H., 'Diplomacy', in Harriss, *Henry V*.

Keen, M. H. and Daniel, M. J., 'English Diplomacy and the Sack of Fougères', *History*, 59 (1974).

Kekewich, M., 'The Attainder of the Yorkists in 1459', *HR*, 55 (1982).

Kekewich, M. *et al.*, *The Politics of Fifteenth-Century England: John Vale's Book* (Richard III and Yorkist History Trust, Stroud, 1995).

Kekewich, M., 'Sir John Fortescue's *Governance of England*', in Kekewich, ed., *John Vale's Book*.

Kendall, P. M., *Warwick the Kingmaker* (1957).

Kermode, J. I., 'Money and Credit in the Fifteenth Century: Some Lessons from Yorkshire', *Business History Review*, 65 (1991).

Kermode, J. I., *Medieval Merchants: York, Beverley and Hull in the Later Middle Ages* (Cambridge, 1998).

Kettle, A. J. and Johnson, D., 'The Cathedral of Lincoln', *VCH Stafford*, 3 (1970).

Kettle, A. J., 'City and Close: Lichfield in the Century before the Reformation', in Barron and Harper-Bill, *Church in Pre-Reformation Society*.

Kieckhefer, R., *Magic in the Middle Ages* (Cambridge, 1989).

Kingsford, C. L., *Prejudice and Promise in Fifteenth-Century England* (Oxford, 1925).

Kingsford, C. L., ed., *Stonor Letters and Papers of the Fifteenth Century*, 2 vols (Camden, 3rd ser., 29 and 30, 1919). Reprinted with an introduction by Carpenter, M. C. (Cambridge, 1990).

Kirby, J. L., 'Calais sous les Anglais, 1399–1413', *Revue de Nord*, 37 (1955).

Kirby, J. L., 'Council and Councillors of Henry IV', *TRHS*, 5th ser., 14 (1964).

Kirby, J. L., *Henry IV of England* (Constable, 1970).

Kirby, J. W., ed., *The Plumpton Letters and Papers* (Camden, 5th ser., 8, 1996).

Knowles, D., *The Religious Orders in England*, vol. 2 (Cambridge, 1955) and vol. 3 (Cambridge, 1959).

Kreider, A., *English Chantries: the Road to Dissolution* (Cambridge, Mass., 1979).

Kumin, B., *The Shaping of a Community: the Rise and Reformation of the English Parish* (Aldershot, 1996).

Labarge, M. W., *Gascony: England's First Colony, 1204–1453* (1980).

Lamb, H. H., *Climate, History and the Modern World* (1982).

Lander, J. R., 'Edward IV: the modern legend and a revision', *History*, 41 (1956).

Lander, J. R., 'The Yorkist Council and Administration 1461–85', *EHR*, 73 (1958).

Lander, J. R., 'Council, Administration and Councillors, 1461–85', *BIHR*, 32 (1959).

Lander, J. R., 'Henry VI and the Duke of York's Second Protectorate, 1455–6', *BJRL* 43 (1960–1).

Lander, J. R., 'Attainder and Forfeiture, 1453–1509', *Historical Journal*, 4 (1961).

Lander, J. R., 'Marriage and Politics in the Fifteenth Century', *BIHR*, 36 (1963).

Lander, J. R., 'The Treason and Death of the Duke of Clarence' *Canadian Journal of History*, 2 (1967).

Lander, J. R., *Conflict and Stability in Fifteenth-Century England* (1969, 1974, 1977).

Lander, J. R., 'Bonds, Coercion and Fear: Henry VII and the Peerage', in Rowe, J. G. and Stockdale, W. H., eds, *Florilegium Historiale: Essays Presented to Wallace K. Ferguson* (Toronto, 1971).

Lander, J. R., 'The Hundred Years' War and Edward IV's 1475 Campaign in France', in Slavin, A. J., ed., *Tudor Men and Institutions: Studies in English Law and Constitution* (Louisiana, 1972).

Lander, J. R., *Crown and Nobility 1450–1509* (1976).

Lander, J. R., *The Limitations of English Monarchy in the Later Middle Ages* (Toronto, 1989).

Lander, J. R., *English Justices of the Peace, 1461–1509* (Gloucester, 1989).

Lawrence, C. H., ed., *The English Church and the Papacy in the Middle Ages* (1965).

Leader, D. R., *A History of the University of Cambridge, I: The University to 1546* (Cambridge, 1988).

Leff, G., *Heresy in the Later Middle Ages* (2 vols, Manchester, 1967).

Lepine, D., *A Brotherhood of Canons serving God: English Secular Cathedrals in the Later Middles Ages* (Woodbridge, 1995).

Leyser, H. A., *Medieval Women: a Social History of Women in England, 450–1500* (1995).

Linnell, C. L. S., 'The Commonplace Book of Robert Reynes of Acle', *Norfolk Archaeology*, 32 (1958–61).

Lloyd, T. H., *England and the German Hanse, 1157–1611* (Cambridge, 1991).

Lomas, R. A., *North-East England in the Middle Ages* (Edinburgh, 1992).

Lomas, R. A., *County of Conflict: Northumberland from Conquest to Civil War* (East Linton, 1996).

Lovatt, R., 'The "Imitation of Christ" in Late Medieval England', *TRHS*, 5th ser. 18 (1968).

Lovatt, R., 'A Collector of Apocryphal Anecdotes: John Blacman Revisited', in Pollard, *Property and Politics* (1984).

Lowe, D. E., 'Patronage and Politics: Edward IV, the Wydvils, and the Council of the Prince of Wales, 1471–83', *Bulletin of the Board of Celtic Studies*, 29 (1980–2).

Luckett, D., 'Crown Office and Licensed Retinues in the Reign of Henry VII', in Archer and Walker, *Rulers and Ruled*.

Luckett, D., 'Crown Patronage and Political Morality in Early Tudor England: the Case of Giles, Lord Daubeney', *EHR*, 110 (1995).

Luckett, D., 'The Thames Valley Conspiracies against Henry VII', *HR*, 68 (1995).

Luckett, D., 'Patronage, Violence and Revolt in the Reign of Henry VII', in Archer, ed., *Crown, Government and People*.

Lutton, R., 'Connections between Lollards, Townsfolk and Gentry in Tenterden in the Late Fifteenth and Early Sixteenth Centuries', in Aston and Richmond, *Lollardy and the Gentry.*

Lydgate's Troy Book, A.D. 1412–20, ed Bergen, H. (EETS, 1906).

Lydon, J. F., *The Lordship of Ireland in the Middle Ages* (Dublin, 1972).

Lydon, J. F., 'Nation and Race in Medieval Ireland', in Forde, *Concepts of National Identity.*

Lytton, E. L. B., *The Last of the Barons* (1843).

McConica, J., *English Humanists and Reformation Politics* (Oxford, 1965).

McConica, J., ed., *The History of the University of Oxford, III, The Collegiate University* (Oxford, 1986).

McCree, B. R., 'Religious Guilds and Regulation of Behaviour in Late-Medieval Towns', in Richmond and Rosenthal, *People, Politics and Community.*

McCulloch, D., *Thomas Cranmer* (1996).

Macdougall, N., *James III* (Edinburgh, 1982).

Macdougall, N., *James IV* (Edinburgh, 1989).

McFarlane, A., *The Rise of English Individualism* (Oxford, 1978).

McFarlane, K. B., *John Wycliffe and the Beginnings of English Nonconformity* (1952).

McFarlane, K. B., *Lancastrian Kings and Lollard Knights* (Oxford, 1972).

McFarlane, K. B., *The Nobility of Later Medieval England* (Oxford, 1973).

McGladdery, C., *James II* (Edinburgh, 1990).

McHardy, A., 'Clerical Taxation in Fifteenth-century England', in Dobson, *Church, Politics and Patronage.*

McHardy, A. K., '*De Heretico Comburendo*, 1401', in Aston and Richmond, *Lollardy and the Gentry.*

McIntosh, M. K., 'Local Change and Community Control in England, 1465–1500', *Huntingdon Library Quarterly*, 49 (1986).

McIntosh, M. K., *Controlling Misbehaviour in England, 1370–1600* (Cambridge, 1998).

McKendick, S., 'Tapestries from the Low Countries in England during the Fifteenth Century' in Barron and Saul, *England and the Low Countries.*

McKenna, J. W., 'The Coronation Oil of the Yorkist Kings', *EHR*, 82 (1967).

McKenna, J. W., 'Piety and Propaganda: the Cult of Henry VI', in Rowland, *Chaucer and Middle English Studies.*

McKenna, J. W., 'The Myth of Parliamentary Sovereignty in Late-Medieval England', *EHR*, 94 (1979).

McKie, J. D., *The Earlier Tudors* (Oxford, 1952).

McNiven, P., 'The Cheshire Rising of 1400', *BJRL*, 52 (1969–70).

McNiven, P., 'The Betrayal of Archbishop Scrope', *BJRL*, 54 (1972).

McNiven, P., 'The Scottish Policy of the Percies and the Strategy of the Rebellion of 1403', *BJRL*, 62 (1980).

McNiven, P., 'Prince Henry and the English Crisis of 1412', *History*, 65 (1980).

McNiven, P., 'Legitimacy and Consent: Henry IV and the Lancastrian Title, 1399–1406', *Medieval Studies*, 8 (1982).

McNiven, P., 'The Problem of Henry IV's Health', *EHR*, 100 (1985).

McNiven, P., *Heresy and Politics in the Reign of Henry IV: the Burning of John Badby* (Woodbridge, 1987).

McNiven, P., 'Rebellion, Sedition and the Legend of Richard II's Survival in the Reigns of Henry IV and Henry V', *BJRL*, 76 (1994).

McSheffrey, S., *Gender and Heresy: Women and Men in Lollard Communities, 1420–1530* (Philadelphia, 1995).

Macrae-Spencer, A., 'Putting Women in their Place', *The Ricardian*, 128 (1995).

Maddern, P., *Violence and Social Order in East Anglia, 1422–1442* (Oxford, 1992).

Maddern, P., 'Friends of the Dead', in Archer and Walker, *Rulers and Ruled.*

Maddicott, J. R., 'The County Community and the Making of Public Opinion in Fourteenth-Century England', *TRHS*, 5th ser., 28 (1978).

Maddicott, J. R., 'Parliament and the Constituencies', in Davies and Denton, eds, *English Parliament.*

Mancini, Dominic, *The Usurpation of Richard III*, ed. Armstrong, C. A. J., 2nd edn (Oxford, 1969).

Martin, J. E., *Feudalism to Capitalism: Peasant and Landlord in English Agrarian Development* (1983).

Mason, R. A., ed., *Scotland and England, 1286–1815* (Edinburgh, 1987).

Massey, R., 'The Land Settlement in Lancastrian Normandy', in Pollard, *Property and Politics.*

Mate, M. E., 'The Economic and Social Roots of Medieval Popular Rebellion: Sussex in 1450–51', *EcHR*, 45 (1992).

Mate, M. E., *Daughters, Wives and Widows after the Black Death: Women in Sussex, 1350–1535* (Woodbridge, 1998).

Mayer, T. F., *Thomas Starkey and the Commonweal: Humanist Politics and Religion in the Reign of Henry VIII* (Cambridge, 1989).

Mayhew, M., 'Population, Money Supply and the Velocity of Circulation, 1300–1770', *EcHR*, 48 (1995).

Meech, S. B. and Allen, H. E., eds, *The Booke of Marjory Kempe* (EETS, 1940).

Mercer, M., 'Lancastrian Loyalism in the South-West: the Case of the Beauforts', *SH*, 19, (1997).

Michalove, S. D., ed., *Estrangement, Enterprise and Education in Fifteenth Century England* (Stroud, 1998).

Miller, E., ed., *The Agrarian History of England and Wales, III: 1348–1500* (Cambridge, 1991).

Milner, J. D., 'The English Enterprise in France, 1412–13', in Clayton, ed., *Trade, Devotion and Governance.*

Monstrelet, E., *La chronique d'Enguerran de Monstrelet*, ed., Douet-d'Arcq, L. (Paris, 1857–62).

Moran, J. A., 'Clerical Recruitment in the Diocese of York, 1340–1530', *JEH*, 34 (1983).

Moran, J. A., *The Growth of English Schooling, 1340–1558* (Princeton, 1985).

More, Thomas, *The History of King Richard III*, ed. Sylvester, R. S., *Yale Edition of the Complete Works of St Thomas More*, vol. 2 (New Haven, 1963).

More, Thomas, *Utopia*, ed. Surtz, E., *Yale Edition of the Complete Works of St Thomas More*, vol. 4 (New Haven, 1965).

More, Thomas, *Utopia*, ed. Surtz, E. (New Haven, 1964).

More, Thomas, *The History of King Richard III*, ed., Sylvester, R. S., (New Haven, 1976).

Moreton, C., *The Townshends and their World* (Oxford, 1992).

Morgan, D. A. L., 'The King's Affinity in the Polity of Yorkist England', *TRHS*, 5th ser., 23 (1973).

Morgan, D. A. L., 'The Individual Style of the English Gentleman', in Jones, *Gentry and Lesser Nobility*.

Morgan, D. A. L., 'The House of Policy: the Political Role of the Late Plantagenet Household, 1422–1485 in Starkey *English Court*.

Morgan, P., *War and Society in Medieval Cheshire, 1277–1403* (Chetham Soc., Manchester, 1987).

Morgan, P., 'Henry IV and the Shadow of Richard II', in Archer, *Crown, Government and People*.

Morgan, P., 'The Death of Edward V and the Rebellion of 1483', *HR*, 68 (1995).

Morice, H., *Mémoires Pour Servir de Preuves a L'Histoire de Bretagne*, iii (1746).

Munro, J. H., *Wool, Cloth and Gold: the Struggle for Bullion in Anglo-Burgundian Trade* (Toronto, 1972).

Musgrove, F., *The North of England; a History from Roman Times to the Present* (Oxford, 1990).

Musson, A. and Ormrod, W. M., *The Evolution of English Justice: Law, Politics and Society in the Fourteenth Century* (1999).

Myers, A. R., ed., *The Household of Edward IV: The Black Book and the Ordinances of 1478* (Manchester, 1959).

Myers, A. R. C., *English Historical Documents, IV, 1327–1485* (1969).

Nauert, C. G., *Humanism and the Culture of Renaissance Europe* (Cambridge, 1995).

Neville, C. J., 'Keeping the Peace on the Northern Marches during the Later Middle Ages', *EHR*, 109 (1994).

Neville, C. J., 'Local Sentiment and the "National" Enemy in Northern England in the Later Middle Ages', *Journal of British Studies*, 35 (1996).

Neville, C. J., *Violence, Custom and Law: the Anglo-Scottish Border Lands in the Later Middle Ages* (Edinburgh, 1998).

Newman, C. M., *Late-Medieval Northallerton: a Small Market Town and its Hinterland, c.1470–1540* (Stamford, 1999).

Nicholls, K. W., 'Gaelic Society and Economy', in Cosgrove, *Medieval Ireland*.

Nichols, G., ed., *Chronicle of the Rebellion in Lincolnshire* (Camden Soc, 1847).

Nichols, D., *Medieval Flanders* (1992).

Nicholson, R., *Scotland: the Later Middle Ages* (Edinburgh, 1974) (Scotland).

Nightingale, P., 'Monetary Contraction and Mercantile Credit in Later Medieval England, *EcHR*, 2nd ser., 43 (1990).

Nightingale, P., 'The Growth of London in the Medieval English Economy', in Britnell and Hatcher, *Progress and Problems*.

Oberman, H. A. and Brady, T. A., eds, *Itinerarium Italicum. The Profile of the Italian Renaissance in the Mirror of its European Transformations* (Leiden, 1975).

Oliva, M., *The Convent and the Community in Late Medieval England: Female Monasticism in the Diocese of Norwich, 1350–1450* (Woodbridge, 1998).

Orme, N., 'Medieval Hunting: Fact and Fancy', in Hanawalt, *Chaucer's England.*

Orme, N., 'The Culture of Children in Medieval England', *PP*, 147 (1995).

Orme, N. and Webster, M., *The English Hospital, 1070–1570* (New Haven, 1995).

Ormrod, W. M., *The Reign of Edward III: Crown and Political Society in England, 1327–1377* (New Haven, 1990).

Ormrod, W. M., *Political Life in Medieval England, 1300–1450* (Macmillan, 1995).

Ormrod, W. M. and Lindley, P., eds, *The Black Death in England* (Stamford, 1996).

Palliser, D. M., 'A Crisis in English Towns. The Case of York, 1460–1640', *NH*, 14 (1978).

Palliser, D. M., 'Urban Decay Revisited', in Thomson, *Towns and Townspeople.*

Palliser, D. M., 'Urban Society', in Horrox, *Fifteenth-Century Attitudes.*

Palmer, J. J., 'The War Aims of the Protagonists and the Negotiations for Peace', in Fowler, *The Hundred Years' War.*

Pantin, W. A., *The English Church in the Fourteenth Century* (Cambridge, 1955).

Payling, S. J., 'The Ampthill Dispute: a Study in Aristocratic Lawlessness and the Breakdown of Lancastrian Government', *EHR*, 104 (1989).

Payling, S. J., *Political Society in Lancastrian England: the Greater Gentry of Nottinghamshire* (Oxford, 1991).

Payling, S. J., 'Murder, Motive and Punishment in Fifteenth-Century England: Two Case Studies', *EHR*, 113 (1998).

Payne, A., 'The Salisbury Roll of Arms, 1463', in Williams, *England in the Fifteenth Century.*

Phythian-Adams, C., *Societies, Culture and Kinship* (Leicester, 1993).

Plumb, D., 'The Social and Economic Spread of Rural Lollardy: a Re-Appraisal', *Studies in Church History*, 23 (1986).

Plummer, C., 'Introduction' to Fortescue, *Governance of England.*

Pollard, A. J., 'The Family of Talbot, Lords Talbot and Earls of Shrewsbury in the Fifteenth Century' (University of Bristol, PhD, 1968).

Pollard, A. J., 'The Northern Retainers of Richard Neville, Earl of Salisbury', *NH*, 11 (1976).

Pollard, A. J., 'Lord FitzHugh's Rising in 1470', *BIHR*, 52 (1979).

Pollard, A.J., *John Talbot and the War in France* (London: Royal Historical Society, 1983).

Pollard, A. J., ed., *Property and Politics: Essays in Late-Medieval English History* (Gloucester, 1984).

Pollard, A. J., 'St Cuthbert and the Hog: Richard III and the County Palatine of Durham, 1471–85', in Griffiths and Sherborne, *Kings and Nobles.*

Pollard, A. J., 'The North-Eastern Economy and the Agrarian Crisis of 1438–40', *NH*, 25 (1989).

Pollard, A. J., *North-Eastern England during the Wars of the Roses* (Oxford, 1990).

Pollard, A. J., *Richard III and the Princes in the Tower* (Stroud, 1991).

Pollard, A. J., 'Dominic Mancini's Narrative of the Events of 1483', *Nottingham Medieval Studies*, 38 (1994).

Pollard, A. J., ed., *The Wars of the Roses* (1995).

Pollard, A. J., 'Society, Politics and the Wars of the Roses', in Pollard, *The Wars of the Roses*.

Pollard, A. J., 'The Lancastrian Constitutional Experiment Revisited: Henry IV, Sir John Tiptoft and the Parliament of 1406', *Parliamentary History*, 14 (1995).

Pollard, A. J., ed., *The North of England in the Age of Richard III* (Stroud, 1996).

Pollard, A. J., 'The Crown and the County Palatine of Durham, 1437–94', in Pollard, *North of England*.

Pollard, A. J., 'The Characteristics of the Fifteenth-Century North', in Appleby and Dalton, *Government, Religion and Society*.

Poos, L. A., *A Rural Society after the Black Death: Essex, 1350–1525* (Cambridge, 1991).

Porter, R. and Teich, M., eds, *The Renaissance in National Context* (Cambridge, 1992).

Post, J. B., 'Crime in Later Medieval England: Some Historiographical Limitations', *Continuity and Change*, 2 (1987).

Powell, E., 'Arbitration and the Law in the Late Middle Ages', *TRHS*, 5th ser., 33 (1983).

Powell, E., 'The Settlement of Disputes by Arbitration in Fifteenth-Century England', *Law and History Review*, 2 (1984).

Powell, E., 'The Restoration of Law and Order', in Harriss, *Henry V*.

Powell, E., 'The Administration of Criminal Justice in Late Medieval England: Peace Sessions and Assizes', in Eales and Sullivan, eds, *The Political Context of Law*.

Powell, E., *Kingship, Law and Society: Criminal Justice in the Reign of Henry V* (Oxford, 1989).

Powell, E., 'After "After McFarlane": the Poverty of Patronage and the Case for Constitutional History', in Clayton, *Trade, Devotion and Governance*.

Powell, E., 'Law and Justice', in Horrox, *Fifteenth-Century Attitudes*.

Powell, E., 'The Strange Death of Sir John Mortimer', in Archer and Walker, *Rulers and Ruled*.

Powell, J. E. and Wallis, K., *The House of Lords in the Middle Ages* (1968).

Power, E. E., *Medieval English Nunneries, c. 1275–1536* (Cambridge, 1922).

Power, E. and Postan, M. M., *Studies in Fifteenth-Century Trade* (1933 and 1961).

Prestwich, M., *The Three Edwards: War and State in England, 1272–1377* (1980).

Pronay, N., 'The Chancellor, the Chancery and the Council at the End of the Fifteenth Century', in Hearder and Loyn, *British Government*.

Pronay, N. and Cox, J., eds, *The Crowland Chronicle Continuations, 1459–1486* (Gloucester, 1986).

Pronger, W. H., 'Thomas Gascoigne', *EHR*, 53 (1938) and 54 (1939).

Pugh, T. B., 'The Magnates, Knights and Gentry', in Chrimes, *Fifteenth-Century England*.

Pugh, T. B., 'Richard Plantagenet (1411–60), Duke of York, as the King's Lieutenant in France and Ireland', in Rowe, *Aspects*.

Pugh, T. B., *Henry V and the Southampton Plot* (Gloucester, 1988).

Pugh, T. B., 'Richard, Duke of York and the Rebellion of Henry Holand, Duke of Exeter, in May 1454', *HR*, 63, 1990.

Pugh, T. B., 'Henry VII and the English Nobility', in Bernard, *Tudor Nobility*.

Putnam, B., *Proceedings before the Justices of the Peace in the Fourteenth and Fifteenth Centuries: Edward III to Richard III* (1936).

Quinn, D. B., 'The Hegemony of the Earls of Kildare, 1494–1520', in Cosgrove, *Medieval Ireland*.

Quinn, D. B., 'Aristocratic Autonomy', in Cosgrove, *Medieval Ireland*.

Raine, J., ed., *The Fabric Rolls of York Minster* (Surtees Soc, xxxv, 1859).

Rawcliffe, C. A., *The Staffords, Earls of Stafford and Dukes of Buckingham, 1394–1521* (Cambridge, 1978).

Rawcliffe, C. A., 'The Great Lord as Peacekeeper: Arbitration by English Noblemen and their Councils in the Later Middle Ages', in Guy and Beales, *Law and Social Change*.

Rawcliffe, C. A., *Medicine and Society in Later Medieval England* (Stroud, 1995).

Rawcliffe, C. A., *The Hospitals of Medieval Norwich* (Norwich: Centre of East Anglian Studies, 1995).

Rawcliffe, C. A., 'The Insanity of Henry VI', *Historian*, 50 (1996).

Rex, R., *Henry VIII and the English Reformation* (1993).

Reynolds, S., *An Introduction to the History of English Medieval Towns* (Oxford, 1977).

Richmond, C. F., 'Fauconberg's Kentish Rising of May 1471', *EHR*, 85 (1970).

Richmond, C. F., *John Hopton: a Suffolk Gentleman in the Fifteenth Century* (Cambridge, 1981).

Richmond, C. F., 'After McFarlane', *History*, 68 (1983).

Richmond, C. F., 'Religion and the English Gentleman', in Dobson, *Politics and Patronage*.

Richmond, C. F., '1485 and All That, or What was going on at the Battle of Bosworth', in Hammond, *Loyalty, Lordship and Law*.

Richmond, C. F., 'Hand and Mouth: Information Gathering and Use in England in the Later Middle Ages', *Journal of Historical Sociology*, 1 (1988).

Richmond, C. F., *The Paston Family in the Fifteenth Century: the First Phase* (Cambridge, 1990).

Richmond, C. F., 'The English Gentry and Religion', in Harper-Bill, *Religious Belief*.

Richmond, C. F., 'An Outlaw and Some Peasants: the Possible Significance of Robin Hood', *Nottingham Medieval Studies*, 36 (1993).

Richmond, C. F., '1483: the Year of Decision', in Gillingham, *Medieval Kingship*.

Richmond, C., 'The Murder of Thomas Dennis', *Common Knowledge*, 2 (1993).

Richmond, C., 'Religion', in Horrox, *Fifteenth-Century Attitudes*.

Richmond, C. F., 'The Visual Culture of Fifteenth-Century England', in Pollard, *The Wars of the Roses*.

Richmond, C. F., *The Paston Family in the Fifteenth Century: Fastolff's Will* (Cambridge, 1996).

Richmond, C. F., 'The Earl of Warwick's Domination of the Channel and the Naval Dimension to the Wars of the Roses, 1456–60', *SH*, 20/21 (1998–9).

Riddy, F., 'Women talking about the things of God', in Meale, Carole, ed., *Women and Literature in England, 1150–1500* (Cambridge, 1993).

Rigby, S. H., 'Urban "Oligarchy" in Late-Medieval England', in Thomson, *Towns and Townspeople.*

Rigby, S. H., *English Society in the Later Middle Ages: Class, Status and Gender* (1995).

Riley, H. T., ed., *Registrum Abbatiae Johannis Whethamstede*, vol. 1 (Rolls Series, 1872).

Rogers, A. R., 'The Political Crisis of 1401', *Nottingham Medieval Studies*, 12 (1968).

Rogers, A. R., 'Henry IV, the Commons and Taxation', *Medieval Studies*, 31 (1969).

Rogers, J. E. T., *Six Centuries of Work and Wages* (1886).

Rosenthal, J. T., 'Lancastrian Bishops and Educational Benefaction', in Barron and Harper-Bill, *Church in Pre-Reformation Society.*

Rosenthal, J. T., *The Purchase of Paradise* (1972).

Rosenthal, J. T. and Richmond, C. F., eds, *People, Politics and Community in the Later Middle Ages* (Gloucester, 1987).

Roskell, J. S., *The Commons and their Speakers in English Parliaments, 1376–1523* (Manchester, 1965).

Roskell, J. S. *et al.*, *History of Parliament: The House of Commons, 1386–1421*, 4 vols (Stroud, 1993).

Ross, C. D., *Edward IV*, (1974).

Ross, C. D., ed., *Patronage, Pedigree and Power in Later Medieval England* (Gloucester, 1979).

Ross, C. D., *Richard III* (1981).

Ross, C. D., 'Rumour, Propaganda and Public Opinion during the Wars of the Roses', in Griffiths, *Patronage, Crown and Provinces.*

Rosser, G., 'Communities of Parish and Guild in the Late Middle Ages', in Wright, *Parish, Church and People.*

Rosser, G., *Medieval Westminster* (Oxford, 1989).

Rosser, G., 'Going to the Fraternity Feast: Commensuality and Social Relations in Late Medieval England', *JBS*, 33 (1994).

Rous, John, *Historia Regum Angliae*, in Hanham, *Richard III and His Early Historians.*

Rowe, J., ed., *Aspects of Government and Society in Later Medieval England: Essays in Honour of J.R. Lander* (Toronto, 1986).

Rowland, B., ed., *Chaucer and Middle English Studies* (1974).

Rowlands, J., *Holbein: the Paintings of Hans Holbein the Younger* (1985).

Rowney, I., 'Arbitration in Gentry Disputes in the Later Middle Ages', *History*, 67 (1982).

Rowney, I., 'The Hastings Affinity in Staffordshire and the Honour of Tutbury', *BIHR*, 57 (1984).

Rowntree, C. C., 'Studies in Carthusian History in Later Medieval England' (University of York, D Phil thesis, 1981).

Rubin, M., 'Corpus Christi Fraternities and Late-Medieval Piety', *Studies in Church History*, 23 (1986).

Rubin, M., *Charity and Community in Medieval Cambridge* (Cambridge, 1987).

Rubin, M., *Corpus Christi: the Eucharist in Late-Medieval Culture* (Cambridge, 1991).

Rubin, M., 'The Poor', in Horrox, *Fifteenth-Century Attitudes*.

Saul, N., 'The Commons and the Abolition of Badges', *Parliamentary History*, 9 (1990).

Saul, N., 'Richard II and the Vocabulary of Kingship', *EHR*, 110 (1995).

Saul, N., *Richard II* (Hew Haven, 1997).

Saul, N., 'The Kingship of Richard II', in Goodman and Gillespie, *Richard II*.

Scarisbrick, J., *The Reformation and the English People* (Oxford, 1984).

Schneider, R., ed., *Das Spätmittelalterliche Königtum im Europäischen Vergleich* (Sigmaringen, 1987).

Schofield, R., 'Taxation and the Political Limits of the Tudor State', in Cross, *Law and Governance*.

Scofield, C. L., *The Life and Reign of Edward the Fourth*, 2 vols (1924).

Secreta Secretorum, ed. Manzaloni, M. A. (EETS, 276,1977).

Sellar, W. C., and Yeatman, R. J., *1066 and All That*, (2nd edn, 1975).

Shahar, S., *Childhood in the Middles Ages* (1990).

Shakespeare, W., *The Tragedy of King Richard II*.

Shakespeare, W., *The Tragedy of King Richard III*.

Shaw, D. G., *The Creation of a Community: the City of Wells in the Middles Ages* (Oxford, 1993).

Sherborne, J. W., 'Perjury and the Lancastrian Revolution of 1399', *Welsh History Review*, 14 (1988).

Sinclair, A. F. J., 'The Beauchamp Earls of Warwick in the Later Middle Ages' (University of London, PhD, 1987).

Smyth, J., *Lives of the Berkeleys*, ed. Maclean, J., vol. 2 (Gloucester, 1883).

Sneyd, C. A., ed., *A Relation, or rather True Account of the island of England*, Camden (37, 1847).

Stapleton, B., ed., *Conflict and Community in Southern England* (Stroud, 1992).

Starkey, D., 'The Age of the Household: Politics, Society and the Arts', in Medcalfe, *Later Middle Ages*.

Starkey, D., 'Which Age of Reform?', in Coleman and Starkey, *Revolution Reassessed*.

Starkey, D., ed., *The English Court from the Wars of the Roses to the Civil War* (1987).

Starkey, D., 'Intimacy and Innovation: the Rise of the Privy Chamber, 1485–1547', in Starkey, *English Court*.

Starkey, D., 'England', in Porter and Teich, *The Renaissance in National Context* (1992).

Starkey, D. and Coleman, C., eds, *Revolution Reassessed: Revisions in the History of Tudor Government and Administration* (Oxford, 1986).

Stevenson, J., ed., *Letter and Papers Illustrative of the Wars of the English in France during the Reign of Henry VI* (2 vols in 3, RS, 1861–4).

Stone, L., *The Crisis of the Aristocracy, 1558–1641* (Oxford, 1965).

Storey, R. L., *The End of the House of Lancaster* (1966).

Storey, R. L., *Thomas Langley and the Bishopric of Durham* (1969).

Storey, R. L., 'Lincolnshire and the Wars of the Roses', *Nottingham Medieval Studies*, 14 (1970).

Storey, R. L., *Diocesan Administration in the Fifteenth Century* (York, Borthwick Paper, 16, 2nd edn, 1972).

Storey, R. L., 'Recruitment of the English Clergy in the Period of the Conciliar Movement', *Annuarium Historiae Conciliorum*, 7 (1975).

Storey, R. L., 'Gentlemen Bureaucrats', in Clough, *Professions, Vocations and Culture*.

Stratford, J., *The Bedford Inventories: The Worldly Goods of John, Duke of Bedford, Regent of France (1389–1435)* (Society of Antiquaries, London, 1993).

Strohm, P., *England's Empty Throne. Usurpation and the Language of Legitimation, 1399–1422* (New Haven, 1998).

Strype, J., *The Life of the Learned Sir Thomas Smith* (Oxford, 1820).

Stubbs, W., *The Constitutional History of England*, vol. 3, 5th edn (Oxford, 1897).

Suetonius, *The Twelve Caesars*, trans. Robert Graves (Harmondworth, 1957).

Summerson, H., *Medieval Carlisle* (Cumberland and Westmorland Antiquarian and Archaeological Society, Extra Series, 25, vol. 2, 1993).

Summerson, H., 'Carlisle and the English West March in the Later Middle Ages', in Pollard, *North of England*.

Sutton, A. F., ' "A Curious Searcher for our Weal public": Richard III, Piety, Chivalry and the Concept of the Good Prince', in Hammond, *Loyalty, Lordship and Law*.

Sutton, A. F., 'The Administration of Justice whereunto we be professed', *The Ricardian*, 53 (1976).

Sutton, A. F., 'Richard III's Tytylle and Right: a New Discovery', *The Ricardian*, 57 (1977).

Sutton, A. F., 'Sir Thomas Cook and his "Troubles" ', *Guildhall Studies in London History*, 3 (1978).

Sutton, A. F. and Hammond, P. W., *The Coronation of Richard III: the Extant Documents* (Gloucester, 1983).

Sutton, A. F. and Visser-Fuchs, L., 'A Most Benevolent Queen', *The Ricardian*, 129 (1995).

Sutton, A. and Visser-Fuchs, L., with Hammond, P. W., *The Reburial of Richard Duke of York, 21–30 July 1476* (Richard III Society, 1996).

Swanson, R. N., 'Universities, Graduates and Benefices in Late Medieval England', *PP*, 106 (1985).

Swanson, R. N., *Church and Society in Late Medieval England* (Oxford, 1989).

Swanson, R. N., *Catholic England: Faith, Religion and Observance before the Reformation* (Manchester, 1993).

Tanner, N. P., *Heresy Trials in the Diocese of Norwich* (Camden, 4th ser., 20, 1977).

Tanner, N. P., *Kent Heresy Proceedings, 1511–12* (Kent Records, 26, Maidstone 1997).

Tanner, N. P., 'Penances imposed on Kentish Lollards by Archbishop Warham, 1511–12', in Aston and Richmond, *Lollardy and the Gentry*.

Taylor, F. and Roskell, J. S., eds, *Gesta Henrici Quinti* (Oxford, 1975).

Taylor, J. and Childs, W., eds, *Politics and Crisis in Fourteenth-Century England* (Gloucester, 1990).

Thomas, H. and Thornley, I. D., eds, *The Great Chronicle of London* (1938).

Thompson, B., ed., *The Reign of Henry VII* (Stamford, 1995).

Thomson, J. A. F., *The Later Lollards, 1414–1520* (Oxford, 1965).

Thomson, J. A. F., 'The Well of Grace: Englishmen and Rome in the Fifteenth Century', in Dobson, *The Church, Politics and Patronage*.

Thomson, J. A. F., *The Transformation of Medieval England, 1370–1529* (Harlow, 1983).

Thomson, J. A. F., ed., *Towns and Townspeople in the Fifteenth Century* (Gloucester, 1988).

Thornton, T., 'Scotland and the Isle of Man, c.1400–c.1625: Noble Power and Royal Presumption in the Northern Irish Sea Province', *SCR*, 87 (1998).

Thurley, S., *The Royal Palaces of Tudor England: Architecture and Court Life, 1460–1547* (New Haven, 1993).

Tillotson, J. H., *Marrick Priory: a Nunnery in Late-Medieval Yorkshire* (Borthwick Paper 75, 1979).

Tillotson, J. H., *Monastery and Society in the Later Middle Ages: Selby Abbey, 1398–1537* (Woodbridge, 1988).

Tuck, J. A., 'Richard II and the Border Magnates', *NH*, 3 (1968).

Tuck, J. A., *Richard II and the English Nobility* (1973).

Tuck, J. A., 'Henry IV and Europe: a Dynasty's Search for Recognition', in Britnell and Pollard, *McFarlane Legacy*.

Tuck, J. A. and Goodman, A., eds, *War and Border Societies in the Middle Ages* (1992).

Tudor-Craig, P., 'Richard III's Triumphant Entry into York', in Horrox, *Richard III and the North*.

Twigg, G., *The Black Death: a Biological Reappraisal* (1984).

Usk, A., *The Chronicle of Adam Usk*, ed. Given-Wilson, C. (Oxford, 1997).

Vale, M. G. A., 'The Last Years of English Gascony', *TRHS*, 5th ser., 19 (1969).

Vale, M. G. A., *English Gascony, 1399–1453* (Oxford, 1970).

Vale, M. G. A., *Piety, Charity and Literacy among the Yorkshire Gentry, 1370–1480* (York, Borthwick Paper 50, 1976).

Vale, M. G. A., 'An Anglo-Burgundian Nobleman and Art Patron', in Barron and Saul, *England and the Low Countries*.

Vaughan, R., *Philip the Bold: the Formation of the Burgundian State* (1962).

Vaughan, R., *John the Fearless: the Growth of Burgundian Power* (1966).

Vaughan, R., *Philip the Good: the Apogee of Burgundy* (1970).

Vergil, Polydore, *Three Books of Polydore Vergil's Histories*, ed. Ellis, H. (Camden Society, 1844).

Vergil, Polydore, *Anglica Historia*, ed. and trans. Hay, D. (Camden, new series, 74, 1950).

Vickers, K. H., *Humphrey, Duke of Gloucester* (1907).

Vickerstaff, J. J., *A Great Revolutionary Deluge?, Education and the Reformation in County Durham* (Teesside Paper in North Eastern History, 2, 1992).

Virgoe, R., 'The Death of William de la Pole, Duke of Suffolk', *BJRL*, 47 (1965).

Virgoe, R., 'William Tailboys and Lord Cromwell: Crime and Politics in Lancastrian England', *BJRL*, 55 (1973).

Virgoe, R., 'Aspects of the County Community in the Fifteenth Century', in Hicks, *Profit, Piety and the Professions.*

Walker, S., *The Lancastrian Affinity, 1361–1399* (Oxford, 1990).

Walker, S., 'Yorkshire Justices of the Peace, 1389–1413', *EHR*, 98 (1993).

Walker, S., 'Political Saints in Later Medieval England', in Britnell and Pollard, *McFarlane Legacy.*

Walker, S., 'Richard II's Views on Kingship,' in Archer and Walker, *Rulers and Ruled.*

Ward, J., *The English Noblewoman in the Middle Ages* (1992).

Warkworth, J., *A Chronicle of the First Thirteen Years of the Reign of King Edward the Fourth*, ed. Halliwell, J. O. (Camden, old series, 10, 1839).

Warner, G., ed., *The Libelle of Englyssche Polycie* (Oxford, 1926).

Watt, J. A., *The Church in Medieval Ireland* (Dublin, 1972).

Watts, J. L., 'When Did Henry VI's Minority End?', in Clayton, *Trade, Devotion and Governance.*

Watts, J. L., 'Polemic and Politics in the 1450s', in Kekewich, *John Vale's Book.*

Watts, J. L., 'Ideas, Principles and Politics', in Pollard, *Wars of the Roses.*

Watts, J. L., 'A New Ffundation of is Crowne: Monarchy in the Age of Henry VII', in Thompson, *Reign of Henry VII.*

Watts, J. L., *Henry VI and the Politics of Kingship* (Cambridge, 1996).

Watts, J. L., ed., *The End of the Middle Ages?* (Stroud, 1998).

Watts, J. L., 'Introduction: History, the Fifteenth Century and the Renaissance', in Watts, *End of the Middle Ages?*

Waugh, S. L., *England in the Reign of Edward III* (Cambridge, 1991).

Waurin, Jean de, *Anchiennes Cronicques d'Engleterre*, ed. Dupont, E., 3 vols (Paris, 1858–63).

Waurin, Jean de, *Receuil des Cronicques et Anchiennes Istories de la Grant Bretaigne*, ed. Hardy, W. and E. L. C. P., 5 vols (Rolls Series, 1864–91).

Wedgwood, J. C., *History of Parliament. Biographies of the Members of the Commons House, 1439–1509* (1936).

Weightman, C., *Margaret of York, Duchess of Burgundy, 1446–1503* (Gloucester, 1989).

Weiss, R., *Humanism in England during the Fifteenth Century*, 2nd edn (Oxford, 1957).

Whiting, R., *The Blind Devotion of the People: Popular Religion and the English Reformation* (Cambridge, 1989).

Wickham, G., *Early English Stages, 1300–1660, Vol. 1, 1300–1576* (1959).

Wilkinson, B., *Constitutional History of England in the Fifteenth Century* (1964).

Wilkinson, B., *The Later Middle Ages in England 1216–1485* (1969).

Wilks, M., 'Predestination, Poverty and Power: Wyclife's Theory of Dominion and Grace', *Studies in Church History*, 2 (1965).

Williams, C. H., 'The Rebellion of Humphrey Stafford in 1486', *EHR*, 43 (1928).

Williams, D., ed., *England in the Fifteenth Century* (Woodbridge, 1987).

Williams, E. C., *My Lord of Bedford, 1389–1435* (1963).

Williams, G., *Recovery, Reorientation and Reformation: Wales, c.1415–1642* (Oxford, 1987).

Williams, G., *Renewal and Reformation: Wales, c.1415–1642* (Oxford, 1992).

Williams, G., *The Welsh Church from Conquest to Reformation* (Cardiff, 1962, 2nd edn. 1987).

Williams, G., *Wales and the Reformation* (Cardiff, 1997).

Wolffe, B. P., 'The Management of the English Royal Estates under the Yorkist Kings', *EHR*, 71 (1956).

Wolffe, B. P., *The Crown Lands 1471–1536: An Aspect of Yorkist and Early Tudor Government* (1970).

Wolffe, B. P., *The Crown Lands, 1461–1536* (1970).

Wolffe, B. P., *The Royal Demesne in English History* (1971).

Wolffe, B. P., 'The Personal Rule of Henry VI', in Chrimes, *Fifteenth-Century England*.

Wolffe, B. P., *Henry VI* (1981).

Wood, C. T., 'Richard III, William, Lord Hastings and Friday the Thirteenth', in Griffiths and Sherborne, *Kings and Nobles*.

Wood, C. T., *Joan of Arc and Richard III: Sex, Saints and Government in the Middle Ages* (Oxford, 1988).

Woodger, L. S., 'Henry Bourgchier, Earl of Essex and his Family' (University of Oxford, DPhil, 1974).

Wood-Leigh, K., *Perpetual Chantries in Britain* (Cambridge, 1966).

Woodruff, D., ed., *For Hilaire Belloc* (1942).

Wright, E., 'Henry IV, the Commons and the Recovery of Royal Finance in 1407', in Archer and Walker, *Rulers and Ruled*.

Wright, N. A. R., 'The *Tree of Battles* of Honoré Bouvet', in Allmand, *War, Literature and Politics*.

Wright, S. M., *The Derbyshire Gentry in the Fifteenth Century* (Derbyshire Record Society, Chesterfield, 1983).

Wright, S. M., ed., *Parish, Church and People: Local Studies in Lay Religion, 1350–1750* (1988).

Wrightson, K., ' "Sorts of People" in Tudor and Stuart England', in Barry and Brooks, *Middling Sort*.

INDEX

Note: the following abbreviations are used in the index: EIV for King Edward IV; EV for King Edward V; HIV for King Henry IV; HV for King Henry V; HVI for King Henry VI; HVII for King Henry VII; HVIII for King Henry VIII; RII for King Richard II; RIII for King Richard III.